Master Dogen's

Shobogenzo

Gudo Nishijima was born in Yokohama, Japan in November 1919, and graduated from the Law Department of Tokyo University in September 1946.

In October 1940 he first met Master Kodo Sawaki, whose teaching he received until Master Kodo's death in December 1965. During this time, he combined the daily practice of Zazen and study of Shobogenzo with a career at the Japanese Ministry of Finance and at a securities financing company. In December 1973 he became a priest under the late Master Renpo Niwa, and in December 1977 he received the transmission of Dharma from the same Master (who subsequently became the abbot of Eihei-ji temple). Shortly thereafter he became a consultant to the Ida Ryogokudo company, and in 1987 established the Ida Ryogokudo Zazen Dojo in Ichikawa City near Tokyo. Now in his eighties, he continues to give instruction in Zazen, and lectures on Master Dogen's works, in Japanese and in English, in Tokyo and Osaka and at Tokei-in temple in Shizuoka prefecture.

Gudo Nishijima's other publications in English include "How to Practice Zazen" (with Joe Langdon), "To Meet the Real Dragon" (with Jeffrey Bailey), "Shinji Shobogenzo" (with Michael Luetchford and Jeremy Pearson) and "A Heart-to-Heart Chat on Buddhism with Old Master Gudo" (with James Cohen). He has published a Japanese translation of Master Nāgārjuna's Mūlamadhyamakakārikā, and is presently at work on an English translation.

Chodo Cross was born in Birmingham, England, in December 1959. He went to Japan in January 1982, following graduation from Sheffield University, met Nishijima Roshi in June 1982, and received the Buddhist precepts in May of the following year. In December 1994 he returned to England in order to train to be a teacher of the F. M. Alexander Technique. In September 1998, having ceased work on the present translation and qualified as an Alexander teacher, he received the transmission of Dharma from Nishijima Roshi. He is currently leading a small group of Alexander colleagues in Zazen practice and welcomes inquiries from anyone interested in participating in Zazen retreats in England.

Master Dogen's

Shobogenzo

Book 1

Translated
by
Gudo Wafu Nishijima
Chodo Cross

Dogen Sangha
www.dogensangha.org

Reprinted, 2006

ISBN 1-4196-3820-3

To order additional copies, please contact
BookSurge, LLC
www.booksurge.com
1-866-308-6235 (USA)
orders@booksurge.com

Front cover: Portrait of Master Dogen Viewing the Moon, reproduced courtesy of Hokyo-ji, Fukui Prefecture.

Back cover: Portion of a scroll of *Fukan-zazengi*, believed to be in Master Dogen's own hand.

Contents

Acknowledgments

This translation and its publication have been made possible by the benevolence of the following sponsors:

The Japan Foundation

Mr. Hideo Ida, President of Ida Ryogokudo Co., Ltd.

Mr. Tadashi Nakamae, President of Nakamae International Economic Research

We should like to thank Michael Luetchford for his efforts in publishing this book, and Jeremy Pearson for his invaluable help at the editing and production stages. Our thanks also go to Yoko Luetchford for her work on inputting and checking the kanji, and to Emma Gibson for her help with proofreading.

Preface

Shobogenzo was written by Master Dogen in the thirteenth century. I think that reading Shobogenzo is the best way to come to an exact understanding of Buddhist theory, because Master Dogen was outstanding in his ability to understand and explain Buddhism rationally.

Of course, Master Dogen did not depart from traditional Buddhist thought. But at the same time, his thought as expressed in Shobogenzo follows his own unique method of presentation. If we understand what this method is, Shobogenzo is not so difficult to read. But unless we understand his method of thinking, it is completely impossible for us to understand what Master Dogen is trying to say in Shobogenzo.

Buddhists revere Buddha, Dharma and Samgha. Buddha means Gautama Buddha. Samgha means those people who pursue Gautama Buddha's truth. Dharma means reality. Master Dogen's unique method of thought is his way to explain what Dharma is.

Basically, he looks at a problem from two sides, and then tries to synthesize the two viewpoints into a middle way. This method has similarities with dialectic method in western philosophy, particularly as used by Hegel and Marx.

Hegel's dialectic, however, is based on belief in spirit, and Marx's dialectic is based on belief in matter. Master Dogen, through the Buddhist dialectic, wants to lead us away from thoughts based on belief in spirit and matter.

Master Dogen recognized the existence of something which is different from thought; that is, reality in action. Action is completely different from intellectual thought and completely different from the perceptions of our senses. So Master Dogen's method of thinking is based on action, and because of that, it has some unique characteristics.

First, Master Dogen recognized that things we usually separate in our minds are, in action, one reality. To express this oneness of subject and object Master Dogen says, for example, *"If a human being, even for a single moment, manifests the Buddha's posture in the three forms of conduct, while [that person] sits up straight in* samādhi, *the entire world of Dharma assumes the Buddha's posture and the whole of space becomes the state of realization."* This sentence, taken from the chapter *Bendowa*, is not illogical, but it reflects a new kind of logic.

Secondly, Master Dogen recognized that in action, the only time that really exists is the moment of the present, and the only place that really exists is this place. So the present moment and this place – the here and now – are very important concepts in Master Dogen's philosophy of action.

The philosophy of action is not unique to Master Dogen; this idea was also the center of Gautama Buddha's thought. All the Buddhist patriarchs of ancient India and China relied upon this theory and realized Buddhism itself. They also recognized the oneness of reality, the importance of the present moment, and the importance of this place.

But explanations of reality are only explanations. In Shobogenzo, after he had explained a problem on the basis of action, Master Dogen wanted to point the reader into the realm of action itself. To do this, he sometimes used poems, he sometimes used old Buddhist stories that suggest reality, and he sometimes used symbolic expressions.

So the chapters of Shobogenzo usually follow a four-phased pattern. First Master Dogen picks up and outlines a Buddhist idea. In the second phase, he examines the idea very objectively or concretely, in order to defeat idealistic or intellectual interpretations of it. In the third phase, Master Dogen's expression becomes even more concrete, practical and realistic, relying on the philosophy of action. And in the fourth phase, Master Dogen tries to suggest reality with words. Ultimately, these trials are only trials. But we can feel something that can be called reality in his sincere trials, when we reach the end of each chapter.

I think this four-phased pattern is related with the *Four Noble Truths* preached by Gautama Buddha in his first lecture. By realizing Master Dogen's method of thinking, we can come to realize the true meaning of Gautama Buddha's *Four Noble Truths.* This is why we persevere in studying Shobogenzo.

Gudo Wafu Nishijima

Ida Zazen Dojo
Tokyo
February 1994

Notes on the Translation

Aim

Several months ago, Nishijima Roshi commented *"I like the translation from which Master Dogen's Japanese can be guessed."* This describes a good aim for the donkeywork of translation: just stick closely to the original Japanese text. Make it Master Dogen's Shobogenzo.

Source text

The source text for chapters 1 to 21 is contained in the first three volumes of Nishijima Roshi's 12-volume *Gendaigo-yaku-shobogenzo (Shobogenzo in Modern Japanese). Gendaigo-yaku-shobogenzo* contains Master Dogen's original text, notes on the text, and the text rendered into modern Japanese. Reference numbers enclosed in brackets in the left margin of this translation refer to corresponding page numbers in *Gendaigo-yaku-shobogenzo,* and much of the material reproduced in the footnotes comes from *Gendaigo-yaku-shobogenzo.*

Gendaigo-yaku-shobogenzo is based upon the 95-chapter edition of Shobogenzo, which was arranged in chronological order by Master Hangyo Kozen, sometime between 1688 and 1703. The 95-chapter edition is the most comprehensive single edition, including important chapters such as *Bendowa* and *Hokke-ten-hokke* which do not appear in other editions. Furthermore, it was the first edition to be printed with woodblocks, in the Bunka era (1804–1818), and so the content was fixed at that time. The original woodblocks are still preserved at Eihei-ji, the temple in Fukui prefecture which Master Dogen founded.

Sanskrit terms

As a rule, Sanskrit words such as *samādhi* (the balanced state), *prajñā* (real wisdom), and *bhikṣu* (monk), which Master Dogen reproduces phonetically with Chinese characters, 三昧 (ZANMAI), 般若 (HANNYA), and 比丘 (BIKU), have been retained in Sanskrit form.

In addition, some Chinese characters representing the meaning of Sanskrit terms which will already be familiar to readers (or which will become familiar in the course of reading Shobogenzo) have been returned to Sanskrit. Examples are 法 (HO; "reality," "law," "method," "things and phenomena"), usually translated as "Dharma" or "dharmas"; 如来 (NYORAI; "Thus-Come"), always translated as *"Tathāgata"*; and 声聞 (SHOMON; "voice-hearer"), always translated as *"śrāvaka."*

There are places in Shobogenzo where Master Dogen himself, relying on his wide familiarity with Chinese sutras, traces the origin of Chinese characters back to Sanskrit words. A prominent example is 道 (DO; "way," "truth") which in the opening paragraph of chapter 70, *Hotsu-bodaishin,* Master Dogen explicitly identifies with the Sanskrit *bodhi.*

Even in translating Chinese terms whose Sanskrit derivation Master Dogen does not explicitly recognize, knowledge of the Sanskrit can still be very helpful. An early example is the adjective 無為 (MUI) used in the opening sentence of chapter 1, *Bendowa,* to describe Zazen. Japanese dictionaries define 無為 (MUI) as "idle" or "inactive," but Nishijima Roshi originally translated it as "natural." In Buddhist sutras, 無為 (MUI) represents the Sanskrit asaṃskṛta, which is defined in the Monier-Williams Sanskrit dictionary as follows: *not prepared, not consecrated; unadorned; unpolished, rude (as speech).* The Sanskrit dictionary definition, while by no means an absolute criterion, supports Nishijima Roshi's interpretation that 無為 (MUI) describes Zazen as natural, or without intention; something as it is.

Another example: The character 漏 (RO), "leakage," appears in the opening sentences of the Lotus Sutra, where it represents the Sanskrit āsrava. The Monier-Williams Sanskrit dictionary defines āsrava as: *the foam on boiling rice; a door opening into water and allowing the stream to descend through it; (with Jainas) the action of the senses which impels the soul towards external objects; distress, affliction, pain.* Thus, in the 2nd paragraph of chapter 10, *Shoaku-makusa,* the noun 無漏 (MURO), "no leakage," appears to describe the state without emotional distress, that is, the balanced and satisfied state of body-and-mind. This does not mean that 無漏 (MURO) should be translated as "the state without emotional distress," or as "the balanced and satisfied state of body-and-mind," but such meaning will hopefully be conveyed by a literal translation such as "[the state] without excess" or "[the state] without the superfluous," supported by a footnote and a cross-reference to the Sanskrit Glossary.

Chinese proper nouns

In general Chinese proper nouns have been romanized according to their Japanese pronunciation – as Master Dogen would have pronounced them for a Japanese audience. Thus, we have let the romanization of all names of Chinese masters follow the Japanese pronunciation, while also adding an appendix showing the Chinese romanization of Chinese masters' names. For other Chinese proper names, we have used Chinese romanization only for terms such as the *Shaolin* temple (in Japanese romanization *Shorin-ji*) whose Chinese romanization may already be familiar to most readers.

Chinese text

Master Dogen wrote Shobogenzo in Japanese, that is to say, using a combination of Chinese characters (squared ideograms usually consisting of many strokes) and the Japanese phonetic alphabet which is more abbreviated. Chinese of course is written in Chinese characters only. Therefore when Master Dogen quotes a passage, or borrows a phrase, from a Chinese text – as he very often does – it is readily apparent to the eye as a string of Chinese ideograms uninterrupted by Japanese squiggles. We have attempted to mirror this effect, to some degree, by using italics for such passages and phrases.

A pattern which occurs frequently in Shobogenzo is a quotation of Chinese characters from a conversation between Zen Masters, or from a sutra, followed by Master Dogen's commentary in which each Chinese character takes on new meaning. An early example is in the 2nd paragraph of chapter 2, where Master Dogen quotes the Great Wisdom Sutra. The Sutra says 竊作是念, lit. "[the monk] secretly makes this thought." As a conventional phrase, this just means "[the monk] secretly thinks." However, individually, the character 竊 (secret) suggests something beyond thinking and sense-perception, that is, something real; the character 作 (make or work) suggests action; the character 是 (this) suggests concrete reality; and the character 念 (thought, idea, mindfulness) suggests not only thought but the monk's real state of mind. So Master Dogen's commentary says that the monk's 竊作是念 *(secretly working concrete mind)* is real wisdom itself.

In this way, Master Dogen emphasizes that the words of the sutras and masters whom he reveres are not meant to convey only conceptual meaning. Those words are trying to bring us back to the reality which is prior to words. This is particularly true with respect to the Lotus Sutra. The Lotus Sutra contains the characters 是経 (ZEKYO), "this Sutra." In several chapters of Shobogenzo (specifically chap. 52, *Bukkyo,* but see also chap. 17, *Hokke-ten-hokke*) the fact emerges that, in Master Dogen's mind, *this Sutra* and the real Universe in which we live are identified. That being so, Master Dogen, in his commentaries, seems to treat the characters of the Lotus Sutra not as a stream of concepts but rather as a series of momentary mirrors, or independent blocks, of real form – to be brought in and re-arranged as Master Dogen sees fit.

In such instances, readers will want to refer to the Chinese characters in question. Fortunately, due to the generosity of Mr. Tadashi Nakamae (who provided the computer) and the industriousness of Michael and Yoko Luetchford (who installed the software and created and input unavailable characters), we have been able to reproduce these Chinese characters in the footnotes and in an appendix of Lotus Sutra references.

Meaning of 正法眼蔵 (SHOBOGENZO), "The Right-Dharma-Eye Treasury"

正 (SHO) means "right" or "true."

法 (HO), "Law," represents the Sanskrit *"Dharma."*

All of us belong to something which, prior to our naming it or thinking about it, is already there. And it already belongs to us. "Dharma" is one name for *what is already there.*

法眼 (HOGEN), "the Dharma-eye," represents the direct experience of what is already there. Because the Dharma is prior to thinking, it must be directly experienced by a faculty which is other than thinking. 眼 (GEN) "eye," represents this direct experience which is other than thinking.

正法眼 (SHOBOGEN), "the right-Dharma-eye," therefore describes the right experience of what is already there.

蔵 (ZO), "storehouse" or "treasury," suggests something that contains and preserves the right experience of what is already there. Thus, Nishijima Roshi has interpreted 正法眼蔵 (SHOBOGENZO), "the right-Dharma-eye treasury," as an expression of Zazen itself.

All who benefit from this translation, myself included, should be profoundly grateful to Nishijima Roshi for his unceasing effort to clarify the real meaning of Shobogenzo.

Chodo Cross
Saitama
February 1994

Shobogenzo

Chapters 1 to 21

開経偈

無上甚深微妙法
百千萬劫難遭遇
我今見聞得受持
願解如来真実義

KAIKYOGE

MUJO-JINSHIN-MIMYO-HO
HYAKU-SEN-MAN-GO-NAN-SOGU
GA-KON-KENMON-TOKU-JUJI
GAN-GE-NYORAI-SHINJITSU-GI

Verse for Opening the Sutras

The supreme, profound, subtle and fine Dharma,
In hundred thousand myriad kalpas is hard to meet.
Now that I see and hear it and am able to receive and retain it,
I desire to understand the real meaning of the Tathāgata's teaching.

[1]

弁道話

Bendowa

A Talk about Pursuing the Truth

***Ben** means "to make an effort" or "to pursue," **do** means "the truth," and **wa** means "a talk" or "story." Master Dogen usually used the word **bendo** to indicate the practice of Zazen, so **Bendowa** means a talk about pursuing the truth, or a talk about the practice of Zazen. This volume was not included in the first edition of Shobogenzo. It was found in Kyoto in the Kanbun era (1661–1673), and added to Shobogenzo when the 95-volume edition was edited by Master Hangyo Kozen in the Genroku era (1688–1704).*

[11] **When the buddha-tathāgatas,**[1] each having received the one-to-one transmission of the splendid Dharma, experience the supreme state of bodhi,[2] they possess a subtle method which is supreme and without intention. The reason this [method] is transmitted only from buddha to buddha, without deviation, is that the *samādhi* of receiving and using the self[3] is its standard. For enjoyment of this *samādhi*, the practice of [Za]zen, in the erect sitting posture, has been established as the authentic gate. This Dharma[4] is abundantly present in each human being, but if we do not practice it, it does not manifest itself, and if we do not experience it, it cannot be realized. When we let go, it has already filled the hands; how could it be defined as one or many? When we speak, it fills the mouth; it has no restriction in any direction. When buddhas are constantly dwelling in and maintaining this state, they do not leave recognitions and perceptions in separate aspects [of reality]; and when living beings are eternally functioning in this state, aspects [of reality] do not appear to them in separate recognitions and percep-

---

1. 諸仏如来 (SHO-BUTSU-NYORAI). The expression derives from the Lotus Sutra (see LS 1.88). 如来 (NYORAI) represents the Sanskrit word *tathāgata* which means "one who has arrived in the state of reality." It is the highest epithet of a buddha. See Glossary.

2. 阿耨菩提 (ANOKU-BODAI), short for 阿耨多羅三藐三菩提 (ANOKUTARA-SANMYAKU-SANBODAI), which is a transliteration of the Sanskrit words *anuttara-samyak-saṃbodhi*. *Bodhi* means "perfect wisdom," "the truth," or "the state of truth." See Glossary.

3. 自受用三昧 (JIJUYO-ZANMAI). 自 (JI) means "self," 受 (JU) means "to receive" and 用 (YO) means "to use." 三昧 (ZANMAI) represents the Sanskrit word *samādhi*. See Glossary. *Samādhi* is explained from many viewpoints in Shobogenzo, for example as 自証三昧 (JISHO-ZANMAI), *samādhi* as self experience; as 法性三昧 (HOSSHO-ZANMAI), *samādhi* as the Dharma-nature; as 海印三昧 (KAI-IN-ZANMAI), *samādhi* as the state like the sea; and as 三昧王三昧 (ZANMAI-O-ZANMAI), the *samādhi* which is king of *samādhis*. 自受用三昧 (JIJUYO-ZANMAI) suggests the state of natural balance which we experience when making effort without an intentional aim.

4. 法 (HO) has a wide range of meanings: Dharma, dharmas (see Glossary), law, things and phenomena, method, reality, et cetera. "This Dharma" suggests the method of Zazen and at the same time the reality of Zazen.

tions.[5] The effort in pursuing the truth[6] that I am now teaching makes the myriad dharmas[7] real in experience; it enacts the oneness of reality on the path of liberation.[8] At that moment of clearing barriers and getting free, how could this paragraph be relevant?

[14] After I established the will to pursue the Dharma, I visited [good] counselors[9] in every quarter of our land. I met Myozen[10] of Kennin [temple]. Nine seasons of frosts and of flowers[11] swiftly passed while I followed him, learning a little of the customs of the Rinzai lineage. Only Myozen had received the authentic transmission of the supreme Buddha-Dharma, as the most excellent disciple of the founding master, Master Eisai[12]—the other students could never compare with him. I then went to the great Kingdom of Sung, visiting [good] counselors in the east and west of Chekiang[13] and hearing of the tradition through the gates of the five lineages.[14] At last I visited Zen Master Nyojo[15] of Dai-byaku-ho mountain,[16] and there I was able to complete the great task of a lifetime of practice. After that, at the beginning of the great Sung era of Shojo,[17] I came home determined to spread the Dharma and to save living beings—it was as if a heavy burden had been placed on my shoulders. Nevertheless, in order to wait for an upsurge during which I might discharge my sense of mission, I thought I would spend some time wandering like a cloud, calling here and there like a water weed, in the style of the ancient sages. Yet if there were any true practitioners who put the will to the truth first, being naturally unconcerned with fame and profit, they might be fruitlessly misled by false teachers and might needlessly throw a veil over right understanding. They might idly become drunk with self-deception, and sink forever into the state of delusion. How would they be able to promote the right seeds of prajñā,[18] or have the opportunity to attain the truth? If I were now absorbed in drifting like a cloud or a wa-

---

5. In the state of Zazen, our consciousness is whole.

6. "Effort" is 功夫 (KUFU). "Pursuing the truth" is 弁道 (BENDO), as in the chapter title *Bendowa*. Master Dogen used the words 功夫弁道 (KUFU-BENDO) to express Zazen itself.

7. 万法 (BANPO), lit. ten-thousand dharmas; in other words, all things and phenomena. See note 4.

8. 出路 (SHUTSURO). 出 (SHUTSU) means "to get out" and 路 (RO) means "path" or "road." *Fukanzazengi* contains the words 出身の活路 (SHUSSHIN *no* KATSURO), "the vigorous road of the body getting out," that is, the state of vigorous action in which our body gets free from intellectual worries and sensory attachments.

9. 知識 (CHISHIKI), short for 善知識 (ZENCHISHIKI), from the Sanskrit *kalyāṇa-mitra* (see Glossary).

10. 全功 (ZENKO). 全 (ZEN) stands for 明全 (MYOZEN). 公 (KO) is an honorific. Master Myozen and Master Dogen set off together in 1223 to investigate Buddhism in China. Master Myozen died on May 5th, 1225, aged 41, in Ryozen-ryo dormitory at Tendo-zan temple. Before becoming the disciple of Master Eisai, Master Myozen had learned the teachings of the Tendai Sect, on Mt. Hi-ei.

11. Autumns and springs.

12. Master Eisai (1141–1215), who went to China and introduced the transmission of the Rinzai sect into Japan.

13. A province in Eastern China, bordering the East China Sea.

14. The so-called Soto, Rinzai, Hogen, Igyo, and Unmon sects. See chap. 49, *Butsudo*.

15. 浄禅師 (JO-ZENJI), Master Tendo Nyojo (1163–1228), successor of Master Seccho Chikan. Usually referred to in Shobogenzo as 先師 (SENSHI), "my late Master."

16. 大白峰 (DAIBYAKUHO), lit. "Great White Peak," is another name for Tendo-zan mountain, where Master Tendo Nyojo led the order from 1224 until his death.

17. The Shojo era was from 1228 to 1233.

18. Real wisdom. See chap. 2, *Maka-hannya-haramitsu*.

ter weed, which mountains and rivers ought they to visit?[19] Feeling that this would be a pitiful situation, I decided to compile a record of the customs and standards that I experienced first-hand in the Zen monasteries of the great Kingdom of Sung, together with a record of profound instruction from a [good] counselor which I have received and maintained. I will leave this record to people who learn in practice and are easy in the truth, so that they can know the right Dharma of the Buddha's lineage. This may be a true mission.

[17] [The sutras] say: The Great Master Śākyamuni at the order on Vulture Peak[20] transmitted the Dharma to Mahākāśyapa.[21] [The Dharma] was authentically transmitted from patriarch to patriarch and it reached the Venerable Bodhidharma.[22] The Venerable One himself went to China and transmitted the Dharma to the Great Master Eka.[23] This was the first transmission of the Buddha-Dharma in the Eastern Lands.[24] Transmitted one-to-one in this manner, [the Dharma] arrived naturally at Zen Master Daikan,[25] the Sixth Patriarch. At that time, as the real Buddha-Dharma spread through the eastern [land of] China, it became clear that [the Dharma] is beyond literary expression. The Sixth Patriarch had two excellent disciples, Ejo of Nangaku[26] and Gyoshi of Seigen.[27] Both of them, having received and maintained the posture of Buddha,[28] were guiding teachers of human beings and gods alike. [The Dharma] flowed and spread in these two streams, and five lineages were established. These are the so-called Hogen Sect, Igyo Sect, Soto Sect, Unmon Sect, and Rinzai Sect. In great Sung [China] today the Rinzai Sect alone holds sway throughout the country. Although there are differences between the five traditions, the posture with the stamp of the Buddha's mind[29] is only one. Even in the great Kingdom of Sung, although from the Later Han Dynasty[30] onwards philosophical texts had been disseminated through the country, and had left some impression, no-one could decide which were inferior and which were superior. After the ancestral Master came from the west, he directly cut to the source of the confusion,[31] and spread the unadulterated Buddha-Dharma. We should hope that the same thing will happen in our country. [The sutras] say that the many patriarchs and the many buddhas, who dwelt in and maintained the Buddha-Dharma, all relied on the

---

19. In order to find a true teacher.

20. Vulture Peak is so called because the silhouette of the mountain resembles a vulture. The Buddha often preached there.

21. Master Mahākāśyapa, the first patriarch in India.

22. Master Bodhidharma (6th century), the twenty-eighth patriarch in India and the first patriarch in China.

23. Master Taiso Eka, the second patriarch in China.

24. 東地 (TOCHI), China. Master Dogen commonly referred to India and China as 西天東地 (SAITEN-TOCHI), "the Western Heavens and Eastern Lands."

25. Master Daikan Eno (638–713), the sixth patriarch in China.

26. Master Nangaku Ejo (677–744).

27. Master Seigen Gyoshi (died 740), the seventh Chinese patriarch in Master Dogen's lineage.

28. 仏印 (BUTSU-IN), lit. "Buddha-seal." 印 (IN) can be interpreted as a seal of approval, that is, certification. Or it can be interpreted as concrete form, or posture.

29. 仏心印 (BUTSU-SHIN-IN), lit. "Buddha-mind-seal." In chap. 72, *Zanmai-o-zanmai,* Master Dogen says that the Buddha-mind-seal is the full lotus posture itself.

30. The Later Han Dynasty was from 25 to 221 A.D.

31. Lit. "cut the roots of the arrowroot and wisteria." These two vines symbolize something confused or complicated. See chap. 46, *Katto.*

practice of sitting erect in the samādhi of receiving and using the self,[32] and esteemed [this practice] as the right way to disclose the state of realization. Human beings who attained the truth in the Western Heavens and Eastern Lands followed this style of practice. This [practice] relies on the mystical and authentic transmission of the subtle method from master to disciple, and the [disciple's] reception and maintenance of the true essence of the teachings.

[20] In the authentic transmission of [our] religion, it is said that this Buddha-Dharma,[33] which has been authentically and directly transmitted one-to-one, is supreme among the supreme. After the initial meeting with a [good] counselor we never again need to burn incense, to do prostrations, to recite Buddha's name, to practice confession, or to read sutras. Just sit and get the state which is free of body and mind. If a human being, even for a single moment, manifests the Buddha's posture in the three forms of conduct,[34] while [that person] sits up straight in samādhi, the entire world of Dharma assumes the Buddha's posture and the whole of space becomes the state of realization. [The practice] thus increases the Dharma-joy that is the original state of the buddha-tathāgatas, and renews the splendor of their realization of the truth. Furthermore, throughout the Dharma-worlds in ten directions, ordinary beings of the three states and the six states[35] all become clear and pure in body-and-mind at once; they experience the state of great liberation,[36] and their original features appear. Then all dharmas experience and understand right realization and myriad things each put their Buddhist body into practice; in an instant, they totally transcend the limits of experience and understanding; they sit erect as kings of the Bodhi tree;[37] in one moment, they turn the great Dharma-wheel[38] which is in the unequaled state of equilibrium;[39] and they expound the ultimate, unadorned, and profound state of prajñā. These balanced and right states of realization also work the other way,[40] following paths of intimate and mystical cooperation, so that this person who sits in Zazen steadfastly gets free of body and mind, cuts away miscellaneous impure views and thoughts [accumulated] from the past, and thus experiences and understands the natural and pure Buddha-Dharma. Throughout each of the infinitesimal, innumerable seats of truth of the buddha-tathāgatas, [the practitioner] promotes the Buddha's work and spreads its influence far and wide over those who have the ascendant makings of buddha, thus vividly uplifting the ascendant real state of buddha. At this time, everything in the Universe in ten direc-

32. 自受用三昧 (JIJUYO-ZANMAI); the state of natural balance, see note 3.

33. 仏法 (BUPPO), "Buddha-Dharma," or "Buddhist Method," in this case means Zazen itself.

34. 三業 (SAN-GO), the three kinds of behavior; that is, behavior of body, speech, and mind.

35. 三途 (SANZU), lit. "the three courses," or the three miserable worlds, are hell, the world of hungry ghosts, and the world of animals. 六道 (ROKUDO), lit. "the six ways" or the six human worlds, are the three miserable worlds plus the worlds of demons, human beings, and gods.

36. 大解脱地 (DAI-GEDATSU-CHI). 大 (DAI) means great. 解脱 (GEDATSU) represents the Sanskrit *vimukti*, which means to get free of all hindrances. 地 (CHI) means state.

37. The Sanskrit *bodhi* means the state of truth. The Buddha attained the truth sitting under a pipal tree (Latin name: *Ficus religiosa*). In Buddhist countries this tree is called the bodhi tree.

38. 天法輪 (TENBORIN), turning of the Dharma-wheel, symbolizes Buddhist preaching. See chap. 74, *Tenborin*.

39. 無等等 (MUTODO), lit. "equality without equal," from the Sanskrit *asamasama*. The expression appears in the Heart Sutra (see chap. 2, *Maka-hannya-haramitsu*), and in the Lotus Sutra (LS 3.270).

40. Towards the practitioner—the practice influences both object and subject.

tions—soil, earth, grass, and trees; fences, walls, tiles, and pebbles—performs the Buddha's work. The people that receive the benefit thus produced by wind and water are all mystically helped by the fine and unthinkable influence of the Buddha, and they exhibit the immediate state of realization. All beings who receive and utilize this water and fire spread the influence of the Buddha in the original state of experience, so that those who live and talk with them also, are all reciprocally endowed with the limitless Buddha-virtue. Expanding and promoting their activity far and wide, they permeate the inside and the outside of the entire Universe with the limitless, unceasing, unthinkable, and incalculable Buddha-Dharma. [The state] is not dimmed by the views of these individuals themselves, however, because the state in the quietness, without intentional activity, is direct experience. If we divide practice-and-experience into two stages, as in the thoughts of common folk, each part can be perceived and understood separately. [But] if perception and understanding are mixed in, that is not the standard state of experience, because the standard state of experience is beyond deluded emotion. Although, in the quietness, mind and external world enter together into the state of experience and pass together out of the state of realization, [those movements] are the state of receiving and using the self.[41] Therefore, [movements of mind and the external world] neither stir a single molecule nor disturb a single form, but they accomplish the vast and great work of Buddha and the profound and fine influence of Buddha. The grass, trees, soil, and earth reached by this guiding influence all radiate great brightness, and their preaching of the deep and fine Dharma is without end. Grass, trees, fences, and walls become able to preach for all souls, [both] common people and saints; and conversely, all souls, [both] common people and saints, preach for grass, trees, fences, and walls. The world of self-consciousness, and [the world] of consciousness of external objects, lack nothing—they are already furnished with the concrete form of real experience. The standard state of real experience, when activated, allows no idle moment. Zazen, even if it is only one human being sitting for one moment, thus enters into mystical co-operation with all dharmas, and completely penetrates all times; and it therefore performs, within the limitless Universe, the eternal work of the Buddha's guiding influence in the past, future, and present. For everyone it is completely the same practice and the same experience. The practice is not confined to the sitting itself; it strikes space and resonates, [like] ringing that continues before and after a bell. How could [the practice] be limited to this place? All concrete things[42] possess original practice as their original features; it is beyond comprehension. Remember, even if the countless buddhas in ten directions, as numerous as the sands of the Ganges, tried with all their power and all their Buddha-wisdom to calculate or comprehend the merit of one person's Zazen, they could not even get close.

[26] Now we have heard how high and great is the merit of this Zazen. [But] some stupid person might doubtingly ask, "There are many gates to the Buddha-Dharma. Why do you solely recommend sitting in Zazen?"[43]

---

41. 自受用の境界 (JIJUYO *no* KYOGAI), lit. "the area of receiving and using self," that is, the state of natural balance. See note 3.

42. 百頭 (HYAKUTO), lit. "hundreds of heads," suggesting miscellaneous concrete things.

43. Questions and answers are not separated in the source text. They have been separated here for ease of reading.

I say: Because it is the authentic gate to the Buddha-Dharma.

[26] [Someone] asks, "Why do you see it as the only authentic gate?"

I say: The Great Master Śākyamuni exactly transmitted, as the authentic tradition, this subtle method of grasping the state of truth, and the tathāgatas of the three times[44] all attained the truth through Zazen. Thus the fact that [Zazen] is the authentic gate has been transmitted and received. Furthermore, the patriarchs of the Western Heavens and the Eastern Lands all attained the truth through Zazen. Therefore I am now preaching [Zazen] to human beings and gods as the authentic gate.

[27] [Someone] asks, "That which relies upon receiving the authentic transmission of the subtle method of the Tathāgata, or upon following the traces of the ancestral masters, is surely beyond the intellect of the common man. Reading sutras and reciting the names of buddhas, however, may naturally become the causes and conditions of enlightenment. But as for just idly sitting without doing anything, how can that be the means of getting enlightenment?"

I say: If you now think that the samādhi of the buddhas, the supreme and great Dharma, is idle sitting without doing anything, you are a person who insults the Great Vehicle.[45] [Such] delusion is so deep that it is like being in the ocean and saying there is no water. [In Zazen] we are already seated, stably and thankfully, in the buddhas' samādhi of receiving and using the self. Is this not the accomplishment of vast and great virtue? It is pitiful that your eyes are not yet open and your mind remains in a drunken stupor. In general, the state of the buddhas is unthinkable: intelligence cannot reach it. How much less could disbelief or inferior wisdom know the state? Only people of great makings and right belief can enter into it. For people of disbelief, even if taught, it is difficult to receive the teaching—even on Vulture Peak there were people [about whom the Buddha said,] *"That they withdraw also is fine."*[46] As a general rule, when right belief emerges in our mind, we should do training and learn in practice. Otherwise, we should rest for a while. Regret the fact if you will, but from ancient times the Dharma has been dry. Further, do you know for yourself any virtue that is gained from practices such as reading sutras and reciting names of buddhas? It is very unreliable to think that only to wag the tongue and to raise the voice has the virtue of the Buddha's work. When we compare [such practices] with the Buddha-Dharma, they fade further and further into the distance. Moreover, we open sutras to clarify the criteria that the Buddha taught of instantaneous and gradual practice,[47] and those who practice according to the teaching are invariably caused to attain the state of real experience. This is completely different from aspiring to the virtue of attainment of bodhi by vainly exhausting the intellect. Trying to arrive at the Buddha's state of truth [only] through action of the mouth, stupidly chanting thousands or tens of thousands of times, is like hoping to reach [the south country of] Etsu by pointing a carriage towards

---

44. 三世 (SANZE), the past, present, and future; eternity.

45. 大乘 (DAIJO), Mahāyāna Buddhism.

46. 退亦佳矣 (TAIYAKUKEI). See LS 1.86-88.

47. 頓漸修行 (TONZEN-SHUGYO). 頓漸 (TONZEN) stands for 頓悟 (TONGO), "instant-aneous realization," and 漸悟 (ZENGO), "gradual realization." These represent two views of realization—as occurring just in the moment of practice, and as a process continuing over a long line of moments—based on the two views of time.

the north. Or it is like trying to put a square peg into a round hole. Reading sentences while remaining ignorant of how to practice [is like] a student of medicine forgetting how to compound medications. What use is that? Those who chant endlessly are like frogs in a spring paddy field, croaking day and night. In the end it is all useless. It is still more difficult for people who are deeply disturbed by fame and gain to abandon these things. The mind that craves gain is very deep, and so it must have been present in the ancient past. How could it not be present in the world today? It is most pitiful. Just remember, when a practitioner directly follows a master who has attained the truth and clarified the mind, and when the practitioner matches that mind and experiences and understands it, and thus receives the authentic transmission of the subtle Dharma of the Seven Buddhas,[48] then the exact teaching appears clearly and is received and maintained. This is beyond the comprehension of Dharma-teachers who study words.[49] So stop this doubting and delusion and, following the teaching of a true master, attain in experience the buddhas' samādhi of receiving and using the self, by sitting in Zazen and pursuing the truth.

[32] [Someone] asks, "The Flower of Dharma[50] and the teaching of the Garland [Sutra],[51] which have now been transmitted into this country, are both ultimate expressions of the Great Vehicle. Moreover, in the case of the Shingon Sect,[52] [the transmission] passed directly from the Tathāgata Vairocana to Vajra-sattva, and so [the transmission from] master to disciple is not at random. Quoting the principles which it discusses, that *"Mind here and now is buddha,"* and *"This mind becomes buddha,"*[53] [the Shingon Sect] proclaims that we realize the right realization of the five buddhas[54] in one sitting, without undergoing many kalpas[55] of training. We can say that this is the ultimate refinement of the Buddha's Dharma. What is so excellent then about the practice which you now solely recommend, to the exclusion of these other [practices]?"

I say: Remember, among Buddhists we do not argue about superiority and inferiority

---

48. The seven ancient buddhas were Vipaśyin, Śikhin, Viśyabhū, Krakucchanda, Kanakamuni, Kāśyapa, and Śākyamuni (see chap. 15, *Busso).* Belief in the Seven Buddhas reflects the belief that the Dharma is eternal, predating the historical Buddha, Śākyamuni.

49. 法師 (HOSSHI). In Master Dogen's time some priests in the Tendai Sect had this title.

50. 法華宗 (HOKKESHU). 法華 (HOKKE) stands for 法華経 (HOKKEKYO), "the Sutra of the Flower of Dharma," the Lotus Sutra. 宗 (SHU) means religion or sect. 法華宗 (HOKKESHU) was the name formerly used for the Tendai Sect. The Tendai Sect was established in China by Master Tendai Chigi based on the Lotus Sutra. It was introduced into Japan by Master Saicho (767–822).

51. 華厳教 (KEGONKYO), lit. "Kegon teaching," means the teaching of the Kegon Sect which was also established in China, based on the Kegon (Garland) Sutra. It was introduced into Japan in 736.

52. 真言宗 (SHINGONSHU). The Shingon Sect is derived from Vajrayāna Buddhism. Master Kukai went to China and brought the teachings of the Shingon Sect back to Japan in 806. Vajrayāna Buddhism reveres Vajra-sattva, the Diamond Buddha, who is said to have received the transmission from Vairocana, the Sun Buddha.

53. "Mind here and now is buddha" is 即心是仏 (SOKU-SHIN-ZE-BUTSU)—the title of chap. 6. "This mind becomes buddha" is 是心作仏 (ZE SHIN-SA-BUTSU).

54. That is, the five Buddhas in the mandala used in the esoteric Buddhism of the Shingon Sect. The mandala would be a picture with Vairocana Buddha in the middle surrounded by buddhas to his north, south, east, and west.

55. 劫 (GO, or KO) represents the sound of the Sanskrit *kalpa,* which means an infinitely long time. A *kalpa* was explained, for example, as the time it would take to wear away a large boulder if an angel rubbed it once every three years with its sleeve.

of philosophies, or choose between shallowness and profundity in the Dharma; we need only know whether the practice is genuine or artificial. Some have entered into the stream of the Buddha's truth at the invitation of grass, flowers, mountains, and rivers. Some have received and maintained the stamp of Buddha by grasping soil, stones, sand, and pebbles. Furthermore, the Vast and Great Word[56] is even more abundant than the myriad phenomena. And the turning of the great Dharma-wheel is contained in every molecule. This being so, the words *"Mind here and now is buddha"* are only the moon in water,[57] and the idea *"Just to sit is to become buddha"* is also a reflection in a mirror. We should not be caught by the skillfulness of the words. Now, in recommending the practice in which bodhi is directly experienced, I hope to demonstrate the subtle truth that the Buddhist patriarchs have transmitted one-to-one, and thus to make you into people of the real state of truth. Moreover, for transmission of the Buddha-Dharma, we must always take as a teacher a person who has experienced the [Buddha's] state. It is never enough to take as our guiding teacher a scholar who counts words; that would be like the blind leading the blind. In this, the lineage of the authentic transmission of the Buddhist patriarchs, we all revere wise masters who have attained the truth and experienced the state, and we cause them to dwell in and to maintain the Buddha-Dharma. This is why, when Shintoists of [the lineages of] yin and yang[58] come to devote themselves, and when arhats who have experienced the effect[59] come to ask for Dharma, we give each of them, without fail, the means of clarifying the mental state. This is something that has never been heard in other lineages. The disciples of the Buddha should just learn the Buddha-Dharma. Furthermore, we should remember that from the beginning we have never lacked the supreme state of bodhi, and we will receive it and use it forever. At the same time, because we cannot perceive it directly,[60] we are prone to beget random intellectual ideas, and because we chase after these as if they were real things, we vainly pass by the great state of truth. From these intellectual ideas emerge all sorts of flowers in space:[61] we think about the twelve-fold cycle[62] and the twenty-five spheres of existence; and ideas of the three vehicles and

---

56. 広大の文字 (KODAI *no* MONJI), lit. "the wide and great characters" suggests Dharma as not only the accumulation of material phenomena but also something which has meaning.

57. An image of the moon, not the moon itself.

58. 冥陽の神道 (MEIYO *no* SHINTO). 冥陽 (MEIYO) means "yin and yang." 神道 (SHINTO), lit. "Way of the Gods" is the ethnic spiritual religion of Japan. The idea of two lineages of Shinto, the yin and the yang, seems to have originated with attempts of the Shingon Sect to reconcile its teachings with indigenous Japanese beliefs.

59. An *arhat* is a person who has attained the ultimate state (the fourth effect) of a śrāvaka, that is, the ultimate level of abstract Buddhist learning. The *arhat* is the subject of chap. 34, *Arakan*.

60. "Perceive it directly" is 承当 (JOTO), short for 承受合当 (JOJU-GATTO), lit. "receiving a hit." Generally, 承当 (JOTO) means to be struck by reality directly in momentary experience. In the last section of the independent work *Gakudo-yojin-shu*, Master Dogen explains 承当 (JOTO), or "receiving a hit," as follows: *"Using this body-and-mind, we directly experience the state of buddha. This is to receive a hit."*

61. 空華 (KUGE), "flowers in space" symbolize images. See chap. 41, *Kuge*.

62. 十二輪転 (JUNI-RINDEN), the twelve-fold cycle of cause and effect, from the Sanskrit *dvādaśāṅga-pratītya-samutpāda* (see Glossary). See, for example, LS 2.56.

the five vehicles[63] or of having Buddha[-nature] and not having Buddha[-nature] are endless. We should not think that the learning of these intellectual ideas is the right path of Buddhist practice. When we solely sit in Zazen, on the other hand, relying now on exactly the same posture as the Buddha, and letting go of the myriad things, then we go beyond the areas of delusion, realization, emotion, and consideration, and we are not concerned with the ways of the common and the sacred. At once we are roaming outside the [intellectual] frame, receiving and using the great state of bodhi. How could those caught in the trap of words compare [with this]?

[37] [Someone] asks, "Among the three kinds of training[64] there is training in the balanced state, and among the six pāramitās[65] there is the dhyāna pāramitā, both of which all bodhisattvas learn from the outset and all bodhisattvas practice, regardless of whether they are clever or stupid. The Zazen [that you are discussing] now is surely [only] one of these. Why do you say that the Tathāgata's right Dharma is concentrated in this [practice of Zazen]?"

I say: The question arises because this right-Dharma-eye treasury, the supreme and great method, which is the one great matter[66] of the Tathāgata, has been called the "Zen Sect." Remember that this title "Zen Sect" was established in China and the east; it is not heard in India. When the Great Master Bodhidharma first stayed at Shaolin temple in the Sung-shan mountains,[67] and faced the wall for nine years, monks and laymen were still ignorant of the Buddha's right Dharma, so they called [Master Bodhidharma] a Brāhman who made a religion of Zazen. Thereafter, the patriarchs of successive generations all constantly devoted themselves to Zazen. Stupid secular people who saw this, not knowing the reality, talked at random of a Zazen Sect. Nowadays, dropping the word "Za," they talk of just the Zen Sect.[68] This interpretation is clear from records of the patriarchs.[69] [Zazen] should not be discussed as the balanced state of dhyāna in the six pāramitās and the three kinds of training. That this Buddha-Dharma is the legitimate intention of the one-to-one transmission has never been concealed through the ages. In the order on Vulture Peak in ancient times, when the Tathāgata gave the

63. 三乗 (SANJO), "the three vehicles," or the three kinds of Buddhist, are explained in chap. 24, *Bukkyo*. They are the *śrāvaka*, who relies on the theory of four philosophies; the *pratyekabuddha*, who relies on the theory of dependent origination (the twelve-fold chain of cause and effect); and the *bodhisattva*, who relies on the six *pāramitās* (the six accomplishments). The five vehicles are these three, plus human beings and gods.

64. 三学 (SANGAKU), from the Sanskrit *tisraḥ śikṣāḥ*, are the precepts, the balanced state, and wisdom.

65. The Sanskrit word *pāramitā* means that which has arrived at the opposite shore, an accomplishment. 六度 (ROKUDO), the six *pāramitās*, are giving, keeping the precepts, patience, diligence, the practice of Zazen (*dhyāna*), and real wisdom. The Sanskrit *dhyāna* was rendered into Chinese and Japanese as 禅 (CH'AN or ZEN).

66. 一大事 (ICHIDAIJI) appears in the Lotus Sutra. See LS 1.88-90 and chap. 17, *Hokke-ten-hokke*.

67. The Sung-shan mountains consist of two main peaks, 太室 (TAISHITSU) to the east, and 少室 (SHOSHITSU) to the west. These mountains contained many Buddhist temples; the Shaolin temple was on Shoshitsu Peak.

68. The Zazen Sect is 坐禅宗 (ZAZENSHU), lit. "Sitting Dhyāna Sect." Dropping the 坐 (ZA) gives 禅宗 (ZENSHU), lit. "Dhyāna Sect."

69. 広語 means 広録 (KOROKU), "broad records," and 語録 (GOROKU), "record of the words." See bibliography.

Dharma to the Venerable Mahākāśyapa, transmitting the right-Dharma-eye treasury and the fine mind of nirvāṇa, the supreme and great method, only to him, the ceremony was witnessed directly by beings among the celestial throng which are present in the world above, so it must never be doubted. It is a universal rule that those celestial beings will guard and maintain the Buddha-Dharma eternally; their efforts have never faded. Just remember that this [transmission of Zazen] is the whole truth of the Buddha's Dharma; nothing can be compared with it.

[40] [Someone] asks, "Why, in discussing entry into the state of experience, do Buddhists recommend us to practice the balanced state of dhyāna solely by sitting, which is [only] one of the four forms of conduct?"[70]

I say: It is difficult to calculate all the ways that buddhas have successively practiced since ancient times to enter the state of real experience. If we want to find a reason, we should remember that what Buddhists practice is reason in itself. We should not look for [a reason] besides this. But an ancestral master has praised [sitting] by saying, *"Sitting in Zazen is the peaceful and joyful gate of Dharma."*[71] So in conclusion the reason may be that, of the four forms of conduct, [sitting is the most] peaceful and joyful. Furthermore, [sitting] is not the way practiced by one or two buddhas; all the buddhas and all the patriarchs possess this way.

[41] [Someone] asks, "In regard to this practice of Zazen, a person who has not yet experienced and understood the Buddha-Dharma may be able to acquire that experience by pursuing the truth in Zazen. [But] what can a person who has already clarified the Buddha's right Dharma expect to gain from Zazen?"

I say: We do not tell our dreams before a fool, and it is difficult to put oars into the hands of a mountaineer; nevertheless I must bestow the teaching. The thought that practice and experience are not one thing is just the idea of non-Buddhists. In the Buddha-Dharma practice and experience are completely the same. [Practice] now is also practice in the state of experience; therefore, a beginner's pursuit of the truth is just the whole body of the original state of experience. This is why [the Buddhist patriarchs] teach, in the practical cautions they have handed down to us, not to expect any experience outside of practice. And the reason may be that [practice itself] is the directly accessible original state of experience. Because practice is just experience, the experience is endless; and because experience is practice, the practice has no beginning. This is how both the Tathāgata Śākyamuni and the Venerable Patriarch Mahākāśyapa were received and used by the practice that exists in the state of experience. The Great Master Bodhidharma and the founding Patriarch Daikan[72] were similarly pulled and driven by the practice that exists in the state of experience. The examples of all those who dwelt in and maintained the Buddha-Dharma are like this. The practice that is never separate from experience exists already: having fortunately received the one-to-one

---

70. 四儀 (SHIGI), walking, standing, sitting, and lying down.

71. 坐禅はすなはち安楽の法門なり。(ZAZEN *wa sunawachi* ANRAKU *no* HOMON *nari.*) These words may originate with Master Choro Sosaku, who was the editor of *Zen-en-shingi (Pure Criteria for Zen Monasteries).* Master Dogen quotes the same words in *Fukan-zazengi* (see Appendix). The words 安楽 (ANRAKU), "peaceful and joyful" or "stable and comfortable" are contained in the title of the 14th chapter of the Lotus Sutra, 安楽行 (ANRAKUGYO), *"Peaceful and Joyful Practice."*

72. Master Daikan Eno. See note 25.

transmission of a share of the subtle practice, we who are beginners in pursuing the truth directly possess, in the state without intention, a share of original experience. Remember, in order to prevent us from tainting the experience that is never separate from practice, the Buddhist patriarchs have repeatedly taught us not to be lax in practice. When we forget the subtle practice, original experience has filled our hands; when the body leaves original experience behind, the subtle practice is operating throughout the body. Moreover, as I saw with my own eyes in great Sung China, the Zen monasteries of many districts had all built Zazen Halls accommodating five or six hundred, or even one or two thousand monks, who were encouraged to sit in Zazen day and night. The leader of one such order[73] was a true master who had received the Buddha's mind-seal. When I asked him the great intent of the Buddha-Dharma, I was able to hear the principle that practice and experience are never two stages. Therefore, in accordance with the teaching of the Buddhist patriarchs, and following the way of a true master, he encouraged [everyone] to pursue the truth in Zazen; [he encouraged] not only the practitioners in his order, but [all] noble friends who sought the Dharma, [all] people who hoped to find true reality in the Buddha-Dharma, without choosing between beginners and late learners, without distinction between common people and sacred people. Have you not heard the words of the ancestral Master[74] who said, *"It is not that there is no practice-and-experience, but it cannot be tainted."* Another [master] said, *"Someone who sees the way practices the way."*[75] Remember that even in the state of attainment of the truth, we should practice.

[44] [Someone] asks, "The masters who spread the teachings through our country in previous ages had all entered Tang China and received the transmission of Dharma. Why, at that time, did they neglect this principle, and transmit only philosophical teaching?"

I say: The reason that past teachers of human beings did not transmit this method was that the time had not come.

[45] [Someone] asks, "Did those masters of former ages understand this method?"

I say: If they had understood it, they would have made it known to all.

[45] [Someone] asks, "It has been said that we should not regret our life and death,[76] for there is a very quick way to get free of life and death. That is, to know the truth that the mental essence is eternal. In other words, this physical body, having been born, necessarily moves towards death; but this mental essence never dies at all. Once we have been able to recognize that the mental essence which is unmoved by birth and decay[77] exists in our own body, we see this as the original essence. Therefore the body is just a temporary form; it dies here and is born there, never remaining constant. [But] the mind is eternal; it is unchangeable in the past, future, or present. To know this is called

---

73. Master Tendo Nyojo.

74. Master Nangaku Ejo. The conversation between Master Daikan Eno and Master Nangaku Ejo is recorded in *Shinji-shobogenzo* pt. 2, no. 1. See also Shobogenzo chap. 7, *Senjo*, chap. 29, *Inmo*, and chap. 62, *Hensan*.

75. *Keitoku-dento-roku*, chap. 5, in the section on Master Honjo.

76. 生死 (SHOJI), lit. "life and death" or "living-and-dying," is the title of chap. 92.

77. 生滅 (SHOMETSU). 生 (SHO) means not only "life" but also "birth" and "appearance." In this paragraph 生滅 (SHOMETSU) has also been translated as "appearance and disappearance."

'to have become free of life and death.' Those who know this principle stop the past [cycle of] life and death forever and, when this body passes, they enter the spirit world.[78] When they present themselves in the spirit world, they gain wondrous virtues like those of the buddha-tathāgatas. Even if we know [this principle] now, [our body] is still the body that has been shaped by deluded behavior in past ages, and so we are not the same as the saints. Those who do not know this principle will forever turn in the cycle of life and death. Therefore we should just hasten to understand the principle that the mental essence is eternal. Even if we passed our whole life in idle sitting, what could we expect to gain? The doctrine I have expressed like this is truly in accord with the truth of the buddhas and the patriarchs, is it not?"

I say: The view expressed now is absolutely not the Buddha's Dharma; it is the view of the non-Buddhist Senika.[79] According to that non-Buddhist view, there is one spiritual intelligence existing within our body. When this intelligence meets conditions, it can discriminate between pleasant and unpleasant and discriminate between right and wrong, and it can know pain and irritation and know suffering and pleasure—all [these] are abilities of the spiritual intelligence. When this body dies, however, the spirit casts off the skin and is reborn on the other side; so even though it seems to die here it lives on there. Therefore we call it immortal and eternal. The view of that non-Buddhist is like this. But if we learn this view as the Buddha's Dharma, we are even more foolish than the person who grasps a tile or a pebble thinking it to be a golden treasure; the delusion would be too shameful for comparison. National Master Echu[80] of great Tang China strongly cautioned against [such thinking]. If we equate the present wrong view that *mind is eternal but forms perish* with the splendid Dharma of the buddhas, thinking that we have escaped life and death when we are promoting the original cause of life and death, are we not being stupid? That would be most pitiful. Knowing that this [wrong view] is just the wrong view of non-Buddhists, we should not touch it with our ears. Nevertheless, I cannot help wanting to save you from this wrong view and it is only compassionate [for me] now [to try]. So remember, in the Buddha-Dharma, because the body and mind are originally one reality, the saying that essence and form are not two has been understood equally in the Western Heavens and the Eastern Lands, and we should never dare to go against it. Further, in the lineages that discuss eternal existence, the myriad dharmas are all eternal existence: body and mind are not divided.[81] And in the lineages that discuss extinction, all dharmas are extinction: essence and form are not divided.[82] How could we say, on the contrary, that the body is

---

78. 性海 (SHOKAI), lit. "essence-ocean."

79. The *Avataṃsaka-sūtra* (called *Kegon-kyo* in Japanese and the *Garland Sutra* in English) records many questions put to the Buddha by a Brahman called Senika. See chap. 6, *Soku-shin-ze-butsu.*

80. Master Nanyo Echu (675?–775), successor of Master Daikan Eno. "National Master" was his title as teacher of the Emperor. See for example chapters 6, 18, 19, and 44.

81. For example, the Sarvāsti-vāda school, rendered into Chinese as 説一切有部 (SETSU-ISSAI-U-BU), or "the School which Preaches the Existence of All Things," held that dharmas have a real existence in the past, present, and future. This school flourished in India for many centuries and was widely studied in China and Japan.

82. "Extinction" is 寂滅 (JAKUMETSU), which was sometimes used as a translation of the Sanskrit *nirvāṇa*, but which here is opposed to 常住 (JOJU), "eternal existence." Thus, "lineages that discuss extinction" roughly correspond to the Śūnyatā school, or 空門 (KUMON), i.e., the school that stressed the teachings of *śūnyatā*, which deny that there can be any static existence.

mortal but the mind is eternal? Does that not violate right reason? Furthermore, we should realize that living-and-dying is just nirvāṇa;[83] [Buddhists] have never discussed nirvāṇa outside of living-and-dying. Moreover, even if we wrongly imagine the understanding that *mind becomes eternal by getting free of the body* to be the same as the Buddha-wisdom which is free of life and death, the mind that is conscious of this understanding still appears and disappears momentarily, and so it is not eternal at all. Then isn't [this understanding] unreliable? We should taste and reflect. The principle that body and mind are one reality is being constantly spoken by the Buddha-Dharma. So how could it be, on the contrary, that while this body appears and disappears, the mind independently leaves the body and does not appear or disappear? If there is a time when [body and mind] are one reality, and another time when they are not one reality, then it might naturally follow that the Buddha's preaching has been false. Further, if we think that life and death are something to get rid of, we will commit the sin of hating the Buddha-Dharma. How could we not guard against this? Remember, the lineage of the Dharma which [asserts that] *in the Buddha-Dharma the essential state of mind universally includes all forms*, describes the whole great world of Dharma inclusively, without dividing essence and form, and without discussing appearance and disappearance. There is no [state]—not even bodhi or nirvāṇa—that is different from the essential state of mind. All dharmas, myriad phenomena and accumulated things, are totally just the one mind, without exclusion or disunion. All these various lineages of the Dharma assert that [myriad things and phenomena] are the even and balanced undivided mind, other than which there is nothing; and this is just how Buddhists have understood the essence of mind. That being so, how could we divide this one reality into body and mind, or into life-and-death and nirvāṇa? We are already the Buddha's disciples. Let us not touch with our ears those noises from the tongues of madmen who speak non-Buddhist views.

[51] [Someone] asks, "Must a person who is devoted to this Zazen always adhere spotlessly to the precepts?"

I say: Keeping the precepts, and pure conduct,[84] are the standard of the Zen lineages and the usual habit of Buddhist patriarchs. [But] those who have not yet received the precepts, or who have broken the precepts, are not without their share [of the benefit of Zazen].

[51] [Someone] asks, "Is there nothing to prevent a person who practices this Zazen from also performing mantra and quiet-reflection practices?"[85]

I say: When I was in China, I heard the true essence of the teachings from a true master; he said that he had never heard that any of the patriarchs who received the authentic

83. The Sanskrit word *nirvāṇa* literally means the extinction of a flame. See Glossary.

84. 持戒梵行 (JIKAI-BONGYO). 梵行 (BONGYO) represents the Sanskrit *brāhma-carya* (see Glossary). 行持 (GYOJI), lit. "Conduct and Keeping" or "Practice and Continuance" is the title of chap. 29.

85. 真言止観の行 (SHINGON-SHIKAN *no* GYO). 真言 (SHINGON), lit. "truth-word" means mantra. The use of a mantra is characteristic of the esoteric Buddhism of the Shingon Sect. 止観 (SHIKAN), lit. "ceasing and reflecting," representing the Sanskrit words *śamatha* (quietness) and *vipaśyanā* (insight, reflection), is a practice of the Tendai Sect: the method of practice is almost the same as the practice of Zazen explained by Master Dogen, but in the Tendai Sect the practice is not regarded as sufficient in itself.

transmission of the Buddha-seal ever performed such practices additionally, in the Western Heavens or in the Eastern Lands, in the past or in the present. Certainly, unless we devote ourselves to one thing, we will not attain complete wisdom.

[52] [Someone] asks, "Should this practice also be undertaken by lay men and lay women, or is it performed only by people who have left home?"

I say: An ancestral master has been heard to say that, with respect to understanding of the Buddha-Dharma, we must not choose between men and women, high or low.

[52] [Someone] asks, "People who leave home get free of all involvements at once, so they have no hindrances in practicing Zazen and pursuing the truth. How can a busy lay person devotedly do training and be at one with the unintentional state of Buddhist truth?"

I say: In general, the Buddhist Patriarch,[86] overfilled with pity, left open a wide and great gate of compassion so that all living beings could experience and enter [the state of truth]; what human being or god could not want to enter? Thus, when we research the past and the present, there are many confirmations of such [experience and entry]. For instance, Daiso[87] and Junso[88] were, as emperors, very busy with affairs of state, [but] they pursued the truth by sitting in Zazen and realized the Buddhist Patriarch's great truth. Both Minister Lee and Minister Bo, serving as [the emperor's] lieutenants, were the arms and legs of the whole nation, [but] they pursued the truth by sitting in Zazen and experienced and entered the Buddhist Patriarch's truth. This [practice-and-experience] rests only upon whether or not the will is present; it does not relate to whether the body stays at home or leaves home. Moreover, any person who profoundly discerns the superiority or inferiority of things will naturally have belief. Still more, those who think that worldly affairs hinder the Buddha-Dharma only know that there is no Buddha-Dharma in the world; they do not know that there are no worldly dharmas in the state of Buddha. Recently in great Sung [China] there was [a man] called Minister Hyo, a high-ranking official who was accomplished in the Patriarch's truth. In his later years he made a poem in which he expressed himself as follows:

When official business allows, I like to sit in Zazen.
I have seldom slept with my side touching a bed.
Though I have now become Prime Minister,
My fame as a veteran practitioner has spread across the four seas.

This was somebody with no time free from official duties but, because his will to the Buddha's truth was deep, he was able to attain the truth. We should reflect on ourselves [in comparison] with him, and we should reflect on the present [in comparison] with those days. In the great Kingdom of Sung, the present generation of kings and ministers, officials and commoners, men and women, all apply their mind to the Patriarch's truth, without exception. Both the military and literary classes are resolved to

---

86. 仏祖 (BUSSO) is the title of chap. 15. Translated as "Buddhist patriarchs," it refers to the Buddhist patriarchs in general; translated as "the Buddhist Patriarch," it usually refers to the Buddha or to Master Bodhidharma.

87. 代宗 (DAISO), a Tang emperor who reigned from 763 to 779, and a student of Master Nanyo Echu.

88. 順宗 (JUNSO), another Tang emperor, who reigned from 805 to 806.

practice [Za]zen and to learn the truth. Those who resolve it will, in many cases, undoubtedly clarify the mental state. Thus, it can naturally be inferred that worldly affairs do not hinder the Buddha-Dharma. When the real Buddha-Dharma spreads throughout a nation the buddhas and the gods guard [that nation] ceaselessly, so the reign is peaceful. When the imperial reign is peaceful, the Buddha-Dharma comes into its own. Furthermore, when Śākyamuni was in the world, [even] people of heavy sins and wrong views were able to get the truth, and in the orders of the ancestral masters, [even] hunters and old woodcutters entered the state of realization, to say nothing of other people. We need only research the teaching and the state of truth of a true teacher.

[56] [Someone] asks, "Even in the present corrupt world in this latter age,[89] is it still possible to realize the state of real experience when we perform this practice?"

I say: Philosophers have occupied themselves with such concepts and forms, but in the real teaching of the Great Vehicle, without discriminating between "right," "imitative," and "latter" Dharma, we say that all those who practice attain the state of truth. Furthermore, in this directly-transmitted right Dharma, both in entering the Dharma and getting the body out, we receive and use the treasure of ourselves. Those who are practicing can naturally know whether they have got the state of real experience or not, just as people who are using water can tell by themselves whether it is cold or warm.

[57] [Someone] asks, "It is said that in the Buddha-Dharma once we have clearly understood the principle that mind here and now is buddha, even if our mouth does not recite the sutras and our body does not practice the Buddha-way, we are not lacking in the Buddha-Dharma at all. Just to know that the Buddha-Dharma originally resides in each of us is the whole of the attainment of the truth. There is no need to seek anything else from other people. How much less need we bother about pursuing the truth in Zazen?"

I say: These words are extremely unreliable. If it is as you say, how could any intelligent person fail to understand this principle once it had been explained to them? Remember, we learn the Buddha-Dharma just when we give up views of subject and object. If knowing that *we ourselves are just buddha* could be called the attainment of the truth, Śākyamuni would not have bothered to teach the moral way in the past. I would like now to prove this through the subtle criteria of the ancient patriarchs:

Long ago, there was a monk called Prior Soku[90] in the order of Zen Master Hogen.[91] Zen Master Hogen asks him, *"Prior Soku, how long have you been in my order?"*

Soku says, *"I have served in the Master's order for three years already."*

---

89. 末代 (MATSUDAI). 末 stands for 末法 (MAPPO), "latter Dharma." The years after the Buddha's death were divided into three periods: 正法 (SHOBO), "right Dharma," the first five hundred years during which the Dharma would flourish; 像法 (ZOHO), "imitative Dharma," the next one thousand years during which the Dharma begins to pale; and 末法 (MAPPO), "latter Dharma," the next ten thousand years during which the Dharma degenerates. See Glossary under *Saddharma.*

90. 則公監院 (SOKUKO-KAN-IN). 則 (SOKU) is the monk's name. 公 (KO) is an honorific used for both priests and laymen, approximately equivalent to *san* in modern Japanese. 監院 (KAN-IN) or 監寺 (KANSU) is one of the six main officers of a big temple.

91. Master Hogen Bun-eki (885–958), successor of Master Rakan Keishin and founder of the Hogen Sect.

The Zen Master says, *"You are a recent member of the order. Why do you never ask me about the Buddha-Dharma?"*

Soku says, *"I must not deceive you, Master. Before, when I was in the order of Zen Master Seiho, I realized the state of peace and joy in the Buddha-Dharma."*

The Zen Master says, *"Relying upon what words were you able to enter?"*

Soku says, *"I once asked Seiho: Just what is the student that is I?*[92] *Seiho said: The children of fire*[93] *come looking for fire."*

Hogen says, *"Nice words. But I am afraid that you may not have understood."*

Soku says, *"The children of fire belong to fire. [So] I understood that their being fire yet looking for fire represented my being myself yet looking for myself."*

The Zen Master says, *"I have become sure that you did not understand. If the Buddha-Dharma were like that, it could never have been transmitted until today."*

At this Soku became embarrassed and distressed, and he stood up [to leave]. [But] on the road he thought, *"The Zen Master is [respected] throughout the country [as] a good counselor, and he is a great guiding master to five hundred people. There must surely have been some merit in his criticism of my wrongness."*

[Soku] goes back to the Zen Master to confess and to prostrate himself in apology. Then he asks, *"Just what is the student that is I?"*

The Zen Master says, *"The children of fire come looking for fire."*

Under the influence of these words, Soku grandly realized the Buddha-Dharma.

Clearly, the Buddha-Dharma is never known with the intellectual understanding that *we ourselves are just buddha.* If the intellectual understanding that *we ourselves are just buddha* were the Buddha-Dharma, the Zen Master could not have guided [Soku] by using the former words, and he would not have admonished [Soku] as he did. Solely and directly, from our first meeting with a good counselor, we should ask the standards of practice, and we should single-mindedly pursue the truth by sitting in Zazen, without allowing a single recognition or half an understanding to remain in our minds. Then the subtle method of the Buddha-Dharma will not be [practiced] in vain.

[61] [Someone] asks, "When we hear of India and China in the past and present, there are those who realized the state of truth on hearing the voice of a bamboo, or who clarified the mind on seeing the colors of the flowers.[94] Furthermore, the Great Teacher Śākyamuni experienced the truth when he saw the bright star, the Venerable Ānanda[95] realized the Dharma when a temple flagpole fell, and not only that: among the five

---

92. 学人の自己 (GAKUNIN *no* JIKO). 学人 (GAKUNIN), student, was used by a student to refer to himself. 自己 (JIKO) means "self." So Soku's question was "What am I?"

93. 丙丁童子 (BYOJO-DOJI). 丙 (BYO or HEI), is the third calendar sign, read as *hinoe* or "older brother of fire." 丁 (JO or TEI) is the fourth calendar sign, read as *hinoto* or "younger brother of fire." The words "The children of fire come looking for fire" suggest real effort of a practitioner to pursue what is already there. 童子 (DOJI) means child.

94. These examples of Buddhist masters realizing the truth are recorded in detail in chap. 9, *Keisei-sanshiki.*

95. Master Ānanda was the second patriarch in India—the successor of Master Mahākāśyapa.

lineages following from the Sixth Patriarch[96] many people have clarified the mental state under the influence of a single word or half a line of verse. Had they all, without exception, pursued the truth by sitting in Zazen?"

I say: We should know that these people of the past and present who clarified the mind on seeing forms and who realized the truth on hearing sounds, were all without intellectual doubt in pursuing the truth, and just in the moment of the present there was no second person.

[62] [Someone] asks, "In India and China, the people are originally unaffected and straight. Being at the center of the civilized world makes them so. As a result, when they are taught the Buddha-Dharma they understand and enter very quickly. In our country, from ancient times the people have had little benevolence and wisdom, and it is difficult for us to accumulate the seeds of rightness. Being the savages and barbarians[97] [of the south-east] makes us so. How could we not regret it? Furthermore, people who have left home in this country are inferior even to the lay people of the great nations; our whole society is stupid, and our minds are narrow and small. We are deeply attached to the results of intentional effort, and we like superficial quality. Can people like this expect to experience the Buddha-Dharma straight away, even if they sit in Zazen?"

I say: As you say, the people of our country are not yet universally benevolent and wise, and some people are indeed crooked. Even if we preach right and straight Dharma to them, they will turn nectar into poison. They easily tend toward fame and gain, and it is hard for them to dissolve their delusions and attachments. On the other hand, to experience and enter the Buddha-Dharma, one need not always use the worldly wisdom of human beings and gods as a vessel for transcendence of the world.[98] When the Buddha was in [the] world, [an old monk] experienced the fourth effect [when hit] by a ball,[99] and [a prostitute] clarified the great state of truth after putting on a kaṣāya;[100] both were dull people, stupid and silly creatures. But aided by right belief, they had the means to escape their delusion. Another case was the devout woman preparing a midday meal who disclosed the state of realization when she saw a stupid old bhikṣu[101] sitting in quietness. This did not derive from her wisdom, did not derive from writings, did not depend on words, and did not depend on talk; she was

96. Master Daikan Eno.

97. 盤夷 (BAN-I). As the center of civilization, the Chinese supposed the existence of four groups of barbarians surrounding them. These included 南蕃 (NANBAN), the savages of the south and 東夷 (TO-I), the barbarians of the east. So the words "savages and barbarians" suggest people living to the south and to the east of China, including the Japanese.

98. 出世 (SHUSSE) can be interpreted either as "to transcend the secular world" or as "to manifest oneself in the world." In the latter usage, the words usually mean to become the master of a big temple.

99. A young monk wanted to play a joke on a stupid old monk who lived in the Buddha's order. So he led the old monk into a dark room and hit him with a ball, saying, *"You have got the first effect."* He hit him again and said, *"You have got the second effect."* Then he hit him a third time and said, *"You have got the third effect."* Finally he hit him one last time and said, *"You have got the fourth effect."* But strangely, when the old monk came out of the dark room he had actually experienced the fourth effect. 四果 (SHIKA), the fourth effect, refers to the state of *arhat*, that is, the ultimate state of Buddhism.

100. The story of the prostitute who put on a kaṣāya (Buddhist robe) as a joke is recorded in chap. 12, *Kesa-kudoku*.

101. A Buddhist monk.

aided only by her right belief. Furthermore, Śākyamuni's teachings have been spreading through the three-thousand-world only for around two thousand or so years. Countries are of many kinds; not all are nations of benevolence and wisdom. How could all people, moreover, possess only intelligence and wisdom, keenness [of ear] and clarity [of eye]? But the right Dharma of the Tathāgata is originally furnished with unthinkably great virtue and power, and so when the time comes it will spread through those countries. When people just practice with right belief, the clever and the stupid alike will attain the truth. Just because our country is not a nation of benevolence or wisdom and the people are dull-witted, do not think that it is impossible for us to grasp the Buddha-Dharma. Still more, all human beings have the right seeds of prajñā in abundance. It may simply be that few of us have experienced the state directly, and so we are immature in receiving and using it.

[65] The above questions and answers have come and gone, and the alternation between audience and speaker has been untidy. How many times have I caused flowers to exist in flowerless space?[102] On the other hand, the fundamental principle of pursuing the truth by sitting in Zazen has never been transmitted to this country; anyone who hoped to know it would have been disappointed. This is why I intend to gather together the few experiences I had abroad, and to record the secrets of an enlightened teacher,[103] so that they may be heard by any practitioner who desires to hear them. In addition there are standards and conventions for monasteries and temples, but there is not enough time to teach them now, and they must not be [taught] in haste.

[66] In general, it was very fortunate for the people of our country that, even though we are situated east of the Dragon Sea and are far separated by clouds and mist, from around the reigns of Kinmei[104] and Yomei,[105] the Buddha-Dharma of the west spread to us in the east. However, confusion has multiplied over concepts and forms, and facts and circumstances, disturbing the situation of practice. Now, because we make do with tattered robes and mended bowls, tying thatch so that we can sit and train by the blue cliffs and white rocks, the matter of the ascendant state of buddha becomes apparent at once, and we swiftly master the great matter of a lifetime of practice. This is just the decree of Ryuge [mountain],[106] and the legacy of Kukkuṭapāda [mountain].[107] The forms and standards for sitting in Zazen may be practiced following *Fukan-zazengi* which I compiled in the Karoku era.[108]

---

102. Here 空華 (KUGE), "flowers in space," represents abstract images as opposed to reality. (In chap. 42, *Kuge,* flowers in space and real flowers are identified.)

103. Master Tendo Nyojo.

104. 539–571.

105. 585–587.

106. Master Ryuge Koton (835–923), successor of Master Tozan Ryokai, lived on Ryuge mountain and made many poems praising the beautiful scenery of nature.

107. Master Mahākāśyapa, successor of the Buddha, is said to have died on Kukkuṭapāda mountain in Magadha.

108. The Karoku era was from 1225 to 1227. Master Dogen came back to Japan in the late summer of 1227 and wrote his first draft of *Fukan-zazengi (The Universal Guide to the Standard Method of Zazen)* shortly after. This initial version is called 真筆本 (SHINPITSU-BON), or "the Original Edition." After revising this edition, Master Dogen, finally arrived at the 流布本 (RUFU-BON), or "the Popular Edition." See Appendix.

[68] Now, in spreading the Buddha's teaching throughout a nation, on the one hand, we should wait for the king's decree, but on the other hand, when we recall the bequest of Vulture Peak, the kings, nobles, ministers, and generals now manifested in hundred myriad koṭis of realms all have gratefully accepted the Buddha's decree and, not forgetting the original aim of earlier lives to guard and maintain the Buddha's teaching, they have been born. [Within] the frontiers of the spread of that teaching, what place could not be a Buddha-land? Therefore, when we want to disseminate the truth of the Buddhist patriarchs, it is not always necessary to select a [particular] place or to wait for [favorable] circumstances. Shall we just consider today to be the starting point? So I have put this together and I will leave it for wise masters who aspire to the Buddha-Dharma and for the true stream of practitioners who wish, like wandering clouds or transient water weeds, to explore the state of truth.

Mid-autumn day, [in the 3rd year of] Kanki.[109]
Written by the śramaṇa[110] Dogen, who entered Sung [China] and received the transmission of the Dharma.

Shobogenzo Bendowa

---

109. The 15th day of the 8th lunar month, 1231.
110. Monk (see Glossary).

[2]

摩訶般若波羅密

MAKA-HANNYA-HARAMITSU

Mahā-prajñā-pāramitā

Maka is a phonetic rendering of the Sanskrit word mahā, which means "great." ***Hannya*** *is a phonetic rendering of the Sanskrit word prajñā which can be translated as "real wisdom" or "intuitive reflection."* ***Haramitsu*** *is a phonetic rendering of the Sanskrit word pāramitā which literally means "to have arrived at the opposite shore," that is, to have accomplished the truth. So* ***maka-hannya-haramitsu*** *means the accomplishment which is great real wisdom. In this chapter, Master Dogen wrote his interpretation of the Mahā-prajñā-pāramitā-hṛdaya-sūtra. Hṛdaya means heart. This short sutra, usually called "the Heart Sutra," represents the heart of the six hundred volumes of the Mahā-prajñā-pāramitā-sūtra. Even though it is very short, the Heart Sutra contains the most fundamental principle of Buddhism. What is the most fundamental principle? Prajñā. What is prajñā? Prajñā, or real wisdom, is a kind of intuitive ability that occurs in our body and mind, when our body and mind are in the state of balance and harmony. We normally think that wisdom is something based on the intellect, but Buddhists believe that wisdom, on which our decisions are based, is not intellectual but intuitive. The right decision comes from the right state of body and mind, and the right state of body and mind comes when our body and mind are balanced and harmonized. So mahā-prajñā-pāramitā is wisdom that we have when our body and mind are balanced and harmonized. And Zazen is the practice by which our body and mind enter the state of balance and harmony. Mahā-prajñā-pāramitā, then, is the essence of Zazen.*

[71] ***When Bodhisattva Avalokiteśvara***[1] *practices the profound prajñā-pāramitā,* the whole body[2] *reflects that the five aggregates*[3] *are totally empty.*[4] The five aggregates are matter, feeling, thinking, enaction, and consciousness. They are five instances of prajñā. Reflection is prajñā itself. When this principle is preached and realized, it is said that *matter is just the immaterial*[5] *and the immaterial is just matter.* Matter is matter, the imma-

---

1. 観自在菩薩 (KANJIZAI-BOSATSU), lit. "Bodhisattva of Free Reflection," is one of the Chinese renderings of Bodhisattva Avalokiteśvara (see chap. 33, *Kannon*, and Lotus Sutra chap. 25). This paragraph begins with the same words as the Heart Sutra.

2. Master Dogen added to the first line of the Heart Sutra the words 渾身 (KONSHIN), "whole body," as the subject of 照見 (SHOKEN), "to reflect."

3. 五蘊 (GO-UN), from the Sanskrit *pañca-skandha*. See Glossary.

4. "Empty" 空 (KU), which represents the Sanskrit *śūnyatā* (see Glossary). As an adjective, 空 (KU) means bare, bald, naked, empty, as it is.

5. "The immaterial" is also 空 (KU), this time used as a noun. In this case, 空 (KU) means the immaterial, that which is empty, or devoid of physical substance; that is, the spiritual or mental face of reality as opposed to matter. In other cases, the noun 空 (KU) means the empty state, that is, the state in which reality is as it is. See chap. 22, *Bussho*.

terial is the immaterial.[6] They are hundreds of things,[7] and myriad phenomena. Twelve instances of prajñā-pāramitā are the twelve entrances [of sense-perception].[8] There are also eighteen instances of prajñā.[9] They are eyes, ears, nose, tongue, body, and mind;[10] sights, sounds, smells, tastes, sensations, and properties;[11] plus the consciousnesses of eyes, ears, nose, tongue, body, and mind. There are a further four instances of prajñā. They are suffering, accumulation, cessation, and the Way.[12] There are a further six instances of prajñā. They are giving, pure [observance of] precepts, patience, diligence, meditation, and prajñā [itself].[13] One further instance of prajñā-pāramitā is realized as the present moment. It is the state of anuttara-samyak-saṃbodhi.[14] There are three further instances of prajñā-pāramitā. They are past, present, and future.[15] There are six further instances of prajñā. They are earth, water, fire, wind, space, and consciousness.[16] And there are a further four instances of prajñā that are constantly practiced in everyday life: they are walking, standing, sitting, and lying down.[17]

[74] In the order of Śākyamuni Tathāgata there is a bhik˘ u[18] who secretly thinks, "*I shall bow in veneration of the profound prajñā-pāramitā. Although in this state there is no appearance and disappearance of real dharmas,*[19] *there are still understandable explanations of all precepts, all balanced states, all kinds of wisdom, all kinds of liberation, and all views. There are*

---

6. The sutra says 色即是空 (SHIKI-SOKU-ZE-KU), "matter is just the immaterial," and 空即是色 (KU-SOKU-ZE-SHIKI), "the immaterial is just matter." Master Dogen added 色是色 (SHIKI-ZE-SHIKI), matter is matter, and 空是空 (KU-ZE-KU), the immaterial is the immaterial.

7. 百艸 (HYAKUSO), lit. "hundreds of weeds."

8. 十二入 (JUNI-NYU), "twelve entrances," from the Sanskrit *dvādaśayatanāni,* are the six sense organs and their objects.

9. 十八界 (JUHACHI-KAI), lit. "eighteen spheres," from the Sanskrit *aṣṭādaśa dhātavaḥ,* are the senses, their objects, and the six corresponding kinds of consciousness. See Glossary under *dhātu-loka.*

10. 身 (SHIN), "body," from the Sanskrit *kāya,* means the body, or the skin, as the organ of touch. 意 (I), "mind," from the Sanskrit *manas,* means the mind as the center of thought, which is placed on the same level as the senses, below *prajñā.*

11. 触 法 (SHOKU, HO) "sensations and properties" from the Sanskrit *sparśa* and *dharma,* represent the objects of body and mind as sense organs.

12. 四諦 (SHITAI), the four philosophies, or The Four [Noble] Truths, are 苦 集 滅 道 (KU, SHU, METSU, DO). These words derive from the Sanskrit *duḥkha-satya* (truth of suffering), *saṃdhaya-satya* (truth of accumulation), *nirodha-satya* (truth of dissolution), and *mārga-satya* (truth of the right way).

13. 六度 (ROKUDO), the six pāramitās. In Sanskrit they are as follows: Giving is *dāna,* explained in detail in chap. 45, *Bodaisatta-shishobo.* Pure [observance of] precepts is *śīla.* Patience is *kṣānti.* Diligence is *vīrya.* Meditation is *dhyāna.* (*Dhyāna* is sometimes represented phonetically in Shobogenzo by the Chinese characters 禅那 (ZEN-NA), but in this case *dhyāna* is expressed as 静慮 (JO-RYO), lit. "quiet thought.") The sixth pāramitā, real wisdom, is *prajñā.*

14. The Sanskrit *anuttara-samyak-saṃbodhi* (see chap. 1, note 2) is rendered into Chinese in the second paragraph of this chapter as 無上正等菩提 (MUJO-SHOTO-BODAI), "the supreme right and balanced state of bodhi." Alternative renderings into Chinese are 無上正等覚 (MUJO-SHOTO-KAKU), "the supreme right and balanced state of truth," and 無上等正覚 (MUJO-TOSHO-KAKU), "the supreme balanced and right state of truth."

15. 三世 (SANZE), the three times.

16. 六大 (ROKUDAI), the six elements. In Sanskrit, *saḍ dhātavaḥ.* See Glossary under *dhātu.*

17. 四儀 (SHIGI), the four forms of behavior.

18. The Sanskrit word *bhikṣu* (originally "mendicant"), means a Buddhist monk.

19. 無諸法生滅 (MU-SHOHO-SHOMETSU, or SHOHO *no* SHOMETSU *nashi*). The Heart Sutra says 是諸法空相。不生不滅。(ZE-SHOHO-KUSO. FUSHO-FUMETSU.)—"*These real dharmas are bare manifestations. They neither appear nor disappear.*"

also understandable explanations of the effect of one who has entered the stream, the effect of [being subject to] one return, the effect of [not being subject to] returning, and the effect of the arhat.[20] *There are also understandable explanations of [people of] independent awakening,*[21] *and [people of] bodhi.*[22] *There are also understandable explanations of the supreme right and balanced state of bodhi. There are also understandable explanations of the treasures of Buddha, Dharma, and Saṃgha. There are also understandable explanations of turning the wonderful Dharma-wheel*[23] *to save sentient beings."* The Buddha, knowing the bhikṣu's mind, tells him, *"This is how it is. This is how it is. The profound prajñā-pāramitā is too subtle and fine to fathom."*[24]

The bhikṣu's *secretly working concrete mind*[25] at this moment is, in the state of bowing in veneration of real dharmas, prajñā itself—whether or not [real dharmas] are without appearance and disappearance—and this is a *venerative bow* itself. Just at this moment of bowing in veneration, prajñā is realized as explanations which can be understood: [explanations] from *precepts, balance, and wisdom,*[26] to *saving sentient beings,* and so on. This state is described as *being without.*[27] Explanations of the state of *being without* can thus be understood. Such is the profound, subtle, unfathomable prajñā-pāramitā.

[76] The God Indra[28] asks the venerable monk Subhuti,[29] *"Virtuous One! When bodhisattva-mahāsattvas*[30] *want to research*[31] *the profound prajñā-pāramitā, how should they research it?"*

---

20. The *śrāvaka,* or intellectual Buddhist, passes through these four stages. In Sanskrit, the first is *srotāpanna,* the second is *sakṛdāgāmin,* the third is *anāgāmin,* and the fourth is *arhat.*

21. 独覚 (DOKU-KAKU), lit. "independently awakened," means a *pratyekabuddha,* a naturalistic Buddhist. The distinction between *śrāvakas, pratyekabuddhas, bodhisattvas,* and *buddhas,* which the Buddha explains in the Lotus Sutra, is described in chap. 24, *Bukkyo.*

22. 菩提 (BODAI), in this case seems to suggest a person who has the state of bodhi, that is, a bodhisattva.

23. 転妙法輪 (TENMYOHORIN), "turning the wonderful Dharma-wheel" means Buddhist preaching. See chap. 74, *Tenborin.*

24. This passage is quoted from the Dai-hannya-kyo, chap. 291, Attachment and Non-attachment to Form.

25. 竊作是念 (SETSU-SA-ZE-NEN). In the sutra, these characters lit. mean "secretly made this thought." But 作 (SA), "make," also means "to act," or "to function;" 是 (ZE), "this," also means "concrete;" and 念 (NEN), "thought," or "image in the mind," also means "mindfulness," or "state of mind." Master Dogen interpreted 念 (NEN) not as a thought but as the monk's state of mind, which is *prajñā* itself, which is the state of action itself.

26. Precepts, balance, and wisdom are 三学 (SANGAKU), the three kinds of training. See Glossary under *tisraḥ śiksāḥ.*

27. 無 (MU, *nashi*) expresses absence. In this paragraph, 無生滅 (MU-SHOMETSU) is translated as "there is no appearance and disappearance" (see note 19), and "without appearance and disappearance." As a noun 無 (MU) means "the state of being without," i.e., the state that is free. This usage is explained in detail in chap. 22, *Bussho.* The character 無 (MU) appears over twenty times in the Heart Sutra.

28. 天帝釈 (TENTAI-SHAKU). 天帝 (TENTAI) is lit. "God-Emperor" and 釈 (SHAKU) stands for Śakra-devānām-indra, which is the Sanskrit name of the god in question. He (sometimes she) was incorporated into Buddhism as a guardian of Buddhist teachings. See Glossary.

29. 具寿善現 (GUJU-ZENGEN). 具寿 (GUJU), or "venerable monk," is derived from the Sanskrit *āyuṣmat,* a term of reverence. 善現 (ZENGEN), lit. "Good Manifestation," is the Chinese rendering of Subhuti, one of the Buddha's disciples.

30. Mahāsattva literally means "great being." Both *bodhisattva* and *mahāsattva* describe a Buddhist

Subhuti replies, *"Kauśika!*[32] *When bodhisattva-mahāsattvas want to research the profound prajñā-pāramitā, they should research it as space."*[33]

So researching prajñā is space itself. Space is the research of prajñā.

[77] The God Indra subsequently addresses the Buddha, *"World-Honored One! When good sons and good daughters receive and retain, read and recite, think reasonably about, and expound to others this profound prajñā-pāramitā that you have preached, how should I guard it? My only desire, World-Honored One, is that you will show me compassion and teach me."*

Then the venerable monk Subhuti says to the God Indra, *"Kauśika! Do you see something which you must guard, or not?"*

The God Indra says, *"No, Virtuous One, I do not see anything here that I must guard."*

Subhuti says, *"Kauśika! When good sons and good daughters abide in the profound prajñā-pāramitā as thus preached, they are just guarding it. When good sons and good daughters abide in the profound prajñā-pāramitā as thus preached, they never stray. Remember, even if all human and nonhuman beings were looking for an opportunity to harm them, in the end it would be impossible. Kauśika! If you want to guard the bodhisattvas who abide in the profound prajñā-pāramitā as thus preached, it is no different from wanting to guard space."*[34]

Remember, to receive and retain, to read and recite, and to think reasonably about [prajñā], are just to guard prajñā. And to want to guard it is to receive and retain it, to read and recite it, and so on.

[78] My late Master, the eternal Buddha, says:

Whole body like a mouth, hanging in space;
Not asking if the wind is east, west, south, or north,
For all others equally, it chatters prajñā:
Chin Ten Ton Ryan Chin Ten Ton.[35]

This is the chattering of prajñā [transmitted] by Buddhist patriarchs from rightful successor to rightful successor. It is prajñā as the whole body, it is prajñā as the whole of others,[36] it is prajñā as the whole self, and it is prajñā as the whole east, west, south, and north.

[79] Śākyamuni Buddha says, *"Śāriputra!*[37] *These many sentient beings should abide in this prajñā-pāramitā as buddhas. When they serve offerings to, bow in veneration of, and consider,*

---

practitioner.

31. 学 (GAKU) includes both the meaning of "learn" and of "practice." Research of *prajñā* as space suggests the concrete practice of Zazen.

32. Kauśika is another name of Indra. See Glossary.

33. 虚空 (KOKU), "empty space," or "space," from the Sanskrit *ākāśa*, is the title of chap. 77, *Koku*.

34. This story is also from the *Dai-hannya-kyo*, chap. 291.

35. This poem about a windbell is from *Nyojo-osho-go-roku (Record of the Words of Master [Tendo] Nyojo)*. The last line of the poem represents the sound of the windbell. The original characters can be read in several other ways in Japanese; for example, *teki cho to ryo teki cho to*. The original Chinese pronunciation is not known.

36. "Others" is 陀 (TA), which sometimes means "others" and sometimes means "the external world." In Master Dogen's commentary it suggests the latter meaning.

37. Śāriputra was one of the Buddha's ten great disciples, and said to be foremost in wisdom. He died while the Buddha was still alive. Much of the *Mahā-prajñā-pāramitā-sūtra* is addressed to Śāriputra.

the prajñā-pāramitā, they should be as if serving offerings to and bowing in veneration of the buddha-bhagavats.[38] *Why? [Because] the prajñā-pāramitā is no different from the buddha-bhagavats, and the buddha-bhagavats are no different from the prajñā-pāramitā. The prajñā-pāramitā is just the buddha-bhagavats themselves, and the buddha-bhagavats are just the prajñā-pāramitā itself. Wherefore? Because, Śāriputra, the apt, right, and balanced state of truth, which all the tathāgatas have, is always realized by virtue of the prajñā-pāramitā. Because, Śāriputra, all bodhisattva-mahāsattvas, the independently awakened, arhats, those beyond returning, those who will return once, those received into the stream, and so on, always attain realization by virtue of the prajñā-pāramitā. And because, Śāriputra, all of the ten virtuous paths of action*[39] *in the world, the four states of meditation,*[40] *the four immaterial balanced states,*[41] *and the five mystical powers*[42] *are always realized by virtue of the prajñā-pāramitā."*

[80] So buddha-bhagavats are the prajñā-pāramitā, and the prajñā-pāramitā is *these real dharmas*. These *real dharmas* are *bare manifestations*: they are *neither appearing nor disappearing, neither dirty nor pure, neither increasing nor decreasing*. The realization of this prajñā-pāramitā is the realization of buddha-bhagavats. We should inquire into it, and we should experience it. To serve offerings to it and to bow in veneration is just to serve and to attend buddha-bhagavats, and it is buddha-bhagavats in service and attendance.

Shobogenzo Maka-hannya-haramitsu

Preached to the assembly at Kannon-dori-in temple on a day of the summer retreat in the 1st year of Tenpuku.[43]

Copied in the attendant monks' quarters at Kippo temple in Etsu-u[44] on the 21st day of the 3rd lunar month in spring of the 2nd year of Kangen.[45]

---

38. Bhagavat is a Sanskrit term of veneration. See Glossary.

39. 十善業道 (JU-ZENGODO), or the ten paths of good action, are followed by refraining from doing the ten kinds of bad conduct, namely: killing, stealing, committing adultery, telling lies, two-faced speech, abusive slander, useless gossip, greed, anger, and devotion to wrong views.

40. 四静慮 (SHI-JORYO), or the "four *dhyānas.*" See chap. 90, *Shizen-biku.*

41. 四無色定 (SHI-MUSHIKI-JO) or "the four balanced states which transcend the world of matter" are as follows: 1) 空無辺処定 (KU-MUHEN-SHO-JO), "balance in infinite space;" 2) 識無辺処定 (SHIKI-MUHEN-SHO-JO), "balance in infinite consciousness;" 3) 無所有処定 (MU-SHO-U-SHO-JO), "balance in not having anything;" and 4) 非想非非想処定 (HISO-HIHISO-SHO-JO), "balance in transcendence of thinking and not-thinking." Such enumeration of concepts is characteristic of Theravada Buddhism.

42. 五神通 (GO-JINZU). The five mystical powers are discussed in chap. 25, *Jinzu.*

43. 1233.

44. Corresponds to present-day Fukui prefecture.

45. 1244.

The Heart Sutra of Mahā-prajñā-pāramitā

Bodhisattva Avalokiteśvara, when practicing the profound prajñā-pāramitā, reflects that the five aggregates are totally empty, and overcomes all pain and wrongdoing. Śāriputra, matter is no different from the immaterial, and the immaterial is no different from matter. Matter is just the immaterial, and the immaterial is just matter. Feeling, thinking, enaction, and consciousness are also like this. Śāriputra, these real dharmas are bare manifestations. They are neither appearing nor disappearing, neither dirty nor pure, neither increasing nor decreasing. Therefore, in the state of emptiness, there is no matter, no feeling, thinking, enaction, or consciousness. There are no eyes, ears, nose, tongue, body, mind; no sights, sounds, smells, tastes, sensations, properties. There is no sphere of eyes, nor any other [elementary sphere]: there is no sphere of mind-consciousness. There is no ignorance, and no ending of ignorance, nor any other [causal process]: there is no aging and death, and no ending of aging and death. There is no suffering, accumulation, cessation, or Way. There is no wisdom, and no attaining—because [the state] is non-attainment. Bodhisattvas rely upon prajñā-pāramitā, and therefore their minds have no hindrance. They have no hindrance, and therefore they are without fear. They leave all confused dream-images far behind, and realize the ultimate state of nirvāṇa. The buddhas of the three times rely upon prajñā-pāramitā, and therefore they attain anuttara-samyak-saṃbodhi. So remember: prajñā-pāramitā is a great and mystical spell; it is a great and luminous spell; it is the supreme spell; it is a spell in the unequaled state of equilibrium. It can clear away all suffering. It is real, not empty. Therefore we invoke the spell of prajñā-pāramitā. We invoke the spell as follows:

Gate, gate, pāragate, pārasangate. Bodhi, svāhā.

The Heart Sutra of Prajñā

[3]

現成公案

GENJO-KOAN

The Realized Universe

***Genjo** means "realized," and **koan** is an abbreviation of **kofu-no-antoku,** which was a notice board on which a new law was announced to the public in ancient China. So **koan** expresses a law, or a universal principle. In Shobogenzo, **genjo koan** means the realized law of the Universe, that is Dharma, or the real Universe itself. The fundamental basis of Buddhism is belief in this real Universe, and in **Genjo Koan** Master Dogen preaches to us the realized Dharma, or the real Universe itself. When the seventy-five chapter edition of Shobogenzo was compiled, this chapter was placed first, and from this fact we can recognize its importance.*

[83] **When all dharmas** are [seen as] the Buddha-Dharma, then there is delusion and realization, there is practice, there is life and there is death, there are buddhas and there are ordinary beings. When the myriad dharmas are each not of the self, there is no delusion and no realization, no buddhas and no ordinary beings, no life and no death. The Buddha's truth is originally transcendent over abundance and scarcity, and so there is life and death, there is delusion and realization, there are beings and buddhas. And though it is like this, it is only that flowers, while loved, fall; and weeds while hated, flourish.

[84] Driving ourselves to practice and experience the myriad dharmas is delusion. When the myriad dharmas actively practice and experience ourselves, that is the state of realization. Those who greatly realize[1] delusion are buddhas. Those who are greatly deluded about realization are ordinary beings. There are people who further attain realization on the basis of realization. There are people who increase their delusion in the midst of delusion. When buddhas are really buddhas, they do not need to recognize themselves as buddhas. Nevertheless, they are buddhas in the state of experience, and they go on experiencing the state of buddha.

[85] When we use the whole body-and-mind to look at forms, and when we use the whole body-and-mind to listen to sounds, even though we are sensing them directly, it is not like a mirror's reflection[2] of an image, and not like water and the moon. While we are experiencing one side, we are blind to the other side.

---

1. 大悟 (DAIGO), "great realization," is the title of chap. 26. Here it is used as a verb, 大悟する (DAIGO *suru*), "greatly realize."

2. やどす (yadosu), lit. means "to accommodate."

[86] To learn the Buddha's truth is to learn ourselves. To learn ourselves is to forget ourselves. To forget ourselves is to be experienced by the myriad dharmas. To be experienced by the myriad dharmas is to let our own body-and-mind, and the body-and-mind of the external world, fall away. There is a state in which the traces of realization are forgotten; and it manifests the traces of forgotten realization for a long, long time.

[87] When people first seek the Dharma, we are far removed from the borders of Dharma. [But] as soon as the Dharma is authentically transmitted to us, we are a human being in [our] original element. When a man is sailing along in a boat and he moves his eyes to the shore, he misapprehends that the shore is moving. If he keeps his eyes fixed on the boat, he knows that it is the boat which is moving forward. Similarly, when we try to understand the myriad dharmas on the basis of confused assumptions about body and mind, we misapprehend that our own mind or our own essence may be permanent. If we become familiar with action and come back to this concrete place, the truth is evident that the myriad dharmas are not self. Firewood becomes ash; it can never go back to being firewood. Nevertheless, we should not take the view that ash is its future and firewood is its past. Remember, firewood abides in the place of firewood in the Dharma. It has a past and it has a future. Although it has a past and a future, the past and the future are cut off. Ash exists in the place of ash in the Dharma. It has a past and it has a future. The firewood, after becoming ash, does not again become firewood. Similarly, human beings, after death, do not live again. At the same time, it is an established custom in the Buddha-Dharma not to say that life turns into death. This is why we speak of *no appearance.*[3] And it is the Buddha's preaching established in [the turning of] the Dharma-wheel that death does not turn into life. This is why we speak of *no disappearance.*[3] Life is an instantaneous situation, and death is also an instantaneous situation. It is the same, for example, with winter and spring. We do not think that winter becomes spring, and we do not say that spring becomes summer.

[89] A person getting realization is like the moon being reflected[4] in water: the moon does not get wet, and the water is not broken. Though the light [of the moon] is wide and great, it is reflected in a foot or an inch of water. The whole moon and the whole sky are reflected in a dew-drop on a blade of grass and are reflected in a single drop of water. Realization does not break the individual, just as the moon does not pierce the water. The individual does not hinder the state of realization, just as a dew-drop does not hinder the sky and moon. The depth [of realization] may be as the concrete height [of the moon]. The longness and shortness of its moment should be investigated in large [bodies of] water and small [bodies of] water, and observed in the width and the narrowness of the sky and the moon.[5]

[90] When the Dharma has not yet satisfied the body-and-mind we feel already replete with Dharma. When the Dharma fills the body-and-mind we feel one side to be lacking. For example, sailing out beyond the mountains and into the ocean, when we look around in the four directions, [the ocean] appears only to be round; it does not appear

3. "No appearance" is 不生 (FUSHO). "No disappearance" is 不滅 (FUMETSU). The words 不生不滅 (FUSHO-FUMETSU)—which appear for example in the Heart Sutra, quoted in chap. 2, *Maka-hannya-haramitsu*—express the instantaneousness of the Universe.

4. Throughout this paragraph, "to be reflected in" is originally やどる (yadoru), lit. "to dwell in."

5. We should investigate realization as concrete facts.

to have any other form at all. Nevertheless, this great ocean is not round, and it is not square. Other qualities of the ocean are inexhaustibly many: [to fishes] it is like a palace and [to gods] it is like a string of pearls.[6] But as far as our eyes can see, it just seems to be round. As it is for [the ocean], so it is for the myriad dharmas. In dust and out of the frame,[7] [the myriad dharmas] encompass numerous situations, but we see and understand only as far as our eyes of learning in practice are able to reach. If we wish to hear how the myriad dharmas naturally are,[8] we should remember that besides their appearance of squareness or roundness, the qualities of the oceans and qualities of the mountains are numerous and endless; and that there are worlds in the four directions. Not only the periphery is like this: remember, the immediate present, and a single drop [of water] are also like this.

[91] When fish move through water, however they move, there is no end to the water. When birds fly through the sky, however they fly, there is no end to the sky. At the same time, fish and birds have never, since antiquity, left the water or the sky. Simply, when activity is great, usage is great, and when necessity is small, usage is small. Acting in this state, none fails to realize its limitations at every moment, and none fails to somersault freely at every place; but if a bird leaves the sky it will die at once, and if a fish leaves the water it will die at once. So we can understand that water is life and can understand that sky is life. Birds are life, and fish are life. It may be that life is birds and that life is fish. And beyond this, there may still be further progress. The existence of [their] practice-and-experience, and the existence of their lifetime and their life, are like this. This being so, a bird or fish that aimed to move through the water or the sky [only] after getting to the bottom of water or utterly penetrating the sky, could never find its way or find its place in the water or in the sky. When we find this place, this action is inevitably realized as the Universe. When we find this way, this action is inevitably the realized Universe [itself].[9] This way and this place are neither great nor small; they are neither subjective nor objective; neither have they existed since the past nor do they appear in the present; and so they are present like this. When a human being is practicing and experiencing the Buddha's truth in this state, to get one dharma is to penetrate one dharma, and to meet one act is to perform one act. In this state the place exists and the way is mastered, and therefore the area to be known is not conspicuous. The reason it is so is that this knowing and the perfect realization of the Buddha-Dharma appear together and are experienced together. Do not assume that what is attained will inevitably become self-conscious and be recognized by the intellect. The experience of

6. This sentence alludes to a traditional Buddhist teaching that different subjects see the same ocean in different ways: To fish it is a palace, to gods it is a string of pearls, to humans it is water, and to demons it is blood or pus. 瓔珞 (YORAKU), "string of pearls," represents the Sanskrit muktāhāra, a name for a string of pearls or jewels worn by royalty and nobility in ancient India.

7. 塵中格外 (JINCHU-KAKUGE), "inside dust, outside the frame," means, the secular world and the world experienced in the Buddhist state.

8. 万法の家風 (BANPO *no* KAFU), lit. "the family customs of the myriad dharmas." 家 (KA) means house, home, or family. 風 (FU) means wind, air, style, behavior, custom.

9. 現成公案 (GENJO-KOAN) is used first as a verb, 現成公案す (GENJO-KOAN *su*), and second as a noun, 現成公案 (GENJO-KOAN).

the ultimate state is realized at once. At the same time, its mysterious existence is not necessarily a manifest realization.[10] Realization is the state of ambiguity itself.[11]

[94] Zen Master Hotetsu[12] of Mayoku-zan mountain is using a fan. A monk comes by and asks, *"The nature of air is to be ever-present, and there is no place that [air] cannot reach. Why then does the Master use a fan?"*

The Master says, *"You have only understood that the nature of air is to be ever-present, but you do not yet know the truth[13] that there is no place [air] cannot reach."*

The monk says, *"What is the truth of there being no place [air] cannot reach?"*

At this, the Master just [carries on] using the fan. The monk does prostrations.[14] The real experience of the Buddha-Dharma, the vigorous road of the authentic transmission, is like this. Someone who says that because [the air] is ever-present we need not use a fan, or that even when we do not use [a fan] we can still feel the air, does not know ever-presence, and does not know the nature of air. Because the nature of air is to be ever-present, the behavior[15] of Buddhists has made the Earth manifest itself as gold and has ripened the Long River into curds and whey.[16]

Shobogenzo Genjo-koan

This was written in mid-autumn[17] in the 1st year of Tenpuku,[18] and was presented to the lay disciple Yo Koshu of Chinzei.[19]

Edited in [the 4th] year of Kencho.[20]

---

10. "Manifest realization" and "realization" (in the next sentence) are originally the same characters: 見成 (GENJO).

11. "The state of ambiguity" is 何必 (KAHITSU). A Chinese sentence beginning with these characters would ask the question, "Why should it necessarily be that...?" or "How can it conclusively be decided that...?"

12. A successor of Master Baso Do-itsu.

13. 道理 (DORI) means truth, principle, or fact. The monk was interested in philosophical theory, but the Master recommended him to notice concrete facts.

14. Shinji-shobogenzo pt. 2, no. 23. According to the story in Shinji-shobogenzo, after the monk's prostration, the Master says, "Useless master of monks! If you got a thousand students, what gain would there be?"

15. 風 (FU). Two meanings of 風 (FU) are relevant in this section. The first is "wind" or "air," as in the story. The second is "customs," "manners," or "behavior," as in this usage. See also note 8.

16. Master Goso Ho-en said in his formal preaching, *"To change the Earth into gold, and to churn the Long River into a milky whey."* 酥酪 (SORAKU), or "curds and whey," was some kind of edible dairy product, like yogurt or cheese. 長河 (CHOGA), lit. "the Long River," is the Chinese name for the galaxy we call "the Milky Way."

17. In the lunar calendar, autumn is the 7th, 8th, and 9th lunar months. As the autumn sky is usually very clear, this is a good time to view the moon. Several chapters of Shobogenzo were written around the time of the autumn equinox on the 15th day of the 8th lunar month.

18. 1233.

19. Corresponds to present-day Kyushu.

20. 1252.

[4]

一顆明珠

IKKA-NO-MYOJU

One Bright Pearl

__Ikka__ means "one," __myo__ means "bright" or "clear," and __ju__ means "pearl." So __ikka no myoju__ means one bright pearl. This chapter is a commentary on Master Gensa Shibi's words that the whole Universe in all directions is as splendid as a bright pearl. Master Dogen loved these words, so he wrote about them in this chapter.

[97] **In [this] sāhā-world,**[1] in the great Kingdom of Sung, in Fuchou province, at Gensa-zan temple, [there lived] the Great Master Shu-itsu, whose Dharma-name [as a monk] was Shibi and whose secular surname was Sha.[2] While still a layman he loved fishing, and he would float down the Nantai river on his boat, following the other fishermen. It may have been that he was not waiting even for the fish with golden scales that lands itself without being fished.[3] At the beginning of the Kantsu[4] era of the Tang Dynasty, suddenly he desires to leave secular society; he leaves his boat and enters the mountains. He is already thirty years old, [but] he has realized the precariousness of the floating world and has recognized the nobility of the Buddha's way. At last he climbs Seppo-zan mountain, enters the order of Great Master Shinkaku,[5] and pursues the truth[6] day and night. One day, in order to explore widely the surrounding districts, he leaves the mountain, carrying a [traveling] bag. But as he does so, he stubs his toe on a stone. Bleeding and in great pain, [Master Gensa] all at once seriously reflects as follows: *"[They say] this body is not real existence. Where does the pain come from?"* He thereupon returns to Seppo. Seppo asks him, *"What is it, Bi of the dhūta?"*[7] Gensa says, *"In the end I just cannot be deceived by others."*[8] Seppo, loving these words very much,

---

1. 娑婆世界 (SHABA-SEKAI). 娑婆 (SHABA) represents the Sanskrit sahā-loka-dhatu, which means the world of human beings.

2. Master Gensa Shibi (835–907), successor of Master Seppo Gison. When monks died they were not referred to by the name used in their lifetime. "Great Master Shu-itsu" is Master Gensa's posthumous title. Shibi is his 法諱 (HOKI), or "Dharma [-name] to be avoided." See also notes to chap. 16, *Shisho*.

3. Even as a layman Master Gensa led a relaxed and peaceful life, without worrying about the results of his efforts.

4. 860 to 873.

5. Master Seppo Gison (822–907), successor of Master Tokuzan Senkan. Great Master Shinkaku is his posthumous title.

6. 弁道 (BENDO) expresses the practice of Zazen.

7. 備頭陀 (BIZUDA). 備 (BI) is from the name Shibi. 頭陀 (ZUDA) is from the Sanskrit word dhūta, which means hard practice. Master Gensa was known for his hard practice, so he got the nickname of 備頭陀 (BIZUDA). The twelve dhūta are listed in chap. 30, *Gyoji*. See also LS 2.310.

8. The expression is ironic. Master Gensa makes it sound as if he would like to be able to learn from others, but in the end it is impossible: he can be satisfied not with second-hand knowledge, but only by

says, *"Is there anyone who does not have these words [inside them]? [But] is there anyone who can speak these words?"* Seppo asks further, *"Bi of the dhūta, why do you not go exploring?"*[9] The Master [Gensa] says, *"Bodhidharma did not come to the Eastern Lands; the Second Patriarch did not go to the Western Heavens."*[10] Seppo praised this very much. In his usual life as a fisherman [Master Gensa] had never seen sutras and texts even in a dream. Nevertheless, profundity of will being foremost, his outstanding resolve made itself apparent. Seppo himself considered [Gensa] to be outstanding among the saṃgha; he praised [Gensa] as the pre-eminent member of the order. [Gensa] used vegetable cloth for his one robe, which he never replaced, but patched hundreds of times. Next to his skin he wore clothes of paper, or wore *moxa*.[11] Apart from serving in Seppo's order, he never visited another [good] counselor. Nevertheless, he definitely realized the power to succeed to the Master's Dharma. After he had attained the truth at last, he taught people with the words that the whole Universe in ten directions is one bright pearl. One day a monk asks him, *"I have heard the Master's words that the whole Universe in ten directions is one bright pearl. How should the student understand [this]?"* The Master says, *"The whole Universe in ten directions is one bright pearl. What use is understanding?"* On a later day the Master asks the question back to the monk, *"The whole Universe in ten directions is one bright pearl. How do you understand [this]?"* The monk says, *"The whole Universe in ten directions is one bright pearl. What use is understanding?"* The Master says, *"I see that you are struggling to get inside a demon's cave in a black mountain."*[12]

[101] The present expression *"The whole Universe in ten directions is one bright pearl"* originates with Gensa. The point is that the whole Universe in ten directions is not vast and great, not meager and small, not square or round, not centered or straight, not in a state of vigorous activity, and not disclosed in perfect clarity. Because it is utterly beyond living-and-dying, going-and-coming,[13] it is living-and-dying, going-and-coming. And because it is like this, the past has gone from this place, and the present comes from this place. When we are pursuing the ultimate, who can see it utterly as separate moments? And who can hold it up for examination as a state of total stillness? *"The whole of the ten directions"* describes the ceaseless [process] of pursuing things to make them into self, and of pursuing self to make it into something. The arising of emotion and the distinctions of the intellect, which we describe as separation, are themselves [as real as] turning the head and changing the face, or developing things and throwing [oneself] into the moment. Because we pursue self to make it into something, the whole of the ten directions is in the ceaseless state. And because [the whole of the ten directions] is a fact before the moment, it sometimes overflows beyond the [our] regulating

---

experiencing things for himself.

9. 徧参 (HENSAN), or "thorough exploration," is the title of chap. 62. Here it is used as a verb, 徧参する (HENSAN *suru*).

10. Master Bodhidharma actually did come to the Eastern Lands (China), but *"Master Bodhidharma did not come to the Eastern Lands"* suggests that he came to China naturally, rather than out of personal intention. The Second Patriarch, Master Taiso Eka, did not go to the Western Heavens (India), and *"The Second Patriarch did not go to the Western Heavens,"* suggests similarly that it was natural for him not to go.

11. Coarse vegetable fiber.

12. *Shinji-shobogenzo*, pt. 1, no. 15.

13. 生死去来 (SHOJI-KORAI), or "living-and-dying, going-and-coming," is an expression of everyday life that appears frequently in Shobogenzo.

ability which is the pivot of the moment.[14] *"The one pearl"* is not yet famous, but it is an expression of the truth. It will be famously recognized. *"The one pearl"* goes directly through ten thousand years: the eternal past has not ended, but the eternal present has arrived. The body exists now, and the mind exists now. Even so, [the whole Universe] is a bright pearl. It is not grass and trees there and here, it is not mountains and rivers at all points of the compass; it is a bright pearl. *"How should the student understand it?"* Even though it seems that the monk is playing with his conditioned intellect[15] in speaking these words, they are the clear manifestation of the Great Activity, which is just the Great Standard itself. Progressing further, we should make it strikingly obvious that a foot of water is a one foot wave: in other words, a yard of the pearl is a yard of brightness. To voice this expression of the truth, Gensa says, *"The whole Universe in ten directions is one bright pearl. What use is understanding?"* This expression is the expression of truth to which buddha succeeds buddha, patriarch succeeds patriarch, and Gensa succeeds Gensa. If he wants to avoid this succession—while it is not true that no opportunity for avoidance exists—just when he is ardently trying to avoid it, [the moment] in which he speaks and lives is the total moment, conspicuously manifest before him. Gensa, on a subsequent day asks the monk, *"The whole Universe in ten directions is one bright pearl. How do you understand [this]?"* This says that yesterday [Master Gensa] was preaching the established rule, but his exhalations today rely upon the second phase: today he is preaching an exception to the established rule. Having pushed yesterday aside, he is nodding and laughing. The monk says, *"The whole Universe in ten directions is one bright pearl. What use is understanding?"* We might tell him: *you are riding your adversary's horse to chase your adversary. When the eternal Buddha preaches for you, he is going among alien beings.*[16] We should turn [back] light and reflect[17] for a while: How many cases and examples of *"What use is understanding?"* are there? We can tentatively say that while teaching and practice are seven dairy cakes and five vegetable cakes, they are also "south of the [River] Sho" and "north of the [River] Tan."[18]

[105] Gensa says, *"I see that you are struggling to get inside a demon's cave in a black mountain."* Remember, the face of the sun and the face of the moon have never changed places since the eternal past. The sun's face appears together with the sun's face, and the moon's face appears together with the moon's face. For this reason, [Master Yakusan Igen said,] *"Even if I say that the sixth moon*[19] *is a very nice time of year, I should not say*

---

14. 機要の管得 (KIYO no KANTOKU). 機要 (KIYO) means the central part of a mechanism; at the same time, 機 (KI) suggests the moment of the present. 管得 (KANTOKU), means "being able to control."

15. 業識 (GOSSHIKI), or "karmic consciousness." The term is discussed in chap. 22, *Bussho*.

16. 異類中行 (IRUI-CHU-GYO), "going among alien beings," is a common expression in Shobogenzo. In this case it suggests the absolute difference between the real understanding of Master Gensa and the intellectual understanding of the monk.

17. 回光遍照 (E-KO-HEN-SHO) describes the state in Zazen. The expression appears in *Fukanzazengi* (see Appendix).

18. The River Sho flows north of the River Tan, and the River Tan flows south of the River Sho. In China the area between the two rivers was used as a symbol of one thing that can be expressed in two ways. In this sentence, cakes symbolize concrete things, and "south of the River Sho" and "north of the River Tan" represent subjective views. In Buddhist teaching and practice, recognition of concrete facts and theoretical understanding are both important.

19. 六月 (ROKUGATSU), or "the sixth lunar month," was an uncomfortably hot time in the South of China.

that my surname is Hot."[20] Thus, this bright pearl's possession of reality and lack of beginning are limitless, and the whole Universe in ten directions is one bright pearl. Without being discussed as two pearls or three pearls, the Whole Body[21] is one right-Dharma-eye, the Whole Body is real substance, the Whole Body is one phrase, the Whole Body is brightness, and the Whole Body is the Whole Body itself. When it is the Whole Body it is free of the hindrance of the Whole Body; it is perfect roundness,[22] and roundly it rolls along.[23] Because the virtue of the bright pearl exists in realization like this, there are Avalokiteśvaras[24] and Maitreyas[25] in the present, seeing sights and hearing sounds; and there are old buddhas and new buddhas manifesting their bodies and preaching the Dharma.[26] Just at the moment of the present, whether suspended in space or hanging inside a garment,[27] whether kept under a [dragon's] chin[28] or kept in a top-knot,[29] [the one bright pearl,] in all cases, is one bright pearl throughout the whole Universe in ten directions. To hang inside a garment is its situation, so do not say that it will be dangling on the surface. To hang inside a top-knot or under a chin is its situation, so do not expect to play with it on the surface of the top-knot or on the surface of the chin. When we are intoxicated, there are close friends[30] who give us a pearl; and we should always give a pearl to a close friend. When the pearl is hung upon us we are always intoxicated. That which *already is like this*[31] is the one bright pearl which is the Universe in ten directions. So even though it seems to be continually changing the outward appearance of its turning and not turning, it is just the bright pearl. The very recognition that the pearl has been existing like this is just the bright pearl itself. The bright pearl has sounds and forms that can be heard like this. Already *having got the state like this*,[32] those who surmise that "I cannot be the bright pearl," should not doubt that they are the pearl. Artificial and non-artificial states of surmising and doubting, attaching and rejecting, are just the small view. They are nothing more than trying to make [the bright pearl] match the narrow intellect. How could we not love the bright pearl? Its colors and light, as they are, are endless. Each color and every ray of light at

---

20. Buddhist monks would customarily avoid giving their family name, and reply instead "It is a nice time of year."

21. 全身 (ZENSHIN), "whole body," sometimes suggests the Universe as the Buddha's whole body. See chap. 72, *Nyorai-zenshin*.

22. "Perfect roundness" is 円陀陀地 (EN-DA-DA-CHI), lit. "circle diagonal-diagonal state." 円 (EN) means circular or perfect. 陀 (DA), repeated for emphasis, mean diagonal; at the same time, it suggests the absence of corners, i.e. roundness. 地 (CHI) means "state."

23. 転轆轆 (TEN-ROKU-ROKU). 転 (TEN) means "to turn" or "to roll." 轆轆 (ROKU-ROKU) is onomatopoeic for a round object rolling.

24. Bodhisattva Avalokiteśvara is the subject of chap. 33, *Kannon*. See also Lotus Sutra chap. 25.

25. The Bodhisattva Maitreya is expected to be born 5,670 million years in the future, to save all living beings who were left unsaved by the Buddha. See, for example, LS 1.62. In this sentence the Bodhisattvas Avalokiteśvara and Maitreya symbolize Buddhist practitioners today.

26. Alludes to the description of Avalokiteśvara (Regarder of the Sounds of the World) in the Lotus Sutra. See LS 3.252.

27. See LS 2.114.

28. Black dragons keep a pearl under their chins. The black dragon's pearl is a symbol of the truth.

29. See LS 2.276.

30. See LS 2.114.

31. 既是恁麼 (KIZE-INMO). At the beginning of chap. 29, *Inmo*, Master Ungo Doyo discusses 既是恁麼人 (KIZE-INMO-NIN), or "a person in the state of already being like this."

32. 得恁麼 (TOKU-INMO). These characters also appear in chap. 29, *Inmo*.

each moment and in every situation is the virtue of the whole Universe in ten directions; who would want to plunder it?[33] No-one would throw a tile into a street market. Do not worry about falling or not falling[34] into the six states of cause and effect.[35] They are the original state of being right from head to tail, which is never unclear,[34] and the bright pearl is its features and the bright pearl is its eyes. Still, neither I nor you know what the bright pearl is or what the bright pearl is not. Hundreds of thoughts and hundreds of negations of thought have combined to form a very clear idea.[36] At the same time, by virtue of Gensa's words of Dharma, we have heard, recognized, and clarified the situation of a body-and-mind which has already become the bright pearl. Thereafter, the mind is not personal; why should we be worried by attachment to whether it is a bright pearl or is not a bright pearl, as if what arises and passes were some person.[37] Even surmising and worry is not different from the bright pearl. No action nor any thought has ever been caused by anything other than the bright pearl. Therefore, forward steps and backward steps in a demon's black-mountain cave are just the one bright pearl itself.

Shobogenzo Ikka-no-myoju

Preached to the assembly at Kannon-dori-kosho-horin-ji temple in the Uji district of Yoshu[38] on the 18th day of the 4th lunar month in the 4th year of Katei.[39]

Copied in the prior's quarters of Kippo-ji temple in Shibi county, in the Yoshida district of Esshu,[40] on the 23rd day of the intercalary 7th lunar month in the 1st year of Kangen,[41] attendant bhikṣu Ejo.

---

33. Master Gensa said, *"It is forbidden for anyone to plunder a street market."* See *Shinji-shobogenzo* pt. 1, no. 38.

34. 不落 (FURAKU), "not falling," and 不昧 (FUMAI), "not being unclear," represent opposing views of cause and effect. See, for example, chap. 76, *Dai-shugyo*.

35. 六道の因果 (ROKUDO *no* INGA) are the six states through which we pass according to the law of cause and effect: the state of beings in hell, the state of hungry ghosts, the state of animals, the state of angry demons, the state of human beings, and the state of gods.

36. 明明の艸料 (MEI-MEI *no* SORYO) 想料 (SORYO) means "idea" or "thinking." In this sentence, Master Dogen substituted 艸 (SO), "weeds" (symbolizing concrete things), for 想 (SO), "idea," in order to allude to the traditional saying 明明百艸頭 (MEI-MEI *taru* HYAKU-SO-TO), "clear-clear are hundreds of weeds" (see chap. 22, *Bussho*).

37. The original word for "some person" is たれ (tare), which means "who?"

38. Corresponds to present-day Kyoto prefecture.

39. 1238.

40. Corresponds to present-day Fukui prefecture.

41. 1243.

[5]

重雲堂式

JU-UNDO-SHIKI

Rules for the Hall of Heavy Cloud

__Ju-undo__ or "the Hall of Heavy Cloud" was the name of the Zazen Hall of Kannon-dori-kosho-horin-ji temple. __Shiki__ means rules. So __Ju-undo-shiki__ means "Rules for the Hall of Heavy Cloud." Kannon-dori-kosho-horin-ji temple was the first temple established by Master Dogen. He built it in Kyoto prefecture in 1233, several years after coming back from China. __Ju-undo__ was the first Zazen Hall to be built in Japan. Master Dogen made these rules for the Hall, and titled them. The chapter was not included in Shobogenzo when the 75-chapter edition was compiled, but was added when the 95-chapter edition was compiled at the end of the 17th century. The inclusion of this chapter is very useful in understanding Shobogenzo, because what is written here represents in a concrete way Master Dogen's sincere attitude in pursuing the truth.

[111] **People who have the will to the truth** and who discard fame and gain may enter. We should not randomly admit those who might be insincere. If someone is admitted by mistake, we should, after consideration, make them leave. Remember, when the will to the truth has secretly arisen, fame and gain evaporate at once. Generally, in [all] the great-thousandfold world,[1] there are very few examples of the right and traditional transmission. In our country, this will be seen as the original source. Feeling compassion for future ages, we should value the present.

[112] The members of the Hall should harmonize like milk and water, and should wholeheartedly promote each other's practice of the truth. Now we are for the present [as] guests and hosts,[2] but in future we will forever be Buddhist patriarchs. So now that each of us is meeting what is hard to meet, and is practicing what is hard to practice, we must not lose our sincerity. This [sincerity] is called *the body-and-mind of the Buddhist patriarchs;* it inevitably becomes buddha and becomes a patriarch. We have already left our families and left our hometowns; we rely on clouds and rely on waters.[3] The benevolence of [the members of] this Saṃgha, in promoting [each other's] health and in promoting [each other's] practice, surpasses even that of a father and mother. A father

1. 大千界 (DAISENKAI) is short for 三千大千世界 (SANZEN-DAISEN-SEKAI), or "the three-thousand-great-thousandfold world." This expression, which derives from the ancient Indian belief that the world comprises many groups of thousands of worlds, occurs frequently in the Lotus Sutra. See for example, LS 2.218-220.

2. 賓主 (HINJU), translated in para. [116] as "members and leaders."

3. In China and Japan monks are commonly referred to as 雲水 (UNSUI), which means "clouds and water."

and mother are only parents for the short span between life and death, but [the members of] this Saṃgha will be friends in the Buddha's truth forever.

[113] **W**e should not be fond of going out. If absolutely necessary, once in one month is permissible. People of old lived in distant mountains or practiced in remote forests. They not only had few human dealings, but also totally discarded myriad involvements. We should learn their state of mind in shrouding their light and covering their tracks. Now is just the time to [practice as if to] put out a fire on our head. How could we not regret idly devoting this time to worldly involvements? How could we not regret this? It is hard to rely on what has no constancy, and we never know where, on the grass by the path, our dew-drop life will fall. [To waste this time] would be truly pitiful.

[114] **W**hile we are in the Hall we should not read the words of even Zen texts. In the Hall we should realize the principles and pursue the state of truth. When we are before a bright window,[4] we can enlighten the mind with the teachings of the ancients. Do not waste a moment of time. Single-mindedly make effort.[5]

[115] **W**e should make it a general rule to inform the leader of the Hall[6] where we are going, whether it is night or day. Do not ramble around at will. That might infringe the discipline of the Saṃgha. We never know when this life will finish. If life were to end during an idle excursion, that would certainly be something to regret afterwards.

[115] **W**e should not strike other people for their mistakes. We should not look on people's mistakes with hatred. In the words of an ancient,[7] *"When we do not see others' wrongness or our own rightness, we are naturally respected by seniors and admired by juniors."* At the same time, we should not imitate the wrongs of others. We should practice our own virtue. The Buddha prevented wrongdoing, but not out of hatred.

[116] **A**ny task, big or small, we should do only after informing the leader of the Hall. People who do things without informing the leader of the Hall should be expelled from the Hall. When formalities between members and leaders are disrupted, it is hard to tell right from wrong.

[116] **I**n and around the Hall, we should not raise the voice or gather heads to converse. The leader of the Hall should stop this.

[117] **I**n the Hall we should not practice ceremonial walking.[8]

[117] **I**n the Hall we should not hold counting beads.[9] And we should not come and go with the hands hanging down.[10]

---

4. Suggests a place, other than the Zazen Hall, suitable for reading.

5. 専一に功夫す (SEN-ITSU *ni* KUFU *su*). These words also appear in *Fukan-zazengi*.

6. 堂主 (DOSHU), "the leader of the Hall," would have been the head monk (not Master Dogen himself).

7. Master Hakuyo Hojun. See *Zoku-dento-roku*, chap. 29.

8. 堂主 (GYODO), ceremonial walking, is a way of serving offerings to the Buddha image, in which the practitioner circles the Buddha image three times, walking around clockwise so that the Buddha remains to the practitioner's right.

9. Some people use a kind of rosary, usually with 108 beads, to count the recitations of Buddha's name, and so on. The Sanskrit term for a rosary is *akṣa-sūtra*. See Glossary.

10. In other words, we should hold the hands in front of the chest in *shashu*, with the right hand

[118] In the Hall we should not chant, or read sutras. If a donor[11] requests the reading of sutras by the whole order, then it is permissible.

[118] In the Hall we should not loudly blow the nose, or loudly hack and spit. We should regret the fact that our moral behavior is still [so] imperfect. And we should begrudge the fact that time is stealing away, robbing us of life with which to practice the truth. It might be natural for us to have minds like fish in a dwindling stream.

[119] Members of the Hall should not wear brocade. We should wear [clothes of] paper, cotton, and so forth. Since ancient times, all the people who clarified the truth have been like this.

[119] Do not come into the Hall drunk. If someone forgetfully [enters] by mistake, they should do prostrations and confess. Also, alcohol should not be brought into [the Hall]. Do not enter the Hall flushed and inebriated.[12]

[120] If two people quarrel, both should be sent back to their quarters, because they not only hinder their own practice of the truth, but also hinder others. Those who see the quarrel coming but do not prevent it are equally at fault.

[120] Anyone who is indifferent towards the instructions for [life] in the Hall should be expelled by the common consent of all members. Anyone whose mind is in sympathy with the transgression is [also] at fault.

[121] Do not disturb the other members by inviting guests, whether monks or lay people, into the Hall. When talking with guests in the vicinity [of the Hall], do not raise the voice. Do not deliberately boast about your own training, greedily hoping for offerings. [A guest] who has long had the will to participate in practice, and who is determined to tour the Hall and do prostrations,[13] may enter. In this case also, the leader of the Hall must be informed.

[121] Zazen should be practiced as in the Monks' Halls [of China].[14] Never be even slightly lazy in attending and requesting [formal and informal teaching], morning and evening.

[122] During the midday meal and morning gruel, a person who drops the accessories for the pātra[15] on the ground should be penalized[16] according to the monastery rules.

---

covering the left fist.

11. "Donor" is originally *dāna* (free-giving), the first of the six *pāramitās*. In this case *dāna* stands for *dānapati*, the Sanskrit word for a person who supports a Buddhist order. The reading of sutras at a donor's request is explained in detail in chap. 21, *Kankin*.

12. "Flushed and inebriated" is originally にらぎのかして *(niragi nokashi te)*. Being written in hiragana, the Japanese phonetic alphabet, this allows alternative interpretations. The interpretation used here is that *niragu* means to temper steel, or to redden, and *nokashi te* means emboldened, or inebriated. The traditional interpretation in Japan has been that *nira* means leeks, *gi* means onions, and *no ka shi te* means smelling, so the sentence would mean "Do not enter the Hall smelling of leeks and onions."

13. 巡礼 (JUNREI) stands for 巡堂礼拝 (JUNDO-RAIHAI), or "to go round the Hall and do prostrations." The method is explained in chap. 21, *Kankin*.

14. In big temples in China the Zazen Hall was called 僧堂 (SODO) or "Monks' Hall," because the monks would live in the hall, not only sitting but also eating and sleeping there.

15. *Pātra* is the Sanskrit word for the Buddhist food bowl. See chap. 78, *Hatsu-u*.

16. "Penalized" is 罰油 (BATSU-YU), lit. "penalty of oil." In the temples of China oil for lamps was scarce, so it is likely that monks were penalized by paying oil from their ration.

[122] In general, we should staunchly guard the prohibitions and precepts of the Buddhist patriarchs. The pure criteria of monasteries should be engraved on our bones, and should be engraved on our minds.

[123] We should pray that our whole life will be peaceful, and that our pursuit of the truth will abide in the state without intent.

[123] These few rules [listed] above are the body-and-mind of eternal buddhas. We should revere them and follow them.

The 25th day of the 4th lunar month in the 2nd year of Rekinin.[17] Set forth by the founder of Kannon-dori-kosho-gokoku-ji temple, sramaṇa Dogen.

17. 1239.

[6]

即心是仏

SOKU-SHIN-ZE-BUTSU

Mind Here and Now Is Buddha

__Soku__ means "here and now." __Shin__ means "mind." __Ze__ means "is." __Butsu__ means "buddha." The principle of __soku-shin-ze-butsu__, or "mind here and now is buddha" is very famous in Buddhism, but many people have interpreted the principle to support the beliefs of naturalism. They say if our mind here and now is just buddha, our conduct must always be right, and in that case, we need not make any effort to understand or to realize Buddhism. However, this interpretation is a serious mistake. The principle __soku-shin-ze-butsu__, "mind here and now is buddha," must be understood not from the standpoint of the intellect, but from the standpoint of practice. In other words, the principle does not mean belief in something spiritual called "mind" but it affirms the time "now" and the place "here" as reality itself. This time and place must always be absolute and right, and so we can call them the truth or "buddha." In this chapter, Master Dogen explained this meaning of __soku-shin-ze-butsu__, or "mind here and now is buddha."

[125] **What every buddha and every patriarch** has maintained and relied upon, without exception, is just *"mind here and now is buddha."* Many students, however, misunderstand that *"mind here and now is buddha"* did not exist in India, but was first heard in China. As a result, they do not recognize their mistake as a mistake. Because they do not recognize the mistake as a mistake, many fall down into non-Buddhism. When stupid people hear talk of *"mind here and now is buddha,"* they interpret that ordinary beings' intellect and sense-perception, which have never established the bodhi-mind, are just buddha. This derives from never having met a true teacher. The reason I say that they become non-Buddhists is that there was a non-Buddhist in India, called Senika, whose viewpoint is expressed as follows: *The great truth exists in our own body now, so we can easily recognize its situation. In other words, [a spiritual intelligence] distinguishes between pain and pleasure, naturally senses cold and warmth, and recognizes discomfort and irritation. [The spiritual intelligence] is neither restricted by myriad things nor connected with circumstances: things come and go and circumstances arise and pass, but the spiritual intelligence always remains, unchanging. This spiritual intelligence is all around, pervading all souls—common and sacred—without distinction. In its midst, illusory flowers in space exist for the time being, but when momentary insight has appeared, and things have vanished and circumstances have disappeared, then the spiritual intelligence, the original essence, alone is clearly recognizable, peaceful, and eternal. Though the physical form may be broken, the spiritual intelligence departs unbroken; just as, when a house burns down in a fire, the master of the house leaves. This perfectly clear and truly spiritual presence is called "the essence of perception and intelligence." It is also described as "buddha," and called "enlightenment." It includes*

both the subject and the object, and it permeates both delusion and enlightenment. [So] let the myriad dharmas and all circumstances be as they are. The spiritual intelligence does not coexist with circumstances and it is not the same as things. It abides constantly through passing kalpas. We might also call the circumstances that exist in the present "real," in so far as they derive from the existence of the spiritual intelligence: because they are conditions arising from the original essence, they are real things. Even so, they are not eternal as the spiritual intelligence is, for they exist and then vanish. [The spiritual intelligence] is unrelated to brightness and darkness, because it knows spiritually. We call this "the spiritual intelligence," we also call it "the true self," we call it "the basis of awakening," we call it "original essence," and we call it "original substance." Someone who realizes this original essence is said to have returned to eternity and is called a great man who has come back to the truth. After this, he no longer wanders through the cycle of life and death; he experiences and enters the essential ocean[1] where there is neither appearance nor disappearance. There is no reality other than this, but as long as this essence has not emerged, the three worlds[2] and the six states[3] are said to arise in competition. This then is the view of the non-Buddhist Senika.

[129] Master Echu, National Master Daisho,[4] of the great Kingdom of Tang, asks a monk, *"From which direction have you come?"*

The monk says, *"I have come from the south."*

The Master says, *"What [good] counselors are there in the south?"*

The monk says, *"[Good] counselors are very numerous."*

The Master says, *"How do they teach people?"*

The monk says, *"The [good] counselors of that quarter teach students directly that mind here and now is buddha. Buddha means consciousness itself. You now are fully endowed with the essence of seeing, hearing, awareness, and recognition. This essence is able to raise the eyebrows and to wink, to come and go, and to move and act. It pervades the body, so that when [something] touches the head, the head knows it, and when something touches the foot, the foot knows it. Therefore it is called 'the true all-pervading intelligence.' Apart from this there is no buddha at all. This body must appear and disappear, but the mental essence has never appeared or disappeared since the limitless past. The appearance and disappearance of the body is like a dragon changing its bones, a snake shedding its skin, or a person moving out of an old house. This body is inconstant; the essence is constant. What they teach in the south is, for the most part, like this."*

The Master says, *"If it is so, they are no different from the non-Buddhist Senika. He said, 'In our body there is a single spiritual essence. This essence can recognize pain and irritation. When the body decays the spirit departs; just as when a house is burning the master of the house departs. The house is inconstant; the master of the house is constant.' When I examine people like*

---

1. 性界 (SHOKAI). See chap. 1, *Bendowa*.

2. 三界 (SANGAI), "the three worlds" or "the triple world," are the worlds of volition, matter, and the immaterial. See chap. 47, *Sangai-yuishin*.

3. 六道 (ROKUDO), the six [miserable] states, are the state of beings in hell, the state of hungry ghosts, the state of animals, the state of angry demons, the state of human beings, and the state of gods.

4. Master Nan-yo Echu (675?–775), successor of Master Daikan Eno. "National Master Daisho" was his title as a teacher of the emperor. Master Dogen often refers to Master Nan-yo Echu simply as the National Master.

this, they do not know the false from the true. How can they decide what is right? When I was on my travels, I often saw this kind. Recently they are very popular. They gather assemblies of three or five hundred people and, eyes gazing towards the heavens, they say 'This is the fundamental teaching of the south.'[5] *They take the Platform Sutra*[6] *and change it, mixing in folk stories, and erasing its sacred meaning. They delude and disturb recent students. How could [theirs] be called the spoken teaching?*[7] *How painful it is, that our religion is being lost. If seeing, hearing, awareness, and recognition could be equated with the Buddha-nature, Vimalakīrti*[8] *would not have said, 'The Dharma is transcendent over seeing, hearing, awareness, and recognition. When we use seeing, hearing, awareness, and recognition, it is only seeing, hearing, awareness, and recognition; it is not pursuit of the Dharma.'"*

[131] National Master Daisho is an excellent disciple of the eternal Buddha of Sokei.[9] He is a great good counselor in heaven above and in the human world. We should clarify the fundamental teaching set forth by the National Master, and regard it as a criterion[10] for learning in practice. Do not follow what you know to be the viewpoint of the non-Buddhist Senika. Among those of recent generations who subsist as masters of mountains in the great Kingdom of Sung, there may be no-one like the National Master. From the ancient past, no counselors to equal the National Master have ever manifested themselves in the world. Nevertheless, people of the world mistakenly think that even Rinzai[11] and Tokuzan[12] might equal the National Master. Only people [who think] like this are great in number. It is a pity that there are no teachers with clear eyes. This *"mind here and now is buddha"* that the Buddhist patriarchs maintain and rely upon is not seen by non-Buddhists and [people of] the two vehicles, even in their dreams. Buddhist patriarchs alone, together with Buddhist patriarchs,[13] possess hearing, action, and experience which have enacted and which have perfectly realized *mind here and now is*

5. Master Nan-yo Echu lived in the north of China which was the center of Chinese civilization at the time of the Tang Dynasty (619–858), so Buddhist philosophy was strong in the north. However, the Buddhism of southern China was thought to be very practical. The government moved south in the Sung Dynasty (960–1279) in response to invasion from the north.

6. 六祖法宝壇経 (ROKUSO-HOBO-DANKYO), "the Platform Sutra of the Sixth Patriarch's Dharma-Treasure," is a collection of the preachings of Master Daikan Eno, the sixth patriarch in China and the master of Master Nan-yo Echu.

7. 言教 (GONKYO), "spoken teaching," suggests the original teaching of the Buddha, which was not recorded in writing until the 1st century B.C., when the Pali canon was written on palm leaves in the monasteries of Sri Lanka.

8. 浄名 (JOMYO), lit. "Pure Name," is a Chinese rendering of Vimalakīrti, a layman of the Buddha's time who was excellent in Buddhist philosophy. Many questions and answers between Vimalakīrti and the Buddha are recorded in the *Vimalakīrti-nīrdeśa*.

9. Master Daikan Eno.

10. "Criterion" is 亀鑑 (KIKAN), lit. "turtle-mirror." In ancient China, fortune-tellers would sometimes heat a turtle shell and divine an appropriate course of action by looking at the crack. Thus, a turtle shell was used like a mirror, as a criterion for making decisions.

11. Master Rinzai Kigen (died 867), founder of the Rinzai Sect, successor of Master Obaku Ki-un. See chap. 49, *Butsudo*.

12. Master Tokuzan Senkan (780–865), successor of Master Ryutan Soshin. See chap. 18, *Shinfukatoku*.

13. 唯仏祖与仏祖 (YUI-BUSSO-YO-BUSSO) is a variation of 唯仏与仏 (YUI-BUTSU-YO-BUTSU), "buddhas alone, together with buddhas." The Lotus Sutra says, *"Buddhas alone, together with buddhas, can perfectly realize that all dharmas are real form."* See LS 1.68.

buddha. Buddhas[14] have continued to pick up and to throw away hundreds of weeds, but they have never represented themselves as a sixteen-foot golden body.[15] *The immediate*[16] Universe[17] exists; it is not awaiting realization,[18] and it is not avoiding destruction. *This concrete*[19] triple world[20] exists; it is neither receding nor appearing, and it is not just mind.[21] *Mind*[22] exists as fences and walls; it never gets muddy or wet, and it is never artificially constructed. We realize in practice that *mind here and now is buddha,*[23] we realize in practice that *the mind which is buddha is this,*[24] we realize in practice that *buddha actually is just the mind,*[25] we realize in practice that *mind-and-buddha here and now is right,*[26] and we realize in practice that *this buddha-mind is here and now.*[27]

[134] Realization in practice like this is just *mind here and now is buddha* picking itself up and authentically transmitting itself to *mind here and now is buddha*. Authentically transmitted like this, it has arrived at the present day. *The mind that has been authentically transmitted* means one mind as all dharmas, and all dharmas as one mind. For this reason, a man of old[28] said, *"When a person becomes conscious of the mind, there is not an inch of soil on the Earth."* Remember, when we become conscious of the mind, the whole of heaven falls down and the whole ground is torn apart. Or in other words, when we become conscious of the mind, the Earth grows three inches thicker. An ancient patriarch

---

14. 仏 (BUTSU) means "buddha." The following four sentences begin with 仏 (BUTSU), "buddha;" 即 (SOKU), "here and now;" 是 (ZE), "is;" and 心 (SHIN), "mind," respectively.

15. The sixteen-foot golden body is the idealized image of the Buddha.

16. 即 (SOKU). 即 can function as an adjective ("here and now," "immediate," "actual"); it can function as a copula, i.e. a linking verb, to express the oneness of two factors (A 即 B = "A, that is, B"); it can function as an adverb ("here and now," "just," "immediately," "directly," "actually"); and it can also function as a conjunction expressing temporal contingency (A 即 B = "A, immediately followed by B").

17. 即公案 (SOKU-KOAN), "the immediate Universe" or "the here-and-now Universe." Here 即 is used as an adjective.

18. 見成 (GENJO). 見成 (GENJO) and 公案 (KOAN) are often associated, as in the title of chap. 3, *Genjo-koan (The Realized Universe).*

19. 是 (ZE), can function as an adjective ("this," "concrete," "this concrete;" or "right," "correct"); it can function as a copula in the same way as 即 ("is," "are," "is just the same as"); it can function as an adverb ("here and now," "actually"); and it can function as a pronoun ("this").

20. 是三界 (ZESANGAI), "this triple world" or "this concrete triple world." Here 是 is used as an adjective.

21. 唯心 (YUISHIN). 三界唯心 (SANGAI YUISHIN), "The Triple World is Just Mind," is the title of chap. 47, *Sangai-yuishin.*

22. 心 (SHIN) means mind.

23. 即心是仏 (SOKU-SHIN ZE BUTSU), as in the title of this chapter. In this case, 即 (here and now) is an adjective and 是 (is) is a copula. The four expressions following this expression represent further combinations of the four characters 即心是仏. See following notes.

24. 心即仏是 (SHIN-SOKU-BUTSU ZE). In this case, 即 (which is) is a copula and 是 (this) is a pronoun.

25. 仏即是心 (BUTSU SOKU ZE SHIN). In this case, 即 (actually) is an adverb and 是 (is just) is a copula.

26. 即心仏是 (SOKU-SHIN-BUTSU ZE). In this case, 即 (here and now) and 是 (right) are both adjectives.

27. 是仏心即 (ZE-BUTSU-SHIN SOKU). In this case also, 是 (this) and 即 (here and now) are both adjectives.

28. Master Chorei Shutaku. His words mean that to know the mind is just to know reality, in which an inch of soil cannot be separated from the whole Earth.

said,[29] *"What is fine, pure, and bright mind? It is mountains, rivers, and the Earth, the sun, the moon, and the stars."* Clearly, "mind" is mountains, rivers, and the Earth, the sun, the moon, and the stars. But what these words say is, when we are moving forward, not enough, and when we are drawing back, too much. Mind as mountains, rivers, and the Earth is nothing other than mountains, rivers, and the Earth. There are no additional waves or surf, no wind or smoke. Mind as the sun, the moon, and the stars is nothing other than the sun, the moon, and the stars. There is no additional fog or mist. Mind as living-and-dying, coming-and-going, is nothing other than living-and-dying, coming-and-going. There is no additional delusion or realization. Mind as fences, walls, tiles, and pebbles is nothing other than fences, walls, tiles, and pebbles. There is no additional mud or water. Mind as the four elements and five aggregates is nothing other than the four elements and five aggregates. There is no additional horse or monkey.[30] Mind as a chair or a whisk[31] is nothing other than a chair or a whisk. There is no additional bamboo or wood. Because the state is like this, *mind here and now is buddha* is untainted *mind here and now is buddha.* All buddhas are untainted buddhas. This being so, *mind here and now is buddha* is the buddhas [themselves] who establish the will, undergo training, [realize] bodhi, and [experience] nirvāṇa. If we have never established the will, undergone training, [realized] bodhi, and [experienced] nirvāṇa, then [the state] is not *mind here and now is buddha.* If we establish the mind and do practice-and-experience even in a single kṣaṇa,[32] this is *mind here and now is buddha.* If we establish the will and do practice-and-experience in a single molecule, this is *mind here and now is buddha.* If we establish the will and do practice-and-experience in countless kalpas, this is *mind here and now is buddha.* If we establish the will and do practice-and-experience in one instant of consciousness, this is *mind here and now is buddha.* If we establish the will and do practice-and-experience inside half a fist, this is *mind here and now is buddha.* To say, on the contrary, that undergoing training to become buddha for long kalpas is not *mind here and now is buddha,* is never to have seen, never to have known, and never to have learned *mind here and now is buddha.* It is never to have met a true teacher who proclaims *mind here and now is buddha*. The term "buddhas" means Śākyamuni Buddha. Śākyamuni Buddha is just *mind here and now is buddha.* When all the buddhas of the past, present, and future become buddha, they inevitably become Śākyamuni Buddha, that is, *mind here and now is buddha*.

29. Master Isan Reiyu asked the question to his disciple Master Kyozan Ejaku. See *Shinji-shobogenzo* pt. 2, no. 68.

30. Horse and monkey allude to the phrase 意馬心猿 (I-BA SHIN-EN) or "horse-will, monkey-mind." The horse represents the restless will and the monkey represents the mischievous intellect.

31. 払子 (HOSSU) is a ceremonial fly-whisk—a wooden stick with a long plume of animal hair—held by a master during a Buddhist lecture.

32. 刹那 (SETSUNA), represents the Sanskrit *kṣaṇa*, "moment." Sixty-five *kṣaṇas* are said to pass in the clicking of the fingers.

Shobogenzo Soku-shin-ze-butsu

Preached to the assembly at Kannon-dori-kosho-horin-ji temple in the Uji district of Yoshu,[33] on the 25th day of the 5th lunar month in the 1st year of En-o.[34]

33. Corresponds to present-day Kyoto prefecture.
34. 1239.

[7]

洗浄

SENJO

Washing

***Sen** means "to wash," and **jo** means "to purify." So **senjo** means "washing." Buddhism is neither idealism nor materialism, but belief in reality, which has both a spiritual side and a material side. So Buddhism insists that to clean our physical body is to purify our mind. Therefore, in Buddhism, cutting our fingernails, shaving our head, and washing our body are all very important religious practices. In this chapter Master Dogen expounds the religious meaning of such daily behavior, and preaches the importance in Buddhism of cleansing our physical body.*

[139] **There is practice-and-experience** that Buddhist patriarchs have guarded and maintained; it is called *not being tainted.*

[140] The Sixth Patriarch[1] asks Zen Master Dai-e[2] of Kannon-in temple on Nangaku-zan mountain, *"Do you rely on practice and experience or not?"*

Dai-e says, *"It is not that there is no practice and experience, but the state can never be tainted."*

The Sixth Patriarch says, *"Just this untainted state is that which buddhas guard and desire. You are also like this. I am also like this. And the ancestral masters of India[3] were also like this..."[4]*

[140] The Sutra of Three Thousand Dignified Forms for Ordained Monks[5] says, *"Purifying the body means washing the anus and the urethra,[6] and cutting the nails of the ten fingers."* So even though the body-and-mind is not tainted, there are Dharma-practices of purifying the body and there are Dharma-practices of purifying the mind. Not only do we clean body-and-mind; we also clean the national land and clean beneath trees.[7] To clean the national land, even though it has never become dirty, is *that which buddhas guard and*

---

1. Master Daikan Eno (638–713), successor of Master Daiman Konin.

2. Master Nangaku Ejo (677–744), successor of Master Daikan Eno. Zen Master Dai-e was his posthumous title.

3. 西天 (SAITEN), "Western Heavens," means India.

4. *Shinji-shobogenzo* pt. 2, no. 1. See also chap. 29, *Inmo*, and chap. 62, *Hensan*.

5. 大比丘三千威儀経 *(Dai-biku-san-zen-yuigi-kyo).*

6. 大小便 (DAISHOBEN). In modern Japanese *daishoben* means "feces and urine," but in this chapter the words suggest the parts of the body where feces and urine emerge: the anus and the urethra. Although it is not common practice nowadays to wash around the urethra after urinating, it seems that Master Dogen recommended us to do so.

7. It is a Buddhist tradition to sit under a tree. The Buddha is said to have realized the truth while sitting under a Bodhi tree.

desire; and even when they have arrived at the Buddhist effect, they still do not draw back or cease. It is hard to fathom this point. To enact the Dharma is the point. To attain the state of truth is to enact the Dharma.

[141] The Pure Conduct chapter of the Garland Sutra[8] says, *"When we relieve ourselves, we should pray that living beings will get rid of impurity and will be free of greed, anger, and delusion. Then, having arrived at the water, we should pray that living beings will progress towards the supreme state of truth and attain the Dharma which transcends the secular world. While we are washing away impurity with the water, we should pray that living beings will have pure endurance, and will ultimately be free of dirt."*

[142] Water is not always originally pure or originally impure. The body is not always originally pure or originally impure. All dharmas are also like this. Water is never sentient or non-sentient, the body is never sentient or non-sentient, and all dharmas are also like this. The preaching of the Buddha, the World-Honored One, is like this. At the same time, [to wash] is not to use water to clean the body; [rather,] when we are maintaining and relying upon the Buddha-Dharma in accordance with the Buddha-Dharma, we have this form of behavior, and we call it *"washing."* It is to receive the authentic transmission of a body-and-mind of the Buddhist Patriarch immediately; it is to see and to hear a phrase of the Buddhist Patriarch intimately; and it is to abide in and to retain a state of brightness of the Buddhist Patriarch clearly. In sum, it is to realize countless and limitless virtues. At just the moment when we dignify body-and-mind with training, eternal original practice is completely and roundly realized. Thus the body-and-mind of training manifests itself in the original state.

[144] We should cut the nails of [all] ten fingers. *Of [all] ten fingers* means the fingernails of both left and right hands. We should also cut the toenails. A sutra says, *"If the nails grow to the length of a grain of wheat, we acquire demerit."* So we should not let the nails grow long. Long nails are naturally a precursor of non-Buddhism. We should make a point of cutting the nails. Nevertheless, among the priests of the great Kingdom of Sung today, many who are not equipped with eyes of learning in practice grow their nails long. Some have [nails] one or two inches long, and even three or four inches long. This goes against the Dharma. It is not the body-and-mind of the Buddha-Dharma. People are like this because they are without reverence for the old traditions[9] of Buddhists; venerable patriarchs who possess the state of truth are never like this. There are others who grow their hair long. This also goes against the Dharma. Do not mistakenly suppose that because these are the habits of priests in a great nation, they might be right Dharma.

[145] My late Master, the eternal Buddha, spoke stern words of warning to priests throughout the country who had long hair or long nails. He said, *"Those who do not un-*

8. The Garland Sutra is 華厳経 (*Kegon-kyo*) in Chinese or Japanese, and the Avataṃsaka-sūtra in Sanskrit. The sutra compares the whole Universe to the realization of Vairocana Buddha. Its basic teaching is that myriad things and phenomena are the oneness of the Universe, and the whole Universe is myriad things and phenomena.

9. "Reverence for the old traditions" is 稽古 (KEIKO), lit. "consideration of the past," or "emulation of the ancients." In modern Japanese *keiko* is the term generally used for training by sumo wrestlers, martial artists, et cetera.

derstand [the importance of] shaving the head[10] *are not secular people, and are not monks; they are just animals. Since ancient times, was there any Buddhist patriarch who did not shave the head? Those today who do not understand [the importance of] shaving the head are truly animals."* When he preached to the assembly like this, many people who had not shaved their heads for years shaved their heads. In formal preaching in the Dharma Hall or in his informal preaching, [the Master] would click his fingers loudly as he scolded them.[11] *"Not knowing what the truth is, they randomly grow long hair and long nails; it is pitiful that they devote a body-and-mind in the south [continent] of Jambudvīpa*[12] *to wrong ways. For the last two or three hundred years, because the truth of the ancestral Master has died out, there have been many people like these. People like these become the leaders of temples and, signing their names with the title of 'Master,' they create the appearance of acting for the sake of the many, [but] they are without benefit to human beings and gods. Nowadays, on all the mountains throughout the country, there is no-one at all who has the will to the truth. The ones who attained the truth are long extinct. Only groups of the corrupt and the degenerate [remain]."* When he spoke like this in his informal preaching, people from many districts who had arbitrarily assumed the title of "veteran master" bore no grudge against him and had nothing to say for themselves. Remember, growing the hair long is something that Buddhist patriarchs remonstrate against, and growing the nails long is something that non-Buddhists do. As the children and grandchildren of Buddhist patriarchs, we should not be fond of such violations of the Dharma. We should clean the body-and-mind, and we should cut the nails and shave the head.

[147] *Wash the anus and the urethra:* Do not neglect this. There was an episode in which, through this practice, Śāriputra[13] caused a non-Buddhist to submit himself. This was neither the original expectation of the non-Buddhist nor the premeditated hope of Śāriputra, but when the dignified behavior of the Buddhist patriarchs is realized, false teaching naturally succumbs. When [monks] practice beneath a tree or on open ground,[14] they have no constructed toilets; they rely on conveniently located river-valleys, streams, and so on, and they clean themselves with pieces of soil. This is [when] there is no ash. They just use two lots of seven balls of soil. The method of using the two lots of seven balls of soil is as follows: First they take off the Dharma-robe and fold it, then they pick up some soil—not black but yellowish soil—and divide it into balls, each about the size of a large soy bean. They arrange these into rows of seven balls, on a stone or some other convenient place, making two rows of seven balls each. After that they prepare a stone to be used as a rubstone. And after that they defecate. After defecating they use a stick, or sometimes they use paper. Then they go to the wa-

---

10. In Master Tendo Nyojo's quotation, "shaving the head" is 浄髪 (JOHATSU), lit. "purifying the hair." In Master Dogen's commentary, the expressions used are 剃頭 (TEITO) lit. "shaving the head," and 剃髪 (TEIHATSU), lit. "shaving the hair."

11. The first quotation in this paragraph is clearly defined in the original text. But it is not totally clear where Master Dogen's own words end and the second quotation begins.

12. Jambudvīpa is the continent south of Mt. Sumeru on which, according to ancient Indian cosmology, human beings live.

13. Śāriputra was one of the Buddha's ten great disciples. There is a story in chap. 35 of *Maka-sogi-ritsu (Precepts for the Great Saṃgha)* that a non-Buddhist was converted to Buddhism on witnessing Śāriputra's method of defecating.

14. 樹下露地 (JUGE-ROJI), "beneath trees and on open ground," suggests the practice of the Buddha and the monks of his time. However, the tense of the Japanese is the present.

terside to clean themselves, first carrying three balls of soil to clean with. They take each individual ball of soil in the palm of the hand and add just a little water so that, when mixed with the water, [the soil] dissolves to a consistency thinner than mud—about the consistency of thin rice gruel. They wash the urethra first. Next, they use one ball of soil, in the same way as before, to wash the anus. And next, they use one ball of soil, in the same way as before, briefly to wash the impure hand.[15]

[149] Ever since [monks] started living in temples, they have built toilet buildings. These are called *tosu* [the east office], or sometimes *sei* [the toilet], and sometimes *shi* [the side building].[16] They are buildings which should be present wherever monks are living. The rule in going to the toilet is always to take the long towel.[17] The method is to fold the towel in two, and then place it over the left elbow so that it hangs down from above the sleeve of your jacket. Having arrived at the toilet, hang the towel over the clothes-pole.[18] The way to hang it is as it has been hanging from your arm. If you have come wearing a kaṣāya of nine stripes, seven stripes, and so on, hang [the kaṣāya] alongside the towel. Arrange [the kaṣāya] evenly so that it will not fall down. Do not throw it over [the pole] hastily. Be careful to remember the mark [on the pole]. *Remembering the mark* refers to the characters written along the clothes-pole; these are written inside moon-shaped circles on sheets of white paper, which are then attached in a line along the pole. So remembering the mark means not forgetting by which character you have put your own gown,[19] and not getting [the places] mixed up. When many monks are present do not confuse your own place on the pole with that of others. During this time, when [other] monks have arrived and are standing in lines, bow to them with the hands folded.[20] In bowing, it is not necessary to face each other directly and bend the body; it is just a token bow of salutation with the folded hands placed in front of the chest. At the toilet, even if you are not wearing a gown, still bow to and salute [other] monks. If neither hand has become impure, and neither hand is holding anything, fold

---

15. It is not clear what was done with the remaining eleven balls of soil.

16. A standard temple in China and Japan faces south. As you approach the temple from the south, the Buddha Hall is directly in front of you, and the Zazen Hall is to the left (west). A toilet building located to the east would be on the far right (furthest east). In certain ages, however, the main toilet building was located to the west. See the Temple Plan in the Appendix.

17. 手布 (SHUKIN). The *shukin* is a piece of cloth, measuring one *jo* plus two *shaku* (total: 3.64 meters) in length, which is used as a towel, and also as a sash to keep up the sleeves. It is one of the eighteen articles a monk is supposed to have. The method of using the *shukin* is explained in detail in chap. 56, *Senmen*.

18. 浄竿 (JOKAN), lit. "pure pole," is a bamboo or wooden pole set up horizontally at about head height.

19. 直裰 (JIKITOTSU), lit. "directly-sewn." Traditionally a monk in China wore a kind of long black cotton jacket, or *hensan*, and a black skirt, or *kunzu*. By Master Dogen's time, it was customary for the jacket and skirt to be sewn together, hence the name *jikitotsu*, or "directly sewn." The *jikitotsu* is the long black gown with wide sleeves commonly worn by priests in Japan today. A monk of Master Dogen's time would usually have worn the following clothes: a white loincloth, white underclothes, a black jacket (*hensan*) and black skirt (*kunzu*), and/or a black gown (*jikitotsu*), and finally the *kaṣāya*. The standard form of the *kaṣāya*, or Buddhist robe, is universal (see chap. 12, *Kesa-kudoku* and chap. 13, *Den-e*), but the other clothes worn by monks have changed according to the climates and customs of different countries and different ages.

20. 叉手 (SHASHU). The left hand is curled into a fist, the fingers covering the thumb, and placed in front of the chest with the palm of the hand facing downwards. The open right hand rests, palm down, on the top of the left hand.

both hands and bow. If one hand is already soiled, or when one hand is holding something, make the bow with the other hand. To make the bow with one hand, turn the hand palm upward, curl the fingertips slightly as if preparing to scoop up water, and bow as if just lowering the head slightly. If someone else [bows] like this, you should do likewise. And if you [bow] like this, others should do likewise. When you take off the jacket[21] and the gown, hang them next to the towel. The way to hang them is as follows: Remove the gown and bring the sleeves together at the back, then bring together the armpits and lift them up so that the sleeves are one over the other. Then, take the inside of the back of the collar of the gown with the left hand, pull up the shoulders with the right hand, and fold the sleeves and the left and right lapels over each other. Having folded the sleeves and lapels over each other, make another fold, down the middle from top to bottom, and then throw the collar of the gown over the top of the pole. The hem of the gown and the ends of the sleeves will be hanging on the near side of the pole. For example, the gown will be hanging from the pole by the join at the waist. Next, cross over the ends of the towel which are hanging down on the near and far sides of the pole, and pull them across to the other side of the gown. [There,] on the side of the gown where the towel is not hanging, cross over [the ends] again and make a knot. Go round two or three times, crossing over [the ends] and making a knot, to ensure that the gown does not fall from the pole to the ground. Facing the gown, join the palms of your hands.[22] Next, take the cord and use it to tuck in the sleeves.[23] Next, go to the wash-stand and fill a bucket with water and then, holding [the bucket] in the right hand, walk up to the toilet. The way to put water into the bucket is not to fill it completely, but to make ninety percent the standard. In front of the toilet entrance, change slippers. Changing slippers means taking off your own slippers in front of the toilet entrance and putting on the straw [toilet] slippers.[24]

[153] Zen-en-shingi[25] says, *"When we want to go to the toilet, we should go there ahead of time. Do not get into a state of anxiety and haste by arriving just in time. At this time, fold the kaṣāya, and place it on the desk in your quarters, or over the clothes-pole."*

[154] Having entered the toilet, close the door with the left hand. Next, pour just a little water from the bucket into the bowl of the toilet. Then put the bucket in its place directly in front of the hole. Then, while standing facing the toilet bowl, click the fingers three times. When clicking the fingers, make a fist with the left hand and hold it against the left hip. Then put the hem of your skirt and the edges of your clothes in order, face the entrance, position the feet either side of the rim of the toilet bowl, squat down, and defecate. Do not get either side of the bowl dirty, and do not soil the front or the back of the bowl. During this time, keep quiet. Do not chat or joke with the person on the other

---

21. 褊杉 (HENSAN). See note 19.

22. 合掌 (GASSHO). In *gassho* the palms are brought together in front of the chest, with the tips of the fingers in line with the nostrils.

23. Lit. "take the *banzu* and wear it on both arms." 袢子 (BANZU), lit. "binding thing," is a long cord tied round the shoulders and armpits (of the under-garment) so that the sleeves can be tucked in, leaving the arms bare.

24. 蒲鞋 (HO-AI), lit. "cattail slippers." 蒲 (HO), "cattail," is a marsh plant with long flat leaves, often used for weaving.

25. *Pure Criteria for Zen Monasteries*. The editing of *Zen-en-shingi* was completed by Master Choro Sosaku in 1103. It was based on Master Hyakujo's *Ko-shingi (Old Pure Criteria)*.

side of the wall, and do not sing songs or recite verses in a loud voice. Do not make a mess by weeping and dribbling, and do not be angry or hasty. Do not write characters on the walls, and do not draw lines in the earth with the shit-stick. The stick is to be used after you have relieved yourself. Another way is to use paper; old paper should not be used, and paper with characters written on it should not be used. Distinguish between clean sticks and dirty sticks. The sticks are eight *sun*[26] long, of triangular section, and the thickness of a thumb. Some are lacquered and some are not lacquered. Dirty [sticks] are thrown into the stick-box. Clean [sticks] originally belong in the stick rack. The stick-rack is placed near the board [that screens] the front of the toilet bowl. After using the stick or using paper, the method of washing is as follows: Holding the bucket in the right hand, dip the left hand well [into the water] and then, making the left hand into a dipper, scoop up the water; first rinsing the urethra three times and then washing the anus. Make yourself pure and clean by washing according to the method. During this time, do not tip the bucket so suddenly that water spills out of the hand or splashes down, causing the water to be used up quickly. After you have finished washing put the bucket in its place, and then, taking [another] stick, wipe yourself dry. Or you can use paper. Both places, the urethra and the anus, should be thoroughly wiped dry. Next, with the right hand, rearrange the hem of your skirt and the corners of your clothes, and holding the bucket in the right hand, leave the toilet, taking off the straw [toilet] slippers and putting on your own slippers as you pass through the entrance. Next, returning to the wash-stand, put the bucket back in its original place. Then wash the hands. Taking the spoon for ash in the right hand, first scoop [some ash] onto a tile or a stone, sprinkle a few drops of water onto it with the right hand, and cleanse the soiled hand. Scrub the [fingers] on the tile or the stone, as if sharpening a rusty sword on a whetstone. Wash like this, using ash, three times. Then wash another three times, putting soil [on the stone] and sprinkling it with water. Next, take a honey locust[27] in the right hand, dip it in a small tub of water, and scrub it between the hands. Wash [the hands] thoroughly, going up to the forearms as well. Wash with care and effort, dwelling in the mind of sincerity. Three lots of ash, three lots of soil, and one honey locust, makes seven rounds altogether; that is the standard. Next, wash [the hands] in the large tub. This time skin cleansers,[28] soil, ash, and so on, are not used. Just wash with water, either cold or hot. After washing once, pour the [used] water into a small bucket, then pour some fresh water [into the tub], and wash the hands again.

[157] The Garland Sutra says, *"When we wash the hands with water, we should pray that living beings will get excellent and fine hands, with which to receive and to retain the Buddha-Dharma."*[29]

[158] To pick up the water ladle, always use your right hand. While doing this, do not

---

26. One *sun* is approximately equal to 1.2 inches.

27. Honey locusts are produced by a tall leguminous tree of the same name (Latin name: *Gleditsia japonica*). They are long twisted pods containing a sweet edible pulp and seeds that resemble beans.

28. 面薬 (MENYAKU), lit. "face medicines."

29. This quotation is from the old translation of the Garland Sutra done by Buddhabhadra in 60 fascicles between 418 and 420. A second translation was done by Śikṣānanda in 80 fascicles between 695 and 699. This is known as the new translation, but there was also a third partial translation done by Prajña in 40 fascicles from 759 to 762.

noisily clatter ladle and bucket. Do not splash water about, scatter honey locusts around, get the washstand area wet, or be generally hasty and messy. Next, wipe the hands on the common towel, or wipe them on your own towel. After wiping the hands, go under the clothes-pole, in front of your gown, and take off the cord and hang it on the pole. Next, after joining hands, untie the towel, take down the gown, and put it on. Then, with the towel hanging over the left arm, apply fragrance. In the common area there is a fragrance-applier. It is fragrant wood fashioned into the shape of a treasure-pot,[30] as thick as a thumb, and as long as the width of four fingers. It is hung from the clothes-pole with a piece of string a foot or more long, which is threaded through a hole bored in each end of the fragrant [wood]. When this is rubbed between the palms, it naturally spreads its scent to the hands. When you hang your cord on the pole, do not hang it on top of another so that cord and cord become confused and entangled. Actions like these all *purify the Buddha's land, and adorn the Buddha's kingdom,* so do them carefully, and do not be hasty. Do not be in a hurry to finish, thinking that you would like to get back. Privately, you might like to consider the principle that *we do not explain the Buddha-Dharma while in the toilet.*[31] Do not keep looking into the faces of other monks who have come there. Cold water is considered better for washing when in the toilet itself; it is said that hot water gives rise to intestinal diseases. [But] there is no restriction against using warm water to wash the hands. The reason that a cauldron is provided is so that we can boil water for washing the hands. Shingi says, *"Late in the evening, boil water and supply oil.*[32]*Always ensure [a] continuous [supply of] hot and cold water, so that the minds of the monks are not disturbed."* So we see that we [can] use both hot and cold water. If the inside of the toilet has become dirty, close the door, and hang up the "dirty" sign. If a bucket has been dropped [into the toilet bowl] by mistake, close the door, and hang up the "fallen bucket" sign. Do not enter[33] a closet on which one of these signs is hung. If, when you are already in the toilet, [you hear] someone outside clicking the fingers, you should leave presently. Shingi says, *"Without washing, we must neither sit on the monks' platform, nor bow to the Three Treasures. Neither must we receive people's prostrations."* The Sutra of Three Thousand Dignified Forms says, *"If we fail to wash the anus and the urethra, we commit a duṣkṛta,*[34] *and we must not sit on a monk's pure sitting cloth*[35] *or bow to the Three Treasures. Even if we do bow, there is no happiness or virtue."*

[162] Thus, at a place of the truth where we strive in pursuit of the truth,[36] we should

---

30. This kind of pot has an oval body, a long neck, and a lid, often with jewels. (So the piece of fragrant wood would have been oval with tapered ends.) In certain Buddhist ceremonies, such pots were used to hold water for sprinkling on practitioners' heads.

31. The characters are in the style of a quotation from a Chinese text, though the source has not been traced.

32. Oil for lamps.

33. "Enter" is originally "ascend." The toilets were raised a little above the ground.

34. Violations of some of the 250 precepts for monks were classed, according to their relative importance, as *duṣkṛta*. Wrongdoings in this category include, for example, failure to observe the seven methods of stopping a quarrel.

35. 坐具 (ZAGU), represents the Sanskrit *niṣīdana*. The *zagu* is a cloth or a mat used to do prostrations on, or to sit on.

36. "A place of the truth where we strive in pursuit of the truth" is 弁道功夫の道場 (BENDO KUFU *no* DOJO). Master Dogen often used the expression 弁道功夫 (BENDO KUFU), "effort in pursuit of the truth," to express Zazen itself. "A place of the truth" is 道場 (DOJO), lit. "truth-place," which represents

consider this behavior to be foremost. How could we not bow to the Three Treasures? How could we not receive people's prostrations? And how could we not bow to others? In the place of truth of a Buddhist patriarch, this dignified behavior is always done, and people in the place of truth of a Buddhist patriarch are always equipped with this dignified behavior. It is not our own intentional effort; it is the natural expression of dignified behavior itself. It is the usual behavior of the buddhas and the everyday life of the patriarchs. It is [Buddha-behavior] not only of buddhas in this world: it is Buddha-behavior throughout the ten directions; it is Buddha-behavior in the Pure Land and in impure lands. People of scant knowledge do not think that buddhas have dignified behavior in the toilet, and they do not think that the dignified behavior of buddhas in the sahā-world[37] is like that of buddhas in the Pure Land. This is not learning of the Buddha's truth. Remember, purity and impurity is [exemplified by] blood dripping from a human being. At one time it is warm, at another time it is disgusting. The buddhas have toilets, and this we should remember.

[163] Fascicle 14 of Precepts in Ten Parts[38] says, *"Śrāmaṇera Rāhula[39] spent the night in the Buddha's toilet. When the Buddha woke up, the Buddha patted Rāhula on the head with his right hand, and preached the following verse:*

You were never stricken by poverty,
Nor have you lost wealth and nobility.[40]
Only in order to pursue the truth, you have left home.
You will be able to endure the hardship."

[164] Thus, there are toilet-buildings in the Buddha's places of practicing the truth. And the dignified behavior done in the Buddha's toilet-building is washing. That the Buddha's behavior, having been transmitted from patriarch to patriarch, still survives, is a delight to those who venerate the ancients. We have been able to meet what is difficult to meet. Furthermore, the Tathāgata graciously preached the Dharma for Rāhula inside the toilet-building. The toilet-building was one [place of] assembly for the Buddha's turning of the Dharma-wheel. The advancing and stillness[41] of that place of truth has been authentically transmitted by the Buddhist patriarchs.

[165] Fascicle 34 of the Mahāsaṃghika Precepts[42] says, *"The toilet building should not be*

---

the Sanskrit *bodhi-maṇḍa*, "seat of truth." See Glossary.

37. The *sahā-world* means the human world. See Glossary.

38. 十誦律 (JU-JU-RITSU), a 61-fascicle translation of the vinaya of the Sarvāstivādin School. It enumerates the 250 precepts of a monk in Hīnayāna Buddhism, and was translated into Chinese by Hannyatara and Kumārajīva.

39. The Sanskrit word *śrāmaṇera*, which means "novice," is a variation of *śramaṇa*, which means "monk." Rāhula was the Buddha's son from his marriage with Yaśodharā. It is said that he became a fully-ordained monk when he was twenty, and that he was foremost among the ten great disciples of the Buddha in meticulous observation of the precepts.

40. Before becoming a monk, the Buddha was the heir to his father's throne, so his son Rāhula was born into the nobility.

41. 進止 (SHINSHI), "progressing and stopping," suggests active and passive behavior, that is, real behavior in daily life.

42. 摩訶僧祇律 (MAKA-SOGI-RITSU), a 40-fascicle version of the vinaya of the Mahāsaṃghika School of Hīnayāna Buddhism. It was translated into Chinese by Buddhabhadra during the Eastern Tsin Dynasty (317–420).

located to the east or to the north. It should be located to the south or to the west. The same applies to the urinal."

[166] We should follow this [designation of] the favorable directions. This was the layout of all the monasteries[43] in India in the Western Heavens, and the [method of] construction in the Tathāgata's lifetime. Remember, this is not only the Buddha-form followed by one buddha; it describes the places of truth, the monasteries, of the Seven Buddhas. It was never initiated; it is the dignified form of the buddhas. Before we have clarified these [dignified forms], if we hope to establish a temple and to practice the Buddha-Dharma, we will make many mistakes, we will not be equipped with the Buddha's dignified forms, and the Buddha's state of bodhi will not yet manifest itself before us. If we hope to build a place of practicing the truth, or to establish a temple, we should follow the Dharma-form which the Buddhist patriarchs have authentically transmitted. We should just follow the Dharma-form which has been authentically transmitted as the right tradition. Because it is the traditional authentic transmission, its virtue has accumulated again and again. Those who are not legitimate successors to the authentic transmission of the Buddhist patriarchs do not know the body-and-mind of the Buddha-Dharma. Without knowing the body-and-mind of the Buddha-Dharma, they never clarify the Buddha-actions of the Buddha's lineage. That the Buddha-Dharma of the Great Master Śākyamuni Buddha has now spread widely through the ten directions is the realization of the Buddha's body-and-mind. The realization of the Buddha's body-and-mind, just in the moment, is like this.

Shobogenzo Senjo

Preached to the assembly at Kannon-dori-kosho-horin-ji temple in the Uji district of Yoshu,[44] on the 23rd day of the 10th lunar month in the winter of the 1st year of En-o.[45]

---

43. 精舎 (SHOJA) is the translation into Chinese characters of the Sanskrit vihāra.
44. Corresponds to present-day Kyoto prefecture.
45. 1239.

[8]

礼拝得随

Raihai-Tokuzui

Prostrating to Attainment of the Marrow

***Raihai** means "to prostrate oneself to," **toku** means "to get," or "to attain," and **zui** means "marrow." So **raihai-tokuzui** means prostrating oneself to attainment of the marrow, in other words, revering what has got the truth. In this chapter Master Dogen preached to us that the value of a being must be decided according to whether or not it has got the truth. So he said, even if it is a child, a woman, a devil, or an animal like a wild fox, if it has got the truth, we must revere it whole-heartedly. In this attitude, we can find Master Dogen's sincere reverence of the truth, and his view of men, women, and animals.*

[169] **In practicing the state of anuttara-samyak-saṃbodhi** the most difficult thing is to find a guiding teacher. Though beyond appearances such as those of a man or a woman, the guiding teacher should be a big stout fellow,[1] and should be someone ineffable.[2] He is not a person of the past and present, but may be a good counselor with the spirit of a wild fox.[3] These are the features of [someone who] has got the marrow;[4] he may be a guide and a benefactor; he is never unclear about cause and effect; he may be you, me, him, or her.[5]

[170] Having met with a guiding teacher, we should throw away myriad involvements and, without wasting a moment of time,[6] we should strive in pursuit of the truth. We should train with consciousness, we should train without consciousness, and we

1. 大丈夫 (DAIJOBU), or "great stout fellow," was originally a concept in Confucianism, suggesting a man of Confucian virtue. The word was used later in Chinese Buddhism, meaning someone who has trained perfectly. In modern Japanese, 大丈夫 (DAIJOBU) is commonly used as an adjective meaning "all right."

2. 恁麼人 (INMONIN). Master Ungo Doyo, quoted in chap. 29, Inmo, says, "If you want to attain the matter of the ineffable, you must have become someone ineffable."

3. 野狐精 (YAKO-ZEI), or "ghost of a wild fox," often suggests criticism that a person's state is too mystical, not practical enough. But in this case, it suggests the presence of something natural and mystical.

4. "Got the marrow" is 得髄 (TOKUZUI). Master Taiso Eka made three prostrations to Master Bodhidharma, and returned to his seat. Master Bodhidharma said, *"You have got my marrow."* The story is recorded in chap. 46, *Katto.*

5. "Him or her" is 渠 (*kare*), which usually means "he" or "him," but which in this context is clearly neutral.

6. 寸陰 (SUN-IN), lit. "an inch of shadow."

should train with semi-consciousness. Thus, we should learn walking on tip-toes[7] to put out a fire on our head.[8] When we behave like this, we are unharmed by abusive demons. The Patriarch who cuts off an arm and gets the marrow[9] is never another, and the master who gets free of body-and-mind[10] is ourself already. Getting the marrow, and receiving the Dharma, invariably come from sincerity and from belief. There is no example of sincerity coming from outside, and there is no way for sincerity to emerge from within. [Sincerity] just means attaching weight to the Dharma and thinking light of [one's own] body. It is to get free from the secular world and to make one's home the state of truth. If we attach even slightly more weight to self-regard for the body than to the Dharma, the Dharma is not transmitted to us, and we do not attain the truth. Those resolute spirits who attach [greater] weight to the Dharma are not unique, and they do not depend upon the exhortation of others, but let us take up, for the present, one or two instances. It is said that those who attach weight to the Dharma, will make the body-and-mind into a seat on the floor,[11] and will serve for countless kalpas [whatever] is maintaining and relying upon the great Dharma, [whatever] has *got my marrow*,[12] whether it is an outdoor pillar, whether it is a stone lantern, whether it is the buddhas, whether it is a wild dog, a demon or a god, a man or a woman. Bodies and minds are easily received: they are [as common] in the world as rice, flax, bamboo, and reeds. The Dharma is rarely met. Śākyamuni Buddha says, *"When you meet teachers who expound the supreme state of bodhi, have no regard for their race or caste,*[13] *do not notice their looks, do not dislike their faults, and do not examine their deeds. Only because you revere their prajñā, let them eat hundreds and thousands of pounds of gold every day, serve them by presenting heavenly food, serve them by scattering heavenly flowers, do prostrations and venerate them three times every day, and never let anxiety or annoyance arise in your mind. When we behave like this, there is always a way to the state of bodhi. Since I established the mind, I have been practicing like this, and so today I have been able to attain anuttara-samyak-saṃbodhi."* This being so, we should hope that even trees and stones might preach to us,[14] and we should re-

---

7. 翹足 (GYOSOKU), lit. "holding up the feet." Legend says the Buddha naturally walked on tip-toes. To learn walking on tip-toes means to learn how to behave like the Buddha.

8. A symbol of sincere behavior.

9. Master Taiso Eka cut off part of his arm to show his sincerity to Master Bodhidharma (see chap. 30, *Gyoji*), and several years later Master Bodhidharma affirmed Master Taiso Eka's state with the words *"You have got my marrow."*

10. 身心脱落 (SHINJIN-DATSURAKU), "getting free of body and mind," was an expression commonly used by Master Tendo Nyojo, Master Dogen's master.

11. A figurative expression suggesting a humble attitude.

12. 吾髄を汝得せるあらば (GOZUI *o* NYOTOKU *seru araba*), lit. "If it has 'you-got' 'my-marrow.'" 吾髄 (GOZUI), means Master Bodhidharma's marrow.

13. In the Buddha's time, Indian society had four castes: *brāhmaṇa* (priests), *kṣatriya* (the ruling nobility), *vaiśya* (workers), and *śūdra* (servants). At the lowest end of the social scale were people without any caste.

14. 若樹若石 (NYAKU-JU NYAKU-SEKI), alludes to a story in the Mahāparinirvāṇa-sūtra. A demon told a child-bodhisattva the first two lines of a four-line poem: *"All actions are in the state without constancy / Concrete existence is the arising and passing of dharmas."* The demon said it was too hungry to tell the child the last two lines, so the child offered his own body as a meal for the demon if it would recite the last two lines. So the demon recited the last two lines: *"After arising and passing have ceased, / The peace and quiet is pleasure itself."* The child preserved the verse for posterity by writing it on some nearby trees and rocks in his own blood, before being eaten by the demon.

quest that even fields and villages might preach to us.[15] We should question outdoor pillars, and we should investigate even fences and walls. There is the ancient [example of the] God Indra[16] prostrating himself to a wild dog as his master, and asking it about the Dharma; his fame as a great bodhisattva has been transmitted. [Fitness to be asked] does not rest upon the relative nobility of one's station. Nevertheless, stupid people who do not listen to the Buddha's Dharma think, *"I am a senior bhikṣu. I cannot prostrate myself to a junior who has got the Dharma." "I have endured long training. I cannot prostrate myself to a recent student who has got the Dharma." "I sign my name with the title of master. I cannot prostrate myself to someone who does not have the title of master." "I am an Administrator of Dharma Affairs.*[17] *I cannot prostrate myself to lesser monks who have got the Dharma." "I am the Chief Administrator of Monks.*[18] *I cannot prostrate myself to lay men and lay women who have got the Dharma." "I am [a bodhisattva] of the three clever stages and ten sacred stages. I cannot prostrate myself to bhikṣuṇīs and other [women], even if they have got the Dharma." "I am of royal pedigree. I cannot prostrate myself to the family of a retainer or to the lineage of a minister, even if they have got the Dharma."* Stupid people like these have heedlessly fled their father's kingdom and are wandering on the roads of foreign lands;[19] therefore, they neither see nor hear the Buddha's truth.

[176] Long ago, in the Tang Dynasty, Great Master Shinsai of Joshu[20] established the mind and set off as a wayfarer.[21] In the story he says, *"I shall question anyone who is superior to me, even a child of seven. And I shall teach anyone who is inferior to me, even a man of a hundred."* The old man[22] is willing to prostrate himself on asking a seven-year-old about the Dharma—this is a rare example of a resolute spirit, and the working of the mind of an eternal buddha. When a bhikṣuṇī who has got the truth and got the Dharma manifests herself in the world,[23] bhikṣus[24] who seek the Dharma and learn in practice will devote themselves to her order, prostrating themselves and asking about the Dharma—this is an excellent example of learning in practice. For instance, it is like the thirsty finding drink.

[178] The Chinese Zen Master Shikan[25] is a venerable patriarch in Rinzai's lineage. Once

15. 若田若里 (NYAKU-DEN NYAKU-RI). These words originate in the Lotus Sutra. See LS 3.72-74.

16. 天帝釈 (TENTAI-SHAKU). See chap. 2, *Maka-hannya-haramitsu,* note 28.

17. 法務司 (HOMUSHI). The title is no longer in use, and the exact nature of the position is unclear. 司 (SHI) means "government official." A monk holding this position would also have been an official in the government.

18. 僧正司 (SOJOSHI). This title has also gone out of use.

19. Alludes to a parable in the *Shinge (Belief and Understanding)* chapter of the Lotus Sutra. See LS 1.236.

20. Master Joshu Jushin. A successor of Master Nansen Fugan. He also studied under Masters Obaku, Hoju, Enkan, and Kassan. Died 897, aged 120. Great Master Shinsai is his posthumous title. See chap. 35, *Hakujushi.*

21. 行脚 (ANGYA), lit. "to go on foot," means to travel from place to place, visiting Buddhist masters, or on a pilgrimage to sacred places.

22. It is said that Master Joshu Jushin was already sixty before he became a Buddhist monk.

23. 出世 (SHUSSE), lit. "manifest oneself in the world," usually means to become the master of a big temple.

24. 比丘僧 (BIKU-SO). 比丘 (BIKU) represents the Sanskrit word *bhikṣu,* which means a male monk. 僧 (SO), usually translated as "monk," is originally neutral in gender. It sometimes represents the Sanskrit word *saṃgha,* as in the case of the Three Treasures, 仏法僧 (BUPPOSO), Buddha, Dharma, and Saṃgha.

25. Master Kankei Shikan (died 895), successor of Master Rinzai. Throughout this paragraph he is

upon a time, Rinzai sees the Master coming [to visit] and holds onto him. The Master says, *"It is understood."*[26] Rinzai lets go and says, *"I will allow you to stop for a while."*[27] From this point on, he has already become Rinzai's disciple. He leaves Rinzai and goes to Matsuzan,[28] at which time Matsuzan asks him, *"Where have you come from?"* The Master says, *"The entrance of the road."* Matsuzan says, *"Why have you come here without anything on?"*[29] The Master has no words. He just prostrates himself, bowing as disciple to teacher. The Master asks a question back to Matsuzan: *"Just what is Matsuzan?"* Matsuzan says, *"[Matsuzan] never shows a peak."*[30] The Master says, *"Just who is the person within the mountain?"* Matsuzan says, *"It is beyond appearances such as those of a man or a woman."* The Master says, *"Then why do you not change [your form]?"* Matsuzan says, *"I am not the ghost of a wild fox. What might I change?"* The Master prostrates himself. Eventually he decides to work as the head of the vegetable garden and works there altogether for three years. Later, when he has manifested himself in the world,[31] he preaches to the assembly, *"I got half a dipper at Old Papa Rinzai's place, and I got half a dipper at Old Mama Matsuzan's place.*[32] *Making a dipper with both [halves], I have finished drinking, and, having arrived directly at the present, I am completely satisfied."* Hearing these words now, I look back on the traces of those days with veneration for the past. Matsuzan is an excellent disciple[33] of Koan Daigu. She has power in her lifeblood, and so she has become Shikan's "Ma." Rinzai is an authentic successor of Obaku [Ki]un.[34] He has power in his efforts, and so he has become Shikan's "Pa." "Pa" means father, and "Ma" means mother.[35] Zen Master Shikan's prostration to and pursuit of the Dharma under Nun Matsuzan Ryonen are an excellent example of a resolute spirit, and integrity that students of later ages should emulate. We can say that he broke all barriers, large and small.

[180] Nun Myoshin is a disciple of Kyozan.[36] Kyozan, on one occasion, is choosing the

---

referred to as "the Master."

26. Master Rinzai wanted Master Kankei to stay in his order. Master Kankei understood Master Rinzai's intention, and agreed.

27. *Shinji-shobogenzo* pt. 3, no. 17: Master Kankei Shikan is coming to visit Master Rinzai. When Master Rinzai sees him, he holds onto him. Master Kankei says, *"Understood."* Master Rinzai lets go of him and says, *"I will allow you to stop for a while."* When Master Kankei becomes the master of his own temple, he preaches to the assembly, *"When I met Master Rinzai, there was no discussion. Arriving directly at the moment of the present, I am completely satisfied."*

28. Nun-Master Matsuzan Ryonen, successor of Master Koan Daigu.

29. Lit. "Why haven't you come here covering yourself?" This suggests that it sometimes better to be polite than to give a terse "Zen" answer.

30. The proper name 末山 (MATSUZAN) is lit. "the Last Mountain," or "the End Mountain."

31. 出世 (SHUSSE), i.e., when he became the master of a big temple. See note 23.

32. "Papa" is 爺爺 (YA-YA). "Mama" is 孃孃 (JO-JO).

33. 神足 (JINSOKU), lit. "mystical foot," is a traditional term for an excellent member of an order. The Chinese commentary *Daichido-ron* (based on the Mahā-prajñā-pāramitopadeśa) explains the term 神足 (JINSOKU) as follows: *"Their fine abilities are difficult to fathom, so we call them mystical; they support many living beings, so we call them feet."*

34. Master Obaku Ki-un (exact dates unknown—died between 855 and 859), successor of Master Hyakujo Ekai.

35. Master Dogen explained the meaning of the Chinese characters 爺 (YA) and 孃 (JO), using the Japanese phonetic alphabet.

36. Master Kyozan Ejaku (807–883), successor of Master Isan Reiyu.

Chief of the Business Office.[37] He asks around the retired officers and others on Kyozan mountain, *"Who is the right person?"* They discuss it back and forth, and eventually Kyozan says, *"Disciple [Myo]shin from the Wai river, though a woman, has the spirit of a big stout fellow.[38] She is certainly qualified to be Chief of the Business Office."* All the monks agree. [So] at length Myoshin is assigned as Chief of the Business Office. The dragons and elephants in Kyozan's order do not resent this. Though the position is in fact not so grand, the one selected for it might need to love herself. While she is posted at the Business Office, seventeen monks from the Shoku district[39] form a group to visit teachers and seek the truth, and, intending to climb Kyozan mountain, they lodge at dusk at the Business Office. In a night-time talk, while resting, they discuss the story of the founding Patriarch Sokei,[40] and the wind and the flag.[41] The words of each of the seventeen men are totally inadequate. Meanwhile, listening from the other side of the wall, the Chief of the Business Office says, *"Those seventeen blind donkeys! How many straw sandals have they worn out in vain? They have never seen the Buddha-Dharma even in a dream."* A temple servant present at the time overhears the Chief of the Business Office criticizing the monks and informs the seventeen monks themselves, but none of the seventeen monks resents the criticism of the Chief of the Business Office. Ashamed of their own inability to express the truth, they at once prepare themselves in the dignified form,[42] burn incense, do prostrations and request [her teaching]. The Chief of the Business Office says, *"Come up here!"* The seventeen monks approach her, and while they are still walking, the Chief of the Business Office says, *"This is not wind moving, this is not a flag moving, and this is not mind moving."* When she teaches them like this, the seventeen monks all experience reflection. They bow to thank her and have the ceremony to become her disciples. Then they go straight back home to western Shoku. In the end, they do not climb Kyozan mountain. Truly the state [demonstrated] here is beyond [bodhisattvas at] the three clever and ten sacred stages;[43] it is action in the truth as transmitted by Buddhist patriarchs from authentic successor to authentic successor. Therefore, even today, when a post as master or assistant-master[44] is vacated, a bhikṣuṇī who has got the Dharma may be requested [to fill it]. Even if a bhikṣu is senior in years and experience, if he has not got the Dharma, what importance does he have? A leader of monks must always rely upon clear eyes. Yet many [leaders] are drowning

---

37. 廨院 (KAI-IN). This office was for dealing with lay people such as government officials, merchants, and donors. The building was usually located lower down the mountain than the main temple buildings.

38. 大丈夫 (DAIJOBU). See note 1. Suggests that she was healthy and vigorous, and had self-control.

39. In present-day Szechuan province.

40. Master Daikan Eno (638–713), successor of Master Daiman Konin.

41. Two monks are having a discussion. One monk says, "The flag is moving." The other monk says, "The wind is moving." Master Daikan Eno says, "The wind is not moving and the flag is not moving. You are moving mind." (Keitoku-dento-roku, chap. 5. See also Shobogenzo chap. 29, *Inmo*.)

42. 威儀を具す (IIGI *o* GU *su*), lit. "to prepare the dignified form," means to wear the *kaṣāya* and to take the *zagu* (prostration cloth).

43. A bodhisattva is said to pass through fifty-two stages on the road to buddhahood. The first group of ten stages is the ten stages of belief. The next three groups of ten stages are the three clever stages. The fifth group of ten stages is the ten sacred stages. The fifty-first stage is 等覚 (TOKAKU), "the balanced state of truth," and the fifty-second stage is 妙覚 (MYOKAKU), "the fine state of truth."

44. 伴座 (HANZA), lit. "half-seat"—a reference to the story that the Buddha shared his seat with Master Mahākāśyapa.

in the body-and-mind of a village bumpkin; they are so dense that they are prone to be derided even in the secular world. How much less do they deserve to be mentioned in the Buddha-Dharma? Moreover, there may be [men] who would refuse to prostrate themselves to women monks who are teachers that have received the Dharma, and who are [the men's] elder-sisters, aunts, and so on.[45] Because they do not know and will not learn, they are close to animals, and far from the Buddhist patriarchs. When the sole devotion of body-and-mind to the Buddha-Dharma is retained deep in [a person's] consciousness, the Buddha-Dharma always has compassion for the person. Even human beings and gods, in their stupidity, have the sympathy to respond to sincerity, so how could the buddhas, in their rightness, lack the compassion to reciprocate sincerity. The sublime spirit which responds to sincerity exists even in soil, stones, sand, and pebbles. In the temples of the great Kingdom of Sung today, if a resident bhikṣuṇī is reputed to have got the Dharma, the government issues an imperial edict for her to be appointed master of a nuns' temple, and she gives formal preaching in the Dharma Hall of her present temple. All the monks, from the Master down, attend [the formal preaching]. They listen to the Dharma, standing on the ground, and questions are also [put by] the bhikṣus, the male monks. This is a traditional standard. A person who has got the Dharma is one individual true eternal buddha here and now, and as such should not be met as someone from the past. When that person looks at us, we meet each other in a new and singular state. When we look at that person, the mutual relation may be *today having to enter today*. For example, when arhats, pratyekabuddhas, and [bodhisattvas at] the three clever and ten sacred stages,[46] come to a bhikṣuṇī who is retaining the transmission of the right-Dharma-eye treasury, to prostrate themselves and to ask her about Dharma, she must receive these prostrations. Why should men be higher? Space is space, the four elements are the four elements,[47] the five aggregates are the five aggregates,[48] and women are also like this. As regards attainment of the truth, both [men and women] attain the truth, and we should just profoundly revere every single person who has attained the Dharma. Do not discuss man and woman. This is one of Buddhism's finest Dharma-standards.

[187] In Sung Dynasty [China], the term *"householder"*[49] refers to gentlemen who have not left their families.[50] Some of them live in houses with their wives, while others are single and pure, but anyway we can say that they are immensely busy with dusty toil.[51]

---

45. Elder sister means a senior female member of one's master's order. Aunt means a senior female member of one's master's order.

46. In the Lotus Sutra the Buddha explains four classes of Buddhists: the *śrāvaka* (intellectual Buddhist), the *pratyekabuddha* (perceptive Buddhist), the *bodhisattva* (practical Buddhist), and the *buddha*. These classes were further sub-divided. An *arhat* is at the fourth and final state of a *śrāvaka*. For further explanation, see chap. 24, *Bukkyo*.

47. Earth, water, fire, and wind; representing the material world.

48. Matter, perception, thinking, enaction, and consciousness; representing the phenomenal world.

49. 居士 (KOJI), "householder," represents the Sanskrit word *gṛhapati*, which means "the master of a household." At the same time, the concept of the *koji* also comes from Confucianism: a man who did not work for the imperial government, but studied Confucianism as a civilian, was called *koji*.

50. 出家 (SHUKKE). 出 (SHUTSU) means "to get out of" or "to transcend." 家 (KE) means a house, a home, or a family; at the same time it suggests the web of social and economic relationships inevitably connected with family life. As a verb, *shukke* means to become a Buddhist monk; as a noun, it means a monk.

51. 塵労 (JINRO), "dusty toil," means secular work.

Nevertheless, if one of them has clarified something, patch-robed monks[52] gather to do prostrations and to ask for the benefit [of his teaching], as to a master who had left home. We also should be like that, even towards a woman, even towards an animal. When [a person] has never seen the truths of the Buddha-Dharma even in a dream, even if he is an old bhikṣu of a hundred years, he cannot arrive at the level of a man or woman who has got the Dharma, so we should not venerate [such a person], but need only bow to him as junior to senior. When [a person] practices the Buddha-Dharma and speaks the Buddha-Dharma, even if a girl of seven, she is just the guiding teacher of the four groups,[53] and the benevolent father of all living beings. We should serve and venerate her as we do the buddha-tathāgatas, and as it was, for example, when the dragon's daughter became a buddha.[54] This is just the time-honored form in Buddhism. Those who do not know about it, and who have not received its one-to-one transmission, are pitiful.

[188] Another case: Since the ancient past in Japan and China, there have been women emperors. The whole country is the possession of such an empress, and all the people become her subjects. This is not out of reverence for her person, but out of reverence for her position. Likewise, a bhikṣuṇī has never been revered for her person, but is revered solely for her attainment of the Dharma. Furthermore, the virtues which accompany the fourth effect all belong to a bhikṣuṇī who has become an arhat.[55] Even [these] virtues accompany her; what human being or god could hope to surpass these virtues of the fourth effect? Gods of the triple world are all inferior to her. While being forsaken [by human beings] she is venerated by all the gods. How much less should anyone fail to venerate those who have received the transmission of the Tathāgata's right Dharma, and who have established the great will of a bodhisattva?[56] If we fail to venerate such a person it is our own wrongness. And if we fail to revere our own supreme state of bodhi, we are stupid people who insult the Dharma. Again, there are in our country, daughters of emperors, or ministers' daughters who become queens consort,[57] or queens who are titled with the names of temples.[58] Some of them have shaved their head, and some of them do not shave their head. In any case, priests who [only] look like bhikṣus and who crave fame and love gain, never fail to run to the house of such [a woman] and strike their head at her clogs. They are far inferior to serfs following a lord. Moreover, many of them actually become her servants for a period of years. How piti-

---

52. 雲衲霞袂 (UN-NO-GA-BEI), lit. "clouds-patches-mist-sleeves." Clouds and mist suggest the free and natural life of a Buddhist monk. Patches and sleeves suggest the Buddhist robe, and the gowns with wide sleeves usually worn by monks in China and Japan.

53. 四衆 (SHISHU): *bhikṣu* (monks), *bhikṣuṇī* (nuns), *upāsaka* (lay men), and *upāsikā* (lay women).

54. See LS 2.224.

55. The four stages of a *śrāvaka*, or intellectual Buddhist, are as follows: *srotāpanna* (stream-enterer), *sakṛdāgāmin* (the state of returning only once again), *anāgāmin* (the state which is not subject to return), and *arhat* (the ultimate state which is the fourth effect). An *arhat* is a *śrāvaka* who has overcome all hindrances and who needs to learn nothing more. In chap. 34, *Arakan*, Master Dogen identifies *arhat* and *buddha*.

56. The will to save others before we ourselves are saved. See chap. 69, *Hotsu-mujoshin*; chap. 70, *Hotsu-bodaishin*; and chap. 93, *Doshin*.

57. The emperor would have several wives, or queens consort. Ministers would be eager to have a daughter made a queen consort.

58. In those days Buddhism was revered highly in Japanese society. So aristocratic women liked to have a titular position in a Buddhist temple.

ful they are. Having been born in a minor nation in a remote land, they do not even know a bad custom like this for what it is. There was never [such ignorance] in India and China, but only in our country. It is lamentable. Forcedly to shave the head and then to violate the Tathāgata's right Dharma must be called deep and heavy sin. Solely because they forget that worldly ways are dreams and illusions, flowers in space, they are bonded in slavery to women. It is lamentable. Even for the sake of a trifling secular livelihood, they act like this. Why, for the sake of the supreme bodhi, do they fail to venerate the venerable ones who have got the Dharma? It is because their awe for the Dharma is shallow, and their will to pursue the Dharma is not pervasive. When [people] are already coveting a treasure they do not think about refusing it just because it is the treasure of a woman. When we want to get the Dharma, we must surpass such resolve. If it is so, even grass, trees, fences, and walls will bestow the right Dharma, and the heavens and the earth, myriad things and phenomena, will also impart the right Dharma. This is a truth which we must always remember. Before we seek the Dharma with this determination, even if we meet true good counselors, we will not be soaked by the benevolent water of Dharma. We should pay careful attention [to this].

[192] Furthermore, nowadays extremely stupid people look at women without having corrected the prejudice that women are objects of sexual greed. Disciples of the Buddha must not be like this. If whatever may become the object of sexual greed is to be hated, do not all men deserve to be hated too? As regards the causes and conditions of becoming tainted, a man can be the object, a woman can be the object, what is neither man nor woman can be the object, and dreams and fantasies, flowers in space, can also be the object. There have been impure acts done with a reflection on water as an object, and there have been impure acts done with the sun in the sky as an object.[59] A god can be the object, and a demon can be the object. It is impossible to count all the possible objects; they say that there are eighty-four thousand objects. Should we discard all of them? Should we not look at them? The precepts[60] say, *"[Abuse of] the two male organs,*[61] *or the three female organs,*[62] *are both* pārājika, *and [the offender] may not remain in the community."*[63] This being so, if we hate whatever might become the object of sexual greed, all men and women will hate each other, and we will never have any chance to attain salvation. We should examine this truth in detail. There are non-Buddhists who have no wife: even though they have no wife, they have not entered the Buddha-Dharma, and so they are [only] non-Buddhists with wrong views. There are disciples of the Buddha who, as the two classes of lay people,[64] have a husband or a wife: even though they have a husband or a wife, they are disciples of the Buddha, and so there are no other beings equal to them in the human world or in heaven above.

[194] Even in China, there was a stupid monk who made the following vow: *"Through every life, in every age, I shall never look at a woman."* Upon what morality is this vow

---

59. References to old Chinese and Japanese stories. *Kojiki (Record of Ancient Matters),* a book of ancient Japanese legends, tells the story of a woman who was sexually stimulated by the rays of the sun.

60. Fascicle 1 of Shibun-ritsu (Precepts in Four Divisions).

61. Male organ and anus.

62. Urethra, female organ, and anus.

63. The Sanskrit word *pārājika* expresses one of the most serious violations of the precepts, which may warrant expulsion from the monastic order.

64. *Upāsaka* (layman) and *upāsikā* (laywoman).

based? Is it based on secular morality? Is it based on the Buddha-Dharma? Is it based on the morality of non-Buddhists? Or is it based on the morality of heavenly demons?[65] What wrong is there in a woman? What virtue is there in a man? Among bad people there are men who are bad people. Among good people there are women who are good people. Wanting to hear the Dharma, and wanting to get liberation, never depend upon whether we are a man or a woman. When they have yet to cut delusion, men and women alike have yet to cut delusion. When they cut delusion and experience the principle, there is nothing at all to choose between a man and a woman. Moreover, if [a man] has vowed never to look at a woman, must he discard women even when vowing to save limitlessly many living beings?[66] If he discards them, he is not a bodhisattva. How much less [does he have] the Buddha's compassion. This [vow] is just a drunken utterance caused by deep intoxication on the wine of the śrāvaka. Neither human beings nor gods should believe this [vow] to be true. Furthermore, if we hate [others] for the wrongs they have committed in the past, we must even hate all bodhisattvas. If we hate like this, we will discard everyone, so how will we be able to realize the Buddha-Dharma? Words like those [of the monk's vow] are the deranged speech of a stupid man who does not know the Buddha-Dharma. We should feel sorry for him. If that monk's[67] vow is true, did Śākyamuni and the bodhisattvas of his time all commit wrongs?[68] And was their bodhi-mind less profound than the will of that monk? We should reflect [on this] quietly. We should learn in practice whether the ancestral masters who transmitted the treasury of Dharma, and the bodhisattvas of the Buddha's lifetime, had things to learn in the Buddha-Dharma without this vow. If the vow of that monk were true, not only would we fail to save women, but also, when a woman who had got the Dharma manifested herself in the world and preached the Dharma for human beings and gods, we would be forbidden to come and listen to her, would we not? Anyone who did not come and listen would be not a bodhisattva, but just a non-Buddhist. When we look now at the great Kingdom of Sung, there are monks who seem to have been in training for a long time, [but] who have only been vainly counting the sands of the ocean[69] and rolling like surf over the ocean of life and death.[70] There are also those who, although women, have visited [good] counselors, made effort in pursuit of the truth, and thus become the guiding teachers of human beings and gods. There are [women] such as the old woman who wouldn't sell her rice cakes [to Tokuzan] and threw her rice cakes away.[71] It was pitiful that although [Tokuzan] was a male

---

65. 天魔 (TENMA) are demons in heaven who govern the world of volition and hinder Buddhism. They symbolize idealistic people. The various classes of demons are discussed in chap. 70, *Hotsu-bodaishin.*

66. The original words are 衆生無辺誓願度 (SHUJO-MUHEN-SEIGAN-DO), or *"Living beings are limitless; I vow to save them."* This is the first of 四弘誓願 (SHI-GU-SEIGAN), the Four Universal Vows: *Living beings are countless; I vow to save them. / Annoyances are endless; I vow to cut them. / The teachings of Dharma are boundless; I vow to learn them. / The Buddha's truth is supreme; I vow to realize it."*

67. "That monk" is なんぢ (*nanji*), or "you." Master Dogen often uses なんぢ (*nanji*) for the third person, when criticizing someone's wrongness.

68. That is, by looking at women.

69. In Master Yoka Gengaku's poem *Shodo-ka (Song of Experiencing the Truth)* there is a line *"Entering the ocean and counting sands, they hinder themselves in vain."* Counting the sands of the ocean symbolizes the difficulty of realizing the Dharma only by reading books.

70. Symbolizes the life of people who do not have any valuable aim.

71. See chaps. 18 and 19, *Shin-fukatoku.*

monk, a bhikṣu, he had been vainly counting the sands of the ocean of philosophy, and had never seen the Buddha-Dharma, even in a dream. In general, we should learn to understand clearly whatever circumstances we meet. If we learn only to fear and to flee [from circumstances], that is the theory and practice of a śrāvaka of the small vehicle. When we abandon the east and try to hide away in the west, the west is also not without its circumstances. Even if we think that we have escaped circumstances, unless we understand them clearly, though they may be distant, they are still circumstances, we are still not in the state of liberation, and the distant circumstances will [disturb us] more and more deeply.

[198] Again in Japan, there is one particularly laughable institution. This is either called a "sanctuary,"[72] or called a "place for practicing the truth of the Great Vehicle," where bhikṣuṇīs and other women are not allowed to enter. The wrong custom has long been handed down, and so people cannot recognize it for what it is. People who emulate the ancients do not rectify it, and men of wide knowledge give no thought to it. Calling it the enactment of people of authority, or terming it the legacy of men of tradition, they never discuss it at all. If one laughed, a person's guts might split. Just who are the so-called people of authority? Are they sages or are they saints? Are they gods or are they devils? Are they [bodhisattvas at] the ten sacred stages or are they [bodhisattvas at] the three clever stages? Are they [bodhisattvas in] the balanced state of truth or are they [bodhisattvas in] the fine state of truth? Moreover, if old [ways] should never be reformed, should we refrain from abandoning incessant wandering through life and death? Still more, the Great Master Śākyamuni is just the supreme right and balanced state of truth itself,[73] and he clarified everything that needs to be clarified, he practiced everything that needs to be practiced, and he liberated[74] all that needs to be liberated. Who today could even approach his level? Yet the Buddha's order when he was in the world included all four groups: bhikṣus, bhikṣuṇīs, upāsakas, and upāsikās, it included the eight kinds of beings,[75] the thirty-seven kinds of beings, and the eighty-four thousand kinds of beings. The formation of the Buddhist order is clearly the Buddhist order itself. So what kind of order has no bhikṣuṇīs, has no women, and has no eight kinds of beings? We should never hope to have so-called sanctuaries which surpass in their purity the Buddhist order of the Tathāgata's lifetime, because they are the sphere of heavenly demons.[76] There are no differences in the Dharma-form of the Buddhist order,

---

72. 結界 (KEKKAI), lit. "bounded area," represents the Sanskrit *sīmā-bandha*,"a depository of rules of morality."

73. 無上正等覚 (MUJO-SHOTO-KAKU). These characters represent the meaning of the Sanskrit *anuttara-samyak-saṃbodhi*. The Sanskrit word *bodhi* is represented by 覚 (KAKU), lit. "awakening," or "awareness;" it suggests the state experienced throughout the body-and-mind in Zazen. *Bodhi* is usually represented by the character 道 (DO), lit. "Way," and it is also sometimes represented phonetically as 菩提 (BODAI).

74. 解脱す (GEDATSU su). 解 (GE) means "to solve," and 脱 (DATSU) means "to get rid of." Here *gedatsu su* is used as a verb.

75. Eight guardians of the Buddha-Dharma: *deva* (gods), *nāga* (dragons), *yakṣa* (demons), *gandharva* (celestial musicians who feed on fragrances), *asura* (evil spirits), *garuḍa* (birds which hunt dragons), *kimnara* (half-horses, half-men), and *mahoraga* (serpents). These fantastic beings existed in ancient Indian legends, so they were utilized in Buddhist sutras to suggest the diversity of the Buddha's audiences. See Glossary and, for example, LS 2.140.

76. 天魔 (TENMA). See note 65.

not in this world or in other directions, and not among a thousand buddhas of the three times.[77] We should know that [an order] with a different code is not a Buddhist order. *The fourth effect*[78] is the ultimate rank. Whether in the Mahāyāna or the Hīnayāna, the virtues of the ultimate rank are not differentiated. Yet many bhikṣuṇīs have experienced the fourth effect. [So] to what kind of place—whether it is within the triple world or in the Buddha-lands of the ten directions—can [a bhikṣuṇī] not go? Who could stand in her path? At the same time, the fine state of truth[79] is also the supreme rank. When a woman has [thus] already become buddha, is there anything in all directions that she cannot perfectly realize? Who could aim to bar her from passing? She already has virtue that *widely illuminates the ten directions;* what meaning can a boundary have? Moreover, would goddesses be barred from passing? Would nymphs be barred from passing? Even goddesses and nymphs are beings that have not yet cut delusion; they are just aimlessly wandering ordinary beings. When they have wrong, they have; when they are without [wrong], they are without. Human women and bestial women, also, when they have wrong, they have; when they are without wrong, they are without. [But] who would stand in the way of gods or in the way of deities? [Bhikṣuṇī] have attended the Buddha's order of the three times; they have learned in practice at the place of the Buddha. If [places] differ from the Buddha's place and from the Buddha's order, who can believe in them as the Buddha's Dharma? [Those who exclude women] are just very stupid fools who deceive and delude secular people. They are more stupid than a wild dog worrying that its burrow might be stolen by a human being. The Buddha's disciples, whether bodhisattvas or śrāvakas, have the following ranks: first, bhikṣu; second, bhikṣuṇī; third, upāsaka; and fourth, upāsikā. These ranks are recognized both in the heavens above and in the human world, and they have long been heard. This being so, those who rank second among the Buddha's disciples are superior to sacred wheel-rolling kings,[80] and superior to Śakra-devānām-indra.[81] There should never be a place where they cannot go. Still less should [bhikṣuṇīs] be ranked alongside kings and ministers of a minor nation in a remote land. [But] when we look at present "places of the truth" which a bhikṣuṇī may not enter, any rustic, boor, farmer, or old lumberjack can enter at random. Still less would any king, lord, officer, or minister be refused entry. Comparing country bumpkins and bhikṣuṇīs, in terms of learning of the truth or in terms of attainment of rank, who is superior and who is inferior, in conclusion? Whether discussing this according to secular rules or according to the Buddha-Dharma, [one would think that] rustics and boors should not be allowed to go where a bhikṣuṇī might go. [The situation in Japan] is utterly deranged; [our] inferior nation is the first to leave this stain [on its history]. How pitiful it is. When the eldest daughters of the compassionate father of the triple world came to a small country, they found places where they were barred from going. On the other hand, fellows who live in

---

77. 三世 (SANZE), past, present, and future; eternity.

78. 四果 (SHIKA), arhathood, the ultimate state in Hīnayāna Buddhism. See note 55.

79. The ultimate state of a bodhisattva in Mahāyāna Buddhism. See note 43.

80. 天輪聖王 (TENRINJO-O), from the Sanskrit *cakravarti-rāja*. In ancient Indian mythology there are four such kings who rule over the four continents surrounding Mount Sumeru. They each have a precious wheel or *cakra*.

81. The God Indra. See note 16 and Glossary.

those places called "sanctuaries" have no fear of [committing] the ten wrongs,[82] and they violate the ten important precepts[83] one after another. Is it simply that, in their world of wrongdoing, they hate people who do not do wrong? Still more, a deadly sin[84] is a serious matter indeed; those who live in sanctuaries may have committed even the deadly sins. We should just do away with such worlds of demons. We should learn the Buddha's moral teaching and should enter the Buddha's world. This naturally may be [the way] to repay the Buddha's benevolence. Have these traditionalists understood the meaning of a sanctuary, or have they[85] not? From whom have they received their transmission? Who has covered them with the seal of approval? Whatever comes into *this great world sanctified by the buddhas*—whether it is the buddhas, living beings, the Earth, or space—will get free of fetters and attachments, and will return to the original state which is the wonderful Dharma of the buddhas. This being so, when living beings step once [inside] this world, they are completely covered by the Buddha's virtue. They have the virtue of refraining from immorality, and they have the virtue of becoming pure and clean. When one direction is sanctified, the whole world of Dharma is sanctified at once, and when one level is sanctified, the whole world of Dharma is sanctified. Sometimes places are sanctified using water, sometimes places are sanctified using mind, and sometimes places are sanctified using space. For every case there are traditions which have been transmitted and received, and which we should know.[86] Furthermore, when we are sanctifying an area, after sprinkling nectar[87] and finishing devotional prostrations[88]—in other words, after making the place pure—we recite the following verse:

This world and the whole world of Dharma,
Naturally are sanctified, pure and clean.

Have the traditionalists and veterans who nowadays usually proclaim sanctuaries understood this meaning, or have they not? I guess they cannot know that the whole world of Dharma is sanctified within [the act of] sanctification itself. Clearly, drunk on the wine of the śrāvaka, they consider a small area to be a great world. Let us hope that they will snap out of their habitual drunken delusion, and that they will not violate the wholeness of the great world of the buddhas. We should prostrate ourselves in veneration of the virtue by which [the buddhas], through acts of salvation and acceptance,

---

82. There are several interpretations of the ten wrongs. One interpretation is that the ten wrongs are as follows: killing, stealing, adultery, telling lies, two-faced speech, abusive slander, useless chatter, greed, anger, and devotion to wrong views.

83. The ten important precepts, or prohibitions, are as follows: not to take life, not to steal, not to lust, not to lie, not to sell liquor, not to discuss the faults of other Buddhists, not to praise oneself, not to begrudge Dharma or possessions, not to get angry, and not to insult the Three Treasures. See chap. 94, *Jukai.*

84. The five deadly sins are to kill one's father, to kill one's mother, to kill an arhat, to spill the Buddha's blood, and to disrupt the Buddhist order.

85. "They" is originally なんぢ (*nanji*–"you"); see note 67.

86. For example, it is traditional to sprinkle water over the area where a precepts ceremony is to be held.

87. 甘露 (KANRO), lit. "sweet dew," from the Sanskrit *amṛta*, which means nectar from heaven. In this case, "nectar" means water.

88. 帰命の礼 (KIMYO *no* RAI), lit. "devotion-of-life bow." In a devotional prostration, the practitioner drops five parts of the body to the ground: left knee, right knee, left elbow, right elbow, forehead.

cover all living beings with their influence. Who could deny that this [prostration] is the attainment of the marrow of the truth?

Shobogenzo Raihai-tokuzui
Written at Kannon-dori-kosho-horin-ji temple
on the day of purity and brightness[89] in [the
2nd year of]
En-o.[90]

89. 清明の日 (SEI-MEI *no* HI). This was the name given to the 15th day after the spring equinox.
90. 1240.

[9]

谿声山色

KEISEI-SANSHIKI

The Voices of the River-Valley and the Form of the Mountains

***Kei** means "river-valley," **sei** means "sound" or "voice," **san** means "mountain," and **shiki** means "form" or "color." So **keisei-sanshiki** means voices of river-valleys and forms of mountains—that is, Nature. In Buddhism, this world is the truth itself, so Nature is a face of the truth. Nature is the material side of the real world, so it is always speaking the truth, and manifesting the law of the Universe every day. This is why it has been said since ancient time that sounds of rivers are the preaching of Gautama Buddha and forms of mountains are the body of Gautama Buddha. In this chapter, Master Dogen preached to us the meaning of Nature in Buddhism.*

[209] **In the supreme state of bodhi,** Buddhist patriarchs who transmitted the truth and received the behavior have been many, and examples of past ancestors who reduced their bones to powder[1] cannot be denied. Learn from the ancestral Patriarch who cut off his arm,[2] and do not differ by a hair's breadth [from the bodhisattva who] covered the mud.[3] When we each get rid of our husk, we are not restricted by former views and understanding, and things which have for vast kalpas been unclear suddenly appear before us. In the here and now of such a moment, the self does not recognize it, no-one else is conscious of it, you do not expect it, and even the eyes of Buddha do not glimpse it. How could the human intellect fathom it?

[210] In the great Kingdom of Sung there lived the Layman Toba, whose name was Soshoku, and who was also called Shisen.[4] He seems to have been a real dragon in the literary world,[5] and he studied the dragons and elephants of the Buddhist world.[6] He swam happily into deep depths, and floated up and down through layers of cloud.[7] Once he visited Lushan.[8] In the story he hears the sounds of a mountain stream flowing

---

1. Symbolizing dogged perseverance in pursuing the truth.
2. Master Taiso Eka. See chap. 30, *Gyoji*.
3. In a past life as a bodhisattva, the Buddha spread his hair over a muddy puddle so that his master, Dīpamkara Buddha, could walk over it.
4. The Chinese poet So Toba (1036–1101). Toba was the poet's pen-name. *Koji* is a title used for a lay Buddhist (see chap. 8, *Raihai-tokuzui*, note 49). Soshoku was his formal name. He also used the name Shisen. Like Buddhist monks, men of literature in China often had many different names.
5. 筆海 (HITSUKAI), lit. "the ocean of the brush."
6. He read the writings of excellent Buddhist masters.
7. Master Dogen praised his ability as a poet.
8. A region of China famed for its beautiful scenery.

through the night, and realizes the truth. He makes the following verse, and presents it to Zen Master Joso:[9]

> *The voices of the river-valley are the [Buddha's] Wide and Long Tongue,*[10]
> *The form of the mountains is nothing other than his Pure Body.*
> *Through the night, eighty-four thousand verses.*
> *On another day, how can I tell them to others?*

When he presents this verse to Zen Master [Jo]so, Zen Master [Jo]so affirms it. [Jo]so means Zen Master Shokaku Joso, a Dharma-successor of Zen Master Oryu Enan.[11] [E]nan is a Dharma-successor of Zen Master Jimyo So-en.[12] Once, when Layman [Toba] met Zen Master Butsu-in Ryogen,[13] Butsu-in gave him a Dharma-robe, the Buddhist precepts, and so on, and the layman always wore the Dharma-robe to practice the truth. The layman presented Butsu-in with a priceless jeweled belt. People of the time said, *"Their behavior is beyond common folk."* So the story of realizing the truth on hearing the river-valley may also be of benefit to those who are later in the stream. It is a pity that, so many times, the concrete form of the teaching, preaching of Dharma by manifestation of the Body,[14] seems to have leaked away. What has made [layman Toba] see afresh the form of the mountains and hear the voices of the river-valley? A single phrase? Half a phrase? Or eighty-four thousand verses? It is a shame that sounds and forms have been hiding in the mountains and waters. But we should be glad that there are moments in which, and causes and conditions whereby, [real sounds and forms] show up in the mountains and waters. The Tongue's manifestation never flags. How could the Body's form exist and vanish? At the same time, should we learn that they are close when they are apparent, or should we learn that they are close when they are hidden? Should we see them as a unity, or should we see them as a half?[15] In previous springs and autumns, [layman Toba] has not seen or heard the mountains and waters, but in moments *through the night*, he is able, barely, to see and to hear the mountains and waters. Bodhisattvas who are learning the truth now should also open the gate to learning [by starting] from mountains flowing and water not flowing.[16] On the day before the night during which this layman has realized the truth, he has visited Zen Master [Jo]so and asked about stories of *the non-emotional preaching Dharma*.[17] Under the words of the Zen Master, the form of his somersaulting is still immature,[18] but when

9. Master Shokaku Joso (1025–1091), successor of Master Oryu Enan.

10. The wide and long tongue is one of the thirty-two distinguishing features of the Buddha.

11. Master Oryu Enan (1002–1069), successor of Master Sekiso So-en. Lived on Mt. Oryu and was regarded as the founder of the Oryu Sect. His posthumous title is Zen Master Fukaku.

12. Master Jimyo (Sekiso) So-en (986–1039), successor of Master Fun-yo Zensho.

13. Master Butsu-in Ryogen (1032–1098). Zen Master Butsu-in is his posthumous title.

14. 現身説法 (GENSHIN-SEPPO), "manifesting body and preaching Dharma." The expression derives from the chapter of the Lotus Sutra on Bodhisattva Avalokiteśvara, who appears in different bodies in order to preach the Dharma to different beings. See LS 3.252.

15. Should we see them (idealistically) as an inclusive whole, or should we see them (materialistically) as a concrete half?

16. In other words, the study of Nature is a gate of entry into Buddhism. 山流水不流 (SANRYU-SUI-FU-RYU), lit. "mountains flow, waters do not flow," expresses the relativity of Nature.

17. 無情説法 (MUJO-SEPPO), is the title of chap. 53, which contains several stories about the preaching of Dharma by the non-emotional (i.e. Nature).

18. His body did not somersault into the state of action under the Master's words.

the voices of the river-valley are heard, waves break back upon themselves and surf crashes high into the sky. This being so, now that the voices of the river-valley have surprised the layman, should we put it down to the voices of the river-valley, or should we put it down to the influence of Shokaku? I suspect that Shokaku's words on *the non-emotional preaching Dharma* have not stopped echoing, but are secretly mingling with the sounds of the mountain stream in the night. Who could empirically affirm this situation as a single gallon?[19] And who could pay homage[20] to it as the whole ocean? In conclusion, is the layman realizing the truth, or are the mountains and waters realizing the truth? How could anyone who has clear eyes not put on their eyes at once [and look] at the manifestation of the Long Tongue, and the Pure Body?

[215] Another case: Zen Master Kyogen Chikan[21] was learning the truth in the order of Zen Master Dai-i Dai-en.[22] On one occasion, Dai-i says, *"You are sharp and bright, and you have wide understanding. Without quoting from any text or commentary, speak a phrase for me in the state you had before your parents were born."*[23] Kyogen searches several times for something to say, but he is not able. He deeply regrets the state of his body-and-mind, and looks through books that he has kept for years, but he is still dumbfounded. In the end, he burns all the writings he has collected over the years, and says, *"A rice cake that is painted in a picture*[24] *cannot stave off hunger. Upon my oath, I shall not desire to understand the Buddha-Dharma in this life. I only want to be the monk who serves the morning gruel and midday meal."* So saying, he spends years and months as a server of meals. *The monk who serves the morning gruel and midday meal* means one who waits upon the other monks at breakfast and the midday meal;[25] he would be like a "liveried waiter"[26] in this country. While he is thus occupied, he says to Dai-i, *"Chikan is dull in body-and-mind and cannot express the truth. Would the Master say something for me?"* Dai-i says, *"I would not mind saying something for you, [but if I did so,] perhaps you would bear a grudge against me later."* After spending years and months in such a state, [Chikan] enters Buto-zan mountain, following the tracks of National Master Daisho,[27] and makes a thatched hut on the remains of the National Master's hermitage. He has planted bamboo and made it his

---

19. 一升 (ISSHO) is a measure of capacity, approximately equal to 1.8 liters.

20. 朝宗 (CHOSHU), lit. "morning homage." The expression derives from the ancient custom in China of making government decisions before the emperor in the morning. In this and the preceding sentence, Master Dogen denies the two extreme views of materialism and idealism: only seeing things as isolated and concrete, and only revering general abstractions.

21. Master Kyogen Chikan (died 898), successor of Master Isan Reiyu. He originally took the precepts under Master Isan's master, Hyakujo Ekai, and later became a student of Master Isan himself. He wrote more than two hundred poems.

22. Master Isan Reiyu (771–853), successor of Master Hyakujo Ekai. Dai-i (or Isan) is the name of the mountain where he lived. The Tang emperor Senso gave him the posthumous title Zen Master Dai-en. He became a monk when he was 15, and became a student of Master Hyakujo when he was 23. He is known as the founder of the Igyo Sect.

23. In other words, on the basis of the reality which transcends past, present, and future.

24. See chap. 40, *Gabyo*.

25. Monks only ate light snacks after the midday meal, so gruel for breakfast and the midday meal were the only two meals.

26. 陪饌役送 (BAISENEKISO). The job of *baisenekiso* was to wait on someone of high rank.

27. Master Nan-yo Echu (died 775), successor of the Sixth Patriarch, Master Daikan Eno. National Master Daisho was his title as the Emperor's teacher. After he retired, he built a hut on Mt. Buto and lived there alone.

friend. One day, while he is sweeping the path, a piece of tile flies up and strikes a bamboo with a crack. Hearing this sound, he suddenly realizes the great state of realization. He bathes and purifies himself, and, facing Dai-i-zan mountain, he burns incense and does prostrations. Then, directing himself to [Master] Dai-i, he says, *"Great Master Dai-i! If you had explained it to me before, how would this thing have been possible? The depth of your kindness surpasses that of a parent."* Finally, he makes the following verse:

At a single stroke I lost recognition.
No longer need I practice self-discipline.
[I am] manifesting behavior in the way of the ancients,
Never falling into despondency.
There is no trace anywhere:
[The state] is dignified action beyond sound and form.
People everywhere who have realized the truth,
All will praise [these] supreme makings.

He presents the verse to Dai-i. Dai-i says, *"This disciple is complete."*[28]

[218] Another case: Zen Master Reiun Shigon[29] is a seeker of the truth for thirty years. One day, while on a ramble in the mountains, he stops for a rest at the foot of a hill and views the villages in the distance. It is spring, and the peach blossoms are in full bloom. Seeing them, he suddenly realizes the truth. He makes the following verse and presents it to Dai-i:

For thirty years, a traveler in search of a sword.[30]
How many times have leaves fallen and buds sprouted?
After one look at the peach blossoms,
I have arrived directly at the present and have no further doubts.

Dai-i says, *"One who has entered by relying on external phenomena will never regress or falter."*[31] This is his affirmation. What person who has entered could not rely on external phenomena? What person who has entered could regress or falter? [Isan's words] are not about [Shi]gon alone. Finally, [Shigon] succeeds to the Dharma of Dai-i. If the form of the mountains were not the Pure Body, how would things like this be possible?

[220] A monk asks Zen Master Chosa [Kei]shin,[32] *"How can we make mountains, rivers, and the Earth belong to ourselves?"* The Master says, *"How can we make ourselves belong to mountains, rivers, and the Earth?"*[33] This says that ourselves are naturally ourselves, and even though ourselves are mountains, rivers, and the Earth, we should never be restricted by belonging.

---

28. *Shinji-shobogenzo* pt. 1, no. 17. The version recorded in *Shinji-shobogenzo,* in Chinese characters, is slightly different from the version in this chapter.

29. Master Reiun Shigon (dates unknown), also a successor of Master Isan Reiyu.

30. Symbolizing something very sharp and definite, or extreme.

31. *Shinji-shobogenzo* pt. 2, no. 55.

32. Master Chosa Keishin (died 868), successor of Master Nansen Fugan. At first he taught Buddhism by moving from place to place, without a temple of his own. After that he lived on Chosa-zan mountain. People at that time called him *Shin Daichu* or "Keishin the tiger," because his teachings were so sharp and fast. Quoted several times in chap. 60, *Juppo.*

33. *Shinji-shobogenzo* pt. 1, no. 16.

[221] Master Ekaku of Roya, [titled] Great Master Kosho,[34] is a distant descendant of Nangaku.[35] One day Shisen,[36] a lecturer of a philosophical sect, asks him, *"How does pure essentiality suddenly give rise to mountains, rivers, and the Earth?"* Questioned thus, the Master preaches, *"How does pure essentiality suddenly give rise to mountains, rivers, and the Earth?"*[37] Here we are told not to confuse mountains, rivers, and the Earth which are just pure essentiality, with *"mountains, rivers and the Earth."* However, because the teacher of sutras has never heard this, even in a dream, he does not know mountains, rivers, and the Earth as mountains, rivers, and the Earth.

[222] Remember, if it were not for the form of the mountains and the voices of the river-valley, picking up a flower could not proclaim anything,[38] and the one who attained the marrow could not stand at his own place.[39] Relying on the virtue of the sounds of the river-valley and the form of the mountains, *the Earth and all sentient beings realize the truth simultaneously,*[40] and there are many buddhas who realize the truth on seeing the bright star. Bags of skin in this state are the wise masters of the past, whose will to pursue the Dharma was very deep. People of the present should research their traces without fail. Now also, real practitioners who have no concern for fame and gain should establish similar resolve. In [this] remote corner in recent times, people who honestly pursue the Buddha-Dharma are very rare. They are not absent, but they are difficult to meet. There are many who drift into the monkhood, and who seem to have left the secular world, but who only use Buddhism as a bridge to fame and gain. It is pitiful and lamentable that they do not regret the passing of this life[41] but vainly go about their dark and dismal business. When can they expect to become free and to attain the truth? Even if they met a true master, they might not love the real dragon.[42] My late [Master, the eternal] Buddha, calls such fellows *"pitiful people."*[43] They are like this because of the bad they have done in past ages. Though they have received a life, they have no will to pursue the Dharma for the Dharma's sake, and so, when they meet the real Dharma, they doubt the real dragon, and when they meet the right Dharma, they are disliked by the right Dharma. Their body, mind, bones, and flesh have never lived

---

34. Master Roya Ekaku, successor of Master Fun-yo Zensho. Great Master Kosho is his posthumous title. Roya is the name of a mountain and of a district.

35. Master Nangaku Ejo (677–744). Master Roya Ekaku belonged to the 11th generation after Master Nangaku Ejo, who was a successor of the Sixth Patriarch, Master Daikan Eno.

36. Chosui Shisen (984–1038). He belonged to the Kegon Sect, which is based on the study of the *Avataṃsaka-sūtra (Garland Sutra).* Before joining the Kegon Sect, he had studied the *Śūraṃgama-sūtra.*

37. Shisen's question and Master Roya's question are exactly the same. Shisen asked about the relation between abstract essence and concrete reality. The Master's rhetorical question suggested that the two factors are not different. See *Shinji-shobogenzo* pt. 1, no. 6.

38. Refers to the story of the transmission between Gautama Buddha and Master Mahākāśyapa. See chap. 68, *Udonge.*

39. Refers to the story of the transmission between Master Bodhidharma and Master Taiso Eka, who prostrated himself three times and then stood at his own place. See chap. 46, *Katto.*

40 The Buddha's description of his realization of the truth, as quoted in several sutras, for example, the second volume of *Shugyo-hongi-kyo.*

41. 光陰 (KOIN), lit. "light and shade," means passing time.

42. Shoko was a man who loved images of dragons. Seeing that Shoko's house was full of dragons, a real dragon decided to pay him a visit. But when Shoko saw the real dragon, he was struck with horror. The story of Shoko and the real dragon is contained in the Chinese book *Soji.*

43. The words are originally from *Ryogon-kyo* (the Chinese translation of the *Śūraṃgama-sūtra*). They were frequently used by Master Tendo Nyojo.

following the Dharma, and so they are not in mutual accord with the Dharma; they do not receive and use [in harmony] with the Dharma. Founders of sects, teachers, and disciples have continued a transmission like this for a long time. They explain the bodhi-mind as if relating an old dream. How pitiful it is that, having been born on the treasure mountain, they do not know what treasure is and they do not see treasure. How much less could they [actually] get the treasure of Dharma? After they establish the bodhi-mind, even though they will pass through the cycle of the six states[44] or the four kinds of birth,[45] the causes and conditions of that cyclical course will all become the actions and vows of the state of bodhi. Therefore, though they have wasted precious time in the past, as long as their present life continues they should, without delay, make the following vow: *"I hope that I, together with all living beings, may hear the right Dharma through this life and through every life hereafter. If I am able to hear it, I will never doubt the right Dharma, and I will never be disbelieving. When I meet the right Dharma, I will discard secular rules and receive and retain the Buddha-Dharma so that the Earth and sentient beings may finally realize the truth together."* If we make a vow like this, it will naturally become the cause of, and conditions for, the authentic establishment of the mind. Do not neglect, or grow weary of, this attitude of mind. In this country of Japan, a remote corner beyond the oceans, people's minds are extremely stupid. Since ancient times, no saint has ever been born [here], nor anyone wise by nature: it is needless to say, then, that real men of learning the truth are very rare. When [a person] tells people who do not know the will to the truth about the will to the truth, the good advice offends their ears, and so they do not reflect upon themselves, but [only] bear resentment towards the other person. As a general rule concerning actions and vows which are the bodhi-mind, we should not intend to let worldly people know whether or not we have established the bodhi-mind, or whether or not we are practicing the truth; we should endeavor to be unknown. How much less could we boast about ourselves? Because people today rarely seek what is real, when the praises of others are available, they seem to want someone to say that their practice and understanding have become harmonized, even though there is no practice in their body, and no realization in their mind. *"In delusion adding to delusion"*[46] describes exactly this. We should throw away this wrong-mindedness immediately. When learning the truth, what is difficult to see and to hear is the attitude of mind [based in] right Dharma. This attitude of mind is what has been transmitted and received by the buddhas, buddha to buddha. It has been transmitted and received as the Buddha's brightness, and as the Buddha's mind. From the time when the Tathāgata was in the world until today, many people have seemed to consider that our concern in learning the truth[47] is to get fame and gain. If, however, on meeting the teachings of a true master, they turn around and pursue the right Dharma, they will naturally attain the truth. We should be aware that the sickness

44. 六趣 (ROKUSHU), the six miserable states through which we pass according to the law of cause and effect: hell (symbolizing the state of suffering), hungry ghosts (symbolizing the state of greed), animals, asura or angry demons, human beings, and gods.

45. 四生 (SHISHO), the four births; birth from the womb, birth from eggs, birth from moisture, and birth from metamorphosis. In Sanskrit, they are: *jarāyu-ja, aṇḍa-ja, saṃsveda-ja, and upapāduka.*

46. 迷中又迷 (MEI-CHU-YU-MEI). Master Dogen used the same expression in the second paragraph of chap. 3, *Genjo-koan.*

47. 学道の用心 (GAKUDO *no* YOJIN), as in Master Dogen's text 学道用心集 (GAKUDO-YOJIN-SHU), or *Collection of Concerns in Learning the Truth.*

described above might be present in the learning of the truth today. For example, among beginners and novices, and among veterans of long training, some have got the makings to receive the transmission of the truth and to pass on the behavior, and some have not got the makings. There may be some who have it in their nature to learn, in veneration of the ancients. There may also be insulting demons who will not learn. We should neither love nor resent either group. [Yet] how can we have no regret? How can we bear no resentment? Perhaps no-one bears resentment because almost no-one has recognized the three poisons as the three poisons.[48] Moreover, we should not forget the determination we had when we began the joyful pursuit of the Buddha's truth. That is to say, when we first establish the will, we are not seeking the Dharma out of concern for others, and, having discarded fame and gain [already], we are not seeking fame and gain: we are just single-mindedly aiming to get the truth. We are never expecting the veneration and offerings of kings and ministers. Nevertheless, such causes of and conditions for [the will to fame and gain] are present today. [Fame and gain] are not an original aim, and they are not [true] objects of pursuit. To become caught in the fetters which bind human beings and gods is [just] what we do not hope for. Foolish people, however, even those who have the will to the truth, soon forget their original resolve and mistakenly expect the offerings of human beings and gods, feeling glad that the merit of the Buddha-Dharma has come to them. If the devotions of kings and ministers are frequent, [foolish people] think, *It is the realization of my own moral way.* This is one of the demons [that hinder] learning of the truth. Though we should not forget the mind of compassion, we should not rejoice [to receive devotion]. Do you remember the golden words of the Buddha, *"Even while the Tathāgata is alive, there are many who have hate and envy."*[49] Such is the principle that the stupid do not recognize the wise, and small animals make enemies of great saints.

[230] Further, many of the ancestral masters of the Western Heavens have been destroyed by non-Buddhists, by the two vehicles,[50] by kings, and so on;[51] but this is never due to superiority on the part of the non-Buddhists, or lack of far-sightedness on the part of the ancestral masters. After the first Patriarch[52] came from the west, he hung up his traveling stick in the Suzan mountains,[53] but neither Bu of the Liang dynasty nor the ruler of the Wei dynasty knew who he was.[54] At the time, there was a pair of dogs known as Bodhiruci Sanzo[55] and Precepts Teacher Kozu. Fearing that their empty fame

48. 三毒 (SANDOKU), the three poisons, are anger, greed, and delusion.

49. Lotus Sutra, *Hosshi (A Teacher of the Dharma)*. See LS 2.152.

50. 二乗 (NIJO), the first two of the four vehicles, which are namely: *śrāvakas* (intellectual Buddhists), *pratyekabuddhas* (sensual Buddhists), *bodhisattvas* (practical Buddhists), and *buddhas*.

51. The Western Heavens means India. It is said that Master Kāṇadeva, the fifteenth Patriarch, was killed by non-Buddhists; Buddhamitra, the teacher of the twenty-first Patriarch Vasubandhu, was defeated by non-Buddhists in a philosophical discussion; and Siṃha-bhikṣu, the twenty-fourth Patriarch, was executed by the king of Kaśmira (present-day Kashmir).

52. Master Bodhidharma. The twenty-eighth patriarch in India, and the first patriarch in China.

53. In Chinese, Sung-shan. The Suzan mountains have two main peaks. The eastern peak is called Taishitsu, and the western peak is called Shoshitsu. There were many Buddhist temples in these mountains. Shorin Temple, where Master Bodhidharma faced the wall in Zazen, was on Shoshitsu Peak.

54. Related stories are in chap. 30, *Gyoji*.

55. A north Indian who arrived in Luoyang in 508 and translated many Sanskrit texts into Chinese. "Sanzo" was a title given to those versed in the tripiṭaka.

and false gain might be thwarted by a right person, they behaved as if looking up at the sun in the sky and trying to blot it out.[56] They are even more terrible than Devadatta,[57] who [lived when the Buddha] was in the world. How pitiful they are. The fame and profit that they[58] love so deeply is more disgusting than filth to the ancestral Master. That such facts occur is not due to any imperfection in the power of the Buddha-Dharma. We should remember that there are dogs who bark at good people. Do not worry about barking dogs. Bear them no grudge. Vow to lead them and to guide them. Explain to them, *"Though you are animals, you should establish the bodhi mind."* A wise master of the past has said, *"These are just animals with human faces."* But there may also be a certain kind of demon which devotes itself and serves offerings to them. A former buddha has said, *"Do not get close to kings, princes, ministers, rulers, brahmins, or secular people."* [59] This is truly the form of behavior that people who want to learn the Buddha's truth should not forget. [When] bodhisattvas are at the start of learning, their virtue, in accordance with their progress, will pile up.

[232] Moreover, there have been examples since ancient time of the God Indra coming to test a practitioner's resolve, or of mārā-pāpīyas[60] coming to hinder a practitioner's training. These things always happened when [the practitioner] had not got rid of the will to fame and gain. When the [spirit of] great benevolence and great compassion is profound, and when the vow to widely save living beings is mature, these hindrances do not occur. There are cases when the power of practice naturally takes possession of a nation. There are cases when [a practitioner] seems to have achieved worldly fortune. At such times, re-examine the case carefully. Do not slumber on without regard to the particular case. Foolish people delight in [worldly fortune] like stupid dogs licking a dry bone. The wise and the sacred detest it as worldly people hate filth and excrement.

[233] In general, a beginner's sentimental thinking cannot imagine the Buddha's truth—[the beginner] fathoms, but does not hit the target. Even though we do not fathom [the truth] as beginners, we should not deny that there is perfect realization in the ultimate state. [Still,] the inner depths[61] of the perfect state are beyond the beginner's shallow consciousness. [The beginner] must just endeavor, through concrete conduct, to tread the path of the ancient saints. At this time, in visiting teachers and seeking the truth, there are mountains to climb and oceans to cross. While we are seeking a guiding teacher, or hoping to find a [good] counselor, one comes down from the heavens, or springs out from the earth.[62] At the place where we meet him, he makes sentient beings

---

56. They reportedly tried to poison Master Bodhidharma.

57. Devadatta was a cousin of the Buddha who became a monk in the Buddha's order, but later turned against him and tried to destroy the Buddhist order in co-operation with King Ajase.

58. なんぢ (*nanji*) is lit. "you"—an impolite form of address that Master Dogen uses for the third person when criticizing.

59. In the *Anraku-gyo (Peaceful and Joyful Practice)* chapter of the Lotus Sutra, the Buddha says to Mañjuśrī: *"A bodhisattva-mahāsattva should not get close to kings, princes, ministers, and administrators."* See LS 2.244.

60. A deadly demon or devil. See Glossary and chap. 70, *Hotsu-bodaishin.*

61. 堂奥 (DO-O), lit. "inner sanctum."

62. 従地湧出 (JU-CHI-YUSHUTSU), "Springing Out from the Earth," is the title of the 15th chapter of the Lotus Sutra.

speak the truth and makes non-sentient beings[63] speak the truth, and we listen with body and listen with mind. *Listening with the ears* is everyday tea and meals, but *hearing the sound through the eyes*[64] is just the ambiguous,[65] or the undecided,[66] itself. In meeting Buddha, we meet ourselves as Buddha and others as Buddha, and we meet great buddhas and small buddhas. Do not be surprised by or afraid of a great buddha. Do not doubt or worry about a small buddha. The great buddhas and small buddhas referred to here are recognized, presently, as the form of the mountains and the voices of the river-valley. In this the Wide and Long Tongue exists, and eighty-four thousand verses exist; the manifestation is *far transcendent,* and the insight is *unique and exceptional.*[67] For this reason, secular [teachings] say *"It gets higher and higher, and harder and harder."*[68] And a past buddha says, *"It pervades*[69] *the sky and pervades the meridians."* Spring pines possess constant freshness, and an autumn chrysanthemum possesses sublime beauty, but they are nothing other than the direct and concrete.[70] When good counselors arrive in this field of earth,[71] they may be great masters to human beings and gods. Someone who randomly affects the forms of teaching others, without arriving in this field of earth, is a great nuisance to human beings and gods. How could [people] who do not know the spring pines, and who do not see the autumn chrysanthemum, be worth the price of their straw sandals? How could they cut out the roots?

[236] Furthermore, if the mind or the flesh grow lazy or disbelieving, we should wholeheartedly confess before the Buddha. When we do this, the power of the virtue of confessing before the Buddha saves us and makes us pure. This virtue can promote unhindered pure belief and fortitude. Once pure belief reveals itself, both self and the external world are moved [into action], and the benefit universally covers sentient and non-sentient beings. The general intention [of the confession] is as follows: *I pray that although my many bad actions in the past have accumulated one after another, and there are causes and conditions which are obstructing the truth, the buddhas and the patriarchs who attained the truth by following the Buddha's Way will show compassion for me, that they will*

---

63. In general, 有情 (UJO), "sentient beings" means, for example, birds, animals, and human beings. 無情 (MUJO), "non-sentient beings," or "the non-emotional," means, for example, grass, trees, and stones. See chap. 53, *Mujo-seppo.*

64. References to Master Tozan's poem, quoted in chap. 53, *Mujo-seppo: "How very wonderful! How very wonderful! The non-emotional preaching Dharma is a mystery. If we listen with the ears, it is ultimately too difficult to understand. If we hear the sound through the eyes, we are able to know it."*

65. 何必 (KAHITSU) or "why should it necessarily be?" See chap. 3, *Genjo-koan,* note 11.

66. 不必 (FUHITSU), or "not necessarily."

67. The words "far transcendent" (廻脱 KEIDATSU) and "unique and exceptional" (独抜, DOKUBATSU) are taken from Master Ungo Doyo's preaching in *Rento-eyo,* chap. 22: *"When a single word is far transcendent, and unique and exceptional, then many words are not necessary. And many are not useful."* 脱 (DATSU), "transcendent," means to get rid of something. So 廻脱 (KEIDATSU), or "far transcendent," suggests the state in which things are as they are, being far removed from the superfluous.

68. From *Rongo,* the fundamental text of Confucianism. Gan-en, a student of Confucius praises Confucius (or his teaching) as follows: *"When I look up at him, he gets higher and higher, and when I bore into him, he gets harder and harder."*

69. "More and more" and "pervades" are originally the same character, 弥 (MI, *iyo-iyo*), used in the first quotation as an adverb (*iyo-iyo*) and in the second quotation as a verb (MI).

70. "The direct and concrete" is 即是 (SOKUZE). These two characters are explained in detail in chap. 6, *Soku-shin-ze-butsu.*

71. 田地 (DENCHI), or "paddy-field," a symbol of the concrete state.

cause karmic accumulations to dissolve, and that they will remove obstacles to learning the truth. May their virtue, and their gates of Dharma, vastly fill and pervade the limitless Dharma-world. Let me share in their compassion. In the past, Buddhist patriarchs were [the same as] us, and in the future we may become Buddhist patriarchs. When we look up at Buddhist patriarchs, they are one Buddhist patriarch, and when we reflect upon the establishment of the mind, it is one establishment of the mind. When [the Buddhist patriarchs] radiate their compassion in all directions,[72] *we can grasp favorable opportunities and we fall upon favorable opportunities. Therefore, in the words of Ryuge,*[73] *"If we did not attain perfection in past lives, we should attain perfection in the present. With this life we can deliver the body which is the accumulation of past lives. The eternal buddhas, before they realized the truth, were the same as people today. After realizing the truth, people today will be eternal buddhas."* Quietly, we should master this reasoning. This is direct experience of realizing the state of buddha. When we confess like this, the mystical help of the Buddhist patriarchs is invariably present. Disclosing the thoughts in our mind and the form of our body, we should confess to the Buddha. The power of confession causes the roots of wrongdoing to dissolve. This is right training of one color;[74] it is right belief in the mind and right belief in the body. At the time of right training, the voices of the river-valley and the form of the river-valley, the form of the mountains and the voices of the mountains, all do not begrudge their eighty-four thousand verses. When the self does not begrudge fame and gain and body and mind, the river-valley and the mountains, similarly, begrudge nothing. Even though the voices of the river-valley and the form of the mountains continue throughout the night to produce, and not to produce, eighty-four thousand verses, if you have not yet understood with all your effort that river-valleys and mountains are demonstrating themselves as river-valleys and mountains, who could see and hear you as the voices of the river-valley and the form of the mountains?

Shobogenzo Keisei-sanshiki

Preached to the assembly at Kannon-dori-kosho-horin-ji temple five days after the start of the retreat in the 2nd year of En-o.[75]

---

72. 七通八達す (SHICHITSU-HATTATSU *su*), lit. "make into seven paths and eight destinations."
73. Master Ryuge Koton (835–923). A successor of Master Tozan Ryokai.
74. "Of one color" means pure, or unadulterated.
75. 1240.

[10]

諸悪莫作

SHOAKU-MAKUSA

Not Doing Wrongs

***Sho** means "many" or "miscellaneous," **aku** means "wrong" or "bad," **maku** means "not" or "don't," and **sa** means "to do." So **shoaku makusa** means "not doing wrong."[1] These words are quoted from a short poem called "the Seven Buddhas' Universal Precept:"[2] "Don't do wrong; do right; then our minds become pure naturally; this is the teaching of the many Buddhas." This poem tells us how closely the teaching of Buddhism is related to morals. In this chapter Master Dogen teaches us the Buddhist theory of morality. Morality or ethics is, by its nature, a very practical problem. But most people are prone to forget the practical character of morality, and usually only discuss it with words or as an abstract theory. However, talking about morality is not the same as being moral. Morality is just doing right or not doing wrong. Here Master Dogen explains real morality, quoting an interesting story about Master Choka Dorin and a famous Chinese poet called Haku Kyoi.*

[3] **The eternal Buddha says,**

> *Not to commit wrongs,[3]*
> *To practice the many kinds of right,[4]*
> *Naturally purifies the mind;[5]*
> *This is the teaching of the buddhas.[6]*

---

1. The meaning of 諸悪莫作 (SHOAKU-MAKUSA) changes in this chapter according to context. It can sometimes be interpreted as the imperative "Don't do wrong" or the ideal "not to do wrong." But sometimes it represents Master Dogen's idea that morality is only a problem of action—the *not-committing* of wrong.

2. 七仏通戒 (SHICHIBUTSU-TSUKAI). 七仏 (SHICHIBUTSU) refers to Śākyamuni Buddha and six legendary buddhas who preceded him. See chap. 15, *Busso.*

3. 諸悪莫作 (SHOAKU-MAKUSA), lit. "Do not commit wrongs." 諸 (SHO) means various, miscellaneous, or all, and sometimes it simply expresses plurality. 悪 (AKU) means evil, bad, wrongdoing, or wrong. 莫作 "wrongs" suggests individual instances of wrongdoing as concrete facts, rather than wrong as an abstract problem. 莫 (MAKU, or *naka[re]*) means "must not" or "Don't!" 作 (SA, or *tsuku[ru]*) means to make, to produce, or to commit—it includes a suggestion of intention. It is useful to distinguish the characters 作 (SA) and 行 (GYO); they both mean to do, but 作 (SA) has more of a feeling of doing intentionally. This chapter contains the idea that, naturally, wrongdoing does not occur; i.e., without our intentional commitment, there is no wrong.

4. 衆善奉行 (SHUZEN-BUGYO), lit. "devoutly practice the many kinds of good," or "good doing of the many kinds of right." 衆 (SHU) means many or many kinds of. 善 (ZEN) means good, or right. 衆善 (SHUZEN), or "the many kinds of right," suggests concrete instances of right as opposed to right as an abstraction. 奉 (BU) is a prefix denoting reverence or devotion. 行 (GYO, or *okona[u]*) means to do, to perform, to enact, or to keep moving along. 奉行 (BUGYO), or "good doing," has a feeling of doing what is natural, as opposed to intentional commitment.

5. 自浄其意 (JIJO-GO-I). According to context, 自 (JI) can be interpreted either as by oneself or as naturally. The interpretation here is that the verse is not a recommendation to be moral, but a proclama-

This [teaching], as the Universal Precept of the ancestral patriarchs, the Seven Buddhas, has been authentically transmitted from former buddhas to later buddhas, and later buddhas have received its transmission from former buddhas. It is not only of the Seven Buddhas: *It is the teaching of all the buddhas.* We should consider this principle and master it in practice. These words of Dharma of the Seven Buddhas always sound like words of Dharma of the Seven Buddhas. What has been transmitted and been received one-to-one is just clarification of the real situation[7] at this concrete place. This already *is the teaching of the buddhas;* it is the teaching, practice, and experience of hundreds, thousands, and tens of thousands of buddhas.

[5] In regard to the *wrongs*[8] which we are discussing now, among *rightness, wrongness,* and *indifference,* there is *wrongness.* Its essence[9] is just non-appearance.[10] The essence of rightness, the essence of indifference, and so on are also non-appearance, are [the state] without excess,[11] and are real form. At the same time,[12] at each concrete place these three properties[13] include innumerable kinds of dharmas. In *wrongs,* there are similarities and differences between wrong in this world and wrong in other worlds. There are similarities and differences between former times and latter times. There are similarities and differences between wrong in the heavens above and wrong in the human world. How much greater is the difference between moral wrong, moral right, and moral indifference in Buddhism and in the secular world. Right and wrong are Time; Time is not right or wrong. Right and wrong are the Dharma; the Dharma is not right or wrong. [When] the Dharma is in balance, wrong is in balance.[14] [When] the Dharma is in balance, right is in balance. This being so, when we learn [the supreme state of] anuttara-samyak-saṃbodhi, when we hear the teachings, do training, and experience

---

tion of the Buddha's teaching that moral conduct is just purification of the mind. Accordingly, 自 (JI) has been translated as "naturally." 浄 (JO) means to purify. 其 (GO, or *so[no]*) means "that," suggesting something concrete and specific. 意 (I) means intention but here the meaning is more practical: it suggests the state of the mind (and body) in action.

6. 是諸仏教 (ZE-SHOBUTSU-KYO). 諸仏 (SHOBUTSU) can be interpreted as "the buddhas" or as "all the buddhas." In Pali, the poem is: *Sabba-pāpass akaraṇam,/ kuselassūpasampada,/ sacitta-pariyodapanaṃ,/ etam buddhana sasanaṃ.*

7. "Clarification of the real situation" is 通消息 (TSUSHOSOKU). 通 (TSU) suggests penetration, clarification, opening up, running through (or universality, as in 通戒 TSUKAI, universal precept). 消息 (SHOSOKU) originally means exhalation and inhalation, and by extension something that is heard from someone, news, actual circumstances, the real situation.

8. 諸悪 (SHO-AKU), as in the original poem.

9. 性 (SHO). In the previous sentence, "rightness" is 善性 (ZENSHO), lit. "good-essence;" "wrongness" is 悪性 (AKUSHO), lit. "bad-essence;" and "indifference" is 無記性 (MUKISHO), lit. "not-described-essence."

10. In this sentence Master Dogen begins his conceptual explanation of right and wrong by introducing the idea of instantaneousness. Non-appearance (無生, MUSHO) describes the state at the moment of the present.

11. 無漏 (MURO), lit. "without leakage," from the Sanskrit (see Glossary under *āsrava*), suggests the state in which things are as they are.

12. Master Dogen is explaining right and wrong as reality. In the previous sentences he began by explaining them as inclusive concepts, in the first or conceptual phase. From here he explains them as concrete, individual, and relative facts, at the second or concrete phase.

13. Rightness, wrongness, and indifference.

14. 法等悪等 (HOTO-AKUTO), or "Dharma in equilibrium, bad in equilibrium," suggests the balanced state in which a bad fact is seen as it is.

the effect, it is profound, it is distant, and it is fine.

[6] We hear of this supreme state of bodhi *sometimes following [good] counselors* and *sometimes following sutras.*[15] At the beginning, the sound of it is *"Do not commit wrongs."* If it does not sound like *"Do not commit wrongs,"* it is not the Buddha's right Dharma; it may be the teaching of demons. Remember, [teaching] that sounds like *"Do not commit wrongs"* is the Buddha's right Dharma. This [teaching]*"Do not commit wrongs"* was not intentionally initiated, and then intentionally maintained in its present form, by the common man: when we hear teaching that has [naturally] become the preaching of bodhi, it sounds like this. What sounds like this is speech which is the supreme state of bodhi in words. It is bodhi-speech already, and so it speaks bodhi.[16] When it becomes the preaching of the supreme state of bodhi, and when we are changed by hearing it, we hope *not to commit wrongs,* we continue enacting *not to commit wrongs,* and wrongs go on not being committed; in this situation the power of practice is instantly realized. This realization is realized on the scale of the whole earth, the whole world, the whole of Time, and the whole of Dharma. And the scale of this [realization] is the scale of *not committing.* For people of just this reality, at the moment of just this reality[17]—even if they live at a place and come and go at a place where they could commit wrongs, even if they face circumstances in which they could commit wrongs, and even if they seem to mix with friends who do commit wrongs—wrongs can never be committed at all. The power of not committing is realized, and so wrongs cannot voice themselves as wrongs, and wrongs lack an established set of tools.[18] There is the Buddhist truth of taking up at one moment, and letting go at one moment.[19] At just this moment, the truth is known that wrong does not violate a person, and the truth is clarified that a person does not destroy wrong.[20] When we devote our whole mind to practice, and when we devote the whole body to practice, there is eighty or ninety percent realization[21] [of not committing wrongs] just before the moment, and there is the fact of not having committed just behind the brain.[22] When you practice by garnering your own body-and-mind, and when you practice by garnering the body-and-mind of *anyone,*[23] the power of practicing with the four elements and the five aggregates is realized at once;[24] but the four elements

15. 或従知識 (WAKU-JU-CHISHIKI) and 或従教巻 (WAKU-JU-KYOGAN). These phrases appear frequently in Shobogenzo.

16. "Bodhi-speech" is 菩提語 (BODAI-GO); "speaking bodhi" is 語菩提 (GO-BODAI). Up to this sentence Master Dogen affirms "Do not do wrong" as words of the truth. From the next sentence, he looks at the concrete reality of practice.

17. 正当恁麼時の正当恁麼人 (SHOTO-INMO-JI *no* SHOTO-INMO-NIN). 正当 (SHOTO), or "exact," suggests exactly this time and place. 正当恁麼時 (SHOTO-INMO-JI) or "at just this moment" is a very common expression in Shobogenzo.

18. Master Dogen emphasizes that if we do not do wrong, there can never be any wrong.

19. 一拈一放 (ICHINEN-IPPO), lit. "one pinch, one release." 拈 (NEN), to twist, pinch, or grasp, symbolizes positive action. 放 (HO), to release, symbolizes passive action.

20. Master Dogen denies the idea that something exists that can be called wrong, bad, or evil outside of our own conduct.

21. 八九成 (HAKKUJO). See chap. 33, *Kannon.*

22. 脳後 (NOGO). The usual expression, which appears in the last sentence of this paragraph, is 機先機後 (KISEN-KIGO), "before the moment, after the moment." The variation 脳後 (NOGO), "behind the brain," suggests the area in which action has taken place already.

23. たれ (*tare*), lit. "who," suggests someone ineffable, or a person whose state cannot be described.

24. The four elements and five aggregates symbolize all physical things and mental phenomena.

and five aggregates do not taint[25] the self. [All things,] even the four elements and five aggregates of today, carry on being practiced; and the power which the four elements and five aggregates have as practice in the present moment makes the four elements and five aggregates, as described above, into practice.[26] When we cause even the mountains, rivers, and the Earth, and the sun, moon, and stars, to do practice, the mountains, rivers, and the Earth, the sun, moon, and stars, in their turn, make us practice.[27] [This is] not a onetime Eye; it is vigorous eyes at many times.[28] Because [those times] are moments in which the Eye is present as vigorous eyes, they make the buddhas and the patriarchs practice, make them listen to the teachings, and make them experience the effect. The buddhas and the patriarchs have never made the teachings, practice, and experience tainted, and so the teachings, practice, and experience have never hindered the buddhas and the patriarchs.[29] For this reason, when [teachings, practice, and experience] compel the Buddhist patriarchs to practice, there are no buddhas or patriarchs who flee, before the moment or after the moment, in the past, present, or future.

[10] In walking, standing, sitting, and lying down through the twelve hours,[30] we should carefully consider the fact that when living beings are becoming buddhas and becoming patriarchs, we are becoming Buddhist patriarchs, even though this [becoming] does not hinder the [state of a] Buddhist patriarch which has always belonged to us. In becoming a Buddhist patriarch, we do not destroy the living being, do not detract from it, and do not lose it; nevertheless, we have got rid of it. We cause right-and-wrong, cause-and-effect, to practice; but this does not mean disturbing, or intentionally producing, cause-and-effect. Cause-and-effect itself, at times, makes us practice. The state in which the original features of this cause-and-effect have already become conspicuous is *not committing*, it is *[the state] without appearance*, it is *[the state] without constancy*, it is *not being unclear*, and it is *not falling down*—because it is the state in which [body and mind] have fallen away.[31]

[11] When we investigate them like this, wrongs are realized as having become com-

---

25. 汚染せず (ZENNA *sezu*), "not tainted," expresses something as is. When we act we have to use physical things, but they do not make us impure.

26. In this sentence, Master Dogen suggests the oneness of concrete circumstances and Buddhist practice.

27. This sentence also suggests the mutual relation between a Buddhist practitioner and nature—in a more poetic style.

28. The Buddhist view is not a once-and-for-all realization, but it appears vigorously at many times.

29. "Unhindered" and "untainted" both express something as it is. Buddhist teachings, practice, and experience exist as they are. Buddhas and patriarchs live freely and independently, as they are.

30. 十二時 (JUNI-JI), lit. "twelve hours," means the twenty-four hours of a day—at that time, the day was divided into twelve periods. See chap. 11, *Uji*.

31. "Not committing" is 莫作 (MAKUSA), as in the poem. "The state without appearance" (無生, MUSHO) and "the state without constancy" (無常, MUJO) suggest concrete reality at the moment of the present from two sides—denial of momentary appearance and denial of continuous existence. "Not being unclear [about cause and effect]" (不昧, FUMAI) and "not falling down into [cause and effect]" (不落, FURAKU) represent opposing viewpoints about the reality of cause-and-effect (see chap. 76, *Dai-shugyo*; chap. 89, *Shinjin-inga*). "Falling away" is 脱落 (DATSURAKU). Master Dogen frequently quoted Master Tendo Nyojo's words that Zazen is 心身脱落 (SHINJIN-DATSURAKU), "the falling away of body and mind."

pletely the same as *not committing*. Aided by this realization, we can penetrate[32] the *not committing* of wrongs, and we can realize it decisively by sitting.[33] Just at this moment—when reality is realized as the *not committing* of wrongs at the beginning, middle, and end—wrongs do not arise from causes and conditions; they are nothing other than just *not committing*.[34] Wrongs do not vanish due to causes and conditions; they are nothing other than just *not committing*. If wrongs are in balance, all dharmas are in balance. Those who recognize that wrongs arise from causes and conditions, but do not see that these causes and conditions and they themselves are [the reality of] *not committing*, are pitiful people. *The seeds of buddhahood arise from conditions* and, this being so, *conditions arise from the seeds of buddhahood*. It is not that wrongs do not exist; they are nothing other than *not committing*. It is not that wrongs exist; they are nothing other than *not committing*. Wrongs are not immaterial; they are *not committing*. Wrongs are not material; they are *not committing*. Wrongs are not *"not committing;"* they are nothing other than *not committing*.[35] [Similarly,] for example, spring pines are neither nonexistence nor existence; they are *not committing*.[36] An autumn chrysanthemum is neither existence nor nonexistence; it is *not committing*. The buddhas are neither existence nor nonexistence; they are *not committing*. Such things as an outdoor pillar, a stone lantern, a whisk, and a staff are neither existence nor nonexistence; they are *not committing*. The self is neither existence nor nonexistence; it is *not committing*. Learning in practice like this is the realized Universe and it is Universal realization—we consider it from the standpoint of the subject and we consider it from the standpoint of the object. When the state has become like this already, even the regret that *"I have committed what was not to be committed"* is also nothing other than energy arising from the effort *not to commit*. But to purport, in that case, that if *not committing* is so we might deliberately commit [wrongs], is like walking north and expecting to arrive at [the southern country of] Etsu. [The relation between] *wrongs* and *not committing* is not only *"a well looking at a donkey;"*[37] it is the well looking at the well, the donkey looking at the donkey, a human being looking at a human being, and a mountain looking at a mountain. Because there is *"preaching of this principle of mutual accordance," wrongs* are *not committing*.

---

32. 見得徹 (KENTOKUTETSU), or "can see thoroughly."

33. 坐得断 (ZATOKUDAN), or "can sit decisively." Master Dogen often uses the words 坐断 (ZADAN), "sit-cut" or "sit away," to mean transcending a problem by practicing Zazen (see for example, chap. 73, *Sanjushichibon-bodai-bunbo*). But in this case, 断 (DAN) is an adverb; "decisively."

34. Master Dogen denies the idea that something called wrongness manifests itself from real circumstances, as if the wrongness and the reality might be two different things. In this paragraph he emphasizes that there is no wrongness separate from the reality of our momentary action.

35. Master Dogen emphasized that wrong is only the problem of not doing wrong.

36. In other words, pine trees in spring exist as they are, without any intentional activity.

37. See *Shinji-shobogenzo*, pt. 2, no. 25. 'Master Sozan asks Ācārya Toku, "It is said that the Buddha's true Dharma-body is just like space, and it manifests its form according to things, like the moon [reflected] in water. How do you preach this principle of mutual accordance?" Toku says, "It is like a donkey looking into a well." The Master says, "Your words are extremely nice words, but they only express eighty or ninety percent." Toku says, "What would the Master say?" Master Sozan says, "It is like the well looking at the donkey."' The story expresses the mutual relation between subject and object.

The Buddha's true Dharma-body[38]
Is just like space.
It manifests its form according to things,
Like the moon [reflected] in water.[39]

Because *not committing* is *accordance with things, not committing* has *manifest form. "It is just like space:" it* is the clapping of hands to the left and the clapping of hands to the right.[40] *"It is like the moon [reflected] in water:"* and the water restricted by the moon.[41] Such instances of *not committing* are the realization of reality which should never be doubted at all.

[14] *"Practice the many kinds of right."*[42] These many kinds of right are [classed] within the three properties[43] as *"rightness."* Even though the many kinds of right are included in *"rightness,"* there has never been any kind of right that is realized beforehand and that then waits for someone to do it.[44] There is none among the many kinds of right that fails to appear at the very moment of doing right. The myriad kinds of right have no set shape, but they converge on the place of doing right faster than iron to a magnet,[45] and with a force stronger than the vairambhaka winds.[46] It is utterly impossible for the Earth, mountains and rivers, the world, a national land, or even the force of accumulated karma, to hinder [this] coming together of right.[47] At the same time, the principle that recognitions differ from world to world,[48] in regard to right, is the same [as in regard to wrong]. What can be recognized [as right] is called right, and so it is *like the manner in which the buddhas of the three times preach the Dharma.* The similarity is that their preaching of Dharma when they are in the world is just temporal. Because their lifetime and body size also have continued to rely totally upon the moment, they *preach the Dharma which is without distinction.*[49] So it is like the situation that right as a charac-

---

38. 法身 (HOSSHIN), from the Sanskrit *dharma-kāya.* In this case, the Dharma-body represents the spiritual or abstract face of reality, and space represents the physical or objective face of reality. The poem suggests the oneness of the two faces.

39. This verse from the *Kon-komyo-kyo,* quoted in the story of Master Sozan and Ācārya Toku, is also quoted in chap. 42, *Tsuki.*

40. In this sentence, space means the place where action is done.

41. The image of the moon can be compared to the individual subject, and the water which surrounds the image can be compared to objective circumstances. Water reflecting the moon symbolizes the oneness of subject and object. The moon restricting the water suggests the fact from the other side, with subject and object reversed.

42. 衆善奉行 (SHUZEN-BUGYO), lit. "devoutly practice the many [kinds of] good," as in the original poem.

43. The three properties are rightness, wrongness, and indifference, as explained in the second paragraph.

44. Even though we can consider rightness abstractly, right itself can only be realized by action in the moment of the present.

45. Even though abstract rightness cannot manifest any form, in action right can manifest itself at once.

46. Very strong winds mentioned in ancient Indian legends.

47. In these opening sentences of the paragraph, Master Dogen affirms the existence of right when realized by action. From the next sentence he explains right as something relative.

48. The usual example is water which fish see as a palace, gods see as a string of pearls, human beings see as water, and demons see as blood or pus.

49. 説無分別法 (MUFUNBETSU [no] HO [o] TOKU), from the *Hoben (Expedient Means)* chapter of the Lotus Sutra. *"In the same manner that the buddhas of the three times / Preach the Dharma, / So now do I also /*

teristic of devotional practice[50] and right as a characteristic of Dharma-practice,[51] which are far removed from each other, are not different things. Or, for example, it is like the keeping of the precepts by a śrāvaka being the violation of the precepts by a bodhisattva. The many kinds of right do not arise from causes and conditions and they do not vanish due to causes and conditions. The many kinds of right are real dharmas, but real dharmas are not many kinds of right. Causes and conditions, arising and vanishing, and the many kinds of right are similar in that if they are correct at the beginning, they are correct at the end. The many kinds of right are *good doing*[52] but they are neither of the doer nor known by the doer, and they are neither of the other nor known by the other. As regards the knowing and the seeing of the self and of the other, in knowing there is the self and there is the other, and in seeing there is the self and there is the other, and thus individual vigorous eyes exist in the sun and in the moon. This state is *good doing* itself. At just this moment of *good doing* the realized Universe exists, but it is not *the creation of the Universe*, and it is not *the eternal existence of the Universe*. How much less could we call it *original practice?*[53] Doing right is *good doing*, but it is not something that can be fathomed intellectually. *Good doing* in the present is a vigorous eye, but it is beyond intellectual consideration. [Vigorous eyes] are not realized for the purpose of considering the Dharma intellectually. Consideration by vigorous eyes is never the same as consideration by other things. The many kinds of right are beyond existence and nonexistence, matter and the immaterial, and so on; they are just nothing other than *good doing*. Wherever they are realized and whenever they are realized, they are, without exception, *good doing*. This *good doing* inevitably includes the realization of the many kinds of right. The realization of *good doing* is the Universe itself, but it is beyond arising and vanishing, and it is beyond causes and conditions. Entering, staying, leaving, and other [concrete examples of] *good doing* are also like this. At the place where we are already performing, as *good doing*, a single right among the many kinds of right, the entire Dharma, the Whole Body,[54] the Real Land, and so on, are all enacted as *good doing*. The cause-and-effect of this right, similarly, is the Universe as the realization of *good doing*. It is not that causes are before and effects are after. Rather, causes perfectly satisfy themselves and effects perfectly satisfy themselves; when causes are in balance the Dharma is in balance and when effects are in balance the Dharma is in balance. Awaited by causes, effects are felt, but it is not a matter of before and after; for the truth is present that the [moment] before and the [moment] after are balanced [as they are].

[19] The meaning of *"Naturally purifies the mind"* is as follows: What is *natural* is *not to commit*, and what *purifies* is *not to commit*. *The* [concrete state][55] is *natural*, and the *mind*[56]

Preach the Dharma which is without distinction." (LS 1.128)

50. 信行 (SHINGYO), or "practice based on belief" suggests, for example, the practice of the Pure Land Sects.

51. 法行 (HOGYO), or "practice based on the teaching of Dharma," suggests, for example, the practice of the so-called Zen sects.

52. 奉行 (BUGYO), or "devout practicing" as in the original poem.

53. 本行 (HONGYO), "original practice," suggests practice done as our original situation, or practice done in the past, or sometimes practice done in past lives. See chap. 17, *Hokke-ten-hokke*. In this case, 本行 (HONGYO) is one example of an abstract understanding of action.

54. 全身 (ZENSHIN). See chap. 71, *Nyorai-zenshin*.

55. "The" is 其 (GO, *sono*), which means "that," suggesting the concrete, real state. See note 5.

is *natural. The [concrete state]* is *not committing,* the *mind* is *not committing.* The *mind* is *good doing,* what *purifies* is *good doing, the [concrete state]* is *good doing,* and what is *natural* is *good doing.* Therefore it is said that *"This is the teaching of the buddhas."* Those who are called *"buddhas"* are, in some cases, like Śiva,[57] [but] there are similarities and differences even among Śivas, and at the same time not all Śivas are buddhas. [Buddhas] are, in some cases, like wheel-rolling kings,[58] but not all sacred wheel-rolling kings are buddhas. We should consider facts like these and learn them in practice. If we do not learn how buddhas should be, even if we seem to be fruitlessly enduring hardship, we are only ordinary beings accepting suffering; we are not practicing the Buddha's truth. *Not committing* and *good doing* are *donkey business not having gone away and horse business coming in."*[59]

[20] Haku Kyo-i[60] of Tang China is a lay disciple of Zen Master Bukko Nyoman,[61] and a second-generation disciple of Zen Master Kozei Daijaku.[62] When he was the governor of Hangzhou[63] district he practiced in the order of Zen Master Choka Dorin.[64] In the story, Kyo-i asks, *"What is the Great Intention of the Buddha-Dharma?"*

Dorin says, *"Not to commit wrongs. To practice the many kinds of right."*[65]

Kyo-i says, *"If it is so, even a child of three can express it!"*

Dorin says, *"A child of three can speak the truth, but an old man of eighty cannot practice it."*

Thus informed, Kyo-i makes at once a prostration of thanks, and then leaves.

[21] Kyo-i, though descended from Haku Shogun,[66] is truly a wizard of the verse who is rare through the ages. People call him one of the twenty-four [great] men of letters.

---

56. "Mind" is 意 (I), lit. "intention." In general, human intention is opposed to the natural way, but the message of this chapter is that the mind of morality is natural.

57. 自在天 (JIZAITEN), "God of Free Will," or "God of Free Movement," represents the god called Śiva in Sanskrit, the god of destruction and regeneration in the Hindu triad of Brahmā (creator), Śiva, and Viṣṇu (preserver). See Glossary.

58. 天輪聖王 (TEN-RIN-SHO-O), from the Sanskrit *cakravarti-rāja.* Master Dogen is urging us to come to a realistic understanding of what buddhas are.

59. Master Chokei asks Master Reiun Shigon "What is the Great Intention of the Buddha-Dharma?" Master Reiun says, *"Donkey business being unfinished, but horse business coming in."* See *Shinji-shobogenzo,* pt. 2, no. 56.

60. Haku Kyo-i, died 846 at the age of 76. Haku was his family name. Kyo-i (lit. Sitting Easy) was one of his pen-names as a poet. He was also called Haku Rakuten. It is said that he attained the truth under Master Bukko Nyoman, after which he became the governor of several districts, visiting masters whose temples were in his district and practicing Zazen.

61. Successor of Master Baso Do-itsu. Dates unknown.

62. Master Baso Do-itsu (704–788), successor of Master Nangaku Ejo. Kozei (or Kiangsi in Chinese pronunciation) was the name of the district where Master Baso lived. Zen Master Daijaku is his posthumous title.

63. Capital of Chekiang, located at the head of Hangzhou Bay (an inlet of the East China sea).

64. Master Choka Dorin, died 824 at the age of 84. He received the Dharma from Master Kinzan Koku-itsu, who belonged to a side lineage (going back to the fourth patriarch Dai-i Doshin, but not going through Master Daikan Eno). Choka means Bird's Nest—it is said that Master Choka practiced Zazen in, and lived in, a tree house.

65. 諸悪莫作, 衆善奉行 (SHOAKU-MAKUSA, SHUZEN-BUGYO), as in the original poem.

66. Hakki, a general of the founder of the Jin dynasty (who reigned from 255 to 250 B.C.). The general was famed for his excellence in military strategy. In this sentence, military ability and ability as a poet are opposed.

He bears the name of Mañjuśrī, or bears the name of Maitreya. Nowhere do his poetical sentiments go unheard and no-one could fail to pay homage to his authority in the literary world. Nevertheless, in Buddhism he is a beginner and a late learner. Moreover, it seems that he has never seen the point of this *"Not to commit wrongs. To practice the many kinds of right,"* even in a dream. Kyo-i thinks that Dorin is only telling him *"Do not commit wrongs! Practice the many kinds of right!"* through recognition of the conscious aim. Thus, he neither knows nor hears the truth that the time-honored[67] [teaching] of the *not committing* of wrongs, the *good doing* of rights, has been in Buddhism from the eternal past to the eternal present. He has not set foot in the area of the Buddha-Dharma. He does not have the power of the Buddha-Dharma. Therefore he speaks like this. Even though we caution against the intentional commitment of wrongs, and even though we encourage the deliberate practice of rights, this should be in the reality of *not committing*. In general, the Buddha-Dharma is [always] the same, whether it is being heard for the first time under a [good] counselor, or whether it is being experienced in the state which is the ultimate effect. This is called *correct in the beginning, correct at the end*, called *the wonderful cause and the wonderful effect*, and called *the Buddhist cause and the Buddhist effect*. Cause-and-effect in Buddhism is beyond discussion of [theories] such as *different maturation* or *equal streams;*[68] this being so, without Buddhist causes, we cannot experience the Buddhist effect. Because Dorin speaks this truth, he possesses the Buddha-Dharma. Even if wrong upon wrong pervade the whole Universe, and even if wrongs have swallowed the whole Dharma again and again, there is still salvation and liberation in *not committing*. Because the many kinds of right are *right at the beginning, in the middle, and at the end,*[69] *"good doing"* has realized *nature, form, body, energy*, and so on, *as they are.*[70] Kyo-i has never trodden in these tracks at all, and so he says *"Even a child of three could express it!"* He speaks like this without actually being able to express an expression of the truth. How pitiful, Kyo-i, you are. Just what are you saying? You have never heard the customs of the Buddha, so do you or do you not know a three-year old child? Do you or do you not know the facts of a newborn baby? Someone who knows a three-year old child must also know the buddhas of the three times. How could someone who has never known the buddhas of the three times know a three-year old child? Do not think that to have met face-to-face is to have known. Do not think that without meeting face-to-face one does not know. Someone who has come to know a single particle knows the whole Universe, and someone who has penetrated one real dharma has penetrated the myriad dharmas. Someone who has not penetrated the myriad dharmas has not penetrated one real dharma. When students of penetration penetrate to the end, they see the myriad dharmas and they see single real dharmas; therefore, people who are learning of a single particle are inevitably learning of the whole Universe. To think that a three-year-old child cannot speak the Buddha-Dharma, and to think that what a

67. 千古万古 (SENKO-BANKO), lit. "thousand-ages old, ten-thousand ages old."

68. The theory that moral and immoral behavior produce different results is represented by the words 異熟 (IJUKU), lit. "different maturation." This expresses the moral viewpoint. The opposing theory is represented by the words 等流 (TORU), lit. "equal streams." This expresses the scientific view of cause and effect; that is, the view which is not concerned with subjective evaluation of cause and effect.

69. 初中後善 (SHOCHUGO-ZEN), from the Introductory chapter of the Lotus Sutra: *"The Dharma which they should preach is good in the beginning, middle, and end."* (LS 1.40; see also chap. 17, *Hokke-ten-hokke*.)

70. Alludes to the *Hoben (Expedient Means)* chapter of the Lotus Sutra. See LS 1.68.

three-year-old child says must be easy, is very stupid. That is because the clarification of life,[71] and the clarification of death, are the *one great purpose*[72] of Buddhists. A master of the past[73] says, *"Just at the time of your birth[71] you had your share of the lion's roar."*[74] *"A share of the lion's roar"* means the virtue of the Tathāgata to turn the Dharma-wheel, or the turning of the Dharma-wheel itself. Another master of the past[75] says, *"Living-and-dying, coming-and-going, are the real human body."* So to clarify the real body and to have the virtue of the lion's roar may truly be the one great matter, which can never be easy. For this reason, the clarification of the motives and actions of a three-year-old child are also the great purpose. Now there are differences between the actions and motives of the buddhas of the three times [and those of children]; this is why Kyo-i, in his stupidity, has never been able to hear a three-year-old child speaking the truth, and why, not even suspecting that [a child's speaking of the truth] might exist, he talks as he does. He does not hear Dorin's voice, which is more vivid than thunder, and so he says, *"Even a child of three could express it!"* as if to say that [Master Dorin himself] has not expressed the truth in his words. Thus [Kyo-i] does not hear the lion's roar of an infant, and he passes vainly by the Zen Master's turning of the Dharma-wheel. The Zen Master, unable to contain his compassion, went on to say, *"A child of three can speak the truth, but an old man of eighty cannot practice it."* What he was saying is this: *A child of three has words which express the truth, and you should investigate this thoroughly. Old men of eighty say, "I cannot practice it," and you should consider this carefully. I leave you to decide whether an infant speaks the truth, but I do not leave the infant to decide. I leave you to decide whether an old man can practice, but I do not leave the old man to decide.*[76] It is the fundamental principle to pursue, to preach, and to honor the Buddha-Dharma like this.

Shobogenzo Shoaku-makusa

Preached to the assembly at Kosho-horin-ji temple on the evening of the moon[77] in the [2nd] year of En-o.[78]

---

71. 生 (SHO), means both birth and life.

72. 一大事の因縁 (ICHIDAIJI *no* INNEN). See chap. 17, *Hokke-ten-hokke*.

73. The quotation is paraphrased from *Daichido-ron,* the Chinese translation of the *Mahā-prajñā-pāramitā-śāstra*. This treatise was largely compiled by Master Nāgārjuna.

74. The Buddha's preaching was said to be like the roar of a lion.

75. Master Engo Kokugon. This quotation also appears in chap. 50, *Shoho-jisso*.

76. A child's expression of the truth and an old man's ability to practice are just reality—they do not rely upon interpretation by the subject.

77. The 15th day of the 8th lunar month, often the day of the year on which the moon is most conspicuous. Many chapters of Shobogenzo were preached on this day.

78. 1240.

[11]

有時

Uji

Existence-Time

***U** means "existence" and **ji** means "time," so **uji** means "existent time," or "existence-time." In this chapter Master Dogen teaches us the meaning of time in Buddhism. As Master Dogen explains in other chapters, Buddhism is realism. Therefore, the view of time in Buddhism is always very realistic. Specifically, time is always related with existence and existence is always related with momentary time. So in reality, the past and the future are not existent time; the present moment is the only existent time—the point at which existence and time come together. Also, time is always related with action here and now. Action can only be realized in time, and time can only be realized in action. Thus, the view of time in Buddhism reminds us of existentialism in modern philosophy. It is very important to understand the Buddhist view of time in order to grasp the true meaning of Buddhism.*

[29] **An eternal Buddha[1] says,**

Sometimes[2] standing on top of the highest peak,
Sometimes moving along the bottom of the deepest ocean.
Sometimes three heads and eight arms,[3]
Sometimes the sixteen-foot or eight-foot [golden body].[4]
Sometimes a staff or a whisk,[5]
Sometimes an outdoor pillar or a stone lantern.[6]
Sometimes the third son of Chang or the fourth son of Lee,
Sometimes the Earth and space.

[30] In this word *"sometimes,"* Time is already just Existence, and all Existence is Time. The sixteen-foot golden body is Time itself. Because it is Time, it has the resplendent

---

1. Master Yakusan Igen. *Keitoku-dento-roku*, chap. 18.

2. 有時 (UJI, or *a[ru]toki*), as in the chapter title. In this case, 有時 is an adverb, read as *a[ru]toki*, and meaning sometimes. In the chapter title, 有時 (UJI) is a compound word, "Existence-Time."

3. This phrase refers to the wrathful images of Buddhist guardian deities, such as *Aizenmyo-o*, the King of Love (in Sanskrit, Rāgarāja), whose statue generally has three angry faces and six arms.

4. 丈六八尺 (JOROKU-HASSHAKU). One *jo* equals ten *shaku*, and one *shaku* is slightly less than a foot. 丈六 (JOROKU) suggests the sixteen-foot golden body, the idealized image of the standing Buddha. 八尺 (HASSHAKU) can be interpreted as representing the balanced image of the sitting Buddha.

5. 拄杖 (SHUJO) is a staff used by Buddhist monks on their travels, and also used in Buddhist ceremonies. 払子 (HOSSU) was originally a fly-whisk, but its function has become ceremonial. These are concrete things which have religious meaning.

6. In China and Japan, temple roofs have long eaves supported by pillars which stand outside of the temple building itself; temple pillars and stone lanterns are thus very common objects.

brightness of Time. We should learn it as the twelve hours[7] of today. The three heads and eight arms are Time itself. Because they are Time, they are completely the same as the twelve hours of today. We can never measure how long and distant or how short and pressing twelve hours is; at the same time, we call it "twelve hours."[8] The leaving and coming of the directions and traces [of Time] are clear, and so people do not doubt it. They do not doubt it, but that does not mean they know it. The doubts which living beings, by our nature, have about every thing and every fact that we do not know, are not consistent; therefore our past history of doubt does not always exactly match our doubt now. We can say for the present, however, that doubt is nothing other than Time. We put our self in order, and see [the resulting state] as the whole Universe. Each individual and each object in this whole Universe should be glimpsed as individual moments of Time.[9] Object does not hinder object in the same way that moment of Time does not hinder moment of Time. For this reason, there are minds which are made up in the same moment of Time, and there are moments of Time in which the same mind is made up. Practice, and realization of the truth, are also like this.[10] Putting the self in order, we see what it is. The truth that self is Time is like this. We should learn in practice that, because of this truth, the whole Earth includes myriad phenomena and hundreds of things, and each phenomenon and each thing exists in the whole Earth. Such toing-and-froing is a first step [on the way] of practice. When we arrive in the field of the ineffable,[11] there is just one [concrete] thing and one [concrete] phenomenon, here and now, [beyond] understanding of phenomena and non-understanding of phenomena, and [beyond] understanding of things and non-understanding of things. Because [real existence] is only this exact moment, all moments of Existence-Time are the whole of Time, and all Existent things and all Existent phenomena are Time. The whole of Existence, the whole Universe, exists in individual moments of Time.[12] Let us pause to reflect whether or not any of the whole of Existence or any of the whole Universe has leaked away from the present moment of Time. Yet in the time of the common man who does not learn the Buddha-Dharma there are views and opinions: when he hears the words *"Existence-Time,"* he thinks, *"Sometimes I became [an angry demon with] three heads and eight arms, and sometimes I became the sixteen-foot or eight-foot [golden body of Buddha]. For example, it was like crossing a river or crossing a mountain. The mountain and the river may still exist, but now that I have crossed them and am living in a jeweled palace with crimson towers, the mountain and the river are [as distant] from me as heaven is from the Earth."* But true reasoning is not limited to this one line [of thought]. That is to say, when I was climbing a mountain or crossing a river, I was there in that Time. There must have been Time in me. And I actually exist now, [so] Time could not have

---

7. 十二時 (JUNI-JI), lit. "twelve times." In Master Dogen's age, one day was divided into twelve periods. Master Dogen suggests that magnificent real time in the balanced state is not different from the ordinary time of concrete daily life.

8. When we are waiting, twenty-four hours is long, and when we are pressed for time, twenty-four hours is short. So the length of a day is relative, but we measure it as "twenty-four hours."

9. "Each individual" is 頭頭 (ZU-ZU), lit. "head-head." "Each object" is 物物 (BUTSU-BUTSU), lit. "thing-thing." "Individual moments of Time" is 時時 (JI-JI), lit. "time-time."

10. Like the will to the truth, Buddhist practice and realization are both real existence and real time.

11. 恁麼の田地 (INMO *no* DENCHI). 恁麼 (INMO) means something ineffable (see chap. 29, *Inmo*). 田 (DEN) means field and 地 (CHI) means earth. 田地 (DENCHI) suggests a concrete area, or real state.

12. "Individual moments of Time" is 時時の時 (JI-JI *no* JI).

departed. If Time does not have the form of leaving and coming, the Time of climbing a mountain is the present as Existence-Time.[13] If Time does retain the form of leaving and coming, I have this present moment of Existence-Time, which is just Existence-Time itself.[14] How could that Time of climbing the mountain and crossing the river fail to swallow, and fail to vomit, this Time [now] in the jeweled palace with crimson towers?[15] The three heads and eight arms were Time yesterday; the sixteen-foot or eight-foot [golden body] is Time today. Even so, this Buddhist principle of yesterday and today is just about moments in which we go directly into the mountains and look out across a thousand or ten thousand peaks; it is not about what has passed. The three heads and eight arms pass instantly as my Existence-Time; though they seem to be in the distance, they are [moments of] the present. The sixteen-foot or eight-foot [golden body] also passes instantly as my Existence-Time; though it seems to be yonder, it is [moments of] the present. This being so, pine trees are Time, and bamboos are Time. We should not understand only that Time flies. We should not learn that "flying" is the only ability of Time. If we just left Time to fly away, some gaps in it might appear. Those who fail to experience and to hear the truth of Existence-Time do so because they understand [Time] only as having passed. To grasp the pivot and express it: all that exists throughout the whole Universe is lined up in a series and at the same time is individual moments of Time.[16] Because [Time] is Existence-Time, it is my Existence-Time.[17] Existence-Time has the virtue of passing in a series of moments.[18] That is to say, from today it passes through a series of moments to tomorrow; from today it passes through a series of moments to yesterday; from yesterday it passes through a series of moments to today; from today it passes through a series of moments to today; and from tomorrow it passes through a series of moments to tomorrow. Because passage through separate moments is a virtue of Time, moments of the past and present are neither piled up one on top of another nor lined up in a row; and, for the same reason, Seigen[19]

---

13. "Time which does not have the form of leaving and coming" means instantaneous time, as opposed to time as a linear progression. If we see Time in this way, even a continuous process—like crossing a mountain—is moments of the present.

14. "Time which retains the form of leaving and coming" means linear time. If we see Time in this way, even though the moment of the present has arrived and it will depart, it exists now. Master Dogen's view of real time embraces both the view of time as a point and the view of time as a line, as well as the view of time as reality itself.

15. Past time swallowing present time suggests the inclusive character of time. Past time vomiting present time suggests the independence of the past and the present.

16. "Individual moments of Time" is 時時 (JI-JI). See note 9 and note 12.

17. 吾有時 (GO-UJI), "my Existence-Time," emphasizes that Existence-Time is not only a concept, but our own real life itself.

18. 経歴 (KYORYAKU or KEIREKI). 経 (KYO or KEI) means passing through, experience, the passage of time: it represents the linear aspect of time. 歴 (RYAKU or REKI) suggests a process through separate, successive stages; it represents the momentary aspect of time.

A note on pronunciation: In Japanese, a Chinese character is read either in its *kun-yomi* form (the native Japanese reading) or in its *on-yomi* form (imitating the Chinese pronunciation). However, the pronunciation of Chinese characters in China varied from age to age, so different readings of the *on-yomi* are possible. *Kyo-ryaku* approximates the pronunciation used in the Wu Dynasty (222–258 A.D.). *Kei-reki* approximates the pronunciation used in the Han Dynasty (206 B.C.–25 A.D.). Buddhist sutras in Japan are usually read according to the pronunciation used in the Wu Dynasty.

19. Master Seigen Gyoshi, died 740.

is Time, Obaku[20] is Time, and Kozei[21] and Sekito[22] are Time.[23] Because subject-and-object already is Time, practice-and-experience is moments of Time. Going into the mud and going into the water[24], similarly, are Time. The view of the common man today, and the causes and conditions of [that] view, are what the common man experiences but are not the common man's Reality.[25] It is just that Reality, for the present, has made a common man into its causes and conditions. Because he understands this Time and this Existence to be other than Reality itself, he deems that *"the sixteen-foot golden body is beyond me."* Attempts to evade [the issue] by [thinking] *"I am never the sixteen-foot golden body"* are also flashes of Existence-Time; they are glimpses of it by a person who has yet to realize it in experience and to rely upon it. The [Existence-Time] that also causes the horse and the sheep[26] to be as they are arranged in the world today, is a rising and falling which is something ineffable abiding in its place in the Dharma. The rat is Time, and the tiger is Time; living beings are Time, and buddhas are Time. This Time experiences the whole Universe using three heads and eight arms, and experiences the whole Universe using the sixteen-foot golden body. To universally realize the whole Universe by using the whole Universe is called *"to perfectly realize."*[27] Enactment of the sixteen-foot golden body[28] by using the sixteen-foot golden body is realized as the establishment of the mind, as training, as the state of bodhi, and as nirvāṇa; that is, as Existence itself, and as Time itself. It is nothing other than the perfect realization of the whole of Time as the whole of Existence; there is nothing surplus at all. Because something surplus is just something surplus, even a moment of half-perfectly-realized Existence-Time is the perfect realization of half-Existence-Time.[29] Even those phases in which we seem to be blundering heedlessly are also Existence. If we leave it utterly up to Existence,[30] even though [the moments] before and after manifest heedless blundering, they abide in their place as Existence-Time. Abiding in our place in the Dharma in

---

20. Master Obaku Ki-un, died between 855 and 859. A second-generation descendant of Master Baso.

21. Master Baso Do-itsu (704–788). See note 42.

22. Master Sekito Kisen (700–790). A successor of Master Seigen Gyoshi. See note 41.

23. The lives of all Buddhist masters are just moments of the present.

24. Symbols of daily struggles.

25. 法 (HO), or Dharma.

26. The twelve hours of the Chinese day were represented by twelve animals: rat (12 midnight), ox (2 a.m.), tiger (4 a.m.), rabbit (6 a.m.), dragon (8 a.m.), snake (10 a.m.), horse (12 noon), sheep (2 p.m.), monkey (4 p.m.), chicken (6 p.m.), dog (8 p.m.), and boar (10 p.m.). These animals were also used to represent directions, the rat indicating north, the horse south, et cetera.

27. The original sentence is constructed with combinations of only three Chinese characters, 尽, 界, 究 (JIN, KAI, GU). "The whole Universe" is 尽界 (JINKAI); 尽 (JIN), "whole," works as an adjective, and 界 (KAI), "world," works as a noun. "Universally realize" is 界尽す (KAI-JIN *su*); 界 (KAI), "universally," works as an adverb and 尽す (JIN *su*), "realize," works as a verb. "Perfectly realize" is 究尽す (GUJIN *su*); 究 (GU), "perfectly," works as an adverb, and 尽 (JIN), "realize," works as a verb. 究尽 (GUJIN) appears in the key sentence of the Lotus Sutra: *"Buddhas alone, together with buddhas, can perfectly realize that all dharmas are real form."* (LS 1.68)

28. 丈六金身する (JOROKU-KONJIN *suru*), lit. "to sixteen-foot golden body"—a noun phrase is used as if it were a verb.

29. 半有時 (HAN-UJI). Master Dogen sometimes uses half to suggest something concrete, individual, or real, as opposed to an ideal (as in the verse in the final paragraph of this chapter).

30. Lit. "If we leave it utterly up to him," i.e., if we let go of subjective worries. "Him" refers to Existence in the previous sentence.

the state of vigorous activity is just Existence-Time. We should not disturb it [by interpreting it] as *"being without,"*[31] and we should not enforceably call it *"Existence."* In regard to Time, we strive to comprehend only how relentlessly it is passing; we do not understand it intellectually as what is yet to come. Even though intellectual understanding is Time, no circumstances are ever influenced by it. [Human] skin bags recognize [time] as leaving and coming; none has penetrated it as Existence-Time abiding in its place: how much less could any experience Time having passed through the gate?[32] Even [among those who] are conscious of abiding in their place, who can express the state of having already attained the ineffable? Even [among those who] have been asserting for a long time that they are like this, there is none who is not still groping for the manifestation before them of the real features. If we leave [even bodhi and nirvāṇa] as they are in the Existence-Time of the common man, even bodhi and nirvāṇa are—[though] merely a form which leaves and comes—Existence-Time.[33]

[38] In short, without any cessation of restrictions and hindrances,[34] Existence-Time is realized. Celestial kings and celestial throngs, now appearing to the right and appearing to the left, are the Existence-Time in which we are now exerting ourselves. Elsewhere, beings of Existence-Time of land and sea are [also] realized through our own exertion now. The many kinds of being and the many individual beings which [live] as Existence-Time in darkness and in brightness, are all the realization of our own effort, and the momentary continuance[35] of our effort. We should learn in practice that without the momentary continuance of our own effort in the present, not a single dharma nor a single thing could ever be realized or could ever continue from one moment to the next.[35] We should never learn that passage from one moment to the next is like the movement east and west of the wind and rain. The whole Universe is neither beyond moving and changing nor beyond progressing and regressing; it is passage from one moment to the next. An example of the momentary passing of time is spring. Spring has innumerable different aspects, which we call "a passage of time."[36] We should learn in practice that the momentary passing of time continues without there being any external thing. The momentary passing of spring, for example, inevitably passes, moment by moment, through spring itself.[37] It is not that *the momentary passing of time* is spring; rather, because spring is the momentary passing of time, passing time

31. 無 (MU), "nonexistence." 有 and 無 (U and MU), "existence and nonexistence," are usually opposed. See for example, chap. 24, *Bussho*.

32. The gate suggests the dualism of illusions and their negation, or idealism and materialism.

33. The fact that all things—even bodhi and nirvāṇa—are Existence-Time does not change, however the fact is interpreted.

34. 羅籠 (RARO), lit. "nets and cages." In China, silk nets 羅 (RA) and bamboo cages 籠 (RO) are used to catch and to keep small birds.

35. "Momentary continuance" and "continue from one moment to the next" are translations of 経歴 (KYORYAKU). See note 18.

36. "The momentary passing of time" and "a passage of time" are also translations of 経歴 (KYORYAKU). Spring has separate momentary aspects: the air is warm, flowers are open, birds are singing, et cetera. At the same time, we see it as an inclusive continuing process.

37. When we think about "passing" we usually imagine a subject passing through an external object, but this does not apply to the passing of time, because the momentary passing of time is complete in itself.

has already realized the truth in the here and now of springtime.[38] We should research [this] in detail, returning to it and leaving it again and again. If we think, in discussing the momentary passing of time, that circumstances are [only] individual things on the outside, while something which can pass from moment to moment moves east through hundreds of thousands of worlds and through hundreds of thousands of kalpas, then we are not devoting ourselves solely to Buddhist learning in practice.[39]

[40] Great Master Yakusan Kodo,[40] the story goes, at the suggestion of Great Master Musai,[41] visits Zen Master Kozei Daijaku.[42] He asks, *"I have more or less clarified the import of the three vehicles and the twelve divisions of the teaching.*[43] *But just what is the ancestral Master's intention in coming from the West?"*[44]

Thus questioned, Zen Master Daijaku says, *"Sometimes*[45] *I make him*[46] *lift an eyebrow or wink an eye, and sometimes I do not make him lift an eyebrow or wink an eye; sometimes to make him lift an eyebrow or wink an eye is right, and sometimes to make him lift an eyebrow or wink an eye is not right."*

Hearing this, Yakusan realizes a great realization and says to Daijaku, *"In Sekito's order I have been like a mosquito that climbed onto an iron ox."*

[42] What Daijaku says is not the same as [what] others [can say]. [His] *eyebrows* and *eyes* may be the mountains and the seas, because the mountains and the seas are [his] *eyebrows* and *eyes*. In his *making himself lift [an eyebrow]*, he may be looking at the mountains; and in his *making himself wink*, he may be presiding over the seas. *Being right* has become familiar to *him*, and *he* has been led by *the teaching*.[47] Neither is *not being right*

---

38. In the first clause, passing time and spring are separated; "the momentary passing of time" means the concept of the season spring, and "spring" means the concrete individual situations of spring—flowers blooming, birds singing, et cetera. In the second clause, Master Dogen suggested the real springtime as the oneness of the conceptual and the concrete.

39. Time is not a factor within the Universe, it is the Universe itself.

40. Master Yakusan Igen (745–828). He became a monk at the age of 17 and eventually succeeded Master Sekito Kisen. Great Master Kodo is his posthumous title.

41. Master Sekito Kisen (700–790). He had his head shaved by Master Daikan Eno and eventually succeeded Master Seigen Gyoshi. He wrote the poem *Sandokai (On Experiencing the State)*, which is often recited in Soto Sect temples. Great Master Musai is his posthumous title.

42. Master Baso Do-itsu (704–788); successor of Master Nangaku Ejo. Kozei was the name of the district where he lived, and Daijaku is his posthumous name. The spread of Buddhism in China in the 8th century sprang from the efforts of Master Sekito and Master Baso.

43. The three vehicles are the ways of the *śrāvaka, pratyekabuddha,* and *bodhisattva,* as outlined by the Buddha in the Lotus Sutra. The twelve divisions of the teachings are as follows: 1) *sūtra,* original texts, sutras; 2) *geya,* verses summarizing the prose content of sutras; 3) *vyākaraṇa,* the Buddha's affirmation that a practitioner is becoming a buddha; 4) *gāthā,* independent verses; 5) *udāna,* spontaneous preaching (usually the Buddha's preaching was prompted by questions from his followers); 6) *nidāna,* historical accounts of causes and conditions; 7) *avadāna,* parables; 8) *itivṛttaka,* stories of past occurrences (especially stories of past lives of the Buddha's disciples); 9) *jātaka,* stories of the Buddha's past lives; 10) *vaipulya,* extensions of Buddhist philosophy; 11) *adbhuta-dharma,* records of miraculous occurrences; 12) *upadeśa,* theoretical discourses. See also Glossary, and chap. 24, *Bukkyo.*

44. The ancestral Master means Master Bodhidharma, who introduced real Buddhism to China from India. See chap. 67, *Soshi-sairai-no-i.*

45. 有時 *(arutoki),* see note 2.

46. 伊 *(kare)* lit. means "him" or "that one." Master Baso thought about his own behavior objectively.

47. "The teaching" is 教 (KYO). In Master Baso's words, 教 is used as an auxiliary causative verb (pronounced *seshimuru).* Master Dogen affirmed that Master Baso's behavior was moral and that he fol-

the same as *not making himself [act]*, nor is *not making himself [act]* the same as *not being right.*[48] All these [situations] are *Existence-Time.* The mountains are Time, and the seas are Time. Without Time, the mountains and the seas could not exist: we should not deny that Time exists in the mountains and the seas here and now. If Time decays, the mountains and the seas decay. If Time is not subject to decay, the mountains and the seas are not subject to decay. In accordance with this truth the bright star appears, the Tathāgata appears, the Eye appears, and picking up a flower appears,[49] and this is just Time. Without Time, it would not be like this.

[44] Zen Master Kisho[50] of the Shoken region is a Dharma-descendant of Rinzai, and the rightful successor of Shuzan.[51] On one occasion he preaches to the assembly:

Sometimes[52] *the will is present but the words are absent,*
Sometimes the words are present but the will is absent,
Sometimes the will and the words are both present,
Sometimes the will and the words are both absent.[53]

[44] The will and the words are both Existence-Time. Presence and absence are both Existence-Time. The moment of presence has not finished, but the moment of absence has come—the will is the donkey and the words are the horse;[54] horses have been made into words and donkeys have been made into will.[55] Presence is not related to having come, and absence is not related to not having come.[56] Existence-Time is like this. Presence is restricted by presence itself; it is not restricted by absence.[57] Absence is restricted by absence itself; it is not restricted by presence. The will hinders the will and meets the will.[58] Words hinder words and meet words. Restriction hinders restriction and meets restriction. Restriction restricts restriction. This is Time. Restriction is utilized

---

lowed the teachings. At the same time, by combining the three characters 是, 伊, and 教, (right, him, and make/teaching), Master Dogen suggested the oneness of Master Baso's words and his state.

48. Immorality is not only inaction—positive action can also be immoral. And inaction is not always immoral—to do nothing is sometimes morally right.

49. The elements of the sentence suggest real situations in the Buddha's life—it is said that he realized the truth on seeing the morning star, and that he transmitted the truth to Master Mahākāśyapa by picking up an udumbara flower. See chap. 68, *Udonge.*

50. Master Shoken Kisho, dates unknown; a successor of Master Shuzan Shonen. Master Shoken was the fourth master in the succession from Master Rinzai, and the ninth master in the succession from Master Nangaku Ejo. It is said that he realized the truth in the order of Master Shuzan when discussing a story about a *shippei* (bamboo stick). Shoken is in modern-day Honan province in East Central China.

51. Master Shuzan Shonen, died 993 at the age of 68. A successor of Master Fuketsu Ensho.

52. 有時 *(arutoki).* See note 2.

53. "Present" is 到 (TO, *ita[rite])* which means to arrive, or to have arrived, to be present. "Absent" is 不到 (FUTO, *ita[ra]zu)* which means not to arrive, or not to have arrived, to be absent.

54. Master Chokei asks Master Reiun Shigon *"What is the Great Intention of the Buddha-Dharma?"* Master Reiun says, *"Donkey business being unfinished, but horse business coming in."* See *Shinji-shobogenzo,* pt. 2, no. 56.

55. The poem seems to be abstract in content, discussing only words and will, but Master Dogen interprets that the poem is also about concrete reality.

56. Presence, or "to have arrived," and absence, or "not to have arrived," are states at the moment of the present; they do not need to be seen as the results of past processes.

57. Presence restricted by itself means real presence as it is, i.e., presence that is not restricted by worrying about absence.

58. Both expressions "the will hinders the will" and "the will meets the will" suggest the real will as it is.

by objective dharmas, but restriction that restricts objective dharmas has never occurred.[59] I meet with a human being, a human being meets with a human being, I meet with myself, and manifestation meets with manifestation. Without Time, these [facts] could not be like this. Furthermore, *the will* is the Time of the realized Universe,[60] *the words* are the Time of the pivot which is the ascendant state,[61] *presence* is the Time of laying bare the substance,[62] and *absence* is the Time of *sticking to this and parting from this.*[63] We should draw distinctions, and should enact Existence-Time,[64] like this. Though venerable patriarchs hitherto have each spoken as they have, how could there be nothing further to say? I would like to say:

The half-presence of will and words is Existence-Time,
The half-absence of will and words is Existence-Time.

There should be research in experience like this.

Making oneself[65] *lift an eyebrow or wink an eye is half Existence-Time,*
Making oneself lift an eyebrow or wink an eye is mixed-up Existence-Time,
Not making oneself lift an eyebrow or wink an eye is half Existence-Time,
Not making oneself lift an eyebrow or wink an eye is mixed-up Existence-Time.

When we experience coming and experience leaving, and when we experience presence and experience absence, like this, that time is Existence-Time.

Shobogenzo Uji

Written at Kosho-horin-ji temple on the 1st day of winter in the 1st year of Ninji.[66]

Copied during the summer retreat in the [1st] year of Kangen[67]—Ejo.

---

59. "Restriction" means being as it is. It is the state which real things already have, it is not something separate which can hinder real things.

60. 現成公案 (GENJO-KOAN). See chap. 3, *Genjo-koan.*

61. 向上関棙 (KOJO-KANREI). 向上 (KOJO), "ascendant," describes the state which is more real than thinking and feeling. See chap. 28, *Butsu-kojo-no-ji.*

62. 脱体 (DATTAI). 脱 (DATSU) means to get free of, or to shed. 体 (TAI) means the body, the substance, the concrete reality.

63. 即此離此 (SOKU-SHI-RI-SHI) suggests real behavior in Buddhist life. This and the three preceding expressions can be interpreted according to four phases: a general expression of reality, the concrete state which is more real than a generalization, the clear establishment of concrete facts in reality, and real action in daily life.

64. "Enact Existence-Time" is 有時す (UJI *su*)—有時 (UJI) is used as a verb.

65. 伊 *(kare)*, as in Master Baso's words. See note 46.

66. The 1st day of the 10th lunar month, 1240.

67. 1243.

[12]

袈裟功徳

KESA-KUDOKU

The Merit of the Kaṣāya

***Kesa** represents the Sanskrit word kaṣāya, or Buddhist robe, and **kudoku** means "virtue" or "merit." So **kesa kudoku** means the merit of the kaṣāya. Being a realistic religion, Buddhism reveres our real life. In other words, Buddhism esteems our real conduct in daily life; wearing clothes and eating meals are very important parts of Buddhist life. In particular, the kaṣāya and pātra, or Buddhist bowl, are the main symbols of Buddhist life. In this chapter Master Dogen explains and praises the merit of the kaṣāya.*

[49] **The authentic transmission into China** of the robe and the Dharma, which are authentically transmitted from buddha to buddha and from patriarch to patriarch, was done only by the founding Patriarch of Sugaku peak.[1] The founding Patriarch was the twenty-eighth patriarch after Śākyamuni Buddha, the transmission having passed twenty-eight times in India from rightful successor to rightful successor. The twenty-eighth patriarch went to China in person and became the First Patriarch [there]. The transmission then passed through five Chinese [masters] and reached Sokei,[2] the thirty-third patriarch, whom we call *the Sixth Patriarch*. Zen Master Daikan, the thirty-third patriarch, received the authentic transmission of this robe and Dharma on Obai-zan mountain[3] in the middle of the night, after which he guarded and retained [the robe] throughout his life. It is still deposited at Horin-ji temple on Sokei-zan mountain. Many successive generations of emperors devoutly asked for [the robe] to be brought to the imperial court, where they served offerings and made prostrations to it, guarding it as a sacred object. The Tang[4] dynasty emperors Chuso, Shukuso, and Daiso[5] frequently had [the robe] brought to the court and served offerings to it. When they requested it and when they sent it back, they would conscientiously dispatch an imperial emissary and issue an edict. The Emperor Daiso once returned the Buddha-robe to Sokei-zan mountain with the following edict: *"I now dispatch the great General Ryu Sokei,[6] Pacifier of the*

---

1. Master Bodhidharma, the twenty-eighth patriarch in India and the first patriarch in China, who introduced the practice of Zazen from India. He lived at the Shaolin temple, one of the many Buddhist monasteries which already existed in the Sung-shan mountains in the north-west of China.

2. Master Daikan Eno (638–713), successor of Master Daiman Konin. Sokei is the name of the mountain where he lived.

3. Obai mountain was where Master Daiman Konin had his Buddhist order.

4. Tang Dynasty (618–907).

5. Chuso (reigned, with an interruption of several years, 684-710) was the fourth emperor of the Tang Dynasty. The emperors Shukuso (reigned 756–763) and Daiso (reigned 763–780) were students of Master Nan-yo Echu (died 775). See for example, chap. 80, *Tashintsu*.

6. Chingoku Dai Shogun Ryu Sokei. 鎮国 (CHINGOKU), lit. "Pacifier of the Nation," was a title given

Nation, to receive with courtesy[7] *and to deliver [the robe]. I consider it to be a national treasure. Venerable priests,*[8] *deposit it according to the Dharma in its original temple. Let it be solemnly guarded only by monks who have intimately received the fundamental teaching. Never let it fall into neglect."* Truly, better than ruling a three-thousand-great-thousandfold realm of worlds as countless as the sands of the Ganges,[9] to see and to hear and to serve offerings to the Buddha's robe as the king of a small country where the Buddha's robe is present, may be the best life among [all] good lives [lived] in life-and-death. Where, in a three-thousandfold world which has been reached by the Buddha's influence, could the kaṣāya not exist? At the same time, the one who passed on the authentic transmission of the Buddha's kaṣāya, having received the face-to-face transmission from rightful successor to rightful successor, is only the ancestral Patriarch of Sugaku peak. The Buddha's kaṣāya was not handed down through side lineages.[10] The transmission to Bodhisattva Bhadrapāla, a collateral descendant of the twenty-seventh patriarch,[11] duly arrived at Dharma-teacher Jo,[12] but there was no authentic transmission of the Buddha's kaṣāya. Again, the Great Master [Doshin], the fourth patriarch in China,[13] delivered Zen Master Hoyu[14] of Gozu-san mountain but did not pass on the authentic transmission of the Buddha's kaṣāya. So even without the transmission from rightful successors, the Tathāgata's right Dharma—whose merit is never empty—confers its wide and great benefit all through thousands of ages and myriads of ages. [At the same time] those who have received the transmission from rightful successors are not to be compared with those who lack the transmission. Therefore, when human beings and gods receive and retain the kaṣāya, they should receive the authentic transmission transmitted between Buddhist patriarchs. In India and in China, in the ages of the Right

---

to generals. 大将軍 (DAI-SHOGUN) means great general.

7. 頂戴 (CHODAI). 頂 (CHO) means the top of the head, and 戴 (DAI) means humbly to receive, so 頂戴 (CHODAI) literally means humbly to receive something upon the head, as a sign of respect.

8. 卿 (KEI), "you," is a term of address for lords, officials of high rank, et cetera.

9. 無量恒河沙 (MURYO-GOGA-SHA) Variations of this expression appear in many places in the Lotus Sutra. See, for example, LS 2.166 and LS 3.214.

10. 傍出 (BOSHUTSU). 傍 (BO), lit. "side," describes a bystander, or something of secondary importance. 出 (SHUTSU) means to depart or to sprout. So 傍出 (BOSHUTSU) means collateral descendants or collateral lineages. Master Dogen revered the one line which he considered to be authentic, and so to some degree, he considered all other lineages of secondary importance. Master Dogen's line is through Master Daikan Eno's successor, Master Seigen Gyoshi. At the same time, Master Dogen revered Master Daikan Eno's other successors, Master Nan-yo Echu and Master Nangaku Ejo. Masters Baso Do-itsu, Nansen Fugan, Joshu Jushin, Hyakujo Ekai, Obaku Ki-un, Rinzai Kigen, Isan Reiyu, Kyogen Chikan, Kyozan Ejaku, and Reiun Shigon were some of the descendants of Master Nangaku Ejo.

11. Master Prajñātara, successor of Master Puṇymitra and master of Master Bodhidharma. An image of a bodhisattva called Bhadrapāla (lit. "Good Guardian") is sometimes kept as a guardian of the temple bath-house.

12. Jo Hosshi, died 414 at the age of 31. 法師 (HOSSHI), "Dharma-teacher" was a title used for Buddhist priest-scholars and teachers of theory. As a layman, Jo worked as a scribe and studied the thoughts of Lao-tsu and Chang-tsu, but after reading the *Vimalakīrti-sūtra* he came to believe in Buddhism and assisted Kumārajiva in the translation of Buddhist sutras.

13. Master Dai-i Doshin, died 651. See chap. 15, *Busso*.

14. Master Gozu Hoyu, died 657 at the age of 64. He was a collateral successor of Master Dai-i Doshin (whose direct successor was Master Daiman Konin). It is said that after living on Gozu mountain and devoting himself to Zazen, Master Hoyu was visited by Master Dai-i Doshin and thereupon attained the truth.

Dharma and the Imitative Dharma,[15] even lay people received and retained the kaṣāya. In this distant and remote land in the present degenerate age, those who shave their beard and hair and call themselves the Buddha's disciples do not receive and retain the kaṣāya. They have never believed, known, or clarified that they should receive and retain [the kaṣāya]; it is lamentable. How much less do they know of the [kaṣāya's] material, color, and measurements. How much less do they know how to wear it.

[54] The kaṣāya has been called, since ancient time, *the clothing of liberation.*[16] It can liberate[16] us from all hindrances such as karmic hindrances, hindrances of affliction, and hindrances of retribution. If a dragon gets a single strand [of the kaṣāya], it escapes the three kinds of heat.[17] If a bull touches [a kaṣāya] with one of its horns, its sins will naturally be extinguished. When buddhas realize the truth they are always wearing the kaṣāya. Remember, [to wear the kaṣāya] is the noblest and highest virtue. Truly, we have been born in a remote land in [the age of] the Latter Dharma, and we must regret this. But at the same time, how should we measure the joy of meeting the robe and the Dharma which have been transmitted from buddha to buddha, from rightful successor to rightful successor? Which [other] lineage has authentically transmitted both the robe and the Dharma of Śākyamuni in the manner of our authentic transmission? Having met them, who could fail to venerate them and to serve offerings to them? Even if, each day, we [have to] discard bodies and lives as countless as the sands of the Ganges, we should serve offerings to them. Indeed we should vow to meet them, humbly to receive them upon the head,[18] to serve offerings to them, and to venerate them in every life in every age. Between us and the country of the Buddha's birth, there are more than a hundred thousand miles of mountains and oceans, and it is too far for us to travel; nevertheless, promoted by past good conduct, we have not been shut out by the mountains and oceans, and we have not been spurned as the dullards of a remote [land]. Having met this right Dharma, we should persistently practice it day and night. Having received and retained this kaṣāya, we should perpetually receive it upon the head in humility and preserve it. How could this only be to have practiced merit under one buddha or two buddhas? It may be to have practiced all kinds of merit under buddhas equal to the sands of the Ganges. Even if [the people who receive and retain the kaṣāya] are ourselves, we should venerate them, and we should rejoice. We should heartily repay the profound benevolence of the ancestral Master in transmitting the Dharma. Even animals repay kindness; so how could human beings fail to recognize kindness? If we failed to recognize kindness, we might be more stupid than animals. The merits of this Buddha-robe and this Buddha-Dharma were never clarified or known by anyone

---

15. Buddhist scholars divided time following the Buddha's death into three periods: 1) 正法 (SHOBO), "Right Dharma," the first five hundred years during which time Buddhism flourished; 2) 像法 (ZOHO), "Imitative Dharma," an intermediate period of one thousand years; and 3) 末法 (MAPPO), "Latter Dharma," the next ten thousand years during which Buddhism degenerates. See Glossary under *saddharma*.

16. 解脱 (GEDATSU), used here first as a noun and then as a verb, represents the Sanskrit word *vimukti* (setting at liberty, release, deliverance, final emancipation).

17. 三熱 (SANNETSU), the three heats, or the three kinds of burning pain. One explanation is as follows: 1) the pain of hot wind and sand being blown against the skin; 2) the pain of the violent wind which takes away jeweled clothes and jeweled ornaments; and 3) the pain of being eaten by a *garuḍa*, a dragon-eating bird.

18. 頂戴 (CHODAI). See note 7.

other than the ancestral Master who transmitted the Buddha's right Dharma. If we want to follow gladly the traces of the buddhas, we should just be glad about this [transmission]. Even after hundred thousand myriads of generations, we should esteem this authentic transmission as the authentic transmission. This [transmission] may be the Buddha-Dharma itself; the proof in due course will become evident. We should not liken [the transmission] to the dilution of milk with water. It is like a crown prince succeeding to the throne. When we want to use milk, if there is no milk other than this diluted milk [described above], although it is diluted milk we should use it. Even when we do not dilute it with water, we must not use oil, we must not use lacquer, and we must not use wine. This authentic transmission may also be like that. Even a mediocre follower of an ordinary master, providing the authentic transmission is present, may be in a good situation to use milk. [But] more to the point, the authentic transmission from buddha to buddha and from patriarch to patriarch is like the succession of a crown prince. Even secular [teaching] says, *"One does not wear clothing different from the official uniform of the previous reign."*[19] How could disciples of the Buddha wear [robes] different from the Buddha's robe?

[58] Since the tenth year of the Eihei era,[20] during the reign of Emperor Komei of the later Han Dynasty,[21] monks and laymen going back and forth between the Western Heavens and the Eastern Lands have followed on each other's heels without cease, but none has claimed to have met in the Western Heavens an ancestral master of the authentic transmission from buddha to buddha and from patriarch to patriarch; none has a record of the lineage of the face-to-face transmission from the Tathāgata. They have only followed teachers of sutras and commentaries, and brought back Sanskrit books of sutras and philosophy. None speaks of having met an ancestral master who is a rightful successor to the Buddha's Dharma, and none mentions that there are ancestral masters who have received the transmission of the Buddha's kaṣāya. Clearly, they have not entered beyond the threshold of the Buddha's Dharma. People like this have not clarified the principle of the authentic transmission by Buddhist patriarchs. When Śākyamuni Tathāgata[22] passed to Mahākāśyapa the right-Dharma-eye treasury and the supreme state of bodhi, he transmitted them together with a kaṣāya received in the authentic transmission from Kāśyapa Buddha.[23] Received by rightful successor from rightful successor, [the kaṣāya] reached Zen Master Daikan of Sokei-zan mountain, the thirty-third generation. The material, color, and measurements [of the kaṣāya] had been transmitted intimately. Since then, the Dharma-descendants of Seigen and Nangaku[24] have intimately transmitted the Dharma, wearing the Dharma of the ancestral patriarchs and keeping the Dharma of the ancestral patriarchs in order. The method of washing [the

---

19. This quotation appears in the book *Kokyo (The Book of Filial Piety)*, a text of Confucianism. It is quoted as an example of reverence of tradition in secular society.

20. 67A.D.

21. The later (or Eastern) Han Dynasty was from 25 to 220A.D. It is said that Buddhist sutras were first translated into Chinese and transmitted into China in 67A.D.

22. 釈迦牟尼如来 (SHAKAMUNI-NYORAI). 釈迦牟尼 (SHAKAMUNI) is the phonetic rendering in Chinese characters of the Sanskrit *Śākyamuni*—sage of the Śākya clan. 如来 (NYORAI), lit. "Thus-Come," represents the Sanskrit *tathāgata*.

23. Kāśyapa Buddha is the sixth of the seven ancient buddhas, Śākyamuni Buddha being the seventh.

24. Master Seigen Gyoshi and Master Nangaku Ejo. See note 10.

kaṣāya] and the method of receiving and retaining [the kaṣāya] cannot be known without learning in practice in the inner sanctum of the legitimate face-to-face transmission of those methods.

[60] *The kaṣāya is said to include three robes. They are the five-stripe robe, the seven-stripe robe, and the large robe of nine or more stripes. Excellent practitioners receive only these three robes, and do not keep other robes. To use just the three robes serves the body well enough. When we are attending to business or doing chores, and when we are going to and from the toilet, we wear the five-stripe robe. For doing good practices among the Saṃgha, we wear the seven-stripe robe. To teach human beings and gods, and to make them devout, we should wear the large robe of nine or more stripes. Or, when we are in a private place we wear the five-stripe robe, when we go among the Saṃgha we wear the seven-stripe robe, and when we go into a royal palace or into towns and villages we should wear the large robe. Or, when it is nice and warm we wear the five-stripe robe, when it is cold we put on the seven-stripe robe as well, and when the cold is severe we also put on the large robe. Once, in ancient times, the weather on a midwinter night was cold enough to split bamboo. As that night fell, the Tathāgata put on the five-stripe robe. As the night passed and it got colder, he put on the seven-stripe robe as well. Later on in the night, when the coldness reached a peak, he also put on the large robe. At this time, the Buddha thought, "In future ages, when the cold is beyond endurance, good sons should be able to clothe their bodies adequately with these three robes."*[25]

[62] The method of wearing the kaṣāya:

To bare only the right shoulder[26] is the usual method. There is a method of wearing [the kaṣāya] so that it goes over both shoulders, a form [followed by] the Tathāgata and veterans who are senior in years and experience: both shoulders are covered, while the chest may be either exposed or covered. [The method of] covering both shoulders is for a large kaṣāya of sixty or more stripes. [Usually,] when we wear the kaṣāya, we wear both sides over the left arm and shoulder. The front edge goes over the left side [of the kaṣāya] and hangs over the [left upper] arm.[27] In the case of the large kaṣāya, [this] front edge passes over the left shoulder and hangs down behind the back. There are various methods of wearing the kaṣāya besides these; we should take time to research them and should inquire into them.

[64] For hundreds of years, through one dynasty after another—Liang, Chen, Sui, Tang, and Sung[28]—many scholars of both the large and the small vehicles have abandoned the work of lecturing on sutras, recognizing that it is not the ultimate, and progressed

---

25. This paragraph is quoted from *Daijogi-sho*.

26. 偏袒右肩 (HENTAN-UKEN). These four characters appear in several places in the Lotus Sutra. See, for example, the opening paragraph of the *Shinge (Belief and Understanding)* chapter (LS 1.222).

27. The folded kaṣāya (folded lengthwise into eight) is first hung over the left shoulder, with the top of the kaṣāya over the front of the body (so that the single string faces the front). The two corners of the top of the kaṣāya are flush with each other. The left hand takes the top left hand corner of the kaṣāya and the right hand takes the top right hand corner of the kaṣāya. The kaṣāya is then opened behind the back, and the right hand brings the top right hand corner of the kaṣāya under the right arm and round to the front, and then hangs it over the left shoulder and left upper arm. So "both sides" means the left and right sides of the top of kaṣāya, and "the front edge" refers to the upper border of the part of the kaṣāya which is held in the right hand.

28. Liang Dynasty (502–556); Chen Dynasty (557–589); Sui Dynasty (589–618); Tang Dynasty (618–907); Sung Dynasty (960–1279).

to learn the authentically transmitted Dharma of the Buddhist patriarchs; when they do so, they inevitably shed their former shabby robes and receive and retain the authentically transmitted kaṣāya of the Buddhist patriarchs. This is indeed the abandonment of the false and the return to the true. [In discussing] the right Dharma of the Tathāgata, [we see] the Western Heavens as the very root of the Dharma. Many teachers of human beings, past and present, have established small views based on the sentimental and parochial thinking of the common man. Because the world of buddha and the world of living beings are beyond being limited and being unlimited, the teachings, practice, and human truths of the Mahāyāna and the Hīnayāna can never fit inside the narrow thoughts of common men today. Nevertheless, [common men] in China, acting at random, have failed to see the Western Heavens as the root, and have considered their newly devised, limited, small views to be the Buddha-Dharma. Such facts should never occur. Therefore if people today who have established the mind want to receive and to retain the kaṣāya, they must receive and retain the kaṣāya of the authentic transmission. They must not receive and retain a kaṣāya newly created according to the idea of the moment. The kaṣāya of the authentic transmission means the one that has been authentically transmitted from Shaolin [temple] and Sokei [mountain],[29] the one that has been received by the Tathāgata's rightful successors without missing a single generation. The kaṣāya worn by their Dharma-children and Dharma-grandchildren is the traditional kaṣāya. What has been newly created in China is not traditional. Now, the kaṣāya worn by the monks who have come from the Western Heavens, in the past and present, are all worn as the kaṣāya authentically transmitted by the Buddhist patriarchs. Not one of these monks [has worn a kaṣāya] like the new kaṣāya being produced in China today by precepts scholars. Dull people believe in the kaṣāya of precepts scholars; those who are clear throw [such robes] away. In general, the merit of the kaṣāya transmitted from buddha to buddha and from patriarch to patriarch is evident and easy to believe in. Its authentic transmission has been received exactly, its original form has been handed down personally, and it exists really in the present. [The Buddhist patriarchs] have received and retained it, and succeeded to each other's Dharma, until today. The ancestral masters who have received and retained [the kaṣāya] are all masters and disciples who experienced the state[30] and received the transmission of Dharma. This being so, we should make [the kaṣāya] properly, according to the method for making the kaṣāya which has been authentically transmitted by the Buddhist patriarchs. This alone is the authentic tradition, and so it has long been experienced and recognized by all common and sacred beings, human beings and gods, and dragons and spirits. Having been born to meet the spread of this Dharma, if we cover our body with the kaṣāya only once, receiving it and retaining it for just a kṣaṇa or a muhūrta,[31] that [experience] will surely serve as a talisman to protect us[32] in the realization of the supreme state of bodhi. When we dye the body-and-mind with a single phrase or a single verse, it be-

---

29. Master Bodhidharma lived at Shaolin temple; Master Daikan Eno lived on Sokei mountain.

30. "Experienced the state" is 証契 (SHOKAI), 証 (SHO) means to experience; 契 (KAI) means to agree or to fit. 証契 (SHOKAI) means to experience the same state as the Buddha.

31. Measurements of time in India. According to one explanation, sixty-four *kṣaṇa* pass in the clicking of the fingers, and thirty *muhūrta* pass in a day. See Glossary.

32. 護身符子 (GOSHIN-FUSHI), lit. "a card to guard the body." Cards bearing lucky words, called *o-mamori* in Japanese, are often sold as talismans at shrines and temples.

comes a seed of everlasting brightness which finally leads us to the supreme state of bodhi. When we dye the body-and-mind with one real dharma or one good deed, it may be *also like this*. Mental images arise and vanish instantaneously; they are without an abode. The physical body also arises and vanishes instantaneously; it too is without an abode. Nevertheless, the merit that we practice always has its time of ripening and shedding. The kaṣāya, similarly, is beyond elaboration and beyond non-elaboration, it is beyond having an abode and beyond having no abode: it is that which *buddhas alone, together with buddhas, perfectly realize.*[33] Nevertheless, practitioners who receive and retain [the kaṣāya] always accomplish the merit that is thus to be gained, and they always arrive at the ultimate. Those without past good conduct—even if they pass through one life, two lives, or countless lives—can never meet the kaṣāya, can never wear the kaṣāya, can never believe in the kaṣāya, and can never clearly know the kaṣāya. In China and Japan today, we see that there are those who have had the opportunity to clothe their body once in the kaṣāya, and there are those who have not. [The difference] depends neither upon high or low status nor upon stupidity or wisdom: clearly it was determined by past good conduct. This being so, if we have received and retained the kaṣāya, we should feel glad about our past good conduct, and should not doubt the accumulation of merit and the piling up of virtue. If we have not got [the kaṣāya] yet, we should hope to get it. We should strive, without delay, to sow the first seeds [of receiving and retaining the kaṣāya] in this life. Those who are prevented by some hindrance from receiving and retaining [the kaṣāya] should repent and confess before the buddha-tathāgatas, and the three treasures of Buddha, Dharma, and Saṃgha. How living beings in other countries must wish, *"If only the robe and the Dharma of the Tathāgata had been authentically transmitted and were intimately present in our country, as they are in China!"* Their shame must be deep, and their sadness tinged with resentment, that the authentic tradition has not passed into their own country. Why are we so fortunate as to have met the Dharma in which the robe and the Dharma of the Tathāgata, the World-honored One, have been authentically transmitted? It is the influence of the great merit of prajñā nurtured in the past. In the present corrupt age of the Latter Dharma, [some] are not ashamed that they themselves have no authentic transmission, and they envy others who possess the authentic transmission. I think they may be a band of demons. Their[34] present possessions and abodes which are influenced by their former conduct, are not true and real. Just to devote themselves[34] to and to venerate the authentically transmitted Buddha-Dharma: this may be their[34] real refuge in learning [the state of] Buddha. In sum, remember that the kaṣāya is the object of the buddhas' veneration and devotion. It is the body of the Buddha and the mind of the Buddha. We call it *the clothing of liberation,*[35] *the robe of a field of happiness,*[36] *the robe without form,*[37] *the*

33. The Lotus Sutra says that *buddhas alone, together with buddhas,* can *perfectly realize* that all dharmas are real form. Master Dogen is emphasizing that the kaṣāya is instantaneous and real, therefore beyond understanding.

34. おのれ (*onore*) also means "our" or "ourselves." These sentences also apply to us.

35. 解脱服 (gedatsu-fuku).

36. 福伝衣 (fukuden-e).

37. 無相衣 (MUSO-E). The kaṣāya is without form in the sense that is a simple rectangular sheet of cloth. These first three phrases all come from the verse which is recited in veneration of the kaṣāya. See para. [105] in this chapter.

supreme robe, the robe of endurance,[38] *the robe of the Tathāgata, the robe of great benevolence and great compassion, the robe which is a banner of excellence,* and *the robe of anuttara-samyak-saṃbodhi.* We should receive and retain it like this, humbly receiving it upon the head. Because it is like this, we should never change it according to [our own] mind.

[71] As material for the robe, we use silk or cotton, according to suitability. It is not always the case that cotton is pure and silk is impure. There is no viewpoint from which to hate cotton and to prefer silk; that would be laughable. The usual method[39] of the buddhas, in every case, is to see rags[40] as the best material. There are ten sorts and four sorts of rags; namely, burned, chewed by an ox, gnawed by rats, from clothes of dead people, and so forth.[41] *The people of the five areas of India*[42] *discarded rags like these in streets and fields, as if they were filth, and so they called them "filthy rags."*[43] *Practitioners picked them up, washed them and sewed them, and used them to cover the body.*[44] Among those [rags] there are various kinds of silk and various kinds of cotton. We should throw away the view [which discriminates between] silk and cotton, and study rags in practice. When, in ancient times[45] [the Buddha] was washing a robe of rags in Lake Anavatapta,[46] the Dragon King praised him with a rain of flowers, and made prostrations of reverence. Some teachers of the small vehicle have a theory about transformed thread,[47] which also may be without foundation. People of the great vehicle might laugh at it. What kind [of thread] is not transformed thread? When those teachers hear of *transformation* they believe their ears, but when they see the transformation itself they doubt their eyes. Remember, in picking up rags, there may be cotton that looks like silk and there may be silk that looks like cotton. There being myriad differences in local customs it is hard to fathom [Nature's] creation—eyes of flesh cannot know it. Having obtained such material, we should not discuss whether it is silk or cotton, but should call it rags. Even if there are human beings or gods in heaven who have survived as rags, they are never sentient beings, they are just rags. Even if there are pine trees or

---

38. 忍辱衣 (NINNIKU-E), lit. "enduring-humiliation robe." 忍辱 (NINNIKU) represents the Sanskrit *kṣānti,* endurance or patience.

39. "Usual method" is 常法 (JOHO). 常 (JO) means constant or eternal, and at the same time usual or common. 法 (HO) means method, or Dharma.

40. "Rags" is 糞掃衣 (FUNZO-E). 糞 (FUN) means excrement, and 掃 (SO, pronounced ZO) means to sweep or "to be swept." 衣 (E) means robe or clothes or clothing. 糞掃 (FUNZO) represents the Sanskrit *pāṃsu-kūla,* which means a dust-heap or a collection of rags out of a dust-heap used by Buddhist monks for their robes. 糞掃衣 (FUNZO-E) has been translated either as "rags" or as "a robe of rags," according to the context.

41. The ten sorts of rags are given in para [117] in this chapter. The first four of these are also known as the four sorts of rags.

42. Lit. "people of the five Indias." Ancient India is said to have been divided into five regions: east, west, central, south, and north.

43. 糞掃衣 (FUNZO-E), see note 40.

44. This section in italics is in the style of a quotation from a Chinese text.

45. Many legends like the one referred to in this sentence appear in stories of the Buddha's past lives as a bodhisattva.

46. Lake Anavatapta was thought to be located north of the Himalayas as the source of the four great rivers of India. It was said to be the home of the king of dragons, and was called the lake where there is no suffering from heat.

47. 化糸 (KESHI), "processed thread." The process of producing silk entails boiling the cocoon while the silkworm is still alive. Some people worried that the production of silk violated the precept of not taking life in vain, and thought that silk should not be used as a material for the kaṣāya.

chrysanthemums that have survived as rags, they are never insentient beings, they are just rags. When we believe the principle that rags are not silk or cotton, and not gold, silver, pearl, or jewel, rags are realized. Before we have got rid of views and opinions about silk and cotton, we have never seen rags even in a dream. On one occasion a monk asks the eternal Buddha,[48] *"Should we see the robe you received on Obai in the middle of the night as cotton, or should we see it as silk? In short, as what material should we see it?"* The eternal Buddha says, *"It is not cotton and it is not silk."* Remember, it is a profound teaching[49] of the Buddha's truth that the kaṣāya is beyond silk and cotton.

[74] The Venerable Śāṇavāsa[50] is third in the transmission of the Dharma-treasury. He has been endowed with a robe since birth. While he is a layman this robe is a secular garment, but when he leaves home[51] it turns into a kaṣāya. In another case, the bhikṣuṇī Śukra,[52] after establishing the will and being clothed in a cotton robe, has been born with a robe in every life and middle existence. On the day that she meets Śākyamuni Buddha and leaves home, the secular robe which she has had since birth changes instantly into a kaṣāya, as in the case of the Venerable Śāṇavāsa. Clearly, the kaṣāya is beyond silk, cotton, and so forth. Moreover, the fact that the virtue of the Buddha-Dharma can transform body-and-mind and all dharmas is as in those examples. The truth is evident that when we leave home and receive the precepts, body-and-mind, object-and-subject, change at once; it is only because we are stupid that we do not know. It is not true that the usual rule[53] of the buddhas applies only to Śāṇavāsa and to Śukra, but not to us; we should not doubt that benefit [accrues] in accordance with individual standing. We should consider such truths in detail and learn them in practice. The kaṣāya that covers the body of [the monks whom the Buddha] welcomes[54] to take the precepts is not necessarily cotton or silk: the Buddha's influence is difficult to consider. The precious pearl within the robe[55] is beyond those who count grains of sand.[56] We should clarify and should learn in practice that which has quantity and that which is

48. The eternal Buddha refers to Master Daikan Eno, who received the kaṣāya from Master Daiman Konin in the middle of the night on Obai mountain. See chap. 30, *Gyoji*.

49. 玄訓 (GENKUN), lit. "black instruction."

50. Born about a hundred years after the death of the Buddha, Master Śāṇavāsa eventually became the third Indian patriarch, succeeding Master Ānanda. The Sanskrit word *śāṇavāsa* lit. means flaxen clothes.

51. 出家 (SHUKKE), lit. "leave home," means to become a monk. See chap. 83, *Shukke*.

52. 鮮白比丘尼 (SENBYAKU-BIKUNI). 鮮白 (SENBYAKU), "Fresh-White" represents the Sanskrit *śukra* which means bright, clear, pure, white, or spotless. Volume 8 of the *Senju-hyaku-en-kyo* says that the *bhikṣuṇī* (Buddhist nun) Śukra was born wearing a pure white robe that never needed washing, and that when she became a nun, the robe changed into a kaṣāya.

53. 常法 (JOHO). See note 39.

54. "Welcomed" is 善来 (ZENRAI), representing the Sanskrit *svāgata;* "Welcome!" The Pali scriptures say that the Buddha accepted his followers into the monkhood simply by saying, *Ehi bhikkhu;* "Welcome, monk."

55. The pearl within the robe alludes to the *Gohyaku-deshi-juki (Affirmation of Five Hundred Disciples)* chapter of the Lotus Sutra, which tells the story of a drunken man whose friend plants a valuable pearl in his clothes. Five hundred arhats compare themselves to the man who unknowingly carries the pearl, because they have been content with inferior wisdom instead of obtaining the Buddha-wisdom (LS 2.114).

56. "Those who count grains of sand" means scholars. The original characters 算沙 (SANSA) "count sand" come from the poem *Shodoka*, by Master Yoka Genkaku. He said, *"They know no respite from analyzing concepts and forms; having entered the ocean, they vainly exhaust themselves by counting grains of sand."*

without quantity, that which has form and that which is without form, in the material, color, and measurements of the kaṣāya of the buddhas. This is what all the ancestral masters of the Western Heavens and the Eastern Lands, past and present, learned in practice and transmitted as the authentic tradition. If someone is able to see and to hear [a master] in whom there is nothing to doubt—the authentic transmission from patriarch to patriarch being evident—but fails, without reason, to receive the authentic transmission from this ancestral master, such smugness would be hard to condone. The extent of [this] stupidity might be due to unbelief. It would be to abandon the real and to pursue the false, to discard the root and to seek after branches. It would be to slight the Tathāgata. People who wish to establish the bodhi-mind should always receive the authentic transmission of an ancestral master. Not only have we met the Buddha-Dharma which is so difficult to meet: also, as Dharma-descendants in the authentic transmission of the Buddha's kaṣāya, we have been able to see and to hear, to learn and to practice, and to receive and to retain [the authentic transmission of the Buddha's kaṣāya]. This is just to see the Tathāgata himself, it is to hear the Buddha's preaching of Dharma, it is to be illuminated by the Buddha's brightness, it is to receive and to use what the Buddha received and used, it is to receive the one-to-one transmission of the Buddha's mind, it is to have got the Buddha's marrow, it is to be covered directly by Śākyamuni Buddha's kaṣāya, and it is Śākyamuni Buddha himself directly bestowing the kaṣāya upon us. Because we follow the Buddha, we have devoutly[57] received this kaṣāya.

[78] The method of washing the kaṣāya:

Put the kaṣāya, unfolded, into a clean tub, then immerse the kaṣāya in fragrant, fully-boiled hot water, and leave it to soak for about two hours.[58] Another method is to soak the kaṣāya in pure, fully-boiled ash-water[59] and to wait for the water to cool. Nowadays we usually use [the] hot ash-water [method]. Hot ash-water is what we call *aku-no-yu* here [in Japan].[60] When the ash-water has cooled, rinse [the kaṣāya] again and again in clean and clear hot water. During the rinsing do not put in both hands to scrub [the kaṣāya] and do not tread on it. Continue until any dirt or grease has been removed. After that, mix aloes, sandalwood,[61] or other incense into some cold water and rinse [the kaṣāya]. Then hang it on a washing pole[62] to dry. After it is thoroughly dry, fold it and put it in a high place, burn incense and scatter petals, walk round it several times [with

57. The Japanese suffix translated as "devoutly" is the honorific *tatematsuru* form, invariably used by Master Dogen to express reverence for the Buddha but usually ignored in this translation due to the lack of a suitable equivalent in English.

58. The day was divided into twelve periods. The original characters 一時 (*hito-toki*) indicate one such period, that is, two hours.

59. 灰水 (AKU). The ash must have been used to make the water more alkaline. In this case the word *aku* is written with the Chinese character for ash (灰) and the Chinese character for water (水), but the word *aku* is originally Japanese, not Chinese.

60. "Hot ash-water" is 灰湯 (KAITO), a Chinese word formed by the character for ash (灰, KAI) and the character for hot water (湯, TO). あくのゆ *(aku-no-yu)* are Japanese words written in *kana,* the phonetic Japanese alphabet. *Aku* means ash-water (see previous note) and *yu* means hot water.

61. 栴檀 (SENDAN) is given in the Kenkyusha dictionary as margosa. At the same time, 栴檀 originally represents the Sanskrit *candana*, sandalwood.

62. 浄竿 (JOKAN), lit. "pure pole," a bamboo or wooden pole suspended horizontally at about head height. See chap. 7, *Senjo.*

the kaṣāya] to the right,[63] and perform prostrations. After making three prostrations, six prostrations, or nine prostrations, kneel up and join the hands,[64] then hold the kaṣāya up with both hands, and in the mouth recite the verse [in praise of the kaṣāya].[65] After that stand up and put on [the kaṣāya] according to the method.

[80] †*"The World-honored One addresses the great assembly: In the ancient past when I was in the order of the Buddha Jewel-Treasury,*[66] *I was the Bodhisattva Great Compassion.*[67] *At that time, the Bodhisattva-Mahāsattva Great Compassion made the following vow before the Buddha Jewel-Treasury:*

"World-honored One! If, after I became a buddha, there were living beings who had entered my Dharma and left home and who wore the kaṣāya—even if they were bhikṣus, bhikṣuṇīs, upāsakas, and upāsikās[68] *who had accumulated heavy sins by violating the grave prohibitions, by enacting false views, or by contemptuously disbelieving the Three Treasures—and in a single moment of consciousness the reverence arose in their mind to honor the saṃghāṭī robe*[69] *and the reverence arose in their mind to honor the World-Honored One or the Dharma and the Saṃgha but, World-honored One, even one among those living beings could not, in [one of] the three vehicles,*[70] *receive affirmation,*[71] *and as a result regressed or went astray, it would mean that I had deceived the buddhas who are present now in the worlds of the ten directions and in countless, infinite asaṃkheya kalpas, and I surely should not realize anuttara-samyak-saṃbodhi.*

World-honored One! After I have become a buddha, if gods, dragons, and demons, and human and nonhuman beings are able to wear this kaṣāya, to venerate, to serve offerings to, to honor, and to praise it, as long as those people are able to see a small part of this kaṣāya, they will be able not to regress while within the three vehicles.

When living beings are afflicted by hunger or thirst—whether they are wretched demons, miserable people, or living beings in the state of hungry ghosts—if they are able to obtain a piece of

---

63. An ancient Indian custom to show reverence for people or sacred objects.

64. 胡跪合掌 (KOKI-GASSHO). 胡 (KO) means foreign and 跪 (KI) means to kneel with the hips extended, as the Chinese noticed that foreigners sometimes kneeled. Joining the hands (*gassho*) means holding the palms together, fingers pointing upwards, fingertips in front of the nostrils.

65. The verse is: 大哉解脱服, 無相福田衣, 披奉如来教, 広度諸衆生. (DAISAI-GEDATSU-FUKU/MUSO-FUKUDEN-E/HIBU-NYORAI-KYO/KODO-SHOSHUJO.) Loosely translated: *"How great is the clothing of liberation. / Though without form it is the robe of real happiness. / Wearing the Buddha's teaching, / I will save living beings everywhere."* See para. [105].

† The following long quotation from the *Hige-kyo* (in Sanskrit, *Karuṇā-puṇḍarīka-sūtra*) is originally one paragraph. It has been divided in translation for ease of reading.

66. 法蔵 (HOZO), from the Sanskrit *Ratnagarbha*. Ratnagarbha Buddha is a legendary past Buddha who appears in the *Hige-kyo*. He encouraged Śākyamuni Buddha and Amitābha Buddha (a symbol of eternal life) to establish the will to the truth.

67. 大悲 (DAIHI), lit. "Great Compassion," from the Sanskrit *Mahākaruṇā*. This is another name of Bodhisattva Avalokiteśvara. See chap. 33, *Kannon*.

68. The four classes of Buddhists: monks, nuns, lay men, and lay women.

69. The Sanskrit root *saṃghāṭ* means to join or fasten together, suggesting the kaṣāya as a robe composed of miscellaneous rags. The *saṃghāṭī* robe (in Japanese 僧伽梨衣, SOGYARI-E) means the large robe.

70. That is, as either a *śrāvaka* (intellectual Buddhist), *pratyekabuddha* (sensory Buddhist), or *bodhisattva* (Buddhist practitioner).

71. "Affirmation" is 記莂 (KIBETSU), from the Sanskrit *vyākaraṇa*. *Vyākaraṇa* is the Buddha's affirmation that a practitioner will become buddha in the future. This sentence includes the first of the five sacred merits mentioned later in the paragraph. The first merit is that all who revere the kaṣāya and the Three Treasures can receive affirmation.

the kaṣāya even as small as four inches,[72] *they will at once be able to eat and drink their fill and to accomplish quickly whatever they wish.*

When living beings offend each other, causing ill will to arise and a fight to develop—or when gods, dragons, demons, gandharva, asura, garuḍa, kiṃnara, mahoraga, kumbhāṇḍa, piśāca,[73] *and human and nonhuman beings are fighting each other—if they remember this kaṣāya, in due course, by virtue of the power of the kaṣāya, they will beget the mind of compassion, soft and flexible mind, mind free of enmity, serene mind, the regulated mind of virtue, and they will get back the state of purity.*

When people are in an armed conflict, a civil lawsuit, or a criminal action, if they retain a small piece of this kaṣāya as they go among these combatants, and if in order to protect themselves they serve offerings to, venerate, and honor it, these [other] people will be unable to injure, to disturb, or to make fools of them; they will always be able to beat their opponents and to come through all such difficulties.

World-honored One! If my kaṣāya were unable to accomplish these five sacred merits,[74] *it would mean that I had deceived the buddhas who are present now in the worlds of the ten directions and in countless, infinite asaṃkheya kalpas, and in future I ought not to accomplish anuttara-samyak-saṃbodhi or to do Buddhist works. Having lost the virtuous Dharma, I would surely be unable to destroy non-Buddhism."*

Good sons![75] *At that time the Tathāgata Jewel-Treasury extended his golden right arm and patted the head of Bodhisattva Great Compassion, praising him with these words:*

"Very good! Very good! Stout fellow! What you have said is a great and rare treasure, and is great wisdom and virtue. When you have realized anuttara-samyak-saṃbodhi, this robe, the kaṣāya, will be able to accomplish these five sacred merits and to produce great benefit."

Good sons! At that time, the Bodhisattva-Mahāsattva Great Compassion, after hearing the praise of that Buddha, jumped endlessly for joy. Then the Buddha [again] extended his golden arm, with its hand of long, webbed fingers[76] *as soft as the robe of a goddess. When he patted the [Bodhisattva's] head, the [Bodhisattva's] body changed at once into the youthful figure of a man of twenty. Good sons! In that order the great assembly of gods, dragons, deities, gandharva, and human and nonhuman beings, with folded hands*[77] *venerated Bodhisattva Great Compassion; they served him offerings of all kinds of flowers; they even made music and offered that; and they*

---

72. Originally, four *sun*. One *sun* is slightly over an inch.

73. Ancient Indian storytellers invented these colorful beings which later found their way into Buddhist sutras. *Gandharva* are fragrance-devouring celestial beings, *asura* are demons which oppose gods, *garuḍa* are dragon-eating birds, *kiṃnara* are half-horses, half-men, *mahoraga* are serpents, *kumbhāṇḍa*, lit. "having testicles like jars," are demons which feed on human energy, and *piśāca* are demons which eat flesh.

74. The five sacred merits are that those who wear, venerate, or retain a piece of the kaṣāya 1) will be able to receive affirmation, 2) will not regress, 3) will be able to satisfy hunger and thirst, and other wishes, 4) will be able to remain peaceful in hostile situations, and 5) will be protected in times of conflict.

75. 善男子 (ZEN-NANSHI), represents the Sanskrit words *kula-putra* with which the Buddha commonly addressed his Buddhist audiences.

76. Webbed fingers and toes are the fifth of the thirty-two distinguishing marks of a Buddha.

77. 叉手 (SHASHU). In *shashu* the fingers of the left hand are curled round the thumb, and the left hand is placed against the chest, the left forearm being held horizontal. The right hand is placed, palm down, on the back of the left hand, the right forearm also being held horizontal.

also praised him in all kinds of ways, after which they abode in silence.'[78]

[86] From the age when the Tathāgata was in the world until today, whenever the merits of the kaṣāya are quoted from the sutras and the vinaya[79] of bodhisattvas and śrāvakas, these five sacred merits are always considered fundamental. Truly, kaṣāyas are the Buddha-robes of the buddhas of the three times. Their merits are measureless. At the same time, to get the kaṣāya in the Dharma of Śākyamuni Buddha may be even better than to get the kaṣāya in the Dharma of other buddhas. The reason, if asked, is that in the ancient past, when Śākyamuni Buddha was in the causal state[80] as the Bodhisattva-Mahāsattva Great Compassion, when he offered his five hundred great vows before the Buddha Jewel-Treasury, he pointedly made the above vows in terms of the merits of this kaṣāya. Its merits may be utterly measureless and unthinkable. This being so, the authentic transmission to the present of the skin, flesh, bones, and marrow of the World-honored One, is the kaṣāya-robe. The ancestral masters who have authentically transmitted the right-Dharma-eye treasury have, without exception, authentically transmitted the kaṣāya. The living beings who have received and retained this robe and humbly received it upon their heads have, without exception, attained the truth within two or three lives. Even when people have put [the kaṣāya] on their body for a joke or for gain, it has inevitably become the causes and conditions for their attaining the truth.

[87] *The ancestral Master Nāgārjuna*[81] *says, 'Further, in the Buddha-Dharma, people who have left family life,*[82] *even if they break the precepts and fall into sin, after they have expiated their sins, they can attain liberation, as the bhikṣuṇī Utpalavarṇā explains in the Jātaka sutra:*[83] *When the Buddha is in the world, this bhikṣuṇī attains the six mystical powers*[84] *and the state of an arhat.*[85] *She goes into the houses of nobles and constantly praises the method of leaving family life, saying to all the aristocratic ladies, "Sisters! You should leave family life."*

The noblewomen say, "We are young and our figures are full of life and beauty. It would be difficult for us to keep the precepts. Sometimes we might break the precepts."

The bhikṣuṇī says, "If you break the precepts, you break them. Just leave family life!"

They ask, "If we break the precepts we will fall into hell. Why should we want to break them?"

She answers, "If you fall into hell, you fall."

The noblewomen all laugh at this, saying, "In hell we would have to receive retribution for our sins. Why should we want to fall [into hell]?"

---

78. *Hige-kyo*, chap. 8 (the chapter on how the bodhisattvas received their affirmation in past lives).

79. *Sūtra* and *vinaya* are two of the three "baskets," or kinds of Buddhist teachings. *Vinaya* means guidance, discipline, instruction, or teaching; that is, the precepts and related writings. The *tripiṭaka*, or three baskets are: *sūtra* (sutras), *vinaya* (precepts), and *abidharma* (commentaries).

80. 因地 (INCHI), "causal state," means the state which caused the Buddha to become a buddha.

81. Master Nāgārjuna was the fourteenth patriarch in India, the successor of Master Kapimala and the teacher of Master Kāṇadeva. He lived sometime around the period 150–250 A.D. This passage is a Chinese translation of the *Mahā-prajñā-pāramitā-śāstra*, which is thought to have been written and compiled mainly by Master Nāgārjuna himself.

82. 出家人 (SHUKKENIN), or "people who have left home"; monks and nuns.

83. 本生経 (HONSHO-KYO), lit. "Past Lives Sutra." Legendary stories of the Buddha's past lives as a bodhisattva.

84. See explanation in the following paragraph.

85. The ultimate state of a *śrāvaka*, or intellectual Buddhist, which is identified with the state of buddha. See chap. 34, *Arakan*.

The bhikṣuṇī says, "I remember in my own past life, once I became a prostitute, wore all sorts of clothes, and spoke in old-fashioned language.[86] *One day I put on a bhikṣuṇī robe as a joke, and due to this as a direct and indirect cause, at the time of Kāśyapa Buddha*[87] *I became a bhikṣuṇī. I was still proud then of my noble pedigree and fine features: vanity and arrogance arose in my mind, and I broke the precepts. Because of the wrongness of breaking the precepts I fell into hell and suffered for my various sins, but after I had suffered retribution I finally met Śākyamuni Buddha, transcended family life, and attained the six mystical powers and the truth of an arhat. Thus, I know that when we leave family life and receive the precepts, even if we break the precepts, due to the precepts as direct and indirect causes we can attain the truth of an arhat. If I had only done bad, without the precepts as direct and indirect causes, I could not have attained the truth. In the past I fell into hell in age after age. When I got out of hell I became a bad person, and when the bad person died, I went back into hell, and there was no gain at all. Now therefore I know from experience that when we leave family life and receive the precepts, even if we break the precepts, with this as a direct and indirect cause we can attain the bodhi-effect."'*[88]

[90] The primary cause of this bhikṣuṇī Utpalavarṇā[89] attaining the truth as an arhat is just the merit of her putting the kaṣāya on her body for a joke; because of this merit, and no other merit, she has now attained the truth. In her second life she meets the Dharma of Kāśyapa Buddha and becomes a bhikṣuṇī. In her third life she meets Śākyamuni Buddha and becomes a great arhat, equipped with the three kinds of knowledge and the six powers. The three kinds of knowledge are supernatural insight, [knowing] past lives, and ending the superfluous. The six powers are the power of mystical transmutation, the power to know others' minds, the power of supernatural sight, the power of supernatural hearing, the power to know past lives, and the power to end the superfluous.[90] Truly, when she was only a wrongdoer she died and entered hell to no avail, coming out of hell and becoming a wrongdoer again. [But] when she has the precepts as direct and indirect causes, although she has broken the precepts and fallen into hell, they are the direct and indirect causes of her attaining the truth at last. Now, even someone who has worn the kaṣāya for a joke can attain the truth in her third life. How, then, could someone who has established pure belief, and who wears the kaṣāya for the sake of the supreme state of bodhi, fail to accomplish that merit? Still further, if we receive and retain [the kaṣāya] throughout our life, humbly receiving it upon the head, the merit might be universal and great beyond measure. Any human being who would like to establish the bodhi-mind should receive and retain the kaṣāya, and humbly receive it upon the head, without delay. To have met this favorable age but not to have sown a Buddhist seed, would be deplorable. Having received a human body on the southern continent,[91] having met the Dharma of Śākyamuni Buddha, and having

---

86. It was the custom in oriental pleasure houses for prostitutes to use old-fashioned language. The custom remained in Japan until the end of the Edo era [1868].

87. See note 23.

88. *Daichido-ron*, chap. 30. This section is also quoted near the beginning of chap. 86, *Shukke-kudoku.*

89. In the Chinese translation of the *Mahā-prajñā-pāramitopadeśa*, the Sanskrit name *Utpalavarṇā*, which means Color of the Blue Lotus, is represented as 優盋羅華 (UBARA-KE). 優盋羅 (UBARA) is a phonetic rendering of *utpala* (blue lotus) and 華 (KE) means flower. Here the name is 漣華色 (RENGE-SHIKI), "Lotus Flower Color."

90. See chap. 25, *Jinzu*, and Glossary under *abhijña*.

91. Ancient Indians imagined a Universe of four continents surrounding a big mountain, with celestial beings in the north and human beings in the south. So the southern continent means the human

been born to meet an ancestral master who is a perfectly legitimate successor to the Buddha-Dharma, if we idly passed up the chance to receive the kaṣāya which has been transmitted one-to-one and which is directly accessible, that would be deplorable. Now, in regard to the authentic transmission of the kaṣāya, the one authentic transmission from the ancestral Master is right and traditional; other masters cannot stand shoulder to shoulder with him. Even to receive and to retain the kaṣāya following a master who has not received the transmission is still of very profound merit. But much more than that, if we receive and retain [the kaṣāya] from a true master who has quite legitimately received the face-to-face transmission, we may really be the Dharma-children and the Dharma-grandchildren of the Tathāgata himself, and we may actually have received the authentic transmission of the Tathāgata's skin, flesh, bones, and marrow. The kaṣāya, in conclusion, has been authentically transmitted by the buddhas of the three times and the ten directions, without interruption; it is what the buddhas, bodhisattvas, śrāvakas, and pratyekabuddhas of the three times and the ten directions have, in like manner, guarded and retained.

[93] Coarse cotton cloth is the standard [material] for making the kaṣāya. When there is no coarse cotton cloth, we use fine cotton cloth. When there is neither coarse nor fine cotton cloth, we use plain silk. When there is neither [plain] silk nor cotton cloth, materials such as patterned cloth[92] or sheer silk may be used; [these are all] approved by the Tathāgata. For countries where there is no plain silk, cotton, patterned cloth, sheer silk, or anything of the kind, the Tathāgata also permits the leather kaṣāya. Generally, we should dye the kaṣāya blue, yellow, red, black, or purple. Whichever color it is, we should make it a secondary color.[93] The Tathāgata always wore a flesh-colored kaṣāya; this was the color of the kaṣāya. The Buddha's kaṣāya transmitted by the First Patriarch was blue-black, and made of the cotton crepe of the Western Heavens. It is now on Sokei-zan mountain. It was transmitted twenty-eight times in the Western Heavens and transmitted five times in China. Now the surviving disciples of the eternal Buddha of Sokei,[94] who have all received and retained the ancient customs of the Buddha's robe, are beyond other monks. Broadly, there are three kinds of robe: *1) the robe of rags, 2) the robe of fur, and 3) the patched robe. Rags* are as explained previously. In *"the robe of fur,"* the fine [down and] hair of birds and beasts is called *"fur." When practitioners cannot obtain rags, they pick up this [fur] and make it into the robe. "The patched robe" describes our sewing and patching, and wearing, [cloth] that has become ragged and worn with age; we do not wear the fine clothes of the secular world.* [95]

[95] ††*'The venerable monk*[96] *Upāli*[97] *asks the World-honored One, "World-honored Bhadanta!*[98]

---

world.

92. 綾 (RYO, *aya*). *Aya* has a pattern woven into a diagonal weave.

93. 壊色 (E-JIKI), lit. "broken color," that is, not a bright, attractive primary color. The kaṣāya is not dyed a primary color.

94. Master Daikan Eno, the sixth patriarch in China.

95. The section in italics is in Chinese characters only, indicating that it was quoted directly from a Chinese text.

†† From here to paragraph [98] is one passage from *Konpon-issai-u-bu-hyaku-ichi-katsuma (101 Customs of the Mūla-sarvāstivādin School)*. In Chinese characters, the Sarvāstivādin School is 説一切有部 (SETSU-ISSAI-U-BU), "the School that Preaches that All Things Exist." Master Dogen esteemed their teaching especially highly. See Glossary and chap. 87, *Kuyo-shobutsu*.

How many stripes does the saṃghāṭī robe have?"

The Buddha says, "There are nine kinds. What are the nine kinds? They are [the saṃghāṭī robe] of nine stripes, eleven stripes, thirteen stripes, fifteen stripes, seventeen stripes, nineteen stripes, twenty-one stripes, twenty-three stripes, and twenty-five stripes. The first three of those kinds of saṃghāṭī robe have two long segments and one short segment [in each stripe], and we should keep [the standard] like this. The next three kinds have three long [segments] and one short, and the last three kinds have four long and one short. Anything with more [segments per] stripe than this becomes an unorthodox robe."[99]

Upāli again addresses the World-honored One, "World-honored Bhadanta! How many kinds of saṃghāṭī robe are there?"

The Buddha says, "There are three kinds: larger, medium, and smaller.[100] *The larger is three cubits long by five cubits wide.*[101] *The smaller is two and a half cubits long by four and a half cubits wide. Anything between these two is called medium."*

Upāli again addresses the World-honored One: "World-honored Bhadanta! How many stripes does the uttarāsaṃga[102] *robe have?"*

The Buddha says, "It has only seven stripes, each with two long segments and one short segment."

Upāli again addresses the World-honored One, "World-honored Bhadanta! How many kinds of seven-striped [robe] are there?"

The Buddha says, "There are three kinds: larger, medium, and smaller. The larger is three cubits by five, the smaller is a half cubit shorter on each side, and anything between these two is called medium."

Upāli again addresses the World-honored One: "World-honored Bhadanta! How many stripes does the antarvāsa[103] *robe have?"*

The Buddha says, "It has five stripes, each with one long segment and one short segment."

Upāli again addresses the World-honored One, "How many kinds of antarvāsa robe are there?"

The Buddha says, "There are three kinds: larger, medium, and smaller. The larger is three cubits

---

96. "Venerable monk" is 具寿 (GUJU), lit. "possessing longevity," which represents the meaning of the Sanskrit *āyuṣmat*, a term of reverence used for the Buddha's disciples. The word *āyuṣmat* lit. means a vital or vigorous person, a person of long life.

97. Upāli was one of the Buddha's ten great disciples, said to be foremost in maintaining the vinaya. Before becoming a monk he was a barber at the royal palace.

98. 大徳世尊 (DAITOKU-SESON), lit. "World-Honored Great Virtuous One." 大徳 (DAITOKU) represents the Sanskrit *bhadanta*—an epithet of the Buddha. See Glossary.

99. 破衲 (HANO), lit. "broken patched-[robe]." 衲 (NO), "patches," suggests the Buddhist robe itself.

100. 上，中，下 (JO, CHU, GE), lit. "upper, middle, and lower."

101. Cubit is 肘 (CHU), lit. "elbow," representing the Sanskrit *hasta*, which means forearm or cubit. The cubit, or *nobechu* in Japanese, is the basic unit of measurement in making a kaṣāya. It is not a fixed distance; it is obtained by measuring the distance from the elbow to the tip of the fist, or the distance from the elbow to the tip of the middle finger, of the person who will wear the kaṣāya.

102. The Sanskrit *uttarāsaṃga* means an upper or outer garment. This robe would be worn for doing prostrations, listening to formal lectures, and the meeting for confession.

103. The Sanskrit *antarvāsa* means an inner or under garment.

by five. The medium and the smaller are as before."[104] *The Buddha says, "There are two further kinds of antarvāsa robe. What are those two? The first is two cubits long by five cubits wide, and the second is two cubits long by four cubits wide."*

The saṃghāṭī is translated as "the double layered robe," the uttarāsaṃga is translated as "the upper robe," and the antarvāsa is translated as "the under robe" or as "the inner robe." At the same time, the saṃghāṭī robe is called "the large robe," and also called "the robe for entering royal palaces" or "the robe for preaching the Dharma." The uttarāsaṃga is called "the seven-striped robe," or called "the middle robe" or "the robe for going among the Saṃgha." The antarvāsa is called "the five-striped robe," or called "the small robe" or "the robe for practicing the truth and for doing work."'

[98] We should guard and retain these three robes without fail. Among saṃghāṭī robes is the kaṣāya of sixty stripes, which also deserves to be received and retained without fail. In general, the length of a [Buddha's] body depends on the span of its lifetime, which is between eighty thousand years[105] and one hundred years.[106] Some say that there are differences between eighty thousand years and one hundred years, while others say that they may be equal. We esteem the insistence that they may be equal as the authentic tradition.[107] The body measurements of buddhas and of human beings are very different: the human body can be measured, but the Buddha-body ultimately cannot be measured.[108] Therefore, in the present moment in which Śākyamuni Buddha puts on the kaṣāya of Kāśyapa Buddha,[109] [the kaṣāya] is not long and not wide. And in the present moment in which Maitreya Tathāgata puts on the kaṣāya of Śākyamuni Buddha, it is not short and not narrow. We should reflect upon clearly, decide conclusively, understand completely, and observe carefully that the Buddha-body is not long or short. King Brahmā,[110] though high in the world of matter, does not see the crown of the Buddha's head. Maudgalyāyana,[111] having gone far into the World of the Bright Banner, does not discern the Buddha's voice: it is truly a mystery that [the Buddha's form and voice] are the same whether seen and heard from far or near. All the merits of the Tathāgata are like this,[112] and we should keep these merits in mind.

[100] As regards [methods of] cutting out and sewing the kaṣāya, there is the robe of

---

104. As in the case of the *uttarāsaṃga* robe, the smaller is a half cubit shorter on each side, and anything between these two is called medium.

105. It is said that Maitreya Buddha will manifest himself in this world when he is eighty thousand years old.

106. The *Fuyo-kyo,* from the Sanskrit *Lalita-vistara-sūtra,* says that the Buddha lived for one hundred years.

107. Master Dogen did not deny the existence of differences in length, but at the same time he suggested that, in the phase of action, relative differences are not important.

108. The Buddha-body is a real state at the moment of the present, not only physical matter.

109. See note 23.

110. The creator deity in Hindu mythology.

111. Maudgalyāyana was one of the Buddha's ten great disciples. It is said that he and Śāriputra, the sons of Brahmin from neighboring villages, were good friends. Maudgalyāyana was said to be foremost in mystical abilities. The World of the Bright Banner is an imaginary western realm where buddhas are living. The *Dai-ho-shaku-kyo* (from the Sanskrit *Mahāratnakūṭa-sūtra*), chap. 10, contains a story in which Maudgalyāyana goes into the World of the Bright Banner.

112. That is, the merits of the Buddha are beyond relative considerations.

separate stripes,[113] the robe of added stripes,[114] the robe of pleated stripes,[115] and the single-sheet robe,[116] each of which is a proper method. We should receive and retain [the kind of robe] that accords with the [material] obtained. The Buddha says, *"The kaṣāya of the buddhas of the three times is invariably backstitched."* In obtaining the material, again, we consider pure material to be good, and we consider so-called "filthy rags" to be the purest of all. The buddhas of the three times all consider [rags] to be pure. In addition, cloth offered by devout donors is also pure. There again, [cloth] bought at a market with pure money is also pure. There are limits on the [number of] days within which the robe should be made,[117] but in the present degenerate age of the Latter Dharma, in a remote country, it may be better for us to receive and to retain [the robe] by doing the cutting and sewing whenever we are promoted by belief. It is an ultimate secret of the Great Vehicle that lay people, whether human beings or gods, receive and retain the kaṣāya. King Brahmā and King Śakra[118] have now both received and retained the kaṣāya, and these are excellent precedents in [the worlds of] volition and matter. Excellent [precedents] in the human world are beyond calculation. All lay bodhisattvas have received and retained [the kaṣāya]. In China, Emperor Bu[119] of the Liang Dynasty and Emperor Yang[120] of the Sui Dynasty both received and retained the kaṣāya. The emperors Daiso and Shukuso[121] both wore the kaṣāya, learned in practice from monks, and received and retained the bodhisattva precepts. Other people such as householders and their wives who received the kaṣāya and received the Buddhist precepts are excellent examples in the past and present. In Japan, when Prince Shotoku[122] received and retained the kaṣāya, and lectured on such sutras as the Lotus Sutra and the Śrīmālā Sutra,[123] he experienced the miraculous omen of precious flowers raining from the heavens. From that time the Buddha-Dharma spread throughout our country. Though [Prince Shotoku] was the regent of the whole country, he was just a guiding teacher to human beings and gods. As the Buddha's emissary, he was father and mother to many living beings. In our country today, although the materials, colors, and measurements

---

113. These names are explanatory rather than accurate translations of the original Chinese characters. "The robe of separate stripes" is 割截衣 (KATSU-SETSU-E), lit. "divided-and-cut robe"; for this robe the individual segments of each stripe are sewn together, then the stripes are sewn together, and finally the borders are sewn, and fastening tapes added.

114. 渫葉衣 (ZECCHO-E), lit. "[unknown character]-leaf robe"; this is basically one large sheet of uncut cloth onto which long thin strips are sewn to create the stripes and borders.

115. 摂葉衣 (SHO-YO-E), lit. "gathered-leaf robe"; this is again one large sheet of uncut cloth, but it is pleated to create the stripes.

116. 縵衣 (MAN-E)—the meaning of the former character is not known; this is a single sheet of cloth, with only the fastening tapes added, and sewn only around the borders.

117. The time-limits were five days for the *saṃghāṭī* robe, four days for the seven-striped robe, and two days for the five-striped robe.

118. Indian legends say that King Brahmā is king of the world of volition, and King Śakra (i.e., Śakra-devānām-indra) is king of the world of matter.

119. Emperor Bu, or Wu, (464–549), reigned from 502 to 549. His conversation with Master Bodhidharma when the latter arrived in China is recorded in chap. 30, *Gyoji.*

120. Emperor Yang (569–617), reigned from 605 to 617.

121. Daiso and Shukuso were emperors of the Tang Dynasty (618–906), who lived at the time of Master Nan-yo Echu. See note 5.

122. Prince Shotoku (573–620) was the primary organizer of the early Japanese state. He promoted Buddhism as the state religion.

123. The full name of the sutra is the *Śrīmālā-devā-siṃhanāda-sūtra*. See Glossary.

of the kaṣāya have all been misunderstood, that we can see and hear the word kaṣāya is due solely to the power of Prince Shotoku. We would be in a sorry state today if, at that time, he had not destroyed the false and established the true. Later, the Emperor Shomu[124] also received and retained the kaṣāya and received the bodhisattva precepts. Therefore, whether we are emperors or subjects, we should receive and retain the kaṣāya and we should receive the bodhisattva precepts without delay. There can be no greater happiness for a human body.

[104] It has been said that *"The kaṣāyas received and retained by lay people are either called 'single-stitched' or called 'secular robes.' That is, they are not sewn with back-stitches."* It is also said that *"When lay people go to a place of [practicing] the truth, they should be equipped with the three Dharma-robes, a willow twig,[125] rinsing water,[126] mealware, and a sitting cloth;[127] they should practice the same pure practices as bhikṣus."[128]*

[105] Such were the traditions of a master of the past.[129] However, [the tradition] that has now been received one-to-one from the Buddhist patriarchs is that the kaṣāyas transmitted to kings, ministers, householders,[130] and common folk, are all backstitched. An excellent precedent is that [Master Daikan Eno] had already received the authentic transmission of the Buddha's kaṣāya as the temple servant Ro.[131] In general, the kaṣāya is the banner of a disciple of the Buddha. If we have already received and retained the kaṣāya, we should humbly receive it upon the head every day. Placing it on the crown of the head, we join the hands and recite the following verse:

Daisai-gedatsu-fuku	*How great is the clothing of liberation,*
Muso-fukuden-e	*Formless, field of happiness, robe!*
Hibu-nyorai-kyo	*Devoutly wearing the Tathāgata's teaching,*
Kodo-shoshujo	*Widely I will save living beings.*

After that we put it on. In the kaṣāya, we should feel like [our] Master and should feel like a tower.[132] We also recite this verse when we humbly receive [the kaṣāya] on the head after washing it.

[107] The Buddha says,

---

124. Emperor Shomu, reigned in Japan from 724 to 749.

125. The use of the willow twig to clean the teeth is explained in chap. 56, *Senmen.*

126. Potable water would be kept in a small corked bottle, for drinking or for rinsing the mouth.

127. The sitting cloth, or *zagu,* is spread on the floor for formal prostrations.

128. Both quotations are from *Maka-shikan-hogyo-den-guketsu,* a Chinese commentary on *Maka-shikan,* which is a record of lectures by the Chinese Master Tendai Chigi, founder of the Tendai Sect.

129. "Master of the past" is 古徳 (KO-TOKU), lit. "ancient merit" or "meritorious person of the past." These words appear frequently in *Maka-shikan.*

130. "Householder" is 居士 (KOJI), see chap. 8, *Raihai-tokuzui.*

131. *Ro* was Master Daikan Eno's name before he became a monk. The story of how he worked as a temple servant in the order of Master Daiman Konin is related in chap. 30, *Gyoji.*

132. These represent the first two of the eight venerative images, or feelings, associated with wearing the kaṣāya: 1) feeling like a tower (because of sitting up straight), 2) feeling like the Buddha ("our Master,") 3) feeling solitude and peace, 4) feeling compassion, 5) feeling veneration, 6) feeling humility, 7) feeling repentance, and 8) feeling as if one has dispelled greed, anger, and stupidity and obtained all the teachings of a monk.

When we shave the head and wear the kaṣāya,
We are protected by the buddhas.
Each person who transcends family life
Is served by gods and men.

Clearly, once we have shaved the head and put on the kaṣāya, we are protected by all the buddhas. Relying on this protection of the buddhas, [a person] can roundly realize the virtues of the supreme state of bodhi. Celestial throngs and human multitudes serve offerings to such a person.

[107] 'The World-honored One says to the bhikṣu Wisdom-Brightness,[133] *"The Dharma-robe has ten excellent merits: 1) It is able to cover the body, to keep away shame, to fill us with humility and to [make us] practice good ways.[134] 2) It keeps away cold and heat, as well as mosquitoes, harmful creatures, and poisonous insects, [so that we can] practice the truth in tranquility. 3) It manifests the form of a śramaṇa[135] who has left family life, giving delight to those who behold it and keeping away wrong states of mind. 4) The kaṣāya is just the manifestation to human beings and gods of a precious flag; those who honor and venerate it are able to be born in a brahma heaven.[136] 5) When we wear the kaṣāya, we feel that it is a precious flag; it is able to extinguish sins and to produce all kinds of happiness and virtue. 6) A fundamental rule in making the kaṣāya is to dye it a secondary color,[137] so that it keeps us free from thoughts of the five desires,[138] and does not give rise to lust. 7) The kaṣāya is the pure robe of the Buddha; for it eradicates afflictions[139] forever and makes them into a fertile field. 8) When the kaṣāya covers the body, it extinguishes the karma of sins and promotes at every moment the practice of the ten kinds of good.[140] 9) The kaṣāya is like a fertile field; for it is well able to nurture the bodhisattva-way. 10) The kaṣāya is also like a suit of armor; for it makes the poisoned arrows of affliction unable to do harm. Wisdom-Brightness! Remember, through these causes, when the buddhas of the three times, and pratyekabuddhas and śrāvakas, and pure monks and nuns, cover the body in the kaṣāya, [these] three groups of sacred beings sit as one on the precious platform of liberation, take up the sword of wisdom to destroy the demons of affliction, and enter together into the many spheres of nirvāṇa which have one taste."* Then the World-honored One speaks again in verse:

Bhikṣu Wisdom-Brightness, listen well!
The great field-of-happiness robe has ten excellent merits:

---

133. 智光 (CHIKO). The Sanskrit name of this monk is not known.

134. "Good ways" is 善法 (ZENHO) lit. "good law." Observance of 善法 (ZENHO), or the moral rule of the Universe, is the second of the three universal bodhisattva precepts (see chap. 94, *Jukai).*

135. The Sanskrit *śramaṇa* means a striver, a mendicant, or a Buddhist monk.

136. The first of the four *dhyāna* heavens in the world of matter is said to consist of three heavens: Brahma-pāriṣadya, Brahma-purohita, Mahābrahman. Beings in these heavens, having left the world of volition, are not troubled by sexual desire.

137. 壊色 (E-JIKI). See note 93.

138. The five desires are desires associated with sight, sound, smell, taste, and touch.

139. 煩悩 (BONNO), representing the Sanskrit *kleśa.*

140. The ten kinds of good are abstention from the ten kinds of wrong: 1) killing, 2) stealing, 3) adultery, 4) lying, 5) two-faced speech, 6) abusive slander, 7) gossip, 8) greed, 9) anger, 10) devotion to wrong views.

Secular clothes increase taintedness from desire,
The Tathāgata's Dharma-attire is not like that;
Dharma-attire fends off social shame,
But fills us with the humility that produces a field of happiness.

It keeps away cold and heat, and poisonous insects;
Firming our will to the truth, it enables us to arrive at the ultimate.

It manifests [the form] of a monk and keeps away greed;
It eradicates the five views[141] *and [promotes] right practice.*

To look at and bow to the kaṣāya's form of a precious banner,
And to venerate it, produces the happiness of King Brahmā.

When a disciple of the Buddha wears the robe and feels like a tower,
This produces happiness, extinguishes sins,
and impresses human beings and gods.

True śramaṇas, of modest appearance, showing respect,
Are not tainted in their actions by secular defilements.

The buddhas praise [the kaṣāya] as a fertile field,
They call it supreme in giving benefit and joy to living beings.
The mystical power of the kaṣāya is unthinkable,
It can cause us to practice deeds that plant the seeds of bodhi,[142]
It makes the sprouts of the truth grow like spring seedlings,
The wonderful effect of bodhi being like autumn fruit.
[The kaṣāya] is a true suit of armor, as hard as a diamond;
The poisoned arrows of affliction can do no harm.
I have now briefly praised the ten excellent merits,
If I had successive kalpas to expound them widely, there would be no end.
If a dragon wears a single strand [of the kaṣāya],
It will escape [the fate of] becoming food for a garuḍa.[143]
If people retain this robe when crossing the ocean,
They need not fear trouble from dragon-fish or demons.
When thunder roars, lightning strikes, and the sky is angry,
Someone who wears the kaṣāya is fearless.
If one clothed in white[144] *is able personally to hold and retain [the kaṣāya],*
All bad demons are unable to approach.
If [that person] is able to establish the will and seeks to leave home,
Shunning the world and practicing the Buddha's truth,
All the demon palaces of the ten directions will quake and tremble,
And that person will quickly experience the body of the Dharma-King.[145,146]

141. 五見 (GOKEN), "five views," represents the Sanskrit *pañca dṛṣṭayaḥ*. See Glossary.

142. The Chinese characters 菩提 (BODAI), "bodhi," and the character 道 (DO), "truth," in the next line are used interchangeably.

143. Lit. "a golden-winged king of birds," that is, a *garuḍa*. See Glossary.

144. 白衣 (BYAKU-E), lit. "a white robe," represents the Sanskrit *avadāta-vāsana*.

145. 法王 (HO-O), "the Dharma King," is an epithet of the Buddha.

146. Vol. 5 of Daijo-honsho-shinchi-kan-kyo.

[113] These ten excellent merits broadly include all the merits of the Buddha's truth. We should explicitly learn in practice the merits present in [these] long lines and [short] verses of praise, not just glancing over them and quickly putting them aside, but researching them phrase by phrase over a long period. These excellent merits are just the merits of the kaṣāya itself: they are not the effect of a practitioner's fierce [pursuit of] merit through perpetual training. The Buddha says, *"The mystical power of the kaṣāya is unthinkable"*; it cannot be supposed at random by the common man or sages and saints. In general, when we *quickly experience the body of the Dharma-King,* we are always wearing the kaṣāya. There has never been anyone, since ancient times, who experienced the body of the Dharma-King without wearing the kaṣāya.

[114] The best and purest material for the robe is rags, whose merits are universally evident in the sutras, precepts, and commentaries[147] of the great vehicle and small vehicle. We should inquire into [these merits] under those who have studied them widely. At the same time, we should also be clear about other materials for the robe. [These things] have been clarified and authentically transmitted by the buddhas and the patriarchs. They are beyond lesser beings.

[115] The Middle Āgama Sutra[148] says, *"Furthermore, wise friends![149] Suppose there is a man whose bodily behavior is pure, but whose behavior of mouth and mind is impure. If wise people see [the impurity] and feel anger they must dispel it. Wise friends! Suppose there is a man whose bodily behavior is impure but whose behavior of mouth and mind is pure. If wise people see [the impurity] and feel anger they must dispel it. How can they dispel it? Wise friends! They should be like a forest bhikṣu[150] with rags, looking among the rags for worn cloth to be thrown away, and for [cloth] soiled by feces or urine, or by tears and spit, or stained by other impurities. After inspecting [a rag, the bhikṣu] picks it up with the left hand and stretches it out with the right hand.[151] If there are any parts which are not soiled by feces, urine, tears, spit, or other impurities, and which are not in holes, [the bhikṣu] tears them off and takes them. In the same way, wise friends, if a man's bodily behavior is impure but the behavior of mouth and mind is pure, do not think about his body's impure behavior. Only be aware of his pure behavior of mouth and mind. If wise people feel anger at what they see, they must dispel it like this."*

[117] This is the method by which a forest bhikṣu collects rags. There are four sorts of rags and ten sorts of rags. When gathering those rags, we first pick out the parts that have no holes. We should then also reject [the parts] that cannot be washed clean, being too deeply soiled with long-accumulated stains of feces and urine. We should select [those parts] that can be washed clean.

[117] The ten sorts of rags:

1) Rags chewed by an ox, 2) rags gnawed by rats, 3) rags scorched by fire, 4) rags

---

147. The *tripiṭaka* (three baskets) of Buddhist teachings. See Glossary.

148. Chu-agon-kyo (*Mādhyamāgama* in Sanskrit and *majjhima-nikāya* in Pali). The *Āgama sutras* relate concrete information about the behavior and speech of the Buddha and his disciples in their daily life.

149. 諸賢 (SHOKEN), "wise ones," or "(ladies and) gentlemen" is a term of respect used when addressing an assembly.

150. 阿練若比丘 (ARANNYA-BIKU). 阿練若 (ARANNYA) represents the Sanskrit *araṇya* which means forest. A forest *bhikṣu* suggests a monk who lives a solitary life in the forest. See also chap. 90, *Shizen-biku.*

151. Traditionally, the right hand is kept pure.

[soiled by] menstruation, 5) rags [soiled by] childbirth, 6) rags [offered at] a shrine, 7) rags [left at] a graveyard, 8) rags [offered in] petitional prayer, 9) rags [discarded by] a king's officers,[152] 10) rags brought back from a funeral.[153] These ten sorts people throw away; they are not used in human society. We pick them up and make them into the pure material of the kaṣāya. Rags have been praised and have been used by the buddhas of the three times. Therefore these rags are valued and defended by human beings, gods, dragons, and so on. We should pick them up to make the kaṣāya; they are the purest material and the ultimate purity. Nowadays in Japan there are no such rags. Even if we search, we cannot find any. It is regrettable that [this] is a minor nation in a remote land. However, we can use pure material offered by a donor, and we can use pure material donated by human beings and gods. Alternatively, we can make the kaṣāya from [cloth] bought at a market with earnings from a pure livelihood. Such rags and [cloth] obtained from a pure livelihood are not silk, not cotton, and not gold, silver, pearls, patterned cloth, sheer silk, brocade, embroidery, and so on; they are just rags. These rags are neither for a humble robe nor for a beautiful garment; they are just for the Buddha-Dharma. To wear them is just to have received the authentic transmission of the skin, flesh, bones, and marrow of the buddhas of the three times, and to have received the authentic transmission of the right-Dharma-eye treasury. We should never ask human beings and gods about the merit of this [transmission]. We should learn it in practice from Buddhist patriarchs.

Shobogenzo Kesa-kudoku

[120] During my stay in Sung China, when I was making effort on the long platform, I saw that my neighbor at the end of every sitting[154] would lift up his kaṣāya and place it on his head; then holding the hands together in veneration, he would quietly recite a verse. The verse was:

Daisai-gedatsu-fuku	*How great is the clothing of liberation,*
Muso-fukuden-e	*Formless, field of happiness, robe!*
Hibu-nyorai-kyo	*Devoutly wearing the Tathāgata's teaching,*
Kodo-shoshujo	*Widely I will save living beings.*

At that time, there arose in me a feeling I had never before experienced. [My] body was overwhelmed with joy. The tears of gratitude secretly fell and soaked my lapels. The reason was that when I had read the Āgama sutras previously, I had noticed sentences about humbly receiving the kaṣāya on the head, but I had not clarified the standards for this behavior. Seeing it done now, before my very eyes, I was overjoyed. I thought to myself, *"It is a pity that when I was in my homeland there was no master to teach this, and no good friend to recommend it. How could I not regret, how could I not deplore, passing so much time in vain? Now that I am seeing and hearing it, I can rejoice in past good*

152. Suggests uniforms discarded by promoted officers.

153. 往還衣 (OKAN-E), lit. "robes of going and returning," that is, cloth used as a funeral shroud and then brought back after the ceremony.

154. "End of sitting" is 開静 (KAIJO), lit. "release of stillness." Traditionally, the clapping of a wooden board at the end of Zazen is called 小開静 (SHO-KAIJO), "small release of stillness," and the ringing of the bell is called 大開静 (DAI-KAIJO), "great release of stillness."

conduct. If I had vainly stayed in my home country, how could I have sat next to this treasure of a monk,[155] *who has received the transmission of, and who wears, the Buddha's robe itself?"* The sadness-and-joy was not one-sided. A thousand myriad tears of gratitude ran down. Then I secretly vowed: *"One way or another, unworthy though I am, I will become a rightful successor to the Buddha-Dharma. I will receive the authentic transmission of the right Dharma and, out of compassion for living beings in my homeland, I will cause them to see and to hear the robe and the Dharma which have been authentically transmitted by the Buddhist patriarchs."* The vow I made then has not been in vain now; many bodhisattvas, in families and out of families,[156] have received and retained the kaṣāya. This is something to rejoice in. People who have received and retained the kaṣāya should humbly receive it upon the head every day and night. The merit [of this] may be especially excellent and supremely excellent. The seeing and hearing of a phrase or a verse may be as in the story of *"on trees and on rocks,"*[157] and the seeing and hearing may not be limited to the length and breadth of the nine states.[158] The merit of the authentic transmission of the kaṣāya is hardly encountered through the ten directions. To [encounter this merit] even if only for one day or for one night may be the most excellent and highest thing.

[123] In the 10th lunar month in the winter of the 17th year of Kajo[159] in great Sung [China], two Korean[160] monks came to the city of Keigen-fu.[161] One was called Chigen and one was called Kei-un. This pair were always discussing the meaning of Buddhist sutras; at the same time they were also men of letters. But they had no kaṣāya and no pātra, like secular people. It was pitiful that though they had the external form of bhikṣus they did not have the Dharma of bhikṣus.[162] This may have been because they were from a minor nation in a remote land. When Japanese who have the external form of bhikṣus travel abroad, they are likely to be the same as Chigen and such. Śākyamuni Buddha received [the kaṣāya] upon his head for twelve years, never setting it aside.[163] We are already his distant descendants, and we should emulate this. To turn the forehead away from prostrations idly done for fame and gain to gods, to spirits, to kings, and to retainers, and to turn instead towards the humble reception upon the head of the

---

155. 僧宝 (SOBO), or "Saṃgha-treasure."

156. 在家出家 (ZAIKE-SHUKKE), lay people and monks.

157. 若樹若石 (NYAKUJU-NYAKUSEKI), "trees and rocks," alludes to the story of the Buddha's past life recorded in the *Mahāparinirvāṇa-sūtra*. When he was "the Child of the Himalayas" pursuing the truth in the mountains, a demon told him the first two lines of a four-line poem: *"Actions are without constancy; / Concrete existence is the arising and passing of dharmas."* The demon said it was too hungry to tell the child the last two lines, so the child offered his own body as a meal for the demon if it would recite the last two lines. So the demon recited the last two lines: *"After arising and passing have ceased, / The stillness is pleasure itself."* The child preserved the verse for posterity by writing it on some nearby trees and rocks in his own blood, before being eaten by the demon.

158. The nine states means China.

159. 1223. The 17th year of the Kajo era was, in fact, 1224. However, the original sentence also identifies the year under the Chinese dating system in which characters from two separate lists are combined. These two characters— 癸 (KI, *mizunoto*), the younger brother of water, or the tenth calendar sign, and 未 (MI, *hitsuji*), the sheep, or the eighth horary sign—identify the year as 1223.

160. "Korean" is 高麗 (KORAI or KOMA). At that time, the Korean peninsular was divided into three states. The state called 高麗 (KORAI) existed from 918 to 1353.

161. Present day Ningpo, in eastern China.

162. They did not have the kaṣāya and pātra.

163. Alludes to a story originally contained in the Āgama sutras. See chap. 13, *Den-e*, para. [143].

Buddha's robe, is joyful.

Preached to the assembly at Kannon-dori-kosho-horin-ji temple, on the 1st day of winter,[164] in the 1st year of Ninji.[165]

---

164. The 1st day of winter means the 1st day of the 10th lunar month.
165. 1240.

[13]

伝衣

DEN-E

The Transmission of the Robe

***Den** means "transmission" and **e** means "robe," so **den-e** means "the transmission of the robe." The content of this chapter is very similar to that of the previous chapter, Kesa-kudoku. Furthermore, the date recorded at the end of each chapter is the same. But whereas the note at the end of Kesa-kudoku says "preached to the assembly at Kannon-dori-kosho-horin-ji temple," the note to this chapter says "written at Kannon-dori-kosho-horin-ji temple..." It thus seems likely that Den-e is the draft of the lecture Master Dogen was to give on October 1st, and Kesa-kudoku is the transcript of the lecture he gave on that day.*

[125] **The authentic transmission into China** of the robe and the Dharma, which are authentically transmitted from buddha to buddha,[1] was done only by the founding Patriarch of Shaolin [temple]. The founding Patriarch was the twenty-eighth ancestral master after Śākyamuni Buddha. [The robe] had passed from rightful successor to rightful successor through twenty-eight generations in India, and it was personally and authentically transmitted through six generations in China; altogether it was [transmitted through] thirty-three generations in the Western Heavens and the Eastern Lands. The thirty-third patriarch, Zen Master Daikan, received the authentic transmission of this robe and Dharma on Obai in the middle of the night, and he guarded and retained [the robe] until his death.[2] It is now still deposited at Horin-ji temple on Sokei-zan mountain. Many generations of emperors in succession requested that it be brought into the palace, where they served offerings to it; they guarded [the robe] as a sacred object. The Tang dynasty emperors Chuso, Shukuso, and Daiso frequently had [the robe] brought to court and served offerings to it. Both when they requested it and when they sent it back, they would dispatch an imperial emissary and issue an edict; this is the manner in which they honored [the robe]. Emperor Daiso once returned the Buddha's robe to Sokei-zan mountain with the following edict: *"I now dispatch the great General Ryu Sokei, Pacifier of the Nation, to receive with courtesy and to deliver [the robe]. I consider it to be a national treasure. Venerable priests, deposit it in its original temple. Let it be solemnly guarded by monks who have intimately received the fundamental teaching. Never let it fall into neglect."*

[127] Thus, the emperors of several generations each esteemed [the robe] as an important

---

1. *Kesa-kudoku* begins 仏仏祖祖 (BUTSU-BUTSU SO-SO), "from buddha to buddha, and from patriarch to patriarch." The difference presumably arose from Master Dogen's feeling on the day.

2. "Until his death" is 生前 (SHOZEN), lit. "life-before." In *Kesa-kudoku* the expression is 一生 (ISSHO), lit. "throughout his life." Again, the difference is incidental.

national treasure. Truly, to retain this Buddha's robe in one's country is a superlative great treasure, which surpasses even dominion over the [worlds] as countless as the sands of the Ganges in a three-thousand-great-thousandfold world. We should never compare it with Benka's gem.[3] [A gem] may become the national seal of state, but how can it become the rare jewel which transmits the Buddha's state? From the Tang dynasty[4] onwards, the monks and laymen[5] who admired and bowed to [the kaṣāya] were all, without exception, people of great makings who believed in the Dharma. If not aided by good conduct in the past, how else would we be able to prostrate this body in admiration to the Buddha's robe which has been directly and authentically transmitted from buddha to buddha? Skin, flesh, bones, and marrow that believe in and receive [the robe] should rejoice; those that cannot believe in and receive [the robe] should feel regret—even though the situation is of their own doing—that they are not the embryos of buddhas. Even secular [teaching] says that to look at a person's behavior is just to look at that person. To have admired and to have bowed now to the Buddha's robe is just to be looking at the Buddha. We should erect hundreds, thousands, and tens of thousands of stūpas and serve offerings to this Buddha-robe. In the heavens above and in the ocean's depths, whatever has mind should value [the robe]. In the human world too, sacred wheel-rolling kings[6] and others who know what is true and know what is superior should value [the robe]. It is pitiful that the people who became, in generation after generation, the rulers of the land, never knew what an important treasure existed in their own country. Deluded by the teachings of Taoists, many of them abolished the Buddha-Dharma. At such times, instead of wearing the kaṣāya, they covered their round heads with [Taoist] caps.[7] The lectures [they listened to] were on how to extend one's life span and to prolong one's years. There were [emperors like this] both during the Tang dynasty and during the Sung dynasty. These fellows were rulers of the nation, but they must have been more vulgar than the common people. They should have quietly reflected that the Buddha's robe had remained and was actually present in their own country. They might even have considered that [their country] was the Buddha-land of the robe. [The kaṣāya] may surpass even [sacred] bones[8] and so on. Wheel-rolling kings have bones, as do lions, human beings, pratyekabuddhas, and the like. But wheel-rolling kings do not have the kaṣāya, lions do not have the kaṣāya, human beings do not have the kaṣāya. Only buddhas have the kaṣāya. We should believe this profoundly. Stupid people today often revere bones but fail to know the kaṣāya. Few know that they should guard and retain [their own kaṣāya]. This situation has arisen

3. Benka was a man in ancient China who found a huge gem, one foot in diameter. He offered it to three kings, but none of them valued the gem at all. In this context, Benka's gem is simply used as an example of something which is very valuable, but not on the same level as the kaṣāya.

4. 619–858.

5. "Monks and laymen" is originally "black and white," symbolizing the clothes of monks and laymen respectively.

6. "Sacred wheel-rolling kings" is 転輪聖王 (TEN-RIN-JO-O), from the Sanskrit *cakravarti-rāja*. These legendary kings were said to govern the four continents east, west, north, and south of Mt. Sumeru. The king with the gold wheel rules all four continents, the king with the silver wheel rules all continents but the north, the king with the copper wheel rules the east and south, and the king with the iron wheel rules only the southern continent.

7. 葉巾 (YOKIN), lit. "leaf-cloth."

8. 舎利 (SHARI), represents the Sanskrit *śarīra*, which literally means bones, but which often suggests the Buddha's relics.

because few people have ever heard of the importance of the kaṣāya, and [even these few] have never heard of the authentic transmission of the Buddha-Dharma. When we attentively think back to the time when Śākyamuni was in the world, it is little more than two thousand years; many national treasures and sacred objects have been transmitted to the present for longer than this. This Buddha-Dharma and Buddha-robe are recent and new. The benefit of their propagation through the *fields and villages*, even if there have been *fifty propagations*, is wonderful.[9] The qualities of those things[10] are obvious [but] this Buddha-robe can never be the same as those things. Those things are not received in the authentic transmission from rightful successors, but this [robe] has been received in the authentic transmission from rightful successors. Remember, we attain the truth when listening to a four-line verse, and we attain the state of truth when listening to a single phrase. Why is it that a four-line verse and a single phrase can have such mystical effect? Because they are the Buddha-Dharma. Now, each robe and [all] nine kinds of robe[11] have been received in the authentic transmission from the Buddha-Dharma itself; [the robe] could never be inferior to a four-line verse, and could never be less effective than a single phrase of Dharma. This is why, for more than two thousand years, all followers of the Buddha—those with the makings of devotional practice and of Dharma-practice—have guarded and retained the kaṣāya and regarded it as their body-and-mind. Those who are ignorant of the right Dharma of the buddhas do not worship the kaṣāya.

[132] Now, such beings as Śakra-devānām-indra and the Dragon King Anavatapta, though they are the celestial ruler of laymen and the king of dragons, have guarded and retained the kaṣāya. Yet people who shave the head, people who call themselves disciples of the Buddha, do not know that they should receive and retain the kaṣāya. How much less could they know its material, color, and measurements; how much less could they know the method of wearing it; and how much less could they have seen the dignified conventions for it, even in a dream?

[133] The kaṣāya has been called since olden times *the clothing that wards off suffering from heat*, and *the clothing of liberation*. In conclusion, its merit is beyond measure. Through the merit of the kaṣāya, a dragon's scales can be freed from the three kinds of burning pain. When the buddhas realize the truth, they are always wearing this robe. Truly, although we were born in a remote land in [the age of] the Latter Dharma, if we have the opportunity to choose between what has been transmitted and what has not been transmitted, we should believe in, receive, guard, and retain [the robe] whose transmission is authentic and traditional. In what lineage have both the robe and the Dharma of Śākyamuni himself been authentically transmitted, as in our authentic tradition? They exist only in Buddhism. On meeting this robe and Dharma, who could be lax in venerating them and serving offerings to them? Even if, each day, we [have to] discard bodies and lives as countless as the sands of the Ganges, we should serve offerings to

---

9. 若田若里 (NYAKUDEN-NYAKURI), "fields and villages," and 五十展転 (GOJU-TENDEN), "fifty propagations," allude to a passage in the 18th chapter of the Lotus Sutra, *Zuiki-kudoku-bon*. See LS 3.72-74.

10. National treasures and sacred relics.

11. The nine kinds of robe are the robes of nine stripes, eleven stripes, thirteen stripes, fifteen stripes, seventeen stripes, nineteen stripes, twenty-one stripes, twenty-three stripes, and twenty-five stripes.

them. Further, we should vow to meet [the robe] and humbly to receive it upon the head in every life in every age. We are the stupid people of a remote quarter, born with a hundred thousand or so miles of mountains and oceans separating us from the land of the Buddha's birth. Even so, if we hear this right Dharma, if we receive and retain this kaṣāya even for a single day or a single night, and if we master even a single phrase or a single verse, that will not only be the good fortune to have served offerings to one buddha or to two buddhas: it will be the good fortune to have served offerings and paid homage to countless hundred thousand koṭis of buddhas. Even if [the servants] are ourselves, we should respect them, we should love them, and we should value them.

[135] We should heartily repay the great benevolence of the ancestral Master in transmitting the Dharma.[12] Even animals repay kindness; how could human beings fail to recognize kindness? If we failed to recognize kindness, we would be inferior to animals, more stupid than animals. People other than the ancestral masters who transmit the Buddha's right Dharma have never known the merit of this Buddha-robe, even in a dream. How much less could they clarify its material, color, and measurements? If we long to follow the traces of the buddhas, we should just long for this [transmission]. Even after a hundred thousand myriads of generations, the authentic reception of this authentic transmission will [still] be just the Buddha-Dharma itself. The evidence for this is clear. Even secular [teaching] says, *"One does not wear clothing different from the clothing of the past king, and one does not follow laws different from those of the past king."* Buddhism is also like that. We should not wear what is different from the Dharma-clothing of past buddhas. If [our clothes] were different from the Dharma-clothing of past buddhas, what could we wear to practice Buddhism and to serve buddhas? Without wearing this clothing, it might be difficult to enter the Buddha's order.

[136] Since the years of the Eihei period,[13] during the reign of Emperor Komei of the later Han Dynasty, monks arriving in the Eastern Lands from the Western Heavens have followed on each other's heels without cease. We often hear of monks going from China to India, but it is not said that they ever met anyone who gave them the face-to-face transmission of the Buddha-Dharma. They [have] only names and forms, learned in vain from teachers of commentaries and scholars of the tripiṭaka.[14] They have not heard the authentic tradition of the Buddha-Dharma. This is why they cannot even report that we should receive the authentic transmission of the Buddha's robe, why they never claim to have met a person who has received the authentic transmission of the Buddha's robe, and why they never mention seeing or hearing a person who has received the transmission of the robe. Clearly, they have never entered beyond the threshold of the house of Buddha. That these fellows recognize [the robe] solely as a garment, not knowing that it is in the Buddha-Dharma [an object of] honor and worship, is truly pitiful. Rightful successors to the transmission of the Buddha's Dharma-treasury also transmit and receive the Buddha's robe. The principle that the ancestral masters who receive the authentic transmission of the Dharma-treasury have never gone without

---

12. Refers to Master Bodhidharma's transmission of the Dharma into China.

13. 58 to 76 A.D.

14. 三蔵 (SANZO), lit. "the three storehouses," represents the Sanskrit *tripiṭaka*, or three baskets, namely: precepts (*vinaya*), sutras (*sūtra*), and commentaries (*abhidharma*).

seeing and hearing[15] the Buddha's robe is widely known among human beings and in the heavens above. This being so, the material, color, and measurements of the Buddha's kaṣāya have been authentically transmitted and authentically seen and heard; the great merits of the Buddha's kaṣāya have been authentically transmitted; and the body, mind, bones, and marrow of the Buddha's kaṣāya have been authentically transmitted, only in the customs of the traditional lineage. [This authentic transmission] is not known in the various schools which follow the teaching of the Āgamas.[16] The [robes] that individuals have established independently, according to the idea of the moment, are not traditional and not legitimate. When our great Master Śākyamuni Tathāgata passed on the right-Dharma-eye treasury and the supreme state of bodhi to Mahākāśyapa, he transmitted them together with the Buddha-robe. Between then and Zen Master Daikan of Sokei-zan mountain, there were thirty-three generations, the transmission passing from rightful successor to rightful successor. The intimate experience and intimate transmission of [the robe's] material, color, and measurements have long been handed down by the lineages, and their reception and retention are evident in the present. That is to say, that which was received and retained by each of the founding patriarchs of the five sects[17] is the authentic tradition. Similarly evident are the wearing [of the robe], according to the methods of former buddhas, and the making [of the robe], according to the methods of former buddhas, which *buddhas alone, together with buddhas*, through generations have transmitted and have experienced as the same state—in some cases for over fifty generations and in some cases for over forty generations—without confusion between any master and disciple. The Buddha's instruction, as authentically transmitted from rightful successor to rightful successor, is as follows:

Robe of nine stripes .... three long [segments], one short [segment];[18] or four long, one short
Robe of eleven stripes .... three long, one short; or four long, one short
Robe of thirteen stripes .... three long, one short; or four long, one short
Robe of fifteen stripes .... three long, one short
Robe of seventeen stripes .... three long, one short
Robe of nineteen stripes .... three long, one short
Robe of twenty-one stripes .... four long, one short
Robe of twenty-three stripes .... four long, one short
Robe of twenty-five stripes .... four long, one short
Robe of two hundred and fifty stripes .... four long, one short
Robe of eighty-four thousand stripes[19] .... eight long, one short

[140] This is an abbreviated list. There are many other kinds of kaṣāya besides these, all

15. "Seeing" means knowing the concrete form, and "hearing" means understanding the principles.

16. Many Hīnayāna Buddhist traditions are based on the teachings of the Āgama sutras.

17. Master Tozan, Master Rinzai, Master Hogen, Master Isan, and Master Unmon. See chap 49, *Butsudo*.

18. That is, three long segments and one short segment in each stripe.

19. In Buddhist sutras, eighty-four thousand signifies a very large number.

of which may be the saṃghāṭī robe. Some receive and retain [the kaṣāya] as lay people, and some receive and retain [the kaṣāya] as monks and nuns. To receive and to retain [the kaṣāya] means to wear it, not to keep it idly folded. Even if people shave off hair and beard, if they do not receive and retain the kaṣāya, if they hate the kaṣāya or fear the kaṣāya, they are celestial demons[20] and non-Buddhists. Zen Master Hyakujo Daichi[21] says, *"Those who have not accumulated good seeds in the past detest the kaṣāya and hate the kaṣāya; they fear and hate the right Dharma."*

[142] *The Buddha says, "If any living being, having entered my Dharma, commits the grave sins or falls into wrong views, but in a single moment of consciousness [this person] with reverent mind honors the saṃghāṭī robe, the buddhas and I will give affirmation, without fail, that this person will be able to become buddha in the three vehicles. Gods or dragons or human beings or demons, if able to revere the merit of even a small part of this person's kaṣāya, will atoonce attain the three vehicles and will neither regress nor stray. If ghosts and living beings can obtain even four inches of the kaṣāya, they will eat and drink their fill. When living beings offend each other and are about to fall into wrong views, if they remember the power of the kaṣāya, through the power of the kaṣāya they will duly feel compassion, and they will be able to return to the state of purity. If people on a battlefield keep a small part of this kaṣāya, venerating it and honoring it, they will obtain salvation."*[22]

[143] Thus we have seen that the merits of the kaṣāya are supreme and unthinkable. When we believe in, receive, guard, and retain it, we will surely get the state of affirmation, and get the state of not regressing. Not only Śākyamuni Buddha, but all the buddhas also have preached like this. Remember, the substance and form of the buddhas themselves is just the kaṣāya. This is why the Buddha says, *"Those who are going to fall into wrong ways hate the saṃghāṭī [robe]."* This being so, if hateful thoughts arise when we see and hear of the kaṣāya, we should feel sorry that our own body is going to fall into wrong ways, and we should repent and confess. Furthermore, when Śākyamuni Buddha first left the royal palace and was going to enter the mountains, a tree god, the story goes, holds up a saṃghāṭī robe and says to Śākyamuni Buddha, *"If you receive this robe upon your head, you will escape the disturbances of demons."* Then Śākyamuni Buddha accepts this robe, humbly receiving it upon his head, and for twelve years he does not set it aside even for a moment. This is the teaching of the Āgama sutras. Elsewhere it is said that the kaṣāya is a garment of good fortune, and that those who wear it always reach exalted rank. In general, there has never been a moment when this saṃghāṭī robe was not manifesting itself before us in the world. The manifestation before us of one moment is an eternal matter,[23] and eternal matters come at one moment. To obtain the kaṣāya is to obtain the Buddha's banner. For this reason, none of the buddha-tathāgatas has ever failed to receive and to retain the kaṣāya. And no person who has received and retained the kaṣāya has failed to become buddha.

---

20. 天魔 (TENMA), celestial demons, symbolize idealistic people who disturb Buddhism.

21. Master Hyakujo Ekai (749–814), a successor of Master Baso Do-itsu. Zen Master Daichi is his posthumous title.

22. This is a summarized list of the five sacred merits of the kaṣāya, from chap. 8 of *Hige-kyo (Karuṇā-puṇḍarīka-sūtra).* A longer enumeration of the five sacred merits, from the same sutra, appears in chap. 12, *Kesa-kudoku* para. [80].

23. 長劫の事 (CHOGO *no* JI), lit. "a matter in long kalpas."

[145] The method of wearing the kaṣāya:
To bare only the right shoulder is the usual method. There is also a method of wearing [the kaṣāya] so that it covers both shoulders. When we wear both sides over the left arm and shoulder, we wear the front edge on the outside and the back edge on the inside.[24] This is one instance of Buddhist dignified behavior. This behavior is neither seen and heard nor transmitted and received by the various groups of śrāvakas: their scriptures on the teaching of the Āgamas do not mention it at all. In general, the dignified behavior of wearing the kaṣāya in Buddhism has been unfailingly received and retained by the ancestral masters who received the transmission of the right Dharma and who are present before us here and now. When receiving and retaining [the kaṣāya], we should unfailingly receive and retain it under such an ancestral master. The traditional kaṣāya of the Buddhist patriarchs has been authentically transmitted from buddha to buddha without irregularity; it is the kaṣāya of former buddhas and of later buddhas, the kaṣāya of ancient buddhas and of recent buddhas. When they transform[25] the state of truth, when they transform the state of buddha, when they transform the past, when they transform the present, and when they transform the future, they transmit the authentic tradition from the past to the present, they transmit the authentic tradition from the present to the future, they transmit the authentic tradition from the present to the past, they transmit the authentic tradition from the past to the past, they transmit the authentic tradition from the present to the present, they transmit the authentic tradition from the future to the future, they transmit the authentic tradition from the future to the present, and they transmit the authentic tradition from the future to the past; and this is the authentic transmission of *buddhas alone, together with buddhas*. For this reason, for several hundred years after the ancestral Master came from the west, from the great Tang to the great Sung [dynasties], many of those accomplished at lecturing on sutras were able to see through their own behavior; and when people of philosophical schools, of precepts, and so on entered the Buddha-Dharma, they threw away the shabby old robes that had formerly been their kaṣāya, and they authentically received the traditional kaṣāya of Buddhism. Their stories appear one after another in Records of the Torch such as *Den[to-roku], Ko[to-roku], Zoku[to-roku], Futo-roku*, and so on.[26] When they were liberated from the small view which is limited thinking about

---

24. When the kaṣāya has been opened behind the back and the strings tied, and the left and right hand are holding the top corners of the kaṣāya, the border running vertically down from the right hand is 前頭 (ZENTO), "the front edge," and the border running vertically down from the left hand is 後頭 (KOTO), "the back edge." The right hand brings the top of the "front edge" around the front of the body and over the left shoulder.

25. "Transform" is 化 (KE). The character often appears in the compound 教化 (KYOKE), lit. "teach-transform," that is, to teach, to educate, or to instruct.

26. Refers to *Goto-roku (The Five Records of the Torch)*, compiled during the Sung period (960–1297), namely: 1) *Dento-roku* or *Keitoku-dento-roku (Keitoku Era Record of the Transmission of the Torch)*, completed by a monk called Dogen in 1004, the first year of the Keitoku era. It contains the histories of 1,701 Buddhists, from the seven ancient buddhas to Master Hogen Bun-eki (855–958). 2) *Koto-roku* or *Tensho-koto-roku (Tensho Era Record of the Widely Extending Torch)*, compiled by the layman Ri Junkyoku during the Tensho era (1023–1031). 3) *Zokuto-roku (Supplementary Record of the Torch)*, completed by Master Ihaku of Bukkoku temple in 1101, during the Kenchu-seikoku era. 4) *Rento-eyo (Collection of Essentials for Continuation of the Torch)*, completed in 1183 and published in 1189. 5) *Futo-roku* or *Katai-futo-roku (Katai Era Record of the Universal Torch)*, compiled by Master Shoju of Rai-an temple during the Katai era (1201–1204).

philosophy and precepts and they revered the great truth authentically transmitted by the Buddhist patriarchs, they all became Buddhist patriarchs. People today also should learn from the ancestral masters of the past. If we would like to receive and to retain the kaṣāya, we should receive the authentic transmission of, and should believe in, the traditional kaṣāya. We should not receive and retain a fake kaṣāya. The traditional kaṣāya means the kaṣāya now authentically transmitted from Shaolin [temple] and Sokei [mountain];[27] its reception from the Tathāgata in the transmission from rightful successor to rightful successor has never been interrupted for even a single generation. For this reason we have exactly received the practice of the truth, and we have intimately obtained, in our own hands, the Buddha's robe; and this is the reason [we should receive the authentic transmission]. The Buddha's [state of] truth is authentically transmitted in the Buddha's [state of] truth; it is not left for lazy people to receive at leisure. A secular proverb says, *"Hearing a thousand times is not as good as seeing once, and seeing a thousand times is not as good as experiencing once."* Reflecting on this, [we can say that] even if we see [the kaṣāya] a thousand times and hear of it ten thousand times, that is not as good as getting it once, and never as good as to have received the authentic transmission of the Buddha's robe. If we can doubt those who have authentic traditions, we should doubt all the more those who have never seen the authentic traditions even in a dream. To receive the authentic transmission of the Buddha's robe may be closer [in experience] than to receive and to hear Buddhist sutras. Even a thousand experiences and ten thousand attainments are not as good as one realization in experience. A Buddhist patriarch is the realization of the same state of experience; we should never rank [a Buddhist patriarch] with common followers of philosophy and precepts. In conclusion, with regard to the merits of the kaṣāya of the Patriarch's lineage, [we can say that] its authentic transmission has been received exactly; [that] its original configuration has been conveyed personally; and [that] it has been received and retained, together with the succession of the Dharma, without interruption until today. The authentic recipients are all ancestral masters who have experienced the same state and received the transmission of Dharma. They are superior even to [bodhisattvas at] the ten sacred stages and the three clever stages; we should serve and venerate them and should bow down to them and humbly receive them upon our heads. If this principle of the authentic transmission of the Buddha's robe is believed just once by this body-and-mind, that is a sign of meeting buddha, and it is the way to learn the state of buddha. [A life] in which we could not accept this Dharma would be a sad life. We should profoundly affirm that if we cover the physical body, just once, with this kaṣāya, it will be a talisman that protects the body and ensures realization of the state of bodhi. It is said that when we dye the believing mind with a single phrase or a single verse we never lack the brightness of long kalpas. When we dye the body-and-mind with one real dharma, [the state] may be *also like this*. Those mental images[28] are without an abode and are irrelevant to what I possess; even so, their merits are indeed as described above. The physical body is without an abode; even so, it is as described above. The kaṣāya, too, is without an origin and also without a destination, it is neither our own possession nor the possession of anyone else; even so, it actually abides at the place

---

27. That is, from Master Bodhidharma and Master Daikan Eno.
28. Of the believing mind described above.

where it is retained, and it covers the person who receives and retains it. The merits acquired [by virtue of the kaṣāya] may also be like this. When we make the kaṣāya, the making is not the elaboration[29] of the common, the sacred, and the like. The import of this is not perfectly realized by [bodhisattvas at] the ten sacred or the three clever [stages]. Those who have not accumulated seeds of the truth in the past do not see the kaṣāya, do not hear of the kaṣāya, and do not know the kaṣāya, not in one life, not in two lives, not even if they pass countless lives. How much less could they receive and retain [the kaṣāya]? There are those who attain, and those who do not attain, the merit to touch [the kaṣāya] once with the body. Those who have attained [this merit] should rejoice. Those who have not attained it should hope to do so. Those who can never attain it should lament. All human beings and gods have seen, heard, and universally recognized that the Buddha's robe is transmitted—both inside and outside the great-thousandfold-world—only in the lineage of the Buddhist patriarchs. Clarification of the configuration of the Buddha's robe also is present only in the lineage of the patriarchs, it is not known in other lineages. Those who do not know it and [yet] do not blame themselves are stupid people. Even if they know eighty-four thousand samādhi-dhāraṇīs,[30] without receiving the authentic transmission of the Buddhist patriarchs' robe and Dharma, without clarifying the authentic transmission of the kaṣāya, they can never be the rightful successors of the buddhas. How the living beings of other regions must long to receive exactly the authentic transmission of the Buddha's robe, as it has been authentically received in China. They must be ashamed, their sorrow in their hearts must be deep, that they have not received the authentic transmission in their own country. Truly, to meet the Dharma in which the robe and the Dharma of the World-Honored Tathāgata have been authentically transmitted is the result of seeds of great merit from past-nurtured prajñā. Now, in this corrupt age of the Latter Dharma, there are many bands of demons who are not ashamed that they themselves lack the authentic transmission, and who envy the authentic transmission [of others]. Our own possessions and abodes are not our real selves. Just authentically to receive the authentic transmission; this is the direct way to learn the state of buddha.

[153] In sum, remember that the kaṣāya is the body of the Buddha and the mind of the Buddha. Further, it is called *the clothing of liberation*, called *the robe of a field of happiness*, called *the robe of endurance*, called *the robe without form*, called *the robe of compassion*, called *the robe of the Tathāgata*, and called *the robe of anuttara-samyak-saṃbodhi*. We must receive and retain it as such. In the great Kingdom of Sung today, people who call themselves students of the precepts, because they are drunk on the wine of the śrāvaka, are neither ashamed, regretful, nor aware that they have received the transmission of a lineage which is alien to their own clan. Having changed the kaṣāya that has been transmitted from the Western Heavens and handed down through the ages from Han to Tang China, they follow small thoughts. It is due to the small view that they are like

29. 作 (SA), to produce, to make, or to do, sometimes represents the Sanskrit *saṃskṛta*, which describes elaboration or artificiality. 作 (SA) thus includes the connotation of intentional effort. See chap. 10, *Shoaku-makusa*. Master Dogen describes Zazen as 無作 (MUSA), "without elaboration," or "unadorned;" that is, natural.

30. *Samādhi* means the balanced state, and *dhāraṇī* means a mystical formula. So *samādhi-dhāraṇīs* are mystical formulae, the incantation of which is supposed to lead the practitioner into the balanced state.

that, and they should be ashamed of [their] small view. Given that they now wear a robe [based on] their own small thinking, they probably lack many [other] of the Buddhist dignified forms. Such things happen because their learning of, and reception of the transmission of, the Buddhist forms, are incomplete. The fact is evident that the body-and-mind of the Tathāgata has been authentically transmitted only in the lineage of the patriarchs, and it has not spread into the customs of those other lineages. If they knew only one Buddhist form in ten thousand they would never destroy the Buddha's robe. Not having clarified even [the meaning of] sentences, they have never been able to hear the fundamental.

[155] There again, to decide that coarse cotton is the only material for the robe runs deeply counter to the Buddha-Dharma; above all it ruins the Buddha-robe. Disciples of the Buddha should not wear [a robe made according to this rule]. Why? [Because] to uphold a view about cloth ruins the kaṣāya. It is pitiful that the views of the śrāvaka of the small vehicle are so tortuous. After their views about cloth have been demolished, the Buddha's robe will be realized. What I am saying about the use of silk and cotton is not the teaching of one buddha or two buddhas; it is the great Dharma of all the buddhas to see rags as the best and purest material for the robe. When, for the present, we list the ten sorts of rags among those [rags], they include silk, cotton, and other kinds of cloth too.[31] Must we not take rags of silk? If we are like that, we go against the Buddha's truth. If we hated silk, we would also have to hate cotton. Where is the reason to hate silk or cotton? To hate silk thread because it is produced by killing is very laughable. Is cotton not the habitat of living things? Sentiment about sentience and insentience is not liberated from the sentiment of the common and sentimental: how could it know the Buddha's kaṣāya? There is further speaking of nonsense by those who bring forth arguments about transformed thread.[32] This also is laughable. Which [material] is not a transformation? Those people believe the ears which hear of *transformation*, but they doubt the eyes which see transformation itself. They seem to have no ears in their eyes, and no eyes in their ears. Where are their ears and eyes at the moment of the present?[33] Now remember, while we are collecting rags, there may be cotton that looks like silk and there may be silk that looks like cotton. When we use it, we should not call it silk and we should not call it cotton; we should just call it rags. Because it is rags it is, as rags, beyond silk and beyond cotton. Even if there are human beings or gods who have survived as rags, we should not call them sentient, [but] they may be rags. Even if there are pine trees or chrysanthemums which have become rags, we should not call them insentient, [but] they may be rags. When we recognize the truth that rags are neither silk nor cotton, and that they are beyond pearls and jewels, rags are realized and we meet rags for the first time. Before views about silk and cotton have withered and fallen, we have never seen rags even in a dream. If we retain views about the cloth—even if we have spent a lifetime receiving and retaining coarse cotton cloth as a kaṣāya—that is not the authentic transmission of the Buddha's robe. At the same time, the various kinds of kaṣāya include cotton kaṣāya, silk kaṣāya, and leather

---

31. The ten sorts of rags are given at the end of para. [165] in this chapter. The point of the classification is to determine how rags were discarded, not their original material.

32. Some people thought that silk is the result of an artificial process, and is therefore not natural.

33. To hear with the eyes and to see with the ears suggests inclusive intuition, as opposed to discriminating intellectual recognition and sensory perception.

kaṣāya: all of these have been worn by buddhas. They have the Buddhist merits of the Buddha's robe, and they possess the fundamental principle that has been authentically transmitted without interruption. But people who are not liberated from common sentiment make light of the Buddha-Dharma; not believing the Buddha's words, they aim blindly to follow the sentiment of the common man. They must be called non-Buddhists who have attached themselves to the Buddha-Dharma; they are people who destroy the right Dharma. Some claim to have changed the Buddha-robe in accordance with the teaching of celestial beings. In that case, they must aspire to celestial buddhahood. Or have they become the descendants of gods? The Buddha's disciples expound the Buddha-Dharma for celestial beings; they should not ask celestial beings about the truth. It is pitiful that those who lack the authentic transmission of the Buddha-Dharma are like this. The view of the celestial multitudes and the view of the Buddha's disciples are very different in greatness, but gods come down to seek instruction in the Dharma from the Buddha's disciples. The reason is that the Buddhist view and the celestial view are very different. Discard, and do not learn, the small views of śrāvakas of precepts sects. Remember that they are the small vehicle. The Buddha says, *"One can repent for killing one's father or killing one's mother, but one cannot repent for insulting the Dharma."*

[160] In general, the way of small views and fox-like suspicion is not the original intention of the Buddha. The great truth of the Buddha-Dharma is beyond the small vehicle. No-one outside of the patriarch's state of truth, which is transmitted with the Dharma-treasury, has known of the authentic transmission of the great precepts of the buddhas. Long ago, [the story goes,] in the middle of the night on Obai, the Buddha's robe and Dharma are transmitted authentically onto the head of the Sixth Patriarch.[34] This is truly the authentic tradition for transmission of the Dharma and transmission of the robe. It is [possible] because the Fifth Patriarch knows a person.[35] Fellows of the fourth effect and the three clever stages, as well as the likes of [bodhisattvas in] the ten sacred stages[36] and the likes of commentary-teachers and sutra-teachers of philosophical schools, would give the [robe and Dharma] to Jinshu;[37] they would not transmit them authentically to the Sixth Patriarch. Nevertheless, when Buddhist patriarchs select Buddhist patriarchs, they transcend the path of common sentiment, and so the Sixth Patriarch has already become the Sixth Patriarch. Remember, the truth of knowing a person and of knowing oneself, which the Buddhist patriarchs transmit from rightful successor to rightful successor, is not easily supposed. Later, a monk asks the Sixth Patriarch, *"Should we see the robe you received in the middle of the night on Obai as cotton, or*

---

34. The story of the transmission between Master Daiman Konin and Master Daikan Eno is contained in chap. 30, *Gyoji*. 頂上に (CHOJO *ni*), "on top of the head," suggests the behavior of placing the kaṣāya on the head in veneration.

35. The ability to know a true person is discussed at the end of chap. 52, *Bukkyo*. At the time of the transmission, Master Daikan Eno was employed as a laborer at the temple.

36. A *śrāvaka* passes through four stages: 1) *srotāpanna* (entry into the stream), 2) *sakṛdāgāmin* (the state of being subject to one return), 3) *anāgāmin* (the state which is not subject to returning), and 4) *arhat* (the fourth effect, which is the ultimate state of the *śrāvaka*). A *bodhisattva* passes through fifty-two stages or states: ten stages of belief, thirty states classified as the three clever stages, ten sacred stages, the balanced state of truth, and finally the fine state of truth.

37. Ācārya Jinshu was the most intelligent monk in Master Daiman Konin's order, accomplished at poetry and revered by emperors. See chap. 22, *Kokyo*.

should we see it as silk, or should we see it as raw silk?[38] *In short, as what material should we see it?"* The Sixth Patriarch says, *"It is not cotton, it is not silk, and it is not raw silk."* The words of the founding Patriarch of Sokei are like this. Remember, the Buddha-robe is not silk, not cotton, and not cotton crepe. Those who, on the contrary, heedlessly recognize [the robe] as silk, as cotton, or as cotton crepe are the sort who insult the Buddha-Dharma. How could they know the Buddha's kaṣāya? Furthermore, there are episodes of the precepts being taken with [the Buddha's] *"Welcome!"* That the kaṣāya gained by these [monks] is utterly beyond discussion of silk and cotton is the Buddha's instruction in the Buddhist truth. In another case, the robe of Śāṇavāsa when he is a layman is a secular garment, but when he leaves family life it becomes a kaṣāya. We should quietly consider this fact. We should not brush it aside as if we did not see or hear it. Moreover, there is a fundamental principle which has been authentically transmitted from buddha to buddha, and from patriarch to patriarch, and which the sort who count words in sentences cannot sense and cannot fathom. Truly, how could the thousand changes and the myriad transformations of the Buddha's truth belong in the limited area of ordinary folk? The [real state of] samādhi exists, and [real practices of] dhāraṇī[39] exist, [but] those who count grains of sand can never find [these] valuable pearls inside their clothes. We should esteem, as the right standard of the kaṣāya of all the buddhas, the material, color, and measurements of the present kaṣāya which has been received in the authentic transmission from Buddhist patriarchs. The precedents for it, in the Western Heavens and the Eastern Lands, going back to ancient times and arriving at the present, are of long standing; and people who have distinguished the right [precedents] from the wrong have already transcended the state of enlightenment. Even though outside of the Buddhism of the patriarchs there are those who claim [to have] the kaṣāya, no original patriarch has ever affirmed [their robes] as the twigs and leaves [of the original kaṣāya]; how could [their robes] germinate the seeds of good roots?[40] How much less could they bear real fruit? We now not only are seeing and hearing Buddha-Dharma that we have not met in vast kalpas; we [also] have been able to see and to hear the Buddha's robe, to learn about the Buddha's robe, and to receive and to retain the Buddha's robe. This just exactly means that we are meeting the Buddha, we are hearing the voice of the Buddha, we are radiating the brightness of the Buddha, we are receiving and using the state received and used by the Buddha, we are receiving the one-to-one transmission of the mind of the Buddha, and we are getting the Buddha's marrow.

[165] For material to make the kaṣāya we invariably use that which is pure. *Pure* describes material offered by a donor of pure faith, or bought at a market, or sent by celestial beings, or donated by dragons, or donated by demons, or donated by kings and ministers, or [even] pure leather. We may use all such material. At the same time, we esteem the ten sorts of rags as pure. The ten sorts of rags are namely:

1) rags chewed by an ox, 2) rags gnawed by rats, 3) rags scorched by fire, 4) rags [soiled by] menstruation, 5) rags [soiled by] childbirth, 6) rags [offered at] a shrine, 7) rags [left at] a graveyard, 8) rags [offered in] petitional prayer, 9) rags [discarded by] a king's of-

38. "Raw silk" means silk that has not been dyed.

39. Master Dogen interpreted *dhāraṇī* as concrete practices which have real power. See chap. 55, *Darani.*

40. 善根 (ZENKON), means good conduct as the root of happiness.

ficers, 10) rags brought back [from a funeral].

[166] We esteem these ten sorts as especially pure material. In secular society they throw them away, [but] in Buddhism we use them. From these customs we can know the difference between the secular world and Buddhism. So when we want pure [material] we should look for these ten sorts. Finding them, we can know what is pure and we can intuit and affirm what is not pure. We can know mind and we can intuit and affirm body. When we obtain these ten sorts, whether they are silk or whether they are cotton, we should consider their purity and impurity. If we understand that the reason we use these rags is to idly make ourselves shabby with shabby robes, that might be extremely stupid. Rags have [always] been used in Buddhism for their splendor and beauty. In Buddhism, what makes our attire shabby is clothes which have come from impurity—[clothes of] brocade, embroidered silk, silk twill, and sheer silk, [clothes of] gold, silver, precious gems, and so on. This is the meaning of shabbiness. In general, whether in the Buddhism of this land or of other worlds, when we use pure and beautiful [cloth], it should be of these ten sorts. Not only has it transcended the limitations of purity and impurity, it also is beyond the limited sphere of the superfluous and the absence of the superfluous.[41] Do not discuss it as matter or mind. It is not connected with gain and loss. [The fact] is only that those who receive and retain the authentic transmission are Buddhist patriarchs; for when we are in the state of a Buddhist patriarch we receive the authentic transmission. To receive and to retain this [transmission] as a Buddhist patriarch does not depend on manifestation or non-manifestation of the body, and does not depend on upholding or non-upholding of the mind, [but] the authentic transmission goes on being received. Absolutely, we should regret that in this country, Japan, monks and nuns of recent ages have, for a long time, gone without wearing the kaṣāya; and we should be glad that we can receive and retain [the kaṣāya] now. Even lay men and women who receive and keep the Buddhist precepts should wear the five-stripe, seven-stripe, and nine-stripe kaṣāya. How then could people who have left family life fail to wear [the kaṣāya]? It is said that [everyone] from King Brahmā and the gods of the six heavens,[42] down to secular men, secular women, and male and female slaves, should receive the Buddhist precepts and wear the kaṣāya; how could bhikṣus and bhikṣuṇīs fail to wear it? It is said that even animals should receive the Buddhist precepts and wear the kaṣāya; how could disciples of the Buddha fail to wear the Buddha's robe? So those who want to become disciples of the Buddha, regardless of whether they are gods above, human beings, kings of nations, or government officials, and irrespective of whether they are lay people, monks, slaves, or animals, should receive and keep the Buddhist precepts and should receive the authentic transmission of the kaṣāya. This is just the direct way to enter authentically into the state of buddha.

[170] *"When washing the kaṣāya, you should mix miscellaneous powdered incense into the water. After drying [the kaṣāya] in the sun, fold it and put it in a high place, serve offerings to it of incense and flowers, and make three prostrations. Then, kneeling up, humbly receive it upon the head and, with the hands joined, render devotion by reciting the following verse:*

---

41. 漏 (RO) and 無漏 (MURO), which represent the Sanskrit *āsrava* and *anāsrava*, suggest the presence and absence of emotional distress.

42. 六天 (ROKUTEN) or 六欲天 (ROKU-YOKU-TEN), are the six heavens of the world of volition, or (as in this case) the gods therein.

How great is the clothing of liberation,
Formless, field of happiness, robe!
Devoutly wearing the Tathāgata's teaching,
Widely I will save living beings.

After reciting [this verse] three times, stand up on the ground and wear [the kaṣāya] devoutly."[43]

[170] During my stay in Sung China, making effort on the long platform, I saw that my neighbor every morning at the time of releasing the stillness, would lift up his kaṣāya and place it on his head; then, holding his hands together in veneration, he would silently recite the verse. At that time, there arose in me a feeling I had never before experienced. [My] body was overfilled with joy, and tears of gratitude secretly fell and moistened the lapels of my gown. The reason was that when I had read the Āgama sutras previously, I had noticed sentences about humbly receiving the kaṣāya upon the head, but I had not clarified the standards for this behavior and had not understood it clearly. Seeing it done now, before my very eyes, I was overjoyed. I thought to myself, *"It is a pity that when I was in my homeland there was no master to teach [me] this, and no good friend to tell [me] of it. How could I not regret, how could I not deplore, passing so much time in vain? Seeing it and hearing it now, I can rejoice in past good conduct. If I had been idly rubbing shoulders in the temples of my home country, how could I have sat shoulder-to-shoulder with this treasure of a monk who is actually wearing the Buddha's robe?"* Sadness and joy were not one-sided. Tears of gratitude fell in thousands and tens of thousands. Then I secretly vowed, *"One way or another, unworthy though I am, I will receive the authentic transmission of the right traditions of the Buddha-Dharma and, out of compassion for living beings in my homeland, I will cause them to see and to hear the robe and the Dharma which have been authentically transmitted from buddha to buddha."* The vow made at that time has not now been in vain; the bodhisattvas, in families and out of families, who have received and retained the kaṣāya are many. This is a matter in which to rejoice. People who have received and retained the kaṣāya should humbly receive it upon their head every day and night. The merit [of this] may be especially excellent and supremely excellent. The seeing and hearing of a phrase or a verse may be as in the story of *"on trees and on rocks,"* [but] the merit of the authentic transmission of the kaṣāya is hardly encountered through the ten directions. In the 10th lunar month, in the winter of the 17th year of Kajo in great Sung [China], two Korean[44] monks came to the city of Keigen-fu. One was called Chigen, the other Kei-un. Both of them were always discussing the meaning of Buddhist sutras, and they were also men of letters. But they had no kaṣāya and no pātra; they were like secular people. It was pitiful that though they had the external form of bhikṣus they did not have the Dharma of bhikṣus. This may have been because they were from a minor nation in a remote land. When people from our country who have the external form of bhikṣus travel abroad, they are likely to be the same as those two monks. Śākyamuni Buddha himself received [the kaṣāya] upon his head

43. This paragraph is in the form of a quotation from a sutra in Chinese. The content is the same as the second half of para. [78] on washing the kaṣāya in the previous chapter. But that paragraph is written in Japanese, whereas this paragraph is written in Chinese characters only.

44. "Korean" is 三韓 (SANKAN), "three-Koreas." In *Kesa-kudoku* the word is 高麗 (KORAI), which was the name of one of the three states comprising the Korean peninsular at that time.

for twelve years, never setting it aside. As already his distant descendants, we should emulate this. To turn the forehead away from prostrations idly done for fame and gain to gods, to spirits, to kings, and to retainers, and to turn it now towards the humble reception upon the head of the Buddha's robe, is a joyful and great happy event.

Shobogenzo Den-e

The 1st day of winter, in the 1st year of Ninji.[45]

Written at Kannon-dori-kosho-horin-ji temple—a śramaṇa who entered Sung [China] and received the transmission of Dharma, Dogen.

45. The 1st day of the 10th lunar month, 1240.

[14]

山水経

SANSUIGYO

The Sutra of Mountains and Water

***San** means "mountains," **sui** means "water"—rivers, lakes, and so on. **Sansui** suggests natural scenery, or Nature itself. **Kyo** or **gyo** means Buddhist sutras. So **Sansuigyo** means mountains and water, or Nature, as Buddhist sutras. Buddhism is basically a religion of belief in the Universe, and Nature is the Universe showing its real form. So to look at Nature is to look at the Buddhist truth itself. For this reason Master Dogen believed that Nature is just Buddhist sutras. In this chapter he explains the real form of Nature, giving particular emphasis to relativity in Nature.*

[175] **The mountains and water of the present** are the realization of the words of eternal buddhas. Both [mountains and water] abide in place in the Dharma, having realized ultimate virtue. Because they are in the state before the kalpa of emptiness, they are vigorous activity in the present. Because they are the self before the sprouting of creation, they are real liberation. The virtues of the mountains are so high and wide that we always realize moral virtue which can ride the clouds by relying on the mountains, and we unfailingly liberate the subtle effectiveness which follows the wind by relying on the mountains.

[176] Master Kai[1] of Taiyo-zan mountain preaches to the assembly, *"The Blue Mountains are constantly walking. The Stone Woman bears children by night."* Mountains lack none of the virtues with which mountains should be equipped. For this reason, they are constantly abiding in stillness and constantly walking. We must painstakingly learn in practice the virtue of this walking. The walking of mountains must be like the walking of human beings; therefore, even though it does not look like human walking,[2] do not doubt the walking of the mountains. The words preached now by the Buddhist Patriarch are already pointing to *walking*, and this is his attainment of the fundamental. We should pursue to the ultimate his preaching to the assembly about *constant walking:* it is

---

1. Master Fuyo Dokai (1043–1118), a Buddhist patriarch in Master Dogen's lineage, the forty-fifth patriarch from the Buddha. Having succeeded Master Tosu Gisei, Master Fuyo preached Buddhism on Mt. Taiyo and elsewhere until he refused a title and a purple robe from the emperor and was banished. When he was eventually pardoned, he built a thatched hut on Mt. Fuyo and lived there in the style of the ancient patriarchs.

2. 行歩 (GYOHO), or "going steps." In the quotation, and elsewhere in Master Dogen's commentary the expression is 運歩 (UNPO), or "transporting steps." Both expressions mean walking.

because [the mountains] are *walking* that they are *constant*.[3] The walking of the Blue Mountains is swifter than the wind, but human beings in the mountains do not sense it or know it. Being *in the mountains*[4] describes the *opening of flowers* in the *[real] world*.[5] People out of the mountains never sense it and never know it—people who have no eyes to see the mountains do not sense, do not know, do not see, and do not hear this concrete fact. If we doubt the walking of the mountains, we also do not yet know our own walking. It is not that we do not have our own walking, but we do not yet know and have not yet clarified our own walking. When we know our own walking, then we will surely also know the walking of the Blue Mountains. The Blue Mountains are already beyond the sentient and beyond the insentient. The self is already beyond the sentient and beyond the insentient. We cannot doubt the present walking of the Blue Mountains. [Though] we do not know how many Dharma-worlds we should use as a scale when taking in the Blue Mountains, we should investigate in detail the walking of the Blue Mountains as well as our own walking. There should be investigation both of backward steps[6] and of stepping backward.[7] We should investigate the fact that just at the moment before the sprouting of creation, and since before the King of Emptiness,[8] walking—in forward steps and backward steps—has never stopped even for an instant. If the walking ceased, the Buddhist patriarchs could not manifest themselves in reality. If there were an end to the walking, the Buddha-Dharma could not reach the present day. Forward walking never ceases, and backward walking never ceases. The moment of forward walking does not oppose backward walking, and the moment of backward walking does not oppose forward walking.[9] We call this virtue *the mountains flowing*, and we call it *the flowing mountains*. The Blue Mountains master in practice the act of walking and the East Mountain learns in practice the act of moving on water; therefore, this learning in practice is the mountains' learning in practice. The mountains, without changing their body-and-mind, with the face and eyes of mountains, have been traveling around learning in practice. Never insult them by saying that the Blue Mountains cannot walk or that the East Mountain cannot move on water. It is because of the grossness of the viewpoint of the vulgar that they doubt the phrase *"the Blue Mountains are walking."* It is due to the poorness of their scant experience that they are astonished

---

3. 常 (JO) means both constant and eternal. Both meanings are relevant here: action makes things balanced (for example, pedaling a bicycle) and action gives things eternal meaning.

4. 山中 (SANCHU). 中 (CHU) means "in" or "in the state of," and Master Dogen sometimes uses the character to mean "in the state of reality." So 山中 (SANCHU) means in the mountains or in the reality of the mountains.

5. 世界裏の華開 (SEKAIRI *no* KEKAI). This alludes to the words of Master Prajñātara, 華開世界起 (KEKAI-SEKAI-KI), "the opening of flowers is the occurrence of the world," suggesting that the real world itself is just the appearance of phenomena. See for example chap. 42, *Kuge*.

6. 退歩 (TAIHO). In *Fukan-zazengi* Master Dogen describes Zazen as 退歩 (TAIHO), a backward step (to our original state). 退歩 (TAIHO) means concrete backward steps.

7. 歩退 (HOTAI) means stepping backward as a principle. We should not only investigate concrete backward steps (for example, by sitting in Zazen, lifting weights, doing prostrations, having a bath, et cetera) but also investigate the meaning of stepping backward (for example, by reading Shobogenzo, researching the function of the autonomic nervous system, drawing inferences from trial and error in daily life, et cetera).

8. 空王 (KU-O) is identified with Bhīṣmagarjitasvara-rāja, or the King of Majestic Voice, the first Buddha to appear in the Kalpa of Emptiness. See chap. 20 of the Lotus Sutra.

9. Each action is done at an independent moment of the present.

at the words *flowing mountains*. Now, not even fully understanding[10] the words *flowing water*, they are drowned in prejudice and ignorance. This being so, they esteem as defining concepts, and esteem as lifeblood, their enumeration of the accumulated virtues [of mountains].[11] The act of walking exists, the act of flowing exists, and moments in which mountains give birth to mountain children exist. By virtue of the fact that mountains become Buddhist patriarchs, Buddhist patriarchs have manifested themselves in reality like this.[12] Though there may be eyes in which grass, trees, soil, stones, fences, and walls are realized, that moment is beyond doubt and beyond disturbance; it is not "total realization." Though moments are realized in which [the mountains] are seen to be adorned with the seven treasures, [those moments] are not "the real refuge." Though visions are realized [of the mountains] as the area in which buddhas practice the truth, [those visions] are not necessarily something to be loved. Though some have got the brains to realize a vision [of the mountains] as the unthinkable merit of the buddhas, reality is not merely this.[13] Every "realization" is an instance of object and subject. We do not esteem such ["realizations"] as the Buddhist patriarchs' action in the state of truth: they are one-sided and narrow views.[14] The moving of circumstances and the moving of mind are criticized by the Great Saint.[15] Explanations of mind and explanations of the nature[16] are not affirmed by the Buddhist patriarchs. Seeing the mind and seeing the nature[17] is the animated activity of non-Buddhists. Staying in words and staying in phrases is not the speech of liberation. There is [a state] which has got free from states like these: it is expressed *"the Blue Mountains are constantly walking"* and *"the East Mountain moves on water."* We should master it in detail.

[182] [In the words] *"The Stone Woman bears children by night"* Time, in which the Stone Woman bears children, is called *night*. In general, there are male stones and female stones, and there are neither male nor female stones, whose practical function supports the heavens and supports the earth. There are heavenly stones and there are earthly stones—as the secular say, but few people know.[18] We should know the facts of child-

10. "Fully understand" is 七通八達 (SHICHITSU-HATTATSU), lit. "pass through seven directions and arrive at eight destinations," suggesting thorough understanding from many viewpoints.

11. Vulgar people do not value the unthinkable reality of mountains, but they esteem the characteristics of mountains which they are able to enumerate.

12. かくのごとく (*kakunogotoku*), "like this," indicates what is already present here and now. かくのごとく (*kakunogotoku*) in Chinese characters is 如是 (NYOZE) which Master Dogen uses as an expression of reality as it is. See chap. 17, *Hokke-ten-hokke*.

13. By denying the four views Master Dogen emphasized the fact that reality cannot be grasped by intellectual thinking.

14. 一隅の管見 (ICHIGU *no* KANKEN), lit. "one-corner pipe-views."

15. "The Great Saint" means the Buddha. Moving circumstances (like a pot) and moving mind (like water) is the theme of a story about Master Nansen Fugan and Master Godai Impo (see chap. 81, *O-saku-sendaba*). Though the words of the story and the words here are slightly different, the point is the same: that separation between subject and object can be transcended by action in the moment of the present.

16. 説心説性 (SESSHIN-SESSHO), or "Expounding the Mind and Expounding the Nature," is the title of chap. 48, *Sesshin-sessho*.

17. 見心見性 (KENSHIN-KENSHO). People in Japan who pursue enlightenment by thinking about *koan* (Buddhist stories) often call the enlightenment they pursue 見性 (KENSHO), "seeing the nature."

18. Subjectively or romantically, we assign gender or other human characteristics to things in Nature. Objectively or scientifically, we do not. Master Dogen's viewpoint is beyond the subjective and objective views. Buddhist knowing of stones is more real than the romantic descriptions found, for ex-

birth: At the time of childbirth, are parent and child both transformed? How could we learn in practice only that childbirth is realized as [the parent] becoming the parent of a child? We should learn in practice, and should penetrate to the end, that the Time of [the child] becoming the child of the parent is the practice-and-experience of the reality of childbirth.

[183] Great Master Unmon Kyoshin[19] says, *"The East Mountain moves on water."* The point realized in these words is that all mountains are an East Mountain, and every East Mountain moves on water.[20] Thus [mountains] such as the nine mountains of Mt. Sumeru have been realized, and they have practiced and experienced.[21] This state is called *"the East Mountain."* Nevertheless, how could Unmon be liberated in the skin, flesh, bones, and marrow, the practice-and-experience, and the vigorous activity of the East Mountain.[22]

[184] At the present time in the great Kingdom of Sung, there is a group of unreliable[23] fellows who have now formed such a crowd that they cannot be beaten by a few real [people]. They say that the present talk of the East Mountain moving on water, and stories such as Nansen's sickle,[24] are stories beyond rational understanding. Their idea is as follows: *"A story which involves images and thoughts is not a Zen story of the Buddhist patriarchs. Stories beyond rational understanding are the stories of the Buddhist patriarchs. This is why we esteem Obaku's use of the stick and Rinzai's shout,[25] which are beyond rational understanding and which do not involve images and thoughts, as the great realization before the sprouting of creation. The reason that the expedient means of many past masters employ tangle[26] cutting phrases is that [those phrases] are beyond rational understanding."* Those fellows who speak like this have never met a true teacher and they have no eyes of learning in

---

ample, in secular Chinese literature.

19. Master Unmon Bun-en (864–949), a successor of Master Seppo Gison, who was a sixth-generation descendant of Master Seigen Gyoshi. It is said that there were never less than a thousand students in Master Unmon's order, and that in his thirty years of spreading Buddhism he produced more than ninety successors. Great Master Kyoshin is his posthumous title as founder of the Unmon sect.

20. An East Mountain means a real mountain.

21. Master Dogen illustrated the principle in the previous sentence with the concrete example of Mt. Sumeru and the eight mountains which surround it.

22. Master Dogen criticizes Master Unmon in, for example, chap. 52, *Bukkyo*.

23. "Unreliable" is 杜撰 (ZUSAN), lit. "edited by Zu [or To]." It is said that poems edited by To Moku of the Sung Dynasty were very irregular and unreliable. Therefore people of the time used the words "edited by Zu (or To)" to represent unreliability.

24. Master Gan of Mt. Nansen in Chishu district [Master Nansen Fugan (748–834)] is doing chores on the mountain. A monk comes by and asks the Master, *"Where does Nansen's road lead?"* The Master holds up his sickle and says, *"I got this sickle for thirty pennies."* The monk says, *"I didn't ask about you paying thirty pennies for the sickle. Where does Nansen's road lead?"* The Master says, *"And now that I can use it, it is really handy."* (*Shinji-shobogenzo*, pt. 2, no. 54). The monk wanted to know what Master Nansen considered to be the aim of his life, but he asked his question as if asking for directions. Master Nansen recommended the monk not to be conscious only of the idealistic aim, but also to recognize concrete facts. The monk insisted that he also wanted to know what the real aim of our life is. Master Nansen's answer was that he was acting in reality.

25. Master Obaku Ki-un (died c. 855) was known for striking his disciples, including Master Rinzai Kigen (c. 815–867), to impress on them that reality is different from thinking and feeling (see for example *Shinji-shobogenzo* pt. 1, no. 27). Master Rinzai used to achieve the same result by yelling *katsu!* (ibid.).

26. 葛藤 (KATTO), "arrowroot and wisteria," "entanglement," or "the complicated," is the title of chap. 46, *Katto*.

practice; they are small dogs who do not deserve to be discussed. For the last two or three hundred years in the land of Sung there have been many such demons and shavelings [like those] in the band of six.[27] It is pitiful that the great truth of the Buddhist Patriarch is going to ruin. The understanding of these [shavelings] is inferior even to that of śrāvakas of the small vehicle; they are more stupid than non-Buddhists. They are not lay people, they are not monks, they are not human beings, and they are not gods; they are more stupid than animals learning the Buddha's truth. What the shavelings call "stories beyond rational understanding" are beyond rational understanding only to them;[28] the Buddhist patriarchs are not like that. Even though [rational ways] are not rationally understood by those [shavelings], we should not fail to learn in practice the Buddhist patriarchs' ways of rational understanding. If ultimately there is no rational understanding, the reasoning which those [shavelings] have now set forth also cannot hit the target. There are many of this sort in all directions of Sung China, and I have seen and heard them before my own eyes. They are pitiful. They do not know that images and thoughts are words and phrases, and they do not know that words and phrases transcend images and thoughts. When I was in China I laughed at them, but they had nothing to say for themselves and were just wordless. Their present negation of rational understanding is nothing but a false notion. Who has taught it to them? Though they lack a natural teacher, they have the non-Buddhist view of naturalism. Remember, this *"The East Mountain moves on water"* is the bones and marrow of the Buddhist patriarchs. Waters are realized at the foot of the East Mountain;[29] thereupon mountains ride the clouds and walk through the sky. The crowns of the waters are mountains, whose walking, upward or downward, is always *on water*.[30] Because the mountains' toes can walk over all kinds of water, making the waters dance, the walking is free in all directions[31] and *practice-and-experience is not nonexistent*.[32] Water is neither strong nor weak, neither wet nor dry, neither moving nor still, neither cold nor warm, neither existent nor nonexistent, neither delusion nor realization. When it is solid it is harder than a diamond; who could break it? Melted, it is softer than diluted milk; who could break it? This being so, it is impossible to doubt the real virtues that [water] possesses. For the present, we should learn in practice the moments in which it is possible to put on the eyes and look in the ten directions at the water of the ten directions. This is not learning in practice only of the time when human beings and gods see water; there is learning in practice of water seeing water.[33] Because water practices and ex-

---

27. 六群禿子 (ROKUGUN-TOKUSHI). The band of six shavelings in the Buddha's order were Nanda, Upananda, Kālodāyin, Chanda, Aśvaka, and Punarvasu. It is said that their misconduct caused the formulation of precepts. 禿子 (TOKUSHI), shaveling (lit. bald child) means someone who becomes a monk in form but who has no will to the truth.

28. The original word, なんぢ (*nanji*), means "you." Master Dogen usually uses this form when directing criticism at someone to whom he does not need to be polite.

29. Rivers, streams, lakes, et cetera are not only an abstraction, but are realized at the foot of a real mountain.

30. In other words, on the basis of reality.

31. 七縦八横 (HICHIJU-HACHI-O), lit. "seven horizontals and eight verticals."

32. 修証即不無 (SHUSHO-SOKU-FU-MU). Master Nangaku Ejo's expression of practice and experience in Zazen. See chap. 7, *Senjo*; chap. 29, *Inmo*; chap. 63, *Hensan*.

33. Master Dogen uses the formula A sees A, A meets A, A restricts A, A succeeds A, et cetera, to suggest the real existence of A.

periences water, there is the investigation in practice of water speaking water. We should manifest in reality the path on which self encounters self. We should advance and retreat along the vigorous path on which the external world exhausts in practice the external world, and we should spring free.

[189] In general, ways of seeing mountains and water differ according to the type of being [that sees them]: There are beings which see what we call water as a string of pearls,[34] but this does not mean that they see a string of pearls as water. They probably see as their water a form that we see as something else. We see their strings of pearls as water. There are [beings] which see water as wonderful flowers; but this does not mean that they use flowers as water. Demons see water as raging flames, and see it as pus and blood. Dragons and fish see it as a palace, and see it as a tower. Some see [water] as the seven treasures and the maṇi gem;[35] some see it as trees and forests and fences and walls; some see it as the pure and liberated Dharma-nature; some see it as the real human body;[36] and some see it as [the oneness of] physical form and mental nature. Human beings see it as water, the causes and conditions of death and life. Thus, what is seen does indeed differ according to the kind of being [that sees]. Now let us be wary of this. Is it that there are various ways of seeing one object? Or is it that we have mistakenly assumed the various images to be one object? At the crown of effort, we should make still further effort. If the above is so, then practice-and-experience and pursuit of the truth also may not be [only] of one kind or of two kinds; and the ultimate state also may be of thousands of kinds and myriad varieties. When we keep this point in mind, although there are many kinds of water, it seems that there is no original water, and no water of many kinds. At the same time, the various waters which accord with the kinds of beings [that see water] do not depend on mind, do not depend on body, do not arise from karma, are not self-reliant, and are not reliant upon others; they have the liberated state of reliance on water itself. This being so, water is beyond earth, water, fire, wind, space, consciousness, and so on. Water is beyond blue, yellow, red, white, or black and beyond sights, sounds, smells, tastes, sensations, or properties; at the same time, as earth, water, fire, wind, space, and so on, water is naturally realized. Because the nations and palaces of the present are like this, it may be difficult to state by what and into what they are created. To assert that they hang on the circle of space and the circle of wind[37] is not true to ourselves and not true to others; it is to speculate on the basis of the suppositions of the small view. People make this assertion because they think that, without somewhere to hang, [dharmas] would not be able to abide.[38]

---

34. Alludes to the metaphor of 一水四見 (ISSUI-SHIKEN), "one water, four views." The goddesses who are sometimes depicted floating in the sky in old Buddhist pictures see water as a string of pearls. Fish see water as a palace or as beautiful flowers. Demons hate water as pus and blood, because it puts out their fires and washes away their impurities. Human beings see water as water. See also chap. 3, *Genjo-koan*.

35. The Sanskrit *maṇi*, which means gem, in this case suggests the *cintāmaṇi*, a fabled gem capable of fulfilling every wish, said to be obtained from the dragon-king of the sea.

36. 真実人体 (SHINJITSU-NINTAI), the words of Master Chosa Keishin. See chap. 37, *Shinjin-gakudo;* chap. 47, *Sangai-yuishin;* chap. 50, *Shoho-jisso;* chap. 62, *Hensan;* chap. 91, *Yui-butsu-yo-butsu*.

37. In ancient Indian cosmology, the physical world is constructed of five elements, called five wheels or five circles (*pañca-maṇḍalaka* in Sanskrit): circles of earth, water, fire, wind, and space. (Interpreting the concepts more broadly: solids, liquids, combustion, gases, and space.)

38. See also discussion of a steelyard in chap. 38, *Muchu-setsumu*.

[193] The Buddha says, *"All dharmas are ultimately liberated; they are without an abode."*[39] Remember, although they are in the state of liberation, without any bonds, all dharmas are abiding in place.[40] Even so, when human beings look at water, the only way we see it is as flowing ceaselessly. This flowing takes many forms, each of which is an example of the human view: [Water] flows over the earth, flows through the sky, flows upward, and flows downward. It flows in a single winding brook, and it flows in the nine [great] depths.[41] It rises up to form clouds, and it comes down to form pools. Bunshi[42] says, *"The way of water is to ascend to the sky, forming rain and dew, and to descend to the earth, forming rivers and streams."* Now even the words of a secular person are like this. It would be most shameful for people who call themselves the descendants of the Buddhist Patriarch to be more ignorant than secular people. We can say that the way of water is beyond the recognition of water, but water is able actually to flow. Water is [also] beyond non-recognition, but water is able actually to flow.

[195] *"It ascends to the sky and forms rain and dew."* Remember, water rises up immeasurably high into the sky above to form rain and dew. Rain and dew are of various kinds corresponding to [the various kinds of] worlds. To say that there are places not reached by water is the teaching of śrāvakas of the small vehicle, or the wrong teaching of non-Buddhists. Water reaches into flames, it reaches into the mind and its images, into wit, and into discrimination, and it reaches into realization of the Buddha-nature.[43]

[195] *"It descends to the earth to form rivers and streams."* Remember, when water descends to the earth, it forms rivers and streams. The vitality of rivers and streams can become sages. Common and stupid folk today assume that water is always in rivers, streams, and oceans. This is not so. Rivers and oceans are realized in water.[44] Thus, water also exists in places which are not rivers and oceans; it is just that when water descends to the earth, it takes effect as rivers and oceans. Further, we must not understand that social worlds cannot exist or that Buddha-lands cannot exist at a place where water has formed rivers and oceans.[45] Even inside a single drop, countless Buddha-lands are realized. This does not mean that there is water within Buddha-lands, and does not mean that there are Buddha-lands inside water. The place where water exists is already beyond the three times and beyond the world of Dharma. Even so, it is the Universe in which water has been realized. Wherever Buddhist patriarchs go water goes, and wherever water goes Buddhist patriarchs are realized. This is why Buddhist patriarchs without exception, when taking up water, have treated it as [their] body-and-mind and have treated it as [their] thinking. This being so, that water rises up is not denied in any text, within [Buddhism] or without. The way of water pervades upward and down-

39. *Dai-ho-shak-kyo*, fascicle 87.

40. 住位 (JU-I), "abide in place," is short for 住法位 (JU-HO-I), "abide in place in the Dharma," which appears in the second sentence of this chapter.

41. 九淵 (KYU-EN) refers to nine famous deep river pools in China.

42. 文子 (BUNSHI) is a Taoist book in ten volumes. The book is said to have been written during the Sui dynasty (581–618) but some scholars suspect that it was written later and falsely dated earlier.

43. Examples such as the humidity of a flame, the dryness of wit, and realization in the sounds of the valley streams, negate the common-sense conception of the scope of water.

44. Rivers and water, or entity and substance, are one.

45. Reality (rivers and oceans) includes both the material (water), and the meaningful (human worlds, Buddhist lands).

ward, vertically and horizontally. At the same time, in the Buddhist sutras, *fire and wind rise upward, earth and water settle downward*. There is something to be learned in practice in this *upward* and *downward*. That is, we [must] learn in practice the Buddha's teaching of *upward* and *downward*, as follows: The place where earth and water go, we think of as *"downward"*[46] We do not think of downward as a place where earth and water go.[47] The place where fire and wind go is *upward*. The *world of Dharma* should not always be related to measurements upward, downward, and in the four diagonals;[48] at the same time, the four elements, the five elements, the six elements, and so on, relying on the concrete place to which they go, just momentarily establish the four-cornered Dharma world.[49] It is not to be assumed that the Heaven of Thoughtlessness[50] is above and that Avīci[51] Hell is below. Avīci is the whole world of Dharma, and Thoughtlessness is the whole world of Dharma. Still, when dragons and fish see water as a palace, they are probably like people looking at a palace, utterly unable to recognize that it is flowing away. If an onlooker were to explain to them *Your palace is flowing water*, the dragons and fish would likely be as startled as we were now to hear the assertion that mountains are flowing. Further, it may also be possible to maintain and to rely upon [the assertion] that there is such preaching in [every] railing, stair, and outdoor pillar of a palace or a mansion. Quietly, we should have been considering this reasoning and we should go on considering it.

[199] If we are not learning the state of liberation at the face of this place, we have not become free from the body and mind of the common man, we have not perfectly realized the land of Buddhist patriarchs, and we have not perfectly realized the palaces of the common man. Although human beings now are profoundly confident that the inner content of the seas and the inner content of the rivers is water, we still do not know what dragons, fish, and other beings view as water and use as water. Do not stupidly assume that every kind of being uses as water what we view as water. When people today who are learning Buddhism want to learn about water, we should not stick blindly in only the human sphere; we should move forward and learn water in the Buddha's state of truth. We should learn in practice how we see the water that Buddhist patriarchs use. Further, we should learn in practice whether there is water or whether there is no water in the houses of Buddhist patriarchs.

[200] Mountains have been the dwelling places of great saints since beyond the past and present. All the sages and all the saints have made the mountains into their inner sanctum and made the mountains into their body-and-mind; and by virtue of the sages and the saints the mountains have been realized. We tend to suppose, with respect to mountains in general, that countless great saints and great sages might be gathered

46. Concepts like "downward" originate with concrete facts like the location of earth and water (see chap. 42, *Tsuki*).

47. We remember that "downward" is only a concept, not an actual place.

48. 四維 (SHI-I), or "four corners"—north-west, south-west, south-east, and north-east.

49. 方隅法界 (HOGU-HOKKAI). 方 suggests 四方 (SHIHO), the four directions—north, south, east, and west. 隅 suggests 四隅 (SHIGU), the four corners. 方隅法界 (HOGU-HOKKAI) suggests concrete reality, as opposed to "the world of Dharma" as a religious concept.

50. 無想天 (MUSOTEN), from the Sanskrit *asaṃjñi-sattvaḥ*, is explained as a group of heavens in the world of matter.

51. *Avīci* is the Sanskrit name for the worst kind of hell.

there; but after we have entered the mountains there is not a single person to meet. There is only the realization of the vigorous activity of mountains. Not even the traces of our having entered remain. When we are in the secular world gazing at the mountains, and when we are in the mountains meeting the mountains, their heads and eyes are very different. Our notion that [the mountains] are not flowing and our view that [the mountains] are not flowing may not be the same as the view of dragons and fish.[52] While human beings and gods, in our own world, are in our element, other beings doubt this [notion and view of ours], or they may not even doubt it. This being so, we should study the phrase *mountains flow* under Buddhist patriarchs; we should not leave it open to doubt.[53] Acting once[54] is just *flowing;* acting once [more] is just *not flowing.* One time round is *flowing;* one time round is *not flowing.* Without this investigation in practice, it is not the right Dharma-wheel of the Tathāgata. An eternal Buddha[55] says, *"If you want to be able not to invite the karma of incessant [hell],*[56] *do not insult the right Dharma-wheel of the Tathāgata."* We should engrave these words on skin, flesh, bones, and marrow, we should engrave them on body-and-mind, on object-and-subject, we should engrave them on the immaterial, and we should engrave them on matter; they are [already] engraved *on trees and on rocks*[57] and they are [already] engraved *in fields and in villages.*[58] We generally say that mountains belong to a country, but [mountains] belong to people who love mountains. Mountains always love their occupiers, whereupon saints and sages, people of high virtue, enter the mountains. When saints and sages live in the mountains, because the mountains belong to these [sages and saints], trees and rocks abound and flourish, and birds and animals are mysteriously excellent. This is because the sages and saint have covered them with virtue. We should remember the fact that mountains like sages and the fact that [mountains] like saints. That many emperors have gone to the mountains to bow before sages and to question great saints is an excellent example in the past and the present. At such times, [the emperors] honor [the sages and saints] with the formalities due to a teacher, never conforming to secular norms. Imperial authority exerts no control whatever over the mountain sages. Clearly, the mountains are beyond the human world. On Kodo[59] [mountain] in the bygone days of Kaho,[60] the Yellow Emperor[61] visited Kosei, crawling on his knees and

52. In the view of dragons and fish, mountains may be flowing.

53. Given that even things which we take for granted are open to doubt, we should rely upon Buddhist patriarchs' teaching.

54. 拈一 (NEN-ITSU), lit."to pick up one." 拈 (NEN) means to pinch, or to pick up; it suggests an action. 一 (ITSU) means one.

55. Master Yoka Gengaku, in his poem *Shodoka*.

56. 無間地獄 (MUGEN-JIGOKU), "Incessant Hell," or "Hell Without Respite," represents the Sanskrit *Avīci*.

57. 若樹若石 (NYAKUJU-NYAKUSEKI). Alludes to the story of the Buddha's past life recorded in the *Mahāparinirvāṇa-sūtra*. See note 157 in chap. 12, *Kesa-kudoku.*

58. 若田若里 (NYAKUDEN-NYAKURI). Alludes to the Lotus Sutra (LS 3.72-74). See note 9 in chap. 13, *Den-e.*

59. The name of a mountain in modern Kansu province in China. The Taoist sage Kosei lived in a cave on Kodo mountain.

60. 華封 (KAHO), lit. "Flower Fiefdom," was a legendary utopian realm.

61. 黄帝 (KOTEI), the Yellow Emperor, was the third of the five rulers in the legendary period of Chinese history (dates estimated as 2852 B.C.– 2205 B.C.). He visited Kosei to ask the secret of immortality. The story is recorded in volume four of the Taoist text 莊子 (SOJI), attributed to Chang-tsu.

kowtowing to beg [instruction]. Śākyamuni Buddha left the palace of his father, the king, to enter the mountains, but his father, the king, did not resent the mountains. The royal father did not distrust those in the mountains who would teach the prince, whose twelve years of training in the truth were mostly spent in the mountains. The revelation of [the prince's] destiny as the King of Dharma also took place in the mountains. Truly, not even the wheel [-rolling] kings hold sway over the mountains. Remember, the mountains are beyond the boundaries of the human world and beyond the boundaries of the heavens above; we can never know the mountains with the human intellect. If [their flowing] is not to be compared with flowing in the human world, who can doubt the flowing, the non-flowing, and the other activities of the mountains?

[205] Again, since the ancient past, there have been from time to time sages and saints who lived by the water. When they live by the water, there are those who fish fishes, those who fish human beings, and those who fish the state of truth. Each of these is in the traditional stream of those who are *in the water*. Going further, there may be those who fish themselves, those who fish fishing, those who are fished by fishing, and those who are fished by the state of truth.[62] In days of old, when Master Tokujo[63] suddenly left Yakusan mountain to live amidst the river's mind, he got the sage[64] of the Katei River. Was this not fishing fishes? Was it not fishing human beings? Was it not fishing water? Was it not fishing himself? A person who is able to meet Tokujo is Tokujo;[65] and Tokujo's *teaching people*[66] is [a human being] meeting a human being. It is not only that there is water in the world; there are worlds in the world of water. And it is not only in water that such [worlds] exist. There are worlds of sentient beings in clouds, there are worlds of sentient beings in wind, there are worlds of sentient beings in fire, there are worlds of sentient beings in earth, there are worlds of sentient beings in the world of Dharma, there are worlds of sentient beings in a stalk of grass, and there are worlds of sentient beings in a staff. Wherever there are worlds of sentient beings, the world of Buddhist patriarchs inevitably exists at that place. We should carefully learn in practice the truth which is like this. In conclusion then, water is the palace of real dragons; it is beyond flowing and falling. If we recognize it as only flowing, the word *flowing* insults water, because, for example, [the word] forces [water] to be what is other than flowing

62. The action of fishing connects subject (fisherman) and object (fish), so Master Dogen uses fishing to suggest the principle of the mutual relation between subject and object in action.

63. Master Sensu Tokujo (dates unknown), a successor of Master Yakusan Igen (745–828). After receiving the Dharma from Master Yakusan he went to live on a river in the Katei valley of the Shushu district, working as a boatman (*Sensu* means boatman), and hoping to find among his passengers a human being with the will to the truth. Master Tokujo's brother disciple Master Dogo Enchi (769–835) recommended Master Kasan Zen-e (805–881) to go and visit Master Tokujo by the river. They had a lively conversation, at the conclusion of which Master Tokujo said that if we fish out all the river's waves (that is, if we do the impossible), we can meet the fish with the golden scales (realize our ideal) for the first time. Master Kasan covered his ears, and thus received Master Tokujo's affirmation. Finally, Master Tokujo told Master Kasan to go deep into the mountains and just teach the Dharma to one student or half a student. Master Dogen quoted at length this story about Master Tokujo and Master Kasan in *Shinji-shobogenzo*, pt. 1, no. 90.

64. Master Kasan Zen-e.

65. In chap. 61, *Kenbutsu*, Master Dogen teaches that a person in the state of buddha is meeting buddha. In this sentence, he substitutes Tokujo for Buddha.

66. 人を接する (*hito o sessuru*), lit. "to receive people." The story in *Shinji-shobogenzo* says 在華亭船上接人, *"he received people on a boat on the Katei river."*

itself. Water is nothing but water's *real form as it is*. Water is just the virtues of water itself; it is beyond *flowing*. When we master the flow and master the non-flow of a single body of water, the perfect realization of the myriad dharmas is realized at once. With mountains too, there are mountains contained in treasure, there are mountains contained in marshes, there are mountains contained in space, there are mountains contained in mountains,[67] and there is learning in practice in which mountains are contained in containment.[68] An eternal Buddha[69] says, *"Mountains are mountains. Water is water."* These words do not say that *"mountains"* are *"mountains;"* they say that mountains are mountains. This being so, we should master the mountains in practice. When we are mastering the mountains in practice, that is effort *in the mountains*. Mountains and water like this naturally produce sages and produce saints.

Shobogenzo Sansuigyo†

Preached to the assembly at Kannon-dori-kosho-horin-ji temple on the 18th day of the 10th lunar month in the 1st year of Ninji.[70]

67. Treasure (value), marshes (nature), space (the stage of action), and mountains (reality) correspond to the four faces of reality outlined in the Buddha's four noble truths.

68. In Zazen, mountains exist as they are.

69. Master Unmon Bun-en says, *"Venerable monks! Do not have delusions. The sky is the sky. The earth is the earth. Mountains are mountains. Water is water. Monks are monks. Laymen are laymen."—Unmon-ko-roku*, Vol. 1.

† Acknowledgment is due to Professor Carl Bielefeldt of Stanford University for his exemplary translation of this chapter.

70. 1240.

[15]

仏祖

Busso

The Buddhist Patriarchs

***Butsu** means "buddha" or "Buddhist," **so** means "patriarch," and therefore **busso** means Buddhist patriarchs. Master Dogen revered Buddhas of the past; he also esteemed the Buddhist transmission from Buddha to Buddha. Furthermore he believed in the continuity of the Buddhist order; the successive leaders of the Buddhist order held an important place in his thought. Here Master Dogen enumerates the names of the Patriarchs of the Buddhist order, and in doing so, he confirms the Buddhist tradition they maintained.*

[209] **The realization of the Buddhist patriarchs**[1] is [our] taking up the Buddhist patriarchs and paying homage to them. This is not of only the past, the present, and the future; and it may be ascendant even to the ascendant [reality] of buddha.[2] It is just to enumerate those who have maintained and relied upon the real features[3] of Buddhist patriarchs, to do prostrations to them, and to meet them. Making the virtue of the Buddhist patriarchs manifest and uphold itself, we have dwelt in and maintained it, and have bowed to and experienced it.

[210] (1) The Great Master[4] Vipaśyin Buddha
—here[5] called Kosetsu
[Universal Preaching]†

(2) The Great Master Śikhin Buddha

---

1. 仏祖 (BUSSO). 祖 (SO), "patriarch," or "ancestor," is originally neuter in gender. However, Master Dogen often uses the term 祖 (SO) for people of the present as well as for people of the past. Therefore, for want of a more neutral alternative, the translation "patriarch" has been preferred throughout the present volume.

2. 仏向上 (BUTSU-KOJO). See chap. 28, *Butsu-kojo-no-ji.*

3. 面目 (MENMOKU), or "face and eyes."

4. "The Great Master" is 大和尚 (DAI-OSHO). The honorific term 和尚 (OSHO) was used in China to address a master directly. The corresponding term in Sanskrit is *upādhyāya* (lit. preceptor, abbot, teacher). In the recitation of the names of the Buddhist patriarchs in Japan, the words *Dai-osho* give a natural rhythm to the reciting. An Appendix shows the standard form of the recitation practiced in Japan.

5. China and Japan.

† The names of the seven ancient buddhas and the first twenty-eight patriarchs (with the exception of the 12th, Master Aśvaghoṣa) are represented by Chinese characters which transliterate the pronunciation of the original Sanskrit name. In general, sources for Sanskrit names and words are 1) Zengakudaijiten, and 2) the Monier-Williams Sanskrit-English Dictionary. These two sources do not give Sanskrit equivalents for the names of the 20th, 22nd, 23rd, and 25th patriarchs. These names were rendered into Sanskrit in Nishijima Roshi's *Gendaigo-yaku-shobogenzo (Shobogenzo in Modern Japanese)* relying on a variety of other sources. The names of the seven ancient buddhas and Master Nāgārjuna are given both in Chinese characters representing Sanskrit pronunciation and in Chinese characters which have meaning.

—here called Ka [Fire]

(3) The Great Master Viśvabhū Buddha
—here called Issai-ji [All Benevolent]

(4) The Great Master Krakucchanda Buddha
—here called Kinsennin [Gold Wizard]

(5) The Great Master Kanakamuni Buddha
—here called Konjikisen [Golden Wizard]

(6) The Great Master Kāśyapa Buddha
—here called Onko [Drinking Brightness]

(7) The Great Master Śākyamuni Buddha
—here called No-nin-jakumoku [Benevolence and Serenity]

[1] The Great Master Mahākāśyapa

[2] The Great Master Ānanda

[3] The Great Master Śāṇavāsa

[4] The Great Master Upagupta

[5] The Great Master Dhītika

[6] The Great Master Micchaka

[7] The Great Master Vasumitra

---

[1] One of the Buddha's ten great disciples, said to be foremost among the ten great disciples in nonattachment, and foremost at *dhūta*, the practice of austerity. He was born into a Brahmin family on the outskirts of Rājagṛha, and became the Buddha's disciple in the third year after the Buddha's realization of the truth. It is said that he entered the state of an arhat after only eight days. After the Buddha's death, Master Mahākāśyapa succeeded the Buddha as leader of the Buddhist order, and organized the First Council at Rājagṛha. At the First Council, in 483 B.C., the Pali canon—consisting of *vinaya* (precepts) and *sūtra* (the Buddha's discourses)—was codified so as to be passed on through recitation to future generations. One hundred years later, in 383 B.C., a Second Council was held to discuss revision of the *vinaya*. Here two traditions emerged: the School of the Elders (Theravadins), and the members of the Great Community (later to develop into the Mahāyāna). A Third Council was held at Patna in 253 B.C. under the patronage of King Aśoka. Here the existing *vinaya* and *sūtra* were supplemented by commentaries which later become known as the *abhidharma*. The three baskets (*tripitaka*) of *vinaya*, *sūtra*, and *abidharma* were later written on palm leaves in the monasteries of Sri Lanka in the first century B.C. Master Mahākāśyapa, having chosen Ānanda as his successor, retired to Kukkuṭapāda Mountain and passed away while sitting in Zazen. See for example chap. 30, *Gyoji*.

[2] Also one of the Buddha's ten great disciples, foremost at remembering the Buddha's preaching. The Buddha's half brother, and only a few days younger than the Buddha himself, he served the Buddha as an attendant monk. Though a monk for forty-four years, he had not realized the truth when the Buddha died. However, he is said to have become an arhat shortly before the First Council at Rājagṛha, where he was to recall the Buddha's discourses for posterity.

[3] See for example chap. 12, *Kesa-kudoku*.

[4] See for example chap. 86, *Shukke-kudoku;* chap. 90, *Shizen-biku*.

[5] A native of the ancient Indian state of Magadha. See for example chap. 86, *Shukke-kudoku*.

[6] A native of central India. His name is written either as Micchaka or as Miccaka.

[8] The Great Master Buddhanandhi

[9] The Great Master Baddhamitra

[10] The Great Master Pārśva

[11] The Great Master Puṇyayaśas

[12] The Great Master Aśvaghoṣa

[13] The Great Master Kapimala

[14] The Great Master Nāgārjuna
– also [called] Ryuju [Dragon-Tree] or Ryusho [Dragon-Excellence] or Ryumo [Dragon-Might]

[15] The Great Master Kāṇadeva

[16] The Great Master Rāhulabhadra

[17] The Great Master Saṃghanandi

[18] The Great Master Geyāśata

---

[7] A native of the northern Indian state of Gandhāra, born at the end of the first century A.D. He is said to have organized, in the Kingdom of Kaniṣka, the Fourth Council, where he compiled the *Abhidharma-mahāvibhāṣā-śāstra*. See for example chap. 77, *Koku*.

[10] A native of central India. He is also said to have presided over the Fourth Council. He was called the Side Saint, because he made a vow never to sleep like a corpse, on his back. See for example chap. 30, *Gyoji*.

[11] A native of the ancient Indian state of Kośala.

[12] The Sanskrit *Aśvaghoṣa* lit. means "Horse Whinny" and in the source text the name is represented not phonetically but by the Chinese characters 馬鳴 (MEMYO), "Horse Whinny." A native of Śrāvastī, he was distinguished in music and in literature. His Buddhist writings include the *Buddhacarita*, a biography of the Buddha in metric form.

[13] A native of the central Indian state of Magadha. It is said that at first he led a non-Buddhist group of three thousand disciples, but later he met Master Aśvaghoṣa, realized the truth, and spread the Dharma through the west of India.

[14] The three Chinese names for Master Nāgārjuna are 竜樹 (RYUJU), 竜勝 (RYUSHO), and 竜盲 (RYUMO). In each case, 竜 (RYU), "dragon," represents the meaning of the Sanskrit *nāga*. In the case of 竜樹 (RYUJU), the Chinese character for tree 樹 (JU) may represent either the sound or the meaning of the Sanskrit *arjuna*, which is the name of a tree.

Master Nāgārjuna lived in the second or third century A.D. He was born into a Brahmin family in southern India. When he became a monk he first studied the Hīnayāna canon, but later journeyed to the Himalayas and learned the teachings of the Mahāyāna from a venerable old bhikṣu. Eventually he succeeded Master Kapimala and compiled many fundamental Mahāyāna texts, including the *Mādhyamaka-kārikā*. The *Mahā-prajñā-pāramitopadeśa* is also attributed to him. See for example, chap. 12, *Kesa-kudoku; chap*. 70, *Hotsu-bodaishin*; chap. 85, *Shime*; chap. 89, *Shinjin-inga*; chap. 90, *Shizen-biku*.

[15] Called Kāṇadeva because of his loss of an eye (the Sanskrit *kāṇa* means one-eyed). Also called Āryadeva. He lived in southern India in the third century and is said to have been killed by a non-Buddhist. See for example chap. 22, *Bussho*.

[16] A native of Kapilavastu, in present day Nepal.

[17] A native of the city of Śrāvasti, the capital of the ancient state of Kośala.

[19] The Great Master Kumāralabdha

[20] The Great Master Gayata†

[21] The Great Master Vasubandhu

[22] The Great Master Manura†

[23] The Great Master Hakulenayasas†

[24] The Great Master Siṃha

[25] The Great Master Vaśasuta†

[26] The Great Master Puṇyamitra

[27] The Great Master Prajñātara

[28] *[1]* The Great Master Bodhidharma

[29] *[2]* The Great Master Eka

[30] *[3]* The Great Master Sosan

[31] *[4]* The Great Master Doshin

---

[19] See for example chap. 84, *Sanji-no-go;* chap. 89, *Shinjin-inga.*

[20] A native of northern India. See for example chap. 84, *Sanji-no-go;* chap. 89, *Shinjin-inga.*

[21] Born in the fifth century in Puruṣapura (close to present-day Peshawar), the capital of Gandhāra. His many works include the *Abidharma-kośa-śāstra.* Master Vasubandhu's brothers Asañga and Buddhasiṃla were also prominent Buddhist philosophers of the time. Their teaching formed the basis of the Yogācāra School. The Yogācāra School and the Mādhayamika School of Master Nāgārjuna are seen as the two major streams of Mahāyāna Buddhism in India.

[22] The son of the King of Nadai (Sanskrit equivalent unknown). Became a monk at the age of thirty.

[23] Born into a Brahmin family. He spread the Dharma in central India.

[24] Born into a Brahmin family in central India. He spread the Dharma in the northern state of Kaśmīra (present-day Kashmir). It is said that he was executed by the king of Kaśmīra. See chap. 84, *Sanji-no-go.*

[25] A native of western India.

[26] A native of southern India.

[27] Born into a Brahmin family in eastern India. See for example chap. 21, *Kankin;* chap. 42, *Kuge.*

[28] The third son of a southern Indian king. Having succeeded Master Prajñātara, he sailed to China during the reign of Emperor Bu (reigned 502–550) of the Liang Dynasty and became the first Buddhist patriarch in China. He went to the Sung-shan mountains in central-northern China to practice Zazen, and transmitted the Dharma to Master Taiso Eka. See for example chap. 30, *Gyoji;* chap. 46, *Katto;* chap. 49, *Butsudo;* chap. 72, *Zanmai-o-zanmai.*

[29] Master Taiso Eka (Ch. Dazu Huike). See for example chap. 30, *Gyoji;* chap. 46, *Katto;* chap. 48, *Sesshin-sessho.*

[30] Master Kanchi Sosan (Ch. Jianzhi Sengcan). It is said that he was already in his forties when he became a disciple of Master Taiso Eka. He wrote *Shinjinmei (Inscription on Believing Mind).* To escape persecution by Emperor Bu (reigned 561–578) of the Northern Chou dynasty, he secluded himself in the mountains for ten years.

[31] Master Dai-i Doshin (Ch. Dayi Daoxin). Became a disciple of Master Kanchi Sosan at the age of fourteen, and succeeded him after nine years. Died in 651.

[32] *[5]* The Great Master Konin

[33] *[6]* The Great Master Eno

[34] *[7]* The Great Master Gyoshi

[35] *[8]* The Great Master Kisen

[36] *[9]* The Great Master Igen

[37] *[10]* The Great Master Donjo

[38] *[11]* The Great Master Ryokai

[39] *[12]* The Great Master Doyo

[40] *[13]* The Great Master Dofu

[41] *[14]* The Great Master Kanshi

[42] *[15]* The Great Master Enkan

[43] *[16]* The Great Master Keigen

---

[32] Master Daiman Konin (Ch. Daman Hongren) (688–761). See for example chap. 22, *Bussho.*

[33] Master Daikan Eno (Ch. Dajian Huineng) (638–713). Spent eight months working as a temple servant at Master Daiman Konin's temple, in which time he received the Master's affirmation and the authentic transmission of the Buddhist robe. After that he lived on Sokei-zan mountain and spread Buddhism from there for forty years. Master Dogen revered Master Daikan Eno very highly as "the founding Patriarch" and "the eternal Buddha." See for example chap. 1, *Bendowa;* chap. 7, *Senjo;* chap. 22, *Bussho;* chap. 30, *Gyoji;* chap. 44, *Kobusshin;* chap. 49, *Butsudo.*

[34] Master Seigen Gyoshi (Ch. Quingyuan Xingsi). Died in 740. See for example chap 49, *Butsudo.*

[35] Master Sekito Kisen (Ch. Shitou Xiqian) (700–790). Had his head shaved by the aged Master Daikan Eno, who advised him to follow Master Seigen Gyoshi. It is said that after succeeding Master Seigen, he built a hut on a rock, earning himself the nickname *Sekito (On Top of the Rock).* He wrote *Sekito-so-an-no-uta (Songs from Sekito's Thatched Hut)* and *Sandokai (Experiencing the State).* See for example chap. 49, *Butsudo.*

[36] Master Yakusan Igen (Ch. Yueshan Weiyan) (745–828). Having become a monk at the age of 17, he learned the sutras and commentaries, kept the precepts, and met Master Sekito Kisen, at whose suggestion he also visited Master Baso Do-itsu. Eventually he became Master Sekito's successor. See for example chap. 27, *Zazenshin.*

[37] Master Ungan Donjo (Ch. Yunyan Tansheng) (782–841). Practiced for twenty years under Master Hyakujo Ekai, after whose death he became the disciple of Master Yakusan. See for example chap. 53, *Mujo-seppo;* chap. 63, *Ganzei.*

[38] Master Tozan Ryokai (Ch. Dongshan Liangjie) (807–869). Became a monk at the age of 21 and traveled around visiting Buddhist masters including Master Nansen Fugan and Master Isan Reiyu. At the latter's suggestion he became the disciple and later the successor of Master Ungan. He wrote *Hokyo-zanmai (Samadhi, the State of a Jewel-Mirror).* See for example chap. 48, *Sesshin-sessho;* chap. 53, *Mujo-seppo;* chap. 63, *Ganzei;* chap. 66, *Shunju.*

[39] Master Ungo Doyo (Ch. Yunju Daoying) (835?–902). Having succeeded Master Tozan, he spread the Dharma from Ungo-zan mountain for thirty years. It is said that his disciples always numbered at least fifteen hundred.

[40] Master Do-an Dofu (Ch. Tongan Daopi). He lived on Hosei-zan mountain in the Koshu district, but his life history is not known.

[41] Master Do-an Kanshi (Ch. Tongan Guanzhi). His life history is unclear.

[42] Master Ryozan Enkan (Ch. Liangshan Yuanguan). His life history is also unclear.

[43] Master Taiyo Keigen (Ch. Dayang Jingxuan) (942–1027). Became a monk under a certain Master

[44] *[17]* The Great Master Gisei

[45] *[18]* The Great Master Dokai

[46] *[19]* The Great Master Shijun

[47] *[20]* The Great Master Seiryo

[48] *[21]* The Great Master Sogyoku

[49] *[22]* The Great Master Chikan

[50] *[23]* The Great Master Nyojo

[222] Dogen, during the summer retreat of the 1st year of the Hogyo era[6] of the great Kingdom of Sung, met and served my late master, the eternal Buddha of Tendo, the Great Master. I perfectly realized the act of prostrating to, and humbly receiving upon my head, this Buddhist Patriarch; it was [the realization of] buddhas alone, together with buddhas.[7]

Chitsu, then traveled around learning Buddhism under various masters before becoming the disciple and eventually the successor of Master Ryozan. When Master Taiyo was about to die, he entrusted his robe, pātra, et cetera to Master Fuzan Ho-en to give to Master Fuzan's disciple Tosu Gisei, thus making Master Tosu his successor. See *Shinji-shobogenzo* pt. 3, no. 43.

[44] Master Tosu Gisei (Ch. Touzi Yiqing) (1032–1083). Became a monk at the age of seven. Later spent about six years in the order of Master Fuzan Ho-en (a member of Master Rinzai's lineage). Receiving the portrait, shoes and other personal effects entrusted by Master Taiyo to Master Fuzan, Master Tosu succeeded Master Taiyo as the tenth-generation descendant in the lineage of Master Seigen Gyoshi. *Go-roku* in two volumes. See for example chap. 53, *Mujo-seppo;* chap. 64, *Kajo.*

[45] Master Fuyo Dokai (Ch. Furong Daokai) (1043–1118). Having realized the Dharma under Master Tosu, he preached on Taiyo-zan and at other temples. The Sung emperor Kiso (reigned 1101–1126) bestowed on him a purple robe and the title Zen Master Josho, but Master Fuyo refused to accept them and was consequently banished. Later he was pardoned and built himself a thatched hut on Fuyo-zan mountain, where he lived in the ancient style. See for example chap. 14, *Sansuigyo;* chap. 64, *Kajo.*

[46] Master Tanka Shijun (Ch. Dangxia Zichun) (1064–117). Having succeeded Master Fuyo, he lived on Tanka-zan mountain, with such disciples as Master Wanshi Shokaku and Master Shinketsu Seiryo. *Go-roku* in two volumes. The six-volume *Kido-shu (The Kido Collection)* is also a record of the words of Master Tanka Shijun. *Kido* (lit. Empty Hall) was probably one of Master Tanka's names.

[47] Master Shinketsu Seiryo (Ch. Zhenxie Qingliao) (1089–1151). *Go-roku* in two volumes.

[48] Master Tendo Sogyoko (Ch. Tiantong Zhongjue). Though he was the grandfather in Buddhism of Master Tendo Nyojo, his life history is not known clearly.

[49] Master Seccho Chikan (Ch. Xuedou Zhijian) (1105–1192). See for example chap. 51, *Mitsugo.*

[50] Master Tendo Nyojo (Ch. Tiantong Rujing) (1163–1228). After realizing the Dharma in Master Chikan's order, he traveled around and taught at temples in many districts for forty years. While living at Jyoji-ji temple, in 1224 he received an imperial edict to become the master of Keitoku-zenji temple on Tendo-zan mountain, where he was to teach Master Dogen. See for example chap. 30, *Gyoji;* chap. 59, *Baike;* chap. 72, *Zanmai-o-zanmai.*

6. 1225.

7. "Perfectly realize" is 究尽 (GUJIN). "Buddhas alone, together with buddhas" is 唯仏与仏 (YUI-BUTSU-YO-BUTSU). These words are from a sentence in the Lotus Sutra which Master Dogen often quoted: *"Buddhas alone, together with buddhas, can perfectly realize that all dharmas are real form."* See LS 1.68.

Shobogenzo Busso

Written at Kannon-dori-kosho-horin-ji temple in the Uji district of Yoshu,[8] Japan, and preached to the assembly there on the 3rd day of the 1st lunar month in the 2nd year of Ninji.[9]

8. Yoshu was the Japanese pronunciation of the name of a district in China. People of the time, looking up to China, borrowed the Chinese name, probably for the district then called *Yamashiro-no-kuni*. The area corresponds to present-day Kyoto prefecture.

9. 1241.

[16]

嗣書

SHISHO

The Certificate of Succession

Shi *means "succession" or "transmission."* ***Sho*** *means "certificate." So* ***shisho*** *means "the certificate of succession." Buddhism is not only theory, but also practice or experience. Therefore it is impossible for a Buddhist disciple to attain the Buddhist truth only by reading Buddhist sutras or listening to a master's lectures. The disciple must live with a master and study the master's behavior in everyday life. After a disciple has learned the master's life and has realized the Buddhist truth in his or her own life, the master gives a certificate to the disciple, certifying the transmission of the truth from master to disciple. This certificate is called* ***shisho****. From a materialistic viewpoint, the certificate is only cloth and ink, and so it cannot hold religious meaning or be revered as something with religious value. But Buddhism is a realistic religion, and Buddhists find religious value in many concrete traditions. The certificate is one such traditional object which is revered by Buddhists. Therefore Master Dogen found much value in this certificate. In this chapter he explains why the certificate is revered by Buddhists, and records his own experiences of seeing such certificates in China.*

[3] **Buddhas, without exception,** receive the Dharma from buddhas, buddha-to-buddha, and patriarchs, without exception, receive the Dharma from patriarchs, patriarch-to-patriarch; this is experience of the [Buddha's] state,[1] this is the one-to-one transmission, and for this reason it is *the supreme state of bodhi*. It is impossible to certify a buddha without being a buddha, and no-one becomes a buddha without receiving the certification of a buddha. Who but a buddha can esteem this state as the most honored and approve it as the supreme? When we receive the certification of a buddha, we realize the state independently, without a master,[2] and we realize the state independently, without our self.[3] For this reason, we speak of buddhas really experiencing the succession, and of patriarchs really experiencing the same state.[1] The import of this truth cannot be clarified by anyone other than buddhas. How could it be the thought of [bodhisattvas in] the ten states or the state of balanced awareness?[4] How much less could it be supposed by teachers of sutras, teachers of commentaries, and the like?

1. 証契 (SHOKAI). 証 (SHO) means experience. 契 (KAI) means pledge, promise, accord, or binding agreement and, by extension, the state which is exactly the same as the state of Gautama Buddha.

2. 無師独悟 (MUSHI-DOKUGO). This expression appears repeatedly in Shobogenzo.

3. 無自独悟 (MUJI-DOKUGO). This is Master Dogen's variation.

4. 十地等覚 (JUCHI-TOGAKU). It is said that bodhisattvas pass through fifty-two stages on the way to Buddhahood. The forty-first to the fiftieth stages are 十地 (JUCHI). The fifty-first stage is 等覚 (TOGAKU) or "balanced awareness," and the ultimate stage is 妙覚 (MYOKAKU) or "subtle awareness."

Even if we explain it to them, they will not be able to hear it, because it is transmitted between buddhas, buddha-to-buddha.

[5] Remember, the Buddha's state of truth is the perfect realization only of buddhas, and without buddhas it has no time. The state is like, for example, stones succeeding each other as stones, jewels succeeding each other as jewels, chrysanthemums succeeding each other, and pine trees certifying each other, at which time the former chrysanthemum and the latter chrysanthemum are each real as they are, and the former pine and the latter pine are each real as they are. People who do not clarify the state like this, even if they encounter the truth authentically transmitted from buddha to buddha, cannot even suspect what kind of truth is being expressed; they do not possess the understanding that buddhas succeed each other and that patriarchs experience the same state. It is pitiful that though they appear to be the Buddha's progeny, they are not the Buddha's children, and they are not child-buddhas.

[6] Sokei,[5] on one occasion, preaches to the assembly, *"From the Seven Buddhas to Eno there are forty buddhas, and from Eno to the Seven Buddhas there are forty patriarchs."*[6] This truth is clearly the fundamental teaching to which the Buddhist patriarchs have authentically succeeded. Among these *Seven Buddhas* some have appeared during the past Kalpa of Resplendence,[7] and some have appeared in the present Kalpa of the Wise.[8] At the same time, to connect in a line the face-to-face transmissions of the forty patriarchs is the truth of Buddha, and is the succession of Buddha. This being so, going up from the Sixth Patriarch to the Seven Buddhas, there are forty patriarchs who are the Buddha-successors, and going down from the Seven Buddhas to the Sixth Patriarch, the forty buddhas must be the Buddha-successors. The truth of buddhas, and the truth of patriarchs, is like this. Without experience of the state, without being a Buddhist patriarch, we do not have the wisdom of a buddha and do not have the perfect realization of a patriarch. Without a buddha's wisdom, we lack belief in the state of buddha. Without a patriarch's perfect realization, we do not experience the same state as a patriarch. To speak of forty patriarchs, for the present, is just to cite those who are close. Thus, the succession from buddha to buddha is profound and eternal; it is without regression or deviation and without interruption or cessation. The fundamental point is this: although Śākyamuni Buddha realizes the truth before the Seven Buddhas, it has taken him a long time to succeed to the Dharma of Kāśyapa Buddha.[9] Although he realizes the truth on the 8th day of the 12th month, thirty years after his descent and birth, [this] is realization of the truth before the Seven Buddhas; it is the same realization of the truth shoulder-to-shoulder with, and in time with, the many buddhas; it is realization of the truth before the many buddhas; and it is realization of the truth after all the many buddhas. There is also the principle to be mastered in practice that Kāśyapa Buddha

5. Master Daikan Eno (638–713), successor of Master Daiman Konin.

6. Master Daikan Eno was the sixth patriarch in China, counting from Master Bodhidharma as the first patriarch in China. He was the thirty-third patriarch, counting from the Buddha's successor, Master Mahakāśyapa as the first patriarch. And he was the fortieth patriarch counting from Vipaśyin Buddha, the first of the seven ancient buddhas.

7. 荘厳劫 (SHOGONKO). The past age extending from the eternal past to Viśyabhū Buddha (the third of the Seven Buddhas), in which one thousand buddhas appeared.

8. 賢劫 (KENGO) from the Sanskrit *bhadra-kalpa*, the age in which we are living now.

9. Kāśyapa Buddha is the sixth of the Seven Buddhas.

succeeds to the Dharma of Śākyamuni Buddha. Those who do not know this principle do not clarify the Buddha's state of truth. Without clarifying the Buddha's state of truth, they are not the Buddha's successors. The Buddha's successors means the Buddha's children. Śākyamuni Buddha, on one occasion, causes Ānanda to ask,[10] *"Whose disciples are the buddhas of the past?"* Śākyamuni Buddha says, *"The buddhas of the past are the disciples of Śākyamuni Buddha."* The Buddhist doctrine of all the buddhas is like this.

[9] To serve these buddhas and to accomplish the succession of Buddha is just the Buddha's truth [practiced by] every buddha. This Buddha's truth is always transmitted in the succession of the Dharma, at which time there is inevitably a certificate of succession. Without the succession of Dharma, we would be non-Buddhists of naturalism. If the Buddha's truth did not dictate the succession of Dharma, how could it have reached the present day? Therefore, in [the transmission] which is [from] buddha [to] buddha, a certificate of succession, of buddha succeeding buddha, is inevitably present, and a certificate of succession, of buddha succeeding buddha, is received. As regards the concrete situation of the certificate of succession, some succeed to the Dharma on clarifying the sun, the moon, and the stars, and some succeed to the Dharma on being made to get the skin, flesh, bones, and marrow;[11] some receive a kaṣāya; some receive a staff; some receive a sprig of pine; some receive a whisk;[12] some receive an udumbara flower; and some receive a robe of golden brocade.[13] There have been successions with straw sandals[14] and successions with a bamboo stick.[15] When such successions of the Dharma are received, some write a certificate of succession with blood from a finger, some write a certificate of succession with blood from a tongue, and some perform the succession of Dharma by writing [a certificate] with oil and milk; these are all certificates of succession. The one who has performed the succession and the one who has received it are both the Buddha's successors. Truly, whenever [Buddhist patriarchs] are realized as Buddhist patriarchs, the succession of the Dharma is inevitably realized. When [the succession] is realized, many Buddhist patriarchs [find that] though they did not expect it, it has come, and though they did not seek it, they have succeeded to the Dharma. Those who have the succession of Dharma are, without exception, the buddhas and the patriarchs.

[12] Since the twenty-eighth Patriarch[16] came from the west, the fundamental principle has been rightly heard in the eastern lands that there is in Buddhism the succession of the Dharma. Before that time, we never heard it at all. [Even] in the Western Heavens, it is neither attained nor known by teachers of commentaries, Dharma-teachers, and the like. It is also beyond [bodhisattvas of] the ten sacred and the three clever states. Teach-

10. Master Ānanda is the second patriarch in India. See chap. 15, *Busso.*

11. Refers to the transmission between Master Bodhidharma and Master Taiso Eka. See chap. 46, *Katto.*

12. 払子 (HOSSU), a whisk usually with a long plume of white animal hair, held by a Buddhist master during a lecture or ceremony, originally used in India to clear insects from one's path (Sk: *vyajana*).

13. Refers to the transmission between the Buddha and Master Mahakāśyapa. See chap. 68, *Udonge.*

14. For example, the succession between Master Taiyo Keigen and Master Tosu Gisei (see notes to chap. 15, *Busso*).

15. 竹篦 (SHIPPEI). A stick about three feet long, made of split bamboo, with a ceremonial handle. It is used, for example, in the ceremony to inaugurate a head monk.

16. Master Bodhidharma. The first patriarch in China.

ers of mantric techniques who intellectually study the tripiṭaka[17] are not able even to suspect that it exists. Deplorably, though they have received the human body which is a vessel for the state of truth, they have become uselessly entangled in the net of theory, and so they do not know the method of liberation and they do not hope for the opportunity to spring free. Therefore, we should learn the state of truth in detail, and we should concentrate our resolve to realize the state in practice.

[13] Dogen, when in Sung [China], had the opportunity to bow before certificates of succession, and there were many kinds of certificate. One among them was that of the veteran master I-ichi Seido[18] who had hung his traveling staff at Tendo [temple]. He was a man from the Etsu district, and was the former abbot of Ko-fuku-ji temple. He was a native of the same area as my late Master. My late Master always used to say, *"For familiarity with the state, ask Ichi Seido!"* One day the Seido said, *"Admirable old [calligraphic] traces are prized possessions of the human world. How many of them have you seen?"* Dogen said, *"I have seen few."* Then the Seido said, *"I have a scroll of old calligraphy in my room. It is a roster. I will let you see it, venerable brother."* So saying, he fetched it, and I saw that it was a certificate of succession. It was a certificate of the succession of Hogen's[19] lineage, and had been obtained from among the robes and pātra[20] of an old veteran monk: it was not that of the venerable I-ichi himself. The way it was written is as follows: *"The first Patriarch Mahākāśyapa realized the truth under Śākyamuni Buddha; Śākyamuni Buddha realized the truth under Kāśyapa Buddha..."* It was written like this. Seeing it, Dogen decisively believed in the succession of the Dharma from rightful successor to rightful successor. [The certificate] was Dharma that I had never before seen. It was a moment in which the Buddhist patriarchs mystically respond to and protect their descendants. The feeling of gratitude was beyond endurance.

[15] The veteran monk Shugetsu, while he was assigned to the post of head monk[21] on Tendo, showed to Dogen a certificate of succession of Unmon's lineage. The master directly above the person now receiving the certificate, and the Buddhist patriarchs of the Western Heavens and the Eastern Lands, were arranged in columns, and under those was the name of the person receiving the certificate. All the Buddhist patriarchs were directly aligned with the name of this new ancestral master. Thus, the more than forty generations from the Tathāgata all converged on the name of the new successor. For example, it was as if each of them had handed down [the Dharma] to the new patriarch. Mahākāśyapa, Ānanda, and so on, were aligned as if [they belonged to] separate lineages.[22] At that time, Dogen asked Head Monk Shugetsu, *"Master, nowadays there are*

---

17. 三蔵 (SANZO), lit. "three storehouses," from the Sanskrit *tripiṭaka,* or three baskets: sutras, precepts, and commentaries.

18. 西堂 (SEIDO), lit. "west hall," is a title of respect for a veteran master who has retired from his own temple and is now living as a guest in (a west hall of) another temple.

19. Master Hogen Bun-eki (885–958), the successor of Master Rakan Keichin, who was a successor of Master Gensa Shibi.

20. A *pātra* is a Buddhist food bowl. Robes and *pātra* symbolize the possessions of a monk.

21. 首座 (SHUSO), lit. "Head Seat." The *shuso* was the leader of the main body of monks in a temple. He was the highest ranking of the six *choshu,* or assistant officers. Ranking above them were the six *chiji,* or main officers.

22. That is, the names of the first and second patriarchs were arranged not in a vertical line, but side by side at the top of their respective columns of historical patriarchs.

slight differences among the five sects[23] *in their alignment [of names]. What is the reason? If the succession from the Western Heavens has passed from rightful successor to rightful successor, how could there be differences?"* Shugetsu said, *"Even if the difference were great, we should just study that the buddhas of Unmon-zan mountain are like this. Why is Old Master Śākyamuni honored by others? He is an honored one because he realized the truth. Why is Great Master Unmon honored by others? He is an honored one because he realized the truth."* Dogen, hearing these words, had a little [clearer] understanding. Nowadays many leaders of the great temples[24] in Kiangsu and Chekiang[25] are successors to the Dharma of Rinzai, Unmon, Tozan, and so on. However, among fellows claiming to be distant descendants of Rinzai a certain wrongness is sometimes contrived; namely, they attend the order of a good counselor, and cordially request a hanging portrait and a scroll of Dharma words,[26] which they stash away as standards of their succession to the Dharma. At the same time, there is a group of dogs who, [prowling] in the vicinity of a venerable patriarch, cordially request Dharma words, portraits, and so on, which they hoard away to excess; then, when they become senior in years, they pay money to government officials and they seek to get a temple, [but] when they are assigned as abbots they do not receive the Dharma from the master [who gave them] the Dharma words and the portrait. They receive the Dharma from fellows of fame and repute of the present generation, or from old veterans who are intimate with kings and ministers, and when they do so they have no interest in getting the Dharma, but are only greedy for fame and reputation. It is deplorable that there are wrong customs like this in the corrupt age of the Latter Dharma. Among people like these, not one person has ever seen or heard the truth of the Buddhist patriarchs, even in a dream. In general, with respect to the granting of Dharma words, portraits, and so forth, they may be given to lecturers of doctrine and laymen and women, and they may be granted to temple servants, tradesmen, and the like. This principle is clear from the records of many masters. Sometimes, when some undeserving person, out of a rash desire for evidence of succession to the Dharma, wants to get a certificate, [a master] will reluctantly take up the writing brush, though those who possess the truth hate to do so. In such a case the certificate does not follow the traditional form; [the master] just writes some brief note saying "succeeded me." The method of recent times is simply to succeed to the Dharma as soon as one attains proficiency in the order of a particular master, with that master as one's master. [That is to say, there are] people who, although they have not received certification from their former master, are occupying the long platform [of another temple] which they have visited only for entry into [the master's] room and formal preaching in the Dharma Hall; [but] when they break open the great matter while staying at [this other] temple, they do not have the time to uphold the transmission of their [original] master; instead they very often take this [new] master as their master. Another matter: there

23. Rinzai, Igyo, Soto, Unmon, Hogen. See chap. 49, *Butsudo.*

24. 大刹 (DAISETSU). 刹 (SETSU) is from the Sanskrit *kṣetra,* which means a sacred spot or district (see Glossary). At the same time, the character appears in Buddhist sutras in the compound 刹竿 (SEKKAN), or "*kṣetra*-pole," that is, a temple flagpole. This led Chinese scholars to interpret that 刹 (SETSU) might be a transliteration of *yaṣṭi,* which means flag-pole. In ancient India a flag announced Buddhist preaching and so Chinese scholars interpreted that a flag-pole symbolized a place of Buddhist preaching, and hence a temple.

25. Provinces in eastern China bordering on the Yellow Sea and the East China Sea, respectively.

26. 法語 (HOGO), calligraphy containing a word or a phrase of Buddhist preaching.

was a certain Library-Chief[27] Den, a distant descendant of Zen Master Butsugen, that is, Master Sei-on of Ryumon.[28] This Library-Chief Den also had a certificate of succession in his possession. In the early years of the Kajo era,[29] when this Library-Chief Den had fallen ill, the Venerable Elder[30] Ryuzen, though a Japanese, had nursed Library-Chief Den with care; so [Library-Chief Den] had taken out the certificate of succession and let [Ryuzen] bow before it to thank him for his nursing work, because his labors had been unremitting. [At that time Library-Chief Den] had said, *"This is something hardly seen. I will let you bow before it."* Eight years later, in the autumn of the 16th year of Kajo,[31] when Dogen first stopped on Tendo-zan mountain, the Venerable Elder Ryuzen kindly asked Library-Chief Den to let Dogen see the certificate of succession. The form of the certificate was as follows: the forty-five patriarchs from the Seven Buddhas to Rinzai were written in columns, while the masters following Rinzai formed a circle in which were transcribed the masters' original Dharma-names[32] and their written seals.[33] The [name of the] new successor was written at the end, under the date. We should know that the venerable patriarchs of Rinzai's lineage have this kind of difference.

[21] My late Master, the abbot of Tendo, profoundly cautioned people against bragging about succeeding to the Dharma. Truly, the order of my late Master was the order of an eternal buddha, it was the revival of the forest.[34] He himself did not wear a patterned kaṣāya. He had a patched Dharma-robe transmitted from Zen Master Dokai of Fuyo-zan mountain,[35] but he did not wear it [even] to ascend the seat of formal preaching in the Dharma Hall. In short, he never wore a patterned Dharma-robe throughout his life as an abbot. Those who had the mind and those who did not know things all praised him and honored him as a true good counselor. My late Master, the eternal Buddha, in formal preaching in the Dharma Hall would constantly admonish monks in all directions, saying, *"Recently many people who have borrowed the name of the Patriarch's truth randomly wear the Dharma-robe and like [to have] long hair, and they sign their name with the title of master as a vessel of promotion. They are pitiful. Who will save them? It is lamentable that the old veterans of all directions have no will to the truth and so they do not learn the state*

---

27. 蔵主 (ZOSU), the monk in charge of storing sutras. The *zosu* was one of the six *choshu,* or assistant officers.

28. Master Ryumon Butsugen (died 1120), a successor of Master Goso Ho-en. He received the title Zen Master Butsugen, together with a purple robe, from the emperor. *Go-roku,* a record of his words, is in eight volumes.

29. 1208–1224.

30. 上座 (JOZA), from the Sanskrit honorific *sthavira,* or in Pali, *thera,* as in *Theravada,* the School of the Elders. See Glossary.

31. 1223.

32. "Original Dharma-name" is 法諱 (HOKI). 法 (HO) means Dharma or Buddhist and 諱 (KI) means "the name to be avoided." After a monk had died, it was customary to avoid using the name the monk had used in his or her lifetime, and to use a posthumous title instead. While living, monks in China and Japan usually have at least two personal names, each written with two Chinese characters. One name is the 法号 (HOGO), "Dharma-title," and another name is the 法名 (HOMYO), "Dharma-name." A *homyo* is always a *hoki,* whereas a *hogo* may be a name used in a monk's lifetime or it may be a posthumous name.

33. 華字 (KAJI). This seal was not stamped, but written with a brush.

34. 叢林 (SORIN), lit. "clump of forest," from the Sanskrit *piṇḍavana,* meaning a large assembly of monks, or a monastery.

35. Master Fuyo Dokai (1043–1118) , the eighteenth patriarch in China and a successor of Master Tosu Gisei. See for example chap. 14, *Sansuigyo;* chap. 29, *Gyoji;* chap. 64, *Kajo.*

of truth. There are few who have even seen and heard of the causes and conditions of the certificate of succession and the succession of the Dharma. Among a hundred thousand people there is not even one! This is [due to] the decline of the Patriarch's truth." He was always admonishing the old veterans of the whole country like this, but they did not resent him. In conclusion, wherever [people] are sincerely pursuing the truth they are able to see and to hear that the certificate of succession exists. *To have seen and heard* may be *learning the state of truth* itself. On the Rinzai certificate of succession, first the [master] writes the name [of the successor], then writes *"Disciple So-and-So served under me,"* or writes *"has attended my order,"* or writes *"entered my inner sanctum,"* or writes *"succeeded me,"* and then lists the former patriarchs in order. [So] it also shows a trace of traditional[36] instruction about the Dharma, the point being for the successor simply to meet a true good counselor, regardless of whether the meeting is in the end or in the beginning: this is the unassailable fundamental principle.[37] Among [certificates of] the Rinzai [lineage], there are some written as described above—I saw them with my own eyes, and so I have written about them.

[24] *"Library-Chief Ryoha[38] is a person of the Ibu[39] district, and now he is my disciple. [I] Tokko[40] served Ko[41] of Kinzan. Kinzan succeeded Gon[42] of Kassan. Gon succeeded En[43] of Yogi. En succeeded Tan[44] of Kai-e. Tan succeeded E[45] of Yogi. E succeeded En[46] of Jimyo. En succeeded Sho[47] of Fun-yo. Sho succeeded Nen[48] of Shuzan. Nen succeeded Sho[49] of Fuketsu. Sho succeeded Gyo of Nan-in.[50] Gyo succeeded Sho[51] of Koke. Sho was the excellent rightful successor of the founding Patriarch Rinzai."[52]*

---

36. "Traditional" is いいきたれる (*ii kitare ru*), lit. "having been spoken."

37. In other words, the most important matter in the transmission is the relation between master and student. This is reflected in the form of the certificate in the Rinzai Sect.

38. Master Musai Ryoha. He was the master of Keitoku-ji temple on Tendo-zan mountain when Master Dogen arrived in China. When Master Ryoha's death was approaching, he sent a letter to Master Dogen's future master, Master Tendo Nyojo, asking him to become the master of the temple.

39. Present-day Fukien, a province of south-east China bordering on the Formosa strait.

40. Master Bussho Tokko (1121–1203). Author of *Sotai-roku, (A Record of Answers to an Emperor)*, one volume.

41. Master Dai-e Soko (b. 1089, died in 1163, 37 years before Master Dogen's birth). He is thought to be the founder of the so-called "koan Zen" of the Rinzai Sect, and as such was criticized by Master Dogen several times in Shobogenzo. See for example chap. 75, *Jisho-zanmai.*

42. Master Engo Kokugon (1063–1135). Edited *Hekigan-roku, (Blue Cliff Record).* Master Engo is quoted in chap. 66, *Shunju*, and chap. 74, *Temborin.*

43. Master Goso Ho-en (1024–1104). *Go-roku,* a record of his words, is in four volumes. He was the third patriarch of the temple on Yogi-zan mountain founded by Master Yogi Ho-e. Master Ho-en is quoted in chap. 74, *Temborin.*

44. Master Kai-e Shutan (1025–1072). Also called Master Haku-un Shutan. (Kai-e and Haku-un are both *hogo*—see note 32).

45. Master Yogi Ho-e (992–1049). Lived on and spread the Dharma from Yogi-zan mountain. *Go-roku* and *Ko-roku,* records of his words, are in one volume each.

46. Master Jimyo So-en (986–1039). Became a monk aged 22.

47. Master Fun-yo Zensho (947–1024). *Go-roku,* a record of his words, is in three volumes.

48. Master Shuzan Shonen (926–993). *Go-roku,* a record of his words, is in one volume.

49. Master Fuketsu Ensho (896?–973).

50. Master Nan-in Egyo (d. 930?).

51. Master Koke Sonsho (830–888).

52. Master Rinzai Gigen (815?–867). A successor of Master Obaku Ki-un. *Go-roku,* a record of his words, is in one volume. His disciples included Master Koke Sonsho, Master Sansho Enen, and Master

[27] Zen Master Bussho Tokko of Aiku-o-zan mountain[53] wrote this and presented it to Musai [Ryo]ha. When [Musai Ryoha] was the abbot of Tendo, my brother monk[54] Chiyu secretly brought it to the Dormitory of Quiescence[55] to show to Dogen. That was the first time I saw it, the 21st day of the 1st lunar month of the 17th year of the great Sung era of Kajo [1224]. How overjoyed I felt! This was just the mystical response of the Buddhist patriarchs. I burned incense and did prostrations, then opened and read it. My asking for this certificate of succession to be brought out [happened as follows]: Around the 7th lunar month of the previous year [1223], in the Hall of Serene Light,[55] Chief Officer[56] Shiko had told Dogen about it in secret. Dogen had asked the Chief in passing, *"Nowadays, what person would have one in their possession?"* The Chief said, *"It seems that the venerable abbot has one in his room. In future, if you cordially request him to bring it out, he will surely show it [to you]."* Dogen, after hearing these words, never stopped hoping, day or night. So in that year [1224], I cordially put my humble request to brother monk Chiyu. I did so with all my heart, and the request was granted. The base on which [the certificate] was written was a lining of white silk, and the cover was red brocade. The rod was precious stone, about nine inches[57] long. [The scroll's] extent was more than seven feet.[58] It was never shown to an idle person. Dogen thanked Chiyu at once, and then went straightway to visit the abbot, to burn incense and to bow in thanks to Master Musai. At that time Musai said, *"This sort of thing is rarely able to be seen or known. Now, venerable brother, you have been able to know of it. This is just the real refuge in learning the truth."* At this Dogen's joy was uncontainable. Later, in the Hogyo era,[59] while traveling as a cloud between Tendai-zan mountain,[60] Gan-zan mountain,

---

Kankei Shikan. See, for example, chap. 49, *Butsudo.*

In this certificate, the names Ryoha and Tokko are *homyo* while Rinzai is a *hogo.* For the other names only the first character of the *homyo* is written. When a master's name is written in full, the name of the master's temple or mountain often precedes the *homyo.* Thus E of Yogi-zan mountain is Master Yogi Ho-e, Nyojo of Tendo-zan mountain is Master Tendo Nyojo, Dogen of Eihei-ji temple is Master Eihei Dogen, et cetera. See note 32.

53. Aiku-o means King Aśoka. In 282 a priest called Ryusaku discovered an old stūpa on this mountain, and guessed that it might be one of 84,000 stūpas said to have been built by King Aśoka of ancient India. So the mountain was named after King Aśoka. It later became one of the five mountains: Mt. Kin, Mt. Hoku, Mt. Tai-haku, Mt. Nan, and Mt. Aiku-o. The government of the Sung Dynasty, promoting Buddhism as part of its political strategy, designated the temples on these five mountains as the most important in China.

54. 小師僧 (SHO-SHI-SO). The term was used for a monk who had not passed ten summer retreats since receiving the precepts.

55. The Dormitory of Quiescence (Ryonen-ryo) and the Hall of Serene Light (Jakko-do) were proper names of these particular buildings on Mt. Tendo.

56. 都寺 (TSUSU), the highest of the six temple officers. The six main officers are 1) 都寺 (TSUSU), chief officer, head of the temple office, comptroller; 2) 監寺 (KANSU), prior; 3) 副司 (FUSU), assistant prior; 4) 堂司 (DOSU) or 維那 (INO), supervisor of monks in the Zazen Hall, rector; 5) 典座 (TENZO), head-cook; and 6) 直歳 (SHISUI), caretaker.

57. Lit. "About nine *sun.*" One *sun* is 1.193 inches.

58. Lit. "more than seven *shaku.*" One *shaku* is ten *sun.*

59. 1225–27.

60. Abbreviated in the original text to 台山 (DAIZAN). The Tendai Sect takes its name from this mountain in Chekiang province in eastern China, where Master Tendai Chigi (538–597) lived. Master Dogen became a monk in the Tendai Sect in Japan while still a teenager.

and so on, Dogen arrived at Mannen-ji temple[61] in the Heiden district. The master of the temple at that time was Master Genshi from Fuchou province. Master [Gen]shi had been assigned following the retirement of the veteran patriarch Sokan and he had completely revitalized the temple. While I was making personal salutations, we had a conversation about the traditional customs of the Buddhist patriarchs, and while quoting the story of the succession from Dai-I[62] to Kyozan,[63] the veteran master said, *"Have you ever seen the certificate of succession [that I have] in my room?"* Dogen said, *"How might I have the chance to see it?"* The veteran master himself immediately rose and, holding aloft the certificate of succession[64] he said, *"I have not shown this even to intimates, or even to those who have spent years serving as attendant monks. That is the Buddhist patriarchs' Dharma-instruction. However, while staying in the city on my usual visit to the city in order to meet the governor of the district, Genshi had the following dream: An eminent monk, whom I supposed to be Zen Master Hojo of Daibai-zan mountain,[65] appeared holding up a branch of plum blossoms and said, 'If there is a real person who has crossed the side of a ship, do not begrudge [these] blossoms.' Thus saying, he gave the plum blossoms to me. Unconsciously, Genshi dreamt of chanting, 'Even before he has stepped over the side of the ship, I would like to give him thirty strokes!' In any event, five days have not passed and I meet you, venerable brother. What is more, you have crossed over the side of a ship. And this certificate of succession is written on cloth patterned with plum blossoms. You must be what Daibai was telling me about. You match the image in the dream exactly and so I have brought out [the certificate]. Venerable brother, would you like to receive the Dharma from me? If you desire it, I will not begrudge it."* Dogen could not contain the belief and excitement. Though he had said that I might request the certificate of succession, I only venerated and served him, burning incense and performing prostrations. Present at that time was a [monk] called Honei, an assistant for the burning of incense; he said that it was the first time he had seen the certificate of succession. Dogen thought inwardly, *"It would be very difficult indeed to see and to hear this sort of thing without the mystical help of the Buddhist patriarchs. Why should a stupid fellow from a remote land be so fortunate as to see it several times?"* My sleeves became damp with the tears of gratitude. At that time the Vimalakīrti Room, the Great Hall,[66] and the other rooms were quiet and empty; there was no-one about. This certificate of succession was written on white silk patterned with plum blossoms fallen on the ground. It was more than nine inches across, and it extended to a length of more than a fathom. The rod was of a yellow precious stone and the cover was brocade. On the way back from Tendai-zan mountain to Tendo, Dogen lodged at the overnight quarters of Gosho-ji temple on Daibai-zan mountain. [Here] I dreamt a mystical dream in which the ancestral Master Daibai came and gave me a branch of plum flowers in bloom. A patriarch's

---

61. A temple established on Mt. Tendai, at the site where Master Tendai Fugan died. Master Fugan was a successor of Master Hyakujo Ekai.

62. Master Isan Reiyu (771–853), a successor of Master Hyakujo Ekai. He had many excellent disciples such as Master Kyozan Ejaku, Master Kyogen Chikan, and Master Reiun Shigon. *Go-roku*, a record of his words, is in one volume.

63. Master Kyozan Ejaku (807–883). *Go-roku*, a record of his words, is in one volume. The story of Master Kyozan's succession is contained in *Goto-egen*, chap. 8.

64. It is usual to place venerated things on the palms of the hands and to hold them up high.

65. Master Daibai Hojo (752–839), a successor of Master Baso Do-itsu. He lived in seclusion on Daibai-zan mountain; see chap. 30, *Gyoji*.

66. Proper names of these particular rooms.

mirror is the most reliable thing there is. The blossoms on that branch were more than a foot in diameter. How could the plum blossoms not have been the flowers of the udumbara?[67] It may be that the state in a dream and the state in waking consciousness are equally real. Dogen, while in Sung [China] and since returning to this country, has not before related [the above] to any person.

[33] Today in our lineage from Tozan [the way] the certificate of succession is written is different from [the way] it is written in the Rinzai and other [lineages]. The founding Patriarch Seigen,[68] in front of Sokei's desk, personally drew pure blood from his finger to copy [the certificate] which the Buddhist Patriarch had kept inside his robe, and [thus] he received the authentic transmission. Legend says that [the certificate] was written and transmitted using a mixture of this finger blood and blood from the finger of Sokei. Legend says that in the case of the First Patriarch and the Second Patriarch also, a rite of mixing blood was performed.[69] We do not write such words as *"My disciple"* or *"Served me."* This is the form of the certificate of succession written and transmitted by the many buddhas and by the Seven Buddhas. So remember that Sokei graciously mixed his own blood with the pure blood of Seigen, and Seigen mixed his own pure blood with Sokei's own blood, and that the founding Patriarch, Master Seigen, was thus the only one to receive the direct certification—it was beyond other patriarchs. People who know this fact assert that the Buddha-Dharma was authentically transmitted only to Seigen.

[34] My late Master, the eternal Buddha, the great Master and Abbot of Tendo, preached the following: *"The buddhas, without exception, have experienced the succession of the Dharma. That is to say, Śākyamuni Buddha received the Dharma from Kāśyapa Buddha, Kāśyapa Buddha received the Dharma from Kanakamuni Buddha, and Kanakamuni Buddha received the Dharma from Krakucchanda Buddha.[70] We should believe that the succession has passed like this from buddha to buddha until the present. This is the way of learning Buddhism."* Then Dogen said, *"It was after Kāśyapa Buddha had entered nirvāṇa that Śākyamuni Buddha first appeared in the world and realized the truth. Furthermore, how could the buddhas of the Kalpa of Wisdom receive the Dharma from the buddhas of the Kalpa of Resplendence?[71] What [do you think] of this principle?"* My late Master said, *"What you have just expressed is understanding [based on] listening to theories. It is the way of [bodhisattvas at] the ten sacred stages or the three clever stages. It is not the way [transmitted by] the Buddhist patriarchs from rightful successor to rightful successor. Our way, transmitted from buddha to buddha, is not like that. We have learned that Śākyamuni Buddha definitely received the Dharma from Kāśyapa Buddha. We learn in practice that Kāśyapa Buddha entered nirvāṇa after Śākyamuni Buddha*

---

67. The udumbara is a species of fig tree whose flowers form a kind of peel, so that there do not appear to be any udumbara flowers. The udumbara flower is a symbol of the transmission of Dharma. See chap. 68, *Udonge*.

68. Master Seigen Gyoshi (660–740) was one of several successors of Master Daikan Eno of Sokei mountain, the sixth patriarch in China. Master Tozan belongs to the lineage of Master Seigen Gyoshi. Master Rinzai belongs to the lineage of another of Master Daikan Eno's successors, Master Nangaku Ejo.

69. Master Bodhidharma and Master Taiso Eka.

70. Krakucchanda Buddha, Kanakamuni Buddha, Kāśyapa Buddha, and Śākyamuni Buddha were the fourth, fifth, sixth, and seventh of the seven ancient buddhas.

71. The Kalpa of Wisdom means the present age. The Kalpa of Resplendence means the eternal past. See note 7.

succeeded to the Dharma. If Śākyamuni Buddha did not receive the Dharma from Kāśyapa Buddha, he might be the same as a naturalistic non-Buddhist. Who then could believe in Śākyamuni Buddha? Because the succession has passed like this from buddha to buddha, and has arrived at the present, the individual buddhas are all authentic successors, and they are neither arranged in a line nor gathered in a group. We just learn that the succession passes from buddha to buddha like this. It need not be related to the measurements of kalpas and the measurements of lifetimes mentioned in the teaching of the Āgamas. If we say that [the succession] was established solely by Śākyamuni Buddha, it has existed for little over two thousand years, [so] it is not old; and the successions [number] little more than forty, [so] they might be called recent. This Buddhist succession is not to be studied like that. We learn that Śākyamuni Buddha succeeded to the Dharma of Kāśyapa Buddha, and we learn that Kāśyapa Buddha succeeded to the Dharma of Śākyamuni Buddha. When we learn it like this, it is truly the succession of the Dharma of the buddhas and the patriarchs." Then Dogen not only accepted, for the first time, the existence of Buddhist patriarchs' succession of the Dharma, but also got rid of an old nest.[72]

Shobogenzo Shisho

Written at Kannon-dori-kosho-horin-ji temple on the 7th day of the 3rd lunar month in the 2nd year of Japan's Ninji era,[73] by [a monk] who entered Sung [China] and received the transmission of the Dharma, sramaṇa Dogen.

The 24th day of the 9th lunar month in [the 1st year of] Kangen.[74] Hung our traveling staffs at old Kippo-ji temple, a thatched cottage in Yoshida district of Echizen.[75] (A written seal)[76]

---

72. The tense of the original Japanese sentence is the historical present. When Master Dogen uses the historical present for a story, we generally try to use the present in translation. But in the many places in this chapter where Master Dogen uses the historical present to describe his own experiences, and in the description of his late Master, the past tense has been used in translation.

73. 1241.

74. 1243. The year is identified, using the Chinese dating system, by the characters 癸卯 (KIBO). 癸 is the tenth calendar sign (the younger brother of water) and 卯 is the fourth horary sign (the rabbit). The year at the end of the chapter is usually expressed in two ways, using the Japanese dating system, and the Chinese dating system (ignored in translation) as a double check. However, in this sentence the words 元年 (GANNEN), "1st year," were abbreviated.

75. Corresponds to present-day Fukui prefecture.

76. It is likely that Master Dogen actually wrote his own seal having arrived at Kippo-ji temple, after which Master Ko-un Ejo, when copying Master Dogen's original text, wrote the words 華字 (KAJI), "written seal" (see note 33).

[17]

法華転法華

HOKKE-TEN-HOKKE

The Flower of Dharma Turns the Flower of Dharma

***Ho** means "Dharma," "the law of the Universe," or the Universe itself. **Ke** means "flowers." So **hokke** means "the Universe which is like flowers." The full title of the Lotus Sutra, **Myoho-renge-kyo**, "The Sutra of the Lotus Flower of the Wonderful Dharma," is usually abbreviated to **Hokke-kyo.** So **hokke** also suggests the wonderful Universe as manifested in the Lotus Sutra. **Ten** means "to turn," or "to move." So **hokke-ten-hokke** means "the wonderful Universe which is like flowers is moving the wonderful Universe which is like flowers itself." This is the Buddhist view of the Universe, and Master Dogen's view. In this chapter, Master Dogen explains this view of the Universe, quoting many words from the Lotus Sutra. The message of the Lotus Sutra is "How wonderful is the Universe in which we are now living!" So here Master Dogen unfolds his view of the Universe, following the theory of the Lotus Sutra.*

[39] ***The content of the Buddha-lands of the ten directions***[1] is the *sole existence*[2] of the *Flower of Dharma.*[3] Herein, *all the buddhas of the ten directions and the three times,*[4] and beings of anuttara-samyak-saṃbodhi,[5] have [times of] turning the Flower of Dharma,[6] and have [times of] the Flower of Dharma turning.[7] This is just the state in which *original practice of the bodhisattva-way*[8] neither regresses nor deviates. It is the *wisdom of the*

1. 十方仏土中 (JUPPO-BUTSUDO-CHU). See LS 1.106.

2. 唯有 (YUI-U). See LS 1.106.

3. 法華 (HOKKE), or (more freely translated) "the Lotus Universe," from the title of the Lotus Sutra. See LS 2.156.

4. "All buddhas" is 一切諸仏 (ISSAI-SHOBUTSU). "Ten directions" is 十方 (JUPPO). "The three times" (past, present, and future; eternity) is 三世 (SANZE). These expressions all derive from the Lotus Sutra. See LS 1.90, LS 1.128.

5. 阿耨多羅三藐三菩提 (ANOKUTARA-SANMYAKU-SANBODAI). These characters, representing the sound of the Sanskrit *anuttara-samyak-saṃbodhi,* appear frequently throughout the Lotus Sutra. See LS 2.156.

6. 転法華 (TENHOKKE). 転 (TEN), is lit. "to turn," "to move," or "to change." Used here as a transitive verb, 転 (TEN) suggests i) to turn a scroll on which the Lotus Sutra is written, and ii) to act in, or upon, the Universe which is identified with the Lotus Sutra. The content of this chapter suggests that to read the Lotus Sutra and to realize the real Universe are the same.

7. 法華転 (HOKKETEN). Used here as an intransitive verb, 転 (TEN) suggests i) a scroll of the Lotus Sutra unrolling naturally, and ii) activity of the Universe independent of the subjective self.

8. 本行菩薩道 (HONGYO-BOSATSUDO). 本 (HON) means "original," and at the same time it suggests the past. 本行 (HONGYO) appears in several places in the Lotus Sutra referring to the practices of bodhisattvas in the eternal past. See LS 2.172, LS 3.20.

buddhas, profound and unfathomable.[9] It is the *calm and clear state of samādhi,*[10] which is *difficult to understand and difficult to enter.*[11] As the Buddha *Mañjuśrī,*[12] it has the *form as it is*[13] of *buddhas alone, together with buddhas,*[14] which is *the great ocean* or *the Buddha-land.* Or as the Buddha *Śākyamuni,*[15] it is *appearance in the world*[16] in the state of *"Only I know concrete form, and the buddhas of the ten directions are also like that."*[17] It is the *one Time*[18] in which he *desires to cause living beings*[19] *to disclose, to display, to realize, and to enter,*[20] [saying] *"I and buddhas in the ten directions are directly able to know these things."*[21] Or it is *Universal Virtue,*[22] *accomplishing* the Dharma-Flower's turning whose *virtue is unthinkable,*[23] and *spreading throughout Jambudvīpa*[24] the *profound and eternal*[25] [truth of] *anuttara-samyak-saṃbodhi,* at which time the earth is able to produce the three kinds of plants, the two kinds of shrubs, and *large and small trees,*[26] and the rain is able to moisten them. In the state in which *an object cannot be recognized,*[27] he is solely *accomplishing the total practice*[28] of the Flower of Dharma turning. While Universal Virtue's spreading [of the truth] is still unfinished, the *great order on Vulture Peak*[29] comes together. Śākyamuni experiences, as the *manifestation of light from his [circle of] white hair,*[30] the coming and

---

9. 諸仏智慧甚深無量 (SHOBUTSU-CHIE-SHINJIN-MURYO). See LS 1.66.

10. 安詳三昧 (ANSHO-ZANMAI). See LS 1.66.

11. 難解難入 (NANGE-NANNYU). See LS 1.66.

12. 文殊師利 (MONJUSHIRI). A symbol of Buddhist wisdom. In Japan the statue in the Zazen Hall is usually the image of Mañjuśrī. The Lotus Sutra describes him as springing out from the great ocean. See LS 2.212-214, LS 2.218.

13. 如是相 (NYOZESO). See LS 1.68.

14. 唯仏与仏 (YUIBUTSU-YOBUTSU). See LS 1.68.

15. 釈迦牟尼 (SHAKAMUNI). The historical Buddha, who was born into the Śākya clan. The Sanskrit Śākyamuni means "Sage of the Śākyas." See LS 2.186-188.

16. 出現於世 (SHUTSUGEN-O-SE). See LS 1.88-90.

17. 唯我知是相, 十方仏亦然 (YUI-GA-CHI-ZE-SO, JUPPO-BUTSU-YAKU-NEN). See LS 1.74.

18. 一時 (ICHIJI). See LS 1.8, and note 146.

19. 欲礼衆生 (YOKU-REI-SHUJO). See LS 1.88-90.

20. 開示悟入 (KAI-JI-GO-NYU). See LS 1.88-90.

21. 我及十方仏乃能知是事 (GA-GYU-JUPPO-BUTSU, NAI-NO-CHI-ZE-JI). See LS 1.70.

22. 普賢 (FUGEN), the Bodhisattva called Samantabhadra in Sanskrit. The last chapter of the Lotus Sutra is *Fugen-bosatsu-kanpotsu (Encouragement of the Bodhisattva Universal Virtue).* The translation into English of Chinese characters representing the names of bodhisattvas has generally followed the translation in LSW.

23. 不可思議の功徳 (FUKASHIGI *no* KUDOKU). See LS 3.210, LS 3.328-330.

24. 閻浮堤に流布せしむる (ENBUDAI *ni* RUFU *se shimuru).* See LS 3.328–330. 閻浮堤 (ENBUDAI) represents the sound of the Sanskrit *Jambudvīpa,* the southern continent upon which, according to ancient Indian cosmology, human beings live.

25. 深大久遠 (SHINDAI-KU-ON). See LS 3.18, LS 3.328–330.

26. 大小諸樹 (DAISHO-SHOJU). See LS 1.274.

27. 所不能知 (SHO-FU-NO-CHI). See LS 1.66.

28. 尽行成就 (JINGYO-JOJU). The characters 成就 (JOJU), "accomplish," appear often in the Lotus Sutra (see LS 1.66, LS 3.328–330). 尽行 (JINGYO) means "total practice" or "all-out action" (see LS 1.66). In this context 尽行 (JINGYO) suggests Universal Virtue's work of realizing the reality of the Lotus Sutra—see LS 3.326.

29. 霊山の大会 (RYOZEN *no* DAI-E). Vulture Peak is a natural platform on the southern slope of Mount Chatha, overlooking the Rājagṛha valley. It was so called because the silhouette of the mountain resembles a vulture. The historical Buddha often preached there. See LS 2.216, LS 3.30.

30. 白毫光相 (BYAKUGO-KOSO). The circle of hair, *ūrṇā* in Sanskrit, is one of the thirty-two distin-

going of Universal Virtue.[31] The Flower of Dharma turns when, before Śākyamuni's *Buddhist assembly is halfway through*, the *consideration*[32] of Mañjuśrī *swiftly* gives *affirmation*[33] to Maitreya. Universal Virtue, the many buddhas, Mañjuśrī, and the great assembly, may all be the *pāramitā of knowing*[34] the Dharma-Flower's turning, which is *good in the beginning, middle, and end.*[35] This is why [the Buddha] has *manifested himself in reality*, calling *sole reliance*[36] on *the one vehicle*[37] *"the one great matter."*[38] Because this *manifestation in reality* is itself *the one great matter*, there are [the words] *"Buddhas alone, together with buddhas, just can perfectly realize that all dharmas are real form."*[39] The method[40] for that is inevitably *the one buddha-vehicle*, and *buddhas alone* necessarily teach its *perfect realization* to *buddhas alone. The many buddhas* and *the Seven Buddhas*[41] teach its *perfect realization* to each individual buddha, buddha-to-buddha, and they cause Śākyamuni Buddha to *accomplish* it.[42] [Every place from] India in the west to China in the east is *in the Buddha-lands of the ten directions*. [For every patriarch] until the thirty-third patriarch, Zen Master Daikan,[43] [this method] is the method which is the *one vehicle* of *buddhas alone*, and which is just *perfect realization* itself. It is *the one buddha-vehicle* in which *sole reliance* is decisively *the one great matter*. Now it is *manifesting itself in the*

---

guishing signs attributed to the Buddha. The Lotus Sutra describes many occasions when the Buddha sent forth a ray of light from between his eyebrows. See LS 1.18, LS 2.176.

31. The final chapter of the Lotus Sutra, *Fugen-bosatsu-kanpotsu*, describes the Bodhisattva Universal Virtue coming from the east to Vulture Peak to hear Śākyamuni's preaching of the Lotus Sutra, and promising to go to any place where people read and recite the Lotus Sutra, in order to serve and to protect them.

32. 惟忖 (YUIJUN). See LS 1.38, LS 1.52.

33. 授記 (JUKI), from the Sanskrit vyākaraṇa. The sixth chapter of the Lotus Sutra and chap. 32 of Shobogenzo have the title *Juki*. Here 授記 (JUKI) refers to Mañjuśrī's affirmation of Maitreya, that is, Mañjuśrī's prediction that Maitreya will become a buddha in future. See LS 1.62.

34. 知見波羅密 (CHIKEN-HARAMITSU). Master Dogen picked up these characters from the Lotus Sutra (see LS 1.68), where they are used as a noun, and he used them as a transitive verb. 知 (CHI) means to know and 見 (KEN) means to see. 知見 (CHIKEN) means knowledge or knowing. Master Dogen sometimes uses the word 知見 (CHIKEN) to represent the intellectual and sensory faculties (e.g. in *Fukan-zazengi:* "How could [dignified behavior] be anything other than criteria that precede knowing and seeing?"), but in this chapter and in the Lotus Sutra, 知見 (CHIKEN) suggests the intuitive wisdom of the mind in action. 波羅密 (HARAMITSU) is from the Sanskrit *pāramitā*, which means "gone to the opposite shore," or "accomplishment." 知見波羅密 (CHIKEN-HARAMITSU) means *prajñā*, or real wisdom experienced throughout the body and mind when the nervous system is set right in Zazen (see chap. 2, *Maka-hannya-haramitsu).*

35. 初中後善 (SHO-CHU-KO-ZEN). See LS 1.40.

36. 唯以 (YUI-I). In the Lotus Sutra, these characters have the meaning of "solely by [reason of...]." See LS 1.88–90.

37. 一乗 (ICHIJO), short for 一仏乗 (ICHI-BUTSUJO). See LS 1.90.

38. 一大事 (ICHIDAIJI). See LS 1.88–90.

39. 唯仏与仏乃能究尽諸法実相 (YUIBUTSU-YOBUTSU-NAINO-GUJIN-SHOHO-JISSO; or read in Japanese, YUI-BUTSU-YO-BUTSU, *sunawachi yoku* SHOHO-JISSO *o* GUJIN *su*) See LS 1.68.

40. The natural method of Zazen.

41. 七仏 (SHICHIBUTSU). See LS 2.96. See also chap. 15, *Busso.*

42. 成就す (JOJU *su*). See note 28.

43. Master Daikan Eno (638–713), a successor of Master Daiman Konin. He was the thirty-third patriarch from Master Mahākāśyapa, and the sixth patriarch in China. He had several excellent disciples including Master Seigen Gyoshi, Master Nangaku Ejo, and Master Nan-yo Echu.

world.[44] It is manifesting itself at this place.[45] That the Buddhist customs of Seigen[46] have been transmitted to the present, and that Nangaku's[47] Dharma-gate has been opened and preached through the world, are totally [due to] the *Tathāgata's real wisdom.*[48] Truly, this [real wisdom] is the *perfect realization* of *buddhas alone, together with buddhas*. The Dharma-Flower's turning may be preaching it[49] as the *disclosure, display, realization, and entering* of buddhas who are rightful successors, and of rightful successors of buddhas. This [real wisdom] is also called *the Sutra of the Lotus Flower of the Wonderful Dharma,*[50] and it is *the method of teaching bodhisattvas.*[51] Because this [real wisdom] has been called *all dharmas, Vulture Peak* exists, *space*[52] exists, the *great ocean*[53] exists, and the *great earth*[54] exists, with the Flower of Dharma as their *national land.*[55] This is just *real form;* it is *reality as it is;*[56] *it is the wisdom of the Buddha;* it is *the constancy of the manifestation of the world;*[57] it is *the real;*[58] it is *the Tathāgata's lifetime;*[59] it is *the profound and unfathomable;*[60] it is *the inconstancy of all actions;*[61] it is *samādhi as [the state of] the Flower of Dharma;*[62] it is *Śākyamuni Buddha;* it is *to turn the Flower of Dharma;*[63] it is *the Flower of Dharma turning;*[64] it is *the right-Dharma-eye treasury and the fine mind of nirvāṇa;*[65]

---

44. 出於現世 (SHUTSUGEN-O-SE). This expression appears many times in the Lotus Sutra with buddhas as the subject (see LS 1.88–90). Here Master Dogen uses it with the Buddhist method, Zazen, as the subject.

45. 出於現此 (SHUTSUGEN-O-SHI). This is Master Dogen's variation on the expression in the Lotus Sutra.

46. Master Seigen Gyoshi (660?–740). The lineages of the Soto, Unmon, and Hogen sects sprang from Master Seigen's descendants.

47. Master Nangaku Ejo (677–744). His history is described in Shobogenzo chap. 62, *Hensan.* The lineages of the Rinzai and Igyo sects sprang from the descendants of Master Nangaku and his successor Master Baso Do-itsu.

48. 如来如実知見 (NYORAI *[no]* NYOJITSU-CHIKEN). See LS 3.18.

49. 法華転すべし (HOKKETEN *su beshi).* Here 法華転す (HOKKETEN *su)* is used as a verb phrase—"the Dharma-Flower's turning preaches."

50. 妙法蓮華経 (MYOHO-RENGE-KYO), the full title of the Lotus Sutra, from the Sanskrit *Saddharma-puṇḍarika-sūtra.* See LS 1.52.

51. 教菩薩法 (KYO-BOSATSU-HO). See LS 1.52.

52. 虚空 (KOKU). See LS 2.286. See also Shobogenzo chap. 77, *Koku.*

53. 大海 (DAIKAI). See LS 2.212–214.

54. 大地 (DAICHI). See LS 2.196–198.

55. 国土 (KOKUDO). See LS 2.286. In this case, 国土 (KOKUDO) suggests a unified realm. Because the Buddha's real wisdom is identified with all things and phenomena in this world, concrete things like Vulture Peak, space, oceans, and the earth form a meaningful whole.

56. 如是 (NYOZE), used here as a noun. See LS 1.68.

57. 世相常住 (SESO-JOJU). See LS 1.120.

58. 如実 (NYOJITSU), as in 如実知見 (NYOJITSU-CHIKEN)—see LS 1.68.

59. 如来寿量 (NYORAI-JURYO), the title of the 16th chapter of the Lotus Sutra.

60. 甚深無量 (SHINJIN-MURYO). See LS 1.66.

61. 諸行無常 (SHOGYO-MUJO). This is the first line of the four-line poem in the *Mahāparinirvāṇa-sūtra,* which a hungry demon tells the child-bodhisattva Himālaya: *"Actions are without constancy. / Concrete existence is the arising and passing of dharmas. / After arising and passing have ceased, / The peace and quiet is pleasure itself."*

62. 法華三昧 (HOKKE-ZANMAI). See LS 3.214.

63. 転法華 (TENHOKKE).

64. 法華転 (HOKKETEN).

65. 正法眼蔵涅槃妙心 (SHOBOGENZO-NEHAN-MYOSHIN). The Buddha said, *"I have the right-Dharma-eye treasury and the fine mind of nirvāṇa; I transmit them to Mahākāśyapa."* See for example chap. 68,

and it is *manifestation of the body to save living beings.*[66] As *affirmation and becoming buddha,*[67] it is maintained and relied upon, and dwelt in and retained.

[47] To the order of Zen Master Daikan[68] at Horin-ji temple on Sokei-zan mountain, in the Shoshu district of Kuangtung,[69] in the great Kingdom of Tang, there came a monk called Hotatsu.[70] He boasts, *"I have recited the Lotus Sutra three thousand times already."*

The Patriarch says, *"Even if [you recite it] ten thousand times, if you do not understand the sutra, you will not be able even to recognize [your] errors."*

Hotatsu says, *"The student is foolish. Until now, I have only been reading [the sutra] aloud following the characters. How could I have hoped to clarify the meaning?"*

The Patriarch says, *"Try reciting a round [of the sutra] and I will interpret it for you."*

Hotatsu recites the sutra at once. When he reaches the *Expedient Means*[71] chapter the Patriarch says, *"Stop! The fundamental point of this Sutra is the purpose of [the buddhas'] appearance in the world.*[72] *Although it expounds many metaphors, [the Sutra] does not go beyond this. What is that purpose? Only the one great matter. The one great matter is just the Buddha's wisdom itself; it is to disclose, to display, to realize, and to enter [the Buddha's wisdom]. [The one great matter] is naturally the wisdom of the Buddha and someone who is equipped with the wisdom is already a buddha. You must now believe that the Buddha's wisdom is simply your own natural state of mind."* He preaches again in the following verse:

When the mind is in delusion, the Flower of Dharma turns.
When the mind is in realization, we turn the Flower of Dharma.
Unless we are clear about ourselves, however long we recite [the sutra],
It will become an enemy because of its meanings.
Without intention the mind is right.
With intention the mind becomes wrong.
When we transcend both with and without,
We ride eternally in the white ox cart.[73]

Udonge.

66. 現身度生 (GENSHIN-DOSHO). See LS 3.252 .

67. 授記作仏 (JUKI-SABUTSU). See for example LS 1.134, LS 1.322.

68. Master Daikan Eno (638–713).

69. 広南東路 (KAINANTORO). This was the name of an administrative area (close to present-day Kuangtung province) created in Southeast China during the reign of the Sung Emperor Kinei (1068–1077).

70. Hotatsu became a monk at the age of seven, and devoted himself to reciting the Lotus Sutra until meeting with Master Daikan Eno and receiving the Master's affirmation.

71. 方便品 (HOBEN-BON), the second chapter of the Lotus Sutra.

72. 因縁出世 (INNEN-SHUSSE). See LS 1.88–90. 因 (IN) means direct or intrinsic causes, and 縁 (EN) means indirect or external causes, connections, or conditions. At the same time, 因縁 (INNEN) represents the Sanskrit *hetu-pratyaya*, which sometimes means "causes" or "purpose."

73. 白牛車 (BYAKUGOSHA). Symbol of the state of Buddhist wisdom. See LS 1.166. The third chapter of the Lotus Sutra, *Hiyu (A Parable),* is the parable of a rich father who lures his children out of a burning house by telling them that there are goat carts, deer carts, and ox carts for them to play with outside the gate. When the children escape the burning house, the father gives them a great cart yoked by white oxen, which is more than they had hoped for. In the same way, buddhas use expedient means to make living beings realize the Buddha's wisdom—even as they discriminate and explain the three vehicles by which śrāvakas, pratyekabuddhas, and bodhisattvas should transcend the triple world, buddhas know that in reality there is only the one Buddha-vehicle which is the real wisdom of Zazen.

Hotatsu, on hearing this poem, addresses the Patriarch again: "*The sutra says that even if all in the great [order], from śrāvakas to bodhisattvas, exhausted their intellect to suppose it,*[74] *they could not fathom the Buddha's wisdom. If you are now saying that the effort to make the common man realize his own mind is just the Buddha's wisdom, unless we are of excellent makings we can hardly help doubting and denying it. Furthermore, the sutra explains the three kinds of cart, but what kind of distinction is there between the great ox cart and the white ox cart? Please, Master, bestow your preaching again.*"

The Patriarch says, "*The intention of the sutra is clear. You are straying off on your own and going against it. When people of the three vehicles cannot fathom the Buddha's wisdom, the trouble is in their supposition itself. Even if together they exhaust their intellects to consider it,*[75] *they will only get further and further away.*[76] *The Buddha originally preaches only for the benefit of the common man; he does not preach for the benefit of buddhas. Some are not fit to believe this principle and withdraw from their seats;*[77] *they do not know that they are sitting in the white ox cart yet still searching outside the gate*[78] *for the three kinds of cart. The words of the sutra are clearly telling you: 'There is neither a second nor a third.'*[79] *Why do you not realize it? The three carts are fictitious, for they belong to the past. The one vehicle is real, for it exists in the present. I only [wish to] make you get rid of the fiction and get back to the reality. When we get back to reality, reality is not a concept. Remember, your possessions are all treasures,*[80] *and they totally belong to you. How you receive and use them is up to you. [The reality of the sutra] is neither the ideas of the father nor the ideas of the children,*[81] *indeed it does not rely upon ideas at all; rather, it is called the Sutra of the Flower of Dharma. From kalpa to kalpa, from noon to night, [our] hands do not put down the sutra, and there is no time when we are not reading it.*" Hotatsu, enlightened already and jumping for joy,[82] presents the following verse of praise:

> *Three thousand recitations of the sutra*
> *With one phrase from Sokei, forgotten.*
> *Before clarifying the import of [the buddhas'] appearance in the world,*
> *How can we stop recurring lives of madness?*
> *[The sutra] explains goat, deer, and ox as an expedient,*
> *[But] proclaims that beginning, middle, and end are good.*
> *Who knows that [even] within the burning house,*
> *Originally we are kings in the Dharma.*

When he presents this verse, the Patriarch says, "*From now on, you may be called the Sutra-reading Monk.*"[83]

---

74. 尽思度量 (JINJI-DORYO). See LS 1.72.

75. 尽思共推 (JINSHI-GUSUI). See LS 1.72.

76. 懸遠 (KEN-ON). See LS 1.128.

77. See LS 1.86.

78. 門外 (MONGE). See LS 1.164.

79. 無二亦無三 (MUNI-YAKU-MUSAN). See LS 1.106.

80. 珍宝 (CHINPO). See LS 1.224.

81. The metaphor of father (the Buddha) and children (his followers) occurs in the parable of the burning house and in several other chapters of the Lotus Sutra.

82. 踊躍歓喜 (YUYAKU-KANKI). This expression occurs repeatedly in the Lotus Sutra. See LS 1.134, LS 1.166.

83. This is Master Daikan Eno's affirmation.

[54] The story[84] of how Zen Master Hotatsu visited Sokei is like this. Hereafter the Flower of Dharma began to be expounded as the Flower of Dharma turning and turning of the Dharma-Flower. [Those terms] were not heard previously. Truly, the clarification of the Buddha's wisdom should always take place under a Buddhist patriarch who may be the right-Dharma-eye treasury itself. [The Buddha's wisdom] cannot be known by literary scholars who vainly count sand and pebbles, as we can see again here in Hotatsu's experience. To clarify the true meaning of the Flower of Dharma, *perfectly realize,* as *only the one great purpose,* that which the ancestral Master *disclosed and displayed.* Do not intend to research other vehicles. The present is the reality as it is[85] of the real form, the real nature, the real body, the real energy, the real causes, and the real effects of the Flower of Dharma turning.[86] This was never heard in China, and it was never present [in China], before the time of the ancestral Master. *"The Flower of Dharma is turning"* means *the mind is in delusion;* the mind being deluded is just the Flower of Dharma turning. Therefore, when the mind is in delusion, we are being turned by the Flower of Dharma. This means that even when mental delusion is in myriad phenomena, *form as it is*[87] is still being turned by the Flower of Dharma. This being turned is not to be rejoiced at, and it is not to be hoped for; it is not gained, and it does not come. Even so, when the Flower of Dharma is turning *there is neither a second nor a third.* Because [the Flower of Dharma turning] is the *sole existence of the one buddha-vehicle,* and because it is the Flower of Dharma with *form as it is,* whether it is the turner or the turned, it is *the one buddha-vehicle,* and *the one great matter.*

† It is just moment by moment of red mind,[88] upon which we *rely solely.* So do not worry about the mind being deluded. *Your actions are the bodhisattva-way itself;*[89] they are *to serve the buddhas*[90] which is *original practice of the bodhisattva way.*[91] What you disclose, display, realize, and enter is, in every case, an instance of the Flower of Dharma turning.

†† There is mental delusion in the burning house, there is mental delusion just at the gate itself, there is mental delusion outside the gate, there is mental delusion just in

---

84. "Story" is 因縁 (INNEN), lit. "causes and conditions;" in this case representing the Sanskrit *nidāna,* which means a primary cause or a historical account. See Glossary and note 72.

85. 如是 (NYOZE), used as a noun. See LS 1.68.

86. 法華転 (HOKKETEN). From here to the end of this long paragraph, Master Dogen explains 法華転 (HOKKETEN), the Flower of Dharma turning. In the following paragraph [62] he explains 転法華 (TENHOKKE), our turning of the Flower of Dharma.

87. 如是相 (NYOZESO). See LS 1.68.

† So far in this paragraph, Master Dogen has outlined in general terms the meaning of "the Flower of Dharma turns" (如是相, HOKKETEN). This short section introduces the concrete or objective phase. The division into sub-paragraphs is only for ease of reading, there being no divisions in the source text.

88. 赤心 (SEKISHIN) means "naked mind," "sincere mind," or "mind as it is."

89.汝等所行, 是菩薩道 (NANJIRA-SHOGYO, ZE-BOSATSU-DO). See LS 1.286.

90. 奉覲於諸仏 (SHOBUTSU *[ni]* BUGON *[suru]),* or to pay homage to the buddhas. See LS 1.300.

91. 本行菩提道 (HONGYO-BOSATSUDO). See LS 2.172, LS 3.20.

†† From here Master Dogen considers the analogy of the burning house on the basis of objective reality, as opposed to idealism. In general, the burning house symbolizes delusion; open ground symbolizes the state of realization; the gate of the house symbolizes the process leading from delusion to realization; the carriages symbolize methods of Buddhist practice; and the white ox-carriage symbolizes practice in the state of Buddhist wisdom, Zazen.

front of the gate, and there is mental delusion within the gate.[92] Mental delusion has created "within the gate" and "outside the gate" and even "the gate itself," "the burning house," and so on; therefore, disclosure, display, realization, and entering may take place even on the white ox-carriage.[93] When we think of entry as *adornment*[94] on this carriage, should we hope for *open ground*[95] as the place to enter, or should we recognize *the burning house* as the place to leave?[96] Should we reach the conclusion[97] that the gate itself is merely a place of momentary passing?[98] Remember, inside the carriage, there is turning [of the Flower of Dharma] which causes us to disclose, to display, to realize, and to enter the burning house; and on the open ground there is turning which causes us to disclose, to display, to realize, and to enter the burning house.[99] There are cases in which the turning activates disclosure, display, realization, and entering through the whole gate as the gate here and now;[100] and there are cases in which the turning activates disclosure, display, realization, and entering through a single gate which is [an instance of] the universal gate.[101] There is turning which discloses, displays, realizes, and enters the universal gate in each instance of disclosure, display, realization, and entering.[102] There are cases in which the turning activates disclosure, display, realization, and entering within the gate,[103] and there are cases in which the turning activates disclosure, display, realization, and entering outside the gate.[104] There are cases of disclosing, displaying, realizing, and entering open ground in the burning house.[105]

---

92. Denial of the idealistic idea that delusion exists only in the burning house.

93. Even people who are in the state of Buddhist wisdom can experience realization by recognizing their thoughts as thoughts.

94. 荘校 (SHOKYO). See LS 1.166.

95. 露地 (ROJI). See LS 1.166.

96. Denial of idealistic interpretations of entering and leaving—reality is where we are already, and so there is no area to be entered and no area to be left.

97. 究尽 (GUJIN), elsewhere translated as "perfectly realize." See LS 1.68.

98. Denial of the idealistic view that the Buddhist process is only a means to an end.

99. Buddhist teaching always affirms the reality of the not-ideal situation, even for those who have real wisdom and are living in the peaceful state.

100. 当門の全門 (TOMON *no* ZENMON), suggests the whole Buddhist process as this moment of the Buddhist process.

101. 普門の一門 (FUMON *no* ICHIMON), suggests the Buddhist process of one individual, at one time and place. The characters 一門 (ICHIMON) appear in the parable of the burning house. See LS 1.162. The characters 普門 (FUMON) are contained in the title of the 25th chapter of the Lotus Sutra, 観世音菩薩普門品 (KANZEON-BOSATSU-FUMON-BON), *"The Universal Gate of the Bodhisattva Regarder of the Sounds of the World."* 門 (MON) means both "gate" and "aspect;" and 普 (FU) means "universal," or "every kind of." The chapter describes how Bodhisattva Avalokiteśvara manifests himself or herself in many different guises (普門, FUMON), in order to save living beings. See LS 3.252 and see Glossary under *Samantamukha*.

102. We usually think that various processes lead us to realization. This suggests, conversely, that realization leads us to realize the Buddhist process.

103. Buddhist wisdom can occur instantaneously, even before the Buddhist process is completed.

104. Buddhist wisdom can still be realized even after the process is complete.

105. We can sometimes realize the peaceful state in painful or emotional circumstances.

††† Therefore the burning house is *beyond understanding*[106] and the open ground is *beyond knowing*.[107] Who could make the turning of the wheel of the triple world[108] into a carriage and ride it as *the one vehicle*? Who could leave and enter disclosure, display, realization, and entering as if they were a gate? If we seek the carriage from the burning house, how many times the wheel must turn! When we look upon the burning house from the open ground, how *deep in the distance*[109] it is! Should we reach the conclusion that Vulture Peak existed *in tranquillity*[110] on open ground? Or should we study in action that the open ground is *balanced and even*[111] on Vulture Peak? *The place where living beings enjoy themselves*[112] has been made into *eternal presence*[113] as *my pure land which is immortal*,[114] and this also we must meticulously perform as *original practice*.[115]

Do we realize in practice that *whole-heartedly wanting to meet Buddha*[116] is about ourselves, or do we realize in practice that it is about others? There are times when the truth is realized as an *individual body*,[117] and there are times when the truth is realized as the *Whole Body*.[118]

Appearance together on Vulture Peak[119] comes from *not begrudging one's own body and life*.[120] There is disclosure, display, realization, and entering in *constantly abiding here preaching the Dharma*,[121] and there is disclosure, display, realization, and entering in, *as an expedient method, manifesting nirvāṇa*.[122] In the state of *being close yet still failing to see*,[123] who could not believe in understanding of non-understanding by *whole-heartedness*?[124]

---

††† This part considers the analogy of the burning house on the practical basis of everyday life.

106. 不会 (FUE). Master Daikan Eno said, "I do not understand the Buddha Dharma." (我不会仏法). See *Shinji-shobogenzo* pt. 1, no. 59.

107. 不識 (FUSHIKI). Alludes to the words of Master Bodhidharma. See chap. 30, *Gyoji* [188], and chap. 20, *Kokyo* [162].

108. 輪転三界 (RINDEN-SANGAI). 輪転 (RINDEN) represents the Sanskrit word *saṃsāra*; lit. "wandering through," or "circuit of mundane existence." 三界 (SANGAI), the triple world, means the world as it is divided in the minds of ordinary people; the ordinary world. The Lotus Sutra teaches us to see the triple world as it really is, as the triple world. See LS 3.18.

109. 深遠 (SHIN-ON). See LS 1.68.

110. 安穏 (ANON). Suggests an ideal situation. See LS 1.146.

111. 平坦 (HEITAN). Suggests the concrete balanced state realized in practice. These characters have not been traced in the Lotus Sutra. An equivalent, though slightly more abstract expression, 平正 (HEISHO), appears many times, often together with 安穏 (ANON). See LS 1.146.

112. 衆生所遊楽 (SHUJO-SHO-YURAKU). See LS 3.32.

113. 常在 (JOZAI). See LS 3.32.

114. 我浄土不毀 (WAGA-JODO-FUKI). See LS 3.32.

115. 本行 (HONGYO), used here as a verb. See note 8, and LS 2.172, LS 3.20.

116. 一心欲見仏 (ISSHIN-YOKU-KENBUTSU). See LS 3.30. See also Shobogenzo chap. 61, *Kenbutsu*.

117. 分身 (BUNSHIN) means "offshoot," suggesting the bodies of individual buddhas as offshoots of the Buddha. See LS 2.176.

118. 全身 (ZENSHIN) sometimes suggests the Universe as the whole body of the Buddha (as in Shobogenzo chap. 71, *Nyorai-zenshin*). See LS 2.154.

119. 倶出霊鷲山 (GUSHUTSU-REIJUSEN). See LS 3.30.

120. 身命を自惜せざる (SHINMYO *o* JISHAKU *se zaru*). See LS 3.30.

121. 常住此説法 (JOJU-SHI-SEPPO). See LS 3.30. See also Shobogenzo chap. 61, *Kenbutsu*.

122. 方便現涅槃 (HOBEN-GEN-NEHAN). See LS 3.30.

123. 而不見の雖近 (SHI-FUKEN *no* SUI-GON). See LS 3.30.

124. 一心 (ISHIN), lit. "one mind;" used in the Lotus Sutra as an adverb ("whole-heartedly"). See LS

The place which is *always filled with gods and human beings*[125] is just the land of Śākyamuni Buddha and of Vairocana,[126] *the eternally peaceful and bright land*[127] itself. We who naturally belong in the *four lands*[128] are just living in *the Buddha's land* which is *real oneness.*[129] When we look at *atoms*[130] that does not mean we fail to see *the world of Dharma.*[131] When we are experiencing the world of Dharma, that does not mean we fail to experience atoms. When the buddhas experience the world of Dharma, they do not exclude us from the experience, which is *good at the beginning, middle, and end.*

This being so, the present is the *form as it is* of the state of experience, and even *alarm, doubt, and fear*[132] are nothing other than reality as it is. With the Buddha's wisdom, this [fear] is only the difference between looking at atoms and sitting in atoms. When we are seated in the world of Dharma it is not wide, and when we are sitting in atoms, they are not confining; therefore, without maintaining and relying upon [reality as it is], we cannot sit, but when we are maintaining and relying upon [reality as it is], there is no alarm or doubt about width and confinement. This is because we have *perfectly realized* the *body* and the *energy* of the Flower of Dharma. So should we think that our own *form* and *nature* now are *originally practicing* in this world of Dharma, or should we think that they are *originally practicing* in atoms? They are without alarm and doubt, and without fear; they are simply the profound and eternal state which is original practice as the Flower of Dharma turning. This seeing atoms and seeing the world of Dharma is beyond conscious action and conscious consideration. Conscious consideration, and conscious action too, should learn Flower of Dharma consideration, and should learn Flower of Dharma action. When we hear of *"disclosure, display, realization, and entering,"* we should understand them in terms of [the Buddha's] *desire to cause living beings.*[133] In other words, that which, as the Flower of Dharma turning, discloses the Buddha's wisdom, we should learn by displaying the Buddha's wisdom. That which, as the Flower of Dharma turning, realizes the Buddha's wisdom, we should learn by entering the

---

3.30.

125. 天人常充満 (TENNIN-JO-JUMAN). See LS 3.32.

126. 毘盧遮那 (BIRUSHANA). Vairocana is the Sun Buddha, not mentioned in the Lotus Sutra itself, but mentioned in 観普賢菩薩行法経 (KAN-FUGEN-BOSATSU-GYOHO-KYO), *the Sutra of Reflection on the Practice of Dharma by Bodhisattva Universal Virtue*, which is included as the third part of the Threefold Lotus Sutra (for example, in LSW).

127. 常寂光土 (JO-JAKU-KO-DO). This sentence is related to the teaching of the Tendai Sect about the four lands (see following note). The Tendai Sect is based on the study of the Lotus Sutra, and Master Dogen spent his teenage years as a monk of the Tendai Sect at a temple on Mt. Hi-ei in Japan.

128. 四土 (SHIDO), are four lands symbolizing the four processes of Buddhist life. They are 1) 凡聖同居土 (BONSHO-DOGO-DO), the land where sacred beings and ordinary people live together; 2) 方便有余土 (HOBEN-UYO-DO), the land of expedient methods where something still remains, that is, the land of those who are led by the Buddha's teachings but who have not yet completely realized the teaching for themselves; 3) 実報無碍土 (JIPPO-MUGE-DO), the land of real results and no hindrances, that is, the land of bodhisattvas who have realized the teaching perfectly; and 4) 常寂光土 (JO-JAKU-KO-DO), the eternally peaceful and bright land, which is the abode of those who have realized the truth.

129. 如一の仏土 (NYOITSU *no* BUTSUDO). See LS 3.158.

130. 微塵 (MIJIN), derived from the Sanskrit *paramāṇu*, which means an infinitesimal portion or atom. See LS 3.130.

131. 法界 (HOKKAI), means inclusive reality.

132. 驚疑怖畏 (KYOGI-FU-I). See LS 2.156–158.

133. 欲令衆生 (YOKU-REI-SHUJO). See LS 1.88–90.

Buddha's wisdom. That which, as the Flower of Dharma turning, displays the Buddha's wisdom, we should learn by realizing the Buddha's wisdom. For each such instance of the Flower of Dharma turning, as disclosure, display, realizing, and entering, we can have ways of perfect realization. In sum, this wisdom-pāramitā[134] of the buddha-tathāgatas is the Dharma-Flower's turning, which is wide, great, profound, and eternal. *Affirmation*[135] is just our own disclosure of the Buddha's wisdom; it is the Flower of Dharma's turning which is never imparted by others. This, then, is [the reality of] *"When the mind is in the state of delusion, the Flower of Dharma turns."*

[62] *"When the mind is in the state of realization, we turn the Flower of Dharma"* describes turning the Flower of Dharma. That is to say, when the Flower of Dharma has *perfectly exhausted*[136] the energy with which it turns us, the *energy as it is*[137] with which we turn ourselves will, in turn, be realized. This realization is to turn the Flower of Dharma. Though the former turning is, even now, without cease, we, reversely, are naturally turning the Flower of Dharma. Though we have not finished donkey business, horse business will still come in.[138] [Here] there exists *sole reliance on the one great purpose* as *real appearance at this place.*[139] The multitudes of the thousandfold world that *spring out of the earth*[140] have long been great honored saints of the Flower of Dharma[141] but they spring out of the earth being turned by themselves and they spring out of the earth being turned by circumstances.[142] In turning the Flower of Dharma we should not only realize springing out of the earth; in turning the Flower of Dharma we should also realize springing out of space.[143] We should know with the Buddha's wisdom not only earth and space but also springing out of the Flower of Dharma itself. In general, in the Time of the Flower of Dharma, inevitably, *the father is young and the son old.*[144] It is neither that the son is not the son, nor that the father is not the father; we should just learn

---

134. 知見波羅密 (CHIKEN-HARAMITSU). See note 34.

135. 授記 (JUKI). See note 33.

136. "Perfectly exhausted" is another translation of 究尽 (GUJIN), usually translated as "perfectly realized." See LS 1.68.

137. 如是力 (NYOZERIKI). See LS 1.68.

138. Master Chokei Eryo asks Master Reiun Shigon, *"Just what is the Great Intent of the Buddha-Dharma?"* Master Reiun says, *"Donkey business being unfinished, but horse business coming in."* See *Shinji-shobogenzo*, pt. 2, no. 56.

139. 出現於此 (SHUTSUGEN-O-SHI). See note 45.

140. 地涌 (CHI-YU). The title of the 15th chapter of the Lotus Sutra is 従地涌出 (JU-CHI-YUSHUTSU), *Springing Out from the Earth.* See LS 2.286.

141. In the *Springing Out from the Earth* chapter, the Buddha is asked to explain why the bodhisattvas who have pursued the truth for a long time in the past have now sprung from the earth and become followers of the Buddha who has only recently realized the truth. See LS 2.318.

142. "Circumstances" is 佗 (TA). This can be interpreted as "circumstances" (as opposed to self), or as "others," or as "him" (the Buddha in the Lotus Sutra—see LS 2.286).

143. 虚空 (KOKU). See LS 2.286. LSW says that the original Sanskrit word in this part of the Lotus Sutra is *ākāśā* (space, ether), which is often used as a synonym for *śūnyatā* (void). In Shobogenzo the Chinese character 空 (KU) includes both these meanings, that is, i) concrete space or the sky, and ii) *śūnyatā* i.e., the state in which there is nothing on our mind, emptiness. But 虚空 (KOKU) usually has a more concrete emphasis (space)—see chap. 77, *Koku.* In this sentence, 転法華す (TENHOKKE *su*) is used as a transitive verb; "to realize... in turning the Flower of Dharma." Compare note 49.

144. 父少而子老 (FUSHO-JI-SHIRO). See LS 2.318.

that the son is old and the father young. Do not imitate *the disbelief of the world*[145] and be surprised. [Even] the disbelief of the world is the Time of the Flower of Dharma. This being so, in turning the Flower of Dharma we should realize the *one Time* in which *the Buddha is living.*[146] Turned by disclosure, display, realization, and entering, we spring out of the earth; and turned by the Buddha's wisdom, we spring out of the earth. At the time of this turning the Flower of Dharma, *mental realization*[147] exists as the Flower of Dharma, and the Flower of Dharma exists as mental realization.[148] For another example, the meaning of *the downward direction* is just *the inside of space.*[149] This *downward,* and this *space,* are just the turning of the Flower of Dharma, and are just the lifetime of the Buddha. We should realize, in turning the Flower of Dharma, that the Buddha's lifetime, the Flower of Dharma, the world of Dharma, and the wholehearted state, are realized as *downward,* and realized also as *space.* Thus, *downward-space* describes just the realization of turning the Flower of Dharma. In sum, at this moment, by turning the Flower of Dharma we can cause the three kinds of grass to exist, and by turning the Flower of Dharma we can cause the two kinds of trees to exist. We should not expect [this] to be a state of awareness, and we should not wonder whether it is a state without awareness. When we turn ourselves and *initiate bodhi,*[150] that is just *the southern quarter.*[151] This realization of the truth is originally present on Vulture Peak, which convenes as an order in the southern quarter. Vulture Peak is always present in our turning the Flower of Dharma. There are Buddha-lands of the ten directions which convene as an order in space, and this is an individual body[152] turning the Flower of Dharma. When we realize it, in turning the Flower of Dharma, as already the Buddha-lands of the ten directions, there is no place into which an atom could enter. There is turning the Flower of Dharma as *"matter just being the immaterial,"*[153] which is beyond *either disappearance or appearance.*[154] There is turning the Flower of Dharma as *"the immaterial just being matter,"*[155] which may be *absence of life and death.*[156] We cannot call it *"being in the world;"*[157]

---

145. 世の不信 (YO *no* FUSHIN). See LS 2.318.

146. 一時仏住 (ICHIJI-BUTSU-JU), taken from the opening words of the Lotus Sutra. See LS 1.8.

147. 心悟 (SHINGO), as in Master Daikan Eno's poem.

148. In general in this paragraph Master Dogen repeatedly suggests the synthesis of two factors: real and mental, objective and subjective, concrete and abstract, the substantial earth and the empty sky, the individual downward direction and all-inclusive space, factual Vulture Peak and the fabulous tower, the historical Buddha and the legendary Tathāgata, and so on.

149. The Lotus Sutra says 下方空中住 (KAHO-KUCHU-JU), "Down below, they live in space." See LS 2.310. Master Dogen read the characters 下方 (KAHO) and 空中 (KUCHU), literally, as noun phrases: "the downward direction," and "the inside of space." He emphasized that we should realize that reality includes both the specific (the downward direction) and the inclusive (space).

150. 発菩提 (HOTSU-BODAI), short for 発菩提心 (HOTSU-BODAISHIN), "to establish the Bodhi-mind." See LS 2.218.

151. 南方 (NANPO), a world free of impurity. See LS 2.224.

152. 分身 (BUNSHIN). See note 117.

153. 色即是空 (SHIKI-SOKU-ZE-KU). Quoted from the Heart Sutra. See Shobogenzo chap. 2, *Maka-hannya-haramitsu*.

154. 若退若出 (NYAKU-TAI-NYAKU-SHUTSU). See LS 3.18.

155. 空即是色 (KU-SOKU-ZE-SHIKI). Also quoted from the Heart Sutra.

156. 無有生死 (MU-U-SHOJI). See LS 3.18.

157. 在世 (ZAISE). See LS 3.18.

and how could it only be in a process of *extinction?*[158] When [a person] is a *close friend*[159] to us, we are also a *close friend* to that person. We must not forget to bow to and to work for a *close friend;* therefore, we must take care to perfectly realize moments of giving *the pearl in the top-knot*[160] and of giving *the pearl in the clothes.*[161] There is turning the Flower of Dharma in the presence *before the Buddha* of a *treasure stūpa,*[162] whose *height is five hundred yojana.*[163] There is turning the Flower of Dharma in the *Buddha sitting inside the stūpa,*[164] whose extent is *two hundred and fifty yojana.* There is turning the Flower of Dharma in springing out from the earth and abiding in the earth, [in which state] mind is without restriction and matter is without restriction. There is turning the Flower of Dharma in springing out from the sky and abiding in the earth, which is restricted by the eyes and restricted by the body.[165] Vulture Peak exists inside the stūpa, and the treasure stūpa exists on Vulture Peak. The treasure stūpa is a treasure stūpa in space, and space makes space for the treasure stūpa.[166] The eternal buddha inside the stūpa takes his seat alongside the buddha of Vulture Peak, and the buddha of Vulture Peak experiences the state of experience as the buddha inside the stūpa.[167] When the buddha of Vulture Peak enters the state of experience inside the stūpa, while object and subject on Vulture Peak [remain] just as they are, he enters into the turning of the Flower of Dharma. When the buddha inside the stūpa springs out on Vulture Peak, while still of the land of eternal buddhas, while still *long extinct,*[168] he springs out. *Springing out,* and *entering into the turning,* are not to be learned under common men and the two vehicles, [but] should follow turning of the Flower of Dharma. *Eternal extinction*[167] is an ornament of real experience that adorns the state of buddha. *Inside the stūpa, before the Buddha, the treasure stūpa,* and *space* are not of Vulture Peak; they are not of the world of Dharma; they are not a halfway stage; and they are not of the whole world. Nor are they concerned with only a *concrete place in the Dharma.*[169] They are simply *different from thinking.*[170] There is turning the Flower of Dharma either in *manifesting the body of Bud-*

---

158. 滅度 (METSUDO). See also LS 3.18.

159. 親友 (SHIN-YU). See LS 2.118.

160. 髻珠 (KEIJU). See LS 2.276.

161. 衣珠 (EJU). See LS 2.118.

162. 仏前に法塔ある (BUTSUZEN *ni* HOTO *aru*) Taken from the opening words of the 11th chapter of the Lotus Sutra, *Ken-hoto (Seeing the Treasure Stupa).* See LS 2.168.

163. 高五百由旬 (KO-GOHYAKU-YUJUN). See LS 2.168. It is said that one yojana is equivalent to the distance an ox can pull a cart in one harnessing—about nine miles (see Glossary). Master Dogen emphasized that even a fabulous tower has its concrete height.

164. 塔中に仏坐 (TOCHU *ni* BUTSUZA). See LS 2.186–188.

165. The Lotus Sutra says the stūpa sprang out from the earth and abode in the sky (see LS 2.168), suggesting phenomenal realization based on the concrete. Master Dogen considered two further cases: concrete realization which is based on the concrete (and which is therefore unrestricted realization), and concrete realization which is based on mental phenomena (and which is therefore realization restricted by the eyes and by the body).

166. Suggests the oneness of an entity and the space which it occupies.

167. The legendary eternal buddha called Buddha Abundant Treasures (Prabhūtaratna Buddha in Sanskrit), and Śākyamuni Buddha who existed as a historical person on Vulture Peak, are on the same level; when we venerate them, we are venerating the same state. See LS 2.186–188.

168. 久滅度 (KUMETSUDO). See LS 2.190.

169. 是法位 (ZE-HO-I). See LS 1.120.

170. 非思量 (HISHIRYO) describes the state in Zazen. See for example chap. 27, *Zazenshin;* chap. 58, *Zazengi;* and *Fukan-zazengi.* The characters also appear in the *Expedient Means* chapter of the Lotus Sutra.

dha and preaching the Dharma for others[171] or in manifesting this body and preaching the Dharma for others. Or turning the Flower of Dharma is the manifestation of Devadatta.[172] Or there is turning the Flower of Dharma in the manifestation of *"to retreat also is fine."*[173] Do not always measure *the waiting, with palms held together and [faces] looking up,*[174] as *sixty minor kalpas.*[175] Even if the length of *wholehearted waiting*[176] is condensed into just a few countless *kalpas*, still it will be *impossible to fathom the Buddha-wisdom.*[177] As how much Buddha-wisdom should we see a wholehearted mind that is waiting? Do not see this turning the Flower of Dharma only as *the bodhisattva-way practiced in the past.*[178] Wherever the Flower of Dharma is a total order the virtue is that of turning the Flower of Dharma, [and it is expressed] as, *"The Tathāgata preaches the Great Vehicle today."*[179] [When] the Flower of Dharma just now is the Flower of Dharma, it is *neither sensed nor recognized,*[180] and at the same time it is *beyond knowing* and *beyond understanding.*[181] This being so, *five hundred [ink] drop [kalpas]*[182] are a brief thousandth [of an instant] of turning the Flower of Dharma; they are the Buddha's lifetime being proclaimed by each moment of red mind.

[70] In conclusion, in the hundreds of years since this Sutra was transmitted into China, to be turned as the Flower of Dharma, very many people, here and there, have produced their commentaries and interpretations. Some, moreover, have attained the Dharma-state of an eminent person by relying on this Sutra. But no-one has grasped the point of *the Flower of Dharma turning*, or mastered the point of *turning the Flower of Dharma*, in the manner of our founding Patriarch, the eternal Buddha of Sokei. Now that we have heard these [points] and now that we have met it, we have experienced the meeting of eternal buddha with eternal buddha; how could [this] not be the land of eternal buddhas? How joyful it is! From kalpa to kalpa is the Flower of Dharma, and from noon to night is the Flower of Dharma. Because the Flower of Dharma is from kalpa to kalpa, and because the Flower of Dharma is from noon to night, even though our own body-and-mind grows strong and grows weak, it is just the Flower of Dharma itself. The reality that exists *as it is* is a *treasure,*[183] is *brightness,*[184] is *a seat of truth,*[185] is

---

See LS 1.88–90.

171. 現仏身而為説法 (GEN-BUSSHIN-JI-I-SEPPO). See LS 3.252

172. Devadatta was a cousin of the Buddha and at one time the Buddha's disciple, but later Devadatta turned against the Buddha, and caused a schism within the Saṃgha. Hence Devadatta is a symbol of bad behavior. See LS 3.282–284. Nevertheless, in the chapter *Devadatta*, the 12th chapter of the Lotus Sutra, the Buddha gives affirmation that Devadatta will become a buddha in future. See LS 2.208.

173. 退亦佳矣 (TAI-YAKU-KE-I). See LS 1.86–88.

174. 合掌瞻仰待 (GASSHO-SENGO-TAI), from Śāriputra's words in the Lotus Sutra, *Hoben*, describing the attitude of the Buddha's disciples waiting for him to preach the Dharma. See LS 1.80. In these sentences Master Dogen praises the attitude of patient waiting.

175. 六十小劫 (ROKUJU-SHOKO). See LS 1.46.

176. 一心待 (ISSHIN-TAI). See LS 1.64.

177. 不能測仏智 (FU-NO-SOKU-BUCCHI). See LS 1.72.

178. 本行菩提道 (HONGYO-BOSATSU-DO). See note 8, and LS 2.172, LS 3.20.

179. 今日如来説大乗 (KONNICHI-NYORAI-SETSU-DAIJO). See LS 1.52.

180. 不覚不知 (FUKAKU-FUCHI). See LS 1.160.

181. 不識、不会 (FUSHIKI, FUE). See notes 106 and 107.

182. 塵点 (JINTEN), short for 塵点劫 (JINTENKO). See LS 2.12-14.

183. 珍宝 (CHINPO). See LS 1.224.

184. 光明 (KOMYO). See LS 2.286. See also chap. 36, *Komyo*.

wide, great, profound, and eternal,[186] is *profound, great, and everlasting,*[187] is *mind in delusion, the Flower of Dharma turning,* and is *mind in realization, turning the Flower of Dharma,* which is really just the Flower of Dharma turning the Flower of Dharma.

[72] *When the mind is in the state of delusion, the Flower of Dharma turns.*
When the mind is in the state of realization, we turn the Flower of Dharma.
If perfect realization can be like this,
The Flower of Dharma turns the Flower of Dharma.

When we *serve offerings to it, venerate, honor, and praise it*[188] like this, the Flower of Dharma is the Flower of Dharma.

Shobogenzo Hokke-ten-hokke

On a day of the summer retreat in the 2nd year of Ninji[189] I have written this and presented it to Zen person Etatsu. I am profoundly glad that he is going to leave home to practice the truth. Just to shave the head is a lovely fact in itself. To shave the head and to shave the head again: this is to be a true child of transcending family life.[190] Leaving home today is the *effects and results as they are* of the *energy as it is* which has turned the Flower of Dharma hitherto. The Flower of Dharma today will inevitably bear the Flower of Dharma's Flower of Dharma fruits. It is not Śākyamuni's Flower of Dharma and it is not the buddhas' Flower of Dharma; it is the Flower of Dharma of the Flower of Dharma. Though *form* is *as it is*, our habitual turning of the Flower of Dharma has been suspended in the state of *neither sensing nor recognizing*. But the Flower of Dharma now is manifesting itself afresh in the state *beyond knowing and beyond understanding*. The past was exhalation and inhalation, and the present is exhalation and inhalation. This we should maintain and rely upon, as the Flower of Dharma which is *too fine to think about.*[191]

Written by the founder of Kannon-dori-kosho-horin-ji temple, a śramaṇa who entered Sung [China] and received the transmission of Dharma, Dogen (His written seal).

The copying was completed at Hogyo-ji temple at the beginning of spring[192] in the 3rd year of Kagen.[193]

---

185. 道場 (DOJO). See LS 1.120.
186. 広大深遠 (KODAI-SHINNON). See LS 1.68.
187. 深大久遠 (SHINDAI-KU-ON). See LS 3.18-20, LS 3.328–330.
188. 供養、恭敬、尊重、讃歎 (KUYO, KUGYO, SONJU, SANDAN). This phrase appears many times in the Lotus Sutra. See LS 1.300.
189. 1241.
190. 真出家児 (SHIN *[no]* SHUKKE-JI), a true monk.
191. 妙難思 (MYONANSHI). See LS 1.82.
192. The 1st month of the lunar calendar.
193. 1305.

[18]

心不可得

SHIN-FUKATOKU

Mind Cannot Be Grasped [The former]

Shin *means "mind,"* ***fu*** *expresses negation,* ***ka*** *expresses possibility, and* ***toku*** *means "to grasp."* ***Shin-fukatoku,*** *or "mind cannot be grasped," is a quotation from the Diamond Sutra. On the basis of our common sense, we usually think that our mind can be grasped by our intellect, and we are prone to think that our mind must exist somewhere substantially. This belief also extends into the sphere of philosophy; Rene Descartes, for example, started his philosophical thinking with the premise "Cogito ergo sum" or "I think therefore I am." The German idealists, for example, Kant, Fichte, von Schnelling, and Hegel, also based their philosophies on the existence of mind. But in Buddhism we do not have confidence in the existence of mind. Buddhism is a philosophy of action, or a philosophy of the here and now; in that philosophy, mind cannot exist independently of the external world. In other words, Buddhism says that all existence is the instantaneous contact between mind and the external world. Therefore it is difficult for us to grasp our mind independently of the external world. In short, Buddhist theory cannot support belief in the independent existence of mind. In this chapter, Master Dogen preached that mind cannot be grasped, explaining a famous Buddhist story about a conversation between Master Tokuzan Senkan and an old woman selling rice cakes.*

[75] **Śākyamuni Buddha says,** *"Past mind cannot be grasped, present mind cannot be grasped, and future mind cannot be grasped."*[1]

This is what the Buddhist Patriarch has mastered in practice. Inside *cannot be grasped* it has scooped out and brought here the caves[2] of the past, present, and future. At the same time it has utilized the cave of [the Buddhist Patriarch] himself, and the meaning of *"self"* here is *mind cannot be grasped.* The present thinking and discrimination is *mind cannot be grasped.* The whole body utilizing the twelve hours is just *mind cannot be grasped.*

[76] After entering the room of a Buddhist patriarch, we understand *mind cannot be grasped.* Before entering the room of a Buddhist patriarch, we are without questions

---

1. Kongo-hannya-haramitsu-kyo or the Diamond Prajñā-pāramitā Sutra, from the Sanskrit Vajracchedikā-prajñā-pāramitā-sūtra. In Japanese the name of the sutra is usually abbreviated to Kongo-kyo or the Diamond Sutra.

2. 窟籠 (KUTSURO), lit. "cave-cage," suggests the regulated and concrete conditions of a buddha's daily life. (This usage is also found in chap. 79, Ango.) The quotation from the Diamond Sutra has exactly described the life of the buddhas of the past, present, and future.

about, we are without assertions about, and we do not see and hear *mind cannot be grasped.* Teachers of sutras and teachers of commentaries, śrāvakas and pratyekabuddhas, have never seen it even in a dream. Evidence of this is close at hand: Zen Master Tokuzan Senkan,[3] in former days, boasts that he has elucidated the Diamond Prajña Sutra.[4] Sometimes he calls himself *Shu, King of the Diamond Sutra.*[5] He is reputed to be especially well-versed in the Seiryu Commentaries,[6] besides which he [himself] has edited texts weighing twelve *tan.*[7] It appears that there is no other lecturer to match him. [In fact,] however, he is the last in a line of literary Dharma-teachers. Once, he hears that there is a supreme Buddha-Dharma, received by rightful successor from rightful successor, and angered beyond endurance he crosses mountains and rivers, carrying his sutras and commentaries with him, until he comes upon the order of Zen Master Shin of Ryutan.[8] On the way to that order, which he intends to join, he stops for a rest. Then an old woman comes along, and she [also] stops for a rest by the side of the road.

Then Lecturer [Sen]kan asks, *"What kind of person are you?"*

The old woman says, *"I am an old woman who sells rice-cakes."*

Tokuzan says, *"Will you sell some rice-cakes to me?"*

The old woman says, *"Why does the Master wish to buy rice-cakes?"*

Tokuzan says, *"I would like to buy rice-cakes to refresh my mind."*[9]

The old woman says, *"What is that great load the Master is carrying?"*

Tokuzan says, *"Have you not heard? I am Shu, King of the Diamond Sutra. I have mastered the Diamond Sutra. There is no part of it that I do not understand. This [load] I am now carrying is commentaries on the Diamond Sutra."*

Hearing this insistence, the old woman says, *"The old woman has a question. Will the Master permit me [to ask] it, or not?"*

---

3. Master Tokuzan Senkan (780–865). After traveling to the south of China he met Master Ryutan Soshin, a third-generation descendant of Master Seigen Gyoshi. It is said that Master Tokuzan received the Dharma from Master Ryutan, and later also met Master Isan Reiyu. He lived for thirty years in the Reiyo district, then fled to Dokufu-zan mountain to escape persecution by the Tang emperor Bu (reigned 841–846), who tried to abolish Buddhism. Finally, in the Daichu era (847–860), the governor of Buryo invited Master Tokuzan to become the master of Kotoku-zen-in temple. Master Tokuzan's successors included Master Seppo Gison.

4. The most popular Chinese translation of the Diamond Sutra is a single-volume version by Kumārajīva. The sutra preaches that all dharmas are bare and without self. Many Chinese masters quoted the Diamond Sutra in their preaching. It was especially highly revered after the time of Master Daikan Eno.

5. 周 (SHU) was Master Tokuzan's family name. At the same time, the character means a complete cycle, and therefore suggests Master Tokuzan's complete understanding of the Diamond Sutra.

6. The Seiryu Commentaries were written by a monk called Do-in at Seiryo-ji temple, under the orders of the Tang emperor Genso (reigned 713–755).

7. One tan is a hundred kin. One kin is equal to about 0.6 kilos.

8. Master Ryutan Soshin. A successor of Master Tenno Dogo, who was the successor of Master Sekito Kisen. It is said that Master Ryutan's family sold rice-cakes for a living, but his life history is not known clearly. He spent his life as a teacher in the Reiyo district.

9. "To refresh my mind" is 点心 (TENJIN), originally used not as a verb but as a noun (lit. I would like to buy a rice-cake and use it as a refreshment). 点 (TEN) means to light, as in to light a candle. 心 (SHIN, JIN) means mind. 点心 (TENJIN) means refreshments—cakes, fruit, or a cup of noodles.

Tokuzan says, *"I give you permission at once. You may ask whatever you like."*

The old woman says, *"I have heard it said in the Diamond Sutra that past mind cannot be grasped, present mind cannot be grasped, and future mind cannot be grasped. Which mind do you now intend somehow to refresh with rice-cakes? If the Master is able to say something, I will sell the rice-cakes. If the Master is unable to say anything, I will not sell the rice-cakes."*

Tokuzan is dumbfounded at this: he does not know how he might politely reply. The old woman just swings her sleeves[10] and leaves. In the end, she does not sell her rice-cakes to Tokuzan. How regrettable it is for a commentator on hundreds of scrolls [of text], a lecturer for tens of years, on merely receiving one question from a humble old woman, to be defeated at once and not even to manage a polite reply. Such things are due to the great difference between [someone] who has met a true teacher and succeeded a true teacher and heard the right Dharma, and [someone] who has never heard the right Dharma or met a true teacher. This is when Tokuzan first says, *"A rice-cake painted in a picture cannot kill hunger."* Now, so they say, he has received the Dharma from Ryutan.

[81] When we carefully consider this story of the meeting between the old woman and Tokuzan, Tokuzan's lack of clarity in the past is audible [even] now. Even after meeting Ryutan he might still be frightened of the old woman. He is just a late learner, not an eternal buddha who has transcended enlightenment. The old woman on this occasion shuts Tokuzan's mouth, but it is still difficult to decide that she is really a true person.[11] The reason is that when she hears the words *mind cannot be grasped,* she thinks only that mind cannot be got, or that mind cannot exist, and so she asks as she does. If Tokuzan were a stout fellow, he might have the power to examine and defeat the old woman. If he had examined and defeated her already, it would also be apparent whether the old woman is in fact a true person. Tokuzan has not yet become Tokuzan, and so whether the old woman is a true person also is not yet apparent.

[82] That the mountain monks of the great Kingdom of Sung today, with their patched robes and wide sleeves,[12] idly laugh at Tokuzan's inability to answer, and praise the old woman's inspired wit, might be very unreliable and stupid. For there is no absence of reasons to doubt the old woman: At the point when Tokuzan is unable to say anything, why does the old woman not say to Tokuzan, *"Now the Master is unable to say something, [so] go ahead and ask [this] old woman. The old woman will say something for the Master instead."* If she spoke like this, and if what she said to Tokuzan after receiving his question were right in expression, it would be apparent that the old woman really was a true person. She has questions, but she is without any assertion. No-one since ancient times has ever been called a true person without asserting even a single word. We can see from Tokuzan's past [experience] that idle boasting is useless, from beginning to end. We can know from the example of the old woman that someone who has never expressed anything cannot be approved. Let us see if we can say something in Tokuzan's place. Just as the old woman is about to question him as she does, Tokuzan

10. A sign of contempt.

11. その人 (sono hito), lit. "that person," or "the very person," or "a person of the fact."

12. 雲衲霞袂 (UN-NO-KA-BEI), lit. "clouds-patches-mist-sleeves." The words suggest the natural life and the usual clothes of a Buddhist monk, and therefore monks themselves.

should tell her at once *"If you are like this, then do not sell me your rice cakes!"* If Tokuzan speaks like this, he might be an inspired practitioner. Tokuzan might ask the old woman, *"Present mind cannot be grasped, past mind cannot be grasped, and future mind cannot be grasped. Which mind do you now intend to refresh with rice-cakes?"* If he questions her like this, the old woman should say at once to Tokuzan, *"The Master knows only that rice-cakes cannot refresh the mind. You do not know that mind refreshes rice-cakes, and you do not know that mind refreshes mind."* If she says this, Tokuzan will surely hesitate. Just at that time, she should take three rice-cakes and hand them over to Tokuzan. Just as Tokuzan goes to take them, the old woman should say, *"Past mind cannot be grasped! Present mind cannot be grasped! Future mind cannot be grasped!"* Or if Tokuzan does not extend his hands to take them, she should take one of the rice cakes and strike Tokuzan with it, saying *"You spiritless corpse! Do not be so dumb!"* When she speaks like this if Tokuzan has something to say [for himself], fine. If he has nothing to say, the old woman should speak again for Tokuzan. [But] she only swings her sleeves and leaves. We cannot suppose that there is a bee in her sleeve, either. Tokuzan himself does not say *"I cannot say anything. Please, old woman, speak for me."* So not only does he fail to say what he should say, he also fails to ask what he should ask. It is pitiful that the old woman and Tokuzan, past mind and future mind, questions and assertions, are solely in the state of *future mind cannot be grasped.* Generally, even after this, Tokuzan does not appear to have experienced any great enlightenment, but only the odd moment of violent behavior.[13] If he had studied under Ryutan for a long time, the horns on his head might have touched something and broken,[14] and he might have met the moment in which the pearl [under the black-dragon's] chin[15] is authentically transmitted. We see merely that his paper candle was blown out,[16] which is not enough for the transmission of the torch.[17] This being so, monks who are learning in practice must always be diligent in practice. Those who have taken it easy are not right. Those who were diligent in practice are Buddhist patriarchs. In conclusion, *mind cannot be grasped* means cheerfully buying a painted rice cake[18] and munching it up in one mouthful.

---

13. See, for example, Shinji-shobogenzo pt. 2, no. 45. 'Tokuzan preaches to an audience, "If you ask a question, there is something wrong. If you do not ask your question, that is also a violation." Then a monk edges forward and prostrates himself. The Master strikes him at once ...'

14. Horns on the head can be interpreted as symbols of Master Tokuzan's high opinion of himself.

15. 頷珠 (GANJU), lit. "chin pearl," means the pearl that a black dragon retains under its chin. The black-dragon's pearl symbolizes the truth.

16. One evening Tokuzan enters Master Ryutan's room, and stands waiting there until late at night. Master Ryutan asks him, "Why don't you retire?" Tokuzan takes his leave but then comes back saying, "It is dark outside." Master Ryutan lights a paper candle and gives it to Master Tokuzan. As soon as Tokuzan touches the candle, Master Ryutan blows it out. Then Master Tokuzan has a sudden great realization and prostrates himself. The story (which suggests that a person cannot find his or her way by relying upon another person's enlightenment) is recorded in Shinji-shobogenzo pt. 2, no. 4, and (a simpler version) in Keitoku-dento-roku, chap. 15.

17. 伝灯 (DENTO) "transmission of the torch," as in 伝灯録 (DENTO-ROKU), "Records of Transmission of the Torch," symbolizes the transmission of the Dharma from Buddhist patriarch to Buddhist patriarch.

18. 画餅 (GABYO), see chap. 40, Gabyo.

Shobogenzo Shin-fukatoku

Preached to the assembly at Kannon-dori-kosho-horin-ji temple, in the Uji district of Yoshu,[19] during the summer retreat in the 2nd year of Ninji.[20]

19. Corresponds to present-day Kyoto prefecture.
20. 1241.

[19]

心不可得

SHIN-FUKATOKU

Mind Cannot Be Grasped [The latter]

The 95-chapter edition of Shobogenzo has two chapters with the same title ***Shin-fukatoku*** *or Mind Cannot Be Grasped. We usually discriminate between the two chapters with the words "the former," and "the latter." The contents of the two chapters are different, but the meaning of the two chapters is almost the same. Furthermore, the end of each chapter records the same date—the summer retreat in 1241. However, while the former chapter says "preached to the assembly" this chapter says "written." So it may be that the former chapter was a short-hand record of Master Dogen's preaching, and the latter was Master Dogen's draft of his lecture. This is only a supposition, and scholars in future may be able to find a more exact conclusion.*

[89] ***Mind cannot be grasped*** is the buddhas; they have maintained it and relied upon it as their own state of anuttara-samyak-saṃbodhi.

[90] The Diamond Sutra says, *"Past mind cannot be grasped, present mind cannot be grasped, and future mind cannot be grasped."*

This is just the realized state of maintaining and relying upon *mind cannot be grasped,* which is the buddhas themselves. They have maintained it and relied upon it as *triple-world mind cannot be grasped* and as *all-dharmas mind cannot be grasped.* The state of maintenance and reliance which makes this clear is not experienced unless learned from buddhas and is not authentically transmitted unless learned from patriarchs. To learn from buddhas means to learn from the sixteen foot body,[1] and to learn from a single stalk of grass.[2] To learn from the patriarchs means to learn from skin, flesh, bones, and marrow,[3] and to learn from a face breaking into a smile.[4] The import of this is that

1. The sixteen-foot golden body of the Buddha, an image of the perfect state.

2. A concrete thing.

3. Master Bodhidharma told his four disciples that they had got his skin, flesh, bones, and marrow. See chap. 46, *Katto.*

when we seek [the truth] under [a teacher who] has evidently received the authentic transmission of the right-Dharma-eye treasury, who has received the legitimate one-to-one transmission of the state in which the mind-seal of the buddhas and the patriarchs is directly accessible, then without fail that [teacher's] bones and marrow, face and eyes, are transmitted, and we receive body, hair, and skin. Those who do not learn the Buddha's truth and who do not enter the room of a patriarch neither see nor hear nor understand this. The method of asking about it is beyond them. They have never realized the means to express it, even in a dream.

[92] Tokuzan, in former days, when not a stout fellow, was an authority on the Diamond Sutra. People of the time called him Shu, King of the Diamond Sutra. Of more than eight hundred scholars, he is the king. Not only is he especially well-versed in the Seiryu Commentaries; he has also edited texts weighing twelve *tan*. There is no lecturer who stands shoulder-to-shoulder with him. In the story he hears that in the south a supreme truth has been received by rightful successor from rightful successor, and so, carrying his texts, he travels across the mountains and rivers. He takes a rest by the left of the road leading to Ryutan, and an old woman comes by.

Tokuzan asks, *"What kind of person are you?"*

The old woman says, *"I am an old woman who sells rice-cakes."*

Tokuzan says, *"Will you sell some rice-cakes to me?"*

The old woman says, *"What does the Master want to buy them for?"*

Tokuzan says, *"I would like to buy some rice-cakes to refresh my mind."*

The old woman says, *"What is all that the Master is carrying?"*

Tokuzan says, *"Have you not heard? I am Shu, King of the Diamond Sutra. I have mastered the Diamond Sutra. There is no part of it that I do not understand. This [load] I am carrying is commentaries on the Diamond Sutra."*

Hearing this, the old woman says, *"The old woman has a question. Will the Master permit me [to ask] it, or not?"*

Tokuzan says, *"I permit it. You may ask whatever you like."*

She says, *"I have heard it said in the Diamond Sutra that past mind cannot be grasped, present mind cannot be grasped, and future mind cannot be grasped. Which mind do you now intend to refresh with my rice-cakes? If the Master is able say something, I will sell the rice-cakes. If the Master is unable to say anything, I will not sell the rice-cakes."*

At this, Tokuzan was dumbfounded; he could not find any appropriate reply. The old woman just swung her sleeves and left. In the end, she did not sell any rice-cakes to Tokuzan. How regrettable it was that a commentator on hundreds of scrolls [of text], a lecturer for tens of years, on receiving one mere question from a humble old woman, promptly fell into defeat. Such things are due to the great difference between those who have received a master's transmission and those who have not received a master's

---

4. Master Mahākāśyapa's face broke into a smile when the Buddha showed his audience an Udumbara flower. See chap. 68, *Udonge*. Master Dogen frequently used the words *skin, flesh, bones, and marrow,* and *a face breaking into a smile* as symbols of the transmission from Buddhist patriarch to Buddhist patriarch.

transmission, between those who visit the room of a true teacher and those who do not enter the room of a true teacher. Hearing the words *"cannot be grasped,"* [some] have simply understood that to grasp is equally impossible both for the former group and for the latter group. They totally lack the vigorous path.[5] Again, there are people who think that we say we cannot grasp it because we are endowed with it originally. Such [thinking] has by no means hit the target. This was when Tokuzan first knew that rice-cakes painted in a picture cannot kill hunger, and understood that for Buddhist training it is always necessary to meet a true person. He also understood that a person who has been uselessly caught up in only sutras and texts is not able to acquire real power. Eventually he visited Ryutan and realized the way of master and disciple, after which he did indeed become a true person. Today he is not only a founding patriarch of the Unmon and Hogen [sects],[6] [but also] a guiding teacher in the human world and in the heavens above.

[95] When we consider this story, it is evident now that Tokuzan in the past was not enlightened. Even though the old woman has now shut Tokuzan's mouth, it is also hard to decide that she is really a true person. In brief, it seems that hearing the words *"mind cannot be grasped,"* she considers only that mind cannot exist, and so she asks as she does. If Tokuzan were a stout fellow, he might have the power of interpretation. If he were able to interpret [the situation], it would also have become apparent whether the old woman was a true person, but because this is a time when Tokuzan was not Tokuzan, whether the old woman is a true person also is not known and not evident. What is more, we are not without reasons to doubt the old woman now. When Tokuzan is unable to say anything, why does she not say to Tokuzan, *"Now the Master is unable to say something, so please go ahead and ask [this] old woman. The old woman will say something for the Master instead."* Then, after receiving Tokuzan's question, if she had something to say to Tokuzan, the old woman might show some real ability. Someone who has the state of effort common to the bones and marrow and the faces and eyes of the ancients, and [common] to the brightness and the conspicuous form of eternal buddhas, in such a situation has no trouble not only taking hold but also letting go of Tokuzan, the old woman, the ungraspable, the graspable, rice-cakes, and mind. The *"Buddha-mind"* is just the three times.[7] Mind and the three times are not separated by a thousandth or a hundredth, but when they move apart and we discuss their separation, then the profound distance [between them] has [already] gone beyond eighty-four thousand.[8] If [someone] says *"What is past mind?"* we should say to that person *"It cannot be grasped."* If [someone] says *"What is present mind?"* we should say to that person *"It cannot be grasped."* If [someone] says *"What is future mind?"* we should say to that

---

5. 活路 (KATSURO). *Fukan-zazengi* contains the words 出身の活路 (SHUSSHIN *no* KATSURO), "the vigorous path of getting the body out."

6. The Unmon Sect traces its lineage back to Master Unmon Bun-en (864–949), a successor of Master Seppo Gison, who was a successor of Master Tokuzan. The Hogen Sect traces its lineage back to Master Hogen Bun-eki (885–958), a successor of Master Rakan Keichin, who was a successor of Master Gensa Shibi, who was a successor of Master Seppo Gison.

7. Past, present, and future; eternal existence.

8. Reality includes all things and phenomena without separation, but if we try to understand it intellectually we lose the state of reality completely.

person *"It cannot be grasped."* The point here is not to say that there is mind, which we provisionally call ungraspable; we are just saying for the present *"It cannot be grasped."* We do not say that it is impossible to grasp mind; we only say *"It cannot be grasped."* We do not say that it is possible to grasp mind; we only say *"It cannot be grasped."* Further, if [someone] says *"What is the state of 'past mind cannot be grasped'?"* we should say *"Living and dying, coming and going."* If [someone] says *"What is the state of 'present mind cannot be grasped'?"* we should say *"Living and dying, coming and going."* If [someone] says *"What is the state of 'future mind cannot be grasped'?"* we should say *"Living and dying, coming and going."* In sum, there is Buddha-mind as fences, walls, tiles, and pebbles, and all the buddhas of the three times experience this as *it cannot be grasped*. There are only fences, walls, tiles, and pebbles, which are the Buddha-mind itself, and the buddhas experience this in the three times as *it cannot be grasped*. Furthermore there is the state of *it cannot be grasped* itself, existing as mountains, rivers, and the Earth. There are [times when] the state of *it cannot be grasped* as grass, trees, wind, and water, is just mind. There are also [times when] *the mind to which we should give rise while having no abode*[9] is the state of *it cannot be grasped.* Still further, mind in the state of *it cannot be grasped* which is preaching eighty thousand Dharma-gates through all the ages of all the buddhas of the ten directions, is like this.

[99] A further example: At the time of the National Master Daisho,[10] Daini Sanzo[11] arrived at the capital[12] from the faraway Western Heavens,[13] claiming to have attained the power to know others' minds.[14] In the story the Tang emperor Shukuso[15] orders the National Master to examine [Sanzo]. As soon as Sanzo meets the National Master, he promptly prostrates himself and stands to the [Master's] right.

At length, the National Master asks, *"Have you got the power to know others' minds, or not?"*

Sanzo says, *"I would not be so bold [as to say]."*[16]

The National Master says, *"Tell me where [this] old monk is now."*

Sanzo says, *"Master, you are the teacher of the whole country. Why are you by the West River watching a boat race?"*

---

9. 応無所住而生其心 (O-MU-SHOJU-JI-SHO-GO-SHIN) or in Japanese pronunciation *(masani jusho naku shi te sono kokoro o shozu beshi)*, lit. "While having no abode still we should cause the mind to arise." These words are from the Diamond Sutra. When Master Daikan Eno happened to hear them recited in a marketplace, he decided at once to leave home and become a monk. See chap. 30, *Gyoji*.

10. Master Nan-yo Echu (675?–775). A successor of Master Daikan Eno. Posthumously titled by the emperor as "National Master Daisho."

11. 三蔵 (SANZO) represents the meaning of the Sanskrit *tripiṭaka*, the three baskets of *sūtra* (scriptures), *vinaya* (precepts), and *abidharma* (commentaries). The title *Sanzo* was given to a person who was accomplished in studying the *tripiṭaka*.

12. The ancient capital of modern-day Luoyang province.

13. 西天 (SAITEN), India.

14. 佗心通 (TASHINTSU). See chap. 80, *Tashintsu*.

15. The third son of the emperor Genso; reigned from 756 until his death in 762; also mentioned in chap. 1, *Bendowa*, and chap. 86, *Shukke-kudoku*.

16. Sanzo suggested that he had the ability, but modesty forbade him from daring to say so.

The National Master, after a while, asks a second time, *"Tell me where the old monk is now."*

Sanzo says, *"Master, you are the teacher of the whole country. Why are you on Tientsin Bridge*[17] *watching [someone] play with a monkey?"*

The National Master asks again, *"Tell me where the old monk is now."*

Sanzo takes a while, but knows nothing and sees nothing. Then the National Master scolds him, saying, *"You ghost of a wild fox,*[18] *where is your power to know others' minds?"*

Sanzo has no further answer.[19]

[101] If we did not know of such an episode, that would be bad, and if we were not informed about it, we might have doubts. Buddhist patriarchs and scholars of the tripiṭaka[20] can never be equal; they are as far apart as heaven and earth. Buddhist patriarchs have clarified the Buddha-Dharma, scholars of the tripiṭaka have never clarified it at all. With regard to [the title] *'scholar of the tripiṭaka,'* indeed, there are cases of even secular people being *'a scholar of the tripiṭaka.'* It represents, for example, the acquisition of a place in literary culture. This being so, even if [Sanzo] has not only understood all the languages of India and China but has also accomplished the power to know others' minds as well, he has never seen the body-and-mind of the Buddhist truth, even in a dream. For this reason, in his audience with the National Master, who has experienced the state of the Buddhist patriarchs, [Sanzo] is seen through at once. When we learn mind in Buddhism, the myriad dharmas are mind itself,[21] and the triple world is mind alone.[22] It may be that mind alone is just mind alone,[23] and that concrete buddha is mind here and now.[24] Whether it is self, or whether it is the external world, we must not be mistaken about the mind of the Buddha's truth. It could never idly flow down to the West River or wander over to Tientsin Bridge. If we want to maintain and to rely upon the body-and-mind of the Buddha's truth, we must learn the power which is the wisdom of the Buddha's truth. That is to say, in the Buddha's truth the whole earth is mind, which does not change through arising and vanishing, and the whole Dharma is mind. We should also learn the whole of mind as the power of wisdom. Sanzo, not hav-

17. Tientsin is a large city and port in Hopeh province, south-east of Beijing.

18. 野狐精 (YAKOZEI). In chap. 8, *Raihai-tokuzui*, "the ghost of a wild fox" symbolizes the natural and mystical quality of a person who has got the Dharma. In this case, it refers to Sanzo's mystical pretensions.

19. This story, together with the comments of the five venerable patriarchs, is also quoted in chap. 80, *Tashintsu*. In the present chapter Master Dogen wrote the story in Japanese; in *Tashintsu* the story is quoted in Chinese characters only. The story is originally recorded in *Keitoku-dento-roku*, chap. 5.

20. "Scholars of the tripiṭaka" is 三蔵 (SANZO). See note 11.

21. 万法即心 (BANPO-SOKUSHIN).

22. 三界唯心 (SANGAI-YUISHIN). See chap. 47, *Sangai-yuishin*. The two expressions in this sentence are traditional expressions.

23. 唯心これ唯心 (YUISHIN *kore* YUISHIN).

24. 是仏即心 (ZEBUTSU-SOKU-SHIN). The two expressions in this sentence are Master Dogen's variations on traditional expressions. In chap. 6, *Soku-shin-ze-butsu*, Master Dogen uses the four characters 即心是仏 in several different combinations. However, the combination used here, 是仏即心 (ZEBUTSU-SOKU-SHIN), does not appear in chap. 6.

ing seen this already, is nothing but the ghost of a wild fox. So, even the first two times, [Sanzo] never sees the mind of the National Master, and never penetrates[25] the mind of the National Master at all. He is a wild fox cub idly playing with no more than the West River, Tientsin Bridge, a boat race, and a monkey—how could he hope to see the National Master? Again, the fact is evident that [Sanzo] cannot see the place where the National Master is. He is asked three times, *"Tell me where the old monk is now,"* but he does not listen to these words. If he could listen, he might be able to investigate [further], [but] because he does not listen, he blunders heedlessly onward. If Sanzo had learned the Buddha-Dharma, he would listen to the words of the National Master, and he might be able to see the body-and-mind of the National Master. Because he does not learn the Buddha-Dharma in his everyday life, even though he was born to meet a guiding teacher of the human world and the heavens above, he has passed [the opportunity] in vain. It is pitiful and it is deplorable. In general, how could a scholar of the tripiṭaka attain to the conduct of a Buddhist patriarch and know the limits of the National Master? Needless to say, teachers of commentaries from the Western Heavens, and Indian scholars of the tripiṭaka, could never know the conduct of the National Master at all. Kings of gods can know, and teachers of commentaries can know, what scholars of the tripiṭaka know. How could what commentary-teachers and gods know be beyond the wisdom of [bodhisattvas at] the place of assignment;[26] or beyond [bodhisattvas at] the ten sacred stages and the three clever stages? Gods cannot know, and [bodhisattvas at] the place of assignment have never clarified, the body-and-mind of the National Master. Discussion of body-and-mind among Buddhists is like this. We should know it and believe it.

[105] The Dharma of our great teacher Śākyamuni is never akin to the ghosts of wild foxes—the two vehicles, non-Buddhists, and the like. Still, venerable patriarchs through the ages have each researched this story, and their discussions have survived:

† A monk asks Joshu,[27] *"Why does Sanzo not see where the National Master is the third time?"* Joshu says, *"He does not see because the National Master is right on Sanzo's nostrils."*

Another monk asks Gensa,[28] *"If [the National Master] is already on [Sanzo's] nostrils, why does [Sanzo] not see him?"* Gensa says, *"Simply because of being enormously close."*

Kai-e Tan[29] says, *"If the National Master is right on Sanzo's nostrils, what difficulty could [Sanzo] have in seeing him? Above all, it has not been recognized that the National Master is inside Sanzo's eyeballs."*

---

25. 通ず (*tsuzu*). The same character, as a noun, appears in the phrase 神通 (JINTSU) "mystical powers," one of which is 佗心通 (TASHINTSU), "the power to know others' minds."

26. 補処 (HOSHO), short for 一生補処の菩薩 (ISSHO-HOSHO *no* BOSATSU), lit. "a bodhisattva at the place of assignment in one life," that is, a bodhisattva who is about to become buddha. In the imagery of ancient India, bodhisattvas live their last life in Tuṣita heaven before descending to the world to become buddha.

† The five following stories are contained in one paragraph in the source text.

27. Master Joshu Jushin (778–897), successor of Master Nansen Fugan. See for example chap. 35, *Hakujushi.*

28. Master Gensa Shibi (835–907), successor of Master Seppo Gison. See for example chap. 4, *Ikka-no-myoju.*

On another occasion, Gensa challenges[30] Sanzo with these words: *"You! Say! Have you seen at all, even the first two times?"* Seccho Ken[31] says *"I am defeated, I am defeated."*

On still another occasion, a monk asks Kyozan,[32] *"Why is it that the third time, though Sanzo takes a while, he does not see where the National Master is?"* Kyozan says, *"The first two times [the Master's] mind is wandering in external circumstances; then he enters the samādhi of receiving and using the self,*[33] *and so [Sanzo] does not see him."*

These five venerable patriarchs are all precise, but they have passed over the National Master's conduct: by only discussing [Sanzo's] failure to know the third time, they seem to permit that he knew the first two times. This is the ancestors' oversight, and students of later ages should know it.

[108] Kosho's[34] present doubts about the five venerable patriarchs are twofold. First, they do not know the National Master's intention in examining Sanzo. Second, they do not know the National Master's body-and-mind.

[109] Now the reason I say that they do not know the National Master's intention in examining Sanzo is as follows: First the National Master says, *"Tell me where the old monk is just now."* The intention expressed [here] is to test whether or not Sanzo has ever known the Buddha-Dharma. At this time, if Sanzo has heard the Buddha-Dharma, he would study according to the Buddha-Dharma the question *"Where is the old monk just now?"* Studied according to the Buddha-Dharma, the National Master's *"Where is the old monk now"* asks *Am I at this place? Am I at that place? Am I in the supreme state of bodhi? Am I in the prajñā-pāramitā? Am I suspended in space? Am I standing on the earth? Am I in a thatched hut?* and *Am I in the place of treasure?* Sanzo does not recognize this intention, and so he vainly offers views and opinions of the common man, the two vehicles, and the like. The National Master asks again *"Tell me where this old monk is just now."* Here again Sanzo offers useless words. The National Master asks yet again, *"Tell me where this old monk is just now,"* whereupon Sanzo takes a while but says nothing, his mind baffled. Then the National Master scolds Sanzo, saying, *"You ghost of a wild fox, where is your power to know others' minds?"* Thus chided, Sanzo still has nothing to say [for himself]. Having considered this episode carefully, the ancestors all think that the National Master is now scolding Sanzo because, even if [Sanzo] knows where the Na-

---

29. Master Kai-e Shutan (1025–1072), successor of Master Yogi Ho-e.

30. 徴す (CHO *su*) means to solicit [an opinion]. At the same time, 徴 (CHO) is sometimes used interchangeably with the character 懲 (also pronounced CHO) which means to chastise.

31. Master Seccho Juken (980–1052), a successor of Master Chimon Koso. His comment is in praise of Master Gensa's comment. Master Seccho is known for promoting the teachings of the Unmon Sect (founded by Master Unmon Bun-en [864–949]). Master Seccho quoted a hundred stories, or *koan*, from *Keitoku-dento-roku* and praised them with poems. Master Engo Kokugon (1063–1135) later based his popular commentary *Hekigan-roku (Blue Cliff Record)* on Master Seccho's book. Master Dai-e Soko (1089–1163), thought to be the originator of so-called *koan zen,* was a student of Master Engo Kokugon. After Master Seccho's death, Master Seccho's disciples compiled his works in *I-roku (Bequeathed Records),* in seven volumes.

32. Master Kyozan Ejaku (803–887). A successor of Master Isan Reiyu. *Go-roku* a record of his words, is in one volume.

33. 自受用三昧 (JIJUYO-ZANMAI), that is, the state of natural balance. See chap. 1, *Bendowa.*

34. 興聖 (KOSHO). At the time, Master Dogen was the master of Kosho-horin-ji temple.

tional Master was the first two times, he does not know the third time. That is not so. The National Master is scolding Sanzo outright for being nothing but the ghost of a wild fox and never having seen the Buddha-Dharma even in a dream. [The National Master] has never said that [Sanzo] knew the first two times but not the third time. His criticism is outright criticism of Sanzo. The National Master's idea is, first, to consider whether or not it is possible to call the Buddha-Dharma *"the power to know others' minds."* Further, he thinks *"If we speak of 'the power to know others' minds' we must take 'others' in accordance with the Buddha's truth, we must take 'mind' in accordance with the Buddha's truth, and we must take 'the power to know' in accordance with the Buddha's truth, but what this Sanzo is saying now does not accord with the Buddha's truth at all. How could it be called the Buddha-Dharma?"* These are the thoughts of the National Master. The meaning of his testing is as follows: Even if [Sanzo] says something the third time, if it is like the first two times—contrary to the principles of the Buddha-Dharma and contrary to the fundamental intention of the National Master—it must be criticized. When [the National Master] asks three times, he is asking again and again whether Sanzo has been able to understand the National Master's words.

[112] The second [doubt]—that [the five venerable patriarchs] do not know the body-and-mind of the National Master—is namely that the body-and-mind of the National Master cannot be known, and cannot be penetrated,[35] by scholars of the tripiṭaka. It is beyond the attainment of [bodhisattvas at] the ten sacred stages and the three clever stages, and it is beyond clarification by [bodhisattvas at] the place of assignment or [in] the state of balanced awareness,[36] so how could the common man Sanzo know it? We must clearly determine [the truth of] this principle. If [people] purport that even Sanzo might know, or might attain to, the body-and-mind of the National Master, it is because they themselves do not know the body-and-mind of the National Master. If we say that people who have got the power to know others' minds can know the National Master, then can the two vehicles also know the National Master? That is impossible: people of the two vehicles can never arrive at the periphery of the National Master. Nowadays many people of the two vehicles have read the sutras of the Great Vehicle, [but] even they cannot know the body-and-mind of the National Master. Further, they cannot see the body-and-mind of the Buddha-Dharma, even in a dream. Even if they seem to read and recite the sutras of the Great Vehicle, we should clearly know that they are totally people of the small vehicles. In sum, the body-and-mind of the National Master cannot be known by people who are acquiring mystical powers or getting practice and experience. It might be difficult even for the National Master to fathom the body-and-mind of the National Master. Why? [Because] his conduct has long been free of the aim of becoming buddha; and so even the Buddha's eye could not glimpse it. His leaving-and-coming has far transcended the nest and cannot be restrained by nets and cages.

---

35. 通ず *(tsuzu)*. See note 25.

36. A bodhisattva is said to pass through fifty-two stages before becoming buddha: ten stages of belief; then thirty states classed as the three clever stages; then ten sacred stages; then the penultimate state; and finally the ultimate state. The penultimate state is 等覚 (TOKAKU), "balanced awareness." The ultimate state is 妙覚 (MYOKAKU), "subtle awareness." The ultimate state is also called 補処 (HOSHO)—see note 26.

[114] Now I would like to examine and defeat each of the five venerable patriarchs. Joshu says that because the National Master is right on Sanzo's nostrils, [Sanzo] does not see. What does this comment mean? Such mistakes happen when we discuss details without clarifying the substance. How could the National Master be right on Sanzo's nostrils? Sanzo has no nostrils. Moreover, although it does appear that the means are present for the National Master and Sanzo to look at each other, there is no way for them to get close to each other. Clear eyes will surely affirm [that this is so].

†† Gensa says, *"Simply because of being enormously close."* Certainly, his *enormously close* can be left as it is, [but] he misses the point. What state does he describe as *enormously close?* What object does he take to be *enormously close?* Gensa has not recognized *enormous closeness,* and has not experienced *enormous closeness.* In regard to the Buddha-Dharma he is the farthest of the far.

Kyozan says, *"The first two times [the Master's] mind is wandering in external circumstances; then he enters the samādhi of receiving and using the self, and so [Sanzo] does not see him."* Though [Kyozan's] acclaim as a little Śākyamuni echoes on high [even] in the Western Heavens, he is not without such wrongness. If he is saying that when [people] see each other [they] are inevitably wandering in external circumstances, then there would seem to be no instance of Buddhist patriarchs seeing each other, and he would appear not to have studied the virtues of affirmation and becoming buddha. If he is saying that Sanzo, the first two times, was really able to know the place where the National Master was, I must say that [Kyozan] does not know the virtue of a single bristle of the National Master's hair.

Gensa demands, *"Have you seen at all, even the first two times?"* This one utterance *"Have you seen at all?"* seems to say what needs to be said, but it is not right because it suggests that [Sanzo's] seeing is like not seeing.[37]

Hearing the above, Zen Master Seccho Myokaku[38] says, *"I am defeated. I am defeated."* When we see Gensa's words as the truth, we should speak like that; when we do not see them as the truth, we should not speak like that.

Kai-e Tan says, *"If the National Master is right on Sanzo's nostrils, what difficulty could [Sanzo] have in seeing him? Above all, it has not been recognized that the National Master is inside Sanzo's eyeballs."* This again discusses [only] the third time. It does not criticize [Sanzo] as he should be criticized, for not seeing the first two times as well. How could [Kai-e] know that the National Master is on [Sanzo's] nostrils or inside [Sanzo's] eyeballs?

[117] Every one of the five venerable patriarchs is blind to the virtue of the National Master; it is as if they have no power to discern the truth of the Buddha-Dharma. Remember, the National Master is just a buddha through all the ages. He has definitely received the authentic transmission of the Buddha's right-Dharma-eye treasury. Schol-

---

†† These five short paragraphs criticizing the five masters are contained in one paragraph in the source text.

37. Master Dogen is concerned with the area beyond seeing and not seeing—that is, realization of the practical state.

38. Another name of Master Seccho Juken. While still living, he was awarded the title Zen Master Myokaku.

ars of the tripiṭaka, teachers of commentaries, and others of the small vehicles, do not know the limits of the National Master at all; and the proof of that is here. "The power to know others' minds," as it is discussed in the small vehicles, should be called "the power to know others' ideas." To have thought that a small-vehicle scholar of the tripiṭaka, with the power to know others' minds, might be able to know a single bristle or half a bristle of the National Master's hair, is a mistake. We must solely learn that a small-vehicle scholar of the tripiṭaka is totally unable to see the situation of the virtue of the National Master. If [Sanzo] knew where the National Master was the first two times but did not know a third time, he would possess ability which is two-thirds of the whole and he would not deserve to be criticized. If he were criticized, it would not be for a total lack [of ability]. If [the National Master] denounced such a person, who could believe in the National Master? [The National Master's] intention is to criticize Sanzo for completely lacking the body-and-mind of the Buddha-Dharma. The five venerable patriarchs have such incorrectness because they completely fail to recognize the conduct of the National Master. For this reason, I have now let the Buddha's teaching of *mind cannot be grasped* be heard. It is hard to believe that people who are not able to penetrate this one dharma could have penetrated other dharmas. Nevertheless, we should know that even the ancestors have [made] such mistakes that are to be seen as mistakes.

[118] On one occasion a monk asks the National Master, *"What is the mind of eternal buddhas?"* The National Master says, *"Fences, walls, tiles, and pebbles."*[39] This also is *mind cannot be grasped.* On another occasion a monk asks the National Master, *"What is the constant and abiding mind of the buddhas?"* The National Master says, *"Fortunately you have met an old monk's palace visit."*[40] This also is mastery of the state of mind which *cannot be grasped.* The God Indra, on another occasion, asks the National Master, *"How can we be free from becoming?"*[41] The National Master says, *"Celestial One! You can be free from becoming by practicing the truth."* The God Indra asks further, *"What is the truth?"* The National Master says, *"Mind in the moment is the truth."* The God Indra says, *"What is mind in the moment?"* Pointing with his finger, the National Master says, *"This place is the stage of prajñā. That place is the net of pearls."* The God Indra does prostrations.

[120] In conclusion, in the orders of the buddhas and the patriarchs, there is often discussion of the body and of the mind in the Buddha's truth. When we learn them both together in practice, the state is beyond the thinking and the perception of the common man and sages and saints. [So] we must master in practice *mind cannot be grasped.*

---

39. See chap. 44, *Kobusshin.* 古仏 (KOBUTSU), lit. means "past/ancient buddhas," but in that chapter, Master Dogen says that 古仏 (KOBUTSU) means buddhas who transcend the past and present and belong directly to eternity.

40. In other words, "Fortunately, you have met the old monk who became master of this temple." 内 (SANDAI), "palace visit," means going to the palace to receive the emperor's permission to become the master of a temple.

41. 有為 (U-I), from the Sanskrit *saṃskṛta*. See Glossary.

Shobogenzo Shin-fukatoku

Written at Kosho-horin-ji temple on a day during the summer retreat in the 2nd year of Ninji.[42]

42. 1241.

[20]

古鏡

KOKYO

The Eternal Mirror

***Ko** means "ancient" or "eternal" and **kyo** means "mirror," so **kokyo** means "the eternal mirror." And what "the eternal mirror" means is the question. In this chapter Master Dogen quoted Master Seppo Gison's words "When a foreigner comes in front of the mirror, the mirror reflects the foreigner." From these words we can understand the eternal mirror as a symbol of some human mental faculty. The eternal mirror suggests the importance of reflection, so we can suppose that the eternal mirror is a symbol of the intuitional faculty. In Buddhist philosophy, the intuitional faculty is called prajñā, or real wisdom. Real wisdom in Buddhism means our human intuitional faculty on which all our decisions are based. Buddhism esteems this real wisdom more than reason or sense-perception. Our real wisdom is the basis for our decisions, and our decisions decide our life, so we can say that our real wisdom decides the course of our life. For this reason, it is very natural for Master Dogen to explain the eternal mirror. At the same time, we must find another meaning of the eternal mirror, because Master Dogen also quoted other words of Master Seppo Gison, "Every monkey has the eternal mirror on its back." Therefore we can think that the eternal mirror means not only human real wisdom, but also some intuitional faculty of animals. So we must widen the meaning of the eternal mirror, and understand it as a symbol of the intuitional faculty which both human beings and animals have. Furthermore Master Seppo Gison said, "When the world is ten feet wide, the eternal mirror is ten feet wide. When the world is one foot wide, the eternal mirror is one foot wide." These words suggest the eternal mirror is the world itself. So we can say that the eternal mirror is not only a symbol of an individual faculty but is also something universal. From ancient times Buddhists have discussed the eternal mirror. In this chapter Master Dogen explains the meaning of the eternal mirror in Buddhism, quoting the words of ancient Buddhist masters.*

[123] **What all the buddhas and all the patriarchs** have received and retained, and transmitted one-to-one, is the eternal mirror. They[1] have the same view and the same face, the same image[2] and the same cast;[3] they share the same state and realize the same experience. A foreigner appears, a foreigner is reflected—one hundred and eight thousand of them. A Chinaman appears, a Chinaman is reflected—for a moment and for ten thousand years. The past appears, the past is reflected; the present appears, the present is reflected; a buddha appears, a buddha is reflected; a patriarch appears, a patriarch is

1. Buddhist patriarchs and the eternal mirror.
2. 像 (ZO), like the English word "image," includes two meanings: (i) a phenomenal form, and (ii) a statue, that is, an image which has been cast from a mold.
3. In Master Dogen's time, mirrors were not made of glass; they were cast from copper and kept highly polished.

reflected.

[125] The eighteenth patriarch, the Venerable Geyāśata, is a man from the kingdom of Magadha in the western regions. His family name is Uzuran, his father's name is Tengai, and his mother's name is Hosho.[4] His mother once has a dream in which she sees a great god approaching her and holding a big mirror. Then she becomes pregnant. Seven days later she gives birth to the Master. Even when he is newborn, the skin of the Master's body is like polished lapis lazuli, and even before he is bathed, he is naturally fragrant and clean. From his childhood, he loves quietness. His words are different from those of ordinary children; since his birth, a clear and bright round mirror has naturally been living with him. *A round mirror* means a round mirror.[5] It is a matter rare through the ages. That it has lived with him does not mean that the round mirror was also born from his mother's womb.[6] The Master was born from the womb, and as the Master appeared from the womb the round mirror came and naturally manifested itself before the Master, and became like an everyday tool. The form of this round mirror is not ordinary: when the child approaches, he seems to be holding up the round mirror before him with both hands, yet the child's face is not hidden. When the child goes away, he seems to be going with the round mirror on his back, yet the child's body is not hidden. When the child sleeps, the round mirror covers him like a flowery canopy. Whenever the child sits up straight, the round mirror is there in front of him. In sum, it follows [all his] movements and demeanors, active and passive. What is more, he is able to see all Buddhist facts of the past, future, and present by looking into the round mirror. At the same time, all problems and issues of the heavens above and the human world come cloudlessly to the surface of the round mirror. For example, to see by looking in this round mirror is even more clear than to attain illumination of the past and illumination of the present by reading sutras and texts. Nevertheless, once the child has left home and received the precepts, the round mirror never appears before him again.[7] Therefore [people of] neighboring villages and distant regions unanimously praise this as rare and wonderful. In truth, though there are few similar examples in this sahā-world, we should not be suspicious but should be broad-minded with regard to the fact that, in other worlds, families may produce such progeny. Remember, there are sutras which have changed into trees and rocks,[8] and there are [good] counselors who are spreading [the Lotus Sutra] in fields and in villages;[9] they too may be a round mirror. Yellow paper on a red rod[10] here and now is a round mirror. Who could think that only

---

4. *Uzuran* is the phonetic representation in Chinese characters of the original name. The derivation of the Chinese characters 天蓋 (TENGAI), "Celestial Canopy," and 方聖 (HOSHO), "Exact and Sacred," is uncertain.

5. 円鑑とは円鏡なり (ENKAN *towa* ENKYO *nari*). Master Dogen explained the less familiar character 鑑 (KAN) with the more familiar character 鏡 (KYO).

6. 同生 (DOSHO) lit. means either "lived with" or "born with." Master Dogen clarified that the meaning here is "lived with."

7. The implication is that after becoming a Buddhist monk he already had the criteria for behavior naturally.

8. "Trees and rocks" alludes to the story of the young "Child of the Himalayas." See note 157 in chap. 12, *Kesa-kudoku*.

9. 若田若里に流布する知識あり (NYAKUDEN-NYAKURI *ni* RUFU *suru* CHISHIKI *ari*). See LS 3.72-74. 知識 (CHISHIKI), lit. knowledge or acquaintance, represents the Sanskrit *kalyāna-mitra*. See Glossary.

10. Yellow paper on a red rod means a Buddhist sutra.

the Master was prodigious?

[129] On an outing one day, encountering the Venerable Saṃghanandi,[11] [Master Geyāśata] directly proceeds before the Venerable [Saṃgha]nandi. The Venerable One asks, *"[That which] you have in your hands is expressing what?"*[12] We should hear *"is expressing What?"* not as a question,[13] and we should learn it as such in practice.

The Master says:

The great round mirror of the buddhas
Has no flaws or blurs, within or without.
[We] two people are able to see the same.
[Our] minds, and [our] eyes, are completely alike.

So how could the great round mirror of the buddhas have been *born together with* the Master? The birth of the Master was the brightness of the great round mirror. Buddhas [experience] the same state and the same view in this round mirror. Buddhas are the cast image of the great round mirror. The great round mirror is neither wisdom nor reason, neither essence nor form. Though the concept of a great round mirror appears in the teachings of [bodhisattvas at] the ten sacred stages, the three clever stages, and so on, it is not the present *great round mirror of the buddhas.* Because *the buddhas* may be beyond wisdom, buddhas have real wisdom, [but] we do not see real wisdom as buddhas. Practitioners should remember that to preach about wisdom is never the ultimate preaching of the Buddha's truth. Even if we feel that the great round mirror of the buddhas is already living with us, it is still a fact that we can neither touch the great round mirror in this life nor touch it in another life; it is neither a jewel mirror nor a copper mirror, neither a mirror of flesh nor a mirror of marrow. Is [the verse] a verse spoken by the round mirror itself or a verse recited by the child? Even if it is the child who preaches this four-line verse, he has not learned it from [other] people, either by *following the sutras* or by *following [good] counselors.* He holds up the round mirror and preaches like this, simply [because] to face the mirror has been the Master's usual behavior since his earliest childhood. He seems to possess inherent eloquence and wisdom. Was the great round mirror born with the child, or was the child born with the great round mirror? It may also be possible that the births took place before or after [each other]. *The great round mirror* is just a virtue of *the buddhas.* Saying that this mirror *has no blurs on the inside or the outside* neither describes an inside that depends on an outside, nor an outside blurred by an inside. There being no face or back, *two individuals*[14] *are able to see the same.* Minds, and eyes, are alike. *Likeness* describes *a human being* meeting *a human being.* In regard to images within, they have mind and eyes, and they are able to see the same. In regard to images without, they have mind and eyes, and they are able to see the same. Object and subject which are manifest before us now are like each other within and like each other without—they are neither I nor anyone else.

---

11. The seventeenth patriarch in India. See chap. 15, *Busso.*

12. Lit. "[That which] you have in your hands has the expression of what?" Master Saṃghanandi invited Master Geyāśata to express his state.

13. "What?" suggests ineffable reality.

14. The poem says 両人 (RYONIN), "two people." This says 両箇 (RYOKO), "two individuals," or "two concrete things:" 箇 (KO) is a counter for inanimate objects.

Such is the meeting of *two human beings*, and the likeness of *two human beings*. That person is called "I," and I am that person. *"Minds, and eyes, are totally alike"* means mind and mind are alike, eyes and eyes are alike. The likeness is of minds and of eyes; this means, for example, that the mind and the eyes of each are alike. What does it mean for mind and mind to be alike? The Third Patriarch and the Sixth Patriarch.[15] What does it mean for eyes and eyes to be alike? The Eye of the truth being restricted by the Eye itself.[16] The principle that the Master is expressing now is like this. This is how [Master Geyāśata] first pays his respects to the Venerable Saṃghanandi. Taking up his principle, we should experience in practice the faces of buddhas and the faces of patriarchs in the great round mirror, which is akin to the eternal mirror.

[134] The thirty-third patriarch, Zen Master Daikan, in former days when toiling in the Dharma-order on Obai-zan mountain, presented the following verse to the ancestral Master,[17] by writing it on the wall:[18]

In the state of bodhi there is originally no tree,
Neither does the clear mirror need a stand.
Originally we do not have a single thing,
Where could dust and dirt exist?

[134] So then, we must study these words. People in the world call the founding Patriarch Daikan "the eternal Buddha." Zen Master Engo[19] says, *"I bow my head to the ground before Sokei,[20] the true eternal Buddha."*[21] So remember [the words] with which the founding Patriarch Daikan displays the clear mirror: *"Originally we do not have a single thing, At what place could dust and dirt exist?" "The clear mirror needs no stand:"* this contains the

15. The third patriarch in China was called 鑑智 (KANCHI), "Mirror Wisdom," and the sixth patriarch in China was called 大鑑 (DAIKAN), "Great Mirror." Both names contain the character 鑑 (KAN), "mirror."

16. In other words, the Buddhist viewpoint realized as it is.

17. Master Daiman Konin (688–761), the thirty-second patriarch (fifth in China). See chap. 15, *Busso*.

18. It was the custom at the temple for a monk who wanted to express an idea to paste up some words on the wall of the southern corridor. In the middle of one night, Ācārya Jinshu, the most intelligent member of the order, secretly took a lantern and posted up the following poem: *"The body is the bodhi tree, / The mind is like the stand of a clear mirror. / At every moment we work to wipe and polish it / To keep it free of dust and dirt."* A boy from the temple recited Jinshu's poem as he passed by the temple servant's cottage where Master Daikan Eno lived and worked, pounding rice for the monks. Hearing the poem, Master Daikan Eno thought that comparing Buddhist practice to keeping a mirror clean was too intellectual or artificial, so he had someone paste up his own poem. All the monks were astonished at the excellence of the laborer's poem. The story is contained in *Rokuso-dankyo (The Sixth Patriarch's Platform Sutra)*.

19. Master Engo Kokugon (1063–1135). A successor of Master Goso Ho-en and an eleventh-generation descendant of Master Rinzai. He received the title of Zen Master Bukka from the Sung emperor Kiso (reigned 1101–1126), and the title Zen Master Engo from the Southern Sung emperor Koso (reigned 1127–1163). His successors included Master Dai-e Soko.

20. Master Daikan Eno. Sokei was the name of the mountain where he lived.

21. Also quoted in chap. 44, *Kobusshin*.

lifeblood; we should strive [to understand it]. All [things in] the clear-clear state[22] are the clear mirror itself, and so we say, *"When a clear head comes, a clear head will do."*[23] Because [the clear mirror] is beyond *any place*, it does not have *any place*.[24] Still more, throughout the Universe in the ten directions, does there remain one speck of dust which is not the mirror? On the mirror itself, does there remain one speck of dust which is not the mirror? Remember, the whole Universe is not lands of dust;[25] and so it is the face of the eternal mirror.

[136] In the order of Zen Master Nangaku Dai-e[26] a monk asks, *"If a mirror is cast into an image,*[27] *to what place does its luster return?"*

The Master says, *"Venerable monk, to what place have the features you had before you became a monk departed?"*

The monk says, *"After the transformation, why does it not shine like a mirror?"*

The Master says, *"Even though it is not shining like a mirror, it cannot delude others one bit."*[28]

[137] We are not sure of what these myriad images[29] of the present are made. But if we seek to know, the evidence that they are cast from a mirror is just [here] in the words of the Master. A mirror is neither of gold nor of precious stone, neither of brightness nor of an image, but that it can be instantly *cast into an image* is truly the ultimate investigation of a mirror.[30] *"To what place does the luster return?"* is the assertion that *the possibility*[31] *of a mirror being cast into an image* is just *the possibility of a mirror being cast into an image;* [it says,] for example, [that] an image returns to the place of an image, and [that] casting can cast a mirror.[32] The words *"Venerable monk, to what place have the features you had before you became a monk departed?"* hold up a mirror to reflect [the monk's] face.[33] At this time, which momentary face[34] might be "my own face"? The Master says,

---

22. 明明 (MEI-MEI), lit. "clear-clear," from 明明百艸頭 (MEI-MEI *[taru]* HYAKU-SO-TO), lit. "hundreds of weeds in the clear-clear state." These are the words of Master Chinshu Fuke, quoted in chap. 22, *Bussho*, suggesting the state in which each miscellaneous concrete thing is conspicuously clear as it is. Master Chinshu Fuke was nicknamed *Hotei* or "Cloth-Bag" because he wandered freely from temple to temple carrying all his belongings in a sack. In Japan the fat laughing monk depicted in "Happy Buddha" statues is called *Hotei*.

23. Also the words of Master Chinshu Fuke, or the Happy Buddha. See *Shinji-shobogenzo* pt. 1 no. 22.

24. "Any place" is いずれのところ *(izure no tokoro)*, Japanese words representing the characters 何処, "where," or "at what place," in the last line of the poem.

25. 塵刹 (JINSETSU), or "lands as numerous as dust-particles."

26. Master Nangaku Ejo (677–744), a successor of Master Daikan Eno. Zen Master Dai-e is his posthumous title.

27. Again, it should be remembered that in those days mirrors were cast from copper which was also used to make images or statues.

28. *Shinji-shobogenzo* pt. 2, no. 16.

29. 万像 (BANSHO), equivalent to 万象 (BANSHO), "myriad phenomena." Here "images" means phenomena; in the rest of this paragraph, "image" means statue. See note 2.

30. Master Dogen praises the monk's viewpoint.

31. "Possibility" is 如 (NYO or *[ga] goto [ki]*), translated in the story as "If..."

32. The monk's question is not only abstract speculation, but it includes recognition of possibilities as they are, of concrete things as they are, and of the state of action which makes all things possible.

33. The monk's question was philosophical, so Master Nangaku brought the discussion back down to the monk's own experience.

34. 面面 (MEN-MEN), lit. "face-face."

"Even though it is not shining like a mirror, it cannot delude others one bit." This means that it cannot shine like a mirror; and it cannot mislead others. Learn in practice that the ocean's drying can never disclose the sea-bed![35] Do not break out, and do not move! At the same time, learn further in practice: there is a principle of taking an image and casting a mirror. Just this moment is miscellaneous bits of utter delusion,[36] in hundred thousand myriads of shining mirror reflections.[37]

[139] Great Master Seppo Shinkaku[38] on one occasion preaches to the assembly, *"If you want to understand this matter,[39] my concrete state is like one face of the eternal mirror. [When] a foreigner comes, a foreigner appears. [When] a Chinaman comes, a Chinaman appears.*

Then Gensa[40] steps out and asks, *"If suddenly a clear mirror comes along, what then?"*

The Master says, *"The foreigner and the Chinaman both become invisible."*

Gensa says, *"I am not like that."*

Seppo says, *"How is it in your case?"*

Gensa says, *"Please, Master, you ask."*

Seppo says, *"If suddenly a clear mirror comes along, how will it be then?"*

Gensa says, *"Smashed into hundreds of bits and pieces!"*

[141] Now the meaning of Seppo's words *"this matter"* should be learned in practice as *"this is something ineffable."*[41] Let us now try to learn Seppo's eternal mirror. In the words *"Like one face of the eternal mirror...," one face* means [the mirror's] borders have been eliminated forever and it is utterly beyond inside and outside; it is the self as a pearl spinning in a bowl.[42] The present *"[when] a foreigner comes, the foreigner appears"* is about one individual red-beard.[43] *"[When] a Chinaman comes, a Chinaman appears:"* although it has been said since the primordial chaos,[44] since [the reign of] Banko,[45] that

---

35. Because if the sea dries up, what was formerly the sea-bed is now land. That the ocean's drying cannot reveal the sea-bed was an expression of reality in China.

36. 瞞瞞点点 (MAN-MAN TEN-TEN), lit. "delusion-delusion, point-point." The characters 瞞 and 点 appear in Master Nangaku's words.

37. "Shining mirror reflections" is 鑑照 (KANSHO), lit. "mirror-shine." These characters also appear in the story ("shine like a mirror"). The last sentence suggests concrete reality which is different from abstract thinking.

38. Master Seppo Gison (822–907), a successor of Master Tokuzan Senkan. Great Master Seppo Shinkaku is the title he received from the emperor Iso (reigned 860–874).

39. 此事 (*kono* JI), or "the matter of this," "the state of reality."

40. Master Gensa Shibi (835–907). *Shinji-shobogenzo* contains many conversations between Master Seppo and Master Gensa, of which this one is typical—with Master Seppo preaching very sincerely and Master Gensa being somewhat cynical.

41. 是什麼事 (*ko[re]* NAN *[no]* JI) alludes to Master Daikan Eno's words 是什麼物恁麼来, "What is it that comes like this?" or "This is something [ineffable] coming like this." See chap. 29, *Inmo* and chap. 63, *Hensan.*

42. A pearl spinning in a bowl symbolizes constant movement (see for example chap. 66, *Shunju,* para. [135]), or in this context, busy daily life.

43. To Chinese people, red-beards were foreigners and foreigners were red-beards. See for example chap. 76, *Dai-shugyo.*

44. 混沌 (KONTON), the state of chaos that existed before the forces of yin and yang had become distinct.

45. Banko appears in the Taoist book *San-go-ryaku-ki (History of the Three [Elements] and Five [Elements]).* He is the Emperor who ruled at the beginning of creation.

this *Chinaman* was created from the three elements and five elements,[46] in Seppo's words now a Chinaman whose virtue is the eternal mirror has appeared. Because the present Chinaman is not 'a Chinaman' *the Chinaman appears*. To Seppo's present words *"The foreigner and the Chinaman both become invisible,"* he might add, *and the mirror itself also becomes invisible*. Gensa's words *"Smashed into hundreds of bits and pieces"* mean *the truth should be expressed like that, but why, when I have just asked you to give me back a concrete fragment, did you give me back a clear mirror?*

[142] In the age of the Yellow Emperor there are twelve mirrors.[47] According to the family legend, they are gifts from the heavens. Alternately, they are said to have been given by [the sage] Kosei of Kodo-zan mountain.[48] The rule for using[49] the twelve mirrors is to use one mirror every hour through the twelve hours, and to use each mirror for a month through the twelve months, [and again] to use the mirrors one by one, year by year through twelve years. They say that the mirrors are Kosei's sutras. When he transmits them to the Yellow Emperor, the twelve hours and so on are mirrors with which to illuminate the past and to illuminate the present. If the twelve hours were not mirrors, how would it be possible to illuminate the past? If the twelve hours were not mirrors, how would it be possible to illuminate the present? The twelve hours, in other words, are twelve concrete sheets [of mirror], and the twelve concrete sheets [of time] are twelve mirrors. The past and present are what the twelve hours use.[50] [The legend] suggests this principle. Even though it is a secular saying, it is in [the reality of] the twelve hours during which *the Chinaman appears*.

[144] *Ken-en,*[51] *the Yellow Emperor, crawls forward on Kodo [mountain] and asks Kosei about the Way. Thereupon, Kosei says, "Mirrors are the origin of yin and yang; they regulate the body eternally. There are naturally three mirrors; namely, the heavens, the earth, and human beings.*[52] *These mirrors are without sight and without hearing.*[53] *They will make your spirit quiet, so that your body will naturally become right. Assured of quietness and of purity, your body will not be taxed and your spirit will not be agitated. You will thus be able to live long.*[54]

[145] In former times, these three mirrors are used to regulate the whole country, and to regulate the great order. One who is clear about this great order is called the ruler of the heavens and the earth. A secular [book][55] says, *"The Emperor Taiso*[56] *has treated human*

---

46. The heavens, the earth, human beings; wood, fire, earth, metal, water.

47. The Yellow Emperor (dates approximated as 2697–2597 B.C.) was the third emperor in the legendary age of the five rulers (2852–2205 B.C.). Volume 8 of the Chinese book 事物原記 (JIBUTSU-GEN-KI), *A Record of the Origins of Things*, says, *"According to the Yellow Emperor's confidential account, when the Emperor met his mother at the royal palace, he cast twelve great mirrors, which he used one month at a time."*

48. Taoist legend says that the Yellow Emperor visited Kosei at Kosei's hermit's cave on Kodo-zan mountain, to ask for the secret of immortality. See chap. 14, *Sansui-gyo*.

49. In the east, the use of a mirror represents the function of decision-making.

50. The idea of past and present is subordinate to the twelve hours of today which, as the ordinary time of concrete daily life, have real substance—in chap. 11, *Uji*, Master Dogen urges us to learn real time as the twelve hours of today.

51. *Ken-en* is the Japanese pronunciation of the Yellow Emperor's personal name.

52. Again it should be stressed that in the orient a mirror means a standard. In this context, for example, the criteria of astrology, geography, and economics could be called mirrors.

53. They are intuitional.

54. Summarized quotation from vol. 4 of the Taoist text *Soji*.

55. *Jokan-seiyo (Jokan Era [Treatise] on the Essence of Government).*

beings as a mirror, and thus he fully illuminates [all problems of] peace and danger, reason and disorder." He uses one of the three mirrors. When we hear that he treats human beings as a mirror, we think that by asking people of wide knowledge about the past and present, he has been able to know when to employ and to discharge saints and sages—as, for example, when he got Gicho and got Bogenrei.[57] To understand it like this is not [truly to understand] the principle which asserts that Emperor Taiso sees human beings as a mirror. Seeing human beings as a mirror means seeing a mirror as a mirror, seeing oneself as a mirror, seeing the five elements[58] as a mirror, or seeing the five constant virtues[59] as a mirror. When we watch the coming and going of human beings, the coming has no traces and the going has no direction: we call this the principle of human beings as a mirror.[60] The myriad diversity of sagacity and ineptitude is akin to astrological phenomena. Truly, it may be as latitude and longitude.[61] It is the faces of people, the faces of mirrors, the faces of the sun, and the faces of the moon. The vitality of the five peaks and the vitality of the four great rivers passes through the world on the way to purifying the four oceans, and this is the customary practice of the mirror itself.[62] They say that Taiso's way is to fathom the universal grid by understanding human beings. [But this] does not refer [only] to people of wide knowledge.

[147] *"Japan, since the age of the gods, has had three mirrors; together with the sacred jewels and the sword they have been transmitted to the present.[63] One mirror is in the Grand Shrines of Ise,[64] one is in the Hinokuma Shrine in Kii-no-kuni,[65] and one is in the depository of the Imperial Court."[66]*

[148] Thus it is clear that every nation transmits and retains a mirror. To possess the mirror is to possess the nation. People relate the legend that these three mirrors were transmitted together with the Divine Throne and were transmitted by the gods. Even so, the perfectly refined copper [of these mirrors] is also the transformation of yin and yang.[67] It may be that [when] the present comes, the present appears [in them], and [when] the past comes, the past appears [in them]. [Mirrors] that thus illuminate the past and present may be eternal mirrors. Seppo's point might also be expressed, *"[When] a Korean comes, a Korean appears; [when] a Japanese comes, a Japanese appears."* Or,

---

56. The second Tang Dynasty emperor, reigned 627–650.

57. Gicho and Bogenrei were two high officials in Emperor Taiso's government.

58. 五行 (GOGYO). Wood, fire, earth, metal, water.

59. 五常 (GOJO). Paternal righteousness, maternal benevolence, friendship as an elder brother, respect as a younger brother, and filial piety.

60. Human beings, as they are, are a criterion; in other words, reality is the criterion.

61. Again, the point is that concrete facts are universal criteria.

62. The five peaks are five mountains in China. The four rivers are the Yellow River, the Yangtse River, and the Waisui and Saisui rivers. The four oceans are the oceans of the north, south, east, and west. This part suggests Master Dogen's optimism about the progress of human society.

63. Refers to Japan's three sacred treasures: the mirrors, the sacred jewels, and the Grass-Mowing Sword.

64. The Inner Shrine at Ise, considered the abode of *Amaterasu*, the Sun-Goddess, still houses one of the sacred mirrors.

65. 紀伊国 (KI-I *no* KUNI), present-day Wakayama prefecture, where the Hinokuma Shrine still houses the second of the three mirrors.

66. The third of the three mirrors, called *Yata-no-kagami*, is still housed in the Imperial Palace in Tokyo. The original text is in the style of a quotation, written in Chinese characters only.

67. It is just a physical substance.

"[When] a god comes, a god appears; [when] a human being comes, a human being appears." We learn appearance-and-coming like this, in practice, but we have not now recognized the substance and details of this appearance: we only meet directly with appearance itself. We should not always learn that coming-and-appearance is [a matter of] recognition or [a matter of] understanding. Is the point here that a foreigner coming is a foreigner appearing? [No,] a foreigner coming should be an instance of a foreigner coming. A foreigner appearing should be an instance of a foreigner appearing. The coming is not for the sake of appearing. Although the eternal mirror is [just] the eternal mirror, there should be such learning in practice.

[149] Gensa steps out and asks, *"What if suddenly it meets the coming of a clear mirror?"*[68] We should research and clarify these words. What might be the scale of the expression of this word *clear*? In these words, the *coming* is not necessarily that of *a foreigner* or of *a Chinaman*. This is the clear mirror, which [Gensa] says can never be realized as *a foreigner* or as *a Chinaman*. Though *a clear mirror coming* is a *clear mirror coming*, it never makes a duality.[69] Though there is no duality, the eternal mirror is still the eternal mirror, and the clear mirror is still the clear mirror. Testimony to the existence of [both] the eternal mirror and the clear mirror has been expressed directly in the words of Seppo and Gensa. We should see this as the Buddha's truth of essence-and-form. We should recognize that Gensa's present talk of the clear mirror coming is totally penetrating,[70] and we should recognize that it is brilliant in all aspects.[71] It may be that in his encounters with human beings, [Gensa] directly manifests [himself], and that in manifesting directness he can reach others. So should we see the clear of the clear mirror and the eternal of the eternal mirror, as the same, or should we see them as different? Is there eternity in the clear mirror, or not? Is there clarity in the eternal mirror, or not? Do not understand from the words *"eternal mirror"* that it must necessarily be clear. The important point is that *"I am like that, and you are also like that."*[72] We should practice without delay, polishing the fact that *"all the patriarchs of India were also like that."* An ancestral Master's expression of the truth[73] says that, for the eternal mirror, there is polishing. Might the same be true for the clear mirror? What [do you say]? There must be learning in practice that widely covers the teachings of all the buddhas and all the patriarchs.

[151] Seppo's words, *"The foreigner and the Chinaman both become invisible"* mean that the foreigner and the Chinaman, when it is the clear mirror's moment, are *both invisible*. What is the meaning of this principle of *both being invisible?* That the foreigner and the Chinaman have already come-and-appeared does not hinder the eternal mirror, so why should they now *both be invisible?* In the case of the eternal mirror, *[when] a foreigner comes a foreigner appears*, and *[when] a Chinaman comes a Chinaman appears*, but *the coming*

---

68. The original story is quoted in Chinese characters only. Here Master Dogen represents Master Gensa's words in Japanese.

69. 二枚 (NIMAI), that is, two mirrors—the eternal mirror, and the clear mirror.

70. 七通八達 (SHICHITSU-HATTATSU), lit. "penetrating the seven directions and arriving at the eight destinations."

71. 八面玲瓏 (HACHIMEN-REIRO). The original meaning of 玲瓏 (REIRO) is the sound of golden bells, and hence something clear, bright, and serene.

72. Master Daikan Eno's words to Master Nangaku Ejo. See *Shinji-shobogenzo* pt. 2, no. 1, and Shobogenzo chap. 7, *Senjo*.

73. See the two stories quoted at the end of this chapter.

of the clear mirror is naturally *the coming of the clear mirror* itself; therefore the foreigner and the Chinaman reflected in the eternal mirror are *both invisible.*[74] So even in Seppo's words there is one face of the eternal mirror and one face of the clear mirror.[75] We should definitely confirm the principle that, just at the moment of *the clear mirror coming,* [the clear mirror] cannot hinder the foreigner and the Chinaman reflected in the eternal mirror.[76] [Seppo's] present assertion, about the eternal mirror, that *"[When] a foreigner comes a foreigner appears,"* and *"[When] a Chinaman comes a Chinaman appears,"* does not say that [the foreigner and the Chinaman] come-and-appear *on the eternal mirror,* does not say that they come-and-appear *in the eternal mirror,* does not say that they come-and-appear *on the exterior of the eternal mirror,* and does not say that they come-and-appear *in the same state as the eternal mirror.* We should listen to his words. At the moment when the foreigner and the Chinaman come-and-appear, the eternal mirror is actually making the foreigner and the Chinaman come. To insist that even when *the foreigner and the Chinaman are both invisible,* the mirror will remain, is to be blind to appearance and to be remiss with regard to coming. To call it absurd would not be going far enough.

[153] Then Gensa says, *"I am not like that."* Seppo says, *"How is it in your case?"* Gensa says, *"Please, Master, you ask."* We should not idly pass over the words *"Please, Master, you ask"* spoken now by Gensa. Without father and son having thrown themselves into the moment, how could the coming of the Master's question, and the requesting of the Master's question, be like this? When [someone] requests the Master's question, it may be that *someone ineffable*[77] has already understood[78] decisively the state in which the question is asked. While the state of the questioner is already thundering, there is no place of escape.

[154] Seppo says, *"If suddenly a clear mirror comes along, how will it be then?"* This question is one eternal mirror which father and son are mastering together.

[155] Gensa says, *"Smashed into hundreds of bits and pieces!"* These words mean smashed into hundred thousand myriads of bits and pieces. What he calls *the moment,*[79] *when suddenly a clear mirror comes along,* is *smashed into hundreds of bits and pieces!* That which is able to experience the state of *smashed into hundreds of bits and pieces* may be the clear mirror. When the clear mirror is made to express itself, [the expression] may be *smashed into hundreds of bits and pieces.* Therefore, the place where smashed bits and pieces are dangling is the clear mirror. Do not take the narrow view that formerly there was a moment of not yet being smashed to bits and pieces and that latterly there may be a moment of no longer being smashed to bits and pieces. [The expression] is simply *smashed into hundreds of bits and pieces!* Confrontation with the hundreds of smashed bits

---

74. The images of the foreigner and the Chinese are no longer relevant.

75. Master Seppo did not only affirm the eternal mirror—both masters affirmed both sides.

76. The simile of the clear mirror does not deny the simile of the foreigner and Chinaman appearing in the eternal mirror. Both similes can co-exist independently.

77. 恁麼人 (INMONIN). See chap. 29, *Inmo.*

78. "Has already understood" is 若会す (NYAKU-E *su*). 若 (NYAKU) originally expresses possibility, but this usage reflects Master Dogen's identification of what is possible and what is already there. Master Dogen explains that 若 (NYAKU) means "already" in chap.22, *Bussho,* [14].

79. 時 (JI, *toki*), means time or moment. In Master Gensa's original question it is translated as "then."

and pieces is a solitary and steep unity.[80] This being so, does this *smashed into hundreds of bits and pieces* describe the eternal mirror, or does it describe the clear mirror?—I would like to ask further for words of transformation.[81] At the same time, it neither describes the eternal mirror nor describes the clear mirror: though [hitherto] we have been able to ask about the eternal mirror and the clear mirror, when we discuss Gensa's words, might it be that what is manifesting itself before us as only sand, pebbles, fences, and walls has become the tip of a tongue, and thus *"smashed into hundreds of bits and pieces?"* What form does *smashing* take? Eternal blue depths; the moon in space.

[157] Great Master Shinkaku of Seppo mountain and Zen Master Enen of Sansho-in temple[82] are walking along when they see a group of apes. Thereupon Seppo says, *"These apes are each backed with one eternal mirror."*[83]

[157] We must diligently learn these words in practice. *Ape* means monkey.[84] How are the apes that Seppo sees? We should ask questions like this, and make effort further, not noticing the passing of kalpas. *"Each is backed with one eternal mirror:"* though the eternal mirror is the face of Buddhist patriarchs, at the same time, the eternal mirror, even in the ascendant state, is the eternal mirror. That it backs each individual ape does not mean that there are big mirrors and small mirrors according to individual differences; it is *one eternal mirror*. As to the meaning of *backed*, for example we say that a painted image of Buddha is *backed* with what we stick behind it. When the backs of apes are backed, they are backed with the eternal mirror. *What kind of paste could have been used?*[85] To speak tentatively, the backs of monkeys might be backed with the eternal mirror. Is the back of the eternal mirror backed with monkeys? The back of the eternal mirror is backed with the eternal mirror, and the backs of monkeys are backed with monkeys. The words that *each back has one face*[86] are never an empty teaching: they are the truth expressed as the truth should be expressed. So apes or eternal mirrors? Ultimately, what can we say? Are we ourselves originally apes? Or are we other than apes? Who can we ask? Whether we are apes is beyond our knowledge and beyond the knowledge of others. Whether we are ourselves is beyond [intellectual] groping.

[159] Sansho says, *"It has been nameless for successive kalpas. Why would you express it as the eternal mirror?"* This is a mirror, a concrete instance, with which Sansho has certified his realization of the eternal mirror. *For successive kalpas* means before a mind or a moment

---

80. 孤峻の一 (KOSHUN *no* ITSU). 一 (ITSU), "one" or "unity," suggests reality as the one, in contrast to Master Gensa's expression which suggests reality as miscellaneous things and phenomena in their own concrete forms. 孤峻 (KOSHUN) expresses the mental aspect (solitude) and concrete aspect (steepness) of the real state.

81. 一転語 (ICHITENGO), lit. "one-turn-words," i.e. words that can change a situation completely. Master Dogen expected the answer "Both the eternal mirror and the clear mirror."

82. Master Sansho Enen (dates unknown), a successor of Master Rinzai.

83. See *Shinji-shobogenzo* pt. 3, no. 95. Also *Hekigan-roku,* no. 68. In the following paragraphs, the rest of the story is quoted line by line.

84. Master Dogen explained the relatively uncommon Chinese characters that appear in the story, 獼猴 (MIKO), with the familiar Japanese word さる *(saru).*

85. The question is written in Chinese characters only, but a source earlier than Master Dogen has not been traced.

86. Master Seppo's words are 一面の古鏡を背せり (ICHIMEN *no* KOKYO *o* HAI *se ri*), lit. "backed with one face of eternal mirror," with 面 (MEN), "face," used as a counter. Master Dogen's comment suggests that all individual things have one reality in common.

of consciousness has ever appeared; it means the inside of a kalpa not having shown its head. *Nameless* describes *the successive kalpas'* sun-faces, moon-faces, and eternal-mirror-faces; and describes the face of the clear mirror. When *the nameless* is really *the nameless,* the *successive kalpas* are never *"successive kalpas."* Given that *the successive kalpas* are not *"successive kalpas,"* Sansho's expression cannot be an expression of the truth. Instead, *before a moment of consciousness has ever appeared* means today. We should train and polish without letting today pass in vain. Frankly, though the fame of this *"nameless for successive kalpas"* is heard on high, it expresses the eternal mirror as what? A dragons' head with a snake's tail![87]

[161] Seppo might now say to Sansho, *The eternal mirror! The eternal mirror!* Seppo does not say that; what he says further is, *"A flaw has appeared,"* or in other words, *"a scratch has emerged."*[88] We are prone to think *how could a flaw appear on the eternal mirror?* At the same time, [in saying that] the eternal mirror has borne a flaw [Seppo] may be calling the expression *"It has been nameless for successive kalpas"* a flaw. The eternal mirror described by *"a flaw has appeared"* is the total eternal mirror. Sansho has not got out of the cave of a flaw appearing on the eternal mirror, and so the understanding which he has expressed is utterly a flaw on the eternal mirror. This being so, we learn in practice that flaws appear even on the eternal mirror and that even [mirrors] on which flaws have appeared are the eternal mirror; this is learning the eternal mirror in practice.

[162] Sansho says, *"What is so deadly urgent that you are not conscious of the story?"*[89] The import of these words is, *Why [are you in] such a deadly hurry?* We should consider in detail and learn in practice whether this *deadly emergency* is [a matter of] today or tomorrow, the self or the external world, the whole Universe in ten directions or [a concrete place] inside the great Kingdom of Tang?[90] As to the meaning of *story* in the words *"You are not conscious of the story,"* there are stories that have continued to be told, there are stories that have never been told, and there are stories that have already been told completely. Now, the truths which are in *the story* are being realized. Has the story itself, for example, realized the truth together with the Earth and all sentient beings?[91] It is never restored brocade.[92] Therefore it is *not conscious;* it is the *non-consciousness* of *"the*

---

87. Master Dogen first of all affirmed Master Sansho's words, because they say that the eternal mirror is never a concept. But in conclusion he was not impressed by Master Sansho calling the eternal mirror "nameless for successive kalpas."

88. Master Dogen explained the meaning of the Chinese character 瑕 (KA, *kizu*) with the Japanese *kana* きず (*kizu*).

89. "Story" is 話頭 (WATO). 話 (WA) means "story." 頭 (TO), "head," is added to make the expression more concrete. In the Rinzai sect, stories (or so-called *koans*) such as those recorded by Master Dogen in *Shinji-shobogenzo,* are called 話頭 (WATO).

90. We should learn whether, in reality, there is anything to be hasty about.

91. The Buddha said that when he realized the truth the Earth and all sentient beings realized the truth at the same time. See for example chap. 69, *Hotsu-mujoshin*. Master Dogen emphasized that the story is not only abstract words, but the representation of something real.

92. The story is not to be fussed and worried over.

man facing the royal personage;"[93] it is being face-to-face without consciousness of each other. It is not that there are no stories; it is just that the concrete situation is *beyond consciousness. Non-consciousness* is red mind in every situation[94] and, further, not-seeing with total clarity.[95]

[163] Seppo says, *"It is the old monk's mistake."* Sometimes people say these words meaning *"I expressed myself badly,"* but [the words] need not be understood like that. *"The old monk"* means the old man who is master in his house;[96] that is to say, [someone] who solely learns in practice the old monk himself, without learning anything else. Though he experiences a thousand changes and ten thousand transformations, heads of gods and faces of demons, what he learns in practice is just the old monk's one move.[97] Though he appears as a buddha and appears as a patriarch, at every moment and for ten thousand years, what he learns in practice is just the old monk's one move. *Mistakes* are his *abundant jobs as temple master.*[98] Upon reflection, Seppo is an outstanding member[99] of [the order of] Tokuzan, and Sansho is an excellent disciple[100] of Rinzai. Neither of the two venerable patriarchs is of humble ancestry: [Seppo] is a distant descendant of Seigen and [Sansho] is a distant descendant of Nangaku.[101] That they have been dwelling in and retaining the eternal mirror is [evidenced] as described above. They may be a criterion[102] for students of later ages.

[165] Seppo preaches to the assembly, *"[If] the world is ten feet*[103] *wide, the eternal mirror is ten feet wide. [If] the world is one foot*[104] *wide, the eternal mirror is one foot wide."*

At this, Gensa, pointing to the furnace, says, *"Tell me then, how wide is the furnace?"*

Seppo says, *"As wide as the eternal mirror."*

---

93. When Master Bodhidharma arrived in China from India, he was presented to Emperor Wu of the Liang Dynasty. The Emperor said to him, *"Who is the man facing the royal personage?"* Master Bodhidharma replied, *"I do not know."* See *Hekigan-roku*, no. 1. In the Emperor Wu story, "I do not know" or "I am not conscious [of myself]" or "I do not understand [myself intellectually]" is 不識 (FUSHIKI), as in Master Sansho's words. Master Sansho's words sound like a complaint that Master Seppo is not listening to him. But Master Dogen interpreted the words 不識 (FUSHIKI) as ironic praise of Master Seppo's state.

94. 条条の赤心 (JOJO *no* SEKISHIN). This is a variation on Master Dogen's usual expression 赤心片片 (SEKISHIN-HENPEN), or "naked mind at every moment."

95. 明明の不見 (MEIMEI *no* FUKEN), lit. "clear-clear not-seeing."

96. That is, his own master, the master of himself.

97. 一著 (ICHIJAKU) means one placement of a stone in a game of go—suggesting one action at one time and place.

98. Sansho asks Seppo, *"The golden-scaled fish that passes through the net: what does it feed on?"* Seppo says, *"When you have got free of the net, I will tell you."* Sansho says, *"The good counselor to fifteen hundred people is not conscious of the story!"* Master Seppo says, *"The old monk's jobs as temple master are abundant."* See *Shinji-shobogenzo* pt. 1, no. 52.

99. 一角 (IKKAKU), lit. one horn.

100. 神足 (JINSOKU), lit. "mystical foot," from the Sanskrit *ṛddipāda*. See Glossary. See also chap. 8, *Raihai-tokuzui*, note 33.

101. Master Seigen Gyoshi (660-740) and Master Nangaku Ejo (677–744) were both disciples of Master Daikan Eno.

102. 亀鏡 (KIKYO), lit. "turtle mirror." Chinese soothsayers used to heat a turtle shell and use the positions of the cracks thus caused to divine a future course of action.

103. 一丈 (ICHIJO). One *jo* is about ten feet.

104. 一尺 (ISSHAKU). One *shaku* is almost exactly one foot, and ten *shaku* equals one *jo*.

Gensa says, *"The Old Master's heels have not landed on the ground."*[105]

[166] He calls ten feet the world; the world is ten feet. He sees one foot as the world; the world is one foot. He describes the ten feet of the present, and describes the one foot of the present, never any other unfamiliar foot or tens of feet. When [people] study this story, they usually think of the width of the world in terms of countless and boundless three-thousand-great-thousandfold worlds or the limitless world of Dharma, but that is only like being a small self and cursorily pointing to beyond the next village. In taking up this world [here and now], we see it as ten feet. This is why Seppo says, *"The width of the eternal mirror is ten feet, and the width of the world is ten feet."* When we learn these ten feet [here and now], we are able to see one concrete part of *the width of the world*. In other cases, when [people] hear the words *"eternal mirror"* they envisage a sheet of thin ice. But it is not like that.[106] The ten foot width [of the eternal mirror] is at one with the ten foot width of the world, but are the form and content [of the eternal mirror and the world] necessarily equal, and are they at one, when the world is limitless?[107] We should consider this diligently. The eternal mirror is never like a pearl. Never hold views and opinions about whether it is bright or dull, and never look at it as square or round. Even though *the whole Universe in ten directions is one bright pearl,*[108] this cannot match *the eternal mirror*. So the eternal mirror, regardless of the coming and the appearance of foreigners or Chinese, is every thing [that happens] through the length and breadth of [this state of] brilliance.[109] [But] it is not numerous and not large. *Width* refers to this [real] quantity; it does not mean extent. *Width* means what is expressed as two or three ordinary inches and counted, for example, in sevens and eights. In calculation of the Buddha's truth, when we calculate it in terms of great realization or non-realization we clarify [a weight of] two pounds or three pounds; and when we calculate it in terms of buddhas and patriarchs we realize five things or ten things.[110] One unit of ten feet is the width of the eternal mirror, and the width of the eternal mirror is one thing.[111] Gensa's words, *"How wide is the furnace?"* are an unconcealed expression of the truth, which we should learn in practice for a thousand ages and for ten thousand ages. To look now into the furnace is to look into [the furnace] having become a person who is *Who?*[112] When we are looking into the furnace, it is not seven feet and it is not eight feet. This [story] is not a tale of agitation and attachment; it is about the realization of a singular

---

105. See *Shinji-shobogenzo* pt. 2, no. 9.

106. Some people think about the eternal mirror too abstractly; others can only conceive it as something material.

107. In Master Seppo's example, the eternal mirror and the world are a unity within the area of ten feet. Master Dogen asked if it would be true if the world were limitless.

108. Master Gensa's expression of the truth. See chap. 4, *Ikka-no-myoju*.

109. 玲瓏 (REIRO), suggests the Universe itself. See note 71.

110. "Thing" is 枚 (MAI), which is used as a counter for thin flat objects such as sheets of paper, layers of clothing, mirrors, et cetera, and sometimes as a counter for generations of Buddhist patriarchs.

111. This sentence can be contrasted with the opening sentence of the paragraph. In this case Master Dogen changed the final element in the sentence from 一丈 (ICHIJO), "one unit of ten feet," to 一枚 (ICHIMAI), "one thing," emphasizing that the eternal mirror is concrete.

112. たれ人 (*tare hito*), a person who has lost self-consciousness, a person whose state is beyond words or understanding.

state in a fresh situation—[as expressed,] for example, *"What is it that comes like this."*[113] When the [meaning of] the words *"what amount of width..."* has come to us, the *"what amount [of width]"* may be different from *"how [wide]"* [as we have understood it] hitherto.[114] We must not doubt the fact of liberation at this concrete place. We must hear in Gensa's words the fundamental point that the furnace is beyond aspects and dimensions. Do not idly allow the one dumpling before you now to fall to the ground. Break it open! This is the effort.

[170] Seppo says, *"As wide as the eternal mirror."* We should quietly reflect on these words. Not wanting to say *the furnace is ten feet wide,* he speaks like this. It is not true that saying *ten feet* would be the fit expression of the truth whereas *"as wide as the eternal mirror"* is an unfit expression. We should research actions that are *as wide as the eternal mirror.* Many people have thought that not saying *the furnace is ten feet wide* was unfitness of expression. They should diligently consider the independence of *width;* they should reflect that *the eternal mirror* is a concrete thing; and they should not let action which is *reality* pass them by.[115] [Seppo] may be *manifesting behavior in the way of the ancients, never falling into despondency.*[116]

[171] Gensa says, *"The Old Man's heels have not landed on the ground."*[117] The point here is, whether we call him *"the Old Man"* or whether we call him *"the Old Master,"* that is not always Seppo himself, because Seppo may be *a [real] Old Man.* As to the meaning of *heels,* we should ask just where they are.[118] We should master in practice just what *heels* means. Does mastering *[heels]* in practice refer to the right-Dharma-eye treasury, or to space, or to the whole ground, or to the lifeblood? How many *[heels]* are there? Is there one? Is there a half? Are there hundred thousand myriads? We should do diligent research like this. *"They have not landed on the ground:"* what kind of thing is *the ground?*[119] We provisionally call the present Earth *"ground,"*[117] in conformance with the view of our own kind. There are other kinds that see it, for instance, as *the Dharma-gate to unthinkable salvation,*[120] and there is a kind that sees [the Earth] as the buddhas' many enactments of the truth. So in the case of the *ground* upon which heels should land, what does [Gensa] see as the *ground*? Is the *ground* the real state of being, or is it the real

---

113. 是什麼物恁麼来 (*ko[re]* SHIMO-BUTSU *[ka]* INMO-RAI). Master Daikan Eno spoke these words to Master Nangaku Ejo when Master Nangaku entered his order. See also note 41.

114. Master Gensa said 闊多少 (*hiroki koto* TASHO, or KATSU-TASHO). In Chinese 多少 (TASHO), lit. "large-small," is the usual way of asking how big something is, how expensive something is, et cetera. However, Master Dogen understood Master Gensa's words not only as an ordinary question, but also as a statement that the furnace was a real quantity.

115. Master Seppo said 如古鏡闊 (NYO-KOKYO-KATSU). Master Dogen considered the real meaning of each of the three elements independently. As an adverb, 如 (NYO) means "as" or "like," but as a noun it means "real state," or "reality,"—for example, in the compound 一如 (ICHINYO), "oneness" or "one reality." Here Master Dogen repeats the character, 如如, for emphasis: reality.

116. The words of Master Kyogen Chikan. See chap. 9, *Keisei-sanshiki.*

117. In the story "ground" is 地 (CHI), "ground" or "earth." "The Earth" is 大地 (DAICHI), "big ground" or "great earth."

118. In general, heels are symbols of the concrete.

119. 地 (CHI) means "ground," or "earth;" at the same time, it means "the concrete," or "concrete state."

120. 不思議解脱法門 (FUSHIGI-GEDATSU-HOMON), the words of Vimalakīrti, a lay student of the Buddha.

state of being without? Further, we should ask again and again, and we should tell ourselves and tell others, whether it is impossible for even an inch or so of what we generally call *"the ground"* to exist within the great order? Is heels touching the ground the right state, or is heels not landing on the ground the right state? What situation leads [Gensa] to say *"they have not landed on the ground?"* When the Earth is without an inch of soil,[121] [the words] *touching the ground* may be immature and [the words] *not having landed on the ground* may be immature.[122] This being so, *the Old Man's heels not having landed on the ground* is the [very] exhalation and inhalation of the Old Man, the [very] moment of his heels.[123]

[174] Zen Master Koto[124] of Kokutai-in temple, on Kinka-zan mountain in the Bushu[125] district, the story goes, is asked by a monk, *"What is the eternal mirror like before being polished?"*[126]

The Master says, *"The eternal mirror."*

The monk says, *"What is it like after being polished?"*

The Master says, *"The eternal mirror."*[127]

[174] Remember, the eternal mirror under discussion now has a time of being polished, a time before being polished, and [a time] after being polished, but it is wholly the eternal mirror. This being so, when we are polishing, we are polishing the eternal mirror in its entirety. We do not polish by mixing in mercury or anything else other than the eternal mirror. This is neither polishing the self nor the self polishing; it is polishing the eternal mirror. Before being polished the eternal mirror is not dull. Even if [people] call it black, it can never be dull: it is the eternal mirror in its vivid state. In general, we polish a mirror to make it into a mirror; we polish a tile to make it into a mirror; we polish a tile to make it into a tile; and we polish a mirror to make it into a tile.[128] There are [times when] we polish without making anything; and there are [times when] it would be possible to make something, but we are unable to polish.[129] All equally are the traditional work of Buddhist patriarchs.

[175] When Baso[130] of Kozei,[131] in former days, was learning in practice under Nan-

---

121. When the earth is realized as it is.

122. "Immature" is 未 (*imadashi*), lit. "not yet." This is the negative used in Master Gensa's original sentence.

123. In this paragraph, Master Dogen urges us to consider what each of Master Gensa's words really expresses. In conclusion, Master Gensa's words describe Master Seppo's real state, his concrete existence.

124. Master Kokutai Koto, a successor of Master Gensa Shibi; dates unknown.

125. A district in Chekiang province in East China.

126. Because in those days mirrors were made of copper, it was natural to think of a mirror as something that needs polishing.

127. See *Shinji-shobogenzo* pt. 2, no. 17.

128. Sometimes our idealism is like polishing a mirror in order to try and make an ideal mirror, sometimes our behavior is as meaningless as trying to polish a tile into a mirror, sometimes we realize concrete things through Buddhist practice, and sometimes our action transcends idealism completely.

129. Two examples of real situations in daily life.

130. Master Baso Do-itsu (709–788). After receiving the Dharma from Master Nangaku Ejo, he lived on Baso-zan mountain in the Jiang-xi district, where he taught more than 130 disciples, including Hyakujo Ekai, Seido Chizo, Nansen Fugan, and Daibai Hojo.

131. 江西, Jiang-xi, a province in Southeast China.

gaku,[132] Nangaku on one occasion intimately transmits to Baso the mind-seal. This is the beginning of the beginning of *polishing a tile.*[133] Baso has been living at Denpo-in temple, sitting constantly in Zazen for a matter of ten or so years. We can imagine what it is like in his thatched hut on a rainy night. There is no mention of him letting up on a cold floor sealed in by snow. Nangaku one day goes to Baso's hut, where Baso stands waiting. Nangaku asks, *"What are you doing these days?"*

Baso says, *"These days Do-itsu just sits."*

Nangaku says, *"What is the aim of sitting in Zazen?"*

Baso says, *"The aim of sitting in Zazen is to become buddha."*[134]

Nangaku promptly fetches a tile and polishes it on a rock near Baso's hut.

Baso, on seeing this, asks, *"What is the Master doing?"*

Nangaku says, *"Polishing a tile."*

Baso says, *"What is the use of polishing a tile?"*

Nangaku says, *"I am polishing it into a mirror."*[135]

Baso says, *"How can polishing a tile make it into a mirror?"*[136]

Nangaku says, *"How can sitting in Zazen make you into a buddha?"*[137]

[178] For several hundred years, since ancient times, most people interpreting this story—great matter that it is—have thought that Nangaku was simply spurring Baso on. That is not necessarily so. The actions of great saints far transcend the states of common folk. Without the Dharma of polishing a tile, how could the great saints have any expedient method of teaching people? The power to teach people is the bones and marrow of a Buddhist patriarch. Although [Nangaku] has devised it, this [teaching method] is a common tool. [Teaching methods] other than common tools and everyday utensils are not transmitted in the house of Buddha. Further, the impression on Baso is immediate. Clearly, the virtue authentically transmitted by the Buddhist patriarchs is directness. Clearly, in truth, when polishing a tile becomes a mirror, Baso becomes buddha. When Baso becomes buddha, Baso immediately becomes Baso. When Baso becomes Baso, Zazen immediately becomes Zazen. This is why the making of mirrors through the polishing of tiles has been dwelt in and retained in the bones and marrow of eternal buddhas; and, this being so, the eternal mirror exists having been made from a tile. While we have been polishing this mirror—in the past also—it has never been tainted. Tiles are not dirty; we just polish a tile as a tile. In this state, the virtue of making a mirror is realized, and this is just the effort of Buddhist patriarchs. If polishing a tile does not make a mirror, polishing a mirror cannot make a mirror either.[138] Who can suppose

132. Master Nangaku Ejo (677–744).

133. 磨瓦 (MASEN). The words first appear in the story of Masters Nangaku and Baso in vol. 5 of *Keitoku-dento-roku*. See also *Shinji-shobogenzo* pt. 1, no. 8.

134. 作仏 (SABUTSU). 作 (SA, *tsukuru, [to] nasu*) means to produce, to make, to become, or to act as.

135. 磨作鏡 (MA-SA-KYO, or *mashi te kagami to nasu*). "Into" represents 作 (SA, *[to] nasu*), as in the preceding note.

136. 成鏡 (JOKYO, or *kagami [to] nasu*). "Make it into" is in this case represented by the character 成 (JO, *nasu*), lit. "to accomplish," "to realize," or "to make."

137. "Make you into a buddha" is 作仏 (SABUTSU), translated previously as "to become buddha."

138. Because polishing makes the mirror—whether the object is a tile or a mirror is not important.

that in this *making* there is [both] *becoming* buddha and *making* a mirror.[139] Further, to express a doubt, is it possible, when polishing the eternal mirror, to mistakenly think that the polishing is making a tile? The real state at the time of polishing is, at other times, beyond comprehension. Nevertheless, because Nangaku's words must exactly express the expression of the truth, it may be, in conclusion, simply that polishing a tile makes a mirror. People today also should try taking up the tiles of the present and polishing them, and they will certainly become mirrors. If tiles did not become mirrors, people could not become buddhas. If we despise tiles as lumps of mud, then we might also despise people as lumps of mud. If people have mind, tiles must also have mind. Who can recognize that there are mirrors in which, [when] tiles come, tiles appear? And who can recognize that there are mirrors in which, [when] mirrors come, mirrors appear?

Shobogenzo Kokyo

Preached to the assembly at Kannon-dori-kosho-horin-ji temple, on the 9th day of the 9th lunar month in the 2nd year of Ninji.[140]

---

139. *Making* and *becoming* are the same character, 作 (SA).
140. 1241.

[21]

看経

KANKIN

Reading Sutras

***Kan** means "to read" and **kin** means "sutras." Many Buddhist sects revere reading sutras, because they think that the Buddhist truth is theory which can be understood through abstract explanation. They think that we can understand Buddhism only by reading sutras. At the same time, there are other sects who deny the value of reading sutras; they say that because Buddhist truth is not a theoretical system, we cannot attain the truth by reading sutras. Master Dogen took the middle way on the problem: rather than deny the value of reading sutras, he said that reading sutras is one way of finding out what Buddhist practice is. He did not believe, however, that we can get the truth by reading sutras; he did not think that reciting sutras might exercise some mystical influence over religious life. In this way Master Dogen's view on reading sutras was very realistic. However, his understanding of "reading sutras" was not limited to written sutras; he believed that the Universe is a sutra. He thought that observing the world around us is like reading a sutra. So for him, grass, trees, mountains, the moon, the sun, and so forth were all Buddhist sutras. He even extended his view of reading sutras to include walking around the master's chair in the middle of the Zazen Hall. This viewpoint is not only Master Dogen's; it is the viewpoint of Buddhism itself. So in this chapter, Master Dogen explains the wider meaning of reading sutras.*

[183] **The practice-and-experience of** anuttara-samyak-saṃbodhi sometimes relies on [good] counselors and sometimes relies on the sutras. *[Good] counselors*[1] means Buddhist patriarchs who are totally themselves. *Sutras* means sutras which are totally themselves. Because the self is totally a Buddhist patriarch and because the self is totally a sutra, it is like this.[2] Even though we call it self, it is not restricted by *me and you.* It is vivid eyes, and a vivid fist.

[184] At the same time,[3] there is the consideration of sutras, the reading of sutras,[4] the reciting of sutras, the copying of sutras, the receiving of sutras, and the retaining of sutras: they are all the practice-and-experience of Buddhist patriarchs. Yet it is not easy to meet the Buddha's sutras: *Throughout innumerable realms, even the name cannot be heard.*[5]

---

1. 知識 (CHISHIKI), short for 善知識 (ZENCHISHIKI), from the Sanskrit *kalyāṇa-mitra,* or "good friend." See Glossary.

2. かくのごとく *(kakunogotoku),* "like this," describes the situation here and now.

3. In the introductory paragraph, Master Dogen explained sutras generally, as self. This signifies a change of viewpoint to the concrete phase.

4. 看経 (KANKIN), as in the chapter title. The original meaning of 看 (KAN) is to see or to watch.

5. This sentence is in the form of a quotation from a sutra, though the source has not been located.

Among Buddhist patriarchs, *even the name cannot be heard.* Amidst the lifeblood, *even the name cannot be heard.* Unless we are Buddhist patriarchs we do not see, hear, read, recite, or understand the meaning of sutras. After learning in practice as Buddhist patriarchs, we are barely able to learn sutras in practice. At this time the reality of hearing [sutras], retaining [sutras], receiving [sutras], preaching sutras, and so on, exists in the ears, eyes, tongue, nose, and organs of body and mind,[6] and in the places where we go, hear, and speak. The sort who *because they seek fame, preach non-Buddhist doctrines*[7] cannot practice the Buddha's sutras. The reason is that the sutras are transmitted and retained on trees and on rocks, are spread through fields and through villages, are expounded by lands of dust, and are lectured by space.

[186] Great Master Kodo[8] the ancestral Patriarch of Yakusan mountain has not ascended [his seat in the Dharma] Hall for a long time. The temple-chief[9] says, *"The monks have long been hoping for your compassionate instruction, Master."*

[Yaku]san says, *"Strike the bell!"*

The temple-chief strikes the bell, and a few of the monks assemble.

[Yaku]san ascends [the seat in the Dharma] Hall and passes a while. Then he gets down from the seat and goes back to the abbot's quarters. The temple-chief follows behind him and says, *"Just before, the Master agreed to preach the Dharma for the monks. Why have you not bestowed a single word upon us?"*

[Yaku]san says, *"For sutras there are sutra-teachers. For commentaries there are commentary-teachers. How could you doubt the old monk?"*[10]

[188] The compassionate instruction of the ancestral Patriarch is that for fists there is a Fist-teacher, and for eyes there is an Eye-teacher. At the same time, with due respect, I would now like to ask the ancestral Patriarch this: I do not deny [your words] *"how can the old monk be doubted?"* but I still do not understand: the Master is a teacher of What.[11]

[188] *The order of the founding Patriarch Daikan[12] is on Sokei-zan mountain in Shoshu district. Hotatsu,[13] a monk who recites the Sutra of the Flower of Dharma,[14] comes to practice there. The founding Patriarch preaches for Hotatsu the following verse:*

The next two sentences Master Dogen probably made himself, substituting "Buddhist patriarchs" and "lifeblood" for "innumerable lands," in order to emphasize the difficulty of meeting Buddhist sutras.

6. 身心塵処 (SHINJIN-JINSHO), the last two of the six sense organs. The body as a sense organ refers to the sense of touch. The mind as a sense organ is the seat of thought. Classing thought as one of six senses emphasizes that it is subordinate to real wisdom. See, for example, LS 3.122: *"Though he has not yet attained faultless real wisdom, his mind-organ is pure like this."*

7. The source of this quotation from a sutra has not been located.

8. Master Yakusan Igen (745–828), successor of Master Sekito Kisen. Great Master Kodo is Master Yakusan's posthumous title.

9. 院主 (INSHU), or "prior," also called *kansu* and *kanin;* one of the six *chiji* or main officers in a temple. See note 54.

10. *Shinji-shobogenzo* pt. 1, no. 79. Also the story is no. 7 in *Wanshi-juko.*

11. "A teacher of What" is 什麼師 (NAN *no* SHI), i.e., a teacher of the ineffable, a teacher whose state and whose teaching cannot be understood intellectually.

12. Master Daikan Eno (638–713).

13. The story of Master Hotatsu and his personal history are explained at length in chap. 17, *Hokke-ten-hokke.*

14. 法華経 (HOKKE-KYO), the Lotus Sutra. See chap. 17, *Hokke-ten-hokke.*

When the mind is in delusion, the Flower of Dharma turns.
When the mind is in realization, we turn the Flower of Dharma.
Unless we are clear about ourselves, however long we recite [the sutra],
It will become an enemy because of its meanings.
Without intention the mind is right.
With intention the mind becomes wrong.
When we transcend both with and without,
We ride eternally in the white ox cart.[15]

[189] So when the mind is in delusion we are turned by the Flower of Dharma; when the mind is in realization we turn the Flower of Dharma. Further, when we spring free from delusion and realization, the Flower of Dharma turns the Flower of Dharma. On hearing this verse Hotatsu jumps for joy and praises it with the following verse:

Three thousand recitations of the sutra
With one phrase from Sokei, forgotten.
Before clarifying the import of [the buddhas'] appearance in the world,
How can we stop recurring lives of madness?
[The sutra] explains goat, deer, and ox as an expedient,
[But] proclaims that beginning, middle, and end are good.
Who knows that [even] within the burning house,
Originally we are kings in the Dharma?

Then the founding Patriarch says, *"From now on, you will rightly be called the Sutra-reading Monk."* We should know that there are sutra-reading monks in Buddhism: it is the direct teaching of the eternal Buddha of Sokei. *Reading* in this [phrase] *"Sutra-reading Monk"* is beyond *having ideas, being without ideas,* and so on.[16] It is *transcendence of both having and being without.* The fact is only that *from kalpa to kalpa the hands never put down the sutra, and from noon to night there is no time when it is not being read.*[17] The fact is only that from sutra to sutra it is never not being experienced.[18]

[191] *The twenty-seventh patriarch is the Venerable Prajñātara*[19] *of eastern India. A king of eastern India, the story goes, invites the Venerable One to a midday meal, at which time the king asks, "Everyone else recites*[20] *sutras. Why is it, Venerable One, that you alone do not recite?"*

---

15. The poem is exactly the same as the one quoted in chap. 17, *Hokke-ten-hokke.*

16. "Reading" and "ideas" are the same Chinese character 念 (NEN). In 念経僧 (NENKINSO), "Sutra-reading Monk," 念 (NEN) is a verb, "reading," suggesting the action of reading the sutra. In the poem 念 (NEN) is a noun, "ideas." 有念 (UNEN), "having ideas," describes the presence of ideas, images, or intention, and 無念 (MUNEN), "being without ideas," describes the absence, or negation, of ideas, images, or intention.

17. Quotation of Master Daikan Eno's words to Hotatsu from *Rokuso-dankyo (The Sixth Patriarch's Platform Sutra).* The next line is Master Dogen's addition.

18. "Sutra" and "experienced" are the same Chinese character 経 (KYO, KIN, or KEI). 経 means (i) sutra, as in the title of this chapter, and (ii) passing through, experience, the passage of time (see note 18 in chap. 11, *Uji*). Master Dogen identified reading sutras and experiencing reality.

19. Master Prajñātara (died 457), was a successor of Master Puṇyamitra and the teacher of Master Bodhidharma.

20. 転ず *(tenzu)* is lit. "to turn," that is, to turn a scroll on which a sutra is written—see chap. 17, *Hokke-ten-hokke.*

The Patriarch says:

> *My[21] out-breath does not follow circumstances,*
> *The in-breath does not reside in the world of aggregates.[22]*
> *I am constantly reciting sutras like this.[23]*
> *Hundred thousand myriad koṭis of scrolls.*
> *Never only one scroll or two scrolls.[24]*

[192] The Venerable Prajñātara is a native of an eastern territory of India. He is the twenty-seventh rightful successor from the Venerable Mahākāśyapa,[25] having received the authentic transmission of all the tools of the Buddha's house: he has dwelt in and retained the brains, the eyes, the fist, and the nostrils; the staff, the pātra, the robe and Dharma, the bones and marrow, and so on. He is our ancestral patriarch, and we are his distant descendants.[26] The words into which the Venerable One has now put his total effort [mean] not only that the out-breath does not follow circumstances, but also that circumstances do not follow the out-breath. Circumstances may be the brains and eyes, circumstances may be the whole body, circumstances may be the whole mind, but in bringing here, taking there, and bringing back here again, the state is just *not following circumstances. Not following* means totally following; therefore it is a state of bustling and jostling. The out-breath is circumstances themselves; even so, *it does not follow circumstances.* For countless kalpas we have never recognized the situation of breathing out and breathing in, but just now the moment has come when we can recognize it for the first time, and so we hear *it does not reside in the world of aggregates* and *it does not follow circumstances.* This is the moment when circumstances research for the first time such things as *the in-breath.* This moment has never been before, and it will never be again: it exists only in the present. *The world of aggregates* means the five aggregates: matter, perception, thought, enaction, and consciousness. The reason he does not reside in these five aggregates is that he is in the world where "five aggregates" have never arrived. Because he has grasped this pivotal point, the sutras he recites are never only one or two scrolls; he is *constantly reciting hundred thousand myriad* koṭis *of scrolls.* Though we say that *hundred thousand myriad* koṭis *of scrolls* just cites for the present an example of a large number, it is beyond only numerical quantity: it assigns the quantity of *hundred thousand myriad* koṭis *of scrolls* to one out-breath's *not residing in the world of aggregates.* At the same time, [the state] is not measured by tainted or faultless wisdom[27] and it is beyond the world of tainted and faultless dharmas.[28] Thus, it is beyond the cal-

---

21. 貧道 (HINDO), lit. "poor way," a humble form used by a Buddhist monk.

22. 蘊界 (UNKAI). 蘊 (UN) represents the Sanskrit *skandha.* The five skandhas are matter, perception, thought, enaction, and consciousness, representing all phenomena in the world. "Circumstances" (衆縁, SHU-EN) in the first line is plural, whereas "the world of aggregates" is singular, but they both suggest the world. The first two lines stress the Master's independence.

23. 如是経 (NYOZE-KYO) means sutras like this, sutras as they are, or sutras as reality.

24. Also quoted in chap. 52, *Bukkyo.*

25. The Buddha's successor, counted as the first patriarch in India.

26. 雲孫 (UNSON), lit. "cloud-grandchildren," a poetic variation of the usual expression 遠孫 (ENSON), lit. "distant grandchildren."

27. 有漏, 無漏智 (URO, MURO-CHI), or "wisdom with excess and without excess," represents the Sanskrit terms *sāsrava-jñāna* and *anāsrava-jñāna.*

28. 有漏, 無漏法 (URO, MURO-HO), or "dharmas with excess and without excess," represents the

culation of wise intelligence, it is beyond the estimation of intelligent wisdom; it is beyond the consideration of non-wise intelligence, and it is beyond the reach of non-intelligent wisdom. It is the practice-and-experience of buddhas and of patriarchs, it is their skin, flesh, bones, and marrow, their eyes, fists, brains, and nostrils, and their staffs and whisks, springing out of the moment.

[196] Great Master Shinsai[29] of Kannon-in temple in Joshu, the story goes, is sent a donation by an old woman, who asks the Great Master to recite the whole of the sutras. The Master descends from the Zazen chair, goes around it once, and says to the messenger, *"I have finished reciting the sutras."* The messenger returns and reports this to the old woman. The old woman says, *"I asked him before to recite the whole of the sutras. Why did the Master only recite half the sutras?"*[30]

[197] Evidently, the recitation of the whole of the sutras or half of the sutras amounts to three scrolls of sutras in the old woman's case.[31] *"I have finished reciting the sutras"* is the whole of Joshu's sutra. In brief, the situation of his reciting the whole of the sutras is as follows: There is Joshu going around the Zazen chair; there is the Zazen chair going around Joshu, there is Joshu going around Joshu, and there is the Zazen chair going around the Zazen chair. At the same time, all instances of reciting the sutras are neither limited to going around a Zazen chair, nor limited to a Zazen chair going around.

[198] Great Master Shinsho[32] of Daizui-zan mountain in Ekishu, whose original Dharma-name was Hoshin,[33] succeeded Zen Master Dai-an[34] of Chokei-ji temple. In the story, an old woman sends a donation and asks the master to recite the whole of the sutras. The Master descends from his Zazen chair, goes around it once, and says to the messenger, *"I have already recited the whole of the sutras."* The messenger returns and reports this to the old woman. The old woman says, *"I asked him before to recite the whole of the sutras. Why did the Master only recite half the sutras?"*[35]

[199] Now, do not study that Daizui is going around the Zazen chair, and do not study that the Zazen chair is going around Daizui. It is not only a grouping together of fists and eyes; his making of a circle is enaction of a circle. Does the old woman have the eyes, or does she not have the eyes [to see it]? Even though she has got the expression *"He only recited half the sutras"* in the authentic transmission from a fist,[36] the old woman should also say, *I asked him before to recite the whole of the sutras. Why did the Master only*

Sanskrit terms *sāsrava-dharma* and *anāsrava-dharma*. See Glossary.

29. Master Joshu Jushin (778–897), was a successor of Master Nansen Fugan, and especially highly revered by Master Dogen (see for example chap. 35, *Hakujushi*). Great Master Shinsai is his posthumous title.

30. *Shinji-shobogenzo* pt. 1, no. 24.

31. Three scrolls of sutras means sutras limited by relative consideration of numbers.

32. Master Daizui Hoshin (dates unknown), a successor of Master Chokei Dai-an. The Emperor sent his emissaries time and time again to invite Master Hoshin to the court, but he always declined. Great Master Shinsho is his posthumous title.

33. Hoshin is the Master's 法諱 (HOKI). This means the name that was avoided after a monk's death, that is, the name a monk used in his lifetime. See notes to chap. 16, *Shisho.*

34. Master Fukushu Dai-an (793–883), a successor of Master Hyakujo Ekai. His posthumous title is Great Master Enju. Quoted in *Shinji-shobogenzo* pt. 2, no. 57.

35. *Rento-eyo,* vol. 10.

36. A practical Buddhist master.

worry his soul?[37] If she spoke like this, even by accident, she would be an old woman with eyes.

[200] [In the order] of the founding Patriarch, Great Master Tozan Gohon,[38] the story goes, there is a government official who prepares the midday meal, offers a donation, and requests the Master to read and recite the whole of the sutras. The Great Master descends from his Zazen chair and bows to[39] the official. The official bows to the Great Master, who leads the official once around the Zazen chair, then bows to the official [again]. After a while he says to the official, *"Do you understand?"* The official says, *"I do not understand."* The Great Master says, *"You and I have read and recited the whole of the sutras. How could you not understand?"*

[201] That *"You and I have read and recited the whole of the sutras"* is evident. We do not learn that to go around the Zazen chair is to read and recite the whole of the sutras, and we do not understand that to read and recite the whole of the sutras is to go around the Zazen chair. All the same, we should listen to the compassionate instruction of the founding Patriarch. My late Master, the eternal Buddha, quoted this story when, while he was residing [as master] on Tendo-zan mountain, a donor from Korea entered the mountain, made a donation for the monks to read the sutras, and requested that my late Master should ascend the lecture seat. When he had quoted [the story], my late Master made a big circle with his whisk and said, *"Tendo today has read and recited for you the whole of the sutras."* Then he threw down the whisk and descended from the seat. We should read and recite now the words spoken by the late Master, never comparing them to [the words of] others. Still, should we think that [Master Tendo], in reading and reciting the whole of the sutras, uses a whole eye or uses half an eye? Do the words of the founding Patriarch and the words of my late Master rely on eyes or rely on tongues? How many [eyes and tongues] have they used? See if you can get to the bottom of it.

[203] The ancestral Patriarch, Great Master Kodo[40] of Yakusan mountain does not usually let people read sutras. One day he is reading a sutra himself. A monk asks him, *"The Master does not usually let others read sutras. Why then are you reading yourself?"*

The Master says, *"I just need to shade my eyes."*

The monk says, *"May I copy the Master?"*

The Master says, *"If you were to read you would surely pierce holes even in ox-hide!"*

[203] The words *"I just need to shade my eyes"* spoken now are words naturally spoken by shaded eyes[41] themselves. *Shading the eyes* describes getting rid of eyes and getting rid

37. 弄精魂 (ROZEIKON), lit. "to play with the soul." This expression usually suggests the practice of Zazen itself ("to play sport with the soul"—see for example chap. 68, *Udonge*), but in this case Master Dogen suggested that the old woman should have said, *The Master need not worry about anything!*

38. Master Tozan Ryokai (807–869), a successor of Master Ungan Donjo. Great Master Gohon is his posthumous title. See chap. 14, *Busso.*

39. 揖す (IU *su*), means to bow the head slightly with the hands in *shashu*—see note 64. Hereafter in this chapter also, "bow" indicates this form of salutation, as opposed to a prostration.

40. Master Yakusan Igen. See note 8.

41. 遮眼 (SHAGAN), "shaded eyes," suggests the balanced and peaceful state of action which is different from the idealistic viewpoint.

of sutras, it describes complete eye shading and completely shaded eyes. *Shading the eyes* means opening the eyes in the shaded state, invigorating the eyes within shade, invigorating shade within eyes, adding an extra eyelid, utilizing the eyes within shade, and eyes themselves utilizing shade. This being so, the virtue of *shading the eyes* is never [mentioned] in any [sutras] other than Eye-sutras. *"You would surely pierce holes even in ox-hide"* describes complete ox-hide and a complete-hide ox, it describes utilizing the ox to become a hide.[42] This is why [possession of] the skin, flesh, bones, and marrow, and horns on the head, and nostrils, has been seen as the vigorous activity of bulls and cows.[43] In *copying the Master,* the ox becomes the Eye—this is described as *shading the eyes.* It is the Eye becoming the ox.

[205] Zen Master Yafu Dosen[44] says:

To serve offerings to buddhas hundred million thousands of times
is boundless happiness,
[But] how can it compare to everyday reading of the old teachings?
On the face of white paper characters are written in black ink.
Open your eyes, I beg you, and look before you.[45]

[206] Remember, serving offerings to olden buddhas and reading the old teachings may be equal in happiness and good fortune and may go beyond happiness and good fortune. *The old teachings* means characters written in black ink on white paper, [but] who can recognize the old teachings as such? We must master just this principle.

[206] [In the order of] Great Master Kokaku[46] of Ungo-zan mountain, the story goes, there is a monk who is reading a sutra in his quarters. The Great Master asks from outside the window, "Ācārya, *what sutra is that you are reading?"*

The monk replies, *"The* Vimalakīrti *Sutra."*

The Master says, *"I am not asking you if it is the* Vimalakīrti *Sutra. That which you are reading is a What Sutra."*[47]

At this the monk is able to enter.[48]

[207] The Great Master's words *"That which you are reading is a What Sutra"* mean that the *state of reading,*[49] in one line, is age-old, profound, and eternal; and it is not desirable to

42. Interpreted simply, Master Yakusan's words mean "Reading sutras will only make your intellect sharper!" But Master Dogen interpreted that the words also include some ironic affirmation of the monk's state—"becoming a hide" suggests realization of the concrete.

43. Oxen sometimes symbolize Buddhist practitioners. In the Lotus Sutra, for example, the ox-cart is the symbol of the bodhisattva-way.

44. Master Yafu Dosen. He realized the truth listening to the preaching of a head monk called Ken of Tosai, after which he changed his name from Tekisan to Dosen. He made commentaries on the Diamond Sutra, and was considered one of seventeen authorities of the age on the Diamond Sutra. He preached on Yafu-zan mountain during the Ryuko era (1163–1164) of the Southern Sung dynasty.

45. Quoted from Master Yafu Dosen's commentary on the Diamond Sutra.

46. Master Ungo Doyo (835?–902), a successor of Master Tozan Ryokai. Great Master Kokaku is his posthumous title. See chap. 14, *Busso.*

47. Master Ungo repeated exactly the words he had said before. He had phrased his words to sound like a simple question, but his idea was that the sutra itself was something ineffable.

48. *Keitoku-dento-roku,* chap. 17.

49. 念底 (NENTEI). In Master Ungo's words, 念底 (NENTEI) means "that which you are reading,"

represent it as "reading." On the road we meet deadly snakes. This is why the question *What Sutra?* has been realized. In meeting as human beings, we do not misrepresent anything. This is why [the monk replies] "*The* Vimalakīrti *Sutra.*" In sum, reading sutras means reading sutras with eyes into which we have drawn together all the Buddhist patriarchs. At just this moment, the Buddhist patriarchs instantly become buddha, preach Dharma, preach buddha, and do buddha-action.[50] Without this moment in reading sutras, the brains and faces of Buddhist patriarchs could never exist.[51]

[209] At present in the orders of Buddhist patriarchs, forms for the reading of sutras are many and varied: for when a donor[52] enters the mountain and requests the whole Saṃgha to read sutras; for when the monks have been requested to read sutras regularly;[53] for when the monks read the sutras of their own volition, and so on. Besides these, there is the sutra-reading by the whole Saṃgha for a deceased monk.

[209] When a donor enters the mountain and requests the monks to read sutras, from breakfast on the day [of the reading] the Hall chief[54] hangs an advance notice of the sutra-reading in front of the Monks' Hall[55] and in all quarters. After breakfast the prostration mat is laid before the [image of the] Sacred Monk.[56] When it is time [for the reading], the bell in front of the Monks' Hall is struck three times, or struck once—according to the instructions of the abbot. After the sound of the bell, the head monk[57] and all the monks put on the kaṣāya and enter the Cloud Hall.[58] They go to their own place[59] and sit facing forward. Then the abbot enters the Hall, goes before the Sacred Monk, bows with joined hands, burns incense, and then sits at the [abbot's] place. Next the child-helpers[60] are told to distribute the sutras. These sutras are arranged before-

---

but here 底 (TEI), lit. "bottom," means "state." The latter usage occurs in *Fukan-zazengi,* in the phrase 不思量底 (FUSHIRYOTEI), "the state beyond thinking."

50. 作仏す (SABUTSU *su*), "become buddha," and 説法す (SEPPO *su*), "preach Dharma," are common compounds. 説仏す (SETSUBUTSU *su*), "preach buddha," and 仏作す (BUTSUSA *su*), "do buddha action," are Master Dogen's variations. In addition, the first three compounds are conventional verb + object compounds, but the fourth 仏作, is unconventional because "to buddha" is not conventionally used as a verb. The effect is to oppose the idealism of "becoming buddha."

51. In other words, if Buddhist sutras cannot be read intuitively, real Buddhism cannot exist—there are only abstract Buddhist patriarchs without heads and faces.

52. 施主 (SESHU) represents the Sanskrit *dānapati.*

53. For example, a lay sponsor bequeaths a sum of money to a monastery, and when the monks read sutras in the morning, they dedicate the reading in accordance with the wishes of that sponsor.

54. 堂司 (DOSU) is the fourth of the six main officers. He is the main officer in charge of daily supervision of the monks. The six main officers are 1) 都寺 (TSUSU), chief officer, head of the temple office, comptroller; 2) 監寺 (KANSU) prior; 3) 副司 (FUSU), assistant prior; 4) 堂司 (DOSU) or 維那 (INO), supervisor of monks in the Zazen Hall, rector; 5) 典座 (TENZO), head-cook; and 6) 直歳 (SHISUI), caretaker.

55. 僧堂 (SODO), the Zazen Hall.

56. 聖僧 (SHOSO), the image in the center of the Zazen Hall, almost always of Mañjuśrī Bodhisattva in Japan. Some halls in China have a Hotei, the Happy Buddha.

57. 首座 (SHUSO), or "chief seat." One of the assistant officers below the main officers.

58. 雲堂 (UNDO), another name for the Zazen Hall.

59. 被位 (HI-I), lit. "the place of their [night]wear," i.e., the place in the Zazen Hall where they sleep.

60. 童行 (ZUNNAN), or "apprentices," are children or youths who generally intend to become monks in future.

hand in the Kitchen Hall, placed in order and made ready to be given out when the time comes. The sutras are either distributed from inside the sutra box, or placed on a tray and then distributed. Once the monks have requested a sutra, they open and read it immediately. During this time, at the [right] moment, the guest-supervisor[61] leads the donor into the Cloud Hall. The donor picks up a hand-held censer just in front of the Cloud Hall and enters the Hall holding it up with both hands. The hand-held censer is [kept] in the common area by the entrance to the Kitchen Hall.[62] It is prepared with incense in advance, and a helper[63] is [instructed] to keep it ready in front of the Cloud Hall. When the donor is about to enter the Hall, [the helper], upon instruction, hands [the censer] to the donor. The guest-supervisor gives the orders regarding the censer. When they enter the Hall, the guest-supervisor leads and the donor follows, and they enter through the southern side of the front entrance to the Cloud Hall. The donor goes before the Sacred Monk, burns a stick of incense, and does three prostrations, holding the censer while doing the prostrations. During the prostrations the guest-supervisor, hands folded,[64] stands to the north of the prostration mat, facing south but turned slightly towards the donor.[65] After the donor's prostrations, the donor turns to the right, goes to the abbot, and salutes the abbot with a deep bow, holding the censer up high with both hands. The abbot remains on the chair to receive the salutation, holding up a sutra with palms held together.[66] The donor then bows to the north. Having bowed, [the donor] begins the round of the Hall from in front of the head monk. During the walk around the Hall, [the donor] is led by the guest-supervisor. Having done one round of the Hall and arrived [again] in front of the Sacred Monk, [the donor] faces the Sacred Monk once more and bows, holding up the censer with both hands. At this time the guest-supervisor is just inside the entrance to the Cloud Hall, standing with hands folded to the south of the prostration mat, and facing north.[67] After saluting the Sacred Monk, the donor, following the guest-supervisor, goes out to the front of the Cloud Hall, does one circuit of the front hall,[68] goes back inside the Cloud Hall proper, and performs three prostrations to the Sacred Monk. After the prostrations, [the donor] sits on a folding chair to witness the sutra-reading. The folding chair is set, facing south, near the pillar to the Sacred Monk's left. Or it may be set facing north near the southern pillar. When the donor is seated, the guest-supervisor should turn to salute

61. 知客 (SHIKA), or "guest prefect," is the assistant officer in charge of supervising guests.

62. 院門 (INMON). In general 院 (IN) represents the Sanskrit *saṃghārāma* or temple. In this case, however, it suggests 庫院 (KU-IN), the Kitchen Hall.

63. 行者 (ANJA) or temple servants, worked as helpers in the temple, not necessarily intending to become monks.

64. 叉手 (SHASHU), hands held horizontally across the chest, with left hand in a fist, thumb inside, and right hand cupped over the left.

65. If you imagine the scene from the front entrance, the prostration mat is directly in front of you, and the donor is facing the mat, his back towards you. The guest-supervisor is to the right of the mat, facing the mat but turned slightly towards the donor and you.

66. 合掌 (GASSHO), palms together, fingertips at the level of the nostrils.

67. Again imagining the scene from the front entrance, the donor is standing between the prostration mat and the sacred image, his back towards you. The guest supervisor is now just in front of you, to the left of the mat and facing right in order to watch the donor.

68. 堂前 (DOZEN) lit. "Hall-front," probably means the *zentan*, the smaller hall which accommodates the temple officers and others who can come and go there without disturbing the main body of monks in the Zazen Hall proper. Or it could indicate the area outside of the Zazen Hall.

the donor, and then go to his or her own place. Sometimes we have a Sanskrit chorus while the donor is walking round the Hall. The place for the Sanskrit chorus is either on the Sacred Monk's right or on the Sacred Monk's left, according to convenience. In the hand-held censer, we insert and burn valuable incense like *jinko* or *sanko*.[69] This incense is supplied by the donor. While the donor is walking around the Hall, the monks join palms. Next is the distribution of donations for the sutra-reading. The size of the donation is at the discretion of the donor. Sometimes things such as cotton cloth or fans are distributed. The donor personally may give them out, or the main officers may give them out, or helpers may give them out. The method of distribution is as follows: [The donation] is placed in front of [each] monk, not put into the monk's hands. The monks each join hands to receive the donation as it is given out in front of them. Donations are sometimes distributed at the midday meal on the day [of the sutra-reading]. If [donations] are to be distributed at lunch time, the head monk, after offering the meal,[70] strikes down the clapper[71] once again, and then the head monk gives out the donations. The donor will have written on a sheet of paper the aim to which [the sutra-reading] is to be directed, and [this paper] is pasted to the pillar on the Sacred Monk's right. When reading sutras in the Cloud Hall, we do not read them out in a loud voice; we read them in a low voice. Or sometimes we open a sutra and only look at the characters, not reading them out in phrases but just reading the sutra [silently]. There are hundreds or thousands of scrolls provided in the common store[72] for this kind of sutra-reading—mostly of the Diamond Prajñā Sutra; the Universal Gate Chapter and the Peaceful and Joyful Practice Chapter of the Lotus Sutra; the Golden Light Sutra,[73] and so on. Each monk goes through one scroll. When the sutra-reading is finished, [the child-helpers] pass in front of the [monks'] seats, carrying the original tray or box, and the monks each deposit a sutra. Both when taking [the sutra] and when replacing it, we join hands. When taking, first we join hands and then we take. When replacing, first we deposit the sutra, then we join hands. After that, each person, palms together, makes the dedication in a low voice. For sutra-readings in the common area,[74] the chief officer or the prior burns incense, does prostrations, goes around the hall, and gives out the donations, all in the same way as a donor, and holds up the censer also in the same way as a donor. If one of the monks becomes a donor and requests a sutra-reading by the whole of the Saṃgha, it is the same as for a lay donor.[75] There is burning of incense, prostrations, going around the Hall, distribution of donations, and so on. The guest-supervisor leads, as in the case of a lay donor.

---

69. *Jinko* means aloes. *Sanko* was a type of incense obtained from the area of Southwest China which is now Cambodia and Vietnam.

70. 施食 (SEJIKI). The method is explained in detail in Master Dogen's *Fu-shukuhan-ho (The Method of Taking Meals).*

71. 椎 (TSUI), a small wooden block used to beat an octagonal wooden pillar.

72. 常住 (JOJU), short for 常住物 (JOJU-MOTSU), tools et cetera available for the monks of a temple to use at any time.

73. 金光明経 (KON-KOMYO-KYO). In Sanskrit, *Suvarṇaprabhāsa-sūtra.*

74. 常住公界 (JOJU-KUGAI). Big temples had a communal hall for reciting sutras.

75. In Master Dogen's time there were monks who came from rich families and who retained their private wealth.

[216] There is a custom of reading sutras for the emperor's birthday. So if the celebration of the birthday of the reigning emperor is on the 15th day of the 1st lunar month, the sutra-readings for the emperor's birthday begin on the 15th day of the 12th lunar month. On this day there is no formal preaching in the Dharma Hall. Two rows of platforms are laid out in front of [the image of] Śākyamuni Buddha in the Buddha Hall. That is to say, [the rows] are laid out facing each other east and west, each running from south to north. Desks are stood in front of the east row and the west row, and on them are placed the sutras: the Diamond Prajñā Sutra, the Benevolent King Sutra, the Lotus Sutra, the Supreme King Sutra,[76] the Golden Light Sutra, and so on. Several monks each day are invited from among the monks in the [Zazen] Hall to partake in refreshments before the midday meal. Sometimes a bowl of noodles and a cup of soup are served to each monk, or sometimes six or seven dumplings with a portion of soup are served to each monk. The dumplings also are served in a bowl, [but in this case] chopsticks are provided; spoons are not provided. We do not change seats to eat, but remain at our seat for the sutra-reading. The refreshments are placed on the desk that the sutras are placed on; there is no need to bring another table. While refreshments are being eaten, the sutras are left on the desk. After finishing the refreshments, each monk rises from his or her seat to [go and] rinse the mouth, then returns to the seat and resumes sutra-reading immediately. Sutra-reading continues from after breakfast until the time of the midday meal. When the lunch time drum sounds three times, we rise from our seats: the day's sutra-reading is limited to before the midday meal. From the first day a board saying *Established as a Practice Place for Celebration of the Emperor's Birthday* is hung in front of the Buddha Hall, under the eastern eaves. The board is yellow. In addition, notice of celebration of the emperor's birthday is written on a *shoji* placard,[77] which is then hung on the eastern front pillar inside the Buddha Hall. This placard [also] is yellow. The name[78] of the abbot is written on red paper or white paper; the two characters [of the name] are written on a small sheet of paper, which is pasted onto the front of the placard, beneath the date. The sutra-reading continues as outlined above until the day of the imperial descent and birth, when the abbot gives formal preaching in the Dharma Hall and congratulates the emperor. This is an old convention which is not obsolete even today. There is another case in which monks decide of their own accord to read sutras. Temples traditionally have a common Sutra Reading Hall. [Monks] go to this hall to read sutras. The rules for its use are as in our present Pure Criteria.[79]

[219] The founding Patriarch, Great Master Kodo[80] of Yakusan mountain, asks Śramaṇera Ko,[81] *"Did you get it by reading sutras, or did you get it by requesting the benefit [of the teaching]?"*[82]

---

76. 最勝王経 (SAISHO-O-KYO). The full name of the Golden Light Sutra is 金光明最勝王経 (KONKOMYO-SAISHO-O-KYO), "Golden Light Supreme King Sutra," from the Sanskrit *Suvarṇaprabhāsottama-rāja-sūtra*, so the Supreme King Sutra and the Golden Light Sutra appear to be one and the same.

77. A placard made of paper stuck to a wooden frame—constructed like the *shoji*, or paper sliding doors, seen in Japanese houses.

78. 名字 (MYOJI) usually means surname, but in this case it means a monk's usual name. In the case of Master Dogen, for example, it would be Dogen.

79. 清規 (SHINGI), "pure criteria," mean a temple's rules and regulations.

80. Master Yakusan Igen. See note 8.

Śramaṇera Ko says, *"I did not get it by reading sutras, and I did not get it by requesting benefit."*

The Master says, *"There are a lot of people who do not read sutras and who do not request benefit. Why do they not get it?"*

Śramaṇera Ko says, *"I do not say that they are without it. It is just that they do not dare to experience it directly."*[83]

[220] In the house of the Buddhist patriarchs, some experience it directly and some do not experience it directly, but reading sutras and requesting the benefit [of the teaching] are the common tools of everyday life.

Shobogenzo Kankin

Preached to the assembly at Kosho-horin-ji temple in the Uji district of Yoshu,[84] on the 15th day of the 9th lunar month in the autumn of the 2nd year of Ninji.[85]

---

81. 高沙弥 (KO-SHAMI). After succeeding Master Yakusan, he built a thatched hut by the roadside and taught Buddhism to passing travelers. 沙弥 (SHAMI) represents the Sanskrit word *śramaṇera* which means novice.

82. 請益 (SHIN-EKI), means listening to the preaching of Dharma and requesting a teacher's personal instruction.

83. *Keitoku-dento-roku*, chap. 14.

84. Corresponds to present-day Kyoto prefecture.

85. 1241.

Appendices

Chinese Masters

Japanese	Pinyin
Baso Do-itsu	Mazu Daoyi
Bukko Nyoman	Foguang Ruman
Bussho Tokko	Fozhao Deguang
Butsu-in Ryogen	Foyin Liaoyuan
Choka Dorin	Niaowo Daolin
Chosa Keishin	Changsha Jingcen
Chorei (Fukushu) Shutaku	Changqing Daan
Dai-e Soko	Dahui Zonggao
Dai-i Doshin	Dayi Daoxin
Daibai Hojo	Damei Fachang
Daikan Eno	Dajian Huineng
Daiman Konin	Daman Hongren
Daizui Hoshin	Taisui Fazhen
Do-an Dofu	Tongan Daopi
Do-an Kanshi	Tongan Guanzhi
Engo Kokugon	Yuanwu Keqin
Fuketsu Ensho	Fengxue Yanzhao
Fukushu (Chokei) Dai-an	Chanqing Daan
Fun-yo Zensho	Fenyang Shanzhao
Fuyo Dokai	Furong Daokai
Gensa Shibi	Xuansha Shibei
Genshi	Yuancai
Goso Ho-en	Wuzu Fayan
Gozu Hoyu	Niutou Fayong
Hogen Bun-eki	Fayan Wenyi
Hotatsu	Foda
I-ichi	Weiyi
Isan Reiyu	Guishan Lingyou
Jimyo (Sekiso) So-en	Shishuang Chuyuan
Joshu Jushin	Zhaozhou Congshen
Kai-e (Haku-un) Shutan	Haihui Shoudan
Kanchi Sosan	Jianzhi Sengcan
Kankei Shikan	Guanxi Zhixian
Koan Daigu	Gaoan Daiyu
Koke Sonsho	Xinghua Congjiang
Kokutai Koto	Guotai Hongdao
Kyogen Chikan	Xiangyan Zhixian
Kyozan Ejaku	Yangshan Huiji
Matsuzan Ryonen	Moshan Liaoran
Mayoku Hotetsu	Magu Baoche

Japanese	Pinyin
Musai Ryoha	Wuji Liaopai
Myoshin	Miaoxin
Nan-in Egyo	Nanyuan Huiyong
Nan-yo Echu	Nanyang Huizhong
Nangaku Ejo	Nanyue Huairang
Nansen Fugan	Nanquan Puyuan
Obaku Ki-un	Huangbo Xiyun
Oryu Enan	Huanglong Huinan
Reiun Shigon	Lingyun Zhiqin
Rinzai Gigen	Linji Yixuan
Roya Ekaku	Langye Huijiao
Ryozan Enkan	Liangshan Yuanguan
Ryuge Koton	Longya Judun
Ryumon Butsugen	Longmen Foyan
Ryutan Soshin	Longtan Chongxin
Sansho Enen	Sansheng Huiran
Seccho Chikan	Xuedou Zhijian
Seccho Juken	Xuedou Chongxian
Seigen Gyoshi	Qingyuan Xingsi
Sekito Kisen	Shitou Xiqian
Sensu Tokujo	Chuanzi Decheng
Seppo Gison	Xuefeng Yicun
Shinketsu Seiryo	Zhenxie Qingliao
Shokaku (Torin) Joso	Donglin Changzong
Shoken Kisho	Yexian Guisheng
Shuzan Shonen	Shoushan Shengnian
Taiso Eka	Dazu Huike
Taiyo Kyogen	Dayang Jingxuan
Tanka Shijun	Danxia Zichun
Tendo Nyojo	Tiantong Rujing
Tendo Sogyoku	Tiantong Zhongjue
Tokuzan Senkan	Deshan Xuanjian
Tosu Gisei	Touzi Yiqing
Tozan Ryokai	Dongshan Liangjie
Ungan Donjo	Yunyan Tansheng
Ungo Doyo	Yunju Daoying
Unmon Bun-en	Yunmen Wenyan
Yafu Dosen	Yefu Daochuan
Yakusan Igen	Yueshan Weiyan
Yogi Ho-e	Yangqi Fanghui

[APPENDIX]

普勧坐禅儀

FUKAN-ZAZENGI

Universal Guide to the Standard Method of Zazen

[Rufu-bon—The Popular Edition[1]]

Now, when we research it, the truth originally is all around: why should we rely upon practice and experience? The real vehicle exists naturally: why should we put forth great effort? Furthermore, the whole body far transcends dust and dirt: who could believe in the means of sweeping and polishing?[2] In general, we do not stray from the right state: of what use, then, are the tip-toes of training?

However, if there is a thousandth or a hundredth of a gap, the separation is as great as that between heaven and earth;[3] and if a trace of disagreement arises, we lose the mind in confusion. Proud of our understanding and richly endowed with realization, we obtain special states of insight; we attain the truth; we clarify the mind; we acquire the zeal that pierces the sky; we ramble through remote intellectual spheres, going in with the head: and yet, we have almost completely lost the vigorous road of getting the body out.

Moreover, we can [still] see the traces of the six years spent sitting up straight by the natural sage of Jetavana park.[4] We can still hear rumors of the nine years spent facing

---

1. There are two main versions of *Fukan-zazengi;* namely, 真筆本 (SHINPITSU-BON), the Original Edition (lit. the edition written in the author's own hand), and 流布本 (RUFU-BON), the Popular Edition. Master Dogen wrote the *Shinpitsu-bon* shortly after returning from China to Japan in 1227. He later revised this edition before settling upon the *Rufu-bon*. Whereas Master Dogen wrote Shobogenzo itself in Japanese, he wrote *Fukan-zazengi* in Chinese characters only. It is originally one long passage; here it has been divided into paragraphs for ease of reading.

2. The words "dust and dirt" (塵埃, JINNAI) and "sweeping and polishing" (払拭, HOSSHIKI) allude to a story about Master Daikan Eno and a monk called Jinshu. Jinshu compared Buddhist practice to making a mirror clean. Master Daikan Eno suggested that there is originally no impurity in the first place. (See chap. 22, *Kokyo*.) Master Dogen picked up the words of the story in these opening lines in which he expresses the fundamentally optimistic idea of Buddhist philosophy.

3. Master Dogen picked up these words from Master Kanchi Sosan's poem *Shinjinmei*. In this part Master Dogen cautions us against falling into the state in which we think too much.

4. Jetavana lit. means "Prince Jeta's Park." This was a park purchased from Prince Jeta, a son of King Prasenajit of Kośala, by a lay disciple of the Buddha called Sudatta or Anāthapiṇḍada, and donated to the Buddha as a place for the rains retreat in Śrāvastī (110km north-east of present-day Lucknow).

the wall by the transmitter of the mind-seal of Shaolin [temple].[5] The ancient saints were like that already: how could people today fail to make effort?

Therefore we should cease the intellectual work of studying sayings and chasing words. We should learn the backward step of turning light and reflecting. Body and mind will naturally fall away, and the original features will manifest themselves before us. If we want to attain the matter of the ineffable, we should practice the matter of the ineffable at once.[6]

In general, a quiet room is good for practicing [Za]zen, and food and drink are taken in moderation. Cast aside all involvements. Give the myriad things a rest. Do not think of good and bad. Do not consider right and wrong. Stop the driving movement of mind, will, consciousness. Cease intellectual consideration through images, thoughts, and reflections. Do not aim to become a buddha. How could [this] be connected with sitting or lying down?[7]

We usually spread a thick mat on the place where we sit, and use a round cushion on top of that. Either sit in the full lotus posture or sit in the half lotus posture. To sit in the full lotus posture, first put the right foot on the left thigh, then put the left foot on the right thigh. To sit in the half lotus posture, just press the left foot onto the right thigh.[8]

Spread the clothing loosely and make it neat.[9] Then put the right hand above the left foot, and place the left hand on the right palm. The thumbs meet and support each other. Just make the body right and sit up straight. Do not lean to the left, incline to the right, slouch forward, or lean backward. The ears must be aligned with the shoulders, and the nose aligned with the navel. Hold the tongue against the palate, keep the lips and teeth closed, and keep the eyes open. Breathe softly through the nose.

When the physical posture is already settled, make one complete exhalation and sway left and right. Sitting immovably in the mountain-still state, *"Think about this concrete state beyond thinking." "How can the state beyond thinking be thought about?" "It is different from thinking."*[10] This is just the pivot of Zazen.

This sitting in Zazen is not learning Zen concentration.[11] It is simply the peaceful and joyful gate of Dharma. It is the practice-and-experience which perfectly realizes the

---

5. 心印 (SHIN-IN), "mind-seal," is an abbreviation of 仏心印 (BUTSU-SHIN-IN) "Buddha-mind-seal." 印 (IN) comes from the Sanskrit word *mudrā* which means "seal." In Shobogenzo Master Dogen identifies 仏心印 (BUTSU-SHIN-IN) with the full lotus posture. Shaolin is the name of the temple where Master Bodhidharma introduced Zazen into China.

6. "Matter of the ineffable" is 恁麼事 (INMO *[no]* JI). Master Tozan preached to the assembly, *"If you want to attain the matter of the ineffable, you must have become someone ineffable. Now that you are already someone ineffable, why worry about attaining the matter of the ineffable?"* See chap. 29, *Inmo*.

7. Sitting and lying down represent the four kinds of behavior: sitting, standing, walking, and lying down. Master Dogen suggested that Zazen is transcendent over the ordinary actions of daily life.

8. Master Dogen gives the left foot on the right thigh as an example. The right foot placed on the left thigh is also the correct lotus posture.

9. Specifically this refers to the custom of not stretching the kaṣāya tightly across the knees.

10. These lines come from a conversation between Master Yakusan Igen and a monk. They are discussed at length in chap. 27, *Zazenshin*.

11. *Sekimon-rinkanroku* relates how historians listed Master Bodhidharma alongside people who were learning Zen concentration (習禅 SHUZEN). See chap. 30, *Gyoji*, para. [193]. In his commentary, Master Dogen says, *"[Master Bodhidharma] sat in stillness facing the wall, but he was not learning Zen concentration."*

state of bodhi. The Universe is conspicuously realized, and restrictions and hindrances[12] never reach it. To grasp this meaning is to be like a dragon that has found water, or like a tiger in its mountain stronghold. Remember, the right Dharma is naturally manifesting itself before us, and darkness and distraction[13] have dropped away already.

If we rise from sitting, we should move the body slowly, and stand up calmly. We should not be hurried or violent. We see in the past that those who transcended the common and transcended the sacred, and those who died while sitting or died while standing,[14] relied totally on this power. Moreover, the changing of the moment, through the means of a finger,[15] a pole,[16] a needle, or a wooden clapper;[17] and the experience of the state,[18] through the manifestation of a whisk,[19] a fist, a staff, or a shout,[20] can never be understood by thinking and discrimination.[21] How could they be known through mystical powers or practice and experience? They may be dignified behavior beyond sound and form.[22] How could they be anything other than criteria that precede knowing and seeing?

Therefore, we do not discuss intelligence as superior and stupidity as inferior. Do not choose between clever people and dull ones. If we single-mindedly make effort [in Zazen] that truly is pursuit of the truth. Practice-and-experience is naturally untainted.[23] Actions are more balanced and constant.[24]

In general, [the patriarchs] of this world and of other directions, of the Western Heavens and of the Eastern Lands, all similarly maintain the Buddha's posture, and solely indulge in the custom of our religion. They simply devote themselves to sitting, and are caught by the still state.

---

12. "Restrictions and hindrances" is 羅籠 (RARO), silk nets and bamboo cages used in China to catch birds and fish.

13. 昏散 (KONSAN), "darkness and distraction," are representative examples of unnatural or imbalanced conditions of body and mind. 昏 (KON) represents the Sanskrit *styāna* and 散 (SAN) represents *vikṣepa*, two of the many defilements listed in Sanskrit commentaries.

14. Master Mahākāśyapa, for example, is said to have died while sitting on Kukkuṭapāda mountain, and Master Kankei Shikan (see chap. 8, *Raihai-tokuzui*), is said to have died while standing up.

15. Master Gutei used to raise one finger to answer a question that could not be answered with words.

16. Master Ānanda realized the truth when a temple flagpole fell to the ground.

17. 鎚 (TSUI), sometimes written 椎 (TSUI). This is a small wooden block used to beat an octagonal wooden pillar. Bodhisattva Mañjuśrī, for example, is said to have preached the truth by using the *tsui*.

18. 証契 (SHOKAI) Lit. "experience-accord," means to experience the same state as Gautama Buddha. See notes on chap. 16, *Shisho*.

19. 払子 (HOSSU), a ceremonial whisk with a wooden handle and a plume of animal hair or other material.

20. Master Baso Do-itsu, for example, was famous for having a very loud yell.

21. Alludes to Lotus Sutra *Hoben-bon (Expedient Means)*. See LS 1.88-90.

22. 声色之外威儀 (SHOSHIKI *no hoka no* IIGI). The same characters appear in a poem by Master Kyogen Chikan, quoted in *chap. 9, Keisei-sanshiki.*

23. Alludes to a conversation between Master Daikan Eno and Master Nangaku Ejo about the oneness of practice and experience. See chap. 7, *Senjo.*

24. 平常 (BYOJO). 平 (BYO, HEI) means level or peaceful. 常 (JO) means constant. As a compound 平常 (BYOJO, HEIJO) means normal. It appears in the phrase 平常心 (BYOJOSHIN, HEIJOSHIN), "balanced and constant mind" or "normal mind." See *Butsu-kojo-no-ji* (28-chapter edition).

Although there are myriad distinctions and thousands of differences, we should just practice [Za]zen and pursue the truth. Why should we abandon our own seat on the floor, to come and go without purpose through the dusty borders of foreign lands?[25] If we misplace one step we pass over the moment of the present. We have already received the essential pivot[26] which is the human body: we must never pass time in vain.[27] We are maintaining and relying upon the pivotal essence[28] which is the Buddha's truth: who could wish idly to enjoy sparks [that fly] from flint? What is more, the body is like a dew-drop on a blade of grass. Life passes like a flash of lightning. Suddenly it is gone. In an instant it is lost.

I beseech you, noble friends in learning through experience, do not become so accustomed to images that you are dismayed by the real dragon.[29] Devote effort to the truth which is directly accessible and straightforward. Revere people who are beyond study and without intention.[30] Accord with the bodhi of the buddhas. Become a rightful successor to the samādhi of the patriarchs. If you practice the state like this for a long time, you will surely become the state like this itself. The treasure-house will open naturally, and you will be free to receive and to use [its contents] as you like.

Fukan-zazengi ends

---

25. Alludes to a parable in the *Shinge (Belief and Understanding)* chapter of the Lotus Sutra about a son who wanders in poverty through foreign lands, unaware that he is the heir to his father's fortune. See LS 1.236.

26. 機要 (KIYO).

27. 莫虚度光陰 (KOIN *munashiku wataru koto nakare).* The same characters appear at the end of the verse *Sandokai* by Master Sekito Kisen.

28. 要機 (YOKI). The words 機要 (KIYO) and 要機 (YOKI) feature prominently in chap. 27, *Zazenshin.* 機 (KI) means mechanism or, sometimes, the state at the moment of the present. 要 (YO) means the main point, important part, pivot.

29. Refers to the story of Shoko, who loved images of dragons but who was terrified to meet a real dragon. The real dragon means Zazen.

30. 絶学無為人 (ZETSU-GAKU-MU-I *[no]* HITO). Master Yoka Genkaku's poem *Shodoka* begins with the words, "Gentlemen, do you not see? A person beyond study and without intention, who is at ease in the truth, does not try to get rid of delusion and does not want to get reality."

[APPENDIX]

仏祖

Busso

The Buddhist Patriarchs

The recitation in Japanese of the names of the Buddhist patriarchs, from the seven ancient buddhas to Master Dogen, is as follows:

(1) Bibashibutsu Dai-osho

(2) Shikibutsu Dai-osho

(3) Bishafubutsu Dai-osho

(4) Kurusonbutsu Dai-osho

(5) Kunagonmunibutsu Dai-osho

(6) Kashobutsu Dai-osho

(7) Shakamunibutsu Dai-osho

[1] Makakasho Dai-osho

[2] Ananda Dai-osho

[3] Shonawasu Dai-osho

[4] Ubakikuta Dai-osho

[5] Daitaka Dai-osho

[6] Mishaka Dai-osho

[7] Basumitta Dai-osho

[8] Buddanandai Dai-osho

[9] Fudamitta Dai-osho

[10] Barishiba Dai-osho

[11] Funayasha Dai-osho

[12] Memyo Dai-osho

[13] Kapimara Dai-osho

[14] Naga-arajuna Dai-osho

[15] Kanadaiba Dai-osho

[16] Ragorata Dai-osho

[17] Sogyanandai Dai-osho

[18] Gayashata Dai-osho

[19] Kumorata Dai-osho

[20] Shayata Dai-osho

[21] Bashubanzu Dai-osho

[22] Manura Dai-osho

[23] Kakurokuna Dai-osho

[24] Shishibodai Dai-osho

[25] Bashashita Dai-osho

[26] Funyomitta Dai-osho

[27] Hannyatara Dai-osho

[28] *[1]* Bodaidaruma Dai-osho

[29] *[2]* Taiso Eka Dai-osho

[30] *[3]* Kanchi Sosan Dai-osho

[31] *[4]* Dai-i Doshin Dai-osho

[32] *[5]* Daiman Konin Dai-osho

[33] *[6]* Daikan Eno Dai-osho

[34] *[7]* Seigen Gyoshi Dai-osho

[35] *[8]* Sekito Kisen Dai-osho

[36] *[9]* Yakusan Igen Dai-osho

[37] *[10]* Ungan Donjo Dai-osho

[38] *[11]* Tozan Ryokai Dai-osho

[39] *[12]* Ungo Doyo Dai-osho

[40] *[13]* Do-an Dofu Dai-osho

[41] *[14]* Do-an Kanshi Dai-osho

[42] *[15]* Ryozan Enkan Dai-osho

[43] *[16]* Taiyo Kyogen Dai-osho

[44] *[17]* Tosu Gisei Dai-osho

[45] *[18]* Fuyo Dokai Dai-osho

[46] *[19]* Tanka Shijun Dai-osho

[47] *[20]* Shinketsu Seiryo Dai-osho

[48] *[21]* Tendo Sogyoku Dai-osho

[49] *[22]* Seccho Chikan Dai-osho

[50] *[23]* Tendo Nyojo Dai-osho

[51] *[24]* Eihei Dogen Dai-osho

The Kaṣāya

A large saṃghāṭī robe made of nine vertical stripes of cloth, with two long segments and one short segment in each stripe. This style of robe is known in Japanese as the *Kassetsu-e.*

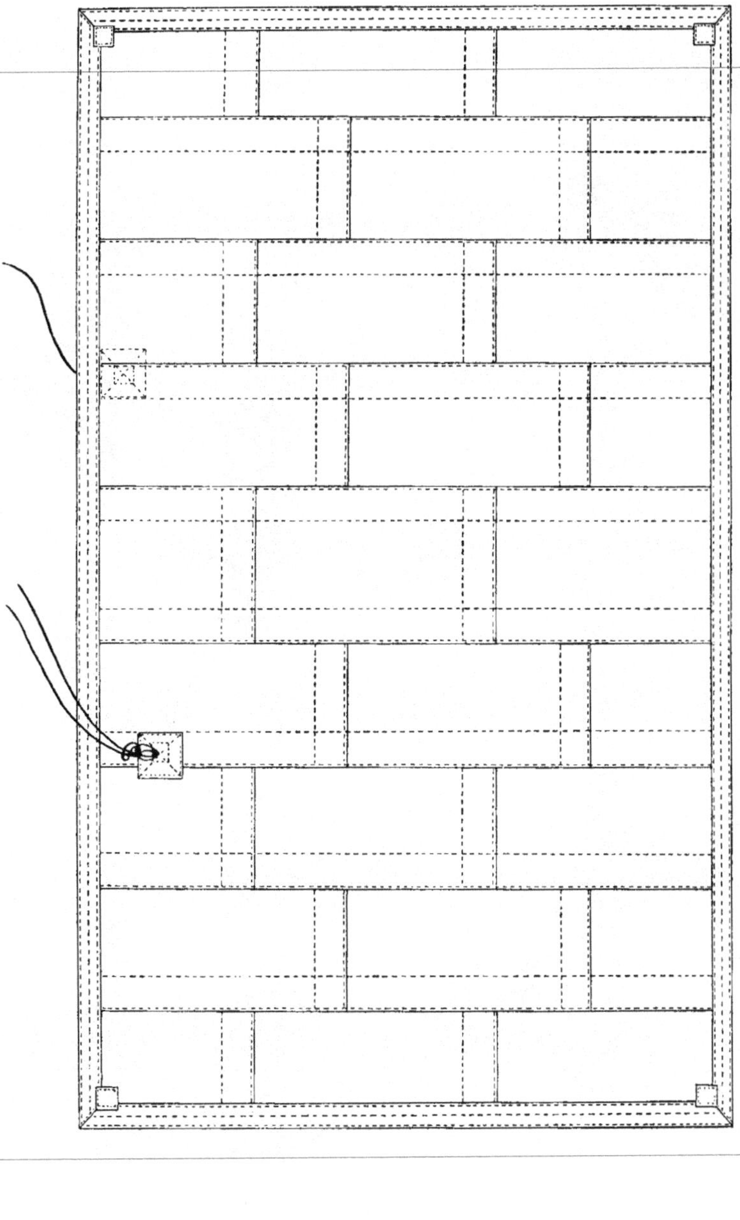

Traditional Temple Layout

The ground plan of 北山景徳霊隠寺 (HOKUZAN-KEITOKU-RYO-ON-JI) in modern-day Hangzhou province, together with a list of *Facilities at Major Buddhist Monasteries in the Southern Sung,* upon which this appendix is based, was obtained by Nishijima Roshi several years ago at a conference of the American Academy of Religions. Unfortunately, the name of the original compiler, to whom acknowledgment is due, is not known.

THE SEVEN MAIN TEMPLE BUILDINGS:

The seven main temple buildings are the Buddha Hall, the Dharma Hall, the Zazen Hall, the Kitchen Hall, the Gate, the Bathhouse, and the Toilet.

In former ages, the Toilet was located to the west and was called 西浄 (SAICHIN), 'West Lavatory,' but later the Toilet was located to the east and Called 東司 (TOSU) 'East Office.' In the original ground plan of 北山景徳霊隠寺 both toilets, east and west, are marked as 東司 (TOSU).

The essential temple layout can be represented in brief as follows:

		(North)		
		Dharma Hall		
(West)	Zazen Hall	Buddha Hall	Kitchen Hall	(East)
	Toilet	Gate	Bathhouse	

FACILITIES AT MAJOR BUDDHIST MONASTERIES IN THE SOUTHERN SUNG:

1.	仏殿 (butsuden)	Buddha Hall
2.	土地堂 (TOCHIDO)	'Lands Hall'; Local Deities Hall
3.	真堂 (SHINDO)	'Trueness Hall;' Hall for Patriarchs' Images
	祖堂 (SODO)	Patriarchs' Hall
4.	羅漢堂 (RAKANDO)	Arhats Hall
5.	正門 (SHOMON)	Main Gate;
6.	水陸堂 (SUIRIKIDO)	All Beings Hall
7.	観音堂 (KANNON-KAKU)	Pavilion of Regarder of the Sounds; Pavilion of Bodhisattva Avalokiteśvara
8.	盧舎那殿 (RUSHANADEN)	Vairocana's Hall
9.	檀那 (DANNA)	Donors' [Hall]
10.	法堂 (HATTO)	Dharma Hall; Lecture Hall
11.	蔵殿 (ZODEN)	'Storage Hall'; Sutra Library
	輪蔵 (RINZO)	'Circle Library'—alludes to a big circular table provided in the library.
12.	看経堂 (KANKINDO)	Sutra Reading Hall;
	経堂 (KYODO)	Sutra Hall
13.	寝堂 (SHINDO)	Abbot's Reception Hall;
	前方丈 (ZEN-HOJO)	'Front of Abbot's Quarters';
	大光明蔵 (DAI-KOMYO-ZO)	'Treasury of Great Brightness'
14.	衆寮 (SHURYO)	Common Quarters; Monks' Dormitories

15.	僧堂 (SODO)	Monks' Hall; Saṃgha Hall
	雲堂 (UNDO)	Cloud Hall;
	坐禅堂 (ZAZENDO)	Zazen Hall
16.	後僧堂 (GOSODO)	Rear Monks' Hall
17.	尼寮 (NIRYO)	Nuns' Quarters
18.	方丈 (HOJO)	'The Square Ten Feet'; Abbot's Quarters
	堂頭 (DOCHO)	The Abbot
19.	侍者寮 (JISHARYO)	Attendant Monks' Quarters
20.	行者堂 (ANJADO)	Temple Servants' Hall
	選僧堂 (SENSODO)	Novice Monks' Hall
21.	庫下行者寮 (KUGE-ANJA-RYO)	Servants' Quarters in the Kitchen Hall
22.	旦過寮 (TANGARYO)	Overnight Lodgings;
	雲水堂 (UNSUIDO)	'Clouds and Water Hall'; Transient Monks' Quarters
23.	客位 (KAKU-I)	Guest Rooms
24.	監司 (KANSU)	'Office of the Prior;'†
25.	都寺 (TSUSU)	Chief Officer
26.	監寺 (KANSU)	Prior
27.	副司 (FUSU)	Assistant Prior
28.	諸頭首寮 (SHO-CHOSHU-RYO)	Assistant Officers' Quarters
29.	知客 (SHIKA)	Guest Supervisor
30.	浴主 (YOKUSU)	Bath Manager
31.	知殿 (CHIDEN)	Supervisor of the Buddha Hall
32.	直歳 (SHISSUI)	Labor Steward
33.	火頭寮 (KAJURYO)	Fire Chief's Quarters; Stove Chief's Quarters
34.	維那司 (INOSU)	Ino; Supervisor of Monks in the Zazen Hall;
	堂司 (DOSU)	Hall Chief
35.	首座 (SHUSO)	Head Monk
36.	蒙堂 (MODO)	'Twilight Hall'; Quarters of Retired Main Officers
37.	前資寮 (ZENSHIRYO)	Former Officers' Quarters; Retired Officers' Quarters
38.	尊長寮 (SONCHORYO)	Retired Abbot's Quarters
	老宿 (ROSHUKU)	'The Old Patriarch'
39.	人力 (NINRIKI)	Laborers
40.	三門 (SANMON)	'Three Gates'—refers to the main entrance and the side entrances on either side of the main entrance.
	山門 (SANMON)	'Mountain Gate'—poetically reproduces the pronunciation of 山門 (SANMON).
41.	外山門 (GAI-SANMON)	'Outer Mountain Gate'; Outer Gate

† In general, 監司 suggests the monk himself or herself, and it may therefore suggest his or her quarters. However, on the present ground plan, no. 24 may be assumed to be the Prior's Office and no. 26 the Prior's Quarters.)

42. 中門 (CHUMON)	Inner Gate
43. 庫堂 (KUDO)	'Pantry Hall'; Kitchen Hall; Administration Hall;
庫院 (KU-IN)	'Pantry Office'
44. 香積厨 (KOSHAKU-CHU)	'Fragrance-Accumulation's Office', Kitchen
45. 延寿堂 (ENJUDO)	'Prolongation of Life Hall'; Infirmary
涅槃堂 (NEHANDO)	Nirvana Hall
省行堂 (SHOGYODO)	'Hall of Reflection of Conduct'
46. 重病閣 (JUBYOKAKU)	Pavilion for the Seriously Ill
47. 浴室 (YOKUSHITSU)	Bathhouse
宣明 (SENMYO)	'Promulgation of Brightness'
48. 洗面処 (SENMENJO)	Washroom; Washstand
水廨 (SUIGE)	'Water Office'
後架 (KOKA)	Rear Stand
49. 東司 (TOSU)	'East Office'; Toilet
西浄 (SAICHIN)	'West Lavatory'; Toilet
50. 尿寮 (SHIRYO)	Urinal
小遣所 (SHOKENJO)	Urinal
51. 把針所 (HASHINJO)	Needlework Room; Sewing Room
52. 洗衣所 (SEN-E-JO)	Laundry
53. 大鍾 (DAISHO)	Big Bell
鐘楼 (SHORO)	Bell Tower
54. 塔 (TO)	Stūpas
55. 廊廡 (ROBU)	Corridors
56. 後槽 (KOSO)	Stable
57. 照堂 (SHODO)	Illuminated Hall
58. 池 (CHI)	Pond

Ground plan of 北山景徳霊隠寺 (HOKUZAN-KEITOKU-RYO-ON-JI) in modern-day Hangzhou province

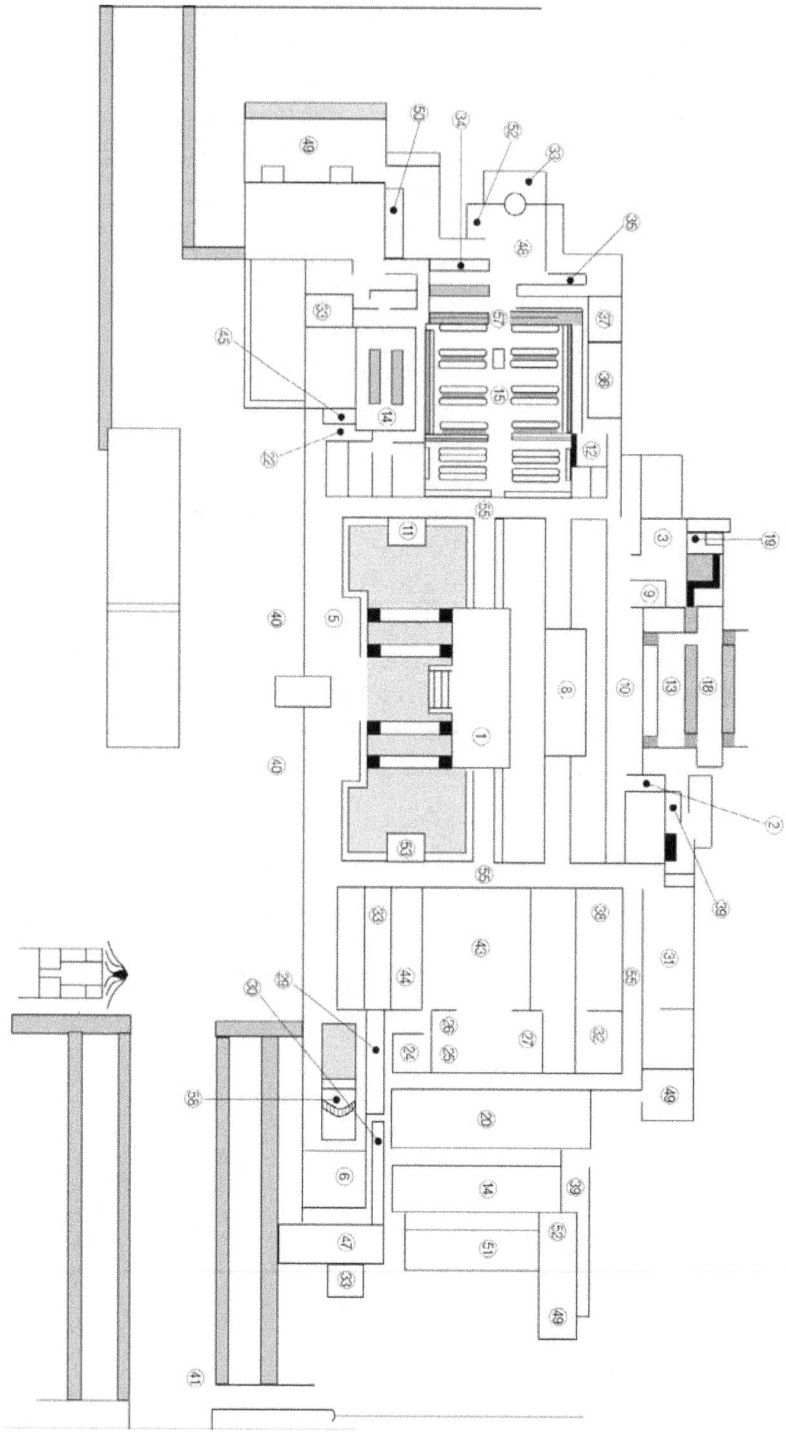

Lotus Sutra References

Saddharma-puṇḍarika-sūtra, The Sutra of the Lotus Flower of the Wonderful Dharma, was translated from Sanskrit into Chinese by Kumārajīva in 406 A.D.

Kumārajīva's translation, 妙法蓮華経 (MYOHO-RENGE-KYO), which Master Dogen quotes in Shobogenzo and which remains the most widely used in Japan, is reproduced in a Chinese/Japanese edition published in three parts by Iwanami Bunko. References below refer to this edition: LS 1.68 means part 1, page 68, of the Iwanami edition.

Kumārajīva's Chinese was rendered into English by Bunno Kato and William Soothill and published in 1930 as *The Sutra of the Lotus Flower of the Wonderful Law*. This *Sutra of the Lotus Flower of the Wonderful Law*, revised by Wilhelm Schiffer and Yoshiro Tamura, forms the core of *The Threefold Lotus Sutra* first published by Weatherhill/Kosei in 1975. The extracts which follow are basically revisions of the Weatherhill/Kosei version.

Chapter One:
Jo (Introductory)

LS 1.8 *SBGZ Ref: ch. 17; ch. 34 [83]*

如是我聞。一時佛住。王舍城。耆闍崛山中。與大比丘衆。万二千人倶。
皆是阿羅漢。諸漏已盡。無復煩悩。逮得己利。盡諸有結。心得自在。

Thus have I heard. At one time the Buddha was living at Rājagṛha. On Mount Gṛdhrakūṭa, he was with twelve thousand great bhikṣus. They were all arhats, having ended all excesses, being without troubles, self-possessed, realizing all bonds of existence, and liberated in mind.

LS 1.14 *SBGZ Ref: ch. 72 [237]*

爾時釋提桓因。與其眷屬。二万天子倶。。。有八龍王。。。各與若干。
百千眷屬倶。

At that time [there was] Śakra-devānām-indra with his following of twenty thousand heavenly sons...There were the eight dragon kings...each with some hundreds or thousands of followers.

LS 1.18 *SBGZ Ref: ch. 17*

爾時佛。放眉間白毫相光。照東方。

At that time the Buddha radiated light from the circle of white hair between his eyebrows, illuminating the eastern quarter.

LS 1.26-28 *SBGZ Ref: ch. 40 [216]*

或有行施　金銀珊瑚 真珠摩尼　硨 磲瑪瑙	There are some who give alms Of gold, silver, and coral, Pearls and jewels, Moonstones and agates.

LS 1.38 *SBGZ Ref: ch. 17*

爾時文殊師利。語彌勒菩薩摩訶薩。及諸大士。如我惟忖。
今佛世尊。欲説大法。

At that time Mañjuśrī spoke to the Bodhisattva-Mahāsattva Maitreya and all the other great beings: *"Good sons! According to my consideration, now the Buddha, the World-honored One, is going to preach the great Dharma."*

LS 1.40 *SBGZ Ref: ch. 11 [21]; ch. 17; ch. 50 [203]*

演説正法。初善。中善。後善。

He proclaimed the right Dharma, which is good in the beginning, good in the middle, and good in the end.

LS 1.42 *SBGZ Ref: ch. 17*

所可説法。初中後善。

The Dharma which they should preach is good in the beginning, middle, and end.

LS 1.42, LS 1.44 *SBGZ Ref: ch. 86 [83]*

其最後佛。未出家時。有八王子。。。是八王子。威徳自在。各領四天下。
是諸王子。聞父出家。得阿耨多羅三藐三菩提。悉捨王位。亦随出家。
発大乗意。常修梵行。皆為法師。已於千万佛所。殖諸善本。

Before the last of those [Sun Moon Light] buddhas left home, he had eight royal sons...These eight princes, unrestricted in their majesty, each ruled four continents. These princes, hearing that their father had left home and attained [the truth of] anuttara-samyak-saṃbodhi, all renounced the throne and, following him, also left home and established the mind of the Great Vehicle. They constantly practiced pure conduct, and all became teachers of Dharma. Under thousands of myriads of buddhas, they had planted many roots of goodness.

LS 1.46 *SBGZ Ref: ch. 17*

時會聴者。亦坐一処。六十小劫。身心不動。

The listeners in that order also remained seated in one place, for sixty minor kalpas, unmoving in body and mind.

LS 1.52 *SBGZ Ref: ch. 17; ch. 52 [21]*

是故惟忖。今日如来。當説大乗経。名妙法蓮華。教菩薩法。佛所護念。

Therefore I consider that the Tathāgata today will preach the sutra of the Great Vehicle, which is called the Lotus Flower of the Wonderful Dharma, the method of teaching bodhisattvas, that which buddhas guard and remember.

LS 1.54 *SBGZ Ref: ch. 36 [126]*

此光照東方　万八千佛土	This light illuminated the eastern quarter Of eighteen thousand Buddha-lands.

LS 1.58 *SBGZ Ref: ch. 50 [214]*

佛説此法華　令衆歓喜已 尋即於是日　告於天人衆 諸法実相義　已為汝等説	When the Buddha [Sun Moon Light] had preached this Flower of Dharma And caused the assembly to rejoice,

Then he, on that very day,
Proclaimed to the assembly of gods and people:
"The truth that all dharmas are real form
Has been preached for you all..."

LS 1.62

SBGZ Ref: ch. 17

是妙光法師　時有一弟子
心常懐懈怠　貧著於名利
求名利無厭　多遊族姓家
棄捨所習誦　廃忘不通利
以是因縁故　号之為求名
亦行衆善行　得見無数佛
供養於諸佛　随順行大道
具六波羅蜜　今見釋師子
其後當作佛　号名曰彌勒

This teacher of Dharma, Mystic Light,
At that time had a disciple
Whose mind was always lazy,
Who was greedily attached to fame and gain,
Who sought fame and gain tirelessly,
Who often found amusement in the
homes of aristocratic families,
Who abandoned what he had learned by heart,
Forgetting everything before he had
understood it clearly,
And who for these reasons
Was called Fame Seeker.
He also by practicing good works
Was able to meet countless buddhas,
To serve offerings to buddhas,
To follow them in practicing the great truth,
And to perfect the six paramitās.
Now he has seen Śākyamuni the lion.
Afterward he will become a buddha.
And will be named Maitreya.

LS1.64

今佛放光明　助発実相義
諸人今当知　合掌一心待

Now the Buddha radiates brightness
To help disclose the meaning of real form.
People, now you must be aware!
Hold palms together and wholeheartedly wait!

Chapter Two:
Hoben (Expedient Means)

LS 1.66

SBGZ Ref: ch. 17

爾時世尊。從三昧安詳而起。告舎利弗。諸佛智慧。甚深無量。其智慧門。難解難入。一切声聞。辟支佛。所不能知。所以者何。佛曾親近。百千万億。無数諸佛。盡行諸佛。無量道法。勇猛精進。名称普聞。成就甚深。未曾有法。随宜所説。意趣難解。

At that time the World-honored One rose calmly and clearly from samādhi and addressed Śāriputra: *"The wisdom of the buddhas is profound and unfathomable. Their lineage of wisdom is difficult to understand and difficult to enter. All śrāvakas and pratyekabuddhas cannot know it. Why? [Because] a buddha has experienced familiarity with countless hundred thousand myriad koṭis of buddhas, and has totally practiced the unfathomable truth and reality of the buddhas; bravely persevering; [letting the buddhas'] names be universally heard; accomplishing the profound unprecedented Dharma; and preaching, as convenience permits, the meaning which is difficult to understand."*

LS 1.68 *SBGZ Ref: ch. 17*

如来方便。知見波羅蜜。皆已具足。舎利弗。如来知見。廣大深遠。

The Tathāgata is perfectly equipped with expediency and the paramitā of wisdom. Śāriputra! The wisdom of the Tathāgata is wide, great, profound, and eternal.

LS 1.68 *SBGZ Ref: ch. 10 [21]; ch. 17; ch. 50 [203]; ch. 54 [98]; ch. 91 [71].*

唯佛與佛。乃能究盡。諸法実相。所謂諸法。如是法。如是性。如是體。
如是力。如是作。如是因。如是縁。如是果。如是報。如是本末究竟等。

Buddhas alone, together with buddhas, are directly able to perfectly realize that all dharmas are real form. What is called *"all dharmas"* is form as it is, the nature as it is, body as it is, energy as it is, action as it is, causes as they are, conditions as they are, effects as they are, results as they are, and the ultimate state of equality of substance and detail, as it is.

LS 1.70 *SBGZ Ref: ch. 17; ch. 50 [210]*

我及十方佛　乃能知是事

I, and buddhas in the ten directions,
Are directly able to know these things.

LS 1.72 *SBGZ Ref: ch. 17*

仮使滿世間　皆如舎利弗
盡思共度量　不能測佛智

Even if the world were full
Of beings like Śāriputra
Who together exhausted their intellects to gauge it,
They could not fathom the Buddha-wisdom.

LS 1.72 *SBGZ Ref: recurrent phrase*

如稲麻竹葦

As [abundant as] rice, hemp, bamboo, and reeds

LS 1.74 *SBGZ Ref: ch. 17; ch. 60 [7]*

唯我知是相　十方佛亦然

Only I know concrete form,
And the buddhas of the ten directions
are also like that.

LS 1.74 *SBGZ Ref: ch. 79 [169]*

爾時大衆中。有諸聲聞。漏盡阿羅漢。阿若 憍 陳如等。千二百人。

At that time in the great assembly, there were śrāvakas, the arhat who had ended excesses Ajñāta-Kauṇḍinya, and others, [altogether] twelve hundred people.

LS 1.80 *SBGZ Ref: ch. 17*

佛口所生子　合掌瞻仰待
願出微妙音　時為如実説

Children born of the Buddha's mouth,
Palms held together, looking up, we wait.
Please send forth the fine sound
And now preach for us [the truth] as it really is.

LS 1.82-84 *SBGZ Ref: ch. 17*

止止不須說　我法妙難思
諸増上慢者　聞必不敬信

Stop, stop, no need to explain.
My Dharma is too fine to think about.
Arrogant people,
If they hear, will surely not believe it with respect.

LS 1.86 *SBGZ Ref: ch. 1 [27]; ch. 17*

說此語時。會中有比丘。比丘尼。優婆塞。優婆夷。五千人等。即從座起。礼佛而退。

When he preached these words, some five thousand bhikṣus, bhikṣuṇīs, upāsakas, and upāsikās in the assembly rose at once from their seats, bowed to the Buddha, and retreated.

LS 1.86 *SBGZ Ref: ch. 23 [117]*

此輩罪根深重。

The roots of wrongdoing of these fellows were deep and heavy.

LS 1.86-88 *SBGZ Ref: ch. 1 [11]; ch. 68*

爾時佛。告舍利弗。我今此衆。無復枝葉。純有貞実。舍利弗。如是増上慢人。
退亦佳矣。汝今善聽。當為汝說。舍利弗言。唯然。世尊。願楽欲聞。
佛告舍利弗。如是妙法。諸佛如来。時乃說之。如優曇鉢華。時一現耳。

Thereupon the Buddha addressed Śāriputra: *"Now in this assembly I am free of twigs and leaves, and only the true and real remain. Śāriputra! That arrogant people like these retreat also is fine. Now listen well and I will preach for you."* Śāriputra said, *"Please do so, World-honored One, I desire joyfully to listen."* The Buddha addressed Śāriputra: *"Wonderful Dharma like this the buddha-tathāgatas preach only occasionally, just as the udumbara flower appears only once in an age."*

LS 1.88-90 *SBGZ Ref: ch. 17; Fukan-zazengi*

是法非思量分別。之所能解。唯有諸佛。乃能知之。所以者何。諸佛世尊。
唯以一大事因緣故。出現於世。舍利弗。云何名諸佛世尊。唯以一大事因緣故。
出現於世。諸佛世尊。欲令衆生。開佛知見。使得清浄故。出現於世。欲示衆生。
佛知見故。出現於世。欲令衆生。悟佛知見故。出現於世。欲令衆生。
入佛知見道故。出現於世。舍利弗。是為諸佛。唯以一大事因緣故。出現於世。

This Dharma cannot be understood by thinking and discrimination. Only buddhas are directly able to know it. Why? The buddhas, the world-honored ones, appear in the world only by reason of the one great purpose. Śāriputra, why do I say that the buddhas, the world-honored ones, appear in the world only by reason of the one great purpose? The buddhas, the world-honored ones, appear in the world because they desire to cause living beings to disclose the wisdom of Buddha which will make them able to become pure. They appear in the world because they desire to show living beings the wisdom of Buddha. They appear in the world because they desire to cause living beings to realize the wisdom of Buddha. They appear in the world because they desire to cause living beings to enter the state of truth which is the wisdom of Buddha. Śāriputra, this is why the buddhas appear in the world only by reason of the one great purpose.

LS 1.90 *SBGZ Ref: ch. 17*

舎利弗。如来但以。一佛乗故。為衆生説法。無有余乗。若二若三。舎利弗。
一切十方諸佛。法亦如是。

Śāriputra. The Tathāgata only by means of the one Buddha-vehicle preaches the Dharma for living beings. There is no other vehicle, neither a second nor a third. Śāriputra, the Dharma of all the buddhas of the ten directions is also like this.

LS 1.98-100 *SBGZ Ref: ch. 34 [87], [91]*

舎利弗。若我弟子。自謂阿羅漢。日辟支佛者。不聞不知。諸佛如来。
但教化菩薩事。此非佛弟子。非阿羅漢。非辟支佛。
又舎利弗。是諸比丘。比丘尼。自謂已得阿羅漢。是最後身。究竟涅槃。
便不復志求。阿耨多羅三藐三菩提。當知此輩。皆是増上慢人。所以者何。
若有比丘。実得阿羅漢。若不信此法。無有此処。

Śāriputra! If any of my disciples, calling themselves arhats or prateyakabuddhas, neither hear nor recognize the fact that the buddha-tathāgatas teach only bodhisattvas, they are not the Buddha's disciples, nor arhats, nor pratyekabuddhas. Again Śāriputra! If these bhikṣus and bhikṣuṇīs think to themselves, *"I have already attained the state of arhat; this is my last life, ultimate nirvana,"* and then they no longer want to pursue [the truth of] anuttara-samyak-saṃbodhi, you should know that these are all people of lofty arrogance. Why? [Because] there is no such thing as a bhikṣu really attaining the state of arhat without believing this teaching.

LS 1.104 *SBGZ Ref: ch. 24 [177]*

我此九部法　随順衆生説	This my Dharma of nine divisions,
入大乗為本　以故説是経	Preached as befits living beings,
	Is the basis for entry into the Great Vehicle.
	Therefore, I preach this Sutra.

LS 1.106 *SBGZ Ref: ch. 17; ch. 29 [99]; ch. 50 [210]; ch. 60 [4]*

十方佛土中　唯有一乗法	In the Buddha-lands of the ten directions,
無二亦無三	There only exists the one-vehicle Dharma.
	There is neither a second nor a third.

LS 1.108 *SBGZ Ref: ch. 50 [213]*

我以相厳身　光明照世間	I, body adorned with signs,
無量衆所尊　為説実相印	And brightness illuminating the world,
	Am honored by countless multitudes
	For whom I preach the seal of real form.

LS 1.116

SBGZ Ref: ch. 87 [150]

若人於塔廟　寶像及畫像
以華香幡蓋　敬心而供養
若使人作楽　擊鼓吹角貝
簫笛琴箜篌　琵琶鐃銅鈸
如是衆妙音　盡持以供養
或以歓喜心　歌唄頌佛徳
乃至一小音　皆已成佛道
若人散乱心　乃至以一華
供養於畫像　漸見無数佛
或有人礼拝　或復但合掌
乃至擧一手　或復小低頭
以此供養像　漸見無量佛
自成無上道　廣土無数衆

If people, to stūpas and shrines,
To jewel images and painted images,
With flowers, incense, flags, and canopies
Reverently serve offerings;
[Or] if they cause others to make music,
To beat drums, to blow horns and conchs,
[To play] panpipes, flutes, lutes, lyres,
Harps, gongs, and cymbals,
And many fine sounds such as these
They serve continually as offerings;
Or [if] with joyful hearts,
They sing the praises of the Buddha's virtue,
Even in one small sound,
They all have realized the Buddha's truth.
If people whose mind is distracted,
With even a single flower
Serve offerings to a painted [Buddha] image,
They will gradually see numberless buddhas.
Again, people who do prostrations
Or who simply join palms,
Even those who raise a hand
Or slightly lower the head,
And thus serve an offering to an image
Will gradually see countless buddhas,
Will naturally realize the supreme truth,
And will widely save numberless multitudes.

LS 1. 120

SBGZ Ref: ch. 17; ch. 29 [99]; ch. 50 [215]

是法往法位　世間相常住
於道場知已　導師方便説

The Dharma abides in its place in the Dharma,
And the form of the world is constantly abiding.
Having recognized this in a place of the truth,
Guiding teachers teach it by expedient means.

LS 1.124

SBGZ Ref: ch. 69 [181]

作是思惟時　十方佛皆現

At the time of this consideration,
The buddhas of the ten directions all appear.

LS 1.128

SBGZ Ref: ch. 10 [14]; ch. 17; ch. 53 [57]

如三世諸佛　説法之儀式
我今亦如是　説無分別法
諸佛興出世　懸遠値遇難
正使出于世　説是法復難

In the same manner that the
buddhas of the three times
Preach the Dharma,
So now do I also
Preach the Dharma that is without distinction.
The appearances of buddhas in the world
Are far apart and hard to meet,
Even when they do appear in the world,
It is still hard for this Dharma to be preached.

Chapter Three:
Hiyu (A Parable)

LS 1.134 *SBGZ Ref: ch. 17*

爾時舍利佛。踊躍歓喜。即起合掌。

At that time, Śāriputra, jumping for joy, stood up at once and joined together the palms of his hands.

LS 1.134 *SBGZ Ref: ch. 17*

我昔従佛。聞如是法。見諸菩薩。受記作佛。

In the past I heard such Dharma from the Buddha and saw bodhisattvas receiving affirmation and becoming buddhas.

LS 1.140-142

心中大驚疑　将非魔作佛	In my mind there was great alarm and doubt:
悩乱我心耶	Was it not a demon acting as Buddha,
	Distressing and confusing my mind?

LS 1.146 *SBGZ Ref: ch. 17*

其土平正。清浄厳飾。安穏豊楽。

The land [of Flower-Light Tathāgata] is level and straight, pure and magnificent, tranquil and prosperous.

LS 1.160 *SBGZ Ref: ch. 17*

我雖能於此。所焼之門。安穏得出。而諸子等。於火宅内。楽著嬉戯。
不覚不知。不驚不怖。

Though I can leave safely through this burning gate, the children in the burning house are absorbed in their play, neither sensing nor knowing, neither alarmed nor afraid.

LS 1.162 *SBGZ Ref: ch. 17*

是舎唯有一門。而復狭小。諸子幼稚。未有所識。恋著戯処。或當堕落。
為火所焼。我當為説。怖畏之事。

This house only has one gate; moreover, it is narrow and small. The children are young and do not yet possess knowledge; they love the places where they play. They may fall into and be burned in the fire. I must explain to them the fearfulness of this matter.

LS 1.164 *SBGZ Ref: ch. 17*

如此種種。羊車。鹿車。牛車。今在門外。可以遊戯。汝等於此火宅。
宜速出来。随汝所欲。皆當與汝。

Many kinds of such goat carts, deer carts, and ox carts are now outside the gate to play with. Come quickly out of this burning house and I will give you all whatever you want.

LS 1.166 *SBGZ Ref: ch. 17*

是時長者。見諸子等。安穏得出。皆於四衢道中。路地而坐。無復障礙。
其心泰然。歓喜踊躍。時諸子等。各白父言。父先所許。玩好之具。
羊車。鹿車。牛車。願途機賜與。舎利弗。爾時長者。各賜諸子。等一大車。

其車高廣。衆寶荘校。。。駕以白牛。

Then the wealthy man sees that his children have got out safely and are all sitting on open ground at the crossroads, with nothing impeding them; his mind is eased and he jumps for joy. Then each of his children says to the father, *"Father, please now give us those lovely playthings you promised us before; the goat carts, deer carts, and ox carts."* Śāriputra! At that time the wealthy man gives to each of his children equally a great cart. The cart is high and wide, adorned with all kinds of treasures... and yoked by white oxen.

LS 1.176 *SBGZ Ref: ch. 17*

汝等速出三界。當得三乘。聲聞。辟支佛。佛乘。我今為汝。保任此事。
終不虛也。汝等但當。勤修精進。

Quickly get out of the triple world and you will attain to the three vehicles, the vehicles of śrāvaka, pratyekabuddha, and Buddha. I now give you my guarantee of this, and in the end it will not be false. You all must solely be diligent and persevere.

LS 1.186-188 *SBGZ Ref: ch. 31 [8]*

於後宅舍　忽然火起
四面一時　其焔倶熾

Whereupon the house
Suddenly catches fire.
In the four directions, all at once,
Its flames are in full blaze.

LS 1.198 *SBGZ Ref: ch. 47 [112]*

一切衆生　皆是吾子
深著世楽　無有慧心
如来已離　三界火宅
寂然閑居　安處林野
今此三界　皆是我有
其中衆生　悉是吾子

All living beings
Are my children
[But] deeply attached to worldly pleasures
They are without wisdom...
The Tathāgata, already free from
The burning house of the triple world
Lives serenely in seclusion
Abiding peacefully in forests and fields.
Now this triple world
All is my possession
And the living beings in it
All are my children.

LS 1.202 *SBGZ Ref: ch. 38 [175]*

乗此寶乗　直至道場

Riding in this precious carriage,
[We] arrive directly at the place of truth.

Chapter Four:
Shinge (Belief and Understanding)

LS 1.222 *SBGZ Ref: ch. 12 [62]*

即從座起。整衣服。偏袒右肩。

Then they rose from their seats, and, arranging their garments, bared only their right shoulders.

LS 1.224 *SBGZ Ref: ch. 17*

不謂於今。忽然得聞。希有之法。深自慶幸。獲大善利。無量珍寶。不求自得。

Without expectation, we now suddenly are able to hear the rarely-encountered Dharma. We profoundly congratulate ourselves on having acquired a great benefit, on having got for ourselves, without seeking it, an immeasurable treasure.

LS 1.224 *SBGZ Ref: ch. 61 [26]; ch. 73 [66]*

譬若有人。年既幼稚。捨父逃逝。

It is like a person who, while still a youth, leaves a father and runs away.

LS 1.236 *SBGZ Ref: ch. 25 [211]*

此是我子。我之所生。於某城中。捨吾逃走。伶 俜 辛苦。五十余年。

This is my son begotten by me. [Since,] in a certain city he left me and ran away, he has been wandering and suffering hardship for over fifty years.

LS 1.260 *SBGZ Ref: ch. 34 [86]*

我等今者　真是聲聞
以佛道聲　令一切聞
我等今者　真阿羅漢

Now we are
Truly voice-hearers,
The voice of the Buddha's truth
We cause all to hear.
Now we are
Truly arhats.

Chapter Five:
Yakuso-yu (Parable of the Herbs)

LS 1.272 *SBGZ Ref: ch. 29 [99]*

破有法王　出現世間
随衆生欲　種種説法
有智若聞　則能信解
無智疑悔　則為永失

The Dharma-King who breaks 'existence,'
Appears in the world
And according to the wants of living beings,
Preaches the Dharma in many ways...
The wise if they hear it,
Are able to believe and understand at once,
The unwise doubt and grieve,
Thus losing it forever.

LS 1.274 *SBGZ Ref: ch. 17*

卉木薬草　大小諸樹
百穀苗稼　甘藷蒲萄
雨之所潤　無不豊足
乾地普洽　薬木竝茂

Plants, shrubs, and herbs;
Large and small trees,
Grain of all kinds, and seedlings,
Sugarcane and grapevines,
Are moistened by the rain,
Without insufficiency.
Dry ground is all soaked,
Herbs and trees flourish together.

LS 1.286 *SBGZ Ref: ch. 17*

汝等所行　是菩薩道
漸漸修学　悉當成佛

Your actions
Are the bodhisattva-way itself.
By gradual practice and learning,
You will all become buddhas.

Chapter Six: *Juki (Affirmation)*

LS 1.300 *SBGZ Ref: ch. 17*

我此弟子。摩訶迦葉。於未来世。當得奉覲。三百万億。諸佛世尊。
供養恭敬。尊重讃歎。廣宣諸佛。無量大法。

This my disciple Mahākāśyapa, in a future age, will be able to serve three hundred myriad koṭis of world-honored buddhas, to make offerings to them, to revere, to honor, and to praise them, and to proclaim widely the limitless great Dharma of the buddhas.

LS 1.322 *SBGZ Ref: ch. 17*

我諸弟子　威徳具足
其数五百　皆當授記
於未来世　咸得成佛

My disciples,
Five hundred in number,
Perfectly equipped with dignified virtues,
All will receive affirmation,
And in a future age,
All will be able to become buddha.

Chapter Seven: *Kejo-yu (The Parable of the Magic City)*

LS 2.12-14 *SBGZ Ref: ch. 17*

如人以力磨　三千大千土
盡此諸地種　皆悉以為墨
過於千国土　乃下一塵点
如是展轉點　盡此諸塵墨
如是諸国土　點與不點等
復盡抹為塵　一塵為一劫

Suppose a person, with [his or her own] power,
Grinds a three-thousand-great-thousandfold land,
And every kind of earth therein,
Entirely into ink,
And, passing through a thousand lands,
Then lets one drop fall.
Dropping them like this as [the journey] proceeds,
[The person] uses up all these specks of ink.
All the countries thus described,
Specked and unspecked alike,
Again are entirely ground to dust,
And one speck is one kalpa.

LS 2.30

捨深禪定楽　為供養佛故

Leaving the profound joy of the immovable state of dhyāna
In order to serve the Buddha.

LS 2.36

聖主天中天　迦陵頻伽聲　　Sacred ruler, god among gods!
With voice of kalavinka

LS 2.56 *SBGZ Ref: ch. 1 [32]*

謂是苦。是苦集。是苦滅。是苦滅道。及廣說十二因縁法。無明縁行。
行縁識。識縁名色。名色縁六入。六入縁觸。觸縁受。受縁愛。愛縁取。
取縁有。有縁生。生縁老死。憂悲苦悩。無明滅則行滅。行滅則識滅。
識滅則名色滅。名色滅則六入滅。六入滅則觸滅。觸滅則受滅。受滅則愛滅。
愛滅則取滅。取滅則有滅。有滅則生滅。生滅則老死憂悲苦悩滅。

He said, *"This is suffering; this the accumulation of suffering; this the cessation of suffering; this the way of cessation of suffering."* And he preached extensively the law of the twelve causal connections: *"Ignorance leads to action. Action leads to consciousness. Consciousness leads to name and form. Name and form lead to the six sense organs. The six sense organs lead to contact. Contact leads to feeling. Feeling leads to love. Love leads to taking. Taking leads to [new] existence. [New] existence leads to life. Life leads to aging and death; grief, sorrow, suffering, and distress. If ignorance ceases, then action ceases. If action ceases, then name and form cease. If name and form cease, then the six sense organs cease. If the six sense organs cease, then contact ceases. If contact ceases, then feeling ceases. If feeling ceases, then love ceases. If love ceases, then taking ceases. If taking ceases, then [new] existence ceases. If [new] existence ceases, then life ceases. If life ceases, then cease aging and death, grief, sorrow, suffering, and distress."*

LS 2.58 *SBGZ Ref: ch. 86 [83]*

十六王子。皆以童子出家。而為沙彌。

The sixteen royal sons, all being youths, left home and became śramaṇeras.

LS 2.60 *SBGZ Ref: ch. 86 [83]*

爾時轉輪聖王。所将衆中。八万億人。見十六王子出家。亦求出家。王即聽許。

At that time, eight myriad koṭis of people among the masses led by the sacred wheel-rolling king, seeing the sixteen royal sons leave home, also sought to leave home, whereupon the king permitted them.

LS 2.62 *SBGZ Ref: ch. 86 [83]*

佛說是経。於八千劫。未曾休廃。說此経已。即入静室。住於禪定。
八万四千劫。是時十六菩薩沙彌。知佛入室。寂然禪定。各昇法座。
亦於八万四千劫。為四部衆。廣說分別。妙法華経。

The Buddha [called Universal Surpassing Wisdom] preached this Sutra for eight thousand kalpas without cessation. When he had finished preaching this Sutra, he at once entered a quiet room and remained in the immovable state of dhyāna for eighty-four thousand kalpas. During this time the sixteen bodhisattva-śramaṇeras, knowing that the buddha had entered the room and was serenely set in dhyāna, each ascended a Dharma-seat and also for eighty-four thousand kalpas widely preached and discriminated to the four groups the Sutra of the Flower of the Wonderful Dharma.

LS 2.66 (Ref. for Katto) *SBGZ Ref: ch. 46 [90]*

其二沙彌。東方作佛。一名阿 閦。在歓喜国。二名須彌頂。

Two of those śramaṇeras became buddhas in the eastern quarter, the first named Akṣobhya who lived in the Land of Joy, the second named Sumeru Peak.

Chapter Eight:
Gohyaku-deshi-juki (The Affirmation of Five Hundred Disciples)

LS 2.96 *SBGZ Ref: ch. 17*

諸比丘。富樓那。亦於七佛。説法人中。而得第一。今於我所。説法人中。
亦為第一。於賢劫中。當来諸佛。説法人中。亦復第一。而皆護持。助宣佛法。

Bhikṣus! Pūrṇa was able to become foremost among Dharma preachers under the Seven Buddhas. Now he has also become foremost among Dharma preachers in my order. He will again be foremost among Dharma preachers under future buddhas in [this] Virtuous Kalpa and will altogether guard, maintain, assist, and proclaim the Buddha-Dharma.

LS 2.112 *SBGZ Ref: ch. 32 [45]*

其五百比丘　次第當作佛
同号曰普明　轉次而授記

Five hundred bhikṣus,
One by one, will become buddha,
With the same title, "Universal Light,"
And one after another, they will give affirmation.

LS 2.114 *SBGZ Ref: ch. 4 [105]; ch. 12 [74]*

世尊。譬如有人。至親友家。酔酒而臥。是時親友。官事當行。
以無価寶珠。繫其衣裏。與之而去。

World-honored One! It is as if some person goes to the house of a close friend, becomes intoxicated, and lies down. Meanwhile the close friend, having to go out on official business, ties a priceless pearl within [that person's] garment as a gift, and departs.

LS 2.118 *SBGZ Ref: ch. 17*

譬如貧窮人　往至親友家
其家甚大富　具設諸肴膳
以無値寶珠　繫著内衣裏

It is like a poor person
Going to the house of a close friend
Whose family is very wealthy
[The friend] serves many fine dishes.
And a priceless pearl,
Ties inside [the poor one's] inner garment.

LS 2.120 *SBGZ Ref: ch. 32 [47]*

我今従佛聞　授記荘厳事
及轉次受決　身心遍歓喜

Now, hearing from the Buddha
Of the wonderful fact of affirmation,
And of the sequential reception of affirmation,
Body and mind are full of joy.

Chapter Nine:
Ju-gaku-mugaku-nin-ki (Affirmation of Students and People Beyond Study)

LS 2.128-130 *SBGZ Ref: ch. 73 [27]*

我常勤精進。是故我已。
得成阿耨多羅三藐三菩提。

I have constantly practiced diligence, and for this reason I have already realized anuttara-samyak-saṃbodhi.

Chapter Ten: *Hosshi (A Teacher of the Dharma)*

LS 2.140 *SBGZ Ref: ch. 32 [50], [52]*

爾時世尊。因薬王菩薩。告八万大士。薬王。汝見是大衆中。無量諸天。
龍王。夜叉。乾闥婆。阿修羅。迦樓羅。緊那羅。摩睺羅伽。人與非人。
及比丘。比丘尼。優婆塞。優婆夷。求聲聞者。求辟支佛者。求佛道者。
如是等類。咸於佛前。聞妙法華経。一偈一句。乃至一念随喜者。
我皆與授記。當得阿耨多羅三藐三菩提。佛告薬王。又如来滅度之後。
若有人。聞妙法華経。乃至一偈一句。一念随喜者。我亦與授。
阿耨多羅三藐三菩提記。

At that time the World-honored One addressed eighty thousand great beings through the Bodhisattva Medicine King: *"Medicine King! You see among this great assembly countless gods, dragon kings, yakṣas, gandharvas, asuras, garuḍas, kiṃnaras, mahoragas, humans and nonhumans, as well as bhikṣus, bhikṣuṇīs, upāsakas, and upāsikās, those who seek to be śrāvakas, those who seek to be pratyekabuddhas, and those who seek the truth of Buddha. When such beings as these are, all before the Buddha, hear a single verse or a single word of the Sutra of the Flower of the Wonderful Dharma and rejoice in it even for a single moment of consciousness, I give affirmation to them all: 'You will attain anuttara-samyak-saṃbodhi.'"* The Buddha addresses Medicine King: *"Moreover, after the Tathāgata's extinction, if there are any people who hear even a single verse or a single word of the Sutra of the Flower of the Wonderful Dharma and rejoice in it for a single moment of consciousness, again, I give affirmation of anuttara-samyak-saṃbodhi..."*

LS 2.152 *SBGZ Ref: ch. 9 [222]*

此経者。如来現在。猶多怨嫉。況滅度後。

This Sutra, even while the Tathāgata is alive, [arouses] much hate and envy; how much more after his extinction!

LS 2.154 *SBGZ Ref: ch. 17; ch. 71 [221]*

薬王。在在処処。若説。若読。若誦。若書。若経巻所住之処。
皆応起七寶塔。極令高廣厳飾。不須復安舍利。所以者何。此中已有。
如来全身。此塔應以。一切華香瓔珞。繒蓋。幢幡。伎楽歌頌。供養恭敬。
尊重讃歎。若有人得見此塔。礼拝供養。當知是等。皆近阿耨多羅三藐三菩提。

Medicine King! In every place where [this Lotus Sutra] is preached, or read, or recited, or copied, or where volumes of the Sutra are kept, we should erect a stūpa of the seven treasures, making it most high, wide, and ornate. [But] there is no need to place bones in it. Why? [Because] in it already there is the whole body of the Tathāgata. This stūpa should be served, revered, honored, and extolled with all kinds of flowers, fragrance, strings of pearls, silk canopies, banners, flags, music, and songs of praise. If any people, being able to see this stūpa, do prostrations and serve offerings to it, know that they are all close to anuttara-samyak-saṃbodhi.

LS 2.156 *SBGZ Ref: ch. 17; ch. 50 [215]*

譬如有人。渇乏須水。於彼高原。穿鑿求之。猶見乾土。知水尚遠。施功不已。
転見湿土。遂漸至泥。其心決定。知水必近。菩薩亦復如是。若未聞未解。
未能修習。是法華経。當知是人。去阿耨多羅三藐三菩提。若得聞解。
思惟。修習。必知得近。阿耨多羅三藐三菩提。所以者何。一切菩薩。
阿耨多羅三藐三菩提。未属此経。此経開方便門。示真実相。

For example, some people are parched and in need of water, for which they search by digging on a plateau. As long as they see dry earth, they know that water is still far away. Making effort unceasingly, in time they see moist earth, and then they gradually reach mud. Their minds are made up. They know that water must be near. Bodhisattvas are also like this. If they have not heard, nor understood, nor been able to practice this Sutra of the Flower of Dharma, we should know that they are still far from [the truth of] anuttara-samyak-saṃbodhi.

If they are able to hear, to understand, to consider, and to practice it, we know for sure that they are close to anuttara-samyak-saṃbodhi. Why? [Because] the anuttara-samyak-saṃbodhi of all bodhisattvas totally belongs to this Sutra. This Sutra opens the door of expedient methods and reveals true and real form.

LS 2.156-158 *SBGZ Ref: ch. 17*

薬王。若有菩薩。聞是法華経。驚疑怖畏。當知是為。新発意菩薩。
若声聞人。聞是経。驚疑怖畏。當知是為。増上慢者。

Medicine King! If a bodhisattva, on hearing this Sutra of the Flower of Dharma, is alarmed, doubting, or afraid, we should know that this is a bodhisattva with recently established intention. If a śrāvaka, on hearing this Sutra, is alarmed, doubting, or afraid, we should know that this is an arrogant person.

LS 2.162

若説此経時　有人悪口罵
加刀杖瓦石　念佛故應忍

If, when they preach this Sutra,
Someone abuses them with an evil mouth,
Or lays upon them swords, sticks, tiles, or stones,
Because they heed the Buddha, they will endure.

LS 2.166 *SBGZ Ref: ch. 61 [31]*

若親近法師　速得菩薩道
随順是師學　得見恒沙佛

If we are close to a teacher of the Dharma,
We at once attain the bodhisattva-way.
And if we learn following this teacher,
We are able to meet buddhas [numerous] as sands of the Ganges.

Chapter Eleven: *Ken-hoto (Seeing the Precious Stupa)*

LS 2.168 *SBGZ Ref: ch. 17*

爾時佛前。有七寶塔。高五百由旬。縦廣二百五十由旬。縦地涌出。住在空中。

At that time, before the Buddha, a stūpa of the seven treasures, five hundred yojanas in height, and two hundred and fifty yojanas in length and breadth, sprang out from the earth and abode in the sky.

LS 2.172 *SBGZ Ref: ch. 17; ch. 87 [160]*

其佛本行菩薩道時。作大誓願。若我成佛。滅度之後。於十方国土。
有説法華経處。我之塔廟。為聴是経故。涌現其前。

When that buddha [Abundant Treasures] was practicing the bodhisattva-way in the past, he had made a great vow: *"After I have realized [the state of] buddha and died, if in the lands of the ten directions there is any place where the Sutra of the Flower of Dharma is preached, my stūpa shall spring up and appear before that place so that I may hear the Sutra..."*

LS 2.176 *SBGZ Ref: ch. 17*

大楽説。白佛言。世尊。我等亦願。欲見世尊。分身諸佛。礼拝供養。
爾時佛放。白毫一光。

[Bodhisattva] Great Eloquence said to the Buddha, *"World-honored One! We also would like to see the many buddhas who are offshoots of the World-honored One, to perform prostrations and to serve offerings to them."* Then the Buddha sent forth a ray of light from [his circle of] white hair.

LS 2.186-188 *SBGZ Ref: ch. 17; ch. 51 [9]*

即時一切衆會。皆見多寶如来。於寶塔中。坐師子座。全身不散。
加入禪定。。。爾時多寶佛。於寶塔中。分半座。與釈迦牟尼佛。而作是言。
釈迦牟尼佛。可就此座。即時釈迦牟尼佛。入其塔中。坐其半座。結跏趺坐。

Then all the assembly saw the Tathāgata Abundant Treasures sitting on the lion seat in the treasure stūpa, his whole body undissipated, as if he had entered the balanced state of dhyāna...Then the Buddha Abundant Treasures, in the treasure stūpa, shared half his seat with Śākyamuni Buddha, and said, *"Śākyamuni Buddha, please take this seat."* Thereupon Śākyamuni Buddha entered inside the stūpa, sat down on the half-seat, and sat in the full lotus posture.

LS 2.190 *SBGZ Ref: ch. 17*

聖主世尊　雖久滅度
在寶塔中　尚為法来

A world-honored sacred lord,
Though long extinct
Inside the treasure stūpa,
Yet comes for the Dharma.

LS 2.194 *SBGZ Ref: ch. 61 [44]*

若説此経　即為見我
多寶如来　乃諸化佛

If they preach this Sutra
Then they will meet me,
The Tathāgata Abundant Treasures,
And many transformed buddhas.

LS 2.196-198 *SBGZ Ref: ch. 17*

若以大地　置足甲上
昇於梵天　亦未為難
佛滅度後　於悪世中
暫読此経　是則為難

To take the great earth,
Put it on a toe-nail,
And ascend to Brahma-heaven:
That also is not hard.
[But] after the Buddha's death,
In a corrupt age,
To read this Sutra even for a moment:
That indeed will be hard.

LS 2.198 *SBGZ Ref: ch. 23 [135]*

我滅度後　若持此経
為一人説　是則為難
於我滅後　聽受此経
問其義趣　是則為難

After my extinction,
To keep this Sutra,
And to preach it to [even] a single person:
That indeed will be hard...
After my extinction,
To listen to and to accept this Sutra,
And to inquire into its meaning:
That indeed will be hard.

Chapter Twelve: *Daibadatta (Devadatta)*

LS 2.208 *SBGZ Ref: ch. 45*

由提婆達多。善知識故。令我是足。六波羅密。慈悲喜捨。三十二相。
八十種好。紫磨金色。十力。四無所畏。四摂法。十八不共。神通道力。
成等正覚。廣度衆生。皆因提婆達多。善知識故。

Through the good counsel of Devadatta, I was caused to obtain the six pāramitās, kindness, compassion, joy, and detachment, the thirty-two signs, the eighty kinds of excellence, a golden complexion with purple luster, the ten powers, the four kinds of fearlessness, the four social methods, the eighteen uncommon [characteristics], the mystical abilities, and bodhi-powers. I realized the balanced and right state of awareness and widely saved living beings, all due to the good counsel of Devadatta.

LS 2.208 *SBGZ Ref: ch. 17; ch. 73 [16]*

提婆達多。却後過無量劫。當得成佛。

Devadatta also, in future, after countless kalpas have passed, will be able to become a buddha.

LS 2.212-214 *SBGZ Ref: ch. 17*

爾時文殊師利。坐千葉蓮華。大如車輪。倶来菩薩。亦坐寶蓮華。
従於大海。娑竭羅龍宮。自然涌出。住虚空中。

Thereupon Mañjuśrī, sitting on a thousand-petal lotus flower as big as a carriage wheel, with the bodhisattvas who accompanied him also sitting on precious lotus flowers, naturally sprang up from the great ocean, out of the palace of the Sāgara Dragon, and abode in space.

LS 2.216

[Bodhisattva Wisdom Accumulation says to Mañjuśrī:]

大智徳勇健　化度無量衆
今此諸大會　及我皆已見
演暢実相義　開闡一乗法
廣導諸羣生　令速成菩提

"Very wise, virtuous, brave, and vigorous one!
You have converted and saved countless beings.
Now this great order
And I, all already have seen
[Your] expounding of the teaching of real form,
Revelation of the one-vehicle Dharma,
And universal guidance of living beings,
Whom you cause swiftly to realize bodhi."

LS 2.218 *SBGZ Ref: ch. 17*

文殊師利言。我於海中。唯常宣説。妙法華経。。。

Mañjuśrī said: *"I, in the sea, am constantly preaching only the Sutra of the Flower of the Wonderful Dharma..."*

LS 2.218 *SBGZ Ref: ch. 17*

文殊師利言。有。娑竭羅龍王女。。。深入禪定。了達諸法。
於刹那頃。発菩提心。得不退転。

Mañjuśrī said: *"There is the daughter of the Dragon King Sāgara... She has profoundly entered the balanced state of dhyāna, and penetrated all dharmas. In a kṣāṇa she established the bodhi-mind and attained the state of not regressing or deviating."*

LS 2.218-220 *SBGZ Ref: ch. 71 [227]*

智積菩薩言。我見釈迦如来。於無量劫。難行苦行。積功累徳。求菩薩道。
未曾止息。観三千大千世界。乃至無有。如芥子許。非是菩薩。
捨身命處。為衆生故。然後乃得。成菩薩道。

The Bodhisattva Wisdom Accumulation said, *"I have seen [how] Śākyamuni Tathāgata, during countless kalpas of hard practice and painful practice, accumulating merit and heaping up virtue, has pursued the bodhisattva-way and has never ceased. I have observed that in the three-thousand-great-thousandfold world, there is no place even the size of a mustard seed where he has not abandoned his body and life as a bodhisattva for the sake of living beings. After acting thus, he was then able to realize the truth of bodhi."*

LS 2.224 *SBGZ Ref: ch. 8 [187]; ch. 17*

皆見竜女。忽然之間。変成男子。具菩薩行。則往南方。無垢世界。
坐寶蓮華。成等正覺。三十二相。八十種好。普為十方。一切衆生。
演説妙法。爾時婆婆世界。菩薩聲聞。天龍八部。人與非人。皆遥見彼。
龍女成佛。普為時會。人天説法。心大歓喜。悉遥敬礼。

All saw the dragon's daughter suddenly become a male, equipped with all the practices of a bodhisattva. She went at once to the southern quarter, the world which is free of impurity, [where she] sat on a precious lotus flower, realizing the balanced and right state of truth, with the thirty-two signs and the eighty kinds of excellence, and preaching the wonderful Dharma for all living beings throughout the ten directions. Then the sahā-world of bodhisattvas, śrāvakas, the eight groups of gods and dragons, and human and nonhuman beings, all seeing from afar the dragon's daughter becoming a buddha and universally preaching the Dharma for the human beings and gods in that order, rejoiced greatly in their hearts and they all bowed from afar in veneration.

Chapter Thirteen: *Kan-ji (Exhortation to Hold Firm)*

Chapter Fourteen: *Anraku-gyo (Peaceful and Joyful Practice)*

LS 2.244 *SBGZ Ref: ch. 9 [230]*

菩薩摩訶薩。不親近。国王王子。大臣。管長。

A bodhisattva-mahāsattva should not get close to kings, princes, ministers, and administrators.

LS 2.258 *SBGZ Ref: ch. 56 [121]*

以油塗身　澡浴塵穢
著新浄衣　内外倶浄

[The bodhisattva] applies oil to the body,
Having bathed away dust and dirt,
And puts on a fresh and clean robe:
Totally clean within and without.

LS 2.266-268 *SBGZ Ref: ch. 56 [122]*

其人雖不問。不信不解是経。我得阿耨多羅三藐三菩提時。
随在何地。以神通力。智慧力。引之令得。住是法中。

Though those people neither hear, nor believe in, nor understand this Sutra, when I attain [the truth of] anuttara-samyak-saṃbodhi, wherever I am, through mystical power and through the power of wisdom, I will lead them and cause them to be able to abide in this Dharma.

LS 2.276-278 *SBGZ Ref: ch. 4 [105]; ch. 17; ch. 76 [115]*

如有勇健　能為難事
王解髻中　明珠賜之
如王解髻　明珠與之
此経為尊　衆経中上
我常守護　不妄開示
今正是時　為汝等説

If there is a brave and vigorous person,
Able to perform difficult deeds,
The king unties from inside his topknot,
The bright pearl, and this he gives...
It is like the king releasing from his topknot
The bright pearl, and giving it.
This Sutra is honored
As supreme among all sutras,
I have always guarded it,
And not revealed it at random.
Now is just the time
To preach it for you all.

LS 2.282 *SBGZ Ref: ch. 61 [34]*

深入禪定　見十方佛

Having profoundly entered
the balanced state of dhyāna,
We meet the buddhas of the ten directions.

LS 2.282 *SBGZ Ref: ch. 38 [187]; ch. 69 [175]; ch. 72 [237]*

諸佛身金色　百福相荘厳
聞方為人説　常有是好夢
又夢作国王　捨宮殿眷屬
及上妙五欲　行詣於道場
在菩提樹下　而處師子座
求道過七日　得諸佛之智
成無上道已　起而轉方輪
為四衆説法　逕千万億劫
説無漏妙法　度無量衆生
後當入涅槃　如煙盡燈滅
若後悪世中　説是第一法
是人得大利　如上諸功徳

The buddhas' bodies, golden colored,
Adorned with a hundred signs of happiness:
In the hearing of Dharma and in preaching for others,
This pleasant dream exists forever.
And in the dream-action, the king of a nation
Forsakes his palace, his followers,
And the five desires for the superior and fine,
And he goes to a place of the truth.
At the foot of a Bodhi tree,
He sits on the lion-seat,
Pursues the truth for seven days,
And attains the wisdom of the buddhas.
Having realized the supreme truth
He arises and turns the wheel of Dharma,
Preaching the Dharma to the four groups
For thousands of myriads of koṭis of kalpas.
He preaches the faultless wonderful Dharma
And saves countless living beings,
After which he naturally enters nirvāṇa
Like a lamp going out when its smoke is spent.
If [anyone] in future corrupt ages
Preaches this paramount Dharma,
That person will obtain great benefit
Such as the virtuous effects [described] above.

Chapter Fifteen: Ju-chi-yushutsu (Springing Out from the Earth)

LS 2.286 *SBGZ Ref: ch. 17*

佛説是時。娑婆世界。三千大千国土。地皆震裂。而於其中。有無量千万億。
菩薩摩訶薩。同時涌出。是諸菩薩。身皆金色。三十二相。無量光明。
先盡在。娑婆世界之下。此界虚空中住。

When the Buddha had preached this, all the earth of the three-thousand-great-thousand lands of the sahā-world quaked and split, and from its midst countless thousand myriad koṭis of bodhisattva-mahāsattvas sprang out together. These bodhisattvas, their bodies all golden, with the thirty-two signs and measureless brightness, had previously all been below the sahā-world, living in the space there.

LS 2.310 *SBGZ Ref: ch. 17; ch. 62 [62]*

阿逸汝當知　是諸大菩薩
從無数劫来　修習佛智慧
悉是我所化　令発大道心
此等是我子　依止是世界
常行頭陀事　志楽於静処
捨大衆憒閙　不楽多所說
如是諸子等　学習我道法
昼夜常精進　為求佛道故
在娑婆世界　下方空中住

Ajita, you should know,
All these great bodhisattvas,
For numberless kalpas,
Have practiced the Buddha's wisdom,
All of them are my converts,
I have caused them to establish
the will to the great truth,
They are my sons.
They remain in this world,
Always practicing the dhūta deeds,
They hope to enjoy quiet places,
Shunning the clamor of crowds,
Taking no pleasure in much explanation.
Sons like these
Are learning the method which is my truth.
They are ever diligent, day and night,
Because they want to get the Buddha's truth.
In the sahā-world,
Down below, they live in space.

LS 2.318 *SBGZ Ref: ch. 17; ch. 47 [112]*

譬如小壮人　年始二十五
示人百歳子　髪白地面皺
是等我所生　子亦說是父
父少而子老　挙世所不信
世尊亦如是　得道来甚近
是所菩薩等　志固無法弱
從無量劫来　而行菩薩道

It is as if a young and strong man,
Just twenty-five years old,
Indicates to others centenarian sons,
With white hair and wrinkled faces,
[Saying], *"These are my offspring,"*
And the sons also saying, *"This is our father"*–
The father young and the sons old.
The whole world does not believe it.
So it is with the World-honored One:
He has attained the truth very recently.
All these bodhisattvas,
Are firm in will, and dauntless,
And for countless ages,
They have practiced the bodhisattva-way.

Chapter Sixteen: *Nyorai-juryo (The Tathāgata's Lifetime)*

LS 3.12-14 *SBGZ Ref: ch. 71 [226]*

善男子。我実成佛已来。無量無辺。百千万億。那由他劫。
譬如五百千万億。那由他。阿僧祇。三千大千世界。假使有人。
抹為微塵。過於東方。五百千万億。那由他。阿僧祇国。乃下一塵。
如是東行。盡是微塵。諸善男子。於意云何。是諸世界。
可得思惟校計。知其数不。

Good sons! It is countless and infinite hundred thousand myriad koṭis of nayutas of kalpas since I actually realized the state of buddha. For instance, suppose there are five hundred thousand myriad koṭis of nayutas of asaṃkheya three-thousand-great-thousandfold worlds; let someone grind them to atoms, pass eastward through five hundred thousand myriad koṭis of nayutas of asaṃkheya countries, and then drop one atom; [suppose the person] proceeds eastward like this [until] all those atoms are used up. Good sons, what do you think? Is it possible, or not, to conceive and compute all those worlds so as to know their number?

LS 3.16 *SBGZ Ref: ch. 83 [21]*

諸善男子。如来見諸衆生。楽於少法。徳薄垢重者。為是人説。我少出家。
阿耨多羅三藐三菩提。然我実成佛已来。久遠若斯。但以方便。
教化衆生。令入佛道。作如是説。

Good sons! Seeing living beings who take pleasure in small things, whose virtue is scant and whose filthiness is accumulated, the Tathāgata to these people states, *'In my youth I transcended family life and attained anuttara-samyak-saṃbodhi.'* And since I actually realized [the state of] buddha, [my] eternity has been such as it is. Only to teach and transform living beings, by expedient means, so that they will enter the Buddhist truth, do I make statements like this.

LS 3.18 *SBGZ Ref: ch. 17; ch. 43 [44]; ch. 47 [110]*

諸所言説。皆実不虚。所以者何。如来如実知見。三界之相。無有生死。
若退若出。亦無在世。及滅度者。非実非虚。非如非異。不如三界。見於三界。

All that he says is real, not empty. Why? [Because] the Tathāgata knows and sees the form of the triple world as it really is, without life and death, or disappearance or appearance; without existence in the world and extinction; neither real nor void; neither thus nor otherwise. It is best to see the triple world as the triple world.

LS3.18-20 *SBGZ Ref: ch. 17; ch. 23 [101]; ch. 50 [215]; ch. 71 [226]*

如是我成佛已来。甚大久遠。寿命無量。阿僧祇劫。常住不滅。
諸善男子。我本行菩薩道。所成寿命。今猶未盡。復倍上数。

Thus, it is very far in the distant past since I realized [the state of] buddha. [My] lifetime is countless asaṃkheya kalpas, eternally existing and not perishing. Good sons! The lifetime which I have realized by my original practice of the bodhisattva-way is not even yet exhausted but will still be twice the previous number [of kalpas].

LS 3.30 *SBGZ Ref: ch. 17 [54]; ch. 60 [44]; ch. 61 [43]*

為度衆生故　方便現涅槃
而実不滅度　常住此説法
我常住於此　以諸神通力
令顛倒衆生　雖近而不見
衆見我滅度　廣供養舎利
咸皆懐恋慕　而生渇仰心

In order to save living beings,
As an expedient method I manifest nirvāṇa,
Yet really I have not passed away,
Constantly abiding here preaching the Dharma,
I am always living at this place,
With mystical powers,

衆生既信伏　質直意柔軟
一心欲見佛　不自惜身命
時我及衆僧　倶出霊鷲山

I make living beings who are upset,
Still fail to see me though I am close.
Many see that I have passed away,
And far and wide they serve offerings to my bones,
All holding romantic yearnings
And bearing thirst in their hearts.
When living beings have believed and submitted,
Being simple and straight, and flexible in mind,
And they wholeheartedly want to meet Buddha,
Without begrudging their own body and life,
Then I and many monks,
Appear together on Vulture Peak.

LS 3.32

SBGZ Ref: ch. 17; ch. 61 [48]; ch. 88 [188]

常在霊鷲山　及余諸住処
衆生見劫盡　大火所焼時
我此土安穏　天人常充満
園林諸堂閣　種種寶荘厳
寶樹他華菓　衆生所遊楽
諸天撃天鼓　常作衆伎楽
雨曼陀羅華　散佛及大衆
我浄土不毀　而衆見焼盡
憂怖諸苦悩　如是悉充満
是諸罪衆生　以悪業因縁
過阿僧祇劫　不聞三寶名
諸有修功徳　柔和質直者
則皆見我身　在此而說法

[I am] eternally present on Vulture Peak,
And in other dwelling places.
Even when living beings see, at the end of a kalpa,
That they are to be burned in a great fire,
This land of mine is tranquil,
Always filled with gods and human beings;
Its parks and many palaces
Are adorned with every kind of treasure;
Precious trees have abundant flowers and fruit:
It is a place where living beings enjoy themselves.
The gods strike celestial drums,
And constantly make theater and music,
Showering mandārava flowers
On the Buddha and the great assembly.
My pure land is immortal,
Yet many view it as to be burned up,
And thus entirely filled
With grief, horror, and agonies.
These living beings of many sins,
With their bad conduct as direct and indirect causes,
Even if they pass asaṃkheya kalpas
Do not hear the name of the Three Treasures.
Beings who practice virtue
And who are gentle, simple, and straight,
All see my body
Existing here and preaching the Dharma.

LS 3.36

SBGZ Ref: ch. 70 [201]

每自作是念　以何令衆生
得入無上道　速成就佛身

Constantly making this my thought:
"How can I make living beings
Able to enter the supreme truth,
And swiftly realize a buddha's body?"

Chapter Seventeen: *Funbetsu-kudoku (Discrimination of Merits)*

LS 3.56 *SBGZ Ref: ch. 61 [39]*

若善男子。善女人。聞我説寿命長遠。深心信解。則為見佛。
常在耆闍崛山。共大菩薩。諸聲聞衆。囲遶説法。又見此娑婆世界。
其他瑠璃。坦然平正。

If good sons and good daughters, hearing my preaching of the eternity of [my] lifetime, believe and understand it with a profound mind, then they will see the Buddha constantly abiding on Mount Gṛdhrakūṭa surrounded by an assembly of great bodhisattvas and many śrāvakas, and preaching the Dharma. And they will see this sahā-world with its land of lapis lazuli, level, normal, and right.

Chapter Eighteen: *Zuiki-kudoku (The Merits of Joyful Acceptance)*

LS 3.72-74 *SBGZ Ref: ch. 8 [70]; ch. 13 [127]; ch. 14 [200]; ch. 20 [125]*

爾時佛告。彌勒菩薩摩訶薩。阿逸多。如来滅後。若比丘。比丘尼。
優婆塞。優婆夷。及餘智者。若長若幼。聞是経。随喜已???。從法會出。
至於餘處。若在僧坊。若空閑地。若城邑巷陌。聚洛田里。如其所聞。
為父母宗親。善友知識。随力演説。是諸人等。聞已隋喜。服行轉教。
餘人聞已。亦随喜轉教。如是展轉。至第五十。

Then the Buddha addressed the bodhisattva-mahāsattva Maitreya: *"Ajita. If, after the Tathāgata's death, bhikṣus, bhikṣuṇīs, upāsakas, and upāsikās, or other wise people, old or young, having heard this Sutra and accepted it with joy, leave the Dharma-order and go elsewhere to stay in monasteries or deserted places, or in cities, streets, hamlets, fields, and villages, to expound [this Sutra] as they have heard it, according to their ability, to their father and mother, relatives, good friends and acquaintances; and all these people, having heard it, accept it with joy and again go on to transmit the teaching; [then] other people, having heard it, also accept it with joy and transmit the teaching, which propagates like this to the fiftieth [generation]..."*

LS 3.88

何況一心聴　解説其義趣 如説而修行　其福不可限	How much more, if we hear [the Sutra] with undivided mind, Elucidate its meaning, And practice according to the teaching: That happiness is beyond limit.

LS 3.90

爾時佛告。常精進菩薩摩訶薩。若善男子。善女人。受持是法華経。
若讀。若誦。若解説。若書寫。是人當得。八百眼功德。千二百耳功德。
八百鼻功德。千二百舌功德。八百身功德。千二百意功德。
以是功德。荘厳六根。皆令清浄。

Then the Buddha addressed the Bodhisattva-Mahāsattva Ever Zealous: *"If any good son or good daughter receives and retains this Sutra of the Flower of Dharma or reads or recites or explains or copies it, that person will obtain eight hundred merits of the eye, twelve hundred merits of the ear, eight hundred merits of the nose, twelve hundred merits of the tongue, eight hundred merits of the body, and twelve hundred merits of the mind; these merits will adorn the six organs making them all pure..."*

Chapter Nineteen:
Hosshi-kudoku (The Merits of a Teacher of the Dharma)

LS 3.122 *SBGZ Ref: ch. 21 [184]*

雖未得。無漏智慧。而其意根。清浄如此。

Though [he or she] has not yet attained faultless real wisdom, his or her mind-organ is pure like this.

Chapter Twenty:
Jofugyo-bosatsu (The Bodhisattva Never Despise)

LS 3.128: *SBGZ Ref: ch. 37 [161]; ch. 52 [23]*

乃往古昔。過無量無邊。不可思議。阿僧祇劫。有佛名威音王。

In the eternal past, countless, infinite, inconceivable asaṃkheya kalpas ago, there was a buddha named King of Majestic Voice.

LS 3.130 *SBGZ Ref: ch. 17*

正法往世劫数。如一閻浮堤微塵。像法住世劫数。如四天下微塵。

The right Dharma remained in the world for a number of kalpas equal to the atoms in one Jambudvīpa. The imitative Dharma remained in the world for a number of kalpas equal to the atoms in four continents.

LS 3.134-136

如此経歴多年。常被罵詈。不生瞋恚。常作是言。汝當作佛。
説是語時。衆人或以。杖木瓦石。而打擲之。避走遠住。猶高聲唱言。
我不敢軽於汝等。汝等皆當作佛。以其常作是語故。増上慢比丘。
比丘尼。優婆塞。優婆夷。号之為常不軽。

Thus he passed many years, constantly abused, never becoming angry, always saying, *"You will become buddhas."* When he said these words, people would sometimes beat him with clubs, sticks, bricks, and stones. He ran away and, keeping his distance, he still called out in a loud voice, *"I dare not despise you. You will all become buddhas."* Because he always spoke these words, arrogant bhikṣus, bhikṣuṇīs, upāsakas, and upāsikās called him "Never Despise."

Chapter Twenty-One:
Nyorai-jinriki (The Mystical Power of the Tathāgata)

LS3.158 *SBGZ Ref: ch. 17; ch. 25 [183]*

于時十方世界。通達無礙。如一佛土。爾時佛告。上行等菩薩大衆。
諸佛神力。如是無量無邊。不可思議。

Thereupon the worlds of the ten directions were realized without hindrance as one Buddha-land. Then the Buddha addressed Eminent Conduct and the other bodhisattvas in the great assembly: *"The mystical powers of the buddhas are like this; countless, infinite, and unthinkable..."*

LS 3.162 *SBGZ Ref: ch. 61 [45]*

能持是経者　則為已見我
亦見多寶佛　及諸分身者

One who is able to keep this Sutra,
Is already meeting me,
And also meeting the Buddha Abundant Treasures,
And those [buddhas] who are [my] offshoots.

Chapter Twenty-Two: *Zoku-rui (The Commission)*

Chapter Twenty-Three: *Yaku-o-bosatsu-honji (The Story of the Bodhisattva Medicine King)*

LS 3.200 *SBGZ Ref: ch. 73 [35]*

如佛為諸法王。此経亦復如是。諸経中王。宿王華。此経能救。
一切衆生者。此経能令。一切衆生。離諸苦悩。此経能大饒益。
一切衆生。充満其願。如清涼池。能満一切。諸渇乏者。如寒者得火。
如裸者得衣。如商人得主。如子得母。如渡得船。如病得医。如暗得燈。
如貧得寶。如民得王。如賈客得海。如炬除暗。此法華経。亦復如是。
能令衆生。離一切苦。一切病痛。能解一切。生死之縛。

As the Buddha is king of all dharmas, so it is also with this Sutra. It is the king of sutras. Star Constellation King Flower! This Sutra can save all living beings. This Sutra can free all living beings from pain and suffering. This Sutra can greatly benefit all living beings and fulfill their desires. Like a clear, cool pool that can satisfy all those who are thirsty; like the cold getting fire; like the naked getting clothing; like [a caravan of] merchants getting a leader; like a child getting its mother; like a crossing getting a ferry; like the infirm getting a doctor; like [those in] darkness getting a light; like the poor getting treasure; like a people getting a king; like traders getting the sea; like a torch dispelling the darkness; so it is also with this Sutra of the Flower of Dharma. It can free living beings from all suffering and all diseases, and can unloose all the bonds of life and death.

LS 3.210 *SBGZ Ref: ch. 17*

汝成就。不可思議功徳。乃能問。釈迦牟尼佛。如此之事。利益無量。一切衆生。

You have accomplished unthinkable virtue, being able to ask Śākyamuni Buddha such things as these, and benefiting all countless living beings.

Chapter Twenty-Four: *Myo-on-bosatsu (The Bodhisattva Wonder Sound)*

LS 3.214 *SBGZ Ref: ch. 17*

得妙幢相三昧。法華三昧。浄徳三昧。宿王戯三昧。無縁三昧。智印三昧。
解一切衆生語言三昧。集一切功徳三昧。清浄三昧。神通遊戯三昧。
慧炬三昧。荘厳王三昧。浄光明三昧。浄藏三昧。不共三昧。
日施三昧。得如是等。百千万億。恒河紗等。諸大三昧。

[Bodhisattva Wonder Sound] had attained samādhi with the form of a wonderful banner, samādhi as the Flower of Dharma, samādhi as pure virtue, samādhi as the sport of the Constellation King, samādhi as the state without involvements, samādhi as the wisdom-seal, samādhi as the state of understanding the words of all living beings, samādhi as the accumulation of all virtues, samādhi as the state of purity, samādhi as the playing of mystical powers, samādhi as the torch of wisdom, samādhi as the king of adornments, samādhi as pure brightness, samādhi as the pure treasury, samādhi as a singular state, and samādhi as the function of the sun. He had attained hundred thousand myriad koṭis of great states of samādhi like these, equal to the sands of the Ganges.

Chapter Twenty-Five: *Kanzeon-bosatsu-fumon (The Universal Gate of the Bodhisattva Regarder of the Sounds of the World)*

LS 3.242 *SBGZ Ref: ch. 33*

善男子。若有無量。百千万億衆生。受諸苦悩。聞是観世音菩薩。
一心称名。観世音菩薩。即時観其音聲。皆説解説。

Good son! If there are countless hundred thousand myriad koṭis of living beings who, suffering from many agonies, hear of this Bodhisattva Regarder of the Sounds of the World and with undivided mind call [the Bodhisattva's] name, the Bodhisattva Regarder of the Sounds of the World will instantly regard their cries, and all will be delivered.

LS 3.252 *SBGZ Ref: ch. 17; allusions in many chapters*

善男子。若有国土衆生。應以佛身。得度者。観世音菩薩。即現佛身。而為説法。應以辟支佛身。得度者。即現辟支佛身。而為説法。應以声聞身。得度者。即現声聞身。而為説法。應以梵王身。得度者。即現梵王身。而為説法。應以帝釈身。得度者。即現帝釈身。而為説法。應以自在天身。得度者。即現自在天身。而為説法。應以大自在天身。得度者。即現大自在天身。而為説法。應以天大将軍身。得度者。即現天大将軍身。而為説法。應以び沙門身。得度者。即現び沙門身。而為説法。應以小王身。得度者。即現小王身。而為説法。應以長者身。得度者。即現長者身。而為説法。應以居士身。得度者。即現居士身。而為説法。應以宰官身。得度者。即現宰官身。而為説法。應以婆羅門身。得度者。即現婆羅門身。而為説法。應以比丘。比丘尼。優婆塞。優婆夷身。得度者。即現比丘。比丘尼。優婆塞。優婆夷身。而為説法。應以長者。居士。宰官。婆羅門婦女身。得度者。即現婦女身。而為説法。應以童男童女身。得度者。即現童男童女身。而為説法。應以天。龍。夜叉。乾闥婆。阿脩羅。迦楼羅。緊那羅。摩 睺 羅伽。人非人等身。得度者。即皆現之。而為説法。應以執金剛神。得度者。即現執金剛神。而為説法。無盡意。是観世音菩薩。成就如是功徳。以種種形。遊諸国土。度脱衆生。是故汝等。應當一心。供養観世音菩薩。是観世音菩薩摩訶薩。於怖畏急難之中。能施無畏。是故此娑婆世界。皆号之為。施無畏者。

Good son! If living beings in any land must be saved through the body of a buddha, the Bodhisattva Regarder of the Sounds of the World manifests at once the body of a buddha and preaches for them the Dharma. To those who must be saved through the body of a pratyekabuddha, [the Bodhisattva] manifests at once the body of a pratyekabuddha and preaches for them the Dharma. To those who must be saved through the body of a śrāvaka, [the Bodhisattva] manifests at once the body of a śrāvaka and preaches for them the Dharma. To those who must be saved through the body of King Brahmā, [the Bodhisattva] manifests at once the body of King Brahmā and preaches for them the Dharma. To those who must be saved through the body of the god-king Śakra, [the Bodhisattva] manifests at once the body of the god-king Śakra and preaches for them the Dharma. To those who must be saved through the body of Īśvara, [the Bodhisattva] manifests at once the body of Īśvara and preaches for them the Dharma. To those who must be saved through the body of Maheśvara, [the Bodhisattva] manifests at once the body of Maheśvara and preaches for them the Dharma. To those who must be saved through the body of a celestial great general, [the Bodhisattva] manifests at once the body of a celestial great general and preaches for them the Dharma. To those who must be saved through the body of Vaiśravaṇa, [the Bodhisattva] manifests at once the body of Vaiśravaṇa and preaches for them the Dharma. To those who must be saved through the body of a minor king, [the Bodhisattva] manifests at once the body of a minor king and preaches for them the Dharma. To those who must be saved through the body of a rich man, [the Bodhisattva] manifests at once the body of a rich man and preaches for them the Dharma. To those who must be saved through the body of a householder, [the Bodhisattva] manifests at once the body of a householder and preaches for them the Dharma. To those who must be saved through the body of a government official, [the Bodhisattva] manifests at once the body of a government official and preaches for them the Dharma. To those who must be saved through the body of a Brāhman, [the Bodhisattva] manifests at once the body of a Brāhman and preaches for them the Dharma. To those who must be saved through the body of a bhikṣu, bhikṣuṇī, upāsaka, or upāsikā, [the Bodhisattva] manifests at once the body of a bhikṣu, bhikṣuṇī, upāsaka, or upāsikā and preaches for them the Dharma. To those who must be saved through the body of the woman of a rich man, householder, official, or Brāhman, [the Bodhisattva] manifests at once the body of a woman and preaches for them the Dharma. To those who must be saved through the body of a boy or a girl, [the Bodhisattva] manifests at once the body of a boy or a girl and preaches for them the Dharma. To those who must be saved through the body of a god, dragon, yakṣa, gandharva, asura, garuḍa, kiṃnara, or mahoraga, a human being or a nonhuman being, [the Bodhisattva], in every case, manifests at once this [body] and preaches for them the Dharma. To those who must be saved through the body of a vajra-holding god, [the Bodhisattva] manifests at once the body of a vajra-holding god and preaches for them the Dharma. Infinite Thought! This Bodhisattva Regarder of the Sounds of the World, accomplishing good effects like these, using all kinds of forms, roams many lands to save living beings. Therefore you all must whole-heartedly serve offerings to Bodhisattva Regarder of the Sounds of the World. This Bodhisattva Regarder of the Sounds of the World, amid fear and distress, is able to give fearlessness. For this reason, in this sahā-world, all call this [Bodhisattva] "Giver of Fearlessness."

LS 3.270 *SBGZ Ref: ch. 1 [20]*

說説是普門品時。衆中八万四千衆生。皆発無等等。阿耨多羅三藐三菩提心。

While the Buddha preached this Universal Gate Chapter, the eighty-four thousand living beings in the assembly all established the will to the unequalled state of equilbrium which is anuttara-samyak-saṃbodhi.

Chapter Twenty-Six:

Darani (*Dhāraṇi*)

LS 3.282-284 *SBGZ Ref: ch. 17*

若不順我呪　悩乱説法者
頭破作七分　如阿梨木枝
如殺父母罪　亦如圧油殃
斗秤欺誑人　調達破僧罪
犯此法師者　當獲如是殃

If anyone fails to heed our spell,
And troubles a preacher of the Dharma,
May their head be split into seven
Like an arjaka sprout.
Their crime is like killing a parent,

Like the sin of pressing oil,
Or cheating people with [false] weights and measures,
Or Devadatta's crime of splitting the Saṃgha.
People who offend such a teacher of the Dharma,
Will acquire similar evil.

Chapter Twenty-Seven: Myo-shogon-o-honji (The Story of the King Resplendent)

LS 3.288-290 *SBGZ Ref: ch. 73 [3]*

是二子。有大神力。福徳智慧。久修菩薩。所行之道。所謂檀波羅密。尸羅波羅密。羼提波羅密。毗梨耶波羅密。禪波羅密。般若波羅密。方便波羅密。慈悲喜捨。乃至三十七品助道法。皆悉明了通達。

These two sons possessed great mystical power, happiness, and wisdom. They had long cultivated the ways practiced by bodhisattvas; that is to say, dāna-pāramitā, śīla-pāramitā, kshānti-pāramitā, vīrya-pāramitā, dhyāna-pāramitā, prajña-pāramitā, and the expedience pāramitā, benevolence, compassion, charity, and the thirty-seven auxiliary bodhi methods—all these they had clearly realized.

LS 3.292-294 *SBGZ Ref: ch. 25 [186]*

於是二子。念其父故。踊在虚空。高七多羅樹。現種種神変。於虚空中。行住坐臥。身上出水。身下出火。身下出水。身上出火。

Thereupon the two sons, because they cared for their father, sprang up into space, to a height of seven tāla trees, and manifested many kinds of mystical transformation, walking, standing, sitting, and lying in space; the upper body emitting water, the lower body emitting fire [or] the lower body emitting water and the upper body emitting fire.

LS 3.302 *SBGZ Ref: ch. 86 [83]*

其王即時。以国付弟。王與婦人二子。并諸眷屬。於佛法中。出家修道。

That king at once gave his kingdom to his younger brother; [then] the king together with his queen, two sons, and many followers, in the Buddha-Dharma, left home to practice the truth.

LS 3.304

此我二子。已作佛事。以下神通変化。轉我邪心。令得安住。於佛法中。得見世尊。此二子者。是我善知識。

These two sons of mine have already done a buddha-deed, with transformations [achieved through] mystical powers, they have changed my wrong mind, enabling me to abide peacefully in the Buddha-Dharma and to meet the World-honored One. These two sons are my friends in virtue.

LS 3.306 *SBGZ Ref: ch. 61 [47]*

大王當知。善知識者。是大因縁。所謂化導。令得見佛。
発阿耨多羅三藐三菩提心。

Remember, great king! A friend of virtue is the great cause which leads us to be able to meet buddha and to establish the will to [the supreme truth of] anuttara-samyak-saṃbodhi.

Chapter Twenty-Eight: *Fugen-bosatsu-kanpotsu* *(Encouragement of the Bodhisattva Universal Virtue)*

LS 3.326 *SBGZ Ref: ch. 17*

若法華経。行閻浮堤。有受持者。応作此念。皆是普賢。威神之力。
若有受持讀誦。正憶念。解其義趣。如説修行。當知是人。行普賢行。

While the Sutra of the Flower of Dharma proceeds on its course through Jambudvīpa, anyone who receives it and retains it should reflect as follows: *"This is all due to the majestic mystical power of Universal Virtue."* If anyone receives and retains it, reads and recites it, rightly remembers it, understands its meaning, and practices as it preaches, we should know that this person is doing the work of Universal Virtue.

LS 3.328-330 *SBGZ Ref: ch. 17*

世尊。我今以神通力故。守護是経。於如来滅後。閻浮堤内。廣令流布。
使不断絶。爾時釈迦牟尼佛讃言。善哉善哉。普賢。汝能護助是経。
令多所衆生。安楽利益。汝已成就。不可思議功徳。深大慈悲。従久遠来。
発阿耨多羅三藐三菩提意。而能作是。神通之願。守護是経。

[The Bodhisattva Universal Virtue said,] *"World-honored One! I now by my mystical power will guard and protect this Sutra. After the death of the Tathāgata, I shall cause it to spread widely throughout Jambudvīpa, and shall never let it cease to exist."* Thereupon Śākyamuni Buddha praised him, saying, *"How excellent, how excellent, Universal Virtue, that you are able to protect and to promote this Sutra, causing peace, joy, and benefit to many living beings. You have already accomplished unthinkable virtue and profound compassion. From the long distant past, you have established the will to [the truth of] anuttara-samyak-saṃbodhi, and have been able to make this vow of mystical power, to guard and to protect this Sutra..."*

LS 3.330 *SBGZ Ref: ch. 61 [37]*

普賢。若有受持。讀誦。正憶念。修習。書寫。是法華経者。
當知是人。則見釈迦牟尼佛。如従佛口。聞此経典。

Universal Virtue! If there is anyone who receives and retains, reads and recites, rightly remembers, practices, and copies this Sutra of the Flower of Dharma, know that this person is meeting Śākyamuni Buddha and hearing this Sutra as if from the Buddha's mouth.

Glossary of Sanskrit Terms

This glossary presents brief dictionary definitions of Sanskrit terms represented in the present volume. Definitions are drawn in general from *A Sanskrit-English Dictionary* by Sir Monier Monier-Williams [MW], (Oxford University Press, 1333 pp.). Also used were *A Sanskrit Dictionary for Students* by A.A. Macdonell [MAC], (Oxford University Press, 382 pp.), *Japanese-English Buddhist Dictionary* [JEBD], (Daito Shuppansha, 456 pp.), and *The Historical Buddha* [HB] by H.W. Schumann (Arkana, 274 pp.).

Chapter references, unless otherwise stated, refer to chapters of Shobogenzo. Arrangement is according to the English alphabet.

Abhidharma ('on Dharma,' prefix for names of Buddhist commentaries)
Represented by 論 (RON), "doctrine, discussion, argument."
[MW] the dogmas of Buddhist philosophy or metaphysics.
abhi: (a prefix to verbs and nouns, expressing) to, towards, into, over, upon.
The literal meaning of *abhidharma* is therefore "that which is directed towards (or additional to) Dharma."
One of the "three baskets," or *tripiṭaka* (q.v.).
Ref: bibliography.

Abhidharma-kośa-śāstra (name of a commentary)
Represented phonetically.
[MW] *kośa*: a cask; a bucket; a box; the interior of a carriage; a store-room; a treasury; a dictionary, lexicon, or vocabulary; a poetical collection, collection of sentences etc.
śāstra: (q.v.): commentary.
Ref: bibliography; ch. 87; ch. 88.

Abhidharma-mahāvibhāṣa-śāstra (name of a commentary)
Represented phonetically.
[MW] *vibhāṣa*: shining brightly, light, luster.
Ref: bibliography; ch. 70; ch. 84; ch. 86.

Abhijña (mystical power, supernatural faculty)
Represented by 神通 (JINZU), "mystical power."
[MW] knowing, skillful, clever; understanding, conversant with; remembrance, recollection; supernatural science or faculty of a Buddha (of which five are enumerated, viz. 1. taking any form at will; 2. hearing to any distance; 3. seeing to any distance; 4. penetrating men's thoughts; 5. knowing their state and antecedents).
Ref: ch. 12 [87]; ch. 25; Lotus Sutra ch. 24.

abhimāna (haughtiness)
Represented by 増上慢 (ZOJOMAN), "lofty arrogance."
[MW] high opinion of one's self, self-conceit, pride, haughtiness.
One of the seven categories of *māna* (arrogance).
Ref: Lotus Sutra ch. 2.

ācārin (practitioner)
Represented phonetically and by 行者 (GYOJA), "practitioner."
[MW] following established practice.
Ref: ch. 12 [64].

ācārya
Represented phonetically.
[MW] 'knowing or teaching the *ācāra* or rules (of good conduct),' a spiritual guide or teacher.
Ref: ch. 21 [206].

acintya (unthinkable)
Represented by 不可思議 (FUKASHIGI), "unthinkable."
[MW] inconceivable, surpassing thought.
Ref: ch. 17; Lotus Sutra ch. 21.

adbhuta-dharma (wonders, marvels)
Represented by 希法 (KIHO), "rare occurrences, marvels" and by 未曾有法 (MI-ZO-U-HO), "unprecedented occurrences."
[MW] 'a system or series of marvels or prodigies.'
One of the 12 divisions of the teachings. See under **anga**.

Ref: ch. 11 [40].

Āgama (name of a group of sutras)
Represented phonetically.
[MW] a traditional doctrine or precept, collection of such doctrines, sacred work; anything handed down and fixed by tradition.
Ref: ch. 12; bibliography.

agaru (aloes)
Represented by 沈香 (JINKO), "aloes."
[MW] the fragrant Aloe wood and tree, Aquilaria Agallocha.
Ref: ch. 12 [78].

ajita (epithet of the Buddha Maitreya)
Represented phonetically.
[MW] not conquered, unsubdued, unsurpassed, invincible, irresistible; name of Viśnu; Śiva; Maitreya or a future Buddha.
Ref: Lotus Sutra ch. 15.

ākāśa (space)
Represented by 虚空 (KOKU), "space."
[MW] a free or open space, vacuity; the ether, sky, or atmosphere.
Ref: ch. 17 [62]; Lotus Sutra ch. 12; ch. 15.

akṣa-sūtra (rosary)
Represented by 数珠 (JUZU), "counting beads," "rosary."
[MW] *akṣa*: a die for gambling; a cube; a seed of which rosaries are made; the Eleocarpus Ganitrus, producing that seed.
sūtra (q.v.): a thread.
Ref: ch. 5.

Akṣobbya (name of a mythical Buddha)
Represented phonetically.
[MW] immovable, imperturbable; name of a Buddha; name of an immense number.
Ref: ch. 46 [90]; Lotus Sutra ch. 7.

Amitābha (name of a mythical Buddha)
Represented phonetically.
[MW] 'of unmeasured splendor,' name of a Dhyāni-buddha.
Ref: ch. 12 [80].

amṛta (nectar)
Represented by 甘露 (KANRO), "sweet dew, nectar."
[MW] immortal, an immortal, a god; a goddess; a spirituous liquor; world of immortality, heaven, eternity; the nectar (conferring immortality, produced at the churning of the ocean), ambrosia.

Ref: ch. 1 [62]; ch. 8 [198].

anāgāmin (the state which is not subject to returning)
Represented phonetically and by 不還果 (FUGEN-KA), "the effect of not returning."
[MW] not coming, not arriving, not future, not subject to returning.
Ref: ch. 2.

Ānanda (name of the Buddha's half-brother and the 2nd patriarch in India)
Represented phonetically and by 慶喜 (KEIKI), "joy."
[MW] happiness, joy, enjoyment.
Ref: ch. 15.

anāsrava (without excess, faultless,)
Represented by 無漏 (MURO), "without leakage."
[MW] *a* (before a vowel *an*): a prefix corresponding to the English *in* or *un*, and having a negative or contrary sense.
āsrava (q.v.): excess, distress.
Ref. ch. 21 [192].

anitya (inconstant)
Represented by 無常 (MUJO), "inconstant."
[MW] not everlasting, transient, occasional, incidental; irregular, unusual; unstable, uncertain.
Ref: ch. 17 [39]; ch. 22.

antarvāsa (inner robe)
Represented phonetically and by 下衣 (GE-E), "under robe," by 内衣 (NAI-E), "inner robe," by 五条衣 (GOJO-E), "5-stripe robe," by 小衣 (SHO-E), "small robe," and by 行道作務衣 (GYODO-SAMU-E), "practice and work robe."
[MW] an inner or under garment.
Ref: ch. 12 [95].

Anāthapiṇḍada or **Anāthapiṇḍika** (a name of Sudatta [q.v.])
[MW] 'giver of cakes or food to the poor.'
Ref: Fukan-zazengi.

Anavatapta (name of a dragon-king and of a lake)
Represented phonetically and by 無熱池 (MUNETSU-CHI), "Lake of No Heat."
[MW] name of a serpent king; of a lake (=Rāvaṇa-hrada).
Ref: ch. 12 [71].

anga (division)
Represented by 分[教] (BUN[KYO]), "divisions [of the teaching]."

[MW] a limb of the body; a subordinate division or department.
The 12 divisions of the teaching are 1) *sūtra*, 2) *geya*, 3) *vyākaraṇa*, 4) *gāthā*, 5) *udāna*, 6) *nidāna*, 7) *avadāna*, 8) *itivṛttaka*, 9) *jātaka*, 10 *vaipulya*, 11) *adbhuta-dharma*, 12) *upadeśa* (q.v.).
Ref: ch. 11 [40]; Lotus Sutra ch. 2.

añjali (salutation with joined hands)
Represented by 合掌 (GASSHO), "joining together of the palms."
[MW] the open hands placed side by side and slightly hollowed (as if by a beggar to receive food; hence when raised to the forehead, a mark of supplication), reverence, salutation.
Ref: ch. 17 [62]; Lotus Sutra ch. 3.

antarā-bhava (the intermediate stage of existence, middle existence)
Represented by 中有 (CHU-U), "middle existence."
[MW] *antarā*: in the middle, inside, within, between; on the way.
bhava: coming into existence; being, state of being, existence, life.
antarā-bhava-sattva: the soul in its middle existence between death and regeneration.
Ref: ch. 12 [74].

anuttara-samyak-saṃbodhi (the supreme right and balanced state of complete truth)
Represented phonetically, and by 無上等正覚 (MUJO-SHOTO-KAKU), "supreme right and balanced state of truth" or by 無上等正覚 (MUJO-TOSHO-KAKU), "supreme balanced and right state of truth."
[MW] *anuttara*: chief, principal, best, excellent. [Supreme.]
samyak: in compounds for *samyañc*.
samyañc: going along with or together, turned together or in one direction, combined, united; turned towards each other, facing one another; correct, accurate, proper, true, right; uniform, same, identical. [Right and balanced.]
sam: a prefix expressing conjunction, union, thoroughness, intensity, completeness. [Complete.]
bodhi: perfect knowledge or wisdom (by which a man becomes a Buddha); the illuminated or enlightened intellect. [State of truth.]
Note: In Shobogenzo, *bodhi* is not intellectual knowledge but a state of body and mind.
Ref: ch. 1; ch. 2; Lotus Sutra ch. 1.

araṇya (forest)
Represented phonetically.
[MW] a foreign or distant land; a wilderness, desert, forest.
Ref: ch. 12 [115].

arhat
Represented phonetically and by 四果 (SHIKA), "the fourth effect."
[MW] able, allowed to; worthy, venerable, respectable; praised, celebrated; the highest rank in the Buddhist hierarchy.
Ref: ch. 1 [62]; ch. 2; Lotus Sutra ch. 1.

arjaka (name of a plant)
Represented phonetically.
[MW] the plant Ocimum Gratissimum.
LSW notes: "It is said that if one touches an arjaka flower its petals open and fall into seven pieces. Kern identifies the plant as Symplocos racemosa, while Monier-Williams dictionary has Ocinum [sic.] gratissimum."
Ref: Lotus Sutra ch. 26.

aśaikṣa (those beyond study)
Represented by 無学 (MUGAKU), "no study."
[MW] 'no longer a pupil,' an Arhat.
Ref: Lotus Sutra ch. 9.

asamasama (the unequalled state of equilibrium)
Represented by 無等等 (MUTOTO), "equality without equal."
[MW] unequalled
Ref: ch. 1 [20]; Lotus Sutra ch. 25.

asaṃjñi-sattvāḥ (Thoughtless Heaven)
Represented by 無想天 (MUSOTEN), "Thoughtless Heaven."
[MW] *asaṃjña*: senseless; not having full consciousness.
Ref: ch. 14 [195].

asaṃkheya (innumerable)
Represented phonetically.
[MW] innumerable, exceedingly numerous.
Ref: ch. 12 [80]; Lotus Sutra ch. 16.

asaṃskṛta (unadorned, without elaboration)
Represented by 無作 (MUSA), "not being produced, not becoming," or by 無為 (MUI), "without artificiality, natural."
[MW] not prepared, not consecrated; unadorned; unpolished, rude (as speech).
Ref: ch. 1 [11]; ch. 12 [64].

Aśoka (name of a great Indian emperor who ruled in the 3rd century B.C.)
Represented phonetically.
[MW] not causing sorrow, not feeling sorrow.
Ref: ch. 15; ch. 45 [73]; bibliography.

āsrava (the superfluous, excess)
Represented by 漏 (RO), "leakage."
[MW] the foam on boiling rice; a door opening into water and allowing the stream to descend through it; (with Jainas) the action of the senses which impels the soul towards external objects; distress, affliction, pain.
Ref: Lotus Sutra ch. 1; ch. 10.

asura (demons)
Represented phonetically and by 非天 (HITEN), "anti-gods."
[MW] an evil spirit, demon, ghost, opponent of the gods.
Ref: ch. 12 [80]; Lotus Sutra ch. 10.

Aśvaghosa (name of a Buddhist patriarch)
Represented by 馬鳴 (MEMYO), "Horse Whinny."
[MW] *aśva*: a horse, stallion.
ghosa: any cry or sound, roar of animals.
Ref: ch. 15.

avadāna (parable)
Represented by 比喩 (HIYU), "metaphor, parable."
[MW] a great or glorious act, achievement (object of a legend, Buddhist literature).
One of the 12 divisions of the teachings. See under **anga**.
Ref: ch. 11 [40]; Lotus Sutra ch. 3.

avadāta-vāsana (clothed in white; lay person)
Represented by 白衣 (BYAKU-E), "white-robe."
[MW] *avadāta*: cleansed, clean, clear; pure, blameless, excellent; of white splendor; dazzling white; white color.
vāsana: covering, clothing, garment, dress.
Ref: ch. 12 [107].

Avalokiteśvara (Regarder of the Sounds of the World)
Represented by 観音 (KANNON), "Regarder of Sounds" and by 観自在 (KAN-JIZAI), "Free in Reflection."
[MW] name of a Bodhisattva worshipped by the northern Buddhists.
avalokita: seen, viewed, observed.
Ref: ch. 2; ch. 33; Lotus Sutra ch. 25.

Avataṇsaka (name of a sutra)
Represented by 華厳 (KEGON), "Flower-Solemnity."
[MW] *avataṇsa*: a garland.
Ref: ch. 1 [32]; ch. 7 [141]; bibliography.

Avīci (name of a particular hell)
Represented phonetically and by 無間地獄 (MUGEN-JIGOKU), "incessant hell."
[MW] waveless; a particular hell.
Ref: ch. 14 [195].

avidyā (ignorance)
Represented by 無明 (MUMYO), "ignorance, darkness."
[MW] unlearned, unwise; ignorance, illusion.
Ref: ch. 2; Lotus Sutra ch. 7.

avyākṛta (indifferent, undifferentiated)
Represented by 無記 (MUKI), "without writing," "blank."
[MW] undeveloped, unexpounded; elementary substance from which all things were created.
Ref: ch. 10.

āyatana (seat [of sense perception])
Represented by 処 (SHO), "place" or 入 (NYU), "entry."
[MW] resting-place, support, seat, place, home, house, abode; (with Buddhists) the five senses and Manas (considered as the inner seats or Āyatanas) and the qualities perceived by the above (the outer Āyatanas).
Ref: ch. 2.

āyuṣmat (venerable monk)
Represented by 具寿 (GU-JU), "possessing longevity" and by 長老 (CHORO), "experienced-old" or "veteran senior."
[MW] possessed of vital power, healthy, long-lived; alive, living; old, aged; 'life-possessing,' often applied as a kind of honorific title (especially to royal personages and Buddhist monks).
Ref: ch. 1 [52]; ch. 2.

bhadanta (Virtuous One)
Represented by 大徳 (DAITOKU), "great virtue."
[MW] term of respect applied to a Buddhist, a Buddhist mendicant.
Ref: ch. 2.

Bhadra-kalpa (the Good Kalpa, the Virtuous Kalpa)
Represented by 賢劫 (KENGO), "Kalpa of the Wise," "Kalpa of the Sages."
[MW] 'the good or beautiful Kalpa,' name of

the present age.
bhadra: blessed, auspicious, fortunate, prosperous, happy; good, gracious, friendly, kind; excellent, fair, beautiful, lovely, pleasant, dear.
kalpa: aeon (q.v.)
Ref: Lotus Sutra ch. 8.

Bhadra-pāla ('Good Guardian,' name of a bodhisattva)
Represented phonetically.
[MW] name of a Bodhi-sattva.
bhadra: good.
pāla: a guard, protector, keeper; an oblong pond (as 'receptacle' of water?).
Ref: ch. 12 [49].

bhagavat
Represented phonetically and by 世尊 (SESON), "World-honored One."
[MW] glorious, illustrious, divine, adorable, venerable; holy (applied to gods, demigods, and saints as a term of address; with Buddhists often prefixed to the titles of their sacred writings); 'the divine or adorable one,' name of a Buddha or a Bodhisattva.
Ref: ch. 2; Lotus Sutra ch. 2.

bhikṣu (monk)
Represented phonetically.
[MW] a beggar, mendicant, religious mendicant; a Buddhist mendicant or monk.
Ref: Lotus Sutra ch. 1.

bhikṣuṇī (nun)
Represented phonetically.
[MW] a Buddhist female mendicant or nun.
Ref: Lotus Sutra ch. 2.

Bhīsma-garjita-ghoṣa-svara-rāja (name of a legendary buddha)
Represented by 威音王 (I-ON-O), "King of Majestic Voice" and by 空王 (KU-O), "King of Emptiness."
[MW] name of a number of Buddhas.
Ref: ch. 14 [176]; Lotus Sutra ch. 20.

bodhi (truth, state of truth)
Represented phonetically and by 道 (DO), "way." See **anuttara-samyak-saṃbodhi**.

bodhicitta (the bodhi-mind, the will to the truth)
Represented by 菩提心 (BODAISHIN), "bodhi-mind" and by 道心 (DOSHIN), "will to the truth."
[MW] *citta* (q.v.): intelligence, mind
Ref: ch. 5 [111]; ch. 69; ch. 70; Lotus Sutra ch. 12.

bodhi-maṇḍa (place of practicing the truth, place of practice, seat of truth)
Represented by 道場 (DOJO), "truth-place," "Way-place," "exercise hall," "gymnasium."
[MW] seat of wisdom (name of the seats which were said to have risen out of the earth under 4 successive trees where Gautama Buddha attained to perfect wisdom).
maṇḍa: the scum of boiled rice (or any grain); ornament, decoration.
Ref: ch. 1 [20]; Lotus Sutra ch. 2.

bodhisattva (Buddhist practitioner)
Represented phonetically.
[MW] 'one whose essence is perfect knowledge [*bodhi*—q.v.].'
sattva: being, existence, entity, reality; true essence, nature, disposition of mind, character.
Ref: Lotus Sutra.

brāhma (moral, pure)
Represented phonetically.
[MW] relating to Brahma, holy, sacred, divine; relating to sacred knowledge.
Ref: ch. 1 [51]; Lotus Sutra ch. 1.

Brahmā (name of the creator deity in the Hindū triad)
Represented phonetically.
[MW] the one impersonal universal Spirit manifested as a personal Creator and as the first of the triad of personal gods.
Ref: ch. 10 [19]; Lotus Sutra ch. 11; ch. 25.

brahma-carya (pure conduct)
Represented by 梵行 (BONGYO), "brahma-conduct."
[MW] study of the Veda, the state of an unmarried religious student, a state of continence and chastity; the unmarried state, continence, chastity; leading the life of an unmarried religious student, practicing chastity.
brahma: in compounds for brahman (the Veda, a sacred text, religious or spiritual knowledge; holy life).
carya: to be practiced or performed; driving (in a carriage); walking or roaming about; proceeding, behavior, conduct; a religious mendicant's life; practicing, peforming.
Ref: ch. 1 [51]; Lotus Sutra ch. 1.

brāhmaṇa (Brāhman, Brahmin)
Represented phonetically.
[MW] one who has divine knowledge, a

Brāhman (generally a priest, but often in the present day a layman although the name is strictly applicable only to one who knows and repeats the Veda).
Ref: ch. 1 [37]; Lotus Sutra ch. 25.

buddha
Represented by 仏 (BUTSU, *hotoke*), "buddha."
[MW] awakened, awake; conscious, intelligent, clever, wise; learnt, known, understood; a wise or learned man, sage; the principal Buddha of the present age (born at Kapila-vastu about the year 500 B.C., his father, Śūddhodana of the Śākya tribe or family, being the Rāja of that district, and his mother, Māyā-devī, being the daughter of Rāja Su-prabuddha; hence he belonged to the Kṣatriya caste and his original name Śākya-muni or Śākya-siṇha was really his family name, while that of Gautama was taken from the race to which his family belonged).
Note: In Shobogenzo, buddha means not only awakened, and not only Gautama Buddha and other historical buddhas, but also the concrete state in Zazen which is the same as the state of Gautama Buddha.

buddha-śāsana (the Buddha's teaching)
Represented by 仏教 (BUKKYO), "Buddha-teaching."
[MW] *śāsana*: punishing; teaching, instructing, an instructor; government, dominion, rule over; an order, command, edict; a writing; any written book or work of authority, scripture; teaching, instruction, discipline, doctrine.
Ref: ch. 1 [68]; ch. 24.

caitya (tomb)
Represented by 塔 (TO), "tower."
[MW] relating to a funeral pile or mound; a funeral monument or Stūpa or pyramidal column containing the ashes of deceased persons.
Ref: ch. 87 [160]; Lotus Sutra ch. 10.

cakra (wheel)
Represented by 輪 (RIN), "wheel."
[MW] the wheel (of a carriage, of the Sun's chariot, of Time); a discus or sharp circular missile weapon; a number of villages, province, district; the wheel of a monarch's chariot rolling over his dominions, sovereignty, realm.

cakravarti-rāja (wheel-rolling king)
Represented by 転輪王 (TEN-RIN-O), "wheel-rolling king."
[MW] *cakravartin*: rolling everywhere without obstruction; a ruler the wheels of whose chariot roll everywhere without obstruction; emperor; sovereign of the world, ruler of a Cakra (or country described as extending from sea to sea).
rāja: king.
Ref: ch. 10 [19]; Lotus Sutra ch. 7.

cakṣus (seeing, eyes)
Represented by 眼 (GEN), "eyes."
[MW] seeing; the act of seeing; faculty of seeing, sight; the eye.
Ref: ch. 2.

caṇḍāla (outcast)
Represented phonetically.
[MW] an outcast, man of the lowest and most despised of the mixed tribes (born from a Śūdra father and a Brāhman mother).
Ref: ch. 8; ch. 84 [26].

candana (sandal[wood])
Represented phonetically.
[MW] sandal (Sirium myrtifolium, either the tree, wood, or the unctuous preparation of the wood held in high estimation as perfumes; hence a term for anything which is the most excellent of its kind).
Ref: ch. 12 [78].

caṅkrama (walking about)
Represented by 経行 (KINHIN), "walking about."
[MW] going about, a walk; a place for walking about.
Ref: ch. 30 [119].

catvāro yonayaḥ (four kinds of birth)
Represented by 四生 (SHISHO), "four [kinds of] birth."
[MW] *catur*: four.
yoni: the womb; place of birth, source, origin, spring, fountain.
The four are *jarāyu-ja* (birth from womb); *aṇḍa-ja* (birth from egg); *saṃsveda-ja* (birth from moisture); and *upapāduka* (metamorphosis).
Ref: ch. 9 [222].

cintāmaṇi (name of a fabulous gem)
Represented by 如意珠 (NYO-I-JU), "the gem of doing as one pleases."
[MW] 'thought gem,' a fabulous gem

supposed to yield its possessor all desires.
Ref: ch. 14 [189].

citta (intelligence)
Represented phonetically and by 心識 (SHINSHIKI) "mental/intellectual consciousness" or by 慮知心 (RYO-CHI-SHIN)," considering and recognizing mind."
[MW] attending, observing; thinking, reflecting, imagining, thought; intention, aim, wish; memory; intelligence, reason.
One of the 3 kinds of mind, the others being *hṛdaya* and *vṛiddha* (q.v.).
Ref: ch. 1 [27]; ch. 70.

citta-manas-vijñana (mind, will, consciousness)
Represented by 心意識 (SHIN-I-SHIKI) "mind, will, consciousness."
[MW] *citta* (q.v.): thought; intelligence.
manas (q.v.): mind, will.
vijñana (q.v.): consciousness.
[JEBD] In Hīnayāna, all three terms are regarded as synonyms for mind.
Ref: Fukan-zazengi.

dāna (giving)
Represented phonetically and by 布施 (FUSE), "alms, charity, giving."
[MW] the act of giving; giving in marriage; giving up; communicating, imparting, teaching; paying back, restoring; adding, addition; donation, gift.
One of the 6 *pāramitās* (q.v.).
Ref: ch. 2; ch. 45; Lotus Sutra ch. 27.

dānapati (donor)
Represented phonetically and by 施主 (SESHU), "alms-lord."
[MW] 'liberality-lord,' munificent man.
dāna: giving.
pati: a master, owner, possessor, lord, ruler, sovereign.
Ref: ch. 5 [118].

dāśa-diś (the ten directions)
Represented by 十方 (JUPPO), "ten directions."
[MW] *diś*: quarter or region pointed at, direction, cardinal point.
Ref: ch. 60; Lotus Sutra ch. 2.

deva (gods)
Represented by 天 (TEN), "gods."
[MW] heavenly, divine; a deity, god.
Ref: Lotus Sutra ch. 1.

dhāraṇī (incantation, enchantment)
Represented phonetically and by 咒 (JU), "spell, incantation."
[MW] a mystical verse or charm used as a kind of prayer to assuage pain etc.
Note: in Shobogenzo, *dhāraṇī* is equated with "personal salutations," i.e., prostrations, with which a practitioner asks a master for the Buddhist teaching.
Ref: ch. 2; ch. 55; Lotus Sutra ch. 26.

dharma (Dharma, dharmas, Reality, method, practice, real dharmas, things and phenomena)
Represented by 法 (HO), "law, method."
[MW] that which is established or firm, steadfast decree, statute, ordinance, law; usage, practice, customary observance or prescribed conduct, duty; right, justice (often as a synonym of punishment); virtue, morality, religion, religious merit, good works; the law or doctrine of Buddhism; nature, character, peculiar condition or essential quality, property, mark, peculiarity.

dharma-cakra (the Dharma-wheel)
Represented by 法輪 (HORIN), "Dharma-wheel."
[MW] the wheel or range of the law; a particular mythical weapon; 'having or turning the wheel of the law,' a Buddha.
Ref: ch. 3 [87]; ch. 74; Lotus Sutra ch. 14.

Dharmagupta (name of a Buddhist school)
Represented by 法蔵部 (HOZO-BU), "Dharma-Storage School."
[MW] *gupta*: protected, guarded, preserved; hidden, concealed, kept secret.
One of the twenty Hīnayāna schools.
Ref: bibliography.

dharma-kāya (Dharma-body)
Represented by 法身 (HOSSHIN), "Dharma-body."
[MW] 'law-body,' name of one of the 3 bodies of a Buddha.
Ref. ch. 10 [11].

dhātu (elements)
Represented by 大 (DAI), "elements" or by 界 (KAI) "spheres."
[MW] layer, stratum; constituent part, ingredient; element, primitive matter (usually reckoned as 5, viz. *kha* or *ākāśa* [space], *anila* [wind], *tejas* [fire], *jala* [water], *bhū* [earth], to which

Buddhists add *vijñāna* [consciousness]); a constituent element or essential ingredient of the body (distinct from the 5 mentioned above...with the southern Buddhists, *dhātu* means either the 6 elements; or the 18 elementary spheres [*dhātu-loka*—q.v.]).
Ref: ch. 2.

dhātu-loka (the [18] elementary spheres)
Represented by 十八界 (JU-HACHI-KAI), "eighteen spheres."
[MW] *dhātu*: elements.
loka: world, sphere [q.v.].
The eighteen elementary spheres are the six *indriyas* (sense-organs): 1. *cakṣur-indriya* (organ of sight, eyes), 2. *śrotrendriya* (organ of hearing, ears), 3. *ghrāṇendriya* (organ of smell, nose), 4. *jihvendriya* (the tongue as a sense organ), 5. *kāyendriya* (the body as sense organ, sense of touch), 6. *manendriya* (mind as a sense center, intelligence); the six *viṣayas* (objects): 1. *rūpa* (forms or colours), 2. *śabda* (sounds), 3. *gandha* (smells), 4. *rasa* (tastes), 5. *sparśa* (sensations), 6. *dharma* (properties); and the six *vijñānas* (consciousnesses): 1. *cakṣur-vijñāna* (visual consciousness), 2. *śrotra-vijñāna* (auditory consciousness), 3. *ghrāṇa-vijñāna* (olfactory consciousness), 4. *jihvā-vijñāna* (taste consciousness), 5. *kāya-vijñāna* (body-consciousness), 6. *mano-vijñāna* (mind-consciousness).
Ref: ch. 2.

dhūta (hard practice, austerity)
Represented phonetically.
[MW] *dhūta*: morality.
dhūta-guṇa: ascetic practice or precept.
Ref: ch. 4; ch. 30; Lotus Sutra ch. 15.

dhyāna (Zen, concentration, meditation)
Represented phonetically by 禅 (ZEN) or 禅那 (ZEN-NA); represented also by 静慮 (JO-RYO), "quiet meditation."
[MW] meditation, thought, reflection, (esp.) profound and abstract religious meditation.
One of the 6 *pāramitās* (q.v.).
Ref: ch. 2 [71]; Lotus Sutra ch. 7; ch. 27.

Dhyāni-Buddha
[MW] a spiritual (not material) Buddha or Bodhi-sattva.

Dignāga (name of a logician)
[JEBD] A native of southern India who lived from the end of the fifth century to the middle of the sixth, and belonged to the school of Vasubandhu. He created a new school of logic using deductive reasoning.

Dīpaṃakara Buddha (name of a Buddha)
Represented by 燃燈仏 (NENTO-BUTSU), "Burning Lamp Buddha."
[MW] 'light-causer,' name of a mythical Buddha.
Ref: ch. 9.

duḥka (suffering)
Represented by 苦 (KU), "suffering."
[MW] uneasy, uncomfortable, unpleasant, difficult; uneasiness, pain, sorrow, trouble, difficulty.
The first of the 4 noble truths.
Ref: ch. 2; Lotus Sutra ch. 7.

duṣkṛta (a class of sins)
Represented phonetically.
[MW] wrongly or wickedly done, badly arranged or organized or applied; a particular class of sins; a wicked deed, wickedness.
Ref: ch. 7 [158].

dvādaśanga-pratītya-samutpāda (twelvefold chain of causation)
Represented by 十二因縁 (JUNI-INNEN) "twelvefold [chain of] causation," or by 十二輪転 (JUNI-RINDEN), "twelvefold cycle."
See *pratītya-samutpāda*.
Ref: ch. 1 [32]; Lotus Sutra ch. 7.

dvādaśayatanāni (twelve seats)
Represented by 十二入り (JUNI-NYU), "twelve entries," or 十二処 (JUNI-SHO) "twelve places."
See under *āyatana*.
Ref: ch. 2.

Ekottarāgama (name of a sutra)
Represented by 増一阿含経 (ZO-ICHI-AGON-KYO), "Āgama Sutras Increased by One."
[MW] name of the fourth Āgama or sacred book of the Buddhists.
ekottara: greater or more by one, increasing by one.
āgama [q.v.]: a traditional doctrine or precept.
Ref: ch. 45; ch. 88; bibliography.

gandha (smell)
Represented by 香 (KO), "fragrance, smell."
[MW] smell, odor; a fragrant substance, fragrance, scent, perfume; the mere

smell of anything, small quantity.
Ref: ch. 2.

Gandhāra (place name)
Represented phonetically.
[JEBD] an ancient country in North India, located north of Punjab and northeast of Kashmir. The capital was Puruṣapura, the present Peshawar.
Ref. ch. 15.

gandharva (fragrance-devouring celestial musicians)
Represented phonetically.
[MW] *gandha*: smell, odor; a fragrant substance, fragrance, scent, perfume. *gandharva*: in epic poetry the Gandharvas are the celestial musicians or heavenly singers who form the orchestra at the banquets of the gods; they follow after women and are desirous of intercourse with them; they are also feared as evil beings.
Ref: Lotus Sutra ch. 10.

garuḍa (king of birds, dragon-devouring bird)
Represented phonetically and by 金羽鳥王 (KIN-SHI-CHO-O), "golden-winged king of birds."
[MW] name of a mythical bird (chief of the feathered race, enemy of the serpent-race).
Ref: ch. 12 [107]; Lotus Sutra ch. 10.

gāthā (poem, independent verse)
Represented phonetically and by 偈 (GE), "verse" or by 諷誦 (FUJU), poetic eulogy."
[MW] a song; a verse, stanza; the metrical part of a Sūtra.
One of the 12 divisions of the teachings. See under **anga**.
Ref: ch. 11 [40]; ch. 24; Lotus Sutra ch. 10.

geya (verse, summarizing verse)
Represented by 応頌 (OJU), "adaptational eulogy," or "additional eulogy."
[MW] being sung or praised [in song].
One of the 12 divisions of the teachings. See under **anga**.
Ref: ch. 11 [40]; ch. 24.

ghrāṇa (nose, smelling)
Represented by 鼻 (BI), "nose."
[MW] smelling, perception of odor; smell, odor; the nose.
Ref: ch. 2.

Gṛdhrakūṭa (Vulture Peak)
Represented phonetically and by 鷲山 (JUSEN), "Vulture Peak," 霊山 (RYOZEN), "sacred mountain," or 霊鷲山 (RYOJUSEN), "sacred Vulture Peak."
[MW] 'vulture-peak,' name of a mountain near Rājāgṛha.
Ref: ch. 17 [54]; Lotus Sutra ch. 1.

gṛhaparti (householder)
Represented by 居士 (KOJI), "lay gentleman."
[MW] the master of a house, householder; householder of peculiar merit.
Ref: ch. 8 [187]; Lotus Sutra ch. 25.

guṇa (virtue, merit)
Represented by 功徳 (KUDOKU).
[MW] a quality, peculiarity, attribute or property; good quality, virtue, merit, excellence.
Ref: ch. 12 [54]; Lotus Sutra ch. 17; ch. 18.

hasta (cubit)
Represented by 肘 (CHU), "elbow."
[MW] the fore-arm (a measure of length from the elbow to the tip of the middle finger = 24 *Āngulas* or about 18 inches).
Ref: ch. 12 [95].

hetu-pratyaya (causes and conditions)
Represented phonetically and by 因縁 (INNEN) "causes and conditions."
[MW] *hetu*: 'impulse,' motive, cause, cause of, reason for.
pratyaya (q.v.): a co-operating cause.
Ref: ch. 1 [32]; Lotus Sutra ch. 2.

Himālaya (the Himalayas)
Represented by 雪山 (SETSUZAN), "snowy mountains."
[MW] 'abode of snow,' the Himalaya range of mountains.
Ref. ch.12; ch. 69.

Hīnayāna (small vehicle)
Represented by 小乗 (SHOJO), "small vehicle."
[MW] 'simpler or lesser vehicle,' name of the earliest system of Buddhist doctrine (opposed to *Mahāyāna*) [q.v.].
Ref: ch. 13 [155].

hṛidaya (heart)
Represented by 心 (SHIN) "heart," and by 草木心 (SOMOKU-SHIN), "the mind of grass and trees."
[MW] the heart, soul, mind; the heart or interior of the body; the heart or center or core or essence or best or dearest or most secret part of anything.
One of the three kinds of mind, the others being *citta* and *vṛiddha* (q.v.).

Ref: ch. 2; ch. 70.

indriya (sense organ)
Represented by 根 (KON), "root."
[MW] fit for or belonging to or agreeable to Indra; power, force, the quality which belongs especially to the mighty Indra; exhibition of power, powerful act; bodily power, power of the senses; faculty of sense, sense, organ of sense; the number five as symbolical of the five senses.
Ref: ch. 2.

itīvṛtaka (stories of past occurrences)
Represented by 本事 (HONJI), "past occurrences."
[MW] *iti*: in this manner, thus (in its original signification, *iti* refers to something that has been said or thought).
vṛt: take place, occur.
One of the 12 divisions of the teachings. See under **anga**.
Ref: ch. 11 [40].

Īśvara ('almighty,' a name of **Śiva**)
Represented by 自在天 (JIZAITEN), "God of Free Will."
[MW] able to do, capable of; master, lord, prince, king, mistress, queen; God; the Supreme Being; the supreme soul (ātman); Śiva.
Ref: ch. 10 [19]; Lotus Sutra ch. 25.

Jambudvīpa (the southern continent)
Represented phonetically.
[MW] the central one of the 7 continents surrounding the mountain Meru (India; named so either from the Jambu trees abounding in it, or from an enormous Jambu tree on Mount Meru visible like a standard to the whole continent).
Jambu: the rose apple tree.
dvīpa: an island, peninsula, sandbank; a division of the terrestrial world (either 7 or 4 or 13 or 18; they are situated around the mountain Meru, and separated from each other by distinct concentric circumambient oceans). *Ref: Lotus Sutra ch. 20.*

jantu (living beings)
Represented by 衆生 (SHUJO), "living beings," and by 群生 (GUNSHO), "miscellaneous beings."
[MW] child, offspring, creature, living being.
Ref: Lotus Sutra ch. 2.

jātaka (past lives)
Represented by 本生 (HONSHO), "past lives."
[MW] engendered by, born under; the story of a former birth of Gautama Buddha.
One of the 12 divisions of the teachings. See under **anga**.
Ref: ch. 11 [40]; bibliography.

jāti-maraṇa (birth and death)
Represented by 生死 (SHOJI), "birth and death," "life and death," "living-and-dying."
[MW] *jāti*: birth, production; re-birth; the form of existence (as man, animal, etcetera).
maraṇa: the act of dying.
Ref: ch. 19 [95]; ch. 92; Lotus Sutra ch. 16.

Jetavana ('Jetṛi's Park,' name of a grove near Śrāvasti)
Represented phonetically.
[MW] *Jeta*: in compounds for 'Jetṛi' ('Victorious'), the name of a son of King Prasenajit of Kośala.
vana: wood, grove.
Ref: Fukan-zazengi.

jihvā (the tongue)
Represented by 舌 (ZETSU), "tongue."
[MW] the tongue.
Ref: ch. 2.

jñāna (knowing)
Represented by 智 (CHI), "wisdom."
[MW] knowing, becoming acquainted with, knowledge, (especially) the higher knowledge (derived from meditation on the one Universal Spirit).
Ref. ch. 21 [192].

kalpa (aeon)
Represented phonetically.
[MW] a fabulous period of time (at the end of a Kalpa the world is annihilated).
Ref: Lotus Sutra ch. 1.

kalyāna-mitra (good friend, good counsellor)
Represented by 善知識 (ZENCHISHIKI), "good acquaintance."
[MW] a friend of virtue; a well-wishing friend; a good counselor.
kalyāna: beautiful, agreeable; illustrious, noble, generous; excellent, virtuous, good.
mitra: friend, companion, associate.
Ref: ch. 21 [183]; Lotus Sutra ch. 12; ch. 18; ch. 27.

kāṇa (one-eyed)
Represented phonetically.
[MW] one-eyed, monoculous.
Ref. ch. 15.

Kaniṣka (name of a king)
Represented phonetically.
[JEBD] A ruler of Northern India and Central Asia. He is said to have been the third important king of the Kuśāṇa dynasty, who lived either in the latter half of the first century or the first half of the second century. He established a country called Gandhāra. Converted by Master Aśvaghosa, he became a great patron of Buddhism.
Ref. ch. 15.

Kapilavastu (name of a city and country)
[JEBD] The capital of the country of the same name. The Buddha was born at Lumbinī on the outskirts of the city. His father, Śuddhodana, was the king of the country.
Ref: ch. 15.

karman (action, form of behavior)
Represented by 業 (GO),
[MW] act, action, performance, business.
Ref: ch. 1 [20]; ch. 84.

karuṇa (compassion)
Represented by 悲 (HI), "sadness, compassion."
[MW] mournful, miserable, lamenting; compassionate.
Ref: ch. 12 [64]; Lotus Sutra ch. 12.

Karuṇa-puṇḍarika-sūtra (The Sutra of the Flower of Compassion)
Represented by 悲華教 (HIGE-KYO), "Flower of Compassion Sutra."
[MW] *karuṇa*: mournful, miserable, lamenting; compassionate.
puṇḍarika: a lotus-flower (especially a white lotus; expressive of beauty).
Ref: ch. 12 [80]; bibliography.

kaṣāya (robe)
Represented phonetically and by 壊色 (EJIKI), "broken color."
[MW] red, dull red, yellowish red (as the garment of a Buddhist Bhikṣu); a yellowish red color; a dull or yellowish red garment or robe.
Ref: ch. 12 [107].

Kauśika
Represented phonetically.
[MW] relating to Kuśika [the father of Viśvāmitra]; name of Indra (as originally perhaps belonging to the Kuśikas [descendants of Kuśika] or friendly to them).
Ref: ch. 2.

kāya (body)
Represented by 身 (SHIN), "body."
[MW] the body; the trunk of a tree; the body of a lute (the whole except the wires).
Ref: ch. 2.

kiṃnara (half horse, half man)
Represented phonetically.
[MW] 'what sort of man?', a mythical being with a human figure and the head of a horse (or with a horse's body and the head of a man; in later times reckoned among the Gandharvas or celestial choristers, and celebrated as musicians).
Ref: Lotus Sutra ch. 10.

kleśa (affliction, trouble)
Represented by 煩悩 (BONNO), "affliction, trouble, hindrance."
[MW] pain, affliction, distress, pain from disease, anguish; wrath, anger; worldly occupation, care, trouble.
Ref: ch. 12 [54]; Lotus Sutra ch. 1.

Kośala (place name)
[HB] Name of an ancient Indian kingdom situated to the north of the river Ganges and containing the cities of Śrāvasti and Vārāṇasī (present-day Benares). One of the two main kingdoms (together with Magadha [q.v.]) determining the political scene in the areas covered by the Buddha in his travels.

koṭi (tens of millions)
Represented by 億 (OKU), "hundred millions."
[MW] the curved end of a bow or of claws, end or top of anything, edge or point; the highest number in the older system of numbers (viz. a Krore or ten millions).
Ref: Lotus Sutra ch. 2.

krośa (a measure of distance)
Represented phonetically.
[MW] a cry, yell, shriek, shout; 'the range of the voice in calling or hallooing,' a measure of distance (= 1/4 Yojana; according to others = 8000 Hastas).

kṣama (confession)
Represented by 懺悔 (SANGE), "*kṣama*-repentance."
[MW] patience, forbearance, indulgence.
Ref: ch. 9 [236].

kśāṇa (moment, instant, instantaneous)
Represented phonetically.
[MW] any instantaneous point of time, instant, twinkling of an eye, moment.
Ref: ch. 1 [134]; ch. 12 [64]; Lotus Sutra ch. 12.

kṣānti (patience, endurance, forbearance)
Represented by 安忍 (ANNIN),"calm endurance," or "bearing patiently."
[MW] patient waiting for anything; patience, forbearance, endurance, indulgence.
One of the 6 *pāramitās* (q.v.).
Ref: ch. 2; Lotus Sutra ch. 27.

kṣatriya (ruling class)
Represented phonetically.
[MW] governing, endowed with sovereignty; a member of the military or reigning order (which in later times constituted the second caste).
Ref. ch. 8.

kṣaya (exhausting, end)
Represented by 尽 (JIN), "exhaust."
[MW] loss, waste, wane, diminution, destruction, decay, wasting or wearing away; removal; end, termination; consumption; the destruction of the universe.
Ref: Lotus Sutra ch. 1.

kṣetra (countries, lands, temple)
Represented phonetically and by 刹土 (SETSUDO), "*kṣetra*-land."
[MW] landed property, land, soil; place, region, country; a house; a town; department, sphere of action; a sacred spot or district, place of pilgrimage; an enclosed plot of ground, portion of space.
Ref: ch. 1 [62].

Kṣudrakāgama (name of a sutra)
Represented by 小阿含経 (SHO-AGON-KYO), "Small Āgama Sutra."
[MW] *kṣudraka*: small, minute.
āgama [q.v.]: a traditional doctrine or precept.
Ref: bibliography.

Kukkuṭapāda (name of a mountain)
Represented by 鶏足 (KEISOKU), "Cock-Foot."
[MW] 'cock-foot,' name of a mountain.
[JEBD] The name of a mountain in Magadha, Central India, where Mahākāśyapa died. Present Kurkeihar, 16 miles northeast of Gayā.
Ref. ch. 1 [66]; ch. 15.

kula-patra (Good sons!)
Represented by 善男子 (ZEN-NANSHI), "good sons."
[MW] a son of a noble family, respectable youth.
kula-patrī: the daughter of a good family, respectable girl.
Ref: ch. 12 [80]; Lotus Sutra ch. 1.

Kumārajīva (name of a translator)
Represented phonetically.
[MW] the plant Putraṃ-jīva.
Ref: Lotus Sutra.

kumbhāṇḍa (name a class of demons)
Represented phonetically.
[MW] 'having testicles shaped like Kumbha,' a class of demons.
kumbha: a jar, pitcher, water-pot.
Ref: ch. 12 [80].

lalita-vistara-sūtra (name of a sutra)
Represented by 普曜経 (FUYO-KYO), "Sutra of the Diffusion of Shining [Artlessness]."
[MW] name of a Sūtra work giving a detailed account of the artless and natural acts in the life of the Buddha.
lalita: artless, innocent; beautiful.
vistara: spreading, extension, diffuseness.
Ref: ch. 12 [98]; bibliography.

loka (world)
Represented by 界 (KAI), "world, sphere."
[MW] free or open space, room, place, scope, free motion; a tract, region, district, country, province; the wide space or world (either 'the universe' or 'any division of it'); the earth or world of human beings; the inhabitants of the world, mankind, folk, people; ordinary life, worldly affairs.
Ref: ch. 2.

Madhyamāgama (name of a sutra)
Represented by 中阿含経 (CHU-AGON-KYO), "Middle Āgama Sutra."
[MW] *madhyama*: middle.
āgama [q.v.]: a traditional doctrine or precept.
Ref: ch. 12 [115]; bibliography.

Mādhyamika or **Mādhyamaka** (name of a school)
Represented by 中観派 (CHUGAN-HA), "Middle View School."
[MW] relating to the middle region; name of a Buddhist school.
[JEBD] One of the two major Mahāyāna schools in India (together with the Yogācāra). The basic statement of the doctrines of this school is found in Master Nāgārjuna's Mādhyamika-kārikā.
Ref. ch. 15.

Mādhyamika-kārikā (name of seminal work by Master Nāgārjuna)
[MW] *Mādhyamika*: relating to the middle region.
kārikā: concise statement in verse of (especially philosophical and grammatical) doctrines.
Ref. ch. 15.

Magadha (place name)
[HB] An ancient state in central India stretching along the southern bank of the Ganges, with its capital at Rājagṛha. One of the two main kingdoms (together with Kośala [q.v.]) determining the political scene in the central Gangetic plain in the 6th century B.C. It was in Magadha that the Buddha realized the truth and first turned the Dharma wheel.
Ref: ch. 20 [125].

Mahāratnakūta-sūtra (name of a sutra)
Represented by 大宝積経 (DAIHO-SHAK-KYO), "Great Treasure Accumulation Sutra."
[MW] *ratna*: treasure.
kūta: a heap.
Ref: ch. 12; ch. 14; ch. 84; bibliography.

Mahāsaṃghika ('Of the Great Saṃgha,' name of a Buddhist school)
Represented phonetically and by 大衆部 (DAISHUBU), "Great Saṃgha School." Together with the Theravāda School, one of the two principal schools of Hīnayāna Buddhism.
Ref: ch. 7 [165].

Mahā-saṃnipāta-sūtra (name of a sutra)
Represented by 大集経 (DAISHUKYO), "Great Aggregation Sutra."
[MW] *saṃnipāta*: falling in or down together, collapse, meeting, encounter; conjunction, aggregation, combination, mixture.
Ref: ch. 86; ch. 88; bibliography.

mahāsattva (great being)
Represented phonetically.
[MW] *mahāsattva*: a great creature, large animal; having a great or noble essence; noble, good (of persons); name of Gautama Buddha as heir to the throne.
mahā: great
sattva: being.
Ref: ch. 2; Lotus Sutra ch. 1.

mahāyāna (Great Vehicle)
Represented by 大乗 (DAIJO), "Great Vehicle."
[MW] great vehicle.
Ref: ch. 8 [198]; Lotus Sutra ch. 1.

Maheśvara (name of Śiva)
Represented by 大自在天 (DAI-JIZAITEN), "Great God of Free Will."
[MW] a great archer; name of Śiva (q.v.).
Ref: ch. 10 [19]; Lotus Sutra ch. 25.

mahoraga (serpent)
Represented phonetically.
[MW] a great serpent (with Buddhists a class of demons).
Ref: Lotus Sutra. ch. 10.

maitreya (benevolence)
Represented phonetically and by 慈 (ZU, JI), "love, affection, pity."
[MW] friendly, benevolent; name of a Bodhisattva and future Buddha (the 5th of the present age).
Ref: ch. 12 [64]; Lotus Sutra ch. 1.

maṇḍala (circle)
See **pañca-maṇḍalaka**.

manas (mind, will)
Represented by 意 (I) "intention."
[MW] *manas*: mind (in the widest sense as applied to all the mental powers), intellect, intelligence, understanding, perception, sense, conscience, will.
Ref: ch. 2; ch. 10.

mandārava (name of a tree and of its flowers)
Represented phonetically.
[MW] The coral tree.
Ref: ch. 42; Lotus Sutra ch. 16.

maṇi (jewel, gem)
Represented phonetically.
[MW] jewel, gem, pearl.
See also **cintāmaṇi**.
Ref: ch. 14 [189].

Mañjuśrī (name of a bodhisattva)
Represented phonetically.
[MW] name of one of the most celebrated Bodhi-sattvas among the northern Buddhists.
Ref: ch. 17 [39]; Lotus Sutra ch. 12.

mantra (mantra)
Represented by 真言 (SHINGON), "truth-word."
[MW] 'instrument of thought,' speech, sacred text or speech, a prayer or song of praise; a Vedic hymn or sacrificial formula; a sacred formula addressed to any individual deity; a mystical verse or magical formula, incantation, charm, spell.
Ref: ch. 1 [51].

Maudgalyāyana (name of a disciple of the Buddha)
Represented phonetically.
[MW] name of a pupil of Gautama Buddha.
Ref: ch. 12 [98].

mārga (the Way)
Represented by 道 (DO), "the Way."
[MW] seeking, search, tracing out, hunting; the track of a wild animal, any track, road, path, way to or through (in compounds), course (also of the wind and the stars); a way, manner, method, custom, usage; the right way, proper course.
The last of the 4 noble truths.
Ref: ch. 2; Lotus Sutra ch. 7.

marā-pāpīyas (deadly demons, demons of death)
Represented phonetically and by 死魔 (SHIMA), "demons of death."
[MW] *marā*: the world of death, killing, the inhabitants of hell.
pāpīyas: worse, lower, poorer, more or most wicked or miserable; (with Buddhists) *mārah-pāpīyān*, the evil spirit, the devil.
Ref: ch. 9 [232]; ch. 70 [216]; Lotus Sutra ch. 3.

moha (delusion, ignorance)
Represented by 痴 (CHI) or 愚痴 (GUCHI), "foolishness."
[MW] loss of consciousness, bewilderment, perplexity, distraction, infatuation, delusion, error, folly; (in philosophy) darkness or delusion of mind; (with Buddhists) ignorance (one of the three roots of vice).
Ref: ch. 8 [194].

mudrā (seal, stamp)
Represented by 印 (IN), "seal."
[MW] a seal or any instrument used for sealing or stamping, a seal-ring, signet-ring, any ring; any stamp or print or mark or impression; an image, sign, badge, token; name of particular positions or intertwinings of the fingers (24 in number, commonly practiced in religious worship, and supposed to possess an occult meaning and magical efficacy).
Ref: ch. 19 [90]; ch. 31; Lotus Sutra ch. 2.

muhūrta (moment, short space of time)
Represented phonetically.
[MW] a moment, instant, any short space of time; a particular division of time, the 30th part of a day, a period of 48 minutes.
Ref: ch. 12 [64].

muktāhāra
Represented by 瓔珞 (YORAKU), "necklace-ornament."
[MW] a string of pearls.
Ref: ch. 3 [90]; Lotus Sutra ch. 10.

mūla (root, fundamental)
Represented by 根 (KON), "root."
[MW] 'firmly fixed,' a root; basis, foundation, cause, origin, commencement, beginning.
Ref: bibliography.

Mūla-sarvāstivādin (name of a school)
Represented by 根本説一切有部 (KONPON-SETSU-ISSAI-U-BU), "Original School of the Preaching that All Things Exist."
[MW] *mūla* (q.v.): fundamental.
sarvāstivāda (q.v.): the doctrine that all things are real.
The prefix "*mūla*" was later added because many schools derived from the Sarvāstivādins.
Ref: ch. 1; bibliography.

nāga (dragon)
Represented by 龍 (RYU), "dragon."
[MW] a snake; a serpent-demon (they are supposed to have a human face with serpent-like lower extremities; with Buddhists they are also represented as ordinary men).
Ref: Lotus Sutra ch. 10.

Nāgārjuna (name of a Buddhist patriarch)
Represented phonetically and by 龍樹 (RYUJU), "Dragon Tree."

[MW] *nāga*: a snake; a serpent-demon.
arjuna: the tree Terminalia Arjuna.
Ref: ch. 12; ch. 15.

naraka (hell)
Represented phonetically and by 地獄 (JIGOKU), "hell."
[MW] hell, place of torment.
Ref: ch. 12 [87].

nayuta (numerical unit, equal to 100 ayuta)
Represented phonetically.
[MW] *ayuta*: 'unjoined, unbounded,' ten thousand, a myriad; in compounds a term of praise.
Ref: Lotus Sutra ch. 16.

nidāna (historical accounts [of causes and conditions])
Represented by 因縁 (INNEN), "causes and conditions."
[MW] a band, rope, halter; a first or primary cause; original form or essence; any cause or motive; pathology.
One of the 12 divisions of the teachings. See under **anga**.
Ref: ch. 11 [40].

nirodha (dissolution, cessation)
Represented by 滅 (METSU), "death, destruction, annihilation."
[MW] confinement, locking up, imprisonment; enclosing, covering up; restraint, check, control, suppression, destruction; (with Buddhists) suppression or annihilation of pain.
Note: in Shobogenzo, the third phase of Master Dogen's 4-phased system is negation of the intellectual views of the first two phases, namely, idealism and materialism. On that basis, *nirodha* may be interpreted not as suppression of pain, but rather as dissolution of, or liberation from, the intellectual restraints of idealism and materialism.
Ref: ch. 2; Lotus Sutra ch. 7.

nirvāṇa (extinction)
Represented phonetically and by 寂滅 (JAKUMETSU), "death, annihilation, extinction, Nirvana."
[MW] blown or put out, extinguished (as a lamp or fire), set (as the sun), calmed, quieted, tamed, dead, deceased (lit. having the fire of life extinguished).
Ref: ch. 1 [45]; Lotus Sutra ch. 2.

niṣīdana (sitting mat, prostration cloth)
Represented by 坐具 (ZAGU), "sitting gear."
[MW] *niṣadana*: sitting down.
Ref: ch. 2 [104].

nitya (eternal)
Represented by 常住 (JOJU), "constantly abiding," "eternal."
[MW] innate, native; continual, perpetual, eternal; constantly dwelling or engaged in, intent upon, devoted or used to; ordinary, usual, invariable; always, constantly, regularly.
Ref: ch. 1 [45]; ch. 14; Lotus Sutra ch. 2.

pada (phrase)
Represented by 句 (KU), "phrase."
[MW] a step, pace, stride; the foot itself; a part, portion, division; a plot of ground; the foot as a measure of length; a portion of a verse, quarter or line of a stanza.
Ref: ch. 1 [9]; Lotus Sutra ch. 10.

pāṃsu-kūla (a dust-heap, rags)
Represented by 糞掃 (FUNZO), "filth-swept."
[MW] a dust heap, (especially) a collection of rags out of a dust-heap used by Buddhist monks for their clothing.
Ref: ch. 12 [71].

pañca dṛṣṭayah (five [wrong] views)
Represented by 五見 (GOKEN), "five views."
[MW] *pañca*: five.
dṛṣṭi: seeing, viewing, beholding; view, notion; (with Buddhists) a wrong view; theory, doctrine, system.
The five are *satkāya-dṛṣṭi*, 身見 (SHINKEN), the personality view; *antagrāha-dṛṣṭi*, 辺見 (HENKEN), extremism; *mithyā-dṛṣṭi*, 邪見 (JAKEN), atheism; *dṛṣṭi-parāmarśa*, 見取見 (KENJU-KEN), dogmatism; *śilavrata-parāmarśa*, 戒禁取見 (KAIGONJU-KEN), attachment to precepts and observances.
Ref: ch. 12 [107].

pañca-maṇḍalaka (the five circles)
Represented by 五輪 (GORIN), "five circles, five wheels."
[MW] *pañca*: five.
maṇḍala: circular, round; a disk; anything round; a circle, globe, orb, ring, circumference, ball, wheel.
Ref: ch. 14 [189].

pañca viṣaya (five objects [of desire])
Represented by 五欲 (GOYOKU), "five desires."
[MW] *pañca*: five.
viṣaya (q.v.): sense-object.
Ref: ch. 12 [107].

pārājika (violation of the precepts warranting expulsion from the community)
Represented phonetically.
[MW] *pāra*: far, distant, beyond, extreme, exceeding.
aj: to drive, propel, throw, cast.
ka: affix added to nouns to express diminution, deterioration, or similarity.
Ref: ch. 8 [192].

paramāṇu (atom)
Represented by 微塵 (MIJIN), "particle."
[MW] an infinitesimal particle or atom.
Ref: ch. 17 [54]; Lotus Sutra ch. 16.

pāramitā (an accomplishment)
Represented phonetically and by 度 (DO), which represents 渡 (DO) "to cross over," or "to have crossed over."
[MW] gone to the opposite shore; crossed, traversed, transcendent, coming or leading to the opposite shore, complete attainment, perfection in (compounds); transcendental virtue, accomplishment (there are 6 or 10, viz. *dāna, śīla, kṣanti, vīrya, dhyāna, prajñā,* to which are sometimes added *satya, adhiṣṭhāna, maitra,* and *upekṣā*).
Ref: ch. 2; Lotus Sutra ch. 27.

pariṇāma (dedication)
Represented by 回向 (EKO), "turning," "[merit]-transference," "dedication."
[MW] change, alteration, transformation into, development, evolution; ripeness, maturity; alteration of food, digestion; result, consequence, issue, end.
Ref: ch. 21 [209].

pari-nirvāṇa (complete extinction)
Represented phonetically.
[MW] completely extinguished or finished.
Ref: ch. 24; bibliography.

parivāra (followers)
Represented by 眷属 (KENZOKU), "kin."
[MW] surroundings, train, suite, dependants, followers.
Ref: ch. 72; Lotus Sutra ch. 1.

parṣad (followers)
Represented by 眷属 (KENZOKU), "kin."
[MW] assembly, audience, company.
Ref: ch. 72; Lotus Sutra ch. 1.

pātra (bowl)
Represented by 鉢盂 (HATSU-U), *pātra-bowl.*
[MW] a drinking vessel, goblet, bowl, cup, dish, pot, plate, utensil, etc, any vessel or receptacle.
Ref: ch. 5 [122]; ch. 78.

piṇḍa-vana (monastery)
Represented by 叢林 (SORIN), "thicket-forest" or "clump of forest."
[MW] *piṇḍa*: any round or roundish mass.
vana: forest, wood, grove, thicket, quantity of lotuses or other plants growing in a thick cluster.
Ref: ch. 1 [65]; ch. 5 [122].

piśāca (name of a class of demons)
Represented phonetically.
[MW] name of a class of demons (possibly so called either from their fondness for flesh [*piśa* for *piśita*] or from their yellowish appearance).
piśita: flesh which has not been cut up or prepared, any flesh or meat.
Ref: ch. 12 [80].

Prabhūtaratna (name of a buddha)
Represented by 多宝 (TAHO), "Abundant Treasures."
[MW] name of a Buddha.
prabhūta: abundant, much, numerous.
ratna: a gift, present, goods, wealth, riches; a jewel, gem, treasure.
Ref: ch. 12 [95]; Lotus Sutra ch. 11.

prajñā (real wisdom)
Represented phonetically and by 知見 (CHIKEN), "knowing," or 慧 (E), "wisdom."
[MW] wisdom, intelligence, knowledge, discrimination, judgment; (with Buddhists) true or transcendental wisdom.
One of the 6 *pāramitās* (q.v.).
Ref: ch. 2; Lotus Sutra ch. 2; ch. 27.

Prasenajit (name of a king)
Represented phonetically.
[HB] The king of Kośala who resided in Śrāvastī (q.v.) and became a lay follower of the Buddha and supporter of the Buddhist order.
Ref. Fukan-zazengi; ch. 59.

pratītya-samutpāda (dependent origination)
Represented by 縁起 (ENGI), "arising from conditions, origin, origination," and by 因縁 (INNEN), "causes and conditions."
[MW] *pratīti*: going towards, approaching; the following from anything (as a necessary result), being clear or intelligible by itself.
samutpāda: rise, origin, production.
Ref: ch. 1 [32]; Lotus Sutra ch. 7.

pratyaya (a co-operating cause)
Represented by 縁 (EN), "relation, connection, circumstance, condition."
[MW] belief, firm conviction, trust, faith, assurance of certainty; proof, ascertainment; (with Buddhists) fundamental notion or idea; consciousness, understanding, intelligence, intellect; analysis, solution, explanation, definition; ground, basis, motive, or cause of anything; (with Buddhists) a co-operating cause; the concurrent occasion of an event as distinguished from its approximate cause.

pratyekabuddha (sensory Buddhist)
Represented phonetically, by 独覚 (DOKU-KAKU), "independent realization" and by 縁覚 (ENGAKU), "realizer of conditions."
[MAC] isolated Buddha who works out his individual salvation only.
Ref: Lotus Sutra ch. 2.

preta (hungry ghosts)
Represented by 餓鬼 (GAKI), "hungry ghosts."
[MW] departed, deceased, dead, a dead person; the spirit of a dead person (especially before obsequial rites are performed), a ghost, an evil being.
Ref: ch. 12 [80].

pṛthag-jana (the common man)
Represented by 凡夫 (BONBU), "the common man."
[MW] a man of lower caste or character or profession.
Ref: ch. 19 [11].

puṇya-kṣetra (field of virtue)
Represented by 福田 (FUKUDEN), "field of good fortune," "field of happiness."
[MW] a holy place, a place of pilgrimage; name of Buddha.
puṇya: auspicious, propitious, fair, pleasant, good, right, virtuous, meritorious, pure, holy, sacred; the good or right, virtue, purity, good work, meritorious act, moral or religious merit.
kṣetra (q.v.): place, sphere of action; plot of ground.
Ref: ch. 12 [120]; ch. 13; ch. 84 [37].

puruṣa (human being)
Represented by 人 (NIN), "person, human being," and by 丈夫 (JOBU), "stout fellow."
[MW] a man, male, human being; a person; a friend; the personal and animating principle in men and other beings, the soul or spirit.
Ref: ch. 8 [169].

Rāgarāja (King of Love)
Represented by 愛染明王 (AIZEN-MYO-O), "the King with the Hue of Love."
[MW] *rāga*: the act of coloring or dyeing; color, hue, tint, dye, (especially) red color, redness; inflammation; any feeling or passion, (especially) love, affection or sympathy for, vehement desire of.
rāja: king.
Ref: ch. 11 [29].

Rājagṛha (name of a city)
Represented by 王舎城 (OSHAJO), "City of Royal Palaces."
[HB] Capital of the ancient Indian kingdom of Magadha, where the Buddha first realized the truth, and the site of the First Council following the Buddha's death.
Ref: Lotus Sutra, ch. 1.

Rāhula (name of a son and disciple of the Buddha)
Represented phonetically.
Ref: ch. 7 [163].

rasa (taste, flavor)
Represented by 味 (MI), "taste."
[MW] the sap or juice of plants, juice of fruit, any liquid or fluid, the best or finest part of anything; taste, flavor (as the principal quality of fluids, of which there are 6 original kinds); any object of taste, condiment, sauce, spice, seasoning; the tongue (as the organ of taste); taste or inclination or fondness for; the taste or character of a work.
Ref: ch. 2.

Ratnagarbha (name of a Buddha)
Represented by 法蔵 (HOZO), "Jewel Treasury."
[MW] filled with precious stones, containing jewels, set with jewels; name of a Bodhi-sattva.
ratna: a jewel, gem, treasure.
garbha: the womb; the inside, middle, interior of anything; an inner apartment, sleeping-room; any interior chamber, adytum or sanctuary of a temple.
Ref: ch. 12 [80].

ṛddipāda (basis of mystical power, excellent disciple)
Represented by 神足 (JINSOKU), "mystical foot."
[MW] one of the four constituent parts of supernatural power.
ṛddi: success; accomplishment, perfection, supernatural power.
pāda (q.v.): foot
Ref. ch.8 [178]; ch. 20 [163].

ṛṣi (hermit, sage)
Represented by 仙 (SEN), "hermit, wizard."
[MW] a singer of sacred hymns, an inspired poet or sage, any person who alone or with others invokes the deities in rhythmical speech or song of a sacred character; [they] were regarded by later generation as patriarchal sages or saints, occupying the same position in Indian history as the heroes and patriarchs of other countries, and constitute a peculiar class of beings in the early mythical system; they are the authors or rather seers of the Vedic hymns.
Ref: ch. 14; ch. 15.

rūpa (matter, form)
Represented 色 (SHIKI), "color, form."
[MW] any outward appearance or phenomenon or color, form, shape, figure; (with Buddhists) material form. One of the 5 *skandhas* (q.v.).
Ref: ch. 2.

śabda (sound)
Represented by 声 (SHO), "sound, voice."
[MW] sound, noise, voice, tone, note; a word; speech, language; the right word, correct expression.
Ref: ch. 2.

saddharma (wonderful Dharma, right Dharma)
Represented by 妙法 (MYO-HO), "wonderful/fine/wonderful Dharma" and by 正法 (SHOBO), "right/true Dharma."
[MW] the good law, true justice; (with Buddhists) designation of the Buddhist doctrines.
sat: being, existing; real, actual, as any one or anything ought to be, true, good, right, beautiful, wise, venerable, honest.
Ref: ch. 1 [11]; ch. 17; Lotus Sutra ch. 1.

saddharma-pratirūpaka ([the age of] imitation of the right Dharma)
Represented by 像法 (ZOBO), "imitative Dharma."
[MW] *saddharma*: right Dharma (q.v.).
pratirūpaka: an image, a picture; forgery; similar, corresponding, having the appearance of anything; a quack, a charlatan.
Ref: ch. 1; Lotus Sutra ch. 20.

Saddharma-puṇḍarika-sūtra (The Sutra of the Lotus Flower of the Wonderful Dharma)
Represented by 妙法蓮華経 (MYO-HO-RENGE-KYO), "The Sutra of the Lotus Flower of the Wonderful Dharma."
[MW] *saddharma*: wonderful Dharma (q.v.).
puṇḍarika: a lotus-flower (especially a white lotus; expressive of beauty).
Ref: ch. 17; Lotus Sutra ch. 1.

saddharma-vipralopa ([the age of] annihilation of the right Dharma)
Represented by 末法 (MAPPO), "the end of the Dharma," "the latter Dharma."
[MW] *saddharma*: right Dharma (q.v.).
vipralopa: destruction, annihilation. *Ref: ch. 1.*

sādhu (Good!)
Represented 善哉 (ZENZAI), "How good!"
[MW] straight, right; leading straight to a goal, hitting the mark, unerring (as an arrow or thunderbolt); straightened, not entangled; well-disposed, kind, willing, obedient; successful, effective, efficient; peaceful, secure; powerful, excellent; fit, proper, right; good, virtuous.
Ref: ch. 12 [80]; Lotus Sutra ch. 28.

sāgara (the ocean)
Represented phonetically.
[MW] the ocean; (plural) the sons of Sagara (a legend asserts that the bed of the ocean was dug by the sons of Sagara [who was a king of the solar race]).
Ref: Lotus Sutra ch. 12.

sahā-loka-dhātu (the human world)
Represented by 娑婆世界 (SHABA-SEKAI), "*sahā-world.*"
[MW] *sahā*: (with Buddhists) name of a division of the world.
loka: world.
dhātu: layer, stratum; part.
Ref: ch. 4; Lotus Sutra ch. 12.

sakṛdāgāmin (the state of returning only once again)
Represented phonetically and by 一来果 (ICHI-RAI-KA), "the effect [which is subject to] one return."
[MW] 'returning only once again.'
Ref: ch. 2.

Śakra-devānām-indra (the God Indra)
Represented phonetically and by 天帝釈 (TENTAI-SHAKU), "the God-Emperor Śakra."
[MW] *Śakra*: strong, powerful, mighty (applied to various gods, but especially to Indra).
deva: heavenly, divine; a deity, god; the gods as the heavenly or shining ones; name of Indra as the god of the sky and giver of rain.
Indra: the god of the atmosphere and sky; the Indian Jupiter Pluvius or lord of rain (who in Vedic mythology reigns over the deity of the intermediate region or atmosphere; he fights against and conquers with his thunderbolt *[vajra]* the demons of darkness, and is in general a symbol of generous heroism; Indra was not originally lord of the gods of the sky, but his deeds were most useful to mankind, and he was therefore addressed in prayers and hymns more than any other deity; in the later mythology Indra is subordinated to the triad Brahman, Vishnu, and Śiva, but remained the chief of all other deities in the popular mind).
Ref: ch. 2; Lotus Sutra ch. 1.

Śākyamuni (name of the Buddha)
Represented phonetically or by 釈尊 (SHAKUSON), "Honored Śākya."
[MW] *Śākya*: the Buddha's family name.
muni: a saint, sage, seer, ascetic, monk, devotee, hermit (esp. one who has taken the vow of silence).
Ref: Lotus Sutra ch. 1.

samādhi (the balanced state, the state)
Represented phonetically or by 定 (JO), "definite, fixed, constant, regular."
[MW] Setting to rights, adjustment, settlement.
Ref: ch. 1 [11]; Lotus Sutra ch. 2; ch. 24.

Samantabhadra (name of a bodhisattva)
Represented by 普賢 (FUGEN), "Universal Wisdom" or "Universal Virtue."
[MW] wholly auspicious; name of a Bodhisattva.
Ref: ch. 17 [39]; Lotus Sutra ch. 28.

Samantamukha (universal gate, all-sidedness)
Represented by 普門 (FUMON), "universal gate" or "all-sidedness."
[MW] *samanta*: 'having the ends together,' contiguous, neighboring, adjacent; 'being on every side,' universal, whole, entire, all.
mukha: the mouth, face, countenance; a direction, quarter; the mouth of spout of a vessel, opening, aperture, entrance into or egress out of.
Ref: ch. 17 [54]; Lotus Sutra ch. 25.

śamatha (quiet)
Represented by 止 (SHI), "ceasing, quieting."
[MW] quiet, tranquility, absence of passion.
Note: 止観 (SHIKAN), "quieting and reflecting," representing the Sanskrit *śamatha* and *vipaśyanā* (q.v.), is a fundamental practice of the Tendai Sect.
Ref: ch. 1 [51].

saṃdhaya (accumulation)
Represented by 集 (SHU), "collection, accumulation."
[MW] to put or join together, unite.
Second of the 4 noble truths.
Ref: ch. 1; Lotus Sutra ch. 7.

Saṃgha (the community)
Represented by 僧 (SO), "monks," and by 衆 (SHU), "the multitude."
[MW] 'close contact or combination,' any collection or assemblage, heap, multitude, quantity, crowd, host, number; any number of people living together for a certain purpose, a society, association, company, community; a clerical community, congregation, church; (esp.) the whole community or collective body or brotherhood of monks.
Ref: ch. 2 [74]; Lotus Sutra ch. 26.

saṃghārāma (temple)
Represented phonetically and by 院 (IN), "temple."
[MW] 'resting place for a company (of monks),' a Buddhist convent or monastery.
Ref: ch. 21 [209]; ch. 84.

saṃghāṭī (the large robe)
Represented phonetically and by 大衣 (DAI-E), "the large robe."

[MW] a kind of garment, a monk's robe.
saṃghāṭa: fitting and joining of timber, joinery.
Ref: ch. 12. [80], [95].

saṃjñā (thinking)
Represented by 想 (SO), "idea, thought."
[MW] agreement, mutual understanding, harmony; consciousness, clear knowledge or understanding or notion or conception. One of the 5 *skandhas* (q.v.).
Ref: ch. 2.

saṃsāra (wandering)
Represented by 流転 (RUTEN), "wandering, constant change," by 輪転 (RINDEN), "turning of the wheel," "revolving," or by 輪廻 (RINNE), "transmigration."
[MW] going or wandering through, undergoing transmigration; course, passage, passing through a succession of states, circuit of mundane existence, transmigration, the world, secular life, worldly illusion.
Ref: ch. 6 [125]; ch. 8 [198]; ch. 17 [54].

saṃskāra (enaction, action)
Represented by 行 (GYO), "doing, acting, carrying out."
[MW] putting together, forming well, making perfect, accomplishment, embellishment, preparation, refining, polishing, rearing; cleansing the body; forming the mind, training, education; correction, correct formation or use of a word; the faculty of memory, mental impression, or recollection; (with Buddhists) a mental conformation or creation of the mind.
However, *saṃskāra* need not always be limited to the mental sphere. *Saṃskāra* is the second link in the twelvefold chain of causation, and one of the 5 *skandhas* (q.v.).
Ref: ch. 2; Lotus Sutra ch. 7.

saṃskṛta (put together, artificial)
Represented by 有為 (U-I), "presence of becoming," "made," "artificial," [opposite of 無為 (MU-I)—see *asaṃskṛta*].
[MW] put together, constructed, well or completely formed, perfected; made ready; prepared, completed, finished; dressed, cooked; purified, consecrated; refined, adorned, ornamented, polished, highly elaborated (especially applied to highly wrought speech).
Ref: ch. 1 [62]; ch. 19 [118].

Saṃyuktāgama (name of a sutra)
Represented by 雑阿含経 (ZO-AGON-KYO), "Miscellaneous Āgama Sutra."
[MW] *sam*: conjunction expressing 'conjunction.'
saṃyukta: joined, united, connected, combined, following in regular succession.
āgama [q.v.]: a traditional doctrine or precept.
Ref: ch. 85; bibliography.

Śāṇavāsa (name of the 3rd patriarch)
Represented phonetically.
[MW] *śāṇa*: made of hemp or Bengal flax, hempen, flaxen, etc.
vāsa: a garment, dress, clothes.
Ref: ch. 12 [74]; ch. 15.

Śāriputra (name of a disciple of the Buddha)
Represented phonetically.
[MW] *Śāri*: from Rūpasārī, the name of Śāriputra's mother.
putra: a son, child.
Ref: ch. 2; Lotus Sutra ch. 2.

śarīra (bones)
Represented phonetically.
[MW] the body, bodily frame, solid parts of the body (pl. the bones); a dead body.
Ref: ch. 71; Lotus Sutra ch. 10.

Sarvāsti-vāda (the doctrine that all is real)
Represented by 説一切有部 (SETSU-ISSAI-U-BU), "School that Preaches that All Things Exist."
[MW] *sarva*: all.
asti: existent, present.
vāda: speaking of or about; speech, discourse, talk, utterance, statement; a thesis, proposition, argument, doctrine.
Sarvāstivāda: the doctrine that all things are real (name of one of the 4 divisions of the Vaibhāṣika system of Buddhism, said to have been founded by Rāhula, son of the great Buddha).
Sarvāstivādin: an adherent of the above doctrine.
Ref: ch. 1 [45]; ch. 87 [171].

sāsrava (having that which is superfluous, tainted)
Represented by 有漏 (URO), "with leakage."
[MW] (with Jainas) connected with the act called *āsrava* (q.v.).
Ref. ch. 21 [192].

śāstra (commentary)
Represented by 論 (RON), "doctrine,

discussion, argument."
[MW] an order, command, precept, rule; teaching, instruction, direction, advice, good counsel; any instrument of teaching, any manual or compendium of rules, any book or treatise.
Ref: bibliography.

satya (truth)
Represented by 諦 (TAI), "clarity, enlightenment, truth," as in 四諦 (SHITAI), "the four [noble] truths."
[MW] truth, reality; speaking the truth, sincerity, veracity; a solemn asseveration, vow, promise, oath; demonstrated conclusion, dogma; the quality of goodness or purity or knowledge.
Ref: ch. 2.

Senika (name of a person)
Represented phonetically.
A non-Buddhist who questions the Buddha in the Garland Sutra.
Ref: ch. 1 [45]; ch. 6.

śikṣā (training, learning)
See **tisraḥ śikṣāḥ**

śīla (moral conduct)
Represented by 浄戒 (JOKAI), "pure [observance of] precepts."
[MW] habit, custom, usage, natural or acquired way of living or acting, practice, conduct, disposition, tendency, character, nature; good disposition or character, moral conduct, integrity, morality, piety, virtue; a moral precept.
One of the 6 *pāramitās* (q.v.).
Ref: ch. 2; Lotus Sutra ch. 27.

sīmā-bandha (sanctuary)
Represented by 結界 (KEKKAI), "bounded area."
[MW] a depository of rules of morality.
Ref: ch. 8 [198].

Śiva (name of the destroying deity in the Hindū triad)
Represented by 自在天 (JIZAITEN), "God of Free Will."
[MW] 'The Auspicious One,' name of the disintegrating or destroying and reproducing deity (who constitutes third god of the Hindū Triad, the other two being Brahmā 'the creator' and Viṣṇu 'the preserver;' in the Veda the only name of the destroying deity was Rudra, 'the terrible god,' but in later times it became usual to give that god the euphemistic name Śiva, 'the auspicious.'
Ref: ch. 10 [19]; Lotus Sutra ch. 25.

skandha (aggregates)
Represented by 蘊 (UN), "accumulations," or by 衆 (SHU) "multitudes."
[MW] the shoulder; the stem or trunk of a tree; a large branch or bough; a troop, multitude, quantity, aggregate; a part, division; (with Buddhists) the 5 constituent elements of being (viz. *rūpa, vedana, saṃjñā, saṃskāra,* and *vijñāna* [q.v.]).
Ref: ch. 2.

smṛti (mindfulness)
Represented by 念 (NEN), "idea, feeling, desire, attention."
[MW] remembrance, reminiscence, thinking of or upon, calling to mind, memory; the whole body of sacred tradition or what is remembered by human teachers; the whole body of codes of law as handed down memoriter or by tradition; desire, wish.
Ref: ch. 2 [74]; ch. 73; Lotus Sutra ch. 1 ["remember"]; ch. 10 ["heed"]; ch. 16 ["thought"]; ch. 27 ["care for"].

sparśa (touch, tangibility, sensation)
Represented by 触 (SOKU), "touch."
[MW] touching, touch, sense of touch, contact; the quality of tangibility (which constitutes the skin's *viṣaya,* q.v.), any quality which is perceptible by touching any object (e.g. heat, cold, smoothness, softness, etc.); feeling, sensation.
Ref: ch. 2.

śramaṇa (striver, monk)
Represented phonetically.
[MW] making effort or exertion, toiling, laboring; one who performs acts of mortification or austerity, an ascetic, monk, devotee, religious mendicant; a Buddhist monk or mendicant (also applied to Buddha himself).
Ref: ch. 1 [68].

śramaṇera (novice)
Represented phonetically.
[MW] (among Buddhists) a pupil or disciple admitted to the first degree of monkhood, a novice.
Ref: ch. 7 [163]; Lotus Sutra ch. 7.

śrāvaka (intellectual Buddhist)
Represented by 声聞 (SHOMON), "voice-hearer."
[MW] hearing, listening to; audible from afar; a pupil, disciple; a disciple of the Buddha (the disciples of the Hinayāna school are sometimes so called in contradistinction to the disciples of the Mahāyāna school; properly only those who heard the law from the Buddha's own lips have the name *śrāvaka*).
Ref: ch. 1 [11]; Lotus Sutra ch. 2.

Śrāvasti (name of a city)
[[JEBD] The capital of Kośala, sometimes treated as an independent country. It is the present Sāhetmātet, Gonda, India.
Ref. ch. 15.

Śrīmālā (name of a district, of a queen, and of a sutra addressed to the queen)
Represented phonetically.
[MW] name of a district and the town situated in it.
Śrīmālā-devī-siṇha-nāda-sūtra: name of a Buddhist Sūtra.
[JEBD] *Śrīmālā*: the daughter of King Prasenajit of Kośala (q.v.). She married the king of Ayodhyā and actively engaged in the propagation of Buddhism in that country.
Ref: ch. 12 [100]; bibliography.

srotāpanna (stream-enterer)
Represented phonetically and by 預流果 (YORU-KA), "the effect which is to have been received beforehand into the stream."
[MW] one who has entered the river (leading to *nirvāṇa*).
Ref: ch. 2.

śrotra (ear, hearing)
Represented by 耳 (NI), "ear."
[MW] the organ of hearing, ear, auricle; the act of hearing or listening to; conversancy with the Veda or sacred knowledge itself.
Ref: ch. 2.

sthavira (elder)
Represented by 上座 (JOZA), "senior seat," and by 長老 (CHORO), "veteran."
[MW] old, ancient, venerable; an old man; an 'Elder' (name of the oldest and most venerable Bhikṣus).
Ref: ch. 16 [15]; ch. 84.

stūpa (tower)
Represented phonetically and by 塔 (TO), "tower."
[MW] a knot or tuft of hair, the upper part of the head, crest, top, summit; a heap or pile of earth or bricks etc., (especially) a Buddhist monument, dagoba (generally of pyramidal or dome-like form and erected over sacred relics of the great Buddha or on spots consecrated as the scenes of his acts); any relic-shrine or relic-casket; any heap, pile, mound.
Note: LSW notes that from the chapter *Hosshi (A Teacher of Dharma)* onwards, the Lotus Sutra stresses the erecting of *caityas* (pagodas for sutras) as opposed to *stūpas* (pagodas for relics). Master Dogen discusses the distinction in Shobogenzo ch. 87. But MW does not distinguish between *stūpas* and *caityas* (q.v.).
Ref: ch. 71; ch. 87 [160]; Lotus Sutra ch. 10.

styāna (sloth)
Represented phonetically and by 惛 (KON) "darkness, stupefaction" and by 惛沈 (KONJIN), "depression."
[MW] grown dense, coagulated; stiffened, become rigid; soft, bland; thick, bulky, gross; density, thickness; idleness, sloth, apathy.
Ref: Fukan-zazengi

Sudatta (name of a person)
[HB] A wealthy gold-dealer and banker of Śrāvastī who become a lay follower of the Buddha and purchased Jetavana park so that the Buddha and Saṃgha could pass the rains retreat near Śrāvastī.
Ref: Fukan-zazengi.

śudra (servants)
Represented phonetically.
[MW] a man of the fourth or lowest of the four original classes or castes (whose only business was to serve the three higher classes).
Ref. ch.8; ch. 82.

Śukra (name of a nun)
Represented by 鮮白 (SENBYAKU), "Fresh-White."
[MW] bright, resplendent; clear, pure; light-colored, white; pure, spotless.
Ref: ch. 12 [74].

Sumeru (also Meru, name of a mountain)
Represented phonetically.
[MW] name of a fabulous mountain (regarded as the Olympus of Hindū mythology and said to form the central

point of Jambu-dvīpa [q.v.]; all the planets revolve around it and it is compared to the cup or seed-vessel of a lotus, the leaves of which are formed by the different Dvīpas).
Ref: ch. 14 [183]; Lotus Sutra ch. 7.

śūnyatā (space, emptiness)
Represented by 空 (KU) , "space," "the sky," "emptiness."
[MW] emptiness, loneliness, desolateness; absence of mind, distraction; vacancy (of gaze); absence or want of; nothingness, non-existence, non-reality, illusory nature of all worldly phenomena.
Note: The latter set of definitions reflects idealistic thought. The philosophical meaning of śūnyatā which emerges in Shobogenzo is emptiness; the bare, bald, naked, raw, or transparent state, that is, the state in which reality is just as it is. At the same time, 空 (KU) can often be interpreted as concrete space.
Ref: ch. 1 [45]; ch. 2; ch. 43; Lotus Sutra ch. 15.

Śūraṃgama-samādhi-nirdeśa (name of a sutra)
Represented phonetically.
[MW] *śūraṃgama*: a particular Samādhi; name of a Bodhi-sattva.
Ref: ch. 43; ch. 74; bibliography.

sūtra (original texts, the sutras)
Represented by 経 (KYO), "sutras," or by 経巻 (KYOGAN), "sutras, volumes of the Sutra."
[MW] a thread, yarn, string, line, cord, wire; that which like a thread runs through or holds together everything, rule, direction; a short sentence or aphoristic rule, and any work or manual consisting of strings of such rules hanging together like threads (these Sūtra works form manuals of teaching in ritual, philosophy, grammar etc; with Buddhists the term Sūtra is applied to original text books as opposed to explanatory works).
One of the "three baskets," or *tripiṭaka* (q.v.); and one of the 12 divisions of the teachings. See under **anga**.

Suvarṇaprabhāsottama-rāja-sūtra (the Golden Light Sutra of the Supreme King)
Represented by 金光明最勝王経 (KON-KOMYO-SAISHO-O-KYO), "Golden Light Supreme King Sutra."
[MW] *suvarṇa*: of a good or beautiful color, brilliant in hue, bright, golden, yellow, gold, made of gold.
prabhāsa: 'splendor,' 'beauty,' name of a Vasu (one who is excellent, good, beneficient).
uttama: uppermost, highest, chief; most elevated; best.
rāja: king.
Ref: ch. 21 [216].

svāgata (well come, welcome)
Represented by 善来 (ZENRAI), "well come, welcome."
[MW] well come; welcome; a greeting, salutation.
Ref: ch. 12 [74].

tāla (palm leaf)
Represented phonetically.
[MW] the palmyra tree or fan-palm (Borassus flabelliformis), producing a sort of spirituous liquor; considered a measure of height.
Ref: Lotus Sutra ch. 27.

tathāgata ('having arrived in the state of reality,' epithet of the Budhha)
Represented by 如来 (NYORAI), "thus-come" or "reality-come."
[MW] being in such a state or condition, of such a quality or nature; he who comes and goes in the same way (as the Buddhas who preceded him).
tathā: in that manner, so, thus.
gata: come.
Ref: ch. 1 [11]; Lotus Sutra ch. 1.

tathātā (reality)
Represented by 如 (NYO), "reality."
[MW] true state of things, true nature.
Appears, for example, in the compound 一如 (ICHI-NYO), "the oneness of reality."
Ref: ch. 1 [11].

tisraḥ śikṣāḥ (three kinds of training, three kinds of learning)
Represented by 三学 (SANGAKU), "three kinds of learning."
[MW] *tisraḥ*: three
śikṣā: desire of being able to effect anything, wish to accomplish; learning, study, knowledge, art, skill in; teaching, training (held by Buddhists to be of three kinds, viz. *adhicitta-śikṣā*, training in the higher thought; *adhiśīla-śikṣā*, training in the higher morality; *adhiprajñā-śikṣā*, training in the higher wisdom).
However, in Japan the three are

traditionally interpreted as 戒, 定, 恵 (RITSU, JO, E), "precepts, balanced state, wisdom," that is, *śīla*, *samādhi*, and *prajñā*.
Ref: ch. 1 [37].

tisro vidyāh (three kinds of knowledge)
Represented by 三明 (SANMYO),"three kinds of clarity."
[MW] *tisro*: three
vidyā: knowledge, science, learning, scholarship, philosophy.
Ref: ch. 12 [90].

tripiṭaka (the three baskets)
Represented by 三蔵 (SANZO), "the three storehouses."
[MW] the 3 baskets or collections of sacred writings (*Sūtra-piṭaka*, *Vinaya-piṭaka*, and *Abhidharma-piṭaka* [q.v.]).
Ref: ch. 2 [136].

Tuṣita (name of a celestial world)
Represented phonetically.
[MW] a class of celestial beings.
Ref: ch. 4 [117].

udāna (spontaneous preaching)
Represented by 自説 (JISETSU), "spontaneous preaching."
[MW] breathing upwards; one of the five vital airs of the human body (that which is in the throat and rises upwards); a kind of snake; joy, heart's joy (Buddhists).
One of the 12 divisions of the teachings. See under **anga**.
Ref: ch. 11 [40].

uḍumbara
Represented phonetically.
[MW] the tree Ficus Glomerata; the fruit of the tree.
Ref: ch. 68; Lotus Sutra ch. 2.

upadeśa (theoretical discourse)
Represented by 論議 (RONGI), "discussion, argument"
[MW] pointing out to, reference to; specification, instruction, teaching, information, advice, prescription; name of a class of writings (Buddhist literature).
One of the 12 divisions of the teachings. See under **anga**.
Ref: ch. 11 [40].

upādhyāya (master)
Represented by 和尚 (OSHO), "master."
[MW] a teacher, preceptor.
Ref: ch. 15.

upasaṃpadā (ordainment)
Represented by 具足戒 (GUSOKU-KAI), "being equipped with the precepts."
[MW] the act of entering into the order of monks.
upasaṃpad: to come to, arrive at, reach, obtain; to bring near to, lead near to, procure, give; to receive into the order of monks, ordain.
Ref: ch. 86 [69].

Upāli
Represented phonetically.
[MW] name of one of the Buddha's most eminent pupils (mentioned as the first propounder of the Buddhist law and as having been formerly a barber).
Ref: ch. 12 [95].

upāsaka (layman)
Represented phonetically.
[MW] serving, a servant; worshipping, a worshipper, follower; a Buddhist lay worshipper.
Ref: Lotus Sutra ch. 2.

upāsikā (laywoman)
Represented phonetically.
[MW] a lay female votary of Buddha.
Ref: Lotus Sutra ch. 2.

upāya-kauśalya (skillful means)
Represented by 善巧方便 (ZENGO-HOBEN), "skillful means, skillful expedient."
[MW] *upāya*: coming near, approach, arrival; that by which one reaches one's aim, a means or expedient, way, stratagem, craft, artifice.
kauśalya: cleverness, skillfulness, experience.
Ref: Lotus Sutra ch. 2.

ūrṇā (circle of hair)
Represented by 白毫 (BYAKU-GO), "white hair."
[MW] wool, a woolen thread, thread; a circle of hair between the eyebrows.
Ref: ch. 17 [39]; Lotus Sutra ch. 2.

utpala (blue lotus)
Represented phonetically.
[MW] the blossom of the blue lotus (Nympaea Caerulea); any water-lily; any flower.
Ref. ch. 12 [90]; ch. 43.

Utpalavarṇā (name of a nun)
Represented phonetically and by 蓮華色 (RENGE-SHIKI), "Lotus-Flower Color."
Ref: ch. 12 [87].

uttarāsanga (outer robe)
Represented phonetically and by 上衣 (JO-E), "upper robe," by 七条衣 (SHICHI-JO-E), "7 stripe robe," by 中衣 (CHU-E), "middle robe," and by 入衆衣 (NYU-SHU-E), "robe for going among the Saṃgha."
[MW] an upper or outer garment.
Ref: ch. 12 [95].

vaiḍūrya (lapis lazuli)
Represented phonetically.
[MW] a cat's-eye gem.
Ref: ch. 20 [125]; Lotus Sutra ch. 17.

vaipulya (extensions [of Buddhist philosophy])
Represented by 方広 (HOKO), "square and wide" or "exact and wide."
[MW] largeness, spaciousness, breadth, thickness; a Sūtra of great extension, Buddhist literature.
One of the 12 divisions of the teachings. See under **anga**.
Ref: ch. 11 [40]; bibliography.

vairambhaka (name of a wind)
[JEBD] an all-destroying wind occurring between kalpas.
Ref: ch. 10 [14].

Vairocana (the Sun Buddha)
Represented phonetically and by 大日如来 (DAI-NICHI-NYORAI), "the Great Sun Tathāgata."
[MW] coming from or belonging to the sun, solar; a son of the sun; name of a Dhyāni-Buddha.
Ref: ch. 1 [32]; ch. 17 [54].

Vaiśravaṇa (a patronymic)
Represented phonetically.
[MW] a patronymic (especially of Kubera and Rāvana).
Ref: Lotus Sutra ch. 25.

vaiśya (working class)
Represented phonetically.
[MW] 'a man who settles on the soil,' a peasant, or 'working man,' agriculturist, man of the third class or caste (whose business was trade as well as agriculture).
Ref. ch.8; ch. 82.

Vajraccedikā-prajñā-pāramitā-sūtra (name of a sutra)
Represented by 金剛経 (KONGO-KYO), "Diamond Sutra."
[MW] *Vajra*: diamond
chedaka: cutting off
Ref: ch. 18; ch. 19; ch. 61; bibliography.

Vajra-sattva (the Diamond Buddha)
Represented by 金剛薩埵 (KONGO-SATTA), "Diamond-sattva."
[MW] *Vajra-sattva*: 'having a soul or heart of adamant,' name of a Dhyāni-Buddha. *Vajra*: 'the hard or mighty one,' a thunderbolt (esp. that of Indra; in Northern Buddhist countries it is shaped like a dumb-bell and called Dorje); a diamond (thought to be as hard as the thunderbolt or of the same substance with it).
Ref: ch. 1 [32].

vandana (worship, prostration)
Represented by 礼拝 (RAIHAI) "worship," "prostration," by 敬礼 (KEIRAI), "venerative bow," and by 稽首 (KEISHU), "striking the head."
[MW] praise, worship, adoration; (with Buddhists) one of the 7 kinds of Anuttara-pūja or highest worship; a mark or symbol impressed on the body (with ashes etc.); the act of praising, praise; reverence (especially obeisance to a superior by touching the feet etc.), worship, adoration.
Ref: ch. 2 [74]; ch. 8.

vārṣika (rains retreat)
Represented by 安居 (ANGO), "the retreat,"
[MW] belonging to the rainy season, rainy; growing in the rainy season or fit for or suited to it; yearly, annual.
Ref. ch. 2 [80]; ch. 79.

vedana (perception, feeling)
Represented by 受 (JU), "accepting, feeling."
[MW] announcing, proclaiming; perception, knowledge; pain, torture, agony; feeling, sensation. One of the 5 *skandhas* (q.v.).
Ref: ch. 2.

vidyā (knowledge)
See **tisro vidyāh**.

vihāra (temple)
Represented by 精舎 (SHOJA), "spiritual building."
[MW] distribution; arrangement; walking for pleasure or amusement, wandering, roaming; sport, play, pastime, diversion, enjoyment, pleasure; a place of recreation, pleasure-ground; (with Buddhists) a monastery or temple (originally a hall where the monks met or walked about; afterwards these

halls were used as temples).
Ref: ch. 7 [166].

vijñāna (consciousness)
Represented by 識 (SHIKI), "consciousness."
[MW] the act of distinguishing or discerning, understanding, comprehending, recognizing, intelligence, knowledge; (with Buddhists) consciousness or thought-faculty.
One of the 5 *skandhas* (aggregates), one of the 6 *dhātus* (elements), and one of the 12 links of the chain of causation (q.v.).
Ref: ch. 2; Lotus Sutra ch. 7.

vikṣepa (distraction)
Represented by 散乱 (SANRAN) or 散 (SAN), "distraction."
[MW] the act of throwing asunder or away or about, scattering, dispersion; casting, throwing, discharging; moving about, waving, shaking; letting loose, indulging; letting slip, neglecting; inattention, distraction, confusion, perplexity.
Ref: Fukan-zazengi.

Vimalakīrti (name of a lay student of the Buddha)
Represented phonetically and by 浄名 (JOMYO), "Pure Name."
[MW] 'of spotless fame,' name of a Buddhist scholar.
Ref: ch. 6 [56]; ch. 73; bibliography.

Vimalakīrti-nīrdeśa (name of a sutra)
Represented by 維摩経 (YUIMA-GYO), "Vimalakīrti Sutra."
[MW] *nīrdeśa*: pointing out, indicating, directing, order, command, instruction; description, specification, special mention, details or particulars.
Ref: ch. 32; ch. 85; bibliography.

vimukti (liberation, salvation)
Represented by 解脱 (GEDATSU), "salvation, emancipation."
[MW] disjunction; giving up; release, deliverance, liberation; release from the bonds of existence, final emancipation.
Ref: ch. 2 [74]; ch. 12; Lotus Sutra ch. 25.

vinaya (discipline, precepts)
Represented by 律 (RITSU), "rules, law, regulation."
[MW] leading, guidance, training (esp. moral training), education, discipline, control, (with Buddhism) the rules of discipline for monks.
One of the "three baskets," or *tripiṭaka* (q.v.).
Ref: ch. 94 [107]; bibliography.

vindhya-vana (monastery)
Represented by 叢林 (SORIN), "thicket-forest" or "clump of forest"—see also **piṇḍa-vana**.
[MW] a forest in the Vindhya.
vindhya: name of a low range of hills connecting the Northern extremities of the Western and Eastern Ghauts, and separating Hindūstan proper from the Dekhan.
vana: forest, wood.
Ref: ch. 5 [122].

vipāka-phala (maturation of effects)
Represented by 異熟果 (IJUKU-KA), "differently maturing effects."
[MW] *vipāka*: ripe, mature; cooking, dressing; ripening, maturing (especially of the fruit of actions), effect, result, consequence.
phala: fruit, consequence, effect, result, retribution (good or bad), gain or loss, reward or punishment.
Ref: ch. 10 [21]; ch. 84.

Vipaśyin (name of a Buddha)
Represented phonetically and by 広説 (KOSETSU), "Universal Preaching."
[MW] name of a Buddha (sometimes mentioned as the first of the seven Tathāgatas or principal Buddhas, the other six being Śikhin, Viśva-bhū, Kraku-cchanda, Kanaka-muni, Kāśyapa, and Śakya-siṇha).
Ref: ch. 15.

vipaśyanā (insight, reflection)
Represented by 観 (KAN), "reflection."
[MW] right knowledge.
vipaś: to see in different places or in detail, discern, distinguish; to observe, perceive, learn, know.
Ref: ch. 1 [51]; ch. 22 [14]; ch. 73.

vīrya (diligence, effort, fortitude)
Represented by 精進 (SHOJIN), "diligence."
[MW] *vīrya*: manliness, valor, strength, power, energy; heroism, heroic deed; manly, vigor, energy, virility.
vīrya pāramitā: highest degree of fortitude or energy.
One of the 6 *pāramitās* (q.v.).
Ref: ch. 2; Lotus Sutra ch. 27.

viṣaya (object)
Represented by 境 (KYO), "boundary, sphere, circumstances" or by 境界 (KYOGAI),

"boundary, environment."
[MW] sphere (of influence or activity), dominion, kingdom; scope, reach (of eyes, ears, mind etc.); an object of sense (there are five in number, the five *indriya* or organs of sense having each their proper *viṣaya* or object viz. 1. *śabda*, 'sound,' for the ear; 2. *sparśa*, 'tangibility' for the skin; 3. *rūpa*, 'form' or 'color' for the eye; 4. *rasa*, 'savor,' for the tongue; 5. *gandha*, 'odor,' for the nose; and these five *viṣayas* are sometimes called the *Guṇas* or 'properties' of the five elements ether, air, fire, water, earth, respectively).
Ref: ch. 2.

Viṣṇu (name of the preserver god in the Hindū triad)
[MW] name of one of the principal Hindū deities (in the later mythology regarded as 'the preserver').
Ref: ch. 10 [19].

vitarka (reflection)
Represented by 覚 (KAKU), "awareness."
[MW] conjecture, supposition, guess, fancy, imagination, opinion; doubt, uncertainty; reasoning, deliberation, consideration; purpose, intention.
vitark: to reflect
Ref: ch. 6 [129].

vṛiddha (experienced)
Represented phonetically and by 積聚精要心 (SHAKUJU-SHOYO-SHIN), "experienced and concentrated mind."
[MW] grown, become larger or longer or stronger, increased, augmented, great, large; grown up, full-grown, advanced in years, aged, old, senior; experienced, wise, learned.
One of the 3 kinds of mind, the others being *citta* and *hṛidaya* (q.v.).
Ref: ch. 70.

vyajana (whisk)
Represented by 払子 (HOSSU), "whisk."
[MW] fanning; a palm-leaf or other article used for fanning, fan, whisk.
Ref: ch. 16 [9]; Fukan-zazengi.

vyākaraṇa (prediction, affirmation)
Represented by 記別 (KIBETSU), "certification-discrimination," and by 授記 (JUKI), "affirmation" or "giving affirmation."
[MW] separation, distinction, discrimination; explanation, detailed description; manifestation, revelation; (with Buddhists) prediction, prophecy.
One of the 12 divisions of the teachings. See under **anga**.
Ref: ch. 11 [40]; ch. 32; Lotus Sutra ch. 3.

yakṣa (demons, devils)
Represented phonetically.
[MW] a living supernatural being, spiritual apparition, ghost, spirit.
Ref: ch. 70 [207]; Lotus Sutra ch. 10.

yaṣṭi (pole, flagpole [as symbol of Buddhist temple])
Represented phonetically.
[MW] 'any support,' a staff, stick, wand, rod, mace, club, cudgel; pole, pillar, perch; a flag-staff.
Ref: ch. 1 [61]; ch. 16 [15].

Yogācāra (name of a school)
[MW] the observance of the Yoga; a particular Samādhi; a follower of a particular Buddhist sect or school; the disciples of that school.
yoga: the act of yoking, joining; a means, expedient, method; undertaking, business, work; any junction, union, combination; fitting together, fitness; exertion, endeavor, diligence.
[JEBD] One of the two major Mahāyāna schools in India (together with the Mādhyamika).
Ref. ch. 15.

yojana (a measure of distance)
Represented phonetically.
[MW] joining, yoking, harnessing; course, path; a stage or Yojana (i.e. a distance traversed in one harnessing or without unyoking; especially a particular measure of distance, sometimes regarded as equal to 4 or 5 English miles, but more correctly = 4 *Krośas* or about 9 miles).
Ref: ch. 17 [62]; Lotus Sutra ch. 11.

Bibliographies

Bibliography One: Main Chinese Sources Quoted by Master Dogen in Shobogenzo

A. Sutras

Attempts at English translations of sutra titles are provisional, and provided only for reference.

Agon-kyo 阿含経 (Āgama Sutras).

In Chinese translation, there are four:

Cho-agon-kyo 長阿含経 (Long Āgama Sutra—in Pali, Digha-nikāya);
Chu-agon-kyo 中阿含経 (Middle Āgama Sutra—in Sanskrit, Madhyamāgama; in Pali, Majjhima-nikāya);
Zo-agon-kyo 雑阿含経 (Miscellaneous Āgama Sutra—in Sanskrit, Saṃyuktāgama; in Pali, Samyutta-nikāya);
Zo-itsu-agon-gyo 増一阿含経 (Āgama Sutras Increased by One—in Sanskrit, Ekottarāgama; in Pali, Aṅguttara-nikāya)
These are supplemented by the **Sho-agon-kyo** 小阿含経 (Small Āgama Sutras—in Sanskrit, Kṣudrakāgama; in Pali, Khuddaka-nikāya), a collection of all the Āgamas beside the four Āgamas. In the Pali canon, Khuddaka-nikāya is the fifth of the five Nikāyas and comprises fifteen short books.

Aiku-o-kyo 阿育王経 (Aśoka Sutra)

Butsu-hongyo-jikkyo 佛本行集経 (Sutra of Collected Past Deeds of the Buddha)

Daibonten-o-monbutsu-ketsugi-kyo 大梵天王問佛決疑経 (Sutra of Questions and Answers between Mahābrahman and the Buddha)

Dai-hannya-kyo 大般若経 (Great Prajñā Sutra), short for **Dai-hannya-haramitta-kyo** 大般若波羅密多経 (Sutra of the Great Prajñā-pāramitā —in Sanskrit, Mahā-prajñā-pāramitā-sūtra)

Daihatsu-nehan-kyo 大般涅槃経 (Sutra of the Great Demise—in Sanskrit, Mahāparinirvāṇa-sūtra)

Dai-hoko-hokyo-gyo 大方廣寶篋経 (The Mahāvaipulya Treasure Chest Sutra)

Dai-hoko-engaku-shutara-ryogi-kyo 大方廣円覚修多羅了義経 (The Mahāvaipulya Round Realization Sutra)

Dai-ho-shak-kyo 大寶積経 (Great Treasure Accumulation Sutra—in Sanskrit, Mahāratnakūta-sūtra)

Daijo-honsho-shinchi-kan-kyo 大乗本生心地観経 (The Mahāyāna Sutra of Reflection on the Mental State in Past Lives)

Daishu-kyo 大集経 (Great Collection Sutra—in Sanskrit, Mahā-saṃnipāta-sūtra)

Engaku-kyo 円覚経 (Sutra of Round Realization)

Fuyo-kyo 普曜経 (Sutra of Diffusion of Shining Artlessness—in Sanskrit, Lalita-vistara-sūtra)

Hige-kyo 悲華経 (Flower of Compassion Sutra—in Sanskrit, Karuṇā-puṇḍarīka-sūtra)

Hokke-kyo 法華経 (Lotus Sutra, Sutra of the Flower of Dharma), short for

Myoho-renge-kyo (Sutra of the Lotus Flower of the Wonderful Dharma—in Sanskrit, Saddharma-puṇḍarīka-sūtra)

Hoku-kyo 法句経 (Sutra of Dharma-phrases—in Pali, Dhammapada)

Honsho-kyo 本生経 (Past Lives Sutra—in Sanskrit, Jātaka)

Ju-o-kyo 十王経 (Ten Kings Sutra)

Kan-fugen-bosatsu-gyobo-kyo 観普賢菩薩行法経 (Sutra of Reflection on the Practice of Dharma by Bodhisattva Universal Virtue)

Kegon-kyo 華厳経 (Garland Sutra—in Sanskrit, Avataṇsaka-sūtra)

Kengu-kyo 賢愚経 (Sutra of the Wise and the Stupid)

Ke-u-koryo-kudoku-kyo 希有校量功徳経 (Sutra of Comparison of the Merits of Rare Occurrences)

Konkomyo-kyo 金光明経 (Golden Light Sutra), short for **Konkomyo-saisho-o-kyo** 金光明最勝王経 (Golden Light Sutra of the Supreme King—in Sanskrit, Suvarṇa-prabhāsottama-rāja-sūtra)

Kongo-kyo 金剛経 (Diamond Sutra), short for **Kongo-hannya-haramitsu-kyo** 金剛般若波羅密経 (Sutra of the Diamond-Prajñā-Pāramitā—in Sanskrit, Vajraccedikā-prajñā-pāramitā-sūtra)

Miroku-josho-kyo 弥勒上生経 (Sutra of Maitreya's Ascent and Birth [in Tuṣita Heaven])

Mizo-u-innen-kyo 未曾有因縁経 (Sutra of Unprecedented Episodes)

Ninno-gyo 仁王経 (Benevolent King Sutra), short for **Ninno-hannya-haramitsu-gyo** 仁王般若波羅密経 (Prajñā-pāramitā Sutra of the Benevolent King)

Senju-hyaku-en-kyo 撰集百縁経 (Sutra of a Hundred Collected Stories)

Shobutsu-yoshu-kyo 諸佛要集経 (Sutra of the Collected Essentials of the Buddhas)

Shuryogon-kyo 首楞厳経 (Śūraṃgama Sutra—in Sanskrit, Śūraṃgama-samādhi-nirdeśa)

Shakubuku-rakan-kyo 折伏羅漢経 (Sutra of the Defeat of the Arhat)

Shugyo-hongi-kyo 修行本起経 (Sutra of Past Occurences of Practice)

Yoraku-hongyo-kyo 瓔珞本起経 (Sutra of Past Deeds as a String of Pearls)

Yuima-gyo 維摩経 (Vimalakīrti Sutra—in Sanskrit, Vimalakīrti-nīrdeśa)

Zuio-hongi-kyo 瑞應本起経 (Sutra of Auspicious Past Occurrences)

B. Precepts

Bonmo-kyo 梵網経 (Pure Net Sutra)

Daibiku-sanzen-yuigi-kyo 大比丘三千威儀経 (Sutra of Three Thousand Dignified Forms for Ordained Monks)

Juju-ritsu 十誦律 (Precepts in Ten Parts), a 61-fascicle translation of the vinaya of the Sarvāstivādin School

Konpon-setsu-issai-u-bu-hyaku-ichi-katsuma 根本説一切有部百一羯磨 (101 Customs of the Mūla-sarvāstivādin School)

Makasogi-ritsu 摩訶僧祇律 (Precepts for the Great Saṃgha), a 40-fascicle translation of the vinaya of the Mahāsaṃghika School of Hīnayāna Buddhism

Shibun-ritsu 四分律 (Precepts in Four Divisions), a 60-fascicle translation of the vinaya of the Dharmagupta School

Zen-en-shingi 禪苑清規 (Pure Criteria for Zen Monasteries)

C. Commentaries

Bosatsuchi-ji-kyo 菩薩地持経 (Sutra of Maintaining the Bodhisattva-State)

Daibibasha-ron 大毘婆沙論 (Abhidharma-mahāvibhāṣa-śāstra)

Daichido-ron 大智度論 (Commentary on the Accomplishment which is Great Wisdom—in Sanskrit, Mahā-prajñā-pāramitopadeśa)

Daijogi-sho 大乗義章 (Writings on the Mahāyāna Teachings)

Hokke-zanmai-sengi 法華三昧懺儀 (A Humble Expression of the Form of the Samādhi of the Flower of Dharma)

Kusha-ron 倶舎論 (Abhidharma-kośa-śāstra)

Maka-shikan 摩訶止観 (Great Quietness and Reflection), a record of the lectures of Master Tendai Chigi, founder of the Tendai Sect

Maka-shikan-hogyo-den-guketsu 摩訶止観輔行伝弘決 (Extensive Decisions Transmitted in Support of Great Quietness and Reflection), a Chinese commentary on *Maka-shikan* by Master Keikei Tannen

D. General Chinese Buddhist Records

Daito-sai-iki-ki 大唐西域記 (Great Tang Records of Western Lands)

Go-to-roku 五燈録 (The Five Records of the Torch), five independent but complimentary collections compiled during the Sung era (960–1279). They are represented in summary form in **Go-to-egen** 五燈会元 (Collection of the Fundamentals of the Five Torches). Namely, the five records are:

Keitoku-dento-roku 景徳伝燈録 (Keitoku Era Record of the Transmission of the Torch)

Tensho-koto-roku 天聖廣燈録 (Tensho Era Record of the Widely Extending Torch)

Zokuto-roku 続燈録 (Supplementary Record of the Torch)

Rento-eyo 聯燈會要 (Collection of Essentials for Continuation of the Torch)

Katai-futo-roku 嘉泰普燈録 (Katai Era Record of the Universal Torch)

Hekigan-roku 碧巌録 (Blue Cliff Record)

Ho-en-shu-rin 法苑珠林 (A Forest of Pearls in the Garden of Dharma), a kind of Buddhist encyclopedia in 100 volumes

Kaigen-shakkyo-roku 開元釈教録 (Kaigen-era Records of Śākyamuni's Teaching)

Kosonshuku-goroku 古尊宿語録 (Record of the Words of the Venerable Patriarchs of the Past)

Rinkan-roku 林間録 (Forest Record), short for **Sekimon-rinkan-roku** 石門林間録 (Sekimon's Forest Record)

So-koso-den 宋高僧伝 (Biographies of Noble Monks of the Sung-era)

Zenmon-shososhi-geju 禪門諸祖師偈頌 (Verses and Eulogies of Ancestral Masters of the Zen Lineages)

Zenrin-hokun 禪林寶訓 (Treasure-Instruction from the Zen Forest)

Zenshu-juko-renju-tsushu 禪宗頌古聯珠通集 (Complete String-of-Pearls Collection of Eulogies to Past Masters of the Zen Sect)

Zoku-dento-roku 続伝燈録 (Continuation of the Record of the Transmission of the Torch), published in China in 1635; sequel to *Keitoku-dento-roku*

Zokukan-kosonshuku-goyo 続刊古尊宿語要 (Summarized Collection of the Words of the Venerable Patriarchs of the Past)

E. RECORDS AND INDEPENDENT WORKS OF CHINESE MASTERS

Baso-Do-itsu-zenji-goroku 馬祖道一禪師語録 (Record of the Words of Zen Master Baso Do-itsu)

Bukka-geki-setsu-roku 佛果擊節録 (Record of Bukka's Attacks on Knotty Problems); [Bukka is an alias of Master Seccho Juken]

Chorei-Shutaku-zenji-goroku 長霊守卓禪師語録 (Record of the Words of Zen Master Chorei Shutaku)

Dai-e-Fugaku-zenji-shumon-buko 大慧普覚禪師宗門武庫 (The War Chest of the School of Zen Master Dai-e Fugaku [Dai-e Soko])

Dai-e-goroku 大慧語録 (Record of the Words of Dai-e [Soko])

Dai-e-zenji-tomei 大慧禪師塔銘 (Inscriptions on the Stūpa of Zen Master Dai-e [Soko])

Engo-zenji-goroku 圜悟禪師語録 (Record of the Words of Zen Master Engo [Kokugon])

Joshu-roku 趙州録 (Records of Joshu [Jushin])

Jugendan 十玄談 (Discussion of the Ten Kinds of Profundity), by Master Do-an Josatsu

Ho-en-zenji-goroku 法演禪師語録 (Record of the Words of Zen Master [Yogi] Ho-en)

Hokyo-zanmai 寶鏡三昧 (Samadhi, the State of a Jewel-Mirror), by Master Tozan Ryokai

Honei-Nin-yu-zenji-goroku 法寧仁勇禪師語録 (Record of the Words of Zen Master Honei Nin-yu)

Hyakujo-roku 百丈録 (Record of Hyakujo), short for **Hyakujo-Ekai-zenji-goroku** 百丈懐海禪師語録 (Record of the Words of Zen Master Hyakujo Ekai)

Koke-zenji-goroku 興化禪師語録 (Record of the Words of Zen Master Koke [Sonsho])

Kido-shu 虚堂集 (The Kido Collection), a collection of the words of Master Tanka Shijun, compiled by Rinsen Jurin

Nyojo-osho-goroku 如浄和尚語録 (Record of the Words of Master [Tendo] Nyojo)

O-an-Donge-zenji-goroku 応菴曇華禪師語録 (Record of the Words of Zen Master O-an Donge)

Rinzai-zenji-goroku 臨済禪師語録 (Record of the Words of Zen Master Rinzai [Gigen])

Rokuso-dankyo 六祖壇経 (The Sixth Patriarch's Platform Sutra), attributed to Master Daikan Eno

Sandokai 参同契 (Experiencing the State), by Master Sekito Kisen

Seccho-Myokaku-zenji-goroku 雪竇明覚禪師語録 (Record of the Words of Zen Master Seccho Myokaku [Seccho Juken])

Sekito-so-an no Uta 石頭草庵歌 (Songs from Sekito's Thatched Hut), by Master Sekito

Kisen
Shodoka 証道歌 (Song of Experiencing the Truth), by Master Yoka Genkaku
Shinjinmei 信心銘 (Inscription on Believing Mind), by Master Kanchi Sosan
Sotai-roku 奏対録 (Record of Answers to an Emperor), by Master Bussho Tokko
Tozan-goroku 洞山語録 (Record of the Words of Tozan [Ryokai])
Unmon-koroku 雲門廣録 (Broad Record of Unmon [Bun-en])
Wanshi-zenji-goroku 宏智禪師語録 (Record of the Words of Zen Master Wanshi [Shokaku])
Wanshi-koroku 宏智廣録 (Broad Record of Wanshi [Shokaku])
Wanshi-juko 宏智頌古 (Wanshi's Eulogies to Past Masters), also known as **Shoyo-roku** 従容録 (The Relaxation Record)
Yafu-Dosen-kongo-kyo 冶父道川金剛経 (Yafu Dosen's Diamond Sutra)

F. CHINESE SECULAR BOOKS ETC.

Confucianist:
Kokyo 孝経 (The Book of Filial Piety)
Rongo 論語 (The Discourses [of Confucius])

Taoist:
Bunshi 文子 from the Chinese *Wen-tzu*, the name of the author to whom the text is ascribed
Kanshi 管子 from the Chinese *Guan-tzu*, the name of the supposed author
Shishi 尸子 from the Chinese *Shi-tzu*, the name of the supposed author
Soji 荘子 from the Chinese *Chuang-tzu*, the name of a disciple of Lao-tzu (the ancient Chinese philosopher regarded as the founder of Taoism)
Inzui 韻瑞 (Rhymes of Good Fortune)
Rikuto 六韜 (Six Strategies)
Sango-ryaku-ki 三五暦記 (History of the Three [Elements] and Five [Elements])

Miscellaneous
Jirui-senshu 事類撰集 (Collection of Matters and Examples)
Jibutsu-gen-ki 事物原記 (Record of the Origin of Things)
Jokan-seiyo 貞観政要 (Jokan Era [Treatise] on the Essence of Government)
Mei-hoki 冥報記 (Chronicles of the Underworld)
Taihei-koki 太平弘記 (Widely Extending Record of the Taihei Era)

Bibliography Two: Other Works by Master Dogen

Fukan-zazengi 普勧坐禅儀 (Universal Guide to the Standard Method of Zazen)
Gakudo-yojin-shu 學道用心集 (Collection of Concerns in Learning the Truth)
Hogyo-ki 寶慶記 (Hogyo Era Record)
Shinji-shobogenzo 真字正法眼蔵 (Right-Dharma-Eye Treasury, in Original [Chinese] Characters); [also known as the **Sambyaku-soku** 三百則]

Eihei-koroku 永平廣録 (Broad Record of Eihei)
Eihei-shingi 永平清規 (Pure Criteria of Eihei):
- **Tenzo-kyokun** 典座教訓 (Instructions for the Cook)
- **Bendo-ho** 辨道法 (Methods of Pursuing the Truth)
- **Fu-shuku-han-ho** 赴粥飯法 (The Method of Taking Meals)
- **Shuryo-shingi** 衆寮清規 (Pure Criteria for the Monks' Dormitory)
- **Tai-taiko-gogejari-ho** 對大己五夏闍梨法 (The Method of Meeting with Veteran Practitioners of Five Summer Retreats)
- **Chiji-shingi** 知事清規 (Pure Criteria for the Temple Officers)

Bibliography Three: Main Japanese References

Bukkyo-jiten:	edited by Ui Hakuju
Bukkyogo-daijiten:	3 volumes edited by Hajime Nakamura
Dai-kanwa-jiten:	13 volumes by Tetsuji Morohashi
Dogen-no-kenkyu:	by Hanji Akiyama
Dogen-zenji-den-no-kenkyu:	by Doshu Ohkubo
Dogen-zenji-no-hanashi:	by Ton Satomi
Hokke-kyo:	published by Iwanami Shoten
Jikai:	edited by Kyosuke Kinta-ichi
Sawaki-Kodo-zenshu:	19 volumes by Master Kodo Sawaki
Shin-bukkyo-jiten:	edited by Hajime Nakamura
Shinshu-kanwa-daijiten:	by Shikita Koyanagi
Shinshu-taisho-daizokyo:	by Daizo Shuppansha
Shobogenzo-chukai-zensho:	10 volumes by Nyoten Jinbo & Bun-ei Ando
Shobogenzo-ji-i:	by Soku-o Eto
Shobogenzo-keiteki:	by Bokuzan Nishi-ari
Shobogenzo-shaku-i:	4 volumes by Kunihiko Hashida
Shobogenzo:	published by Iwanami Shoten, commentary by Nishi-o, Kagamishima, Sakai, and Mizuno
Shoten-zoku-cho:	by Master Osen Mujaku
Sogo-rekishi-nenpyo:	edited by Kenzo Nakajima
Tetsugaku-jiten:	published by Heibon Sha
Tetsugaku-shojiten:	published by Iwanami Shoten
Watsuji-tetsuro-zenshu (vols. 4, 5):	by Tetsuro Watsuji
Zengaku-daijiten:	edited by scholars of Komazawa University
Zengaku-jiten:	by Nyoten Jinbo & Bun-ei Ando

(Texts printed in Taiwan)

Keitoku-dento-roku:	Shin Zen Bi Shuppansha
Zoku-zokyo:	Collection of Buddhist Sutras not included in Shinshu-taisho-daizokyo

Shobogenzo in Modern Japanese:

Gendaigo-yaku-shobogenzo 現代語訳正法眼蔵 (Shobogenzo in Modern Japanese) by G. W. Nishijima, twelve volumes plus a one-volume appendix

Shobogenzo-teisho-roku 正法眼蔵提唱録 (Record of Lectures on Shobogenzo), by G. W. Nishijima, thirty-four volumes

These volumes are obtainable from the publisher:

Kanazawa Bunko Co. Ltd., Sumitomo Ichigaya Bldg., Honmura-cho 1-1, Ichigaya, Shinjuku-ku, Tokyo
Tel: (03) 3235-7060
Fax: (03) 3235-7135

Bibliography Four:
Main English References:

Kenkyusha's New Japanese–English Dictionary: editor in chief, Koh Masuda

Japanese Character Dictionary: Andrew Nelson, published by Charles Tuttle

Japanese Character Dictionary: Mark Spahn & Wolfgang Hadamitzky, published by Nichigai Asssociates

Japanese–English Buddhist Dictionary [JEBD]: published by Daito Shuppansha

A Sanskrit–English Dictionary [MW]: Sir Monier Monier-Williams, Oxford University Press

The Threefold Lotus Sutra [LSW]: Kato and Soothill, published by Weatherhill

The Historical Buddha [HB]: H. W. Schumann, published by Arkana

CPSIA information can be obtained
at www.ICGtesting.com
Printed in the USA
LVHW101311040821
694531LV00016B/320

9 781419 638206